HEARING AND DOING THE WORD

HEARING AND DOING THE WORD

The Drama of Evangelical Hermeneutics in Honor of Kevin J. Vanhoozer

Edited by
Daniel J. Treier and Douglas A. Sweeney

LONDON • NEW YORK • OXFORD • NEW DELHI • SYDNEY

T&T CLARK

Bloomsbury Publishing Plc

50 Bedford Square, London, WC1B 3DP, UK
1385 Broadway, New York, NY 10018, USA
29 Earlsfort Terrace, Dublin 2, Ireland

BLOOMSBURY, T&T CLARK and the T&T Clark logo are trademarks of
Bloomsbury Publishing Plc

First published in Great Britain 2021
Paperback edition published 2023

Copyright © Daniel J. Treier, Douglas A. Sweeney, and contributors, 2021

Daniel J. Treier, Douglas A. Sweeney, and contributors have asserted their right under the
Copyright, Designs and Patents Act, 1988, to be identified as Authors of this work.

For legal purposes the Acknowledgments on p. viii constitute an extension
of this copyright page.

Cover image: *Allegory On the Fall and Redemption of Man*, Lucas Cranach the Younger. Oil
on panel, German 16th century. Bob Jones University.

All rights reserved. No part of this publication may be reproduced or transmitted
in any form or by any means, electronic or mechanical, including photocopying,
recording, or any information storage or retrieval system, without prior permission
in writing from the publishers.

Bloomsbury Publishing Plc does not have any control over, or responsibility for, any
third-party websites referred to or in this book. All internet addresses given in this
book were correct at the time of going to press. The author and publisher regret any
inconvenience caused if addresses have changed or sites have ceased to exist, but can
accept no responsibility for any such changes.

A catalogue record for this book is available from the British Library.

Library of Congress Cataloging-in-Publication Data
Names: Vanhoozer, Kevin J., honouree. |
Treier, Daniel J., 1972– editor. | Sweeney, Douglas A., editor.
Title: Hearing and doing the Word : the drama of evangelical hermeneutics in
honor of Kevin J. Vanhoozer / edited by Daniel J. Treier and Douglas A. Sweeney.
Description: London, UK ; New York, NY, USA : T&T Clark, 2021. |
Includes bibliographical references and index. | Identifiers:
LCCN 2021000834 (print) | LCCN 2021000835 (ebook) |
ISBN 9780567702197 | ISBN 9780567662637 (hb) |
ISBN 9780567662644 (epub) | ISBN 9780567662651 (epdf)
Subjects: LCSH: Bible–Hermeneutics. |
Bible–Criticism, interpretation, etc. | Evangelicalism.
Classification: LCC BS476 .H38 2021 (print) | LCC BS476 (ebook) |
DDC 220.601–dc23
LC record available at https://lccn.loc.gov/2021000834
LC ebook record available at https://lccn.loc.gov/2021000835

ISBN: HB: 978-0-5676-6263-7
PB: 978-0-5677-0219-7
ePDF: 978-0-5676-6265-1
ePUB: 978-0-5676-6264-4

Typeset by Newgen KnowledgeWorks Pvt. Ltd., Chennai, India

To find out more about our authors and books visit www.bloomsbury.com
and sign up for our newsletters.

CONTENTS

Acknowledgments — viii
Abbreviations — ix

INTRODUCTION: EVANGELICAL HERMENEUTICS IN DIALOGUE
WITH KEVIN J. VANHOOZER — 1
   Daniel J. Treier

Part I
THE BIBLICAL SCRIPT

Chapter 1
WILL THE GOOF PREVAIL? THE HERMENEUTICS OF
TEXTUAL CRITICISM — 23
   Iain Provan

Chapter 2
READING BETWEEN THE LINES: ON DISCERNING THE IMPLICIT
MESSAGES OF SCRIPTURE — 37
   V. Philips Long

Chapter 3
NEW TESTAMENT QUOTATIONS OF THE OLD AS DIVINE
SPEECH ACTS — 51
   Karen H. Jobes

Chapter 4
READING JOHN'S GOSPEL AS A THEODRAMATIC PREVIEW OF
COMING ATTRACTIONS — 65
   Robert H. Gundry

Chapter 5
THE GREAT ANTAGONIST — 79
   Graham A. Cole

Chapter 6
MARTYRDOM: MARTIN ALBERTZ'S NEGLECTED NEW
TESTAMENT THEOLOGY AND THE IMPORTANCE OF A THEOLOGICAL
CATEGORY — 93
   Robert W. Yarbrough

Part II
GREAT PERFORMANCES

Chapter 7
THE SPIRIT IN BIBLICAL INTERPRETATION: BASIL OF CAESAREA AND
MODERN DISCUSSION OF MEANING AND SIGNIFICANCE 113
   Darren Sarisky

Chapter 8
AUGUSTINE AND SCRIPTURE 127
   Gregory W. Lee

Chapter 9
THOMAS AQUINAS AND THE BOOK OF JEREMIAH 143
   Matthew Levering

Chapter 10
JOHN CALVIN AND THE THEOLOGICAL INTERPRETATION
OF SCRIPTURE 157
   Scott M. Manetsch

Chapter 11
"THE WHOLE SCOPE AND TENOR OF SCRIPTURE":
HERMENEUTICS, WHOLENESS, AND HOLINESS IN
WESLEYAN THEOLOGICAL INTERPRETATION OF SCRIPTURE 173
   Thomas McCall

Chapter 12
"FANTASTIC!" KARL BARTH, AMERICAN EVANGELICALS,
AND THE STRANGE NEW WORLD OF THEOLOGY 187
   Stephen M. Garrett

Part III
THEODRAMA TODAY

Chapter 13
BAPTIZED BIBLICAL INTERPRETATION: THE PLACE AND
FUNCTION OF THE CREED 205
   Scott R. Swain

Chapter 14
THE TRIUNE GOD 221
   Michael Allen

Chapter 15
HOW GOD DOES THINGS WITH WORDS IN THE CHURCH 235
   Michael Horton

Chapter 16
THE DRAMA OF (IMPUTATION) DOCTRINE: ORIGINAL GUILT AS
BIBLICAL AND SYSTEMATIC THEOLOGY 253
   Hans Madueme

Chapter 17
"BORN OF WATER AND THE SPIRIT": DIVINE AGENCY IN
INTERPRETATIONS OF JOHN 3 AND BAPTISM IN ACTS 271
   Elizabeth Y. Sung

Chapter 18
SCRIPTURE IN SOUND 287
   Jeremy Begbie

CONCLUSION 303
   Douglas A. Sweeney

Publications by Kevin J. Vanhoozer 311
Works Cited 321
List of Contributors 343
Index 345

ACKNOWLEDGMENTS

We are thankful for the opportunity to work with Anna Turton and her team at T&T Clark, and in particular for their willingness to help with preserving a modicum of surprise for this volume's honoree, Kevin J. Vanhoozer, as long as possible.

Jonathan Taylor and then Dr. Vanhoozer's teaching assistant, Matthew Wiley, helped with gathering a list of his publications. Joel Miles helped with the bibliography. Colby Brandt and Samuel Hagos compiled the index. Various Vanhoozer students and colleagues offered quiet encouragement along the way. Since we initiated this project in 2013, the roster of willing and fitting contributors certainly expanded, and we appreciate the forbearance of those we could not include. We also grieve the death of John Webster, who was originally slated to contribute a chapter on Karl Barth.

We are thankful for the enthusiasm and patience of our families regarding this project, and for convivial dinners we enjoyed with the Vanhoozers along the way. Indeed, this opportunity to collaborate only deepened our friendship, yet another gift that Kevin has given to us. We are especially grateful to Kevin's wife Sylvie, daughter Emma, and daughter Mary and son-in-law Josh for trusting us with this endeavor and making helpful recommendations. We hope that it will make a fitting contribution to the celebration of Kevin's sixty-fifth birthday, embodying our love and esteem for him.

ABBREVIATIONS

AB	Anchor Bible
ACCSNT	*Ancient Christian Commentary on the New Testament*, ed. Thomas C. Oden (Downers Grove: IVP, 2001–10)
ACCSOT	*Ancient Christian Commentary on the Old Testament*, ed. Thomas C. Oden (Downers Grove: IVP, 2000–7)
ANF	*Ante-Nicene Fathers* (10 vols.; various editions)
AugSt	*Augustinian Studies*
BETL	Bibliotheca ephemeridum theologicarum lovaniensium
BHS	*Biblia Hebraica Stuttgartensia*
Bib	*Biblica*
CD	Karl Barth, *Church Dogmatics*, ed. G. W. Bromiley and T. F. Torrance, 4 vols. in 14 parts (Edinburgh: T&T Clark, 1956–75)
CNTC	Calvin's New Testament Commentaries, trans. Ross Mackenzie (Grand Rapids: Eerdmans, 1960)
CO	John Calvin, *Ioannis Calvini opera omnia quae supersunt*, ed. G. Baum, E. Cunitz, and E. Reuss, 59 vols. (Brunsvigae: C. A. Schwetschke, 1863–1900)
CTS	*Calvin's Commentaries*, Calvin Translation Society edition [1843–1855], 26 vols. (reprint: Grand Rapids: Baker, 1989)
EBR	*Encyclopedia of the Bible and Its Reception*, ed. Christine Helmer et al., vol. 17 (Berlin: De Gruyter, 2019)
ESV	English Standard Version
ExpTim	*Expository Times*
FRLANT	Forschungen zur Religion und Literatur des Alten und Neuen Testaments
GKC	*Gesenius' Hebrew Grammar*, ed. E. Kautzsch, revised and trans. A. E. Cowley (Oxford: Clarendon, 1910)
HSM	Harvard Semitic Monographs
HTR	*Harvard Theological Review*
IBMR	*International Bulletin of Mission Research*
ICC	International Critical Commentary
IJST	*International Journal of Systematic Theology*
JETS	*Journal of the Evangelical Theological Society*
JPS	Jewish Publication Society
JR	*Journal of Religion*
JSOTSup	*Journal for the Study of the Old Testament*, Supplement Series
JTS	*Journal of Theological Studies*
LCC	Library of Christian Classics
LCL	Loeb Classical Library
MT	Masoretic Text
NCB	New Century Bible

NICNT	New International Commentary on the New Testament
NICOT	New International Commentary on the Old Testament
NIDNTT	*New International Dictionary of New Testament Theology*, ed. Colin Brown, 4 vols. (Grand Rapids: Zondervan, 1975–85)
NIGTC	New International Greek Testament Commentary
NIV	New International Version
NLT	New Living Translation
NPNF	*Nicene and Post-Nicene Fathers* (2 series of 14 vols. each; various editions)
NT	New Testament
NTS	*New Testament Studies*
OT	Old Testament
PNTC	Pillar New Testament Commentary
RSV	Revised Standard Version
SBLDS	SBL Dissertation Series
SJT	*Scottish Journal of Theology*
TOTC	Tyndale Old Testament Commentaries
TS	*Theological Studies*
TynBul	*Tyndale Bulletin*
VC	*Vigiliae christianae*
WBC	Word Biblical Commentary
WSA	*The Works of St. Augustine: A Translation for the 21st Century*, 49 planned vols. (Hyde Park, NY: New City, 1990–)
WTJ	*Westminster Theological Journal*
WUNT	Wissenschaftliche Untersuchungen zum Neuen Testament
ZAW	*Zeitschrift für die alttestamentliche Wissenschaft*

INTRODUCTION: EVANGELICAL HERMENEUTICS IN DIALOGUE WITH KEVIN J. VANHOOZER

Daniel J. Treier

Kevin J. Vanhoozer is today's leading evangelical theologian of biblical interpretation, exercising substantial influence both in contemporary hermeneutics and in academic theology. In this book, Dr. Vanhoozer's students and friends address the current state of evangelical hermeneutics in light of his work. Whether or not authors agree entirely with Kevin or each other, this volume addresses a subject near to his mind and dear to his heart, hoping that further dialogue with his evangelical hermeneutics will foster faithful hearing and doing of God's Word.

This introductory chapter narrates and synthesizes Vanhoozer's account. First, the situation of evangelical hermeneutics from the 1960s onward sets the stage. Next, the chapter sketches a three-act drama of Vanhoozer's own development: an early dialogue in the 1980s and 1990s with hermeneutical philosophy, focused on understanding what it means to be biblical; after the turn of the millennium, a middle dialogue with the motif of drama, focused on understanding Scripture interpretation more theologically; more recently, ongoing dialogue with Christian dogmatics, focused on putting theological interpretation of Scripture into evangelical practice. Finally, the chapter presents preliminary suggestions for dialogue with Vanhoozer's work, setting an agenda for the rest of this book and beyond.

Setting the Stage

At the middle of the twentieth century, evangelicals wrote relatively little about hermeneutics in general or biblical exegesis in particular. As a discipline, hermeneutics—the effort to understand how humans understand, especially "texts"—remained preeminently a European enterprise. Evangelicals continued to approach the Bible as Scripture, mixing popular and pastoral study, yet their scholarly engagement had not accelerated along with others'. They continued to study and teach from particular passages, read in light of the whole canon; many, though not all, evangelical leaders could engage the texts' original languages of Hebrew and Greek; yet few contributed scholarly publications regarding the historical study of particular texts or theoretical discussions of broader hermeneutical challenges.

By the 1960s, a new evangelical generation of biblical scholars began to earn university PhD degrees and to publish in mainstream academic venues. Before long, these scholars brought the fruits of their labors back home to the evangelical market. New commentary series appeared at popular, preaching-focused, and academic levels. Semipopular Bible study courses and materials proliferated, often presenting a triad of observation, interpretation, and application. In emerging colleges and seminaries, more sophisticated classes combined exegetical skills with a basic hermeneutical theory.

This dominant theory came from a 1967 book by E. D. Hirsch Jr. (1928–), a secular American literature professor.[1] Hirsch's *Validity in Interpretation* insisted that the author's intention is the only valid criterion for determining a text's meaning. Texts have manifold significance—multiple "applications," in evangelical parlance—as their meaning is appropriated for various contexts and purposes. But they have one "meaning," fixed by what the author intends to convey through conventional uses of language. This author-oriented approach has underwritten the historical focus of most evangelical biblical scholarship ever since.

Admittedly, there have been minority reports. Hirsch's later work did not maintain the position of *Validity* quite so clearly; yet it received little evangelical attention. Some evangelical hermeneutics borrowed from literary formalism, a prime source of opposition to authorial intention as an interpretive criterion;[2] yet evangelical borrowers typically incorporated such literary practices within a historically and authorially dominated approach. Evangelical scholars outside biblical studies—notably in literature and philosophy—began to challenge Hirsch's position in favor of Hans-Georg Gadamer (1900–2002), Paul Ricoeur (1913–2005), and other thinkers who oriented hermeneutics around texts and their histories of effects in human lives. Hirsch's treatment of Gadamer particularly came under fire; yet Hirsch's criterion still reigned over evangelical biblical interpretation, extending its influence through numerous textbooks.[3]

---

1. E. D. Hirsch Jr., *Validity in Interpretation* (New Haven: Yale University Press, 1967). On the twentieth-century evangelical renaissance of biblical scholarship, see Mark A. Noll, *Between Faith and Criticism: Evangelicals, Scholarship, and the Bible in America* (New York: Harper, 1986); for an overview of the wider context, including the emergence of new scholarly professions and institutions, see Daniel J. Treier and Craig Hefner, "Twentieth- and Twenty-First Century American Biblical Interpretation," in *The Oxford Handbook of the Bible in America*, ed. Paul C. Gutjahr (New York: Oxford University Press, 2017), 129–48.

2. See Kevin J. Vanhoozer, "Intention/Intentional Fallacy," in *Dictionary for Theological Interpretation of the Bible*, ed. Kevin J. Vanhoozer (Grand Rapids: Baker Academic, 2005), 327–30.

3. E.g., Walter C. Kaiser Jr. and Moisés Silva, *An Introduction to Biblical Hermeneutics: The Search for Meaning* (Grand Rapids: Zondervan, 1994), esp. 34–41.

Despite literary and philosophical complexity, historical scholarship seeking the author's intended meaning has obviously generated significant results. Admittedly, evangelical scholars remain a minority in that realm, and even their views are disparate regarding the proper approaches and boundaries for a host of historical-critical questions. Yet evangelicals now comprise a substantial minority, while much of their biblical scholarship is clearly excellent and ecumenically helpful. A noteworthy example is the emerging consensus embracing "inaugurated eschatology"—that the kingdom of God currently has both "already" and "not yet" dimensions in Christ—which has diminished the polarization between covenant and dispensationalist theologies. Simply by attaining historical and literary excellence, biblical scholars became vital pioneers in a wider evangelical renaissance of cultural and intellectual engagement.

Two hermeneutical flies lurked in this evangelical ointment, though. One involved wider hermeneutical trends. Hirsch's argument was aggressive but defensive; as evangelical philosophers and literary scholars joined biblical scholars in pioneering an intellectual renaissance, they often appreciated text- and reader-oriented alternatives that produced tension with biblical scholars. Another challenge involved the identity of the hermeneutically definitive author. Hirsch's argument was secular, applying to texts for whom an author could be known or posited. As evangelical scholars undertook exegesis in the service of developing a biblical theology, they encountered texts for which an author could not be clearly identified or the original context was contested (e.g., Hebrews), and for which multiple intentions might be pertinent (e.g., the Gospels' authors vis-à-vis Jesus' sayings and deeds). They also encountered tensions stemming from the evangelical commitment to Scripture's dual authorship—divine and human—with the wider biblical canon and its witness to a unified redemptive history complicating the identification of the relevant historical author(s) and literary context(s).

In the early 1980s a British evangelical NT scholar, Anthony Thiselton (1937–), began to publish sophisticated treatments of continental European hermeneutics. Thiselton not only introduced evangelicals to better treatments of Gadamer and others, but his hermeneutical work also gained wider scholarly esteem. Without denigrating the significance of historical authors or advocating relativistic pluralism, Thiselton directed new attention to text- and reader-oriented elements. Thiselton went beyond demonstrating his encyclopedic grasp of philosophical and literary currents to deploy this expertise exegetically and theologically.[4]

Then, in the later 1980s, Vanhoozer began to engage hermeneutical theory as a young theologian. His Cambridge doctoral thesis became a landmark on *Biblical*

---

4. See, e.g., Anthony C. Thiselton, *The First Epistle to the Corinthians: A Commentary on the Greek Text*, NIGTC (Grand Rapids: Eerdmans, 2000); idem, *Interpreting God and the Postmodern Self: On Meaning, Manipulation, and Promise* (Grand Rapids: Eerdmans, 1995). Perhaps the most comprehensive consolidation of his hermeneutical contribution is *New Horizons in Hermeneutics: The Theory and Practice of Transforming Biblical Reading* (Grand Rapids: Zondervan, 1992).

Narrative in the Philosophy of Paul Ricoeur (1990). Amid three sojourns teaching at Trinity Evangelical Divinity School, interrupted by eight years at the University of Edinburgh and three years at Wheaton College, Vanhoozer has authored major treatments of general hermeneutics and biblical interpretation (*Is There a Meaning in This Text?*, 1998), theological prolegomena (*The Drama of Doctrine*, 2005), and the doctrine of God (*Remythologizing Theology*, 2010). These four major books shape the narrative structure of the present essay. Vanhoozer has also edited several works, including the award-winning *Dictionary for Theological Interpretation of the Bible* (2005), while authoring legions of essays and other books. Thus, nearly all evangelical biblical scholars and theologians today interact with Vanhoozer's work, and many are broadly sympathetic to his approach. If Thiselton is evangelical hermeneutics' senior statesman and encyclopedic resource, then Vanhoozer is its senior theologian and a primary source of its operational vocabulary.

Therefore, the present book fosters a dialogue about the state of evangelical hermeneutics in light of Vanhoozer's work.[5] His hermeneutics is dialogical in both theory and practice. At the risk of oversimplification, we can trace three distinct periods, each influenced by a particular dialogue partner.

Being Biblical: Early Dialogue with Hermeneutical Philosophy (1986–98)

The chief dialogue partner of Vanhoozer's early period was hermeneutical philosophy. As he says in the major book that closed this period, "My interest in hermeneutics initially arose out of my attempt as a theologian to clarify the role of Scripture in theology. What does it mean to be 'biblical'?"[6] This initial interest elicited an MDiv honors thesis at Westminster Theological Seminary on the special status of the Bible for James Barr (1924–2006), Brevard Childs (1923–2007), and David Kelsey (1932–). Then Vanhoozer's first scholarly publication, from 1986, concerned "The Semantics of Biblical Literature: Truth and Scripture's Diverse Literary Forms." To illustrate the hermeneutical dialogue, this major essay contains epigraphs from ordinary language philosophers J. L. Austin (1911–1960) and Ludwig Wittgenstein (1889–1951); Vanhoozer addresses objections to propositional revelation in response to Barr and Kelsey while appealing to Northrop Frye's (1912–1991) literary criticism, Hans Frei's (1922–1988) arguments about biblical narrative, and C. S. Lewis's (1898–1963) approach to reading.

---

5. There are few substantial treatments of Vanhoozer's hermeneutics, and hardly any with wide influence. One useful sketch of Vanhoozer's theological influence briefly highlights similar characteristics to hermeneutical themes traced here: see Mark Bowald, "A Generous Reformer: Kevin Vanhoozer's Place in Evangelicalism," *Southeastern Theological Review* 4, no. 1 (2013): 3–9.

6. Kevin J. Vanhoozer, *Is There a Meaning in This Text? The Bible, the Reader, and the Morality of Literary Knowledge* (Grand Rapids: Zondervan, 1998; subsequent citations are from the 2nd ed., 2009), 9.

This initial essay concludes with five implications that introduce an early set of enduring commitments: (1) "God reveals himself in the Bible through inscribed discourse acts"; (2) "Exegetes should not make a priori decisions about biblical genres"; (3) "Scripture does many things with words and hence its authority is multifaceted"; (4) "Infallibility means that Scripture's diverse illocutionary forces will invariably achieve their respective purposes"; and (5) "Theology is 'ordinary literature' analysis of an extraordinary book."[7] Apparent here, first, is a commitment to having Scripture's *diverse literary forms* shape theology's substance. While Scripture's truth involves cognitive content that can be paraphrased or sometimes directly reiterated in propositional form, the personal dimensions of divine revelation require treating biblical texts as more than raw materials for theological system-building. The Bible's literary forms accomplish varied speech acts—"illocutionary" acts such as promising, warning, and the like. Texts do more than make assertions; they seek to change the world and our responses to it. Given the focus of this early essay, then, broader Christian doctrine informs the argument less overtly than Vanhoozer's hermeneutical dialogue partners.

Other early works reflect a second commitment: Engaging the Bible fosters truly *Christian humanism*. Soon, for instance, Vanhoozer published essays on aesthetic theology and culture vis-à-vis hermeneutics, while continuing to engage Ricoeur's work. Hermeneutical philosophy offered a resource for analyzing, appropriating, and avoiding cultural trends—with special reference to biblical interpretation. As Vanhoozer asserted in 1998, working on hermeneutical theology—how Christians ought to understand the Bible—pointed to theological hermeneutics, relating biblical interpretation to questions about understanding in general. He came "to think that the way individuals and communities interpret the Bible is arguably the most important barometer of larger intellectual and cultural trends," so that debates about postmodernity and interpretation "were really *theological* issues."[8] Indeed, an initial Christian humanism interested Vanhoozer in relating literary theory to the Bible, which then illuminated how cultures embrace and embody literary theories. Simultaneously, the Bible's own literary forms and content enhanced Vanhoozer's commitment to Christian humanism.

While Vanhoozer's interest in Ricoeur stemmed partly from that philosopher's interest in biblical interpretation and the idea of divine revelation, a third early commitment is also pertinent: *theological dialogue with both "analytic" and "Continental" philosophy*. Ricoeur uniquely engaged both streams of philosophy along with literary interests. Somewhat contrastively, Yale theologian Frei claimed that modernity's newfound historical consciousness and philosophical commitments led critical scholars to obsess over the historical veracity of biblical

---

7. Kevin J. Vanhoozer, "The Semantics of Biblical Literature: Truth and Scripture's Diverse Literary Forms," in *Hermeneutics, Authority, and Canon*, ed. D. A. Carson and John Woodbridge (Grand Rapids: Zondervan, 1986), 49–104, esp. 93–104.

8. Vanhoozer, *Is There a Meaning?*, 9 (original emphasis).

narratives, to the detriment of their literary meaning.[9] Theological conservatives reacted by defending the narratives' truth, to the similar detriment of their meaning. Frei became allergic to general theories of history, meaning, and truth, championing Christian particularity regarding biblical narratives.[10] It would be easy to treat Ricoeur's philosophical theorizing as Frei's polar opposite. Yet Vanhoozer noticed some shared concerns, even crucial resemblances between Frei and Ricoeur.[11] Both thinkers critiqued theologians for obscuring the literary particularity of revelation with abstract concepts. Frei applied "realistic narrative" to the biblical Gospels, with their stories rendering Jesus' identity as an agent—and definitively an agent of God, since without the climax of the resurrection the stories would render a different protagonist.[12] This attention to agency overlapped with Ricoeur's interest in how self-identity works out in literary time.[13]

A fourth commitment is manifest in Vanhoozer's approach to the previous three: authentically *evangelical reform*. He engaged diverse literary forms vis-à-vis the evangelical doctrines of Scripture and revelation; he promoted Christian humanism vis-à-vis Scripture's own forms and content; he pursued philosophical dialogue vis-à-vis the significance of narrative for biblical revelation. Such early Vanhoozer essays appeared in collections shaped by his Trinity Evangelical Divinity School colleagues. Like Frei, Vanhoozer applied H. Richard Niebuhr's (1894–1962) fivefold typology of approaches to Christ and culture to the relation between theology and philosophy.[14] Somewhat unlike Frei, who critiqued evangelical Carl F. H. Henry's (1913–2003) philosophical approach, Vanhoozer clearly retained Scripture's final authority to undergird theology's reign as queen of the sciences, and he sketched a "ministerial" role for philosophy as a servant of queen theology. Throughout these early essays, then, Vanhoozer defended fairly traditional evangelical positions, while pursuing creative reforms in light of contemporary challenges.

---

9. Hans W. Frei, *The Eclipse of Biblical Narrative: A Study in Eighteenth and Nineteenth Century Hermeneutics* (New Haven: Yale University Press, 1974).

10. See also Hans W. Frei, *Types of Christian Theology*, ed. George Hunsinger and William C. Placher (New Haven: Yale University Press, 1992).

11. Kevin J. Vanhoozer, *Biblical Narrative in the Philosophy of Paul Ricoeur: A Study in Hermeneutics and Theology* (Cambridge: Cambridge University Press, 1990), chs. 7–8.

12. Hans W. Frei, *The Identity of Jesus Christ: The Hermeneutical Bases of Dogmatic Theology* (reprint, Eugene, OR: Wipf & Stock, 1997), esp. ch. 13.

13. Paul Ricoeur, *Oneself as Another*, trans. Kathleen Blamey (Chicago: University of Chicago Press, 1992).

14. Compare Kevin J. Vanhoozer, "Christ and Concept: Doing Theology and the 'Ministry' of Philosophy," in *Doing Theology in Today's World: Essays in Honor of Kenneth S. Kantzer*, ed. John D. Woodbridge and Thomas Edward McComiskey (Grand Rapids: Zondervan, 1991), 99–146, with H. Richard Niebuhr, *Christ and Culture* (New York: Harper, 1956) and Frei's *Types of Christian Theology*.

Accordingly, a fifth commitment involved *hermeneutical fidelity to Scripture's divine and human discourse.* By appropriating speech-act philosophy, Vanhoozer sought to overcome an impasse between Scripture only "being" the Word of God, in a static sense tied to propositional revelation, and Scripture only "becoming" the Word of God, in a dynamic sense tied to personal encounter. Evangelicals could not accept a "postmodern" death of the author, yet they must account better for the privileges and responsibilities of cruciform readers. The Holy Spirit, whose inspiration gives meaning to the Bible's humanly authored words, superintends their understanding beyond the common grace that accompanies texts in general. Literary and philosophical concerns can foster a form of biblical theology that more faithfully reflects the conceptual unity and diversity in Scripture.

Is There a Meaning in This Text? brought this chapter of Vanhoozer's work to its culmination. The first section, "Undoing Interpretation: Authority, Allegory, Anarchy," sketches "postmodern" challenges to which the second section, "Redoing Interpretation: Agency, Action, Affect," responds. Contra undoing the author (ch. 2), Vanhoozer rehabilitates a concept of "intention" that is rooted in action theory: intentions make events the kinds of actions for which we hold agents responsible; thus, meaning involves the author's communicative action (ch. 5). Contra undoing the book (ch. 3), Vanhoozer rehabilitates a concept of "meaning" that is determinate while incorporating pluriform understanding: Communicative acts make literary knowledge possible (ch. 6). Contra undoing the reader (ch. 4), Vanhoozer rehabilitates the "morality" of literary knowledge: If we approach texts entirely in terms of ideology and violence, we ironically fail to love authors as "others" or readers as responsible agents who can deploy and develop interpretive virtue (ch. 7).

The theological foundations of this account are Trinitarian and Augustinian. Augustinianism undergirds Vanhoozer's Christian humanism—faith seeking understanding of not just biblical revelation but also, *thereby,* texts in general. Admittedly, some people object that the related treatment of "postmodern" thinkers and themes is too negative, summarily dismissing them for "undoing" despite Vanhoozer's extensive engagement with their texts. Others object that the move from biblical to general hermeneutics is theologically inappropriate, neglecting Scripture's distinctiveness.[15] Trinitarianism undergirds Vanhoozer's account of communicative action—suggesting an analogy between God the Father and the author's originating locution, God the Son and the text's embodied communicative action, and God the Spirit and the reader's responsive understanding. In each case, the latter, communicative reality participates in divine action that is economically appropriated to the former, a Person of the triune God.

This communicative analogy has an Augustinian pedigree, as in the triad of a Lover, the Beloved, and Love itself—not to mention a Barthian precursor, as in the triad of the Revealer, the Revealed, and Revealedness. For Vanhoozer, this

---

15. E.g., R. W. L. Moberly, "Review of Kevin J. Vanhoozer, *Is There a Meaning in This Text?,*" *ExpTim* 110, no. 5 (February 1999): 154, highlights God's distinctiveness as a speaker.

economically appropriated divine action grounds both special hermeneutics for the Spirit's speaking in the Scriptures and general hermeneutics for the Spirit's life-giving common grace. To some eyes, this communicative analogy appears to be forced by extra-theological commitments. Yet Vanhoozer's fifth early commitment—hermeneutical fidelity to Scripture's divine and human discourse—implies a twofold response. First, Scripture's divine discourse has a Trinitarian shape, so the communicative analogy originates in a theology of Word and Spirit rather than speech-act theory. Second, Scripture's human discourse is unique, but not so unique as to eliminate any analogy between the Bible and the reading of other books; on this account, we may find hermeneutical vestiges of the Trinity without falling into modalism or forfeiting Scripture's uniqueness as the Word of God.

In the tenth-anniversary edition of this seminal book, a new preface, "Of Marks and Landmarks," provides a few clarifications. To begin with general hermeneutics, the "backdrop" for engaging with postmodernity was Vanhoozer's eight-year teaching stint at the University of Edinburgh, including interaction with literature students, with literary theory in a biblical interpretation seminar, and with the Church of Scotland's internal debates. As for the "analogy of reading" between general and special hermeneutics, such theological analogies always involve even greater dissimilarities, about which Vanhoozer concedes that his book could have been clearer. As for his account of authorial intention vis-à-vis Hirsch's, Vanhoozer defends a form of determinate meaning in terms of authorial action, not a phenomenological account of consciousness. This focus on action can account more fully for interpreters and their communities.

The final sections of this preface address special hermeneutics in terms of the relation between philosophy and theology as well as a subsequent trajectory toward theological interpretation of Scripture. Vanhoozer deflects the charge of prioritizing speech-act theory over Trinitarian theology, while conceding that he could have been clearer about the modest, ministerial role played by philosophical concepts. Maintaining "an analogy of authorship" between the triune God and human beings, so that "we should begin our thinking about meaning and interpretation as Christians with the paradigm of the triune God in communicative action," Vanhoozer admits, "Much of my academic life subsequent to *Is There a Meaning?* has been spent doing penance for its sins of omission," including explorations of the unique nature of the Bible's authorship and the related doctrine of God.[16]

Thus, the five commitments sketched here reached their full preliminary shape in Vanhoozer's 1998 book: diverse literary forms as vehicles of truth; Christian humanism; dialogue with both major streams of philosophy; evangelical reform; and hermeneutical fidelity to Scripture's divine and human discourse. At the same time, the book anticipated the "hermeneutical theology" to which Vanhoozer initially aspired.[17] Other essays that were published or prepared concurrently

---

16. Vanhoozer, *Is There a Meaning?*, 6–7.
17. Ibid., 9.

signaled a transition toward more overtly theological writing that would draw preeminently upon Christian doctrine. Undoubtedly this trajectory reflects a natural career path for a young systematic theologian. Still, 1998 marks a watershed transition in which Vanhoozer's passion to understand "being biblical" came to fruition—only to foster becoming more overtly theological.

Becoming More Theological: Middle Dialogue with the Drama Motif (1998-2005)

As a transitional year, 1998 also involved returning to the faculty of Trinity Evangelical Divinity School. Vanhoozer returned from Edinburgh just as *Is There a Meaning in This Text?* arrived on bookstore shelves and he was profiled in *Christianity Today*.[18] Several works prepared at Edinburgh attained publication in these middle years, expressing the five commitments sketched above—including edited volumes on mission and epistemology, God's love, and postmodern theology. Some of these, along with the unifying motif of the collection *First Theology: God, Scripture, Hermeneutics*, manifest increasingly overt theological interests.

Joining the five early commitments in this middle period are three newly prominent themes. If the present account of Vanhoozer's development is correct, then these themes should be consistent with prior commitments yet more explicitly connected to biblical theology and Christian doctrine—which is what we find. Thus, covenant, discourse, and wisdom come into new prominence amid Vanhoozer's creative engagement with drama as a biblical and theological motif.

First, *covenant* undergirds a lengthy essay that recapitulated the approach of *Is There a Meaning in This Text?* for the "Scripture and Hermeneutics" seminar series led by Craig Bartholomew (1956–). The essay still addresses both general ("the covenant of discourse") and special ("the discourse of the covenant") hermeneutics theologically. The master concept, covenant, establishes "our properly *theological* responsibility to hear, and to understand, what God and neighbor are saying/doing when they address us."[19] Speech acts remain prominent, but the essay reflects an emerging focus on "Scripture acts." Its first thesis appeals to creation: "Language has a 'design plan' that is inherently covenantal."[20] This covenantal design is rooted, second, in Trinitarian theology. Theses follow regarding meaning, the literal sense, proper understanding of illocutionary acts, interpretation as a process of inference and ascription of authorial acts, and the necessity for properly perlocutionary

---

18. Tim Stafford, "The New Theologians," *Christianity Today* 43, no. 2 (February 8, 1999): 30–50. The others were Ellen Charry (1947–), Richard Hays (1948–), Miroslav Volf (1956–), and N. T. Wright (1948–).

19. Kevin J. Vanhoozer, "From Speech to Scripture Acts: The Covenant of Discourse and the Discourse of the Covenant," in *After Pentecost: Language and Biblical Interpretation*, ed. Craig Bartholomew, Colin Greene, and Karl Möller (Grand Rapids: Zondervan, 2001), 3.

20. Ibid., 10.

effects to unfold from genuine understanding. These third through seventh theses address general hermeneutics theologically, applying speech-act theory with more explicit covenantal overtones. The last three theses move to special hermeneutics, relating covenant to canon: Illocutionary acts also arise from the Scriptures as a whole, so that canon functions almost like a distinctive genre; the Spirit speaks in and through Scripture by rendering efficacious the illocutionary acts at all levels—including the canonical; and covenanting with humanity is the triune God's large-scale illocutionary act in Scripture.

Accordingly, second, *discourse* connects the covenant concept with earlier hermeneutical interests in literary genre, speech-act philosophy, and the like. As Vanhoozer extends Ricoeur's definition of discourse—someone saying something to someone about something—it becomes more communal. Beyond subject matter and authorial agency, reader responses and shared interests emerge. Soon Vanhoozer would appropriate drama as a motif that could develop the implications of the covenant and discourse themes for theological prolegomena—ultimately in the monograph that closed this middle period, *The Drama of Doctrine: A Canonical-Linguistic Approach to Christian Theology*. As we shall see, the "canonical-linguistic" language offers an appreciative alternative to the "cultural-linguistic" paradigm of another Yale theologian, George Lindbeck (1923–2018), yet overtones of interest in "discourse" are present too.

Third, *wisdom* specifies the aim, and to some degree an essential ingredient, of human participation in God's drama of redemption. Vanhoozer's dramatic approach incorporates both "scientific" and "sapiential" aspects. Canonical-linguistic theology is (1) "postpropositionalist," affirming the propositional along with literary, personal, and pluriform dimensions of divine revelation; (2) "postconservative," affirming the Bible's fully authoritative truth along with the imaginative importance of form for dialogic understanding; and (3) "postfoundationalist," affirming Scripture's final authority over the church along with the need for cognitive maps that mediate reality to us. These more objective or "scientific" aspects already incorporate the knowing subject, so theology must foster literary sensibility, biblical imagination, and churchly reflection. Hence, three additional aspects focus on theology as a form of *sapientia*—wisdom that is (4) "prosaic," attentive to cultural particularity beyond the mere translation of abstract "principles"; (5) "phronetic," attentive to virtue and improvisation within narrative frameworks; and (6) "prophetic," attentive to the ways in which resurrection hope confronts sinful accommodation to culture. *Phronēsis*, the Greek term for such practical wisdom, was already a hermeneutical aim in Vanhoozer's earlier work; here it becomes a theological ingredient as well.

Vanhoozer resists making churchly wisdom into a straightforward theological norm, contrasting his "canonical-linguistic" approach with Lindbeck's "cultural-linguistic" account of doctrine. Lindbeck characterized the church's classic approach as "cognitive-propositionalist": that is, doctrine involves truth claims conveying cognitive content. The modern liberal antithesis was "experiential-expressivist": that is, doctrine interprets expressions of human religious experience according to broader philosophical truth. The classic view tends to thwart ecumenical endeavors by insisting on identical formulations of doctrine; the liberal view tends to thwart ecclesial integrity by interpreting doctrine as God-talk without direct reference to God. Lindbeck proposed that a "cultural-linguistic" view could distinguish between first-order language use—say, prayer and praise—and second- or third-order grammatical regulation of that language, via doctrine. Ecumenical gains might arise from allowing different second-order doctrinal language while maintaining identifiably Christian first-order practice.[21]

Vanhoozer worries that Lindbeck's view supplants the canonically authoritative language of Scripture with the cultural-linguistic practice of present-day churches. Yet he welcomes appropriate contemporary interest in community, virtue, language use, and narrative. So he develops an account of doctrine as emerging from the Scriptures themselves in the drama of the church's faith seeking understanding. Here the concept of covenant becomes more specific within the framework of a drama, in which discourse and dialogue carry the action forward. Thus, Part One sketches the "Theodrama" in terms of (1) the gospel and the divine voice, (2) theology and the human voice, and (3) the resulting nature of doctrine. Part Two frames the nature and function of Scripture as "The Script," in which (4) the canon is the covenant document and (5) Scripture and tradition relate through performance interpretation over time, yet (6) tradition does not overwhelm the covenant document with ecclesial authority and (7) the Spirit is at work not only in terms of perlocutionary effects (Vanhoozer's earlier emphasis) but also in the apprehension of canonical practices themselves. Part Three treats the theologian as "The Dramaturge," (8) a critic or expert who advises the director (the pastor) and the performers (God's people) about the script's meaning. Here Vanhoozer lays out the (9) scientific and (10) sapiential aspects of his approach sketched above. Finally, Part Four addresses "The Performance": (11) how the actors learn their spiritual identity and vocation, (12) how the church functions as the acting company, and in conclusion how masterpiece (creedal), regional (confessional), and local (congregational) theater (theology) stage their scenes.

Drama weaves together Vanhoozer's covenant and discourse themes with a theological orientation toward wisdom—personal knowledge that is narratively shaped, communally learned, and imaginatively practiced. This dramatic orientation toward wisdom relates biblical interpretation and theology in a reciprocal rather than linear fashion; each may inform the other. As the Word of God, Scripture is theology's final authority, but its interpretation involves the drama of seeking wisdom in Jesus Christ by the Holy Spirit. This reciprocity of biblical interpretation and theology led Vanhoozer to serve as general editor for another book published in 2005, the *Dictionary for Theological Interpretation of the Bible* (*DTIB*). "Theological exegesis" and "theological hermeneutics" appeared occasionally in the work of earlier figures like Karl Barth (1886–1968), but such terminology rose to new prominence in the 1990s. Students of Childs's "canonical" approach to the OT, advocates of the church's interpretive virtues, and evangelical

---

21. George A. Lindbeck, *The Nature of Doctrine: Religion and Theology in a Postliberal Age* (Philadelphia: Westminster, 1984).

scholars of biblical theology all began to use such terminology and came to speak of "theological interpretation" of Scripture.[22] The award-winning *DTIB* codified a stage of this emerging conversation, which coincided with Vanhoozer's focus on becoming more theological and his corresponding emphasis upon wisdom.

The prime years of Vanhoozer's second sojourn at Trinity Evangelical Divinity School were very fruitful. While the abundant publications of those years were the natural harvest of a gifted and maturing scholar, this fruit also reflected a new season. Earlier literary, humanist, and philosophical seeds, with Vanhoozer's evangelical and biblical cultivation, deepened their roots. Drama offered a conceptual environment within which theological themes of covenant, discourse, and wisdom could flower into a holistic account of Scripture and Christian doctrine. Thus, in a third major season, Vanhoozer could focus on participating in the drama of doctrine primarily as a dogmatic theologian rather than a hermeneutical theorist.

Practicing Evangelical Exegesis: Ongoing Dialogue with Dogmatics (2005–)

This third phase of Vanhoozer's work proceeds from the 2005 publication of *The Drama of Doctrine* and the *DTIB*, takes initial shape in the major 2010 monograph *Remythologizing Theology*, and continues to the present. In our exhaustive bibliography of Vanhoozer's publications, his early commitments make ongoing appearances: (1) Literary, (2) cultural, and (3) philosophical interests persist in coedited volumes and articles. (4) Pursuit of a genuinely evangelical identity epitomizes numerous projects, from engaging Barth on Scripture through evaluating evangelical Trinitarianism and expounding biblical inerrancy all the way to elucidating programmatic proposals regarding Protestant biblical authority and evangelical theology. (5) Preoccupation with being biblical obviously persists as well, and in this vein some articles incorporate new attention to global theology. In addition to these early themes, the middle themes of covenant, discourse, and wisdom continue to appear, especially in expositions of a theodramatic model for doctrine. The new development launching this third phase was that model's application to a dogmatic locus, the doctrine of God, in *Remythologizing Theology: Divine Action, Passion, and Authorship*.[23] Like *Is There a Meaning in This Text?* and *The Drama of Doctrine*, *Remythologizing Theology* is a mammoth tome. While *Remythologizing* has broader theological implications, hermeneutically speaking, Vanhoozer extends the scope of two previous emphases that are worth highlighting.

---

22. See the relevant narrative and sources treated in Daniel J. Treier, "Theological Hermeneutics, Contemporary," in *DTIB*, 787–93; Treier, *Introducing Theological Interpretation of Scripture: Recovering a Christian Practice* (Grand Rapids: Baker Academic, 2008).

23. Cambridge Studies in Christian Doctrine (Cambridge: Cambridge University Press, 2010).

First, not only is dialogue a mode of theological practice that Vanhoozer distinctively embodies, *dialogism* is also a theoretical emphasis. The Russian literary thinker Mikhail Bakhtin (1895–1975) fascinated Vanhoozer, thanks to a dialogical approach inspired by novelist Fyodor Dostoevsky (1821–1881). Bakhtin reveled in "polyphony" with numerous drafts, notebooks, and an open-ended style.[24] Bakhtin was a creative, not naïve, realist: The real and represented worlds are "indissolubly tied up with each other and find themselves in continual mutual interaction."[25] Typical speech circumstances relate language and life in corresponding "genres"; understanding is "dialogic" because truth is eventful, "always develop[ing] *on the boundary between two consciousnesses, two subjects*."[26] Meaning must be actualized in time.[27] The union of art and life occurs in a participant's "answerability."[28]

Bakhtin fascinated Vanhoozer by blending respect for authorial agency with literary interest in how meaning stretches as a chain of events across "great time": Shakespeare's works transcend their epoch because of latent meaning that is dialogically actualized. The desired wholeness of meaning lies in the "utterance," consisting of a speaker saying "*everything* he wishes to say" and thus evoking "the responsive position of the *other* speaker."[29] Understanding the subject matter has the text as its "point of departure," moving backward to past contexts and forward in anticipation of future contexts.[30] Yet "without *one's own* questions one cannot creatively understand anything other or foreign (but, of course, the questions must be serious and sincere)."[31] Dostoevsky's novels are paradigmatic for Bakhtin's

---

24. Mikhail Bakhtin, *Problems of Dostoevsky's Poetics*, ed. and trans. Caryl Emerson, Theory and History of Literature 8 (Minneapolis: University of Minnesota, 1984), 39. See Barbara Green, *Bakhtin and Biblical Scholarship* (Atlanta: SBL, 2000), for an overview of initial secondary literature.

25. Mikhail Bakhtin, *The Dialogic Imagination*, ed. Michael Holmquist, trans. Caryl Emerson and Michael Holmquist (Austin: University of Texas, 1981), 253–4.

26. Mikhail Bakhtin, *Speech Genres and Other Late Essays*, trans. Vern W. McGee (Austin: University of Texas, 1986), 106 (emphasis original).

27. Mikhail Bakhtin, *Toward a Philosophy of the Act*, ed. Vadim Liapunov and Michael Holquist, trans. Vadim Liapunov (Austin: University of Texas, 1993), 58.

28. Mikhail Bakhtin, *Art and Answerability: Early Philosophical Essays*, ed. Michael Holmquist and Vadim Liapunov, trans. Vadim Liapunov and Kenneth Brostrom (Austin: University of Texas, 1990), 2.

29. Bakhtin, *Speech Genres*, 74, 82 (emphases original).

30. Ibid., 161–2.

31. Ibid., 7 (emphasis original). While Bakhtin's dialogism has obvious resonances with Gadamer's *Truth and Method*, 2nd rev. ed., trans. Joel Weinsheimer and Donald Marshall (New York: Crossroad, 1989)—which led theologians like David Tracy toward hermeneutics of "classic" texts—Bakhtin blames dialectic for stripping dialogue of particular voices and cramming concepts into a single abstract consciousness (*Speech Genres*, 147). Hence, Bakhtin favors no "fusion of horizons"; Gadamer's dialectic is somewhat dialogical, though, likewise emphasizing the importance of questions.

polyphony, having characters fully speak their minds without betraying authorial preferences, thus entering into genuine dialogue with various readers and perspectives.

Dialogue has been hermeneutically integral for Vanhoozer throughout his career. His classes are characterized by extensive outlines of dialogue partners, striving to describe their positions in ways they would approve if they were present. His publications are characteristically long because he extensively lays out problems and positions to which he responds. Given his voracious reading, a form of scholarly sprawl can ensue, but Vanhoozer approaches theology as a traditioned community of inquiry that requires doing justice to other voices. Bakhtin's dialogism supports this approach without subordinating authors' agency or texts' integrity to readers' subjectivity. For Scripture specifically, Bakhtin helps Vanhoozer to articulate both how we remain answerable to the divine Word in the human words and why we should appreciate creative understanding. As with speech-act theory from early on and drama theory later, Vanhoozer appropriates these literary and philosophical concepts on an ad hoc basis to help with articulating theological truth. Yet Reformed humanism leads Vanhoozer to appropriate such extrabiblical concepts dialogically, expecting that in particular cases they can enhance biblical understanding and cultural engagement.

Remythologizing Theology extends the scope of dialogism from hermeneutics to divine providence. Vanhoozer suggests that God created humans for dialogical understanding; hence, as much as possible, God acts communicatively—in, with, and under human understanding—rather than achieving desired ends immediately or strategically. Accordingly, *Remythologizing* explores authorship as a possible analogy for divine action. On this account God sovereignly creates, rules, and consummates the world's history with provision for human freedom and character development. Like other theological analogies, dialogic authorship would involve significant dissimilarities alongside the modest similarity in view. If the analogy is legitimate, though, then a "post-Barthian Thomism" ensues, in which classical theism can be retained but reworked in terms of communicative action. God's action is sometimes, but typically not, strategic; that is, God rarely produces unilateral effects in human agents apart from eliciting their understanding. In this way, Vanhoozer has more deeply integrated hermeneutics with theology proper.

A second emphasis for which Vanhoozer has recently expanded the hermeneutical scope is *Trinitarian theology*. This emphasis further manifests Vanhoozer's turn toward creative dialogue with dogmatic theology, appearing in a two-part essay on Scripture ("Triune Discourse") along with *Remythologizing Theology*. As with dialogue, Vanhoozer's appeal to Trinitarian theology is hardly brand new; near the end of his early period, he coordinated an Edinburgh conference and an edited volume on the subject. As we saw above, he integrated a Trinitarian analogy with speech-act categories in *Is There a Meaning in This Text?*. So, when this current Vanhoozer act puts Trinitarian theology closer to front and center, the new spotlight shines on some conflict in the plot along with quality lines.

Remythologizing Theology discusses supposed recoveries of Trinitarian theology as a prelude to addressing divine relationality. Vanhoozer criticizes recent "Trinitarian" trends that together count as "the new kenotic–perichoretic relational ontotheology": that is, against the classic "ontotheological" concept of a Most Perfect Being, many theologians today champion a God of passionate self-giving. Vanhoozer questions whether this concept of passionate self-giving is any less of a cultural imposition, or any more biblical, than the older Most Perfect Being. Instead, the Christian God in three persons is "one who lights and lives in love"; Father, Son, and Spirit are communicative agents in immanent relation. Yes, theirs is a dialogical agency that is expressed, *ad extra*, in granting creaturely freedom and relating passionately with those creatures. Yet this passion is analogical, more dissimilar than similar to its human analogue: God not only communes and communicates with but also ultimately authors humanity. Vanhoozer's hermeneutics and dogmatics come together: "biblical reasoning" as "the formal principle of divine communicative action," and "triune authorship" as its "material principle."

In "Triune Discourse" Vanhoozer articulates more fully his evangelical account of Scripture's formal authority and its material relationship to Trinitarian dogma. Initially highlighting the confessional requirements of the Evangelical Theological Society—the doctrine of the Trinity and the inerrancy of Scripture—Vanhoozer ponders their coherence, suggesting that "the ultimate authority for Christian faith, life and thought" is "*the triune God speaking in and through the Scriptures.*"[32] The formal principle is biblical truth, and the material principle is the triune God of the gospel. Modernity challenged both of these principles, and evangelical theologians have struggled to respond. Some have approached biblical inspiration in terms of divine providence, but potential deism lurks there. Others have approached biblical inspiration on analogy with the Incarnation, but the former involves personal presence and not personhood. Still others have approached biblical inspiration as an aspect of divine revelation, but perennial debates over propositional, personal, and poetic emphases loom, and the concept may not be distinctively Christian.

Vanhoozer evaluates Karl Barth's Trinitarian theology of the Word and Nicholas Wolterstorff's analytic philosophy of divine discourse as contemporary alternatives to traditional accounts. Appreciating Barth's focus on Jesus Christ as the Logos, nevertheless Vanhoozer finds that Barth's concept of divine freedom is overly allergic to identifying the human texts of the Bible as God's Word. Appreciating Wolterstorff's use of speech-act theory, nevertheless Vanhoozer finds that Wolterstorff's concept of divine discourse is overly generic—neglecting the special revelation of the triune God. Thus, Vanhoozer locates the gospel within "the economy of communication," with the triune God being in "communicative

---

32. "Triune Discourse: Theological Reflections on the Claim That God Speaks," in two parts in *Trinitarian Theology for the Church: Scripture, Community, Worship*, ed. Daniel J. Treier and David Lauber (Downers Grove: IVP Academic, 2009), 27.

action for communion" that unites revelation and redemption.³³ The Incarnation resists bifurcating divine transcendence and human language; God can and does speak, for God has spoken—quite personally. Scripture fits within the economy of communication as "a fully human phenomenon subject to the contingencies of language, culture and society" and requiring historical understanding, but also as "*God's communicative work, complete with divine ethos, logos and pathos: God-voiced, God-worded, God-breathed.*"³⁴ The logos of Scripture is covenantal; its ethos involves personal divine agency and presence; its pathos elicits human participation in response. Thus relating Scripture to the Incarnation without drawing an analogy between them, this Trinitarian framework enables providence, revelation, and sanctification to take their rightful places as complementary doctrines.

Scripture's ontology as the Word of the triune God not only establishes its truth but also entails that its rightful reading depends upon the Holy Spirit's illumination. In three theses, Vanhoozer summarizes the character of God's communicative action: (1) "*The Bible is a gracious word, a self-communicating work of triune love*"; (2) "*The Bible is a truthful word, a knowledge-giving work of triune light*"; and (3) "*The Bible is a sanctifying word, a freeing work of triune life.*"³⁵ In view of this divine love, light, and life, he concludes,

> Perhaps the most radical part of my thesis is its implicit claim (now explicit!) that any future evangelical doctrine of Scripture ought to include an account of the reader's interpretive agency and action ... The theological interpretation of Scripture is not an afterthought but lies at the heart of the action, for the interpreter is a co-worker in the field of triune communicative action.³⁶

Evangelical accounts of Scripture's truthfulness have sometimes failed to make their Trinitarian theology explicit and preeminent. They could foster biblical interpretation that failed to make the Holy Spirit's illumination explicit or the interpretive community's growth in virtue prominent. In addressing this problematic tendency, Vanhoozer has integrated his early commitments and middle themes into ongoing engagement with dogmatic theology. Hence, through his theodramatic turn he has extended the hermeneutical scope of his theological emphases upon dialogue and Trinitarian theology. Along the way, he has increasingly practiced the evangelical exegesis he preaches, variously undertaking theological interpretation of Scripture in many of his engagements with dogmatic theology.

Continuing the Dialogue

Like many of Vanhoozer's writings (though not as clever), this introduction to his *oeuvre* is growing lengthy. For brevity's sake, the title of this volume can suggest

---

33. Ibid., 51.
34. Ibid., 64 (emphasis original).
35. Ibid., 77 (emphases original).
36. Ibid., 78.

the key themes with which to conclude—and around which to organize ongoing dialogue with Vanhoozer's hermeneutics.

First, *the drama of evangelical hermeneutics*: Has Vanhoozer wisely improvised his part? The preceding narrative has highlighted his mediating role vis-à-vis major schools of philosophy, philosophy and theology (including general and special hermeneutics), America and the world (particularly the United Kingdom), evangelicals and non-evangelicals, Hirschian author-oriented and Ricoeurian text- or reader-oriented approaches (with historical and literary interests), and so forth. In the ensuing evangelical dialogue, some biblical scholars ask whether Vanhoozer's mediating approach clouds the hermeneutical primacy of authorial intention.

Most basically, some ask whether hermeneutical theory obscures what should instead be clarified in exegetical practice: Here theology *clouds* the actual interpretation of Scripture. In one sense, this concern is easily addressed, on two grounds. First, Vanhoozer's work contains numerous examples of exegetical engagement, both interpreting difficult texts and wrestling with biblical-theological tensions involving multiple texts. Second, the very essays raising this concern ironically contain no biblical exegesis. Rather than a severe flaw, this exegetical dearth may simply reflect unavoidable contingencies. Everyone operates with hermeneutical commitments that need to be periodically articulated and evaluated rather than merely transcended; biblical scholars write hermeneutical essays too. Such essays typically face word limits and other constraints that preclude exegetical detail.[37]

More subtly, others ask whether Vanhoozer's hermeneutical theorizing produces distinct exegetical practices or results: Here theology *does not change* the actual interpretation of Scripture. This concern surfaces in a revealing dialogue about going "beyond" the Bible to theology. Notably, Vanhoozer is the only theologian involved; the other interlocutors are biblical scholars. Indeed, the dialogue was initially prompted by a biblical scholar's essay and a response from Vanhoozer.[38]

---

37. For examples of (relatively sympathetic) biblical scholars critiquing theological interpretation of Scripture on this score, see Markus Bockmuehl, "Bible versus Theology: Is 'Theological Interpretation' the Answer?" *Nova et Vetera* 9, no. 1 (2011): 27–47; D. A. Carson, "Theological Interpretation of Scripture: Yes, But...," in *Theological Commentary: Evangelical Perspectives*, ed. R. Michael Allen (London: T&T Clark International, 2011), 187–207. For examples of Vanhoozer's exegetical engagement, see *Remythologizing*, ch. 1; and "Imprisoned or Free? Text, Status, and Theological Interpretation in the Master/Slave Discourse of *Philemon*," in *Reading Scripture with the Church: Toward a Hermeneutic for Theological Interpretation*, by A. K. M. Adam, Stephen E. Fowl, Kevin J. Vanhoozer, and Francis Watson (Grand Rapids: Baker Academic, 2006), 51–94.

38. Gary T. Meadors, ed., *Four Views on Moving Beyond the Bible to Theology*, Counterpoints (Grand Rapids: Zondervan, 2009). The concern arises especially from Walter C. Kaiser Jr. but lurks in others' responses. This dialogue responds to I. H. Marshall, *Beyond the Bible: Moving from Scripture to Theology* (Grand Rapids: Baker Academic, 2004), in which Vanhoozer contributes "Into the Great 'Beyond': A Theologian's Response to the Marshall Plan," 81–95.

Beyond this dialogue, the major evangelical hermeneutics textbooks, symposia, and the like have been generated by biblical scholars rather than theologians; even Thiselton, the aforementioned senior statesman (whose hermeneutics might not be author-oriented enough for Vanhoozer's critics), trained as a biblical scholar.[39] Furthermore, within a dialogue focused on moving from Bible to theology, the exegetical examples concern ethical rather than doctrinal appropriation of Scripture. To be sure, distinguishing between ethics and doctrine risks creating a false dichotomy, but the dialogue's focus on examples like women in ministry rather than Christology (for instance) is noteworthy.[40]

In this context, then, concern arises over the clarity of theology's hermeneutical contribution. Yet the purported lack of clarity reflects particular expectations. Scholarly genres and disciplinary incentives have not encouraged theologians to publish extensive biblical exegesis or biblical scholars to read theological works. Admittedly, Vanhoozer's hermeneutical contribution might have become more concrete if he had the opportunity to complete a projected theological commentary; his perspective may shift subtly as he interprets particular texts for dogmatic projects. Even so, biblical scholars frequently remain unaware of theological categories or theologians' existing exegesis,[41] while insisting upon how hermeneutics must relate to specific exegetical decisions probably reflects modern disciplinary expectations.

Simultaneously, many biblical scholars ask whether theological interests compete with the hermeneutical priority of human authorial intentions and original historical contexts: Here theology *corrupts* the actual interpretation of Scripture. Whereas theological hermeneutics might seek to articulate more concrete implications for exegetical practice, biblical scholars often worry about eisegesis when theological categories affect interpretive decisions. Here is genuine

---

39. E.g., Jeannine K. Brown, *Scripture as Communication: Introducing Biblical Hermeneutics* (Grand Rapids: Baker Academic, 2007); J. Scott Duvall and J. Daniel Hays, *Grasping God's Word: A Hands-On Approach to Reading, Interpreting, and Applying the Bible*, 3rd ed. (Grand Rapids: Zondervan, 2012); William W. Klein, Craig L. Blomberg, and Robert L. Hubbard Jr., *An Introduction to Biblical Interpretation*, 3rd ed. (Grand Rapids: Zondervan, 2017); the Scripture and Hermeneutics series edited by Craig Bartholomew (albeit with some coeditors of particular volumes coming from other disciplines).

40. For additional comments on this ethical versus doctrinal focus in evangelical hermeneutics, especially regarding the OT, see Daniel J. Treier, "The Freedom of God's Word: Toward an 'Evangelical' Dogmatics of Scripture," in *The Voice of God in the Text of Scripture: Explorations in Constructive Dogmatics*, ed. Oliver D. Crisp and Fred Sanders (Grand Rapids: Zondervan, 2016), 21–40.

41. E.g., to document lack of exegetical awareness regarding David Yeago's theological treatment of Philippians 2, see Daniel J. Treier, "Christology and Commentaries: Examining and Enhancing Theological Exegesis," in *On the Writing of New Testament Commentaries: Festschrift for Grant R. Osborne on the Occasion of His 70th Birthday*, ed. Stanley E. Porter and Eckhard J. Schnabel (Leiden: Brill, 2013), 299–316.

dramatic tension, with no immediate resolution likely.⁴² Accordingly, Vanhoozer's role in the dialogue has been twofold. On one hand, many biblical scholars have appreciated his defenses of doing justice to authors and maintaining evangelical commitments to biblical authority. In contexts where those commitments are unpopular, he has increased their scholarly prominence and theological viability. On the other hand, Vanhoozer has articulated those commitments with fresh nuance. In evangelical contexts, then, his work has surfaced lurking tensions over the relationship(s) between history and redemptive history, Scripture's human and divine authorship, historical and literary and conceptual analysis, and the like. For some, addressing such tensions theologically has risked clouding, corrupting, or at least not sufficiently changing exegetical practice. For many others, though, Vanhoozer's articulation of a robustly evangelical and Trinitarian framework has applied a healing balm to hermeneutical brokenness within biblical scholarship.

Second, then, *hearing and doing the Word* enhances the drama of evangelical hermeneutics by introducing theological voices that address performance interpretation.⁴³ Vanhoozer's early work introduced speech-act categories as a way of maintaining both propositional and personal aspects of revelation. His subsequent work embraced a modest form of performance interpretation. Maintaining Hirschian hermeneutics instead, some traditionalist evangelicals prioritize propositional revelation in a way that locates "hearing and doing" the Word as a separate step of "application" to undertake only after "interpretation" is initially complete. Other Wesleyan, Pentecostal, and Barthian evangelicals, as well as "postliberals," promote different priorities: Rather than determinate meaning, propositional revelation, and/or a sequential account of interpretation and application, they highlight the Holy Spirit's experiential illumination, Christian virtues, and/or the church's cultural-linguistic influence.⁴⁴ Thus, for some,

---

42. With his inimitable dialogism, Vanhoozer has articulated the mutual suspicions in play; see "Interpreting Scripture between the Rock of Biblical Studies and the Hard Place of Systematic Theology: The State of the Evangelical (dis)Union," in *Renewing the Evangelical Mission*, ed. Richard Lints (Grand Rapids: Eerdmans, 2013), 201–25.

43. We secretly proposed this book title in 2014. Vanhoozer confirmed its propriety by publishing *Hearers and Doers: A Pastor's Guide to Making Disciples through Scripture and Doctrine* (Bellingham: Lexham, 2019).

44. For a Wesleyan example, see Joel B. Green, *Seized by Truth: Reading the Bible as Scripture* (Nashville: Abingdon, 2007); for Pentecostal examples, see Kevin L. Spawn and Archie T. Wright, eds., *Spirit and Scripture: Exploring a Pneumatic Hermeneutic* (London: T&T Clark, 2012), and Craig S. Keener, *Spirit Hermeneutics: Reading Scripture in Light of Pentecost* (Grand Rapids: Eerdmans, 2016); for a "postliberal" example, see several works by Stephen E. Fowl (including an essay in *Reading Scripture with the Church*, mentioned above). For Vanhoozer's interaction with pneumatological hermeneutics, see "The Spirit of Light after the Age of Enlightenment: Reforming/Renewing Pneumatic Hermeneutics via the Economy of Illumination," in *Spirit of God: Christian Renewal in the Community of Faith*, ed. Jeffrey W. Barbeau and Beth Felker Jones (Downers Grove: IVP Academic, 2015), 149–67.

Vanhoozer's theodramatic model and special Trinitarian hermeneutics go either too far or not far enough. "Hearing and doing" raises questions about how the Spirit accompanies the Word and how God works in the church community as well as individual interpreters.

Vanhoozer's contributions in this dialogue, then, reflect Reformed as well as evangelical commitments: celebrating the unity of Word and Spirit, yet with the Spirit's hermeneutical ministry preeminently involving internal testimony concerning the Word. Vanhoozer's theodramatic model incorporates performance interpretation more readily than earlier evangelical accounts, yet more restrainedly than contemporary alternatives: hermeneutically connecting hearing with doing, yet clearly norming Christian doctrine with canonical judgments rather than communal practices or personal experience. Vanhoozer's Reformed commitments encourage deeper appreciation for doctrinal and liturgical traditions than other evangelical accounts of performance interpretation might embrace. At the same time, Vanhoozer's evangelical commitments encourage deeper dialogue with non-Reformed accounts than some Reformed accounts might engage.

In the end, Vanhoozer has played a paradigmatic role in the drama of evangelical hermeneutics. Postwar evangelicals began their return to academic life in biblical studies; the starting point, understandably, was *being biblical*. As other evangelicals made their way into history, philosophy, literature, and beyond, they encountered broader hermeneutical challenges and opportunities; the subsequent need, understandably, was *becoming more theological*. Once evangelicals became established in biblical scholarship and engaged with general hermeneutics, they needed a theological—more holistically and emphatically Trinitarian—account of special hermeneutics. Having provided such an account, Vanhoozer has turned toward *practicing evangelical exegesis*. Legions of biblical scholars have done so for over a generation, leaving a treasure trove for theologians to appropriate. Many of these exegetical diamonds in the rough need polishing for their theological beauty to shine clearly. Kevin Vanhoozer's vocation has been helping evangelicals to hear the Word more clearly and do the Word more faithfully, so that "all the treasures of wisdom and knowledge" hidden in Christ (Col. 2:3) may reflect the glory of God in human lives transformed by the gospel.

Part I

THE BIBLICAL SCRIPT

Chapter 1

WILL THE GOOF PREVAIL? THE HERMENEUTICS OF TEXTUAL CRITICISM

Iain Provan

The origins of this essay, which I am delighted to contribute to this well-deserved Festschrift for Kevin J. Vanhoozer, lie deep in the mists of time—that is, during the earliest years of our friendship. Having got to know Kevin first as a graduate student in Cambridge in the early 1980s, I became reacquainted with him in the early 1990s as a colleague at New College in the University of Edinburgh. In this context, one morning, a document crossed my desk. It was a new course proposal, originating with Kevin and forwarded to me as the person responsible for editing such documents and passing them on for publication. This particular proposal described a series of introductory lectures on Christian theology, and I was particularly struck by one of the titles: "Will the Goof Prevail? The Meaning of Divine Providence."

Now we all know how easy it is, working under pressure, to make typing mistakes. My first reaction, therefore, was to wonder whether I was encountering an example of textual corruption. Presumably Kevin had meant to write, "Will the Good Prevail?," and his finger had slipped sideways from the letter "d" to the letter "f" on his keyboard. On the other hand, the colleague whom we honor in the present volume is noted for his literary flair. He was already well known at New College for producing eye-catching titles of lectures. So my second thought was that perhaps this was not a mistake after all—that the wording was deliberate. The sentence made perfect sense as written. It indicated a lecture about the providence of God in overruling evil—taking account of all the "goofs" perpetrated by mortal beings and then working all things together for good.

I was trapped in a readerly dilemma. How could I tell the difference between textual corruption, on the one hand, and literary artistry, on the other? Which text should I prefer, as representing Kevin's communicative intent? For present purposes, the truth of the matter in this particular case is not important; the interested reader can get the answer straight from the author, if *he* even remembers now what his intention *was*. As Robert Browning is (apocryphally) reported once to have said to Elizabeth Barrett about one of his poems, "My dear, when I wrote that, only myself and God knew what it meant; now only God knows." The point of my reminiscence is this: that pausing for second thoughts in such matters is a good practice. I was right not simply to assume that textual corruption had taken place, but to consider the alternatives. It would have been quite improper and unwise simply to proceed to "repair" the text according to my first intuitions, without considering whether those intuitions were reliable. If I *had* "repaired" it, indeed, I might well have missed something important about what its author wanted to say.

This brings me directly to the subject of this essay, which concerns the necessary interface between textual and literary criticism in the study of the consonantal MT of the OT—the basis for both modern scholarly work on the biblical text and modern Protestant (and more recently Roman Catholic) translations of the same.[1] My proposal is simple, but (I believe) important. One frequently gets the impression from scholars carrying out text-critical work on the MT that they have failed to engage in sufficiently deep thought about initially puzzling texts before proposing emendations. They may well agree in principle with Ernst Würthwein's words concerning their discipline:

> Textual criticism, like any other science, cannot achieve convincing results if it does not hold to a methodology which is appropriate to its subject matter and defined by it. An arbitrary procedure which hastily and unnecessarily dismisses the traditional text and puts one's own ideas in its place leads to a subjective form of the text which is uncertain historically and can claim no theological relevance.[2]

Yet in practice scholars have often proceeded in precisely such a hasty and unnecessary manner, favoring emendations that permit texts to make immediate sense to the critics rather than pursuing with sufficient rigor the possible senses of texts as they stand, as pieces of ancient literary art. Evangelical scholars themselves have not always avoided this same tendency, despite holding a self-consciously "high view" of Scripture that one might have expected to generate pronounced hesitancy about emending the biblical text without very strong grounds for doing so. We should all commit to doing better, recognizing that critical methodology *does indeed* need to be "appropriate to its subject matter and defined by it"—which means that the excellent text critic requires always to be, at the same time, an accomplished literary critic.

Truth and Rhetoric

Undoubtedly one of the underlying causes of this tendency toward overly hasty emendation lies in the often-sharp distinction drawn in modernity between truth

---

1. It is quite right that it *should have been* so, and it is important that it *remains* so, both in scholarship in general and in Christian scholarship in particular; see Iain Provan, *The Reformation and the Right Reading of Scripture* (Waco: Baylor University Press, 2017), 27–279, 641–48.

2. Ernst Würthwein, *Der Text des Alten Testaments: Eine Einführung in die Biblia Hebraica*, 4th ed. (Stuttgart: Wurttembergische Bibelanstalt, 1973), 109 (my translation).

and rhetoric. Plato has in this respect (as in others) cast a long shadow over Western intellectual history, stressing as he did the importance of penetrating behind the appearance of things to their bedrock reality—moving beyond "opinion" about the world, founded on sense-perception, to the attainment of "knowledge" by way of rational contemplation. He took this position over against the Sophists of his own time, who tended toward relativism when it came to questions of truth and virtue, and who taught rhetoric simply as a set of skills to be deployed in pursuing the speaker's goals, whatever they might be. In the late nineteenth and early twentieth centuries, as many scholars became less interested in the transcendent and more so in the immanent, and as Plato's rationalism was replaced in much prevailing philosophy by a commitment to empirical inquiry, this same dichotomy between truth and rhetoric nevertheless reappeared in a certain kind of academic biblical scholarship. Bible readers driven by a conviction that the *rhetorically shaped text as we have it now* *obscures* the True and the Good thought it right and proper to disregard it in pursuit of the real history of Israel and of the Church, and of the Bible's real message. Rigorous scientific method, they believed, would get modern scholarship to its goal of secure knowledge, as it probed beneath the surface of the traditional but quite "unsatisfactory" text in pursuit of "the facts." In a scholarly world dominated by source and form criticism, it was *generally* true by the late 1930s that "on almost all sides the final form of the Hexateuch ha[d] come to be regarded as a starting-point barely worthy of discussion, from which the debate should move away as rapidly as possible in order to reach the real problems underlying it"; this remained the prevailing mood in many quarters for decades afterward, and with respect to much more of Scripture than the Hexateuch.[3] It is not surprising that in this context a significant amount of text-critical work gives the impression of viewing the MT only as a "starting-point barely worthy of discussion," quickly and without good reason departing from it in pursuit of a "better" text that might have existed earlier.

Meshech and Kedar

Let us take as our opening example Ps. 120:5 as it is treated in the third edition of *Biblia Hebraica*, published from 1929 to 1937 (hereafter *BH*³). The MT is straightforward: אוֹיָה־לִי כִּי־גַרְתִּי מֶשֶׁךְ שָׁכַנְתִּי עִם־אָהֳלֵי קֵדָר. We may translate in this way: "Woe is me, for I have sojourned in Meshech, I have dwelt among Kedar's tents." Despite the text's straightforwardness, however, *BH*³ suggests in its apparatus that we might wish to read MT's מֶשֶׁךְ (Meshech) instead as מַשָּׂא (Massa), introducing the name of one of Ishmael's sons from Gen. 25:14. Alternatively, *BH*³ proposes, we might read מֹשְׁךְ as a participle preceding a now-missing noun: קֶשֶׁת מֹשְׁכֵי, "those

---

3. Gerhard von Rad, "The Form-Critical Problem of the Hexateuch," in *The Problem of the Hexateuch and Other Essays*, trans. E. W. Trueman Dicken (New York: McGraw-Hill, 1966), 1–78 (1).

who draw the bow." The reference given in respect of this suggestion is Isa. 21:15, 17. In these other contexts from Genesis and Isaiah, the "Kedar" mentioned at the end of Ps. 120:5 is also found:

> These are the names of the sons of Ishmael, listed in the order of their birth: Nebaioth the firstborn of Ishmael, *Kedar*, Adbeel, Mibsam, Mishma, Dumah, *Massa*. (Gen. 25:13-14)

> They flee from the sword, from the drawn sword, from the bent bow and from the heat of battle. This is what the Lord says to me: "Within one year, as a servant bound by contract would count it, all the splendor of *Kedar* will come to an end. The survivors of the archers, the warriors of *Kedar*, will be few." (Isa. 21:15-17)

But why is the emendation of Psalm 120 on the basis of these other "Kedar texts" necessary at all? It is not because of the versional evidence, although that has something of a tendency toward interpreting משך as a verb referring to the idea of prolongation.[4] The editor of the *BH*[3] text evidently did not, however, think that this evidence was actually worth citing. The emendation appears to be premised rather on the view that "Meshech" is unexpected alongside Kedar. Why might someone think so? It is a matter of geography. Ancient Meshech was located in the area between the Black Sea and the Caspian Sea to Israel's far north, while Kedar was one of the nomadic tribes of the Arabian Peninsula to the far south, and we know that this kind of "contradiction" vexed some of our forebears. How could the psalm's author have lived in both places at the same time? Since he could not have done so, MT must be wrong, and it should be emended. Hermann Gunkel, for example, believed exactly this.[5] The way in which the MT can be dismissed in such biblical scholarship with virtually a wave of the hand is nicely illustrated by Charles Briggs's comment in the second volume of his ICC commentary on the Psalms, dating from 1907: "Meshek, referring to the Moschi of the region of the Black Sea, is a later conjecture of MT, and improbable."[6]

Of course, this approach begs a huge question: Granted that from a particular perspective the text is "unexpected," why should we not adjust our expectations rather than the text? What is to prevent us from reading the "geography" of Psalm 120 in terms *not* of the poet's physical abode(s) but of his spiritual landscape? Nothing in fact prevents us from doing this. The psalmist's enemies, from north to south, are no better than hostile barbarians, the text tells us, employing *merismus* to say so. This is a figure of speech whereby two extremes are mentioned as a way of including everything in between: "from a to b, from east to west, from the heavens to the world of the dead." The barbarians in question, we note, are of a particular kind: they are accomplished bowmen. This is already clear from

---

4. Charles A. Briggs, *The Book of Psalms*, ICC, vol. 2 (Edinburgh: T&T Clark, 1907), 445.
5. Hermann Gunkel, *Die Psalmen* (Gottingen: Vandenhoek und Ruprecht, 1926), 539.
6. Briggs, *Psalms*, 2:444.

the reference to Kedar, but Meshech too was renowned for this skill. It was the homeland of the Scythians, bowmen of proverbial cruelty (2 Macc. 4:47). The very noun מֶשֶׁךְ itself reminds us of the verb מָשַׁךְ, "to draw a bow." This is important, because there is a sustained play throughout the psalm on the idea of the *words* of the psalmist's enemies as *arrows*. We note the ambiguous root רמה in vv. 2 and 3, for example, which can refer both to deceit or treachery, particularly of words, and to the shooting of an arrow. Notice further the word שְׁנוּנִים, "sharp," used of arrows in v. 4, which is related to the Hebrew שֵׁן, "tooth," associated with the mouth whence the words are "fired." Here, then, are the psalmist's enemies about whom he laments in Psalm 120, with their "lying lips" and "deceitful tongue." They are like well-known bowmen in the psalmist's world who attach "burning coals of the broom bush" to their arrow tips in order to inflict maximum damage—the wood of the broom plant being particularly well suited to the manufacture of charcoal.

In short, textual criticism has not produced in this case anything approaching "convincing results," precisely because it has not held "to a methodology which is appropriate to its subject matter and defined by it." It is impossible to imagine that any scholar, having expended a modicum of effort in trying to understand Psalm 120 as a piece of rhetorical art, could possibly have arrived at the textual emendation proposed in *BH*³.[7]

The Wall of Daughter Zion

To its credit, the fourth edition in the *Biblia Hebraica* series recognizes that this is the case, and refrains from repeating *BH*³'s proposal about Ps. 120:5 in its own textual apparatus. This is *Biblia Hebraica Stuttgartensia* (hereafter *BHS*), which was first published in fascicles between 1968 and 1976, and then in its initial one-volume form in 1977, since when it has been the standard edition used in teaching and research in OT studies. Its refusal to repeat this particular proposal is consistent with its overall commitment to what Karl Elliger and Wilhelm Rudolph describe in the single volume's preface as "considerable restraint in conjectures and retranslations from the ancient versions"—one of the important differences that they identify between *BHS* and its precursor. They hope that this "will contribute to a greater usefulness for the work."[8]

---

7. Further evidence of artistic skill is the nice example of "step parallelism" in vv. 5-7, whereby the language of the second line of one verse is picked up in the first line of the next: "Woe to me that I dwell in Meshek, that I *live* among the tents of Kedar! Too long have I *lived* among those who hate *peace*. I am for *peace*; but when I speak, they are for war." The effect is to impress upon the reader that the thoughts of this lamenting psalmist in exile are already turning to the "steps" he will take on his ascent up to Jerusalem, the city of peace—the journey described in Psalm 121.

8. Karl Elliger and Willhelm Rudolph, eds., *Biblia Hebraica Stuttgartensia* (Stuttgart: Deutsche Bibelgesellschaft, 1977), xi–xii.

How considerable *is* this "restraint," though? For we encounter on numerous occasions in *BHS* precisely the same lack of literary sensitivity that we find in *BH*³, leading to the same kind of unjustifiable emendations. Consider, for example, Lam. 2:18a. Here the MT reads as follows: צעק לבם אל־אדני חומת בת־ציון. We may translate the first part thus: "Their heart [i.e., that of the inhabitants of Jerusalem] cries out to the Lord." The second part we may then render either as "the wall of daughter Zion" (referring to Yahweh), or "O wall of daughter Zion," beginning an address to the city that continues in the remainder of v. 18 and into v. 19.[9] If the second way is correct, then we have an example of synecdoche, wherein the wall stands for the city as a whole. The *BHS* note, however, proposes that we substantially depart from the MT at this point, and many modern commentators on the text, as well as many of the English translations, do offer a different reading. This is not because of the versional evidence, which cannot be construed as offering any substantially different text.[10] The main "problems" with the MT are rather twofold. First of all, "verse 18b through to v. 19c comprises a series of imperatives and prohibitions where Zion is addressed"; the first part of v. 18a does not fit this context.[11] The proposed emendation in *BHS* with respect to the opening verb of v. 18 is designed to address this problem, creating an imperative where none currently exists. Second, as to the latter part of the verse—as Rudolph himself argues in his commentary on Lamentations—one cannot make sense of חומת in its current position.[12] On the one hand, it is impossible in the context of the remainder of Lamentations 2 to understand "the wall of daughter Zion" as standing in apposition to Yahweh, especially since v. 8 has already *distinguished* Yahweh from this wall, which in that context he was determined to "tear down." On the other hand, the idea that the "physical" wall of daughter Zion is *addressed* in the latter part of v. 18a is also problematic; the wall cannot have been personified to such an extent that one could really have spoken of its tears, eyeball, heart, hands, and children (as vv. 18 and 19 go on to do). So we arrive at a "translation" like the one found in the RSV: "Cry aloud to the Lord! O daughter of Zion!" Here the opening verb is represented as an imperative, and the wall has simply disappeared.

These judgments, however, cannot withstand critical scrutiny. First, sudden changes in the form of address are a literary feature of the entire book of Lamentations, as the author now addresses the reader, now Zion, sometimes differentiating himself from his people, sometimes identifying himself with them. One simply has to take this broader literary context into account when dealing

---

9. For the latter, see Adele Berlin, *Lamentations*, Old Testament Library (Louisville: Westminster John Knox, 2002), 65, 75: "The wall that was earlier destroyed [2:8] is now bidden to cry out to God."

10. Iain Provan, *Lamentations*, NCB (London: Marshall Pickering, 1991), 75–76.

11. R. B. Salters, *Lamentations*, ICC (London: T&T Clark International, 2010), 170.

12. Wilhelm Rudolph, *Das Buch Ruth, Das Hohe Lied, Die Klagelieder, Kommentar zum Alten Testament* (Gütersloh: Gerd Mohn, 1962), 220.

with individual lines. Here in Lam. 2:18, it is perfectly possible to interpret at least the first part of the first line as a pause in the author's exhortation to Zion, drawing the reader into the situation as he does in so many other places in these poems. Second, Rudolph never actually makes clear why the wall of daughter Zion could not have been personified in the way that he describes: he simply takes it to be self-evident. It is, however, not self-evident at all. In any case, it is probably the better option of the two ways of reading the "wall" to understand it as a way of referring to Yahweh, as in Zech. 2:5 (MT 2:9): "I myself will be a wall of fire around [Jerusalem]." Contrary to what Rudolph suggests, third, to read the "wall" in this latter way is entirely unproblematic in the context of Lamentations 2. It makes perfect sense, since Yahweh has himself just destroyed Zion's natural wall in v. 8, that he should be described in v. 18 as her real wall—her only real security.

As in Ps. 120:5, then, there is no need, and no real justification, for emending the text of MT Lam. 2:18a. It is fine just as it is. It is rather startling, therefore, to find one recent commentator simply dismissing "arguments for the retention of the MT as original" as "unconvincing, doctrinaire and tortuous," even while *acknowledging* that "the Versions strongly support MT."[13]

At Every Street Corner

Another example of a dubious *BHS* note is found in Lam. 2:19, where the fourth line further describes the children mentioned in the third line, who "faint from hunger at every street corner" (NIV): העטופים ברעב בראש כל־חוצות. Here *BHS* advises the reader, without any further explanation, that the line is a later addition and not a part of the original text. Again, the versional evidence provides no justification at all for any emendation. What is brought to bear at this point is a set of convictions about "proper" meter and line length in Hebrew poetry. Most of the stanzas in Lamentations 1–2 have three lines; therefore, we must lose one line from Lam. 2:19. There is nothing more sophisticated going on here than that. *BHS* is on the whole more conservative than earlier scholars in its use of this criterion, but apparently it cannot resist appealing to the "rule" when it finds an "obvious" case. The problem is, of course: To whom it is obvious? The way that David Noel Freedman or Adele Berlin looks at Hebrew poetry, for example, enables them to cope with this four-line stanza quite comfortably.[14] Then again, the reader has already encountered another four-line stanza at Lam. 1:7, where there is just as little versional justification for any emendation. Are they *both* corrupt texts? *BHS* thinks that they are. But to misquote Oscar Wilde: To gain one extra line might be considered unfortunate, but to gain two looks like overzealousness. In terms of their literary form, both of the longer stanzas hang together very nicely. Indeed, removing Lam. 2:19d spoils the rather

---

13. Salter, *Lamentations*, 170.
14. David. N. Freedman, "Acrostics and Metrics in Hebrew Poetry," *Harvard Theological Review* 65 (1972): 367–92; Berlin, *Lamentations*, 2–7, 65.

clever double use of ראש in the first and fourth lines ("the beginning of the watches ... the head of every street"). Are we really to mutilate the verse merely on the grounds of speculation about how the ancient Hebrews might have used what we call meter and line length in their composition of poetry?

A Weaned Child beside Me

Before concluding with a *narrrative* example, let us return briefly to two further poetic examples from the Psalms. Consider first of all Ps. 131:2, where we find in the second part of the verse the following: כגמל עלי אמו כגמל עלי נפשי. "Like a weaned child at its mother's side," the psalmist tells us, "like a weaned child beside me is my soul." Here again the *BHS* editor, finding himself unhappy with the second כגמל עלי in the line, offers us an emendation that has no versional support. But what is actually wrong with the text? Perhaps the editor would agree with Briggs, when in his commentary he asserts that the second phrase "is essentially repetition without good reason for emphasis upon the simile, and leaves it unexplained."[15] One might well ask, however: what is repetition *with* good reason? And how much explanation does one need? I can think of various explanations as to why a poet might repeat a word or a phrase, not the least of which is to bring intensity to a line. There is certainly no shortage of other examples of this kind of phenomenon in the OT. Consider, for example, Lam. 1:16: עיני עיני ירדה מים. Lamenting, the poet tells us: "My eye, my eye flows with water." This sentence clearly has a pathos that is not shared by RSV's more straightforward "My eyes flow with tears" (cf. along the same lines NIV: "my eyes overflow with tears"). Predictably, *BHS* pronounces this line in Lamentations corrupt as well—although at least in this case we are dealing with manuscript and versional evidence that *might* be taken to support the emendation.[16] But generally there is a woodenness evident in this kind of reading that cannot do justice to biblical texts—a prosaic pedantry that fails even while engaging in literary criticism to appreciate the nature of the *literature*. One is reminded of something that John Barton once wrote concerning Alfred Lord Tennyson's poem *In Memoriam*: that we could not without great loss replace this poem with a sentence such as "I am extremely sorry that my friend has died."[17] Indeed so—but the loss is apparently lost on many textual critics.

Grass on the Housetops

All the poetic texts discussed thus far display what one might call normal grammar and syntax. What about texts that are by common consent corrupt *precisely in terms*

---

15. Briggs, *Psalms*, 2:467.
16. Yet note the cautionary remarks of Salter, *Lamentations*, 84–5.
17. John Barton, *Reading the Old Testament* (London: Darton, Longman and Todd, 1984), 159.

of grammar and syntax? Psalm 129:6 reads thus: יהיו כחציר גגות שקדמת שלף יבש. The line is generally translated more or less as follows: "Let them be like the grass on the housetops, which withers before it grows up" (RSV). Most commentators locate the real difficulty of this verse in its second half. קדמת is apparently the construct of the noun קדמה, "antiquity, former state," but only here in Psalm 129 is it used in the sense of "before." Moreover, שלף is elsewhere used to mean "to draw out, to draw off"—for example, to draw a sword or take off a sandal. Only here in Psalm 129 is it used of grass, and what it means in this context is said to be unclear. Textual corruption is, therefore, suspected, and *BHS* suggests emending שקדמת שלף to תשדף שקדם, "which the east wind scorches/blights." The final יבש is then redundant and must be deleted. There is no versional evidence in support of this move. It is simply a matter of making "better sense" of a text that is allegedly difficult to understand.

The first thing to be said about this proposal, however, is that it destroys what one could well argue is a deliberate play on words between the first word in v. 5 (יבשו) and the last word of v. 6 (יבש): "May they be turned back in shame ... may they be like grass that withers." The reader who is familiar with the Psalms' literary artistry will not readily surrender up יבש in v. 6, under such circumstances, as a mistake. We saw a similar play on words earlier, in Lam. 2:19, involving the use of ראש in the first and fourth lines ("the beginning of the watches ... the head of every street")—a wordplay also destroyed in that context by a proposed emendation.

It is unwise, second, to place great emphasis on the "unusual" employment of קדמה in this psalm. In the first place, the word only appears in three other places in the OT, which does not exactly provide much basis for any decisions about its "normal use." Moreover, we certainly know of other examples in biblical Hebrew where a noun in the construct state is followed by a perfect verb, particularly in cases where time determination is involved.[18] The use of קדמת in Psalm 129 may be unusual, but it cannot for that reason simply be dismissed as "incorrect."

Finally, what of שלף? Certainly this represents a bold use of language. But we must bear in mind that the *enemies* are being likened to grass in this verse. The idea, I believe, is that they wither like grass—they die—before they are able to draw their swords. The metaphor is helped, of course, by the fact that grass as it grows does in a sense "unsheath itself," as the new growth emerges from within the stalk. The language is unusual, but it is not beyond the bounds of poetic license to use it so. Indeed, I have a hunch that something even more sophisticated is going on in this verse, and that what makes the final link between the ideas of swords/grass and shame/withering is another play on words that is not explicitly expressed in the poem, but perhaps lies in the background: a play on the words חרב, "sword," and חרב, "to be dry, dried up." Given my own understanding of Hebrew poetry in general, and of the literary artistry of the Psalter and Lamentations in particular, such sophistication is hardly beyond the biblical authors' capabilities. Poetry is often highly allusive, and it requires a well-tuned ear to pick up its allusions.

---

18. See GKC §130d.

The Kingdom of Yaudi

In sum, *BHS* does not avoid "restraint in conjectures" with respect to the poetry of the MT quite as much as one might have expected based on what its preface claims about the volume. This lack of restraint is also generally evident in many commentaries and in some English translations. Hitherto we have not blamed any explicitly *evangelical* translation for egregious behavior along such lines. We must now make up for the omission by considering a narrative example—the strange case of the rendering of 2 Kgs 14:28 in the NIV translation of 1984.

The relevant part of the MT runs as follows: השיב את־דמשק ואת־חמת ליהודה בישראל. We may translate the line thus: "he [King Jeroboam II] recovered Damascus and Hamath for Judah in Israel." NIV, however, "translates" it in this way: "he recovered for Israel both Damascus and Hamath, which had belonged to Yaudi." That is to say, NIV proposes that Jeroboam recovered this territory for *Israel* and not *Judah*; indeed, NIV erases Judah from the verse entirely, substituting in its place "Yaudi." A footnote on the latter word then concedes that readers could just as well put "Judah" back into the text in place of "Yaudi," giving the impression that the decision represents something of a coin toss. What has happened here?

What appears to have occurred is this. The NIV translator has discovered that the MT does not make satisfactory sense to him. How are we to conceive of Judah in the south ever having possessed control of two Syrian cities far to her north? Even if Judah once did control them, why would King Jeroboam of northern Israel now restore these two cities to *Judah*, rather than taking them for himself? Further, what are we to make of the strange reference to "Judah in Israel"? The text is problematic. Could it perhaps *once* have made much better sense, but now have become corrupt? It is in pursuit of this "once upon a time" text that the reordering of the current version takes place. In the process Jeroboam of Israel is discovered, much more predictably, to have gained control of territory just to *his* north. This was territory that Israel had previously held, but that at some point (on this theory) had come under the control of Sam'al, a conveniently located Neo-Hittite city-state in the foothills of the Anti-Taurus Mountains in south-central Turkey, which is also referred to "in its indigenous inscriptions … as *Y'dy*."[19] In the later eighth century BC Sam'al became allied with the Assyrian emperor Tiglath-pileser III, and it was eventually absorbed into the Assyrian Empire. Some scholars have suggested that *Ia-u-da-a-a* in Assyrian texts can refer not only to Judah but also to Sam'al ("Yaudi"). Evidently the NIV translator was convinced that confusion of a similar kind between these two kingdoms must have occurred at some early point in the transmission of the Hebrew text of 2 Kgs 14:28. So he has read יהודה in this verse as "Yaudi" (Sam'al).

There are several significant problems with this move. In the first place, the general theory that cuneiform *Ia-u-da-a-a* can refer to Sam'al rather than Judah

---

19. Edward Lipiński, *Studies in Aramaic Inscriptions and Onomastics II*, Orientalia Lovaniensia Analecta 57 (Leuven: Peeters, 1994), 203 n. 2.

is unlikely to be correct. Sam'al is in fact consistently referred to in Assyrian records as *Sam'al(la)*, and as such it is consistently differentiated from *Ia-u-da-a-a*, "Judah"—as in the following inscription from Tiglath-pileser III's reign, dating from around 729 BC:

> [I received the tribute] of Kushtashpi, the Kummuhite ... *Panammuwa, the Sam'alite* ... Sanipu, Ammonite, Salamanu, Moabite, ... [Mi]tinti, the Ashkelonite, *Jehoahaz (Ahaz) the Judahite*.[20]

Even if the general theory were correct, second, there is not a scrap of actual textual evidence supporting the idea of a similar confusion in 2 Kgs 14:28. "Judah" (יהודה) clearly appears in the MT, and no manuscript or versional evidence suggests that the text ever said otherwise. Third, the proposed emendation destroys a clear literary connection between this verse and what precedes it in v. 22, where we read that King Azariah of Judah consolidated his father Amaziah's gains in Edom by reclaiming the port-city of Elath (2 Kgs 14:22; cf. 1 Kgs 9:26). He rebuilt the city and "restored it to Judah" (וישבה ליהודה)—the same vocabulary that is used in v. 28. In other words, there is a common theme of territory "restored to Judah" in these verses.

We are entirely in the realm of ungrounded speculation when it comes to NIV's "reading" here—speculation that not even the frequently speculative *BHS* endorses. It is not surprising, then, that NIV 2011 drops at least the proposal about "Yaudi," while still failing unfortunately to attend to the connection between vv. 22 and 28 in respect of Judah. That is, NIV persists in making Israel *rather than Judah* the beneficiary of the "recovery": "he recovered for Israel both Damascus and Hamath, which had belonged to Judah."

This is an altogether striking *narrative* example of a translator who fails to understand a text subsequently *bailing* on that text, creating a different one. Is it really impossible to come up with any plausible theory about the text as it stands, however? How might we understand the key words "Judah in Israel"? What might the authors of 1–2 Kings be seeking to communicate in this unusual usage?

Here we must remember that, from their perspective, the Davidic dynasty in Jerusalem remained the chosen dynasty even after the division of the kingdoms described in 1 Kings 12, and Judah remained the heartland of the kingdom that rightly belonged to that dynasty, which one day would be returned to it in its entirety (1 Kgs 11:39). Jeroboam II may appear to be a "second Solomon" in the text, in terms of the territory he rules in the north, renewing Israel's dominion over much of southern Syria in a manner analogous to the previous Solomonic dominion: He "restored the boundaries of Israel from Lebo Hamath to the Dead

---

20. William W. Hallo, ed., *The Context of Scripture*, 3 vols. (Leiden: Brill, 1997–2002), 2:289.

Sea" (2 Kgs 14:25).[21] However, by referring to Israel as "Judah in Israel" the authors remind the reader to whom this territory really belonged: the Davidic king.

Perhaps it was especially important to underline this message when Judah had just suffered a major reverse at Israel's hands and may have been effectively a vassal state of Israel for some time. It all began when Amaziah of Judah unwisely confronted Jeroboam's predecessor Jehoash, subsequently suffering an important defeat at Beth-shemesh, about twenty miles west of Jerusalem. Judah's capital was then attacked, and a section of its wall was broken down; plunder was removed from the temple and palace, and hostages were taken away to ensure future good behavior (14:8-14). The way in which the story is told implies that Amaziah may himself have been kept as one of the hostages, and Judah may have been effectively governed by Israel in the period after the battle. We are never told in Kings that Amaziah was *released* followed his capture (14:13), but we *are* informed in further unusual wording that he "lived" (rather than "reigned") for fifteen years after the death of Jehoash (14:17). Moreover, just before we read of Amaziah's demise, we find the concluding regnal formulae for *Jehoash* repeated (14:15-16; cf. 13:12-13), right in the midst of *Amaziah's* story.

Then again, we must note that this *first* account in Kings of the foreign capture of Jerusalem is very reminiscent of the *second from last* (24:8-17), where we also read of a king (Jehoiachin) being taken captive with hostages, and of both temple and palace being plundered. That king went on "living" (Hebrew היח, as in 14:17) in Babylon for many years afterwards—still called "king" by the authors of Kings, even though the king of Babylon effectively ruled over Judah (25:27-30). Precisely in that context, the deportation of Judean kings, we begin to find the regnal years of a *foreign* king being cited (the king of Babylon: 24:12; 25:8)—the ruler who was really in control.

Adding all this together, we are justified in reading 2 Kgs 14:13-20 as presenting the king of *Israel* as the effective ruler of *Judah* in the period after the battle of Beth-shemesh, both at the point of Jehoash's death and for at least fifteen years thereafter, during the reign of his son Jeroboam II. By the end of that period, at least, we know that Amaziah had returned to Jerusalem, since the biblical texts tell us that he fell victim to a conspiracy there and was subsequently assassinated (14:19; 2 Chron. 25:27).[22]

All this is to say that the unusual phrase "Judah in Israel" may be directly connected with the politics of this time period in Israel—with claims and

---

21. In 1 Kgs 8:65 the phrase "from Lebo Hamath to the Wadi of Egypt" seems to be intended as a designation of the whole Solomonic empire, analogous to the phrases "from the River to the land of Philistines, as far as the border of Egypt" and "from Tiphsah to Gaza" in 1 Kgs 4:21, 24 (contrast the designation of Israel proper in 4:25—"from Dan to Beesheba"). Iain Provan, V. Philips Long, and Tremper Longman III, *A Biblical History of Israel*, 2nd ed. (Louisville: Westminster John Knox, 2015), 362 n. 71.

22. It seems likely that in *Judah* Amaziah's infant son Azariah was already regarded as "king" during his father's exile. This would help to explain the very large total of Azariah's

counterclaims about sovereignty. Even if it is not, however, there is still no excuse for setting it aside and preferring a pure invention. The right thing to do with a puzzling text like this is to translate it as it stands, whether or not we can solve the puzzle—waiting for further information to emerge that might help us in the future.

Conclusion

In sum, not every modern textual critic has followed "a methodology which is appropriate to [the discipline's] subject matter and defined by it," if we mean by this Hebrew poetry and narrative that artistically and rhetorically are shaped with great care. The consequence has *indeed* been that all too often a "subjective form of the text" has emerged to replace the real one. If we wish to apprehend more consistently what OT Scripture has to say in its rhetorical artistry, we need more patience, and indeed more self-doubt, than some of our forebears have been capable of. We require self-doubt in respect of our convictions concerning what ancient texts "ought" to look like, and we need patience in wrestling with them longer than we might prefer in the form in which we actually find them. Pausing for a second thought along these lines, as we participate in "the drama of evangelical hermeneutics," offers considerable hope of continuing significant advances in our understanding both of the technique and method of our Hebrew authors, and of the texts that they have produced. This is crucially important to "hearing and doing the Word" (the title of our volume), from the point of view that both Kevin and I share concerning the nature of right biblical hermeneutics. We insist that the divine address through Scripture is heard in and through illocutionary acts performed by authors working in various contexts—linguistic, cultural, canonical, and so on. If we misunderstand the illocutionary act, we shall miss the meaning of the communication. I only wish to point out in this essay some of the ways in which it is already possible to miss it at the level of textual criticism, well before we proceed to other kinds.

---

regnal years in 2 Kgs 15:2 (fifty-two); it includes the sixteen years from the battle of Beth-shemesh to the death of his father. Second Kings, when noting that Azariah himself in the later period of his reign was relieved of responsibility for government even though he was still alive, speaks of this event in a manner that may imply that he also was regarded as effectively dead (2 Kgs 15:5). "Dead" men do not, strictly speaking, occupy regnal years. See Iain Provan, *1 & 2 Kings*, Understanding the Bible (Grand Rapids: Baker, 1995), 240. This interpretation helps to explain the curious wording of 2 Kgs 14:22, where Azariah is reported as consolidating Amaziah's gains in Edom at some point after Jehoash's death (as it seems from the Hebrew; ibid., 237).

Chapter 2

READING BETWEEN THE LINES: ON DISCERNING THE IMPLICIT MESSAGES OF SCRIPTURE

V. Philips Long

Kevin J. Vanhoozer and I became friends long ago and far away. The time was the early 1980s, and the place was Cambridge, England, where we were both pursuing PhDs at the University. I learned much from Kevin in those formative years, and not just in our occasional French and German reading sessions, where we respectively corrected one another's pronunciation. The fields of biblical studies and theology were in those days in a state of ferment. The hegemony of traditional methods was being challenged by works advocating more synchronic literary approaches to the Bible. Robert Alter's now well-known *The Art of Biblical Narrative*[1] was just bursting onto the scene, followed a couple of years later by Adele Berlin's *Poetics and Interpretation of Biblical Narrative*,[2] and in 1985 by Meir Sternberg's landmark tome *The Poetics of Biblical Narrative: Ideological Literature and the Drama of Reading*.[3] A particularly timely work for the development of my own thinking was Kevin's "The Semantics of Biblical Literature: Truth and Scripture's Diverse Literary Forms."[4] In the decades following that early essay, Kevin enriched the field of biblical interpretation with numerous publications that will doubtless be listed elsewhere in the present volume. Given what I have learned from Kevin over the years, both in personal conversation and through his more public contributions, I am grateful to have the opportunity to write an essay in his honour.

---

1. Robert Alter, *The Art of Biblical Narrative* (New York: Basic, 1981).
2. Adele Berlin, *Poetics and Interpretation of Biblical Narrative* (Sheffield: Almond, 1983).
3. Meir Sternberg, *The Poetics of Biblical Narrative: Ideological Literature and the Drama of Reading* (Bloomington: Indiana University Press, 1985).
4. Kevin J. Vanhoozer, "The Semantics of Biblical Literature: Truth and Scripture's Diverse Literary Forms," in *Hermeneutics, Authority, and Canon*, ed. D. A. Carson and J. D. Woodbridge (Grand Rapids: Zondervan, 1986), 49–104.

Early Reactions to the "Newer Literary Approaches"

As with all new approaches, the synchronic readings advocated by the authors mentioned above initially met with mixed reviews. For some, the sensibleness of focusing attention on the texts at hand, rather than on how these texts might or might not have come to be, seemed obvious. After all, for many decades biblical texts had been analyzed into so many pieces that they seemed hardly able to "speak" anymore. In such a context, renewed interest in the extant form of biblical texts was welcomed by many. Reading them in their final form allowed the texts to regain their "voice." As they did so, they regained their ability to address readers on a variety of levels.

But not all were so sanguine about the new approaches. Despite the apparent common sense of reading texts in their extant form, some scholars worried that the newer literary approaches might reduce the biblical texts to little more than literature, unhinged from history or even theology. It is now clear that these worries were at least partly justified. In the decades following the 1980s, some scholars began to assume the biblical texts to be just literature, pure and simple, with little or nothing to say beyond their fictive worlds. Such reductionist readings, however, are neither necessary nor warranted by the evidence. Various other scholars, from the beginning, sought to improve their literary competence in reading ancient texts precisely because they were interested in what these texts might offer with respect to historical and, in the case of the Bible, theological concerns.

Among the ways in which taking a more literary approach promised to improve Bible reading was in its recognition that sophisticated literature—a label justly applied to much of the Bible—requires readers to notice not only what a text states *explicitly* but also what it communicates *implicitly*. In other words, the newer literary approaches reminded readers that they must not only read the lines of the text but also read *between the lines*. Sternberg put it this way: "If the biblical truth is explicit, then the whole truth is implicit; and the more you bring to this art of implication, the more secrets and prizes it yields."[5] This makes excellent sense, as a few examples from the book of Samuel can illustrate. Consider the narrator's mention of Eli's weight and dim-sightedness, Absalom's prized head of hair, Saul's height and handsomeness, and so forth. None of these physical details constitutes an explicit statement about Eli's self-indulgence and spiritual dim-sightedness, or about Absalom's vanity and ambition, or about Saul's external prowess but internal poverty. But each detail typifies the character in such a way that the attentive reader perceives the larger point.

The call of the newer literary approaches to pay attention to the implicit messages of texts—to *read between the lines*—is apt. But here is the rub. Attempts to read between the lines can go astray, particularly when interpreters are insufficiently constrained by the lines themselves. In the opinion of the present writer, some recent interpretations that have sought to read between the lines have, in fact, read

---

5. Sternberg, *Poetics*, 52.

outside the lines—that is, outside the boundary lines established by what the text explicitly says. The burden of the present essay is to show how this can happen and to suggest how such misreadings might be avoided.

When "Reading between the Lines" Becomes a Liability: Some Examples

Having just completed a commentary on 1 and 2 Samuel,[6] I am particularly sensitive to what appear to me to be inadequate treatments of key characters in the book. In my judgment, Samuel, Saul, David, and ultimately Yahweh are each mischaracterized in a range of recent writings.

Let's take Samuel as a first example. What does the text explicitly tell us about Samuel? In 1 Sam. 3:19-20, Samuel is described as "a trustworthy prophet of the Yahweh," recognized as such throughout the land "from Dan to Beersheba."[7] In the dark days of Eli's priesthood, when the word of Yahweh was rare, Yahweh chose to do a new thing through Samuel and, as he grew, Yahweh let "none of his words fall to the ground." This was not a one-time occurrence, as 3:21 makes clear: "Yahweh continued to appear at Shiloh, for Yahweh revealed himself to Samuel at Shiloh by the word of Yahweh." In short, Yahweh established Samuel as a "trustworthy prophet" and continued to engage with him as such on an ongoing basis.

Despite these explicit statements about Samuel's auspicious beginning and his standing as a reliable prophet of Yahweh, some recent writers present the mature Samuel rather differently: a "resentful, crotchety old man"[8]; "an implacable, irascible man, and often a self-interested one as well," "proud, imperious, histrionic," who will be content with nothing less than reducing Saul to "a puppet king"[9]; a "petulant," "peevish" prophet who "plays a daring, brutal game with Saul's faith, Saul's career, and eventually Saul's sanity."[10] All this prompts the reader, according to Walter Brueggemann, to wonder "about Samuel (who appears to be unprincipled) and about Yahweh."[11]

If Samuel is viewed rather negatively in some recent writings, Saul, by contrast, is viewed more positively than has traditionally been the case. As Brueggemann's

---

6. V. Philips Long, *1 and 2 Samuel*, TOTC (Downers Grove: IVP Academic, 2020).

7. Unless otherwise indicated, all translations of biblical or other foreign language texts cited in this essay are my own.

8. J. Richard Middleton, "Samuel Agonistes: A Conflicted Prophet's Resistance to God and Contribution to the Failure of Israel's First King," in *Prophets, Prophecy, and Ancient Israelite Historiography*, ed. M. J. Boda and L. M. W. Beal (Winona Lake: Eisenbrauns, 2013), 88.

9. Robert Alter, *The David Story: A Translation and Commentary of 1 and 2 Samuel* (New York: Norton, 1999), xv–xvi.

10. Walter Brueggemann, *First and Second Samuel*, Interpretation (Louisville: John Knox, 1990), 101.

11. Ibid.

remarks above indicate, Saul is now regarded by some as mainly a victim. There is no denying, of course, that Saul in some sense comes across as a victim. When he sets out in 1 Samuel 9 in response to his father's directive, Saul is in search of lost livestock, not power, and certainly not a kingdom. Nevertheless, it is he whom Yahweh chooses to be Israel's first king in response—we should note—to the Israelite elders' insistent request for "a king to lead us [or "judge us"] such as all the other nations have" (1 Sam. 8:5). Yahweh has Samuel anoint Saul to fill that role (8:19-21; 9:16). Soon enough, however, in narrative time at least, Yahweh rejects Saul for what to many appear to be trivial offences (1 Samuel 13). Brueggemann remarks that when Saul speaks to Samuel in 13:11-12, "Saul could hardly be more deferential."[12] In his influential book *The Fate of King Saul*, David Gunn presents Saul as very much the victim in the biblical story and does not shrink back from assigning the role of villain to Yahweh himself. He writes:

> At the level of the reader's "overview," questions about the moral basis of Yahweh's actions are inescapable. If we are to condemn Saul for his jealous persecution of David, how much more is Yahweh to be condemned for his jealous persecution of Saul! And the question is one that lies before us in the story not only in our puzzlement (not to speak of Saul's) at the judgement scenes but repeatedly, from then on, in the striking disparity of treatment between Saul and David. Yahweh manipulates Saul mercilessly, and he does so for what, on most men's terms, must count as less than honourable motives. He is insulted, feels jealous, is anxious to justify himself. It is tempting to say that this is the human face of God—but to say that is perhaps to denigrate man, and that is not something this Old Testament story does; rather we might say that here we see the dark side of God.[13]

From this quotation, one can quickly see that how one understands the character of Samuel and of Saul directly influences how one understands the character of Yahweh. Saul and his story are complex, to be sure, and it is little wonder that readers have long found the fate of King Saul to be perplexing. But do recent attempts to read Saul as victim, with Yahweh and Samuel as villains, do full justice to the text of 1 Samuel? We shall return to this question in due course, but first a word about David.

If both Samuel and Saul are today being read rather differently than in the past, it comes as no surprise that David is as well. Some earlier readings assumed a pervasively positive view of David. They acknowledged, of course, the glaring exception in 2 Samuel 11 involving David's sexual exploitation of Bathsheba, his murder of her husband Uriah, and his vain attempt to cover up his crimes. But apart from this major lapse, they viewed David as almost too good to be true. Some more recent interpreters see things differently. Both Steven McKenzie[14] and

---

12. Ibid., 99.
13. David M. Gunn, *The Fate of King Saul: An Interpretation of a Biblical Story*, JSOTSup 14 (Sheffield: JSOT, 1980), 128–9.
14. Steven L. McKenzie, *King David: A Biography* (Oxford: Oxford University Press, 2000), 32–34.

Baruch Halpern,[15] for instance, describe David as not just a murderer (which the text readily admits) but as a "serial killer," responsible for many deaths that the book of Samuel ascribes to others.[16] Granted, some of David's own contemporaries despised him as a "man of blood" (Shimei, for instance, in 2 Samuel 16). But the biblical writers themselves take a much more qualified view. They portray David as a deeply flawed individual—and not just in the Bathsheba-Uriah affair—but, even so, a man of genuine faith in Yahweh.

Halpern himself is too good a reader not to recognize the brilliance of the biblical depiction: "1 and 2 Samuel furnish a circumstantial character history whose complexity makes even the most sophisticated ancient biography seem like a cartoon by comparison." With justifiable hyperbole, Halpern continues, "David, in a word, is human, fully, four-dimensionally, recognizably human. He grows, he learns, he travails, he triumphs, and he suffers immeasurable tragedy and loss. He is the first human being in world literature."[17] In short, "The narrative of David's career is one of the great accomplishments of Israel's culture. … From youth to dotage, it follows David as a human being, never fearing to underscore shortcomings, nor to stress peculiarities."[18] But if this is Halpern's view, how can he write in the preface to his book that "the biblical version, in the books of Samuel, presents a man who never did exist, a ruler altogether too good to be true"?[19] Is Halpern perhaps confusing the David of popular imagination with the David of the biblical texts? In the popular imagination, David may at times appear too good to be true, but not in "the biblical version"! Recall Halpern's "never fearing to underscore shortcomings." Halpern's apparent inconsistency at this point leads to a characterization of David (and of the biblical texts) that misses the mark. It is precisely the biblical version in the books of Samuel that presents not only David's strengths but also his very evident weaknesses.

How is it, then, that such astute readers can get things wrong? To this question we now turn.

Direction and Indirection in Biblical Narratives

Everyone must grant that the books of Samuel do not *explicitly* describe Samuel as crotchety, peevish, or unprincipled. Nor do they explicitly say that Saul was a victim of Yahweh and his messenger. Nor do they explicitly charge David with being a serial killer. All these characterizations come from interpreters seeking—we

---

15. Baruch Halpern, *David's Secret Demons: Messiah, Murderer, Traitor, King* (Grand Rapids: Eerdmans, 2001), 73–103.

16. For my description and evaluation of the "serial killer" view, see Iain Provan, V. Philips Long, and Tremper Longman III, *A Biblical History of Israel*, 2nd ed. (Louisville: Westminster John Knox, 2015), 292.

17. Halpern, *David's Secret Demons*, 5 and 6, respectively.

18. Ibid., 53.

19. Ibid., xvi.

must assume—to "read between the lines." All of these characterizations arise only by inference, not from explicit statements in the texts. In principle, there is nothing wrong with seeking out Scripture's implicit messages. Indeed, as we have already observed, inferential "reading between the lines" is what biblical narratives require, if they are to be read for all they are worth. We have observed that biblical narrators often portray their characters through artful indirection. We have agreed with Sternberg[20] that we must attend to the "art of implication" that pervades sophisticated narratives such as those in the book of Samuel. But this is only part of what Sternberg says. Biblical truth, Sternberg insists, is established by *both* explicit and implicit means—perhaps, we could say, by both direction and indirection. The problem in some recent readings of the book of Samuel and its characters is that in seeking to "read between the lines" interpreters end up "reading outside the lines"—that is, outside what the text makes explicit. Seeking to be attentive to indirection, they end up reading the text in the wrong direction.

One brief example may suffice for now. In his essay entitled "Samuel Agonistes: A Conflicted Prophet's Resistance to God and Contribution to the Failure of Israel's First King," Richard Middleton lays the blame for Saul's failure and ultimate rejection in 1 Samuel 13–15 at the feet—or more precisely in the mouth—of Samuel. He summarizes his reading as follows:

> I have argued that God did not initiate a decision to find someone to replace Saul (chap. 13); the reference to someone after God's heart was an extemporaneous utterance by the prophet, made in anger. Nor did God give a command through Samuel for Saul to destroy the Amalekites (chap. 15); that was Samuel's own invention. However, God clearly ends up backing Samuel on both counts.[21]

All but the last sentence of this summary rest on Middleton's attempt to "read between the lines" of 1 Samuel 13–15. The final sentence, though, rests on more explicit indications within the texts. Taken together, these two perspectives are in significant tension. Middleton seeks to resolve the tension of Yahweh's "backing Samuel" (with respect to pronouncements Samuel purportedly made in fits of personal anger) by simply citing the statement in 1 Sam. 3:19 that Yahweh "let none of his [Samuel's] words fall to the ground." Middleton's view seems to be that, having early committed himself to Samuel, Yahweh has no choice but to endorse Samuel's words, whether divinely authorized or not. Middleton goes on to suggest that Yahweh learned from his mistake:

> I propose that YHWH came to the realization through the experience with Samuel that one resentful, crotchety old man (who has the status of an authoritative prophet, whose word God is committed to supporting) can undermine God's

---

20. Sternberg, *Poetics*, 52.
21. Middleton, "Samuel Agonistes," 87.

own long-term purposes for the covenant people. So God decides to put his relationship with the next king on a different (unconditional) footing.[22]

Overall, Middleton's proposed reading of Samuel's character and his role in the rejection of Saul, though clever, seems strained and carries little conviction, particularly if a better reading presents itself whereby what the text presents *implicitly* is in line with what it presents *explicitly*. My contention is that just such a reading is possible and that it must begin with what Middleton in a 2018 SBL presentation referred to as the "doozy of all contradictions" in the book of Samuel. Only when the supposed contradiction between 1 Sam. 10:7 and 10:8 is sorted out will we be in a position to understand Samuel's interaction with Saul in 1 Samuel 13.

On the Seeming Contradiction between Verses 7 and 8 of 1 Samuel 10

Motivations for the readings introduced above doubtless vary from scholar to scholar. But whatever the *motivations*, it appears that the *justifications* of many against-the-grain readings rest in one way or another on a misunderstanding of 1 Sam. 10:7-8. These two verses recount Samuel's pronouncement of Yahweh's charge to Saul at the time of his anointing. It is not surprising that contemporary interpreters find them troubling, for they have long been regarded as problematical. In v. 7, Samuel appears to give Saul divine authorization to do whatever should come his way, while in v. 8 Samuel charges him to go to Gilgal and wait for Samuel to arrive in order that he might offer sacrifices and tell Saul what to do. What v. 7 authorizes, v. 8 seems to take away—or at least this is the impression that many interpreters get. Older commentators sometimes conjectured that v. 7 was the more original command, while v. 8 was a "prophetic correction" arising from a concern among later prophetic circles that the newly appointed leader not be given *carte blanche*. More recent commentators who are less inclined to seek a diachronic solution simply assume that Samuel is being obtuse and unfair to Saul by uttering confusing and contradictory instructions.

Both of these understandings—the prophetic correction view and the perverse prophet view—are, I believe, mistaken and unnecessary. Ironically, both arise precisely from a failure to read appropriately "between the lines" in the story of Saul's anointing. I have worked out my own understanding of this crucial episode in several published studies,[23] so I shall rehearse here only a few key points for the sake of readers unfamiliar with those earlier studies.

---

22. Ibid., 88–9.
23. E.g., V. Philips Long, *The Reign and Rejection of King Saul: A Case for Literary and Theological Coherence*, SBLDS 118 (Atlanta: Scholars, 1989); Long, "How Did Saul Become King? Literary Reading and Historical Reconstruction," in *Faith, Tradition and History*, ed. A. R. Millard, J. K. Hoffmeier, and D. W. Baker (Winona Lake: Eisenbrauns, 1994), 271–84;

My contention is that vv. 7 and 8 are not contradictory but together constitute a *two-part first charge* to Saul, given at the time of his anointing. In v. 7, the prophet articulates Saul's first duty: "When all these signs come to you, do what[24] your hand finds to do." Verse 8, then, states what Saul is to do next, after he has done the first thing: "Then[25] go down ahead of me to Gilgal, and look, I am coming down to you to offer burnt offerings and to sacrifice peace offerings. Seven days you shall wait until I come to you and tell you what you shall do." Understood sequentially, vv. 7 and 8 are neither confused nor contradictory, and they evidence neither a prophetic correction nor a capricious prophet. Samuel gives Saul his first assignment—what his hand will find to do—and then tells him what he is to do when that first assignment is accomplished.

This raises a key question. What precisely should Saul's hand find to do? Here the reader is called upon to read "between the lines." In vv. 5-6, Samuel states that the third of three signs confirming Saul's anointing will take place at Gibeah Elohim ("Hill of God"). He notes also that there is a Philistine garrison at that place. Many commentators make little of the reference to the Philistine garrison, and some even regard the reference as out of place.[26] Saul will almost certainly have been familiar with Gibeah Elohim and with the Philistine garrison located there. So why does Samuel mention what Saul already knows? I believe that Samuel's purpose is to suggest to Saul specifically what his hand should find to do. As soon as the three signs of 1 Samuel 10 are fulfilled, Saul is to attack the Philistine garrison at Gibeah Elohim.

This understanding of the significance of v. 5 is attested at least as far back as the medieval rabbi and commentator David Kimchi (1160–1235), who observes that in mentioning the Philistines, Samuel is "hinting to him [Saul] that he should remove them from there and save Israel out of their hands."[27] This understanding requires the reader to connect some dots, to read between the lines. But once the dots are connected, a clearer picture begins to emerge. Samuel does not charge Saul to do whatever whenever. He does not give him *carte blanche*. In response to

---

Long, *The Art of Biblical History*, ed. M. Silva, Foundations of Contemporary Interpretation vol. 5 (Grand Rapids: Zondervan, 1994), ch. 6; Provan, Long, and Longman, *Biblical History*, 276–85 (q.v. for a succinct and up-to-date discussion).

24. The tendency of numerous English translations to read "whatever" is not warranted by the Hebrew text (*'ăśê lěkā 'ăšer*, "do for yourself what …") and likely arises from a lack of understanding of what Saul is being asked to do.

25. The Hebrew *weqāṭal*-form that launches v. 8 supports a consecutive sense: "Then go …" (so ESV, NLT; cf. JPS, "Afterward, you are to go down …").

26. P. K. McCarter, for example, dismisses the reference as "immaterial at this point and probably secondary, having been added along with the instructions in v 8 as preparation for c 13" (*I Samuel: A New Translation with Introduction and Commentary*, AB [Garden City, NY: Doubleday, 1980], 182).

27. For bibliography and further discussion, see Long, *Reign and Rejection*, 53–4.

Saul's *designation* by anointing and its confirmation by three signs, Saul is to attack the Philistine garrison. This will *demonstrate* to Saul's fellow Israelites that he is the one around whom they should rally and whom they should ultimately *confirm* as their new leader, the king they demanded in 1 Samuel 8.[28]

The significance of v. 5 for understanding what v. 7 is asking of Saul is, unfortunately, generally overlooked, though some few have made the connection in one way or another. Adolphe Lods, for instance, recognizes that it was "the seer who gave Saul the idea of attacking the triumphal stele of Gibeah."[29] Rudolf Kittel, in commenting on Jonathan's later attack on a Philistine garrison at Geba in 1 Sam. 13:3, writes, "Here lay for Saul in truth 'what his hand should find to do,' as Samuel mysteriously but understandably had intimated to him."[30] C. J. Goslinga notes that the juxtaposition of "hill of God" with "garrison of the Philistines" must be meant to prompt Saul to drive the latter from the former.[31] Klaas Smelik remarks that "by mentioning the Philistine occupation there, Samuel underscores Saul's task to deliver Israel."[32]

If this line of interpretation is correct, then the implicit message of the text is that Saul's first action following the third of the three signs confirming his anointing should be to attack the garrison of the Philistines at Gibeah Elohim. Attacking a garrison will not defeat the Philistines, of course, but it will provoke them. Thus, Samuel issues the second part of Saul's first charge: "Then go down to Gilgal" where you are to "wait until I come to you and make known to you what you are to do" (1 Sam. 10:8). Far from being in contradiction with one another, vv. 7 and 8 constitute a two-part charge or command to Saul, the execution of part two being contingent on the prior execution of part one.

---

28. On the notion that ancient Near Eastern and biblical accessions to power often involved three stages—designation, demonstration, and confirmation—see B. Halpern, *The Constitution of the Monarchy in Israel*, HSM 25 (Chico: Scholars, 1981); Halpern, "The Uneasy Compromise: Israel between League and Monarchy," in *Traditions in Transformation: Turning Points in Biblical Faith*, ed. B. Halpern and J. D. Levenson (Winona Lake: Eisenbrauns, 1981), 59–96; D. V. Edelman, "Saul's Rescue of Jabesh-Gilead (1 Sam 11:1–11): Sorting Story from History," *ZAW* 96 (1984): 195–209; Long, *Reign and Rejection*, 183–94; and, most recently and conveniently, Provan, Long, and Longman, *Biblical History*, 279–83.

29. Adolphe Lods, *Israel from its Beginnings to the Middle of the Eighth Century*, trans. S. H. Hooke (London: Kegan Paul, Trench, Trubner, 1932), 353. Whether "garrison," "governor," or "stele" is the proper understanding of Heb. *nṣby* in 1 Sam. 10:5 (or possibly sg. *nṣyb*; cf. 13:3) is debated and makes no difference to our overall understanding here.

30. Rudolf Kittel, *Geschichte des Volkes Israel*, 7th ed., 3 vols. (Gotha: Klotz, 1925), 2:82.

31. C. J. Goslinga, *Het eerste boek Samuel*, Commentaar op het Oude Testament (Kampen: J. H. Kok, 1968), 223. For the original German and Dutch of Kittel and Goslinga, respectively, see Long, *Reign and Rejection*, 53.

32. Klaas A. D. Smelik, *Saul, de voorstelling van Israels eerste Konig in de Masoretische tekst van het Oude Testament* (Amsterdam: Drukkerij en Uitgeverij P. E. T., 1977), 107 (my translation).

As it happens, Saul does not "do what lies at hand," and the process is forestalled. A right understanding of Saul's first charge not only explains the gravity of his failure to wait for Samuel in 1 Samuel 13 but also helps to clarify the intervening episodes leading up to ch. 13, which most commentators have regarded as failing to tell a sensible story. In brief, the episodes between Saul's anointing and his accession may be understood as follows. When Saul, in the immediate aftermath of his anointing, fails to attack the Philistine garrison, Samuel resorts to a lot-casting at Mizpah in order to bring Saul to public attention (10:17-27). Not surprisingly, some naysayers are unimpressed by Saul, despite his commanding physique, for he has just been dragged out of hiding (10:22-23) and has yet to do anything to distinguish himself. Their query has some force, "how can this man save us?" (10:27). The next episode, in which Saul leads a successful military operation against the Ammonites (11:1-15), effectively silences his detractors, and the kingship process is "renewed" (put back on track; 11:14). Chapter 11 concludes with the notice that "Saul and all the Israelites held a great celebration" (v. 15). Samuel, however, is not mentioned as joining the celebration. Instead, he warns the people that kingship can succeed or fail, depending on whether they and their king follow the Lord (12:14-15, 20-25). Clearly, some kind of test remains, and the flow of the text suggests that this test relates to Saul's first charge and the Philistine menace (recall 9:16).

It is no surprise, therefore, that the events of the next chapter correspond to the two stages of Saul's first charge in 10:7-8. In 1 Samuel 13, Saul's son Jonathan does what Saul should have done much earlier. He attacks a Philistine garrison (13:3; cf. 10:7). As expected, this provokes a reaction from the Philistines, and Saul repairs to Gilgal and waits seven days, according to "the time set by Samuel" (13:8; cf. 10:8). He does not wait until Samuel arrives, however, and this is adjudged to be an act of folly (13:13).

Briefly stated, Saul fails in the execution of his first charge. But this raises a further question. Why is this such a grave offence? To answer this question, we must understand the purpose of Saul's first charge. It was designed not only to begin dealing with the Philistines but also, more importantly, to test whether Saul would prove suitable to be king in Israel. Specifically, would he assume the posture of a vassal obedient to the instructions of the Great King, or would he be nothing more than a king "such as all the other nations have"? The nations' kings fed and housed their gods and then expected their gods to assist them in their own initiatives, military or otherwise.[33] Yahweh was not such a god. He was not beholden to the king. The relationship was the reverse. Yahweh gave the instructions. He was the initiator, and the king was to respond. Saul's first charge was crafted in such a way as to test whether he understood and was willing to abide by this relationship. Would he value the word of the Lord above all else? Saul's folly in 1 Samuel 13 showed that, when push came to shove, he would not. By commencing battle preparations in Samuel's absence and without receiving divine instructions, Saul showed that he was not the kind of king Yahweh desired for his people, even if he was the kind of king the people desired for themselves.

---

33. John H. Walton, "A King Like the Nations: 1 Samuel 8 in Its Cultural Context," *Bib* 96 (2015): 179–200.

If all this has led us to a better understanding of Saul's first charge as comprising two parts and as designed to test Saul's capacity to serve as Yahweh's vassal king, then we begin to understand that Saul's failure in 1 Samuel 13 was not a trivial matter. Nor was his rejection by Samuel a case of peevishness but, rather, of prophetic duty.

Our Assessment of Characters in Samuel

What difference does this make for our assessment of characters in Samuel? To begin, we return to the question of whether Saul is presented in 1 Samuel as a victim of Yahweh or at least of his prophet Samuel. The short answer is no. Outside the book of Samuel, the Chronicler attributes Saul's failure and death not to his victimization but to his own unfaithfulness: "So Saul died for his unfaithfulness; he was unfaithful to the LORD in that he did not keep the command of the LORD; moreover, he had consulted a medium, seeking guidance, and did not seek guidance from the LORD" (1 Chron. 10:13-14, NRSV). By the time of the Endor incident in 1 Samuel 28, Saul's dynastic hopes had been dashed (1 Sam. 13:13-14) and his very right to remain on the throne abolished (15:28). Why then does the Chronicler single out Saul's consultation of the witch of Endor? Perhaps he does so to highlight the quintessential and culminating evidence of Saul's long-term and progressive neglect of the word of Yahweh. As I argue elsewhere, "in [1 Sam.] 13:8–9 Saul waits until the last minute before taking matters into his own hands, in 14:18–19 he calls for the oracle but breaks off the inquiry in mid-stream, and finally in 14:36 he must even be reminded that divine inquiry is necessary."[34] By 1 Samuel 28, Yahweh no longer responds to Saul (cf. the divine silence predicted in 8:18 with respect to those dismissive of Yahweh).

This brings us to yet another concern that has been raised in respect of the story of Saul. Some commentators have suggested that we have too many explanations of why Saul was rejected. Was he rejected for proceeding with sacrifices before Samuel arrived in Gilgal (1 Samuel 13), or for failing to execute the ban against the Amalekites (1 Samuel 15), or for consulting a medium (1 Samuel 28)? Upon reflection, it seems best to regard these incidents not as competing explanations but as correlative symptoms of a deeper illness. At its heart, Saul's illness, as portrayed in the book of Samuel, is simply "unfaith," just as the Chronicler maintains, and a failure to give due weight to Yahweh and his word. The gravity of this illness is signaled already near the beginning of the book of Samuel, in the story of Eli: "Those who honor me (give me weight) I will honor (give weight to), but those who slight me will be lightly esteemed" (1 Sam. 3:30b; my paraphrase).[35] To the

---

34. Long, *Reign and Rejection*, 41; cf. 123.

35. The significance of the highly theologized explanation of Eli's rejection should not be overlooked in seeking to understand Saul's rejection, nor should the difference in their responses to their rejections be missed (contrast Eli's submissive acceptance in 1 Sam. 3:18 with Saul's resistance in 20:31 and *passim*).

extent that Saul does not prize the word of Yahweh, he is responsible for his own fate. To the extent that he is a victim, he is a victim of the people, who similarly discount the word of Yahweh (see, e.g., 1 Sam. 8:7-9, 19-21). The text does not present Saul as a victim of Yahweh or his prophet. The people wanted a king like other nations had, and that is what they got.[36]

What about Samuel? Are we to understand him as a petulant, peevish, self-protective power broker, toying with Saul's career and ultimately his sanity? The short answer is no. The text does not present him as a "perfect person," but it does present him as a "true prophet" (recall our earlier discussion of 1 Sam. 3:19-21). To be sure, Samuel sometimes gets things wrong. For instance, he initially misreads the elders' request for a "king to judge us" as a bid to replace him as judge, when in fact the offence is much greater (8:4-7). Or, to cite another example, he initially assumes wrongly that the physically commanding Eliab must be the son of Jesse destined to replace Saul (16:6). Another prophet in the book of Samuel, Nathan, also gets something wrong when he gives David the go-ahead to build a temple for Yahweh (2 Sam. 7:1-3). In each of these cases, however, Yahweh quickly and directly *corrects the prophet* (see 1 Sam. 8:7; 16:7; 2 Sam. 7:4-17, respectively). This is a fundamentally important point.

The notion that Samuel is to be read as a crotchety old man, harassing Saul with prophetic words of his own invention and only backed by Yahweh because the latter had earlier committed himself to let none of Samuel's words "fall to the ground" does not fly. Were Samuel's words of instruction and sanction in 1 Samuel 13 and 15 exclusively his own, not Yahweh's, he would qualify as false prophet par excellence (cf. Deut. 18:20 and *passim*). True prophets were first and foremost "messengers" of Yahweh. To neglect this point and cast Samuel as a political animal is not just a failure to read between the lines in the book of Samuel, but a failure to read the lines themselves. Samuel's pivotal role was in service to Yahweh as Great King. Samuel is not presented as seeking to reduce Saul to his own personal puppet but, rather, as seeking to position Saul properly as a vassal to Israel's divine King. Furthermore, Saul's failure to prove suitable did not bring Samuel joy, but quite the opposite (1 Sam. 15:35–16:1). As Brueggemann remarks, Saul's rejection, "however justified, brings with it deep grief. That is where Saul's tale ends, not in hostility or in anger but in grief, for both Samuel and perhaps for Yahweh."[37]

Now to David. Once we have a clearer view of Saul's failure and of Samuel's function, we can come to a better understanding of David. The text of Samuel makes it clear that Saul came to fear David (1 Sam. 18:8-9, 12, 15, 29; 19:1). For interpreters who regard Saul as essentially a victim, Saul's fear of David must be explained as deriving *not* from some deficiency in Saul but from some wrongful action taken by David. Thence arise theories such as the notion that David must

---

36. Yahweh's displeasure with the people's attitude in seeking such a king may be reflected, at a later date, in Hos. 13:10-11.

37. Brueggemann, *First and Second Samuel*, 118.

have attempted a coup.³⁸ The text, however, makes no mention of a coup. Nor does it imply one. To the contrary, the text tells us of two opportunities that David had to kill Saul, and on each occasion David refuses to lift his hand against the "Lord's anointed" (1 Sam. 24:6-7, 10; 26:9-11, 23). It also tells us of David's growing popularity with Saul's own children and all the people (see, e.g., 1 Samuel 18). Saul's fear of David, according to pointers in the text, arises not from aggressive actions on David's part but from Saul's progressive realization that David is the "neighbor" who is better than he and to whom the kingdom rightly belongs (1 Sam. 15:28; also 18:8; 20:31).

Just as Saul is presented in the book of Samuel as the people's king, David is presented as God's king. In response to the elders' demand for a king such as other nations have, Yahweh instructed Samuel to make "for them" a king (1 Sam. 8:22). This turned out to be Saul (9:16). Later, Yahweh tells Samuel, "I have seen/chosen from among his [Jesse's] sons *for me* a king" (1 Sam. 16:1; my emphasis). This turns out to be David (16:12-13). David is "the one" (16:12) anticipated already in 1 Sam. 13:14, the "man of God's own choosing," or the "man after God's own heart."³⁹ David's privileged status does not mean that he is perfect. Far from it. The text makes this painfully clear. No attempt is made to hide David's shameful (criminal) behaviors in the Bathsheba-Uriah affair of 2 Samuel 11. Nor does the text hide the fact that, after his catastrophic fall, David never fully recovers his balance, although he is forgiven by God. He remains disoriented in some of his judgments⁴⁰ and distant from his children.⁴¹ Even before his moral collapse in 2 Samuel 11, hints of David's human failings emerge. His first recorded words in the book of Samuel—"What will be done for the man who kills this Philistine and removes this disgrace from Israel?" (1 Sam. 17:26a)—may be suggestive of political ambition.⁴² His very next words, however, counter the notion that personal ambition is David's primary motivation: "Who is this uncircumcised Philistine that he should defy the armies of the living God?" (17:26b). In this one verse, then, we catch a glimpse of both David's political ambition and his piety. Hints in the text of David's failings could easily be multiplied. All things considered, the text offers a candid portrait of David as a fully, fallibly human king. It is honest about David, "never fearing to underscore shortcomings, nor to stress peculiarities."⁴³ But it also presents David

---

38. Cf. McKenzie, *King David*, 86-7; see my response in Provan, Long, and Longman, *Biblical History*, 298-9.

39. Both renderings of the Heb. *'iš kilbābô* capture something of the sense of the expression in 13:14. Cf. the similar usage in 1 Sam. 14:7.

40. Note, e.g., his failure to adjudicate between the conflicting stories of Ziba and Mephibosheth (2 Sam. 19:29).

41. The details of his failures in respect of Amnon, Tamar, Absalom, and Adonijah are too numerous to be discussed here, but see Long, *1 and 2 Samuel*, 376-428. Note also the comment in 1 Kgs 1:6 that David never rebuked Adonijah or questioned his actions.

42. See Alter, *David Story*, ad 1 Sam. 17:26.

43. Halpern, *David's Secret Demons*, 53.

as a man profoundly devoted to Yahweh and his word. It presents him as a king who prays, at least much of the time (see, e.g., 1 Sam. 23:1-12; 30:7-8; 2 Sam. 2:1-4; 5:19). When he fails to pray, disaster often follows, if not for himself (1 Samuel 27), then for others (1 Samuel 21–22). But when he enquires of Yahweh, when he pursues the divine initiative rather than the inclinations of his own heart, success in carrying out his mission follows. David is presented as one for whom Yahweh is the fundamental reality, the one from whom David gains his bearings. In short, David, for all his flaws and failings, cared about Yahweh and sought to "honor" him, to "give him weight." It was this Godward orientation (and consequent desire to hear the word of Yahweh) that fundamentally distinguished David from Saul and made him a king suited to the throne of Israel.

Conclusion

The call of the newer literary criticism to "read between the lines" is welcome. But interpreters must read "between the lines" in two senses. They must seek to discern the text's implicit messages, but they must also take care that their readings are indeed "between the lines," that is, constrained by the text's more explicit messages. Earlier we noted Sternberg's insistence that biblical texts make their points *both* explicitly and implicitly. When attempts to read between the lines arrive at interpretations that stand in conflict with the lines themselves, it is time to pause and rethink. In the present essay, I have argued that some recent treatments of major characters in Samuel are, wittingly or unwittingly, guilty of reading *outside the lines*. The results of such readings are not trivial. When Saul is read as a victim of Yahweh and his prophet, Samuel, as vindictive and petty, and David as treacherous and hypocritical, in the end Yahweh becomes abhorrent. But as we have seen, to the extent that Saul is a victim, it is of the people and of his own "unfaith." To the extent that David is "better" than Saul, it is in his fidelity to Yahweh and his word, despite his very human failings. To the extent that Samuel seeks to subordinate Saul, it is not because of some self-protective desire to have a "puppet king" but, rather, because Israel's king, to succeed, must *not* be like the kings of other nations. Israel's king must assume a properly subordinate position in relationship to Yahweh, the Great King, and be obedient to the divine initiative. The ubiquitous testimony of Scripture is that "Yahweh is righteous in all his ways and faithful in all his doings" (Ps. 145:17). Rightly read, the book of Samuel—both in the lines and between the lines—adds its voice to this profession.

Chapter 3

NEW TESTAMENT QUOTATIONS OF THE OLD AS DIVINE SPEECH ACTS

Karen H. Jobes

When speech-act theory is applied to biblical interpretation, it is often used to examine individual statements and passages, such as prophecy, parable, assertion, and so forth. That is well and good, but as Kevin J. Vanhoozer defines it, "Scripture is itself a mighty speech act by which God reveals himself in his Son Jesus Christ."[1] The entire Bible is God's speech act that establishes a covenant in which God promises a relationship with humankind that is redemptive and eternal because of Christ's death and resurrection. So the many and various illocutionary acts performed throughout the locution of Scripture "are also the ingredients of a larger, testament, illocutionary act: covenanting."[2] (Here I use "locution" to refer to the text of Scripture and "illocution" to refer to what the text is doing or putting into effect.) Theologians have long recognized the covenantal nature of God's revelation, and Vanhoozer's consideration of this revelation as Trinitarian divine speech acts has been especially fruitful in understanding special revelation as such.

One feature of the NT divine speech act of covenanting includes hundreds of quotations, allusions, and echoes of the OT. It is commonly understood that NT writers quote the OT to provide authority for their arguments, and this is no doubt true in general. The illocutionary intent of quoting the OT was to persuade NT readers of the truth and respectability of the Christian faith. The NT writers wanted to explain how the gospel of Jesus Christ and the Christianity that developed around it were not new inventions but the culmination of the work and Word of God as inscripturated in the Hebrew sacred texts. However, a consideration of the theory of how quotations function in general suggests that authority is but one dimension of the rhetorical, sociolinguistic, and religious use of quotations of the OT in the NT. The case of quotations in Hebrews is particularly interesting because of the frame introduced in Heb. 1:2 that declares the Son to be a new speech act of God: "In the past God spoke to our ancestors through the prophets

---

1. Kevin J. Vanhoozer, *First Theology: God, Scripture and Hermeneutics* (Downers Grove: InterVarsity, 2002), 157.
2. Ibid., 194.

at many times and in various ways, but in these last days he has spoken to us by his Son." To say that God speaks is to say, at the least, that God communicates with illocutionary intentions that are achieved through the words of Scripture because, even though the Son himself is God's full and final act of revelation, it is only through the preservation of the life and significance of Jesus in the NT texts that this revelation is communicated. Therefore, Richard Briggs, citing Nicholas Wolterstorff, argues, "The locutions of the Bible may serve as the vehicles of divine illocutions, thus securing the literal claim that God speaks, since to speak is to engage in the production of illocutionary acts."[3] Vanhoozer also considers the text of Scripture to be God's Word, saying, "God the Father's locution is the result of his providential involvement in the lives of the human authors of Scripture."[4]

So the book of Hebrews in its entirety is the Father's locution. However, it also appears that the second act of divine revelation in the Son suggested to the author of Hebrews a novel discursive strategy for relativizing the old Sinai covenant and establishing the new covenant in Christ. This strategy involves putting divine speech, comprising OT quotations, into the mouths of the Father, the Son, and the Spirit.

As Meir Sternberg explains, quotation brings together two discourse events, the original expression and that in which it is cited by another author, forming "two separate and independent events."[5] This causes the network of illocutionary intentions of the original quotation within its source to be subordinated "to another network [of intentions, attitudes, and acts] which represents the potential illocutionary force expressed by the quoter."[6] Gillian Lane-Mercier also points out that proof of authority or truth is only one of two uses of quotation, the second being quotation as play, which affords the quoter a discursive space in which to revise, advance, dismiss, parody, even reverse or otherwise engage the source text. Here "play" refers to the space in which a mechanism can move, such as in the statement, "There's too much play in this steering wheel." Quotation as play creates a discursive space in which the quoter may engage the quote for his or her own purposes. In other words, "the already said is used to promote the as-yet-unsaid."[7] The NT use of the OT is arguably a paramount example of this principle.

---

3. Richard S. Briggs, *Words in Action: Speech Act Theory and Biblical Interpretation: Toward a Hermeneutic of Self-Involvement* (Edinburgh: T&T Clark, 2001), 15, citing Nicholas Wolterstorff, *Divine Discourse: Philosophical Reflections on the Claim That God Speaks* (Cambridge: Cambridge University Press, 1995), 75–94.

4. Vanhoozer, *First Theology*, 154.

5. Meir Sternberg, "Proteus in Quotation-Land: Mimesis and Forms of Reported Discourse," *Poetics Today* 3, no. 2 (1982): 107–56, esp. 107, 108.

6. Gillian Lane-Mercier, "Quotation as a Discursive Strategy," *Kodikas* 14 (1991): 199–214, esp. 205, quoting M. Van Overbeke, *Le langage en context: etudes philosophiques et linguistiques de pragmatique*, ed. H. Perret (Amsterdam: John Benjamins, 1980), 471.

7. Lane-Mercier, "Quotation as a Discursive Strategy," 201, 206–7.

As Sternberg puts it, "to quote is to recontextualize" even if the exact words of the original are accurately reproduced.[8] To recontextualize a prior source is to disturb its meaning, because of the difference between the quoter's and the quotee's contexts, in the most inclusive sense of that term.[9] In addition, the textual context framing a quotation is the quoter's creation for his or her own purposes and cannot help but trigger a different set of thoughts than the inset quotation did in its original context. The use of the Psalms in Hebrews is an excellent example, for the frame of a second divine speech act in the Son afforded the opportunity for play that supported the author's purposes even when the quotation was rendered in its exact form, as we shall see below.

The author of Hebrews employs both quotation as proof and quotation as play, often simultaneously, affording him the opportunity to explain both the continuity of the old Sinai covenant with the new covenant (quotation as proof) and the discontinuity as he explains the newness of the covenant in Christ's blood (quotation as play). He quotes the (Greek) OT extensively, sometimes with amazing accuracy, sometimes with intriguing differences, but in all cases he recontextualizes the quotations for a post-resurrection era. Even though Heb. 1:2 is referring to the person of the Son as God's full and final revelation, the words of the inspired NT writers explain the Son and are thereby an integral part of God's new speech act in the Son. The author of Hebrews creates a discourse with new illocutionary intent: to explain the new covenant of Christ and to persuade readers to remain faithful to it.

Despite the new context, in multiple senses, the constant factor for the author of Hebrews is God's speaking, in the past through the OT writers and once again in the Son. This theological premise is the basis for both Hebrews's use of quotation as proof and at the same time quotation as play to achieve a marvelous conversation between God and the Son, as discussed below.

Since both the OT and NT texts are divine speech acts in their own right, when the NT quotes the OT there is an appropriation of a previous speech act of God in a new speech act that potentially, and in fact often, does not have the same illocutionary purpose as the original, although the locution (the quoted text) may be identical or nearly so. The interaction between the discourse that frames the quotation and the quotation itself may in effect change perspective (by putting the quotation in a different mouth), participants (by making antecedents of pronouns ambiguous or reassigning them), tone (by how words that occur in the quotation are used in the frame), and so forth.

Conceptualizing quotations of the OT in the NT as new, divine speech acts may clear the way for seeing how quotations, primarily from the LXX or other Greek versions, can carry normative, divine authority even and especially when they do not agree with the corresponding extant Hebrew text.[10] Christian debates

---

8. Sternberg, "Proteus in Quotation-Land," 130.
9. Ibid.
10. Here I use "LXX" in a general sense to refer to a Greek translation of any part of the Hebrew OT canon.

over whether the LXX was inspired or not, which date back at least to the time of Augustine and Jerome, assume that the authority of the *Greek* quotation is derived from its origin in the inspired *Hebrew* text. Particular tensions arise when the NT writers quote the OT in wording that does not seem to correspond with what God said in the OT. For Hebrews, "authority lies in God speaking" in the Son.[11] Locutions once spoken by God in the past are spoken anew. So rather than assuming that the NT quotation's authority derives from the inspiration of its source text, it is perhaps better to see its authority resulting from its being included in a new, divine speech act that happens to include a locution from previous revelation. The quotation may or may not be composed of the expected, translated wording of the Hebrew; its wording may or may not agree precisely with known ancient Greek translations, and it may or may not be used in a way that matches its contribution to the OT context. But if we consider its authority as a new, fresh locution of God with possibly (probably?) different illocutionary intent, the relationship of the authority of the quotation and its source text is loosened, if not freed.

This means that the divine inspiration of the quotation, presented in Greek translation, does *not* depend on its relationship to the Hebrew. The question of whether the Greek translators were inspired becomes moot, as does the question of how the form of the Greek quotation originated. This is not to say that the relationship of the Greek to its Hebrew is not an interesting and important question. Nor is it to deny that it is exegetically significant to determine if the form of the quotation was created by the NT author or was simply the text in the Greek OT available to him. But *theologically*, God's restatement in the NT of a previous locution of the OT, whether in exactly the same or in a different form, is not a threat to the doctrine of inspiration. Therefore, we need not fret over the use of the uninspired LXX text as an authoritative source in the NT.

This notion of considering the NT quotations of the OT as new, divine speech acts happens to be consistent with how Hebrews presents the quotations of the OT: as if they are not quotations at all. Whether the Father, Jesus Christ, or the Holy Spirit speaks from the OT, it is presented as a new locution directly from the triune God, often using the present tense, as if the OT text previously did not even exist. Indeed, if we were not already aware that the quotation is from the OT (perhaps only because of the way the words are typeset) then we might not know it, for there often is no formula in Hebrews as found elsewhere in the NT indicating that a quotation is being introduced (e.g., "it is written," as such and such a prophet said, etc.). As Daniel Treier observes, "Without subscribing to any particular theory on the relationship of tense morphology and temporal reference, it is clear enough that [Heb.] 3:7-11, 15, and 4:7 indicate contemporary divine address through the text: God is speaking (12:25) afresh 'today.'"[12] Clearly the author of Hebrews believes that previous locutions of God are spoken anew to a new audience in the new context of the Son's appearance in history.

---

11. Daniel J. Treier, "Speech Acts, Hearing Hearts, and Other Senses: The Doctrine of Scripture Practiced in Hebrews," in *The Epistle to the Hebrews and Christian Theology*, ed. Richard Bauckham et al. (Grand Rapids: Eerdmans, 2009), 339.

12. Ibid., 338-9.

The progressive nature of divine revelation entails that subsequent revelation be organically related to what God previously said. Because time is ever-moving, any subsequent revelation is given in a later historical, geopolitical, and (in the case of the NT) cultural and linguistic context. Because redemptive history moves on, normative texts can, and must, "enact new divine speech-acts" if they are to remain normative.[13] Of greatest importance to the NT's historical context is the astounding fact of Jesus Christ's death, resurrection, and ascension, which provided a new lens through which to view God's covenantal acts (both speech and otherwise) of the OT era. It should not be surprising that God's locutions in the NT should both refer to and reinterpret his previous covenantal acts, with the illocutionary intent of revealing Christ and evoking redemptive faith in readers.

Although the Son through whom God now speaks is clearly identified as Jesus Christ, amazingly we find in the book of Hebrews not one word of Jesus' teaching, parables, sermons, conversations, or any of the statements found in the Gospels. When Heb. 1:2 refers to God's Word revealed by the Son, it refers to the *event* of the Incarnation more than any verbal message spoken by Jesus.[14] Nevertheless, in Hebrews we do find speech attributed to Father, Son, and Holy Spirit. This essay focuses on the locutions in Hebrews made by God the Father to the Son (Heb. 1:5, 8, 10, 13; 5:5, 6; 7:21), by Jesus Christ to the Father (2:12, 13; 10:5-7), and by the Holy Spirit (3:7-11; 10:16-18). When these divine locutions that Hebrews puts directly into the mouth of the Father, the Son, and the Spirit are examined, some interesting points are observed:

1. All of these divine locutions are composed *only* of words quoted from the OT Scriptures.
2. Even where God speaks exactly the words of OT Scripture, its sense is recontexualized to refer to the new covenant in Christ.
3. Father, Son, and Spirit speak only OT Scripture as it had been translated by the LXX.

It is striking that the triune God who speaks (Heb. 1:1) in the book of Hebrews speaks locutions composed of *only* words of OT Scripture, which for the writer of Hebrews were authoritative. This is in contrast to, for instance, the Synoptic Gospels where extemporaneous words of divine speech are found (e.g., Mt. 3:17; 17:5; Mk 1:11; 9:7; Lk. 3:22; 9:35; Jn 12:28). No such extemporaneous words of divine speech are found on the lips of the God who speaks in Hebrews. The author of Hebrews views the words of the Jewish Scriptures "as the literal and historical words of God ... with little regard for the fact that these words are in texts written by human authors."[15]

---

13. Ibid., 350.
14. So also Ken Schenck, "God Has Spoken: Hebrews' Theology of the Scriptures," in *The Epistle to the Hebrews and Christian Theology*, ed. Richard Bauckham et al. (Grand Rapids: Eerdmans, 2009), 322.
15. Ibid., 324.

The OT quotations put in God's mouth that are the focus of this study are not the only OT quotations in Hebrews, for there are places where the author simply quotes OT texts without putting the words into God's mouth (Heb. 2:5-8; 3:15; 10:37, 38). For present purposes, though, the instances of direct speech by God the Father, the Son, and the Spirit will be considered from Vanhoozer's perspective of the triune God's speech acts.[16] I will not discuss the various textual forms of the LXX quotations or the text-critical issues involved,[17] nor will I fully exegete the use of these OT quotations in the argument of Hebrews.[18] Rather, the focus will be on the relevant theological inferences that may be drawn for the evangelical doctrine of Scripture.

The Conversation between the Father and the Son in Hebrews

Not only is divine speech in Hebrews Trinitarian in nature, and exclusively composed of quotations from the OT, but it also allows the reader to overhear an amazing inner-Trinitarian dialogue between the Father and the Son that establishes the covenant. In Hebrews God the Father speaks to the Son using words of the OT, and Jesus Christ speaks *only* to the Father, not to the readers, also using only words of OT Scripture. Unlike the Synoptic Gospels' teachings from Jesus, Hebrews has no "But I say to you ..." use of second-person plural pronouns. The divine revelation referenced in Heb. 1:1, 2 is not what Jesus Christ has *said* in his teaching during his earthly ministry but is the incarnate Son himself, in all that he said and did. For Hebrews, the purpose of the Incarnation was to establish a covenant of redemption in which Jesus is both sacrifice and high priest.

---

16. Kevin J. Vanhoozer, "Triune Discourse: Theological Reflections on the Claim That God Speaks (Parts I and II)," in *Trinitarian Theology for the Church: Scripture, Community, Worship*, ed. Daniel J. Treier and David Lauber (Downers Grove: IVP Academic, 2009), 25–78; Vanhoozer, *First Theology*. The literature on OT quotations in Hebrews is vast. See Gert J. Steyn, *A Quest for the Assumed LXX Vorlage of the Explicit Quotations in Hebrews*, FRLANT 235 (Göttingen: Vandenhoeck & Ruprecht, 2011); Susan E. Docherty, *The Use of the Old Testament in Hebrews*, WUNT 260 (Tübingen: Mohr Siebeck, 2009); George H. Guthrie, "Hebrews," in *Commentary on the New Testament Use of the Old Testament*, ed. G. K. Beale and D. A. Carson (Grand Rapids: Baker Academic, 2007), 919–95; Radu Georghita, *The Role of the Septuagint in Hebrews: An Investigation of Its Influence with Special Consideration to the Use of Hab. 2:3–4 in Heb. 10:37–38*, WUNT 2/160 (Tübingen: Mohr Siebeck, 2003); Simon Kistemaker, *The Psalms Citations in the Epistle to the Hebrews* (Amsterdam: Wed. G. van Soest, 1961).

17. Steyn, *A Quest for the Assumed LXX Vorlage*.

18. For my previous work on the exegesis of Christ's words in Hebrews, see Karen H. Jobes, "The Function of Paronomasia in Hebrews 10:5–7," *Trinity Journal* 13ns (1992): 181–91; Jobes, "Rhetorical Achievement in the Hebrews 10 'Misquote' of Psalm 40," *Bib* 72 (1991): 387–96.

The OT quotations put into the mouths of the Father and the Son in Hebrews seem to have the effect of constructing a conversation that centers on establishing this new covenant of redemption, creating the impression that readers are overhearing inner-Trinitarian dialogue without the imposition of the historical OT source text. God's speech in Hebrews 1 is covenantal language declaring the Son to be both God and messianic king; in Hebrews 2 and 10 we find the Son's response to the Father's declarations, and we overhear Christ accepting his sacrificial role in establishing the covenant. Harold Attridge speaks of this "conceit" that readers can actually hear God speaking as the most creative theological work of Hebrews.[19] This dialogue between God and the Son forms a pattern that invites readers to respond similarly in obedience.[20]

This construction of an inner-Trinitarian conversation using OT quotations may explain that ambiguous introductory formula in 2:6, "there is a place where someone has testified," followed by a quotation from Ps. 8:4-6. The author could have written "as the psalmist testified," or even "as David has testified." But that would have brought another personal voice into the conversation, interrupting the flow of dialogue between the Father and Christ. The author of Hebrews no doubt thought Psalm 8 was also God's Word, accurately reflecting God's interpretation of humanity's failure to reach its destiny.[21] But as a discursive strategy Hebrews selects only quotations that represent the conversation between the Father and the Son concerning establishment of the new covenant.

Speech Acts of the Father

In Hebrews 1 God makes declarations about and to the Son primarily quoting Psalms, but without identifying them as such and without referring to a human writer. If we consider the Father's locutions in Hebrews 1 as speech acts, two are rhetorical questions intended to assert the Son's superiority to the angels (Heb. 1:5, 13). Hebrews 1:5 simultaneously introduces the relationship of God to "the Son," previously mentioned as his Father ("my Son … your Father" in 1:1; "his Father … my Son" in 1:3). Perhaps the most theologically interesting of these speech acts is God's declaration of the Son to be God, by taking locutions that had been directed toward Yahweh in the OT, putting them in God's mouth, and directing them to the Son. We find in Heb. 1:5-13 statements that God speaks to the Son in the second-person singular ("you" and "your"), even addressing the Son with the vocative "O God" (ὁ θεὸς) in Heb. 1:8 and "Lord" (κύριε) in 1:10.

---

19. Harold W. Attridge, "God in Hebrews," in *The Epistle to the Hebrews and Christian Theology*, ed. Richard Bauckham et al. (Grand Rapids: Eerdmans, 2009), 104.

20. Harold W. Attridge, *Essays on John and Hebrews*, WUNT 264 (Tübingen: Mohr Siebeck, 2010), 314–15.

21. Schenck, "God Has Spoken," 326. See there more discussion of this interesting introduction of a quotation.

Amazingly in Heb. 1:8 the Son is addressed as God by God ("Your throne, O God, will last for ever and ever"). Although in its OT context the vocative of this statement was assumed to address God the Father, when these same words are put in the mouth of the Father as he addresses the Son, the illocutionary intent clearly changes to become God's pronouncement that the Son is God who will reign forever.

Using the words of LXX Ps. 101:26-28 (Heb./Eng. 102:25-27), God furthermore pronounces in Heb. 1:10-12 the Son's role "in the beginning" at creation, addressing the Son as "you, Lord" (σύ, κύριε) using the vocative κύριε, which is not found in the corresponding Hebrew verse (Heb./Eng. Ps. 102:22). The author of Hebrews puts a reference to God the Father in the OT source text into the mouth of God, thereby changing the referent of κύριε from the LORD to the Son, the Lord. And the vocative with which God addresses the Son comes from a *translation* of the Psalm, including a word not found in the corresponding MT. The illocutionary intent is that God the Father reveals the Son to be God by declaring him to be so—a mighty speech act indeed! Furthermore, God refers to the Son as he who was involved with, and who will survive, the creation—as he who is eternal.

God's speech acts in Hebrews 1 declare that (1) God himself is the Father of the Son, (2) the Son is God, (3) the Son is the messianic king, and (4) the Son's reign as messianic king is eternal. This epoch-making theological declaration was achieved by locutions that are unacknowledged quotations from the OT, where the referents, but not the locutions, have been changed simply by being spoken by a different person to a different person. This is a good example of Sternberg's principle that a quotation and its original expression are "two separate and independent events," in which the quote is subordinated to the purposes of the one quoting it, regardless of how accurately the quotation is reproduced.[22] Despite using exact quotations from the OT Psalms, Hebrews manages to declare the divinity of Christ and identify him as the messianic king.

These divine speech acts in Hebrews 1 are a powerful example of Vanhoozer's idea that

> Scripture is neither simply the recital of the acts of God nor merely a book of inert propositions. Scripture is rather composed of divine-human speech acts that, through what they say, accomplish several authoritative cognitive, spiritual, and social functions. ... The Bible, I shall argue, is a diverse collection of God's mighty speech acts which communicate the saving Word of God.[23]

These speech acts of God the Father are pronouncements that do something mighty indeed: They define the reality shared by the author of Hebrews and his readers by revealing it. The Son's relationship to the Father and his role in the covenant are revealed and effected by God's declaration that it is so. This is not

---

22. Sternberg, "Proteus in Quotation-Land," 107, 108.
23. Vanhoozer, *First Theology*, 131.

to deny that the Son was eternally preexistent with the Father, but to reveal that relationship by a divine declaration in the new post-resurrection moment. Thus, it becomes so in the minds of those who read Hebrews, and thereby in Christian theology.

The Son's Speech Acts

The next explicitly divine locution in Hebrews is found in 2:12, 13, where Jesus, the incarnate Son, declares his allegiance to God the Father with words found in LXX Ps. 21:23 (Heb./Eng. 22:23). The words of the psalmist leading ancient Israel's worship of Yahweh are put in the mouth of Jesus, the incarnate Son. This speech act declares both Jesus' allegiance to the God of the OT, who is the referent of the second person singular pronouns ("your name ... your praises") and Jesus' identification with humankind ("my brothers and sisters"). Jesus declares his trust in the Father with the words of Isa. 8:17 in Heb. 2:13a, "I will put my trust in him," where the pronoun refers to "the LORD" previously mentioned in Isa. 8:17. This declares Jesus' trust in the Father even through suffering (Heb. 2:10), and continues in Heb. 2:13b with a statement originally made by the prophet Isaiah about the children the LORD gave him as signs and symbols (with a probable echo of Isa. 53:10-11). As a locution in Jesus' mouth, it becomes a statement of Jesus' solidarity with those who stand with him, "Abraham's descendants" (Heb. 2:16), binding the redemption of Jesus' "brothers and sisters" to the new covenant.

The "misquote" of LXX Ps. 39:7-9 (Heb./Eng. Ps. 40:6-8) in Heb. 10:5-7 continues the divine conversation between the Son and the Father and declares the basis of the new covenant. Hebrews introduces the quotation within the context of the insufficiencies of animal sacrifices. Here again we find two speech acts separated by a thousand years of redemptive history: A thousand years after David spoke the psalm, Christ speaks it "coming into the world" (εἰσερχόμενος εἰς τὸν κόσμον λέγει). Although the major English translations render the present participle of εἰσέρχομαι as temporal, "when he came," it is not necessary to read it as something Christ literally uttered at some point of the Incarnation. It is hard to imagine when that might be. Rather, it is consistent grammatically and exegetically in this context to consider it a modal ("by coming into the world he says ...") participle. The Incarnation *is* a statement of the Son's willingness to be the ultimate redemptive sacrifice, making the quotation an interpretation of Christ's mission.[24] Within the conversation between God and the Son this statement establishes the need for the Incarnation and is consistent with the author's thought that the Son himself is God's locution. The author of Hebrews is showing that by coming into the world Christ embraces the new covenant that God declares, even though it means becoming human (2:17), suffering (2:10), and experiencing death (9:11-14). Here we hear the Son's "yes!" to the Father's plan of redemption.

---

24. See Schenck, "God Has Spoken," 333.

In this speech act the differences between the NT quotation of Heb. 10:5-7 and its source text are intriguing:

1. σῶμα (body) is found in v. 5c instead of ὠτία (ears);
2. ὁλοκαυτώματα (burnt offerings, plural) is substituted in v. 6 for the singular form ὁλοκαύτωμα;
3. εὐδόκησας (you were pleased) is substituted for ᾔτησας (you demanded) in v. 6;
4. ὁ θεός and τὸ θέλημά σου are transposed in v. 7c.

The remainder of the verse is omitted, making the articular infinitive τοῦ ποιῆσαι the purpose for the coming (I have come to do …) instead of the object of ἐβουλήθην (I desire to do …). It would be a mistake to consider each of these differences independently in text-critical analysis for, when considered together, these differences achieve *paronomasia*, a rhythmic arrangement of style based on phonetic assonance that was highly valued and frequently practiced in the ancient world (Quintillian, *Institutio Oratoria* 9.3.66).[25]

Moreover, while putting this locution into Christ's mouth signals continuity with the Davidic monarchy, the differences signal the discontinuity. For instance, Heb. 10:1, 4 remind the reader that the many sacrificial offerings of animals, repeated endlessly year after year, were insufficient to deal once and for all with sin. In conformity to this thought, the plural form ὁλοκαυτώματα in Heb. 10:5 achieves paronomasia with *σῶμα δέ*, rhetorically contrasting God's redemptive displeasure toward the many burnt offerings with Christ's singular body as the basis of the new covenant. Christ's body, not the many previous animal sacrifices, was "pleasing" to God (εὐδοκέω with its redemptive connotations). In God's prior speech act through the psalmist, David says, "To do your will, my God, I desire." But David's desire exceeded David's ability. In God's new speech act in Hebrews the previous locution is put in Christ's mouth, with the transposition and truncation of the quotation highlighting the *accomplishment* of God's will as the purpose for the preceding "I have come." Christ says, "I have come to do, O God, your will." What David could only desire, Christ accomplished. The transposition and truncation introduce an efficacy and finality to Christ's words that are appropriately lacking in David's.

Divine Speech in Translation

It is often observed in support of the evangelical doctrine of Scripture that by putting text from the OT into God's mouth the author of Hebrews must have believed the OT words to be God's words. What is less often discussed is that by

---

25. See Jobes, "The Function of Paronomasia," 181–91; Jobes, "Rhetorical Achievement," 387–96.

putting *text from the LXX* into God's mouth the author of Hebrews must have believed the words of the Greek *translation* to be appropriate as God's words.

Hebrews allows readers to listen in on dialogue between the Father and the Son, dialogue that is composed solely of *locutions taken from the Greek translation* of various OT verses. In Hebrews the triune God speaks only OT Scripture *as it had been translated* into Greek, implying that the translation of Scripture nevertheless efficaciously functions as word of God for the purposes of Hebrews. Clearly the author of Hebrews saw the Jewish Scriptures to be the authoritative word of God. It is less clear that he could read those Scriptures in their proto-Masoretic Hebrew form; even if he could, he chose to quote the Greek translation of those Scriptures.

Above I argued that, in theological principle, if we consider the NT as a second, independent divine speech act, the source of quotations should not really be an issue. However, that approach is not completely satisfying where the Greek translation of verses that do not agree with the corresponding Hebrew operates as authoritative Scripture within an NT passage. If we think that the NT quotation of the OT must correspond identically to the extant Hebrew text, we are assuming that the MT is *always* more representative of the inspired Hebrew autograph than is a translation of any particular verse. That assumption should probably be questioned, especially in light of the times when the LXX has been shown to preserve an older Hebrew reading that is probably closer to the autograph than is the MT.

But the problem is much broader, for, in fact, only a tiny minority of Bible readers has read the Hebrew and Aramaic Scriptures and the Greek NT; the vast majority of Bible readers throughout history have read in translation, and that is certainly true of the church today. So it is worthwhile to consider how a translation—whether it be the LXX or the ESV, or any other—can efficaciously function as God's Word. That broader topic lies beyond the scope of this work, and so we will limit our consideration to the LXX because it is the translation quoted authoritatively in the NT.

Vanhoozer positions translation within the larger scope of redemptive history, beginning with the incarnation as God's definitive act of translating "divinity into the form of Jesus' humanity" and the Word into "the vernacular context of human history."[26] The nature of Jesus' person and the significance of his work have been preserved in the texts of the NT, which have been received as Scripture by the Christian church. Furthermore, the linguistic translation of Scripture is largely responsible for the success of the gospel's translation into various cultural contexts. In fact, we see that success in the book of Acts, as the gospel of Jesus Christ crosses from predominantly Jewish, Semitic culture and language into the larger Hellenistic, Greek-speaking cultures of the Roman Empire.

Regarding the authority of the LXX as a translation, Vanhoozer's ensuing concept of *ipse*-identity (as opposed to *idem*-identity) may be particularly useful.

---

26. Kevin J. Vanhoozer, *The Drama of Doctrine: A Canonical-Linguistic Approach to Christian Theology* (Louisville: Westminster John Knox, 2005), 318, 322.

The transmission of tradition, of which Bible translation is a particular type, is concerned with the preservation of the same concepts and meaning as the original through constancy and continuity. Vanhoozer points to Paul Ricoeur's distinction between two senses of identity, *idem*-identity ("the identity of sameness or permanence in time") and *ipse*-identity (a sameness that allows for "development, growth, perhaps even a certain degree of change") as a way of preserving theological tradition that nevertheless allows for the differences required by new times, places, and (I would add) languages.[27] Translation by its very definition is incapable of preserving *idem*-identity because the semantic range of words in two different languages is seldom identical, the syntax of expression differs, and cultural idioms and referents are almost invariably different. Only by simply restating a sentence in the same language can *idem*-identity be preserved; translating it into another language requires the goal of preserving *ipse*-identity.

To this we might add Vanhoozer's emphasis on the Holy Spirit as the executor of the Word, meaning both the living Word, who is Christ, and the inscripturated Word.[28] Using Calvin's division of Trinitarian labor, Vanhoozer defines the Spirit to be "the power, that is, the source of the *efficacy*" of the Father's actions and the Son's agency. As Christ's literary executor, the Spirit inspires the human authors of Scripture; as executor of Christ's life, he ministers that life to the church, a process that involves translating Scripture into the languages and cultures of the world, for the transformation of human lives occurs through the ministry of the Word. "Tradition" (and I would add translation) "transmits the gospel not by wooden repetitions but by a communicative *constancy* and *continuity* that stands in *ipse*-identity with Scripture. ... The Spirit is the empowering presence who preserves the constancy of the word even as its meaning is related to new contexts and situations."[29]

The principle of the sufficiency of Scripture for God's purposes comes to mind. *Ipse*-identity of translations requires not an exacting precision that language translation is unable to achieve, but sufficiency, and sufficiency for God's purposes, not ours. Citing Isa. 55:11, Vanhoozer points out that "Scripture is sufficient for everything for which it was divinely given. ... The Bible is sufficient for the use that God makes of it, not for every use to which *we* may want it put."[30]

When we consider the quotations of the Greek OT in the NT, we must consider the use of those specific quotations as evidence of God's purpose. The production of the Greek versions of the Hebrew Scriptures by uninspired translators does not fall outside the purview of God's purposes. And if the Holy Spirit can coopt fallible English translations as efficacious enough to make conversion to Christ and a life

---

27. Ibid., 127, 130–1.
28. Ibid., 198.
29. Ibid., 318, 202–3 (emphases original in these quotations).
30. Kevin J. Vanhoozer, *Biblical Authority after Babel: Retrieving the* Solas *in the Spirit of Mere Protestant Christianity* (Grand Rapids: Brazos, 2016), 114 (emphasis original).

of faith possible today, then cooption of the fallible LXX into a new divine speech act should not scandalize us. As Vanhoozer reminds us,

> To be sure the biblical texts have a "natural history"; they have human authors [and, I would add, translators]. Yet these human testimonies are caught up in the triune economy of word-acts and so ultimately become divine testimonies ... God has, as it were, *elected* (annexed, appropriated, inspired) just these texts as the media of his communicative acts. ... It is the divine illocutions—God's use—that constitute biblical authority.[31]

Therefore, using Vanhoozer's concept of divine speech acts combined with his understanding of the place of translation in God's purposes as executed by the Holy Spirit, we can understand the quotations of the Greek versions of the OT in the NT as fully authoritative for God's communicative purposes.

---

31. Vanhoozer, *Drama of Doctrine*, 177–8, 179 (emphasis original).

Chapter 4

READING JOHN'S GOSPEL AS A THEODRAMATIC PREVIEW OF COMING ATTRACTIONS

Robert H. Gundry

As widely (though not universally) agreed and as will be assumed here, Mark wrote his Gospel first, Matthew second, Luke third, John last of all; and these evangelists pick up the story of Jesus at successively earlier points:

- Mark at John the Baptist's introduction of Jesus onto the public stage;
- Matthew at Jesus' birth;
- Luke at the prior birth of John the Baptist; and
- John the evangelist at the beginning, prior even to creation.

John's starting at an earlier point than all the rest sets the stage for an analogous dating of events earlier than they occur in the Synoptic Gospels.

According to Matthew and Mark, Jesus described his coming death as a sacrifice not until he had passed the midpoint of his public ministry, and did so only in private to his disciples: "even to give his life as a ransom in substitution for many" (Mk 10:45; Mt. 20:28). In John's Gospel Jesus is publicly proclaimed to be a sacrifice already by the Baptist: "Look! The lamb of God that takes away the world's sin!" (1:29, 36).

In Mark, no human being recognizes and declares the divine sonship of Jesus till his death—and then only, though importantly, on the part of a centurion: "Truly this human being was God's Son" (Mk 15:39; similarly Mt. 27:54 with the addition of the centurion's fellow guardsmen). But in Matthew, eleven of the twelve disciples recognize and declare it on their own already upon Jesus' walking on the Sea of Galilee: "Truly you are God's Son" (Mt. 14:33).[1] (In Luke, no human being is ever said to recognize and declare Jesus' divine sonship.) On the other hand, John has the Baptist recognize and declare Jesus' divine sonship even before Jesus started his public ministry: "I have seen and testified that this one ['Jesus'] is the Son of

---

1. "The ones in the boat" who confessed Jesus as truly God's Son refers naturally to the disciples who had not been out on the water with Jesus and Peter; for otherwise we would expect Matthew to have written, as usual, "the disciples" so as to include Peter.

God" (1:34). Only two days later Nathanael follows suit and adds a declaration of Jesus' kingship over Israel: "Rabbi, you are the Son of God; you are the king of Israel" (1:49; cf. 1:45), Jesus' kingship not being declared elsewhere by disciples till Palm Sunday ("Favored [is] the one coming—[i.e.] the king—in the Lord's name" [Lk. 19:38; similarly Jn 12:13]).

John likewise dates Jesus' attraction of disciples—initially Andrew and an unnamed one, then Simon, Philip, and Nathanael—back to the Baptist's testimony, even before Jesus' going to Galilee: "[The Baptist's] two disciples heard him speaking and followed Jesus" (1:35-42). In the Synoptics, Jesus does not attract disciples—Simon and Andrew, James and John—till the start of his Galilean ministry (Mk 1:16-20; Mt. 4:18-22; Lk. 5:1-11). Naturally, then, John omits this Synoptic episode.

In the Synoptics, not until the midpoint of Jesus' ministry does Peter confess Jesus to be the Christ: "You are the Christ" (Mk 8:29; Mt. 16:16; Lk. 9:20). By way of contrast, John advances the confession of Jesus' messiahship to a point prior to his going to Galilee and attributes the confession to Andrew, Peter's brother: "We have found the Messiah, which is translated 'Christ'" (1:41). So Peter is later quoted as confessing Jesus to be "God's Holy One" instead of "the Christ" (6:68-69).

Yet again before his going to Galilee Jesus is said by John to have nicknamed Simon as Cephas/Peter: "Jesus said, 'You are Simon the son of John; you will be called "Cephas," which is translated "Peter"'" (1:42), whereas in Mark and Luke the nicknaming appears to have occurred at the appointment of the Twelve later on in Galilee: "And he [Jesus] appointed the Twelve and put on Simon the name Peter" (Mk 3:16; Lk. 6:14).[2] And because John does not record a post-baptismal temptation of Jesus by the devil (for how could the Word who was both God and God's Holy One be tempted to do evil? Think *non posse peccare*), Jesus' going to Galilee appears to occur earlier than it does in the Synoptics, where he does not go to Galilee till "after John [the Baptist] was given over [i.e., arrested and imprisoned]" (Mk 1:14; Mt. 4:12; cf. Lk. 4:14).

John's Jesus identifies himself as the Son of Man on the first day of his Galilean ministry: "Amen, amen I tell you, you will see the heaven opened and the angels of God ascending and descending on the Son of Man" (1:51). This self-identification comes not till later in the Synoptics (at the healing of a paralytic in Mk 2:10 and Lk. 5:24; after the Sermon on the Mount in Mt. 8:20). In the Fourth Gospel Jesus' first miracle, which John calls a "sign," occurs the day after he arrives in Galilee (1:35, 43; 2:1) and consequently antedates and displaces Jesus' use of wine at the Last Supper as an emblem of his sacrificial blood (2:1-11; 13:1-11) as well as drawing this emblem close to the Baptist's declaration that Jesus is God's lamb that takes away the sin of the world (1:29, 36). And whereas the Synoptics record only Jesus'

---

2. Though mentioning the nickname in Mt. 10:2; 16:18, the First Evangelist appears not to have located the nicknaming chronologically (see Robert H. Gundry, *Peter—False Disciple and Apostate according to Saint Matthew* [Grand Rapids: Eerdmans, 2015], 6-7, 16 n. 3).

going to Jerusalem for the Passover festival during which he died, John has him going to it several times, starting already in 2:13, and thus continues to elaborate the meaning of the Baptist's declaration. The same goes not only for John's placement of Jesus' cleansing the temple at this early point but also and even more strikingly for Jesus' driving out of the temple the sacrificial animals being sold there (2:14-22). Now that God's lamb has appeared on the scene, according to the Baptist, there is no more need for those animals, according to John. The Synoptics say nothing about Jesus' having driven them out (Mk 11:15-17; Mt. 21:12-13; Lk. 19:45-46).

At his cleansing of the temple (τὸ ἱερόν) in John, Jesus predicts the destruction of "this temple" (τὸν ναὸν τοῦτον). ("Predicts" is to be taken loosely here since, strictly speaking, Jesus *challenges* the Jews to destroy this temple.) In view of John's well-known penchant for using synonyms without distinction and in view of the Jews' using in their answer ὁ ναὸς οὗτος for the whole temple complex that "has been a-building for forty-six years," it remains uncertain whether to understand a distinction between the complex and the sanctuary proper. In either case, the Synoptic Jesus does not predict a destruction of the complex till Passion Week (Mk 13:1-2; Mt. 24:1-2; Lk. 21:5-6). By backdating the same or a similar prediction to an early cleansing of the temple, by interpreting the prediction in terms of the Jews' putting Jesus to death (he was speaking about "the temple [consisting] of his body"), and by adding to that interpretation his coming resurrection, John elaborates further the Baptist's recent proclamation of Jesus as God's sacrificial lamb and makes unnecessary—and therefore will omit—

- the passion-and-resurrection predictions that are found later in the Synoptics (Mk 8:31; 9:31; 10:33-34; Mt. 16:21; 17:22-23; 20:18-19; Lk. 9:22, 43; 17:25; 18:31-33);
- the Olivet Discourse that was triggered by Jesus' later prediction of the temple's destruction (Mk 13:3-36; Matthew 24–25; Lk. 21:5-36); and
- the accusation during Jesus' Synoptic trial, or hearing, before the Sanhedrin that he said he would destroy "the temple" (τὸν ναόν) and then build it in three days (Mk 14:58; Mt. 26:61).

According to Mt. 19:28, the cosmic "regeneration" (παλιγγενεσία) will happen "when the Son of Man sits on his glorious throne." The Johannine Jesus individualizes this regeneration, changes it into a birth "from above" (ἐὰν μή τις γεννηθῇ ἄνωθεν) rather than (merely) a second (δεύτερον) birth, and shifts it away from the Son of Man's future coming and back into the present age (3:3, 7).

Though retaining a future judgment (Jn 5:29; 12:48), which appears often in the Synoptics (Mk 12:40; Mt. 10:15; 11:22, 24; 12:36, 40, 41, 42; 23:33; Lk. 10:14; 11:31, 32; 20:47), John also brings forward the judgment into present time: "The one not believing has been judged already, because he has not believed in the name of the one-and-only Son of God," and "The judgment of this world is now" (3:18b-c and 12:31a; see also 5:30; 8:16; 9:39).

In Mt. 28:19 Jesus projects into the future the disciples' activity of baptizing people ("On going, therefore, disciple all nations by baptizing them"), as then happens throughout Luke's book of Acts. John has the disciples baptizing people on behalf of Jesus even before the Baptist's martyrdom, which took place early in Jesus' ministry (3:22, 26; 4:1-2).

Properly, eternal life means life in the age to come, as in Lk. 18:30: ἐν τῷ αἰῶνι τῷ ἐρχομένῳ ζωὴν αἰώνιον, "in the coming age eternal life" (see also Mk 10:17, 30; Mt. 19:16, 29; 25:46; Lk. 10:25; 16:9; 18:18). For believers, however, John has the experience of eternal life start already in the present age, most clearly in 5:24: "Amen, amen I tell you [Jesus is speaking] that the one hearing my word and believing the one who sent me has eternal life and is not going into judgment, but has transferred (μεταβέβηκεν) out of death into life." Perhaps equally clear are both 3:14-18, where a believer's having eternal life antithetically parallels an unbeliever's having been judged ἤδη, "already" (the antithesis lying not between life as future and judgment as present, but between life and judgment as such, both being present), and also 17:3, which defines eternal life as knowing God and Jesus Christ as his Sent One (see also 3:36; 4:14; 6:40, 47, 54; 10:28). Naturally, then, "everyone living" by virtue of now having eternal life through believing in Jesus "will by no means die forever" (οὐ μὴ ἀποθάνῃ εἰς τὸν αἰῶνα [11:26]). The wrath of God, which the Synoptics say is coming in the future ("the wrath to come" according to Mt. 3:7; Lk. 3:7; cf. Lk. 21:23), correspondingly rests right now, according to Jn 3:36b-c, on the person who through unbelief in Jesus is disobedient: "But the one who disobeys the Son will not see life; rather, the wrath of God abides on him."

Although one of ten healed lepers happens to have been a thankful Samaritan according to Lk. 17:11-19, in Lk. 9:51-55 a village of Samaritans refuses to give Jesus hospitality on his last pilgrimage to Jerusalem; according to Mt. 10:5 Jesus went so far as to prohibit the Twelve from entering any city of the Samaritans when he sent them on their evangelistic mission throughout Galilee: "You should not go into a city of the Samaritans." A Samaritan mission will take place not until he has ascended to heaven according to Acts 1:6-11; 8:1, 4-25; 9:31; 15:3. In Jn 4:1-42, though, Jesus himself evangelizes Samaritans after the first of his three pilgrimages to Jerusalem for the Passover (see especially 4:35, 38, addressed by him to his disciples: "You say, don't you, 'It is yet four months and the harvest comes'? Behold, I tell you, lift up your eyes and look at the fields in that they are already white for harvest. ... I have sent you to reap what you have not labored on. Others have labored [on it], and you have entered into their labor").

In the Synoptics, the Jewish temple in Jerusalem remains a proper place to worship God; for in those Gospels Jesus cleanses the temple so that it may be "a house of prayer" (Mk 11:17; Mt. 21:13 [cf. 5:23-24]; Lk. 19:45). In John, by contrast, Jesus tells the Samaritan woman, "Believe me, woman, that an hour is coming when you [plural] will worship the Father neither on this mountain [Gerizim] nor in Jerusalem. ... An hour is coming, *and now is*, when true worshipers will worship the Father in Spirit and Truth [probably referring to the Holy Spirit and Jesus as the Truth (cf. 14:6)]" (4:21, 23). Accordingly, salvation through Jesus is already for "the world," as the Samaritans said (4:42; cf. 1:29; 3:16-17), not just for

4. John's Gospel as a Theodramatic Preview

"the lost sheep of the house of Israel" at least for the time being, as the Synoptic Jesus said (Mt. 10:6; 15:24; cf. Lk. 24:21; Acts 1:6).

In Jn 6:30-35, 47-58, after feeding the five thousand, Jesus

- proclaims himself the bread of life;
- identifies his flesh as true food;
- adds the identification of his blood as true drink;
- makes the eating of his flesh and the drinking of his blood through faith the condition of participating in his (eternal) life;
- thereby advances in somewhat revised form the Words of Institution, which in the Synoptics do not come up until the Last Supper (Mk 14:22-25; Mt. 26:26-29; Lk. 22:17-20; cf. 1 Cor. 11:23-25); and
- consequently omits the institution of the Lord's Supper in his forthcoming account of the Last Supper (Jn 13:1-30; cf. John's antedating and displacing Jesus' use of wine at the Last Supper with the "sign" of turning water to wine in 2:1-11).

According to Mk 13:9 and Mt. 10:17; 23:34, Jesus predicts that his disciples will be beaten and flogged *in* synagogues. By way of modification and intensification, the Johannine Jesus predicts they will be cast *out* of synagogues (16:2). But the casting out of the man born blind, who had been healed by Jesus that very Sabbath day, antedates those future expulsions from synagogues (9:22, 34).

In the Synoptics it is demanded of Jesus that he say whether he is the Christ, and this on the occasion of his trial, or hearing, before the Sanhedrin: "Again the high priest was questioning him and says to him, 'Are you the Christ, the Son of the Blessed One?'" (Mk 14:61; similarly Mt. 26:63; Lk. 22:66-67). John advances the demand to the earlier Feast of Dedication: "Therefore the Jews encircled him and were saying to him, 'Until when are you keeping us in suspense? If you are the Christ, tell us outright'" (10:22-24). Hence, no such demand appears in John's later account of the Jewish high priest's interrogation of Jesus (18:19-21).

John likewise advances the accusation that Jesus has committed blasphemy. In the Synoptics the high priest levels the accusation at Jesus' trial, or hearing: "You [my fellow Sanhedrinists] have heard the blasphemy [spoken by Jesus]" (Mk 14:64); "He has blasphemed!" (Mt. 26:65). Again John puts the accusation at the earlier Feast of Dedication and ascribes it to the Jews: "The Jews answered him, 'We are not trying to stone you for a good work, but for blasphemy, even because you, though you are a human being, are making yourself God'" (10:33-36). So John omits the accusation from his account of the Jewish high priest's interrogation of Jesus (18:19-24).

The Synoptics consistently portray the general resurrection as occurring in the future: "The Ninevite men will be resurrected at the judgment ... The queen of the South will be raised at the judgment" (Mt. 12:41-42; see also Mk 12:18-27; Mt. 22:23-33; Lk. 11:31-32; 14:14; 20:27-40). In John's Gospel, Martha tells Jesus that she knows her brother Lazarus "will rise in the resurrection at the last day" (11:24). But Jesus tells her that he himself *is* the resurrection, so that resurrection has already arrived.

As a result, every believer in him has resurrected life right now and therefore will escape eternal death even though dying at the end of present mortal life: "I am the resurrection and the life. The one believing in me will live even though he dies. And everyone living and believing in me will by no means die forever" (11:25-26).

In Mk 11:18 and Lk. 19:47-48, the Jewish chief priests and scribes in Jerusalem determine to do away with Jesus because of his temple-cleansing and popular teaching: "They were seeking how they might destroy him" (cf. Mk 12:13; Mt. 21:46; Lk. 20:19). Mark dates their determination to the day after Palm Sunday: "the next day" (Mk 11:12). In 11:46-57 of his Gospel, however, John backdates this determination to some time not only prior to Palm Sunday but also prior to Jesus' unspecified period of sojourn in "a city called Ephraim," located outside Judea in "a region near the wilderness" (11:54). Furthermore, John does not attribute the determination to Jesus' temple-cleansing and popular teaching, as in Synoptic tradition—rather, to Jesus' performance of "many signs," most recently and dramatically the raising of Lazarus from the dead (11:1-46). So far as Palm Sunday is concerned, John's quoting the Pharisees as saying to one another, "Look! The *world* has gone after him!" (12:19; emphasis added), and following up with the request of "some Greeks" to see Jesus (12:20-21), look like a Johannine advancement of evangelistic success during the church age right into Jesus' lifetime (cf. the foregoing comments on the advancement of Christian baptism and the evangelization of Samaritans in 4:1-42).

Though the transfiguration of Jesus, occurring as it did in the middle of his ministry, offered a private foregleam of his public glory at the second coming according to the Synoptics (see in particular Lk. 9:31-32), they regularly locate the public glorification of Jesus not until the second coming, "when he comes in the glory of his Father with the holy angels" (Mk 8:23; see also 10:37; 13:26; Mt. 16:27; 19:28; 24:30; 25:31; Lk. 9:26; 21:27; 24:26). John, however, dates Jesus' glory back to his preincarnate state (12:41; 17:24) and portrays the glory as publicly visible already through the incarnation (1:14) and Jesus' signs (2:11; 11:4). Moreover, John distinctively and ingeniously advances the event of Jesus' glorification from the second coming to his being lifted up on a cross, as opposed to being knocked down by way of two Jewish attempts to stone him to death: "The hour has come for the Son of Man to be glorified" (12:23); "Father, the hour has come; glorify your Son" (17:1; see also 8:59; 10:31; 12:16, 32-34; 13:31-32; 17:5). In view of these backdates of Jesus' glorification from the second coming to the crucifixion and long before, John dispenses with the transfigurational preview.

The Synoptic Son of Man will be coming (ἐρχόμενον) and his elect will be gathered not until after the great tribulation yet in the future: "after that tribulation" (Mk 13:24-27; Mt. 24:29-31; Lk. 21:25-28). Though Jn 21:22-23 carries a reference to that coming, Jn 14:1-3; 16:16-22; 20:19, 24, 26; and 21:13 not only backdate the coming to a time right after Jesus' resurrection but also pluralize it into several comings, as shown by the following analysis:

- The abiding of individual disciples *in Christ*, of which 15:4-7 speaks, defines *as Christ himself* the many abodes of which 14:1-3 speaks. Note well the cognate relationship of μοναί, "abodes" (14:2), and μένω, "abide" (15:4-7; cf. also the

statement in 14:23 that Jesus and his Father will make their μονήν, "abode," with obedient believers).
- By referring to the interval of Jesus' crucifixion, burial, and resurrection, the "little while" (μικρόν) of Jesus' disappearance from the disciples (16:16-19) defines his going to prepare a place for each of them—that is, abodes for them in himself—as his imminent salvific work through death and resurrection here on earth, not some figurative sort of carpentry up in heaven later on.
- Therefore, Jesus' "com[ing] again" (πάλιν ἔρχομαι) looks forward, not to what we usually call the second coming, but to the several comings of Jesus to his disciples right after his resurrection. *For John is the only one of the evangelists to use the verb "come" (ἔρχομαι) in connection with Jesus' resurrection-appearances, and he does so four times for three such appearances*: "Therefore when it was evening that day, the first of the week ... Jesus *came* and stood in the midst [of 'the disciples']" (20:19); "But Thomas, one of the Twelve, the one called Didymus, was not with them when Jesus *came*" (20:24); "And after eight days his disciples were inside again, and Thomas [was] with them. Though the doors were locked, Jesus *comes* and stood in the midst [of them]" (20:26); "Jesus *comes* and takes the bread and gives [it] to them, and the fish likewise" (21:13).
- Apparently Mary Magdalene was not present at the Last Supper and therefore was not among "the Twelve" (6:67, 70, 71; 20:24), to eleven of whom Jesus said he would come again and take to himself, so that John omits to use the verb "come" in relating Jesus' resurrection-appearance to Mary (20:14-17).
- Jesus' telling the disciples that *he* will see *them* after a little while rather than, as would be expected, that *they* will see *him* (16:22), plus his threefold bestowal of "Peace" on them when seeing them (20:19, 21, 26), granting them the Holy Spirit by breathing into them (20:22: ἐνεφύσησεν), and calling them his "brothers" and calling God their "Father" and their "God" as well as his own (20:17)—together these actions of Jesus constitute a collective fulfillment of the promise to receive the disciples to himself in order that where he is, they too may be (14:23).

There is no need, then, to mention a yet-future gathering of the elect, as in the Synoptics. Disciples are already with Jesus by abiding in him.

According to Mk 14:26-42; Mt. 26:30-46; and Lk. 22:39-46, on the Mount of Olives and after the Last Supper, which took place in the Upper Room, Jesus uttered his final prayer before crucifixion. In John's Gospel, the Last Supper starts at 13:1-2. Though Jesus says in 14:31, "Get up. Let's go from here," not till 18:1 does he actually go out with his disciples "across the Kidron Ravine to where a garden was." So his last prayer before crucifixion, appearing as it does in ch. 17, is uttered earlier than in the Synoptics. By putting it earlier and therefore at the Last Supper, John has Jesus praying self-composedly for his disciples in their immediate presence rather than apart from them, as the Synoptics have him, in an agonizing sweat of emotional turmoil over his own fate. (How else would we expect God-in-the-flesh [1:14] to behave than with confident self-composure?)

Now John follows up by advancing Jesus' death from the day after the Passover meal, when it occurs in the Synoptics (Mk 14:12-25 with 15:1; Mt. 26:17-29 with 27:1-2; Lk. 22:7-14 with 23:1),[3] to the afternoon when Passover lambs were slain (Jn 13:1; 18:28; 19:14-16). Not only does 13:1 place the Last Supper "before the Festival of Passover," but also the Jewish authorities who led Jesus to Pilate's praetorium did not enter it "lest they be defiled—rather, [that] they might eat the Passover" (18:28); and "it was the Preparation of the Passover [i.e., the Friday when they slaughtered and roasted the Passover lambs in preparation for eating the Passover meal that evening]" when Pilate gave Jesus over to the Jewish authorities "that he might be crucified" (19:14-16). As a result, John's Jesus dies as God's lamb whom the Baptist proclaimed him to be (1:29, 36)—indeed, as a Passover lamb whose bones were not to be broken (Exod. 12:46; Num. 9:12; cf. Ps. 34:20), just as Jesus' bones were not broken (Jn 19:33-36). No wonder, then, the unparalleled command to Judas Iscariot, "What you are doing do very quickly" (13:27). The Johannine Jesus determines his death to take place at the proper time for a Passover sacrifice, not a day too late as in the Synoptics.

An Excursus on the Last Supper in John

In a highly touted book Brant Pitre has elaborated a traditional interpretation of Jesus' Last Supper in John as a Passover meal, just as in the Synoptics.[4] If correct, this interpretation would mean that, contrary to the foregoing, John did not backdate Jesus' crucifixion so as to portray Jesus as God's true Passover lamb who sacrificed himself on the very afternoon when a Passover lamb was supposed to be slain, that is, prior to the following Passover meal.

Pitre correctly defines "Passover" (πάσχα) as carrying any one of several possible meanings, depending on context: Passover lamb, Passover meal, Passover peace offering, or Passover week. He also refutes effectively the Essene hypothesis, which posits the use of different Jewish liturgical calendars in the Synoptic and Johannine accounts, respectively, and he effectively defends the historicity of the Last Supper as a Passover meal, in accordance with the Synoptic accounts. But Pitre's arguments that the Johannine account likewise portrays a Passover meal need refutation.

Pitre infers that the reference in Jn 13:1 to "the festival of the Passover" implies a Passover meal in v. 2 and he argues that if John had wanted to avoid that implication he would have written "*one day* before the Passover" in v. 1 after the pattern of 12:1-2: "*six days* before the Passover." But if "the festival of the Passover" in 13:1 were meant to qualify δείπνου in 13:2 as the Passover meal, we might have

---

3. The Synoptics declare repeatedly and unequivocally the Last Supper to have been a Passover meal, so that in them Jesus was not crucified on the afternoon when Passover lambs were sacrificed (Mk 14:12, 14, 16; Mt. 26:17, 18, 19; Lk. 22:7, 8, 11, 13).

4. Brant Pitre, *Jesus and the Last Supper* (Grand Rapids: Eerdmans, 2015), 251–373.

expected τοῦ δείπνου, "*the* meal," with which the Passover festival started. As it is, the lack of a definite article with δείπνου is reminiscent of a similarly anarthrous δεῖπνον in 12:2, where people made a non-Passover meal, and thereby suggests another non-Passover meal in 13:2 (cf. the Synoptists' using δεῖπνον eight times, but never for the Passover meal). In 13:1, moreover, we might have expected "before *the Passover*" rather than "before *the festival* of the Passover" if John had meant to identify the meal in 13:2 with the Passover, as the Synoptists regularly do (cf. John's connecting πάσχα, whatever its referent, with eating in 18:28). On more than one count, then, John seems to avoid an identification of the meal in 13:2 as a Passover.

Also, according to Jn 13:1 Jesus "loved" his disciples "to the end." When? "Before the festival of the Passover." Pitre then interprets John to mean that Jesus loved his disciples to the end "*just* before the Passover meal." But the intensifying "just" has no basis in the Greek text, and Pitre omits the following bulk of v. 1: "Jesus, knowing that his hour had come for him to transfer out of this world to the Father, having loved his own [who were] in the world, loved them to the end." This omission combines with the addition of "just" to make the chronological phrase "before the festival of the Passover" seem closer to "meal" than it actually is in John's text.

Next, Pitre appeals to Passover-like elements in the Last Supper as described by John: the diners' reclining, Jesus' dipping of a morsel, and some of the disciples' supposing he had told Judas Iscariot to make a last-minute purchase for the feast or to make a charitable contribution to the poor. These elements do indeed reflect the tradition of a Passover meal. But just as John took over the tradition of Jesus' cleansing the temple yet backdated it so that it no longer galvanized the Jewish authorities' determination to do away with Jesus, and then fitted out the episode with material not found in the Synoptic accounts (2:13-22), so John takes over the tradition of Jesus' hosting a Passover meal yet backdates it so that despite carrying over Passover-like elements it no longer qualifies as such, and then fits out the episode with material not found in the Synoptic accounts. In short, we would *expect* a carryover of Passover-like elements in the backdating of what was originally a Passover meal.

According to Jn 18:28 the Jewish authorities did not enter Pilate's praetorium "lest they be defiled—rather, [that they] might eat the Passover." Pitre identifies this Passover with peace offerings eaten throughout the week following the Passover meal. But this interpretation rests on the foregoing argument that 13:1-2 "has already identified the Last Supper [in John] as the initial Jewish Passover meal." Given the weakness of that argument (dealt with above), 18:28 provides no further argument. Put another way, by arguing as he does on 13:1-2 Pitre *has* to take 18:28 as referring to Passover peace offerings.

Passover week did not start till sundown after the slaying of Passover lambs, and the Jews used "Preparation" (παρασκευή) for Friday because on that day they prepared meals for the Sabbath. So Pitre argues that in referring to the day of Jesus' crucifixion, παρασκευὴ τοῦ πάσχα in Jn 19:14 means the Friday of Passover *week* and therefore the day after the slaying of Passover lambs. But the phrase could equally well refer to the Friday when Passover *meals* were prepared, starting with the sacrifice of Passover lambs, which would put Jesus' self-sacrifice at the right time for a Passover sacrifice.

Pitre argues further that since Passover sacrifices did not start being slaughtered till 3:00 p.m. or a little earlier, and since Pilate delivered Jesus to the Jews for crucifixion at "about the sixth hour [taken as noon]" (Jn 19:14), John must not have intended his audience to think of Jesus' death as the true Passover sacrifice. But it was Jesus' death later in the afternoon, not his delivery for crucifixion, that corresponded to the death of Passover lambs.

John 19:31 describes the Sabbath following Good Friday as "great." Why? Because it was the day of the Sheaf Offering, according to Pitre, rather than because it was the second half of Passover day. Pitre allows the latter understanding as "possible," yet asks why then John did not identify that Sabbath with "Passover." But to Pitre's understanding it might be asked why John did not identify that Sabbath with "Sheaf" (δράγμα).

It remains highly problematic for Pitre's view that in contrast to the Synoptics, John carries no explicit identification of the Last Supper as a Passover meal. And though mentioning 1:29 ("Look! The lamb of God that takes away the world's sin!") a couple of times,[5] Pitre neither refutes nor discusses the widespread interpretation of that declaration as a reference to Jesus as God's Passover lamb. More astonishingly, Pitre does not even mention the non-breaking of Jesus' bones in fulfillment of the Mosaic law concerning the slaughter of Passover lambs, as noted explicitly and uniquely in Jn 19:31-37.

* * *

The Synoptists do not record the disciples' reception of the Holy Spirit. Luke 24:49 alludes to it, however, as happening after the disciples have stayed in Jerusalem for a period of time: Jesus told the disciples, "And behold, I am sending on you the Father's promise. But you—sit [tight] in the city till you are clothed with power from the height [of heaven]." But the reception is recorded in Luke's companion volume as having happened seven weeks later on the Day of Pentecost (Acts 2:1-4). John backdates the reception to the evening of the first Easter Sunday: "Therefore when it was evening that day, the first day of the week ... he [Jesus] breathed into [the disciples] and tells them, 'Receive the Holy Spirit'" (20:19, 22). Earlier, John editorialized that "the Spirit was not yet [received], because Jesus had not yet been glorified" (7:39). The first Easter Sunday morning Jesus told Mary Magdalene not to hold him, because he had not yet ascended to the Father, which ascension was to complete the glorification that started with his being lifted up on a cross (20:11-17). He was about to ascend to the Father, and he did so during the rest of that first Easter Sunday. For breathing the Holy Spirit into the disciples during the evening signaled that the prerequisite of glorification had reached completion.

---

5. Ibid., 315, 326.

Jesus' somewhat later invitation to Thomas, "Reach out your finger here and see my hands, and reach out your hand and thrust [it] into my side" (20:27), also implies the completion of Jesus' glorification and thus both a rescinding of the command not to hold Jesus and a confirming of what we might call an early Pentecost in the Fourth Gospel.

Though Mary Magdalene, Mary the mother of James, and Salome went to Jesus' empty tomb "very early in the morning," according to Mk 16:2, they did not go till "the sun had risen." Similarly, in Mt. 28:1 "Mary Magdalene and the other Mary" went to the tomb "later than the Sabbath, as [night] was twilighting into the first [day] of the week" (ὀψέ ... σαββάτων, τῇ ἐπιφωσκούσῃ εἰς μίαν σαββάτων); and in Lk. 24:1 the women went there "on the first [day] of the week at deep (βαθέως) dawn." Though it was early, in other words, the light of dawn was already shining. But we read in Jn 20:1 that Mary Magdalene came to the tomb so "early on the first [day] of the week" that "it was still dark" (σκοτίας ἔτι οὔσης). John has advanced her coming to a point of time prior to dawn. So when Mary sees Jesus, he will appear to her as the true sun, the just-risen light of the world who banishes the darkness of sin and judgment. John 11:9 has made clear that, literally speaking, "the light of the world" means the sun: "If anyone walks around during the day, he does not stumble, because he sees the light of this world." And 8:12 made clear that Jesus compared himself to sunlight: "I am the light of the world" (see also 1:4-5; 12:35-36, 46; 1 Jn 2:8; and cf. John's omitting the darkness that according to the Synoptics obscured the sun on Good Friday afternoon, because the uplifted light of the world was shining from a cross).

In the Synoptics, only Lk. 24:51 mentions Jesus' ascension into heaven ("he departed from them and was being carried up into heaven"; see also Acts 1:9-11). But it is generally agreed that there is a special connection of one sort or another between Luke and John. So it is worth noting that whereas the ascension occurred forty days after Passion Week in Luke-Acts (see, in particular, Acts 1:3, 6-11), in John the ascension not only started with the lifting up of Jesus on a cross (see earlier comments) but also reached completion on the first Easter Sunday: "Jesus tells her, 'Do not hold me, for I have not yet ascended to the Father. But go to my brothers and tell them I am ascending to my Father and your Father, and [to] my God and your God'" (Jn 20:17).

According to Lk. 24:44-51 ("You are witnesses") and Acts 1:6-11 ("You shall be my witnesses") Jesus delivered the Great Commission not until the day of his ascension from the Mount of Olives. Matthew 28:16-20 ("Disciple all the nations") locates the delivery on a mountain in Galilee after the disciples have gone there to see the risen Jesus. According to Jn 20:19-23, on the other hand, he delivered the Great Commission ("Just as the Father sent me, I too am sending you") already on the evening of the first Easter Sunday—and in direct connection with breathing the Holy Spirit into his disciples. No waiting around for the Spirit's descent at Pentecost seven weeks later.

If then the Gospels present what the honoree of this volume, Kevin J. Vanhoozer, calls a "theodrama," John's habit of backdating would appear to make his version of the theodrama a preview of coming attractions. Several hermeneutical questions follow therefrom. The first has to do with historicity. Apart from problems of harmonizing the Synoptics with each other, does not Johannine chronology often look unhistorical in comparison with Synoptic chronology (if not vice versa as well)? If so, a question of literary genre arises: Are we to understand at least John as narrative fiction to a significant extent? That question raises in turn a question concerning scriptural inspiration or, more exactly (on the basis of belief in the Gospels' canonicity), the nature of scriptural inspiration. At the level of language's "natural meaning," which Vanhoozer favors, can such inspiration allow outright conflict between John and the Synoptics? Given a conflict at the level of natural meaning, questions of interpretation then arise: What is the *meaning* in this or that Johannine text? Does John intend his backdating to be taken as historically more accurate than the Synoptics' chronology? Or only, but importantly, as theologically "thicker" and therefore richer than that of the Synoptics? Finally, what kind of theodramatic performance on the part of John's audience does the backdating call for?

As to the question of historicity, Vanhoozer has noted Paul Ricoeur's denial of a sharp dichotomy between history and fiction, has warned that this denial risks a loss of the distinction between historical truth and fictional fantasy, and has cited the Rule of Faith as "a 'construal' of Scripture as a *unified* narrative."[6] Yet "*the authority of the Rule depends on its conforming to the Scriptures*," writes Vanhoozer.[7] So how can we think of Scripture as a unified narrative if at the level of natural meaning both the chronological language of John and its associated material disagree with both the Synoptics' chronological language and its associated material? Or is it that the Rule's conformity to Scripture requires making room for some fiction in John's narrative, some "apostolic creative imagination,"[8] whatever our own predilections when it comes to the meaning of "natural language"?

Hence the question of literary genre. Here Vanhoozer comes down firmly in favor of variety, even in regard to the issue of historicity: "The historical intent of the Gospels need not mean that they refer to actuality *tout court*."[9] He also allows the possibility that the book of Jonah is a "combination" of "history" and "fiction" (among other things) and affirms that not "all narratives" in the Bible are "accurate historical records."[10] So it is "essentially" a "*modern* theory of meaning and truth that generates literalistic interpretations and harmonizations where all parts of the Bible are read as though the primary intent were to state historical facts."[11]

---

6. Kevin J. Vanhoozer, *The Drama of Doctrine: A Canonical-Linguistic Approach to Christian Theology* (Louisville: Westminster John Knox, 2005), 204 (emphasis added); see also Vanhoozer, *Biblical Narrative in the Philosophy of Paul Ricoeur: A Study in Hermeneutics and Theology* (Cambridge: Cambridge University Press, 1990), 11–12, 149–50, 262–6.

7. Vanhoozer, *Drama of Doctrine*, 206–7 (emphasis original).

8. Ibid., 92 (but, differently from here, in reference to "the account of Jesus' resurrection").

9. Vanhoozer, *Biblical Narrative*, 282.

10. Kevin J. Vanhoozer, *Is There a Meaning in This Text? The Bible, the Reader, and the Morality of Literary Knowledge* (Grand Rapids: Zondervan, 1998), 328, 424–5.

11. Ibid., 426 (emphasis original); see also p. 296.

Consequently, reconstructing John's intentions, whether theologically historical or theologically fictional or a mixture of both, depends in Vanhoozer's language "both on our grasp of the text as a whole *and on our knowledge of facts outside the text*."[12] The facts outside John's text include the Synoptic texts. So, apart from engaging in unlikely harmonizations, backdatings in the Fourth Gospel often look either like intentionally historical contradictions of the Synoptics or, as seems more likely, intentionally theological though unhistorical elaborations. Despite treating the whole Bible as a unified theodrama, then, Vanhoozer's recognition of "the diverse speech-acts that together make up the Bible" and of "*the various illocutions in Scripture*" appears to make room for a plurality of theodramas exhibiting different proportions of factual history and "lyric" theology within the consequently multifaceted, overarching theodrama.[13]

So what of the "Reformation insight" that "the infallible rule of interpretation of Scripture is Scripture itself"?[14] Must we conform John to the Synoptics? Or vice versa? To do either would effectively rob one or the others of their divine inspiration and canonicity. And to propose unlikely harmonizations, or to plead ignorance of harmonizations presently beyond our ken, would effectively rob *both* John *and* the Synoptics of their communicative value and thereby attenuate their divine inspiration and canonicity. Far better, then, to posit different kinds of illocutions and preserve the canon as fully "normative for Christian theology."[15] But does this position create, or recognize, an "ugly ditch" between "publicly ascertainable history" in Synoptic chronology, on the one hand, and "privately valued belief" in Johannine chronology, on the other hand?[16] No, because the chronologies remain both individually and conjointly open to public ascertainment and private evaluation alike.

But Vanhoozer is not content to let matters rest in the biblical "script," even if it is understood correctly. He wants performance on stage. So what kind of performance does John's scripted backdating call for? I might offer a suggestion or two. But as a former teacher of Kevin (as I shall now call him) I used to give him homework assignments, and here is my last chance to do so again. So, Kevin, if directing a stage performance of John's theodrama, with particular attention to the element of backdating, how would you have your actors express in word and deed, to our "world" (a favorite term in the Fourth Gospel) as culturally exegeted by you, the meaning and significance of the backdating surveyed above?

---

12. Ibid., 259 (emphasis added).

13. Vanhoozer, *Drama of Doctrine*, 67–8 (emphasis original). Cf. Clement of Alexandria's describing John's Gospel as "spiritual" in contradistinction to the Synoptics as presenting "external facts" (*apud* Eus. *Hist. eccl.* 6.14.7).

14. *Westminster Confession of Faith*, 1.9, cited in Vanhoozer, *Is There a Meaning in This Text?*, 305.

15. Vanhoozer, *Drama of Doctrine*, 135.

16. For the quoted phrases, see Kevin J. Vanhoozer, "Introduction: What Is Theological Interpretation of the Bible?" in *Dictionary for Theological Interpretation of the Bible*, ed. Kevin J. Vanhoozer (Grand Rapids: Baker Academic, 2005), 20.

Chapter 5

THE GREAT ANTAGONIST

Graham A. Cole

Introduction

Broadly speaking, there are two kinds of scholars. First, there are the very few creative scholars who contribute fresh methods, frameworks, and perspectives to their disciplines. Second, there are the interpretive scholars who take the insights of the creative farther, deepening and applying them in innovative ways. Of course, there are creative scholars who are also great interpreters of others—such as Kevin J. Vanhoozer, who has contributed so much to both the academic guild and the church. The notion of theodrama, as he understands it, is one such contribution.[1] His *Drama of Doctrine* especially comes to mind. For some, Vanhoozer and theodrama belong in the same sentence. Indeed, the language of theodrama and allied terms (e.g., scripts, performance) are now quite commonplace in the circles in which I move.

The idea of theodrama conjures up associations with literature and the theater. In a feat of theological imagination, Vanhoozer has been able to rearticulate comprehensively an intelligent orthodoxy in fresh language drawn from the world of theater. He is not the first to see theology in theodramatic terms. Hans Urs von Balthasar is the chief case in point, and Vanhoozer acknowledges his debts to Balthasar.[2] What Vanhoozer offers is a creative appropriation of some of Balthasar's leading ideas.

---

1. Hans Urs von Balthasar captures the essence of his *Dramatik* in his *My Work in Retrospect*, trans. John Saward (San Francisco: Ignatius, 1993), 97–9. Others have used the notion of drama simpliciter as a lens through which to view the biblical witness (e.g., B. B. Warfield, Dorothy Sayers, Bernard Anderson, inter alia). The systematic way in which Vanhoozer, as an evangelical, has done it makes his work stand out.

2. E.g., see Kevin J. Vanhoozer, *The Drama of Doctrine: A Canonical Linguistic Approach to Christian Theology* (Louisville: Westminster John Knox, 2005). There are twenty-eight mentions of Balthasar in this work.

This contribution in Vanhoozer's honor explores one aspect of theodrama. To do so we will adopt a canonical reading strategy as we offer a theological interpretation of a crucial element in the biblical plotline.

Every Great Drama Has One

One what? An antagonist.[3] Not all stories need an antagonist but drama does. Not all stories need conflict but drama does.[4] Think of Shakespeare and the evil Lady Macbeth in Macbeth or J. K. Rowling's Lord Voldemort in the Harry Potter books or Darth Vader in the Star Wars saga.[5] The same is true of the biblical storyline. Of course, opponents of God's purposes are found in both the OT and NT. In the OT, one thinks of Ahab and Jezebel, and in the NT Herod the Great. However, by the time the canon has been read in its entirety, one figure stands out: Satan.[6] Traditionally, Satan is identified as a fallen angel, although Karl Barth had his doubts.[7] This figure goes by many additional names and descriptors in the biblical deposit. Millard J. Erickson lists them as they are found in the NT:

3. For a brief explanation of the concept of the antagonist and the relation of the antagonist to the protagonist, see Leland Ryken, *A Complete Handbook of Literary Forms in the Bible* (Wheaton: Crossway, 2014), 23. In theater and film terms, the protagonist is the lead actor.

4. The antagonist need not be human. The great white shark plays that role in the film *Jaws*.

5. For a survey of the best villains in literature, see https://lithub.com/40-of-the-best-villains-in-literature/ (accessed February 13, 2019). For a survey of the best film villains, see https://www.empireonline.com/movies/features/best-movie-villains/ (accessed February 13, 2019).

6. Significant literature on the devil includes the following: Philip C. Almond, *The Devil: A New Biography* (Ithaca: Cornell University Press, 2014); Darren Oldridge, *The Devil: A Very Short Introduction* (Oxford: Oxford University Press, 2012); Jeffrey Burton Russell, *Satan: The Early Christian Tradition* (Ithaca: Cornell University Press, 1987); Miguel A. De La Torre and Albert Hernandez, *The Quest for the Historical Satan* (Minneapolis: Fortress, 2011); Gregory A. Boyd, *Satan and the Problem of Evil: Constructing Trinitarian Warfare Theodicy* (Downers Grove: IVP Academic, 2001); Sharon Beekmann and Peter G. Bolt, *Silencing Satan: Handbook of Biblical Demonology* (Eugene, OR: Wipf and Stock, 2012). This work also has an extensive bibliography. See further Peter G. Bolt, ed., *Christ's Victory over Evil: Biblical Theology and Pastoral Ministry* (Nottingham: Inter-Varsity, 2009); Richard Beck, *Reviving Old Scratch: Demons and the Devil for Doubters and the Disenchanted* (Minneapolis: Fortress, 2016). Peter Kreeft, *Angels and Demons: What Do We Really Know about Them?* (San Francisco: Ignatius, 1995), provides a Roman Catholic perspective on the questions surrounding angels, Satan, and demons.

7. For a discussion of the identity of Satan and (to my mind) Karl Barth's idiosyncratic view of the devil, see *CD*, III/3, 369–531. Barth claims that Satan was never an angel. This work also discusses the devil's entourage, namely, the demons.

Several other terms are used of him less frequently: tempter (Matt. 4:3; 1 Thess. 3:5), Beelzebul (Matt. 12:24, 27; Mark 3:22; Luke 11:15, 19), enemy (Matt. 13:39), evil one (Matt. 13:19, 38; 1 John 2:13; 3:12; 5:18), Belial (2 Cor. 6:15); adversary (1 Peter 5:18), deceiver (Rev. 12:9), great dragon (Rev. 12:3), father of lies (John 8:44), murderer (John 8:44), sinner (1 John 3:8).[8]

To the list we can add the god of this world (2 Corinthians 4) and perhaps "Apollyon" (Rev. 9:11, meaning "destroyer").[9]

The role of this antagonist in the theodrama merits exploration, which Vanhoozer has begun.[10] In his discussion of the Gospel Theater, he includes Satan and his messengers as rebellious cast members. In this brief but insightful treatment of Satan and his demons, Vanhoozer uses speech-act theory to refresh the language about the evil one and his followers. Satan and his minions, he argues, "possess a peculiarly improper or corrupt kind of communicative agency" as they seek to sow "covenantal discord and division."[11] Indeed, he describes Satan as a "counterfeit communicative" agent, who "is largely responsible for the conflict that propels the drama forward."[12] Satan's medium of mischief consists of words, which Vanhoozer describes "as nothing short of an assault on the Creator and created order alike."[13]

Much more remains to explore, as this present chapter attempts to do by interacting more extensively with the biblical theodrama's plotline.

The Great Antagonist

Among Aristotle's myriad curiosities, he wrote about stories:

> A [story that is] whole is that which has a beginning, middle, and end. A beginning is that which does not itself follow necessarily from something else, but after which a further event or process naturally occurs. An end, by contrast, is that which itself naturally occurs, whether necessarily or usually, after a preceding event, but need not be followed by anything else. A middle is that which both follows a preceding event and has further consequences. Well-constructed plots,

---

8. Millard J. Erickson, *Christian Theology*, 3rd ed. (Grand Rapids: Baker Academic, 2013), 417.

9. J. I. Packer, *Concise Theology: A Guide to Historic Christian Beliefs* (Wheaton: Tyndale, 1993), 69. Others distinguish Apollyon from Satan and argue that Apollyon is a great demon ruler but an underling of Satan. See Merrill F. Unger, *Biblical Demonology: A Study of Spiritual Forces Today* (Grand Rapids: Kregel, 1994), 73-4, for this view.

10. Kevin J. Vanhoozer, *Faith Speaking Understanding: Performing the Drama of Doctrine* (Louisville: Westminster John Knox, 2014), 87-9.

11. Ibid., 87.

12. Ibid., 87-8.

13. Ibid., 88.

therefore, should neither begin nor end at an arbitrary point, but should make use of the patterns stated.[14]

Canonization has produced a biblical plotline and thus a narrative with a beginning, a middle, and an end. So let us first consider the beginning before shifting our focus to the end of the story. The middle will briefly occupy our attention in this section, but more so in the next one.

The first appearance of the chief antagonist to God's Word and ways is found in Genesis 3 and the fall narrative. This figure plays the role of the spoiler of paradise. In a dialogue with Eve, the serpent, who is later identified in the canon as Satan, raises questions about the actual content of God's speech and the integrity of the divine character. The serpent asks (Gen. 3:1), "Did God really say, 'You must not eat from any tree in the garden'?" Before long, the serpent blatantly contradicts God and by implication impugns God's character (Gen. 3:4-5): "You will not certainly die," the serpent said to the woman. "For God knows that when you eat from it your eyes will be opened, and you will be like God, knowing good and evil." Eve succumbs to the primal temptation to disobey the Word of God concerning the tree of the knowledge of good and evil. Adam joins her in this folly. Jacques Ellul rightly describes the result as Le Rupture, for the result is relational catastrophe. There are now ruptures in the relations between the first pair of humans and their Creator (flight, not fellowship), between the male and the female (blame shifting), within the human psyche (fear and shame), and between the humans and the environment (thorns and thistles). The ejection of the man and woman from the garden paradise is an exile that lacks any possibility of ending until the Christ endures exile on the cross on behalf of humankind.

Although Satan rarely appears in the OT part of the canon, conflict is found in numerous places.[15] In Act One, as it were, the great conflict that is a precursor to the NT antagonism between Christ and Satan runs between Pharaoh and the gods of Egypt, on the one hand, and Moses and the God of Abraham, Isaac, and Jacob, on the other. The account of the conflict occupies the script of the first fifteen chapters of the book of Exodus. The *protevangelium* (Gen. 3:15) and the subsequent promises to Abram are under threat (Gen. 12:1-3). The children of Abraham are in bondage in Egypt. The Lord hears and responds (Exodus 1-2, especially 2:23-25). God's kingdom agent is Moses, who in numerous encounters with the Pharaoh represents the divine interests (Exodus 3). God demands that Pharaoh let the people of Israel go so that they might serve ("serve" means "worship" in context) their God (cf. Exod. 8:1; 10:24-25). In miracle after miracle, Pharaoh is discomforted; after the climactic death of the Egyptian firstborn, including Pharaoh's own son, he reluctantly lets Israel go, only to pursue them with his army

---

14. Aristotle, *Poetics* 1450b25-33, here quoting *Aristotle: Poetics, Longinus: On the Sublime, Demetrius: On Style*, trans. Stephen Halliwell, et al., rev. Donald A. Russell, LCL 199 (Cambridge, MA: Harvard University Press, 1995), 55.

15. To explore all the instances of conflict is well beyond the scope of this exercise.

(Exodus 7–12, 14). The sea parts and Israel escapes (Exodus 14). Pharaoh's army, however, does not escape being drowned as the waters return (Exodus 14). God has triumphed over Pharaoh as the Song of Moses shows (Exod. 15:1): "I will sing to the LORD, for he is highly exalted. Both horse and driver he has hurled into the sea." Importantly, God has triumphed over the gods of Egypt as well (Exod. 12:12). This is the exodus story so dear to observant Jews even to this day.

In the middle and at its center is Jesus Christ. The coming of Christ as the light of the world exposes the depths of devilish darkness. The paucity of OT references to Satan gives way to a relative flood of NT revelation, as we shall see in the next part of our discussion. To anticipate, in Act Two the conflict climaxes in the story of the cross and subsequent vindication of Christ. Importantly for our purpose, Jesus understood what he was to accomplish in Jerusalem and by his cross in exodus terms, as the account of the Transfiguration shows (Lk. 9:31). For now, what we are to note in the NT writings is the characterization of Satan as the blinder of minds (2 Cor. 4:4), an angel of light (2 Cor. 11:14), and a roaring lion (1 Pet. 5:8). As the Christian wears the armor of God (Eph. 6:11-13), the devil is to be opposed with the Word of God, which is the sword of the Spirit (Eph. 6:17) and prayer (Eph. 6:18-20). The language of "stand" and "withstand" found in Ephesians suggests that the Christian is in a defensive posture. There is no NT mandate to seek out the evil one and confront him. Such is life in the now-but-not-yet.

The last appearance of the opponent of God's purposes is in Rev. 20:1-10. In this mysterious NT book, there is a description of a millennial period of shalom until there is an outbreak of evil at its end. The devil figures in this picture as the great deceiver, echoing the primal deception as the *modus operandi* of this evil character. The fate of the antagonist is sealed by divine judgment. The lake of fire sees to that. The programmatic statement found in Gen. 3:15 is fulfilled; the serpent's head is indeed crushed.

Now the question may be asked: Is this canonical reading strategy unscholarly eisegesis of OT texts such as Genesis 3, reading later materials into much earlier ones? After all, the OT has little to say about the serpent and indeed Satan. This is a fair question. What is the way forward then? Stephen G. Dempster provides an answer when he writes, "The fact of canonization creates a new literary context for all the individual texts involved, and this fact makes one text out of many."[16] Dempster quotes Harry Gamble with approval: "In the nature of the case, canonization entails a recontextualization of the documents incorporated into the canon. They are abstracted from both their generative and traditional settings and redeployed as parts of a new literary whole; henceforth they are read in terms of this collection. In this way their historically secondary context becomes their hermeneutically primary context."[17] A robust understanding of the divine

---

16. Stephen G. Dempster, "Geography and Genealogy, Dominion and Dynasty: A Theology of the Hebrew Bible," in *Biblical Theology: Retrospect and Prospect*, ed. Scott J. Hafemann (Downers Grove: InterVarsity, 2002), 68.

17. Ibid., n. 8.

inspiration of the Scriptures and the role of the Holy Spirit in their production undergirds these notions.

The Great Antagonist's Desideratum

What motivates the devil to be the spoiler? Perhaps the best clue to the diabolical agenda is found in the temptation of Christ. Having been anointed by the Spirit and baptized by John, the Spirit drives Jesus into the wilderness. The devil tempts Jesus three times. Each temptation, if embraced, would lead to Jesus' abandoning his obedience to the Father. He would become like two other sons of God. He would fail like Adam did in the garden (Genesis 3) and Israel did in the wilderness (Psalm 95). However, Jesus stays true. He proves to be all that Adam should have been and all that Israel should have been.

The third temptation is the most revealing. We read in Mt. 4:9-10:

> Again, the devil took him to a very high mountain and showed him all the kingdoms of the world and their splendor. "All this I will give you," he said, "if you will bow down and worship me."
>
> Jesus said to him, "Away from me, Satan! For it is written: 'Worship the Lord your God, and serve him only.'"

As with the earlier temptations, Jesus shows himself to be the supreme hermeneut. He counters the devil with yet another quote from Deuteronomy, as apposite as the previous two quotes from the same OT text he had used to counter the devil (Mt. 4:3-7).

The devil wants worship. He wants center stage, the place that only God should occupy. (Indeed, Satan wants to replace the lead actor and control the script, the stage direction, and the cast.) In this he apes the divine agenda, which is to reclaim true worship throughout creation. Jesus made the divine agenda clear to the woman at the well in Samaria (Jn 4:21-24):

> "Woman," Jesus replied, "believe me, a time is coming when you will worship the Father neither on this mountain nor in Jerusalem. You Samaritans worship what you do not know; we worship what we do know, for salvation is from the Jews. Yet a time is coming and has now come when the true worshipers will worship the Father in the Spirit and in truth, for they are the kind of worshipers the Father seeks. God is spirit, and his worshipers must worship in the Spirit and in truth."

That agenda is realized in the world to come when all becomes sacred space and redeemed humanity worships God and the Lamb (Rev. 22:1-5). The original divine intent is actualized. Adam was a king and a priest; so too redeemed humankind. In the world to come, God's image bearers will both worship and reign.

The Christus Victor Response

The divine response to the great rupture was one of both grace and judgment. The grace can be seen in God's provision of coverings for the naked pair, and exile from the garden may have been gracious too. Some argue that if the couple had eaten of the tree of life they would have been locked into their predicament. To use a phrase from C. S. Lewis, exile may have been a "severe mercy."[18] Judgment is seen in the pronouncement of curses and in exclusion from the divine presence. The scene is not without hope, however. A promise is made. The serpent will be held accountable, as Gen. 3:15 (the *protevangelium* mentioned earlier) makes plain: "And I will put enmity between you and the woman, and between your offspring and hers; he will crush your head, and you will strike his heel." The future signals a divine intervention through a human agent.

The Johannine literature is particularly revealing as to both the identity of this agent and the task before him. He is both God and human (Jn 1:1-14). He bridges heaven and earth. He embodies Jacob's ladder (Jn 1:51). He is the revealer of God the Father (Jn 1:18) and the Lamb of God who definitively deals with the sin of the world (Jn 1:29). Importantly, he was manifested to destroy the works of the devil (1 Jn 3:8). The divine intention in the incarnation and atoning sacrifice of the Son of God is manifold.

The coming of the Son of God is met with the challenge from the darkness. The threat of evil starts at the beginning. Herod the Great goes on a rampage against the male infants of Bethlehem and the region. He brooked no rival king. However, an angelic messenger warned Jesus' family to escape the slaughter of the innocents (Mt. 2:16-18). The devil is not named; even so, the threat of evil in opposition to the divine intention is patent. The temptations bring the devil into focus. His evil machinations are defeated by the faithfulness of Christ (Mt. 4:1-11). Jesus' exorcisms and healings are demonstrating the overthrow of the strongman and the spoiling of his goods; that is how Jesus saw it (Mk 3:27). Indeed, to ascribe Jesus' mighty works to the devil is to run the risk of an unpardonable sin (Mk 3:28-30). Peter sums up Jesus' ministry in his address to Cornelius in terms of conflict with the devil (Acts 10:38): "how God anointed Jesus of Nazareth with the Holy Spirit and power, and how he went around doing good and healing all who were under the power of the devil, because God was with him."

In the Johannine account, with the prospect of the cross looming before him, Jesus made the connection between his death and the defeat of the devil (Jn 12:31-33): "'Now is the time for judgment on this world; now the prince of this world will be driven out. And I, when I am lifted up from the earth, will draw all people to myself.' He said this to show the kind of death he was going to die." The passion narrative further makes darkness visible in the Johannine explanation of Jesus' betrayal by Judas. In John's account, the upper room discourse throws light on the ultimate causal agent of the betrayal (Jn 13:2): "The evening meal was in

---

18. See Sheldon Vanauken, *A Severe Mercy* (London: Hodder and Stoughton, 1992), 209.

progress, and the devil had already prompted Judas, the son of Simon Iscariot, to betray Jesus." This NIV translation is somewhat anemic. "Prompted" is too weak. The ESV translation is rightly stronger concerning the devil's role. The devil "put [*beblēkotos*, perfect aspect] it [the idea of betrayal] into the heart [*eis tēn kardia*] of Judas." The ESV captures the point that the devil's nefarious intervention affected the very core of Judas's being.

Jesus' death on the cross is replete with dramatic irony.[19] The audience knows what the devil does not know. His engineering of Jesus' death is to bring about his own defeat. The book of Hebrews captures the irony (Heb. 2:14-15): "Since the children have flesh and blood, he too shared in their humanity so that by his death he might break the power of him who holds the power of death—that is, the devil—and free those who all their lives were held in slavery by their fear of death." Jesus died our death. That is to say, he stood in our place and took the judgment we deserve. The devil's power lies in the very human fear of judgment after death. That death and subsequent resurrection of Christ provide a very different future for those in union with him. That future is nothing less than being led to glory (Heb. 2:10).

The resurrection, ascension, and enthronement of Jesus placed him in the position of executive power in God's kingdom. He is declared to be the Son of God by his resurrection from the dead (Rom. 1:4). He is at the right hand of the Father as both Lord and Christ (Acts 2:36). He is vindicated by the Spirit (1 Tim. 3:16). The risen, ascended, and glorified Christ commissions Paul on the Damascus road to be his agent against the devil's kingdom. Paul preached to King Agrippa (Acts 26:17-18): "I will rescue you from your own people and from the Gentiles. I am sending you to them to open their eyes and turn them from darkness to light, and from the power of Satan to God, so that they may receive forgiveness of sins and a place among those who are sanctified by faith in me."

Oscar Cullmann characterized the now and not yet of NT eschatology in an intriguing way with a well-known analogy.[20] He compared the victory of the cross over evil to the D-Day of the Second World War. D-Day in June 1944 was the turning point in the European theater of war; the allies landed at Normandy and the retaking of Europe had begun. The Nazis were not finally defeated until May 1945; that final victory is celebrated as VE Day (Victory in Europe). The now of D-Day was the not yet of VE Day. His analogy is especially apposite with regard to the devil. The cross was the judgment of the prince of this world (Jn 16:7-11, especially v. 11), the event that disarmed the principalities and powers (Col. 2:13-15). It is also the deed that undoes the power of the devil over those who fear death, as the book of Hebrews argues: "Since the children have flesh and blood, he too shared in their humanity so that by his death he might break the power of him who holds the power of death—that is, the devil—and free those who all their

---

19. On dramatic irony, see Ryken, *A Complete Handbook of Literary Forms*, 67.

20. Oscar Cullmann, *Christ and Time: The Primitive Christian Conception of Time and History*, trans. Floyd F. Filson (Philadelphia: Westminster, 1964), 84.

lives were held in slavery by their fear of death." However, final victory awaits. In the in-between time, we wait and work. We redeem the time as people who understand their eschatological setting (Eph. 5:15-16).

While We Wait

There are a number of ways in which the NT writers characterize the in-between time. Paul locates his Romans readers within the space of a groaning creation longing to be set free (Rom. 8:18-25). He locates his Galatian readers within the time frame of this present evil age (Gal. 1:4). He also writes of living in the end of the ages (1 Cor. 10:11). He also places his readers in the *regnum Christi* (1 Cor. 15:25). There is a day coming when God will be all in all (1 Cor. 15:28). The writer to the Hebrews writes of "these last days" (Heb. 1:1-2). The book of Revelation ends with expectation (Rev. 22:21): "Come, Lord Jesus!"

So what is the task of God's people in the in-between time? For a start, believers need to avoid what Paul G. Hiebert described as "the flaw of the excluded middle." He argued that Western Christians had excluded a whole kind of creature from their worldview. This middle consisted of spirits of various kinds (e.g., angels and demons). Hiebert wrote,

> The reasons for my uneasiness with the biblical and Indian worldviews should be clear. I had excluded the middle level of supernatural this-worldly beings and forces from my own worldview. As a scientist I had been trained to deal with the empirical world in naturalistic terms. As a theologian I was taught to answer ultimate questions in theistic terms. For me the middle zone did not really exist. Unlike Indian villagers, I had given little thought to spirits of this world, to local ancestors and ghosts, or to the souls of animals. For me these belonged to the realm of fairies, trolls, and other mythical beings.[21]

Rudolf Bultmann serves as an example of the blind spot that Hiebert identified. Bultmann famously wrote, "We cannot use electric lights and radios and, in the event of illness, avail ourselves of modern medical and clinical means and at the same time believe in the spirit and wonder world of the New Testament."[22] Recently, Miguel A. De La Torre and Albert Hernandez evidence a similar skepticism when they write,

---

21. Paul G. Hiebert, *Anthropological Reflections on Missiological Issues* (Grand Rapids: Baker, 1994), 196.

22. Rudolf Bultmann, "The New Testament and Mythology: The Problem of Demythologizing the New Testament Proclamation," quoted in *The New Testament and Mythology and Other Basic Writings*, ed. and trans. Schubert Ogden (Philadelphia: Fortress, 1984), 4. Craig S. Keener's magisterial *Miracles: The Credibility of New Testament Accounts*, 2 vols. (Grand Rapids: Baker Academic, 2011) is a worthy answer to Bultmann-like skepticism.

We have ended the quest for the historical Satan by finding him in the mirror. We have seen Satan, and much too often over the past twenty centuries he has been us Christians. The real quest that now lies before us is finding a way to exorcize this Satan and the demonic legions lodged within the heart of and mind of an exclusivist and persecuting tradition.[23]

The gospel may be spoiled in a myriad of ways. The work of Christ can be added to; this appears to have been the problem in Galatia, with Moses added to Christ. The person of Christ can be subtracted from. John's first letter describes those who deny that Christ came in the flesh; their Christ had no real humanity. Christ's mediatorship can be lost or obscured by interposing other figures in between God and ourselves, which seems to have been the case at Colossae with angelic figures. Finally, the gospel can be spoiled through disproportion; a biblical truth can be given weight that the canon does not give. The promise of Christ's return was bent out of shape by some of the Thessalonians, who stopped work to await it. So the figure of Satan—and the demonic realm—can consume too much attention (the very thing Satan craves). A handy rule of thumb is to ask: Having read the NT, would I have expected this much emphasis?

Also to be avoided is so redescribing Satan in a reductionist way that his malevolence is depersonalized. Walter Wink is a case in point. Wink, through numerous works, brought the theological world's attention to the deleterious role of demonic forces in society. He understood the Pauline references to "principalities and powers" as referring to impersonal forces at work through human institutions in destructive ways. The Apartheid regime in South Africa illustrated his thesis. In a 2010 interview, he relates having heard striking language from black South Africans: "When I was in South Africa, I actually heard South African people use the phrase, 'The system is at the door. Sneak out the back.'"[24] Apartheid evidenced a power producing an inhuman injustice in white-dominated South African society. He explains, "When a particular Power becomes idolatrous, placing itself above God's purposes for the good of the whole, then that power becomes demonic."[25] But what of Satan per se? Wink argues, "Perhaps in the final analysis Satan is not even a 'personality' at all, but rather a function in the divine process, a dialectical movement in God's purpose which becomes evil only when humanity breaks off the dialectic by refusing creative choice."[26] This does not do justice to the NT witness.[27]

---

23. De La Torre and Hernandez, *The Quest for the Historical Satan*, 220–1.

24. Walter Wink, interview by Steve Holt. Available online: https://www.slideshare.net/smh00a/sojourners-walter-amp-june-wink-interview (accessed February 17, 2021).

25. Walter Wink, *Naming the Powers: The Language of Power in the New Testament* (Philadelphia: Fortress, 1984), 5.

26. Quoted in Stephen F. Noll, *Angels of Light, Powers of Darkness: Thinking Biblically about Angels, Satan, and Principalities* (Eugene, OR: Wipf and Stock, 1998), 123.

27. Although I have a number of criticisms of Wink's theology of the principalities and powers as too reductionist, he is to be applauded for drawing attention to the structural realties of sin.

The NT presents various ways of responding to the devilish threat. Peter sees the devil as the roaring lion seeking prey. He has persecution in mind. In that light, Peter counsels resistance (1 Pet. 5:8-9). Being alert and watchful and having a firm faith are the crucial elements in so resisting. Paul is more expansive. In his second letter to the Corinthians he draws their attention to Eve's story. Paul portrays the devil as the seducer and sees the primal story as analogous to the threat facing the Corinthians' faith. False apostles and deceitful workers are the clear and present danger. These are described as servants of Satan, who disguises himself as an angel of light (2 Cor. 11:1-15). In his letter to the Ephesians, Paul writes of the need to stand against and withstand the devil. The whole armor of God is needed to do so: the belt of truth, the breastplate of righteousness, shoes for the feet made ready by the gospel of peace, the shield of faith, the helmet of salvation, and the sword of the Spirit. The devil is referred to twice in the passage. First, the whole armor of God is needed to stand against the devil's schemes. Second, the shield of faith extinguishes the devil's fiery darts. Again, the posture is defensive. The desiderata are to stand and withstand. There is no suggestion that the Ephesian believers are to engage in search and destroy.

The Definitive Denouement

Lesslie Newbigin captures the divide between the major world religions in terms of those that are road religions and those that are wheel religions.[28] Wheel religions employ the wheel as their organizing metaphor (e.g. Hinduism). Existence is cyclical. Eternal recurrence is the fate of all things. History is without meaning, without a telos. You will be reading this chapter yet again in another cycle. Biblical religion is a road religion. There is a beginning, a middle, and an end. (Recall Aristotle on the structure of stories.) In the beginning, there is a garden paradise; in the end, there is the new world with its city of God, the New Jerusalem. God is there, the Lamb is there, believers are there, but what about Satan?

A minority report in the history of Christian theology finds place for a saved devil in the world to come. The great restoration of all things (*apokatastasis*) will include the devil himself. The protagonist and the antagonist are reconciled on this view. Origen was the speculative genius of early Christianity and the chief contributor to this minority report. In some places, he envisaged salvation for all, even for the devil.[29] A key NT text for Origen was found in 1 Cor. 15:23-28. He understood the defeat of death and the demonic as not only their subjugation but, in the case of the demonic, also their becoming part of a community headed by Christ.[30] However, in his Letter to Friends in Alexandria, he denies the claim that

---

28. Lesslie Newbigin, *The Finality of Christ* (Richmond: John Knox, 1969), 65.

29. J. N. D. Kelly, *Early Christian Doctrines*, 5th ed. (London: Adam and Charles Black, 1977), 474.

30. John R. Sachs, "Apocatastasis in Patristic Theology," *TS* 54 (1993): 621-2.

he held such a hope. Indeed, he argued that only lunatics would hold such a view.[31] Even so, the fifth ecumenical council (AD 553) condemned this view as heresy. The twelfth anathema was explicitly directed at Origen's idea that the devil and evil spirits will be united to Christ in the end:

> If anyone shall say that the heavenly Powers and all men and the Devil and evil spirits are united with the Word of God in all respects, as the Νοῦς which is by them called Christ and which is in the form of God, and which humbled itself as they say; and [if anyone shall say] that the Kingdom of Christ shall have an end: let him be anathema.[32]

Gregory of Nyssa also contributed to the minority report on the *apokatastasis*. He shared some of Origen's perspectives.[33] Divine judgment would not be punitive, but pedagogical and purifying.[34] Like Origen, he appealed to 1 Cor. 15:25-28, but in addition he appealed to Phil. 2:10, which speaks of every knee bowing to Christ.[35] Noted Orthodox theologian Kallistos Ware argues that Gregory of Nyssa wrote on *apokatastasis* in a more guarded way than Origen and thus escaped ecclesial condemnation.[36]

The majority report down through the ages is consistent. The devil will be judged and experience the torment of eternal fire as in Rev. 20:10: "And the devil, who deceived them, was thrown into the lake of burning sulfur, where the beast and the false prophet had been thrown. They will be tormented day and night for ever and ever." It is hard to escape both the definitive and durative nature of this claim.[37] There is no happy ending in the script of the theodrama for the devil and his minions.

Conclusion

This is a strange time in the West. Supernaturalism is under attack from secularism (e.g., Richard Dawkins, Christopher Hitchens, and Sam Harris).

---

31. Ibid., 622.

32. Second Council of Constantinople, quoted in Henry R. Percival, ed., *The Seven Ecumenical Councils*, NPNF 2, ed. Philip Schaff and Henry Wace vol. 14 (n.p.: Charles Scribner's Sons, 1900; reprint, Peabody: Hendrickson, 1999), 319.

33. Kelly, *Early Christian Doctrines*, 484.

34. Sachs, "Apocatastasis in Patristic Theology," 637.

35. Ibid., 634–5.

36. Bishop Kallistos Ware, *How Are We Saved? The Understanding of Salvation in the Orthodox Tradition* (Minneapolis: Light and Life, 1996), 84.

37. Some attempt to escape the durative nature of the devil's fate. Michael Green argues for the annihilation of the devil (*I Believe in Satan's Downfall* [London: Hodder and Stoughton, 1999], 218). However, he fails to deal at all with "day and night for ever and ever" (Rev. 20:10) in his discussion.

Yet the entertainment industry is filled with offerings of supernatural contests between good and evil. The devil is often the chief antagonist in film and TV shows. In biblical perspective, the devil is no figure of fun or entertainment. He is the opponent of God's good character, word, and ways. So the biblical account is amenable to being read in dramatic terms, with drama a most useful lens through which to view the canonical story. Drama means conflict. In a drama there are protagonists and antagonists. Without these elements there is no drama. The canon of Scripture has all these elements: a chief protagonist (Jesus Christ, Son of God), a chief antagonist (the devil), and conflict from Genesis 3 to Revelation 20. However, as Cornelius Plantinga argues, "Nonetheless, Satan is no match for Jesus Christ the exorcist, the destroyer of the destroyer, the one who rebukes, plunders, and intimates Satan."[38] In the end, Satan and his minions are ejected from the theater.

---

38. Cornelius Plantinga Jr., *Not the Way It's Supposed to Be: A Breviary of Sin* (Grand Rapids: Eerdmans, 1995), 74.

Chapter 6

MARTYRDOM: MARTIN ALBERTZ'S NEGLECTED NEW TESTAMENT THEOLOGY AND THE IMPORTANCE OF A THEOLOGICAL CATEGORY

Robert W. Yarbrough

And I heard a voice from heaven saying, "Write this: Blessed are the dead who die in the Lord from now on." "Blessed indeed," says the Spirit, "that they may rest from their labors, for their deeds follow them!"[1]

The first goal of this essay is to call attention to commendable passages that speak of martyrdom in the published works of this volume's honoree, Kevin J. Vanhoozer. This topic deserves greater attention once we consider that some 90,000 Christians perish annually from persecution—247 per day, or about 10 persons each hour. A second, somewhat less central goal is to survey the concept of martyr and martyrdom as it has played out over the centuries in several traditions, lending ballast and perspective to our discussion. A third goal is to highlight a neglected NT theology, written by a little-known scholar who escaped martyrdom under the German Nazis, though he was not spared lengthy prison time; who observed the lethal persecution of colleagues and students from close range; and who probably suffered a shortened life span due to the rigors of his treatment by the Nazis for sheltering Jews and other non-Aryans. His name and major published work are found in this essay's title.

The three sections below attend to these three goals in turn.

Kevin Vanhoozer's Focus on Martyrdom

Alarming numbers regarding the annual tally of murdered Christians were cited above. The 90,000-per-year figure is projected to rise to 100,000 per year by 2025 and to hold steady at that level through 2050.[2] Given recent developments in Hong

---

1. Revelation 14:13. Unless otherwise indicated, Scripture references in this chapter are from the ESV.
2. Todd M. Johnson, Gina A. Zurlo, Albert W. Hickman, and Peter Crossing, "Christianity 2017: Five Hundred Years of Protestant Christianity," *IBMR* 41, no. 1 (January 2017): 50. These martyrdom statistics are explained and defended in Johnson et al., "Christianity

Kong and China, where state oppression of churches and Christians has increased dramatically,[3] these numbers could be low. Persecution of Christians in China, where growth of the church has been prodigious since the 1950s, touches millions. It is also on the rise in other countries.

The sum of human fatalities by martyrdom in just the 2017–50 time span, in any case, will rival the six million victims associated with Hitler's Holocaust. More than that have died in preceding recent decades. The human suffering and tragedy reflected in such numbers have to date been widely neglected in mainstream Western media.[4] It is of little concern to Western university pedagogy, where the Bible's facticity is mostly rejected, in contrast to most martyrs' conviction that it is true—hence their willingness to die for the God whom they associate with the Bible, which they regard as God's Word. To the contrary, martyrdom from NT times through church history has been minimized if not trivialized by a leading Notre Dame scholar, Candida Moss, in *The Myth of Persecution: How Early Christians Invented a Story of Martyrdom*.[5] But others have stepped forward to counterbalance this portrait. Two representative dissenting voices deserve mention. First, Clayton Croy's careful review of the historical facts concludes:

> While conservative Christian rhetoric is sometimes guilty of excesses, this book swings hard in the opposite direction, revising history and denying much of the evidence for early Christian persecution. Modern ideology drives Moss's thesis more than ancient testimony, and the result is a distortion of history more severe than the caricature she wants to expose.[6]

While Croy casts doubt on Moss's handling of the sources, Eckhard Schnabel methodically traces out the biblical passages that speak of persecution of Jesus' followers. He details twenty-seven incidents from a wide range of geographical locations. Not all end in martyrdom, but some do; he finds that in the NT

2018: More African Christians and Counting Martyrs," *IBMR* 42, no. 1 (January 2018): 21, 27. For the most recent numbers, see Gina A. Zurlo, Todd M. Johnson, and Peter Crossing, "World Christianity and Mission 2020: Ongoing Shift to the Global South," *IBMR* 44, no. 1 (January 2020): 8–19, esp. 17.

3. See, e.g., https://evangelicalfocus.com/world/7311/chinese-churches-turned-into-cultural-centers-by-the-government (accessed July 31, 2020).

4. A notable exception, with more reception in its German original than in English translation, is Martin Mosebach, *The 21: A Journey into the Land of Coptic Martyrs* (Walden, NY: Plough, 2019).

5. Candida Moss, *The Myth of Persecution: How Early Christians Invented a Story of Martyrdom* (San Francisco: HarperOne, 2013).

6. N. Clayton Croy, "Review of Candida Moss, *The Myth of Persecution: How Early Christians Invented a Story of Martyrdom*," *Review of Biblical Literature* 10 (2013). Available online: (http://www.bookreviews.org/bookdetail.asp?TitleId=9158&CodePage=8587,9158 (accessed July 10, 2020).

"persecution" describes "the aggressive harassment and deliberate ill-treatment of the followers of Jesus, ranging from verbal abuse, denunciation before local magistrates, initiating court proceedings to beatings, flogging, banishment from a city, execution, and lynch killings."[7]

Schnabel disagrees with the claim of James A. Kelhoffer and others like Moss that NT reports (e.g., by Luke) should be discounted because they are "stereotypical," "artificially construed," or "focused on a single theme."[8] Nor is it wise to imply that Acts engages in anti-Jewish polemic in depicting persecutors in Acts as "usually Jewish" when nearly a third of the times when Acts mentions persecution it involves non-Jewish figures.[9] This could reflect historical reality rather than Lukan propaganda. If Jesus and his first followers were Jewish, and they ran afoul of suppression from Jewish authorities in governments and synagogues across the Roman Empire, then it follows that a true account of this suppression would point to persecutors who would have been "usually Jewish," though not (as Luke's account appears faithfully to report) exclusively Jewish by any means.

We conclude, then, that a theologian today would be justified in highlighting martyrdom as a significant theological category, despite media indifference to current martyrs and some scholars' claims that historically speaking the threat of lethal persecution for Christian confession has been overblown. Kevin Vanhoozer has stepped forward as one such theologian.

Vanhoozer, like Schnabel, takes seriously the NT disciples of Jesus and his subsequent followers (like the late-second-century Scillitan martyrs) as enduring examples of faithful confessors.[10] Jesus' chosen first followers were "disciples in the dock" (i.e., under trial) whose martyrdom constituted their "covenant identity."[11] "Genuine discipleship and authentic Christian identity always involve martyrdom—bearing witness—in life and, if necessary, in death."[12] Vanhoozer recognizes that lexically, in the first century, μάρτυς did not mean a person killed for their conviction but merely a "witness" or testifier to something. In the case of early Christian believers, this something was a life (or if need be death) that indicated *"what is in Christ."*[13] Vanhoozer continues: "Martyrdom is indeed the authentic vocation of followers of Jesus and, indeed, of all human creatures and

---

7. Eckhard Schnabel, "The Persecution of Christians in the First Century," *JETS* 61, no. 3 (2018): 525.

8. Ibid., 546, referring to James A. Kelhoffer, *Persecution, Persuasion and Power: Readiness to Withstand Hardship as a Corroboration of Legitimacy in the New Testament*, WUNT 270 (Tübingen: Mohr Siebeck, 2010).

9. Schnabel, "Persecution of Christians," 547, referring to Kelhoffer, *Persecution, Persuasion and Power*, 286.

10. Kevin J. Vanhoozer, *Faith Speaking Understanding: Performing the Drama of Doctrine* (Louisville: Westminster John Knox, 2014), 70.

11. Ibid., 108.

12. Ibid., 71.

13. Ibid., 70, emphasis original.

followers of Jesus: to bear witness to the great things God has done in all creation and preeminently in the history of Jesus Christ."[14]

But to act as a witness (μάρτυς) has often led to suffering for that witness, even to the point of death, at which point a witness of proclamation of life in Christ comes at the cost of termination of life for Christ. This is a central insight underlying two of Vanhoozer's key works.

First, in *The Drama of Doctrine*,[15] Vanhoozer envisions "A Theater of Martyrdom" (subsection title) as the venue in which the church in our day reflects the atonement in personal and corporate living. This subsection appears at a climactic juncture near the book's end. Vanhoozer calls on the church and its members to "embody the cross" and enter into "the cruciform life" in the way they "speak, act, live—and, as we shall see, suffer."[16]

This "theater of martyrdom" consists first in "a *mimēsis* of martyrs."[17] Living out "the doctrine of the atonement involves living well and dying well for the truth in creative imitation of Christ," who is "the chief martyr."[18] This does not mean that Christ's death is *only* a "witness," for his was the unique self-sacrifice of the Son of God.[19] But it does mean that his followers have his pattern of self-giving to follow (1 Pet. 2:21). Suffering for Christ, which is often the effect of faithful witness, is important not only as a means of speaking up and out but also as "a means of being conformed to Christ's image."[20] Vanhoozer thus calls martyrdom a practice that is Christological, canonical, and traditional. He cements the traditional claim by referring to the hundreds and thousands of sixteenth-century martyrs,[21] who for consolation and courage in their hour of testing often identified with biblical martyrs whose reward for faithfulness was death ("Jonah for drowning, Stephen for stoning, John the Baptist for beheading, Daniel's three friends for burning").[22]

But if a *mimēsis* of martyrs (above) describes the *form* of daily life for believers under the cross, "a martyrdom of life"[23] describes its *focus*, which is twofold. For one thing, an everyday lifestyle of martyrdom cannot be reduced either to sincerity or even suffering: "*the martyrdom that is the proper end of doctrine involves suffering for one's witness to the truth.*"[24] This is not a form of fanaticism but

---

14. Ibid.

15. Kevin J. Vanhoozer, *The Drama of Doctrine: A Canonical Linguistic Approach to Christian Theology* (Louisville: Westminster John Knox, 2005), 428.

16. Ibid.

17. Ibid., 429–30.

18. Ibid., 429.

19. See ibid., 431: "Only Christ's death is redemptive."

20. Ibid., 430.

21. Vanhoozer cites Brad S. Gregory, *Salvation at Stake: Christian Martyrdom in Early Modern Europe* (Cambridge, MA: Harvard University Press, 1999).

22. Vanhoozer, *Drama of Doctrine*, 430.

23. Ibid., 431–4.

24. Ibid., 431, emphasis original.

a rational expression of faithfulness to biblical teaching, confessional ethics, and Christ's evangelistic mandate. For another, martyrdom is the glue of true Christian community. Paul's characterization of the Philippians' deepest unity has analogies in the body of Christ in all times and places: "It has been granted to you that for the sake of Christ you should not only believe in him but also suffer for his sake" (Phil. 1:29). Believers thereby can not only "know him and the power of his resurrection" but also "may share his sufferings, becoming like him in his death" (3:10). Their individual participation in this dynamic forms the core of community identity and effectiveness. If Vanhoozer is correct, lack of such participation means superficial if not hypocritical community.

While death is the lamentable end of faithful witness in too many times and places, Vanhoozer stresses that all Christians may embrace "a kind of martyrdom," which he calls "the martyrdom of life," when they "suffer the pain of social ostracism or ridicule for a cruciform life that is perceived to be culturally out of sync."[25] "There is an everyday martyrdom of life, as well as the extraordinary martyrdom of death." [26]

Second, in Vanhoozer's essay "The Trials of Truth: Mission, Martyrdom, and the Epistemology of the Cross,"[27] he explores "parallels and contrasts between the narrative of the trial of Jesus and the contemporary trials of truth by the postmodern masters of suspicion."[28] His goal is to stake a claim[29] for the truth of an evangelical construal of Christian theology, especially in tandem with the (virtue) ethics that such theology calls for. His discussion eventuates in a comparison between Socrates and Jesus and highlights the importance of "testimony"— μάρτυς. For martyrdom in that sense is "the whole speech act of testifying, not only the proposition, that ultimately communicates truth claims about the way of wisdom."[30] Elsewhere Vanhoozer writes of interpreters' call "to become not masters but 'martyrs' on behalf of [Scripture's] meaning, not only hearers but doers, and perhaps sufferers, of the Word."[31]

Notoriously, since the European Enlightenment (and particularly Kant), the relationship between knowledge and Christian faith (which affirms a knowledge of God denied by Kant) has been problematized. Speaking to that problem at present, Vanhoozer observes, "In a postmodern setting it is no longer enough

---

25. Ibid., 433.

26. Kevin J. Vanhoozer, *Pictures at a Theological Exhibition: Scenes of the Church's Worship, Witness and Wisdom* (Downers Grove: IVP Academic, 2016), 242.

27. In *First Theology: God and Scripture and Hermeneutics* (Downers Grove: InterVarsity, 2002), 337–73.

28. Ibid., 337.

29. See the book in which this essay first appeared: J. Andrew Kirk and Kevin J. Vanhoozer, eds., *To Stake a Claim: Mission and the Western Crisis of Knowledge* (Maryknoll: Orbis, 1999), 120–56.

30. Vanhoozer, *First Theology*, 351.

31. Ibid., 202.

to justify truth claims propositionally,"³² especially when it comes to theological matters. But such claims may be justified "when held by a person with epistemic virtue: one who knows of what she speaks and is willing to suffer on its behalf."³³ Testimony (witness) by such a person in such a way may yield "not mere opinion" (contra Plato and Locke) "but evidence, even a way of knowing."³⁴ Jesus' death exemplifies and establishes this. While its main aim was to atone for sin, he also told Pilate, "For this purpose I was born and for this purpose I have come into the world—to bear witness to the truth. Everyone who is of the truth listens to my voice" (Jn 18:37). The main direct effect and benefit of Jesus' death may have been propitiatory, but he offered himself within a nexus of testimony to himself, by himself, and through his disciples about himself: "you will be my witnesses" (Acts 1:8). This could also be understood as "witnesses of me." The apostolic witnesses did not merely serve under Jesus' aegis: he was the substance of their testimony.

In the end, epistemologically and experientially, martyrological expression and if need be oppression limn the calling and conduct of all who seek to think and live theologically in the historic Christian vein:

> The vocation of the Christian theologian is to be an interpreter-martyr: a truth-teller, a truth-doer, a truth-sufferer. Truth requires evangelical passion, not postmodern passivity; personal appropriation, not calculation. The theologian is to embody in his or her own person the core of Christian culture, in order to provide a focus for Christian wisdom. Making Christian truth claims is ultimately not a crusade nor a pilgrimage nor even a missionary journey, but rather a *martyrological* act. Genuine theology is not only about the art of reasoning well (rationality) but living well (wisdom) and dying well (martyrdom). Martyrdom is a form of indirect epistemology that arises from acts of intellectual virtue (e.g., humility, conviction) motivated by a passion for the truth.³⁵

The job description above is not just for theologians per se. "A martyr is one who suffers because of his or her witness. All Christians are called to bear witness to their identity in Christ, and this often means rejecting alternative ways of realizing our identity or securing social status."³⁶ But precisely through this rejecting one may lay hold of that for which one has been laid hold of in Christ (Phil. 3:12). In a harrowing historical moment when Christ-confessors are dying by brutal means,³⁷ in staggering numbers, and with generally little regard from Western

---

32. Ibid., 356; see also 361.

33. Ibid. For a refutation of the view that martyrs are necessarily misguided fanatics, see 369–71.

34. Ibid., 359.

35. Ibid., 372–3.

36. Vanhoozer, *Pictures at a Theological Exhibition*, 280.

37. Note, e.g., a typical journalistic communique from Nigeria: https://evangelicalfocus.com/world/7286/nigerian-pastor-among-10-christians-killed-in-herdsmen-attacks (accessed July 30, 2020).

thinkers whose status, security, incomes, and daily life breath are not imperiled either by their adherence to historical Christian faith or their divergence from it, Vanhoozer's work stands as a compelling testimony to the contours and the cost of Christian faith through the centuries down to the present, not inevitably at all times but steadily in too many.

Mainstreaming Martyrdom: Cultural and Historical Reminders

In the postmodern relativistic and pluralistic West, Christian martyrdom could seem to be a throwback to times and a mentality when people believed unprovable convictions too easily and deeply, engaged in mortal conflict over the unknowable,[38] and suffered unnecessarily for their misplaced zeal. What does pursuit of God have to do with killing and dying? Today's hegemonic "we" knows better and pursues faith expressions, if any, felt to assure flourishing rather than expose adherents to lethal danger. But history's testimony to martyrdom is too widespread and recurrent to discount. Vanhoozer has urged "a critical realism of testimony" that "recognizes the value of multiple perspectives or voices and insists that through serious interpretation the reader can make cognitive contact with that to which the witnesses testify."[39]

In this section we survey some perspectives that remind attentive interpreters of both culture and Scripture that, like the poor, the martyrs we always have with us. Not all may have died wisely, but the cumulative weight of their shed blood justifies mainstreaming, not marginalizing, the sobering news of the cost of discipleship in a world often unfriendly to those whose loyalty to the otherworldly pushes a putatively tolerant generation past its breaking point.

To begin with the history of film, Rosanne Morici[40] has pointed to Christian martyrdom as the theme or backdrop in many movies, from the silent film *The Passion of Joan of Arc* (1920) to *The Sign of the Cross* (1932) and *Quo Vadis* (1951). More recently, films like *The Mission* (1986) and *Silence* (2016) prompt moral reflection as characters' "suffering tests the ideal that true faith is expressed through willingness to die and is lost in compromised survival" (col. 1100). *Of Gods and Men* (2010) recounts the 1996 murder of seven Trappist monks who "choose to stay in Algeria rather than abandon their neighbors even as the inevitable violence of war closes in on them" (ibid.). Elements of Christian martyrdom inform the

---

38. Recall the final lines of Matthew Arnold's Victorian-era poem "Dover Beach": "And we are here as on a darkling plain/ Swept with confused alarms of struggle and flight,/ Where ignorant armies clash by night."

39. Vanhoozer, *First Theology*, 363.

40. "VIII. Film," in *EBR*, cols. 1098–101. Column numbers in the text of this section refer to this volume and its lengthy series of articles on the "Martyr, Martyrdom" theme (cols. 1064–101). A sizable portion covers Jewish (cols. 1066–79) and Islamic martyrdom (cols. 1090–2), both of which lie outside this essay's purview.

imagery of *Gladiator* (2000). Here the protagonist Maximus "achieves victory through an act of mercy as he spares the life of Commodus, and he achieves salvation through his embrace of noble death as he joins his family in the afterlife" (col. 1099).

Esther Mulders[41] explores martyrdom in the visual arts, where biblical instances and symbols of dying for the faith "are frequent and find their way into art in various forms" (col. 1096). Symbols like the palm branch (see Ps. 92:12: "The righteous flourish like the palm tree") and the laurel crown (see Rev. 2:10: "Be faithful unto death, and I will give you the crown of life") are utilized to suggest victory over death in paintings, mosaics, and other art forms. Although Mulder thinks it "unlikely" that Herod the Great slaughtered the holy innocents (Mt. 1:16), and they are not truly martyrs since their death "cannot have been an act of free will for any cause" (col. 1097), numerous artistic works depict the massacre as a martyrdom event. This is true as well of Stephen's stoning and James the son of Zebedee's beheading. Mulder points to "Bill Viola's video altar piece Martyrs (Earth, Air, Fire, Water) which was opened in May 2014 at St. Paul's Cathedral in London" (col. 1098) as a contemporary depiction of four figures martyred by each of the four elements. "At the height of their violent assault through death each of them passes into light" (ibid.).

Mary Claire Gibson[42] points to martyrs and martyrdom in modern literature, where "it is used in a secular sense … as it is experienced worldwide and is not solely related to Christian beliefs" (col. 1093). She finds martyrological imagery in writers as varied as James Joyce, Gustave Flaubert, Victor Hugo, Stephen King, Shusako Endo, David Diop, Shakespeare, Louisa May Alcott, and Molière. In Suzanne Collins's *The Hunger Games* (2008) and *Catching Fire* (2009), "notions of martyrdom are connected to the traditional meanings of martyrdom drawn from the Bible" (col. 1095). Jean Valjean in Hugo's *Les Misérables* voices a martyr's true confession as he lays a crucifix on a table just before his death: "It is nothing to die; it's awful to not live" (cols. 1093–4).

Echoes and images of martyrdom in film, art, and literature are extensions of deeper focus on it in the history of Christianity.[43] Origen and Cyprian of Carthage pointed to Eleazer the priest and the seven Maccabee brothers and their mother (2 Maccabees, 4 Maccabees) as exemplars for Christian martyrs (col. 1080), among whom was Origen's own father. Other patristic accounts of martyrdom (*Martyrdom of Polycarp*, *Martyrdom of Dasius*) often drew on the Gospels for "a paradigm through which later events were experienced, interpreted, and remembered" (col. 1081). It is hardly surprising that dying for Christ generated accounts that found analogies in the death of Christ. Augustine pointed to the faithful suffering of the apostles in contrast to what he saw as false martyrs among the Donatists (col. 1082).

---

41. "VII. Visual Arts," *EBR* 17, 1096–8.
42. "VI. Literature," *EBR* 17, 1093–6.
43. David L. Eastman, "A. Patristics and Orthodox Churches," *EBR* 17, cols. 1079–83.

Many Christians died taking the gospel to then-pagan northern and eastern Europe, as Boniface and fifty-three other Christians earned their martyrs' crowns in Frisia in AD 754 (col. 1083).[44] Jan Hus, Jerome of Prague, and Hieronymous Savonarola were executed as heretics prior to the Reformation, during and after which many more lost their lives. "In the Netherlands some 1300 followers of Calvin, as well as the English Bible translator William Tyndale, earned execution for the faith by the Habsburg government before 1566" (col. 1084). Anabaptists, Thomas More, the Huguenots, and others likewise paid for their faith with their lives.

The twentieth century, however, has been called "the century of the martyrs" (col. 1085), particularly in Protestant and Orthodox quarters.[45] Far from martyrdom fading from view, it has become more frequent and widespread in a century of unprecedented Christian expansion alongside the rise of ideologies in the hands of dictators (e.g., Stalin, Hitler, Mao) wielding rationales and means to eliminate unwanted segments of their populations. Today, "around 1,100 20th-century martyrs have been canonized in the Russian-Orthodox church, roughly three times as many as in the church's history prior to the 20th century" (col. 1086). As indicated earlier, martyrs worldwide fall at the rate of about 90,000 per year currently.

The prevalence of death for Christian belief and practice in some regions has led to rediscovery of "approaches ... rooted in a Bible-based historic view of martyrdom that has been widely forgotten in Western Christianity" (cols. 1088–9).[46] South Korean theologian Young Kee Lee sees in Christian martyrs an expression of cosmic conflicts described in Scripture; "at times, martyrdom looks like a defeat (cf. Heb 11:35b-40), but finally it will be part of Christ's victory" (col. 1089). Coptic bishop Anba Youannis draws on Tertullian's dictum regarding the blood of the martyrs to suggest that the witness of faithful Christian deaths "is more important for the spreading of the Christian message than preaching or education" (ibid.), a statement that may only make sense if one has lived in Coptic regions with their lengthy history of suppression by the Islamic majority. In many locales, seeking to preach or teach the Christian message will immediately result in injury or death.

Romanian pastor Joseph Ton is only one of many Christian confessors who has reflected on persecution, and witnessed the martyrdom of colleagues, to arrive at reflections on suffering and death for the faith that are not normally glimpsed in settings where churches are not beleaguered like Romanian churches were under communist dictator Nicolae Ceaușescu (ibid.). Jesuit theologian Jon Sobrino has written extensively on Latin American loss of life in pursuit of social justice ideals informing liberation theology (col. 1090). But he is willing to define martyrs more in terms of victims' political convictions and goals rather than their personal faith

---

44. Robert Kolb, "B. Medieval Times and Reformation Era," *EBR* 17, cols. 1083–5.
45. Thomas Martin Schneider, "C. Modern Europe and America," *EBR* 17, cols. 1085–7.
46. Wolfgang Häde, "E. World Christianity," *EBR* 17, cols. 1088–90.

in and identification with Christ as their Savior and Lord, which for many would be a departure from historic understanding of martyrdom.

Martin Albertz and His New Testament Theology of Martyrdom

The prominence of martyrdom in the hermeneutical horizon of Martin Albertz is glimpsed in the subtitle of his sizable (632 pages) biography that appeared in 2001: *Martin Albertz (1883-1956)—Eigensinn und Konsequenz: das Martyrium als Kennzeichen der Kirche im Nationalsozialismus*.[47] This can be translated as *Martin Albertz (1883-1956)—Tenacious Resolve and Outcome: Martyrdom as Mark of the Church under National Socialism*. The remainder of this essay will comment on (1) his life and work with a view to his fidelity in upholding the biblical and historical motif of martyrdom, and (2) factors contributing to the neglect of his work in the scholarly subdiscipline (NT theology) to which he made the greatest contribution.

Albertz's Life and Work

In some ways Albertz resembles the much better known Rudolf Bultmann (1884–1976): born about the same time; son of a pastor like Bultmann; a university student under the same doyens (e.g., Adolf von Harnack, Hermann Gunkel) that were part of the air all German theological students breathed; a pioneer of NT form criticism (following Gunkel's OT lead) alongside Bultmann, Martin Dibelius, and Karl Ludwig Schmidt;[48] and author of a NT theology, though Albertz's (two volumes in four parts) *Die Botschaft des Neuen Testaments*[49] is twice as long as Bultmann's celebrated *Theologie des Neuen Testaments*[50] (704 pages to Albertz's 1,475 pages).

In contrast to Bultmann, however, Albertz affirmed the Christian faith instilled in him by his parents and Reformed church. He deepened in his commitment to what he viewed as biblical Christianity over the decades during which he served as pastor, theological educator, and church overseer. In the very years of the Second World War and Hitler's Holocaust when Bultmann was calling for "demythologizing" the Bible, Albertz was serving three different imprisonments for following the Bible as he (with others) gave assistance to non-Aryans (many of them Jewish) and resisted Nazi pressure. Bultmann's hermeneutic was destined to become a paradigm and springboard for NT interpretation in the rest of the twentieth century and beyond; late in life Albertz wrote an essay in which he pinned on Bultmann the final blame for NT theology "dying a deserved death, because

---

47. By Peter Noss (Neukirchen-Vluyn: Neukirchener Verlag, 2001).
48. Ibid., 5.
49. Zollikon–Zürich: Evangelischer Verlag, 1947–57. The title translated: *The Message of the New Testament*.
50. First edition 1948–53. Translated into English as *Theology of the New Testament* (1951–5).

and to the extent that it does not submit itself to critique before God and Christ but rather draws its standards for criticism [of Scripture] from the surrounding culture."[51] This was of course a culture that proved amenable to Hitler's designs for Jews and others he deplored, among whom were thousands of Christians of Jewish descent—in other words, Jews who had converted to Christianity. Albertz biographer Peter Noss puts their number in Germany at the time of Hitler's rise to power at some four hundred thousand,[52] noting that about five hundred Jews annually were being baptized into the church in that era.[53] Protestant church leaders abandoned these putative brothers and sisters in the faith to Nazi machinations from the 1930s onward.[54] Trained theologians in Germany who defended them can apparently be counted on one hand. Among them was Albertz.

At peril to himself and many associates, Albertz (with Hermann Maas) initiated and led *the first and only agency in the entire German Protestant church* to offer assistance to this persecuted segment of the German population.[55] He also oversaw the founding of a school for educating the children of these families caught between the Nazis who persecuted them for their Jewishness and their Jewish kin who disowned them because of their profession of Christian faith.[56]

Biographical insight on Albertz is available at the website of the German Resistance Memorial Center (*Die Gedenkstätte Deutscher Widerstand*) in Berlin.[57] It honors the memory of some 608 persons who "took action against the National Socialist dictatorship from 1933 to 1945 and made use of what freedom of action they had" for the sake of Jews.[58] It is remarkable that almost no academic theologians are mentioned; the total number comes to two (Karl Barth, Dietrich Bonhoeffer). Biblical scholars seem to be limited to a total of one: Martin Albertz.

---

51. Martin Albertz, "Die Krisis der sogenannten neutestamentlichen Theologie," *Zeichen der Zeit* 8 (1954): 375.

52. Petre Noss, "Theologische 'Leuchttürme' im Protestantismus und die Schicksale der Christen jüdischer Herkunft 1933–1945," in *Nationalprotestantische Mentalitäten: Konturen, Entwicklungslinien und Umbrüche eines Weltbildes*, ed. Manfred Gailus and Hartmut Lehmann (Göttingen: Vandenhoeck & Ruprecht, 2005), 309.

53. Ibid., 315.

54. Ibid., 311 n. 16: Noss notes that in 1933 church leaders and theologians were "everything but prepared" to deal with Hitler's singling out of people of Jewish descent, including thousands of Christian church members. "Only a few" theologians "reacted critically." For their part, "the church leaders failed."

55. Ibid., 324.

56. Ibid., 315.

57. https://www.gdw-berlin.de/en/home/. Two other biographical sources (in addition to the Noss biography above (n. 47)): Kurt Scharf, "Martin Albertz zum 70. Geburtstag," in *Theologia Viatorum V: Jahrbuch der Kirchlichen Hochschule Berlin 1953–54*, ed. Harald Kruska (Berlin: Lettner-Verlag, 1954), 9–20; Noss, "Theologische 'Leuchttürme' im Protestantismus," 318–26.

58. Noss, "Theologische 'Leuchttürme' im Protestantismus," 315.

Albertz was in trouble with the Nazi secret police ("Gestapo," from *Geheime Staatspolizei*) and often imprisoned from 1934 until the end of the war. Kurt Scharf recounts the harrowing drama, much of it rooted in the treachery of fellow churchmen, with 75 percent of his church council belonging to the Nazi-aligned "German Christians" c. 1933.[59] Scharf quotes an official summary of Albertz's criminality: "As a cleric stripped [by the Nazis in the mid-1930s] of his church ordination, he continued [when not incarcerated] to lead the church, preach, and baptize. Moreover, his preaching opposed Hitler's claim to total allegiance with the demand for total allegiance to Jesus Christ."[60] Scharf also lauds Albertz's aplomb, poise, indifference to personal danger, and fearless, compassionate witness for Christ even toward those who arrested and interrogated him.[61]

Noss takes up the question of why there were so few Christian theologians[62] who "went against the trend of the overwhelming majority of Christians in the Third Reich in the years of the Nazi regime."[63] In particular, why were there so few who "from their theology drew consequences for their ethical action and urged these [consequences] on others"?[64] The only "theologische Leuchttürme" ("theological lighthouses") he finds to analyze are Albertz, Barth, Bonhoeffer, and a pastor with an academic doctorate named Hans Ehrenberg who was of Jewish descent.

Albertz was not martyred in the course of his defiance of state authority. But his persistence and concrete actions could have led to his martyrdom (as for many on the German Resistance Memorial Center list). What are some possible contributing factors to his neglect down to the present?

---

59. Scharf, "Martin Albertz zum 70. Geburtstag," 17–18.

60. Ibid., 18.

61. Ibid., 19.

62. Noss, "Theologische 'Leuchttürme' im Protestantismus." Noss does not include in this definition three Protestant pastoral leaders (Martin Niemoller, Paul Schneider, and Theophil Wurm) who appear among the roster of 608 German Resistance Memorial Center names. While they defied the Nazis, they were not "theologians" in the technical sense of having completed the German university *Habilitation* (second dissertation required for recognition as a professor). That there are only three pastors (not counting Catholic priests, of which likewise there are only a few) is perhaps a tribute to the training most pastors received from their university professors, some of whom supported state ideology, many more who kept a low profile for the sake of their own reputation and safety, and perhaps none whose teaching and convictions instilled a willingness to defend Jews or Jewish Christians against a totalitarian regime, even if it threatened the mainstream Protestant and Catholic churches too. But perhaps churches whose leaders lacked conviction to stand up for the Jews were perceived by Nazi leaders as a minimal threat to their reign.

63. Ibid., 307.

64. Ibid.

Factors Contributing to Albertz's Neglect

That Albertz has been so thoroughly overlooked is curious. Surely he is more significant than innumerable obscure figures found in the prodigious thirty-volume *Encyclopedia of the Bible and Its Reception*. But in the column in volume one where "Albertz" would appear, one reads merely of Heinrich Albert (1604–1651), "the organist at the cathedral of Königsberg" (col. 710). Martin Albertz's absence is glaring.

From NT studies too he has vanished. Peter Stuhlmacher's magisterial volume lists twenty-seven NT theologies going back to 1948 and Bultmann; Albertz's four volumes are absent.[65] William Baird's three volumes seem never to mention him.[66] He is likewise absent from Stephen Neill's and Tom Wright's well-known work.[67] Why has it been expedient so thoroughly to ignore the only German NT theologian who actively opposed the Nazis and put his own welfare on the line for the sake of providing open support and protection for Christians of Jewish descent?

One reason is a mythology that arose after the Second World War, which has since been debunked:

> The German Protestant legend of the Church Struggle as a valiant fight against Nazism, which was propagated after the war mainly by pastors and theologians bent on painting their actions and that of their churches in the most sympathetic light, has been demythologized. Many of the churches in fact cooperated with Hitler, in effect (and in many cases in actuality) promulgating Nazi ideology, including antisemitism.[68]

The same source recognizes the role of "the Grüber office" in aiding Jews.[69] Located in Berlin, this office "provided Jews (including Jews who converted to Christianity) who were under grave threat from the Reich with advice about emigration, finding employment abroad, social assistance, legal matters, and educational support."[70]

---

65. Peter Stuhlmacher, *Biblical Theology of the New Testament*, ed. and trans. Daniel P. Bailey (Grand Rapids: Eerdmans, 2018), xxxiii–xxxiv.

66. William Baird, *History of New Testament Research*, 3 vols. (Minneapolis: Fortress, 1992–2013).

67. Stephen Neill and Tom Wright, *The Interpretation of the New Testament 1861–1986*, 2nd ed. (Oxford: Oxford University Press, 1988).

68. Christopher J. Probst, *Demonizing the Jews: Luther and the Protestant Church in Nazi Germany* (Bloomington: Indiana University Press, 2012), 10. As Noss writes, "Christian anti-Judaism in theology and the church, which mirrored a widespread social mentality fed by 'demonizing stereotypes of outsiders and enemies,' prepared the soil for the National Socialist politics of depriving Jews of legal standing. It did this actively and passively, consciously and unconsciously" ("Theologische 'Leuchttürme' im Protestantismus," 314). Not only the German Christians but also the Confessing Church were complicit.

69. Probst, *Demonizing the Jews*, 10, 116, 173.

70. Ibid. 10.

This was the office headed by Albertz.[71]

Given Albertz's insight into the real gravity of the times, his reading of the Bible that taught resistance was required, and his ethical courage in putting his theology into costly practice, it may be time to give Albertz's publications a fresh look in light of the biography that is now available[72] and a more truthful understanding of the Bultmann heyday than he and his followers generated when it comes to complicity in church structures that abetted Hitler. If "it was almost forty years—from 1956 to 1995—before a German court finally saw clear to declare posthumously that Bonhoeffer had been innocent,"[73] it is not too late to exhume and review the buried treasure of Albertz's NT theology in view of its dramatic historical and biographical context.[74]

A second reason for neglect of Albertz's work is doubtless its biblical realism. Bultmann took a dim view of a historic Christian reading of the NT and was revered for his genius. At the same time, what we would today call a "cancel culture" of colleagues loyal to Bultmann condescendingly set Albertz's four volumes aside as offering "only profound and often at points valid meditations under systematic categories."[75] Albertz affirmed Scripture as the voice of God and of the Holy Spirit.[76] He argued for the authenticity of the NT writings.[77] Unlike Bultmann, he affirmed Christ's resurrection.[78] He singled out the call to witness/martyrdom frequently when he encountered these in the course of his exposition,[79] reflecting its presence in the text and also his own *Sitz im Leben*, which he portrayed as analogous to oppression faced by NT authors who wrote from prison: "At the time when the preparation of the manuscript" of his first volume was supposed to begin, Albert

---

71. For background and details see Noss, *Martin Albertz (1883-1956)—Eigensinn und Konsequenz*, 353-64.

72. I.e., Noss, *Martin Albertz (1883-1956)—Eigensinn und Konsequenz*.

73. Martin E. Marty, *Dietrich Bonhoeffer's Letters and Papers from Prison: A Biography* (Princeton: Princeton University Press, 2011), 187-8.

74. A small start was made some years ago: see Robert W. Yarbrough, *The Salvation Historical Fallacy? Reassessing the History of New Testament Theology* (Leiden: Deo, 2004), 299-316.

75. Otto Merk, *Biblische Theologie des Neuen Testaments in ihrer Anfangszeit: Ihre methodischen Probleme bei Johann Philipp Gabler und Georg Lorenz Bauer und deren Nachwirkungen* (Marburg: N. G. Elwert, 1972), 263 nn. 166-7. Albertz saw the New Testament as unified by its message. Merk faults him for failing to concur (with the consensus of German scholars) that the New Testament writings are largely isolated from, or even in opposition to, each other (cf. F. C. Baur). To treat them, with the historic church, as unified is to set oneself outside the de facto and rival *ecclesia* of true scholars. Hence Albertz deserves to be dismissed. For helpful background, see Michael Legaspi, *The Death of Scripture and the Rise of Biblical Studies* (Oxford: Oxford University Press, 2011).

76. Albertz, *Die Botschaft des Neuen Testaments*, I/1: 18-19.

77. Ibid., 28-9.

78. Ibid., 30-1 and passim.

79. See ibid., 31; I/2: 18-23, 66, 67, 170-1, 206, 246-7; 316, 333, 344, 350-2.

was "arrested and sentenced to 1½ years of prison because of his involvement in the Theological Examination Office and Teaching Office of the Confessing Church."[80] This was followed by ten more months of the same (1944-5). Albertz notes, "The plan of this book and a part of its execution were carried out, therefore, in prison just like a portion of the epistles of the New Testament."[81]

In an era where Bultmannian skepticism was the order of the day for biblical scholars in the German university, Albertz's open integration of Trinitarian confessional Christianity with his exegesis guaranteed that his NT theology would be regarded as an outlier. The core of Albertz's exposition of the NT *Botschaft* was "the grace of our Lord Jesus Christ,"[82] "the love of God,"[83] and "the fellowship of the Holy Spirit."[84] While a student in Berlin, Bultmann complained in a letter about dogmatics lectures from Julius Kaftan: "What rubbish is contained in terms like 'revelation,' 'Trinity,' 'miracle,' 'God's attributes'—it's appalling!"[85] He remained dismissive of confessional Christianity throughout his career.

A third consideration in the neglect of Albertz is the death of many of his students in the war years or thereafter. Many threw themselves into ministry selflessly as Albertz did and paid the price. Few remained to do research under his oversight or otherwise carry on his heritage. Exemplary in this connection is Ilse Fredrichsdorff (1915-1945), a student and eventually pastoral leader whom Albertz assisted at numerous points, including helping to arrange her travel and study with Barth in 1938. Her story is in some ways more dramatic than Albertz's, though it is virtually unknown outside specialist circles.[86] Following theological study, she taught in Albertz's school for non-Aryan Christian children and eventually became a de facto pastor[87] of congregations northeast of Berlin, where the battle against the Russians was the fiercest as the war drew to a close. Having buried some one hundred of her own parishioners, she died of the same hunger and disease (typhoid) that wracked her congregation in the starvation zone of Russia-occupied Germany.[88] It is fair to call her a martyr to ministry, a practitioner

---

80. Ibid., I/1: 12.

81. Ibid.

82. Ibid., II/1: 155-315.

83. Ibid., II/2: 19-103.

84. Ibid., 104-251.

85. Konrad Hammann, *Rudolf Bultmann—Eine Biographie* (Tübingen: Mohr Siebeck, 2009), 23.

86. The fullest account I have encountered is Renate Schatz-Hurschmann, "Eine Frau ist immer im Dienst: Das Leben der Ilse Fredrichsdorff," in *Frauen in dunkler Zeit*, ed. Susi Hausammann, Nicole Kuropka, and Heike Scherer (Köln: Rheinland-Verlag, 1996), 121-59.

87. At that time women in the German Protestant church could not receive the official recognition of ordination.

88. For which reason Albertz, who conducted her memorial service, dedicated volume II/1 of *Die Botschaft des Neuen Testaments* to her memory (along with the memory of another of his students). He outlines her wrenching story on pp. 13-14 of that volume.

of the sometimes fatal μάρτυς model upheld by Vanhoozer, displayed in church history, and highlighted by Albertz. Her story, like his NT theology, deserves a wider audience.

Conclusion

This essay has focused on Christian martyrdom, in large measure by calling attention to the prominent place it plays in the writings of this volume's honoree and in the life and writings of Martin Albertz. Is there any convergence between these two writers despite their varied disciplines, emphases, and social locations? The following four similarities may be suggested.

Both Albertz and Vanhoozer are "martyrs" solely in the sense of being "witnesses" to Christ as Lord and Savior. Neither of their professions of faith resulted in their deaths (in Vanhoozer's case: so far). Yet both stand out in their times as academics whose Bible interpretation calls for the practical faithfulness that may and does result in death for those who embrace it. Albertz's own summary of this theological and ecclesial work was the following: "Theology is wisdom in an enormously practical [i.e., lived-out] sense."[89] Vanhoozer insists that theological truth results in a tangible "way of wisdom, a truth for which we can live and die."[90]

They are also comparable in their shared emphasis on the continuing viability, indeed necessity, of creedal Christianity with an emphasis on Jesus' saving death. Both Albertz and Vanhoozer uphold a high view of Christ and the Bible. Albertz called the appearance of the NT "more important for world history than even the Roman empire."[91] Vanhoozer's analogous convictions are implicit in the statements of faith to which he has subscribed as a faculty member at confessional institutions.

Both scholars embrace, when called for, a contrarian willingness to defy conventions of their academic disciplines when guild loyalties stray from the historical and theological truth that Christ and Scripture embody and commend. Albertz's criticism of biblical criticism reaches a highpoint in his essay on the history of German NT theology, with the provocative "so-called" in the title.[92] Vanhoozer, while invariably courteous and positive in expression, takes on the whole world of deconstructive postmodernism with his robustly Trinitarian outlook in which "the triune God is a personal and transcendent communicative agent."[93]

Both Martin Albertz and Kevin J. Vanhoozer commend and model an ecclesial commitment despite the real or possible cost. Through both men's writings, and perhaps more significantly through the lives of their students, the ultimate

---

89. Noss, "Theologische 'Leuchttürme' im Protestantismus," 318.
90. Vanhoozer, *First Theology*, 340.
91. Albertz, *Die Botschaft des Neuen Testaments*, I/2: 496.
92. Albertz, "Die Krisis der sogenannten ["so-called"] neutestamentlichen Theologie."
93. Vanhoozer, *First Theology*, 13.

alternative community has been aided and abetted in ways that only eternity will reveal. Words of an Albertz student and later protégé serve to characterize the literary legacy of both:

> His academic publications as they stand serve as weapons which the Christian and the church can employ and apply, whether church leadership or faculty at academic or ecclesial institutions, or whether the preacher or the catechumen being grounded in the faith. [The one who comes to Albertz's writings, and Vanhoozer's too] need not fear that the sword of the Word that is handed to him is dull or fragile, or that the proffered shield and armor might not suffice to ward off the fiery arrows of the evil one.[94]

---

94. Scharf, "Martin Albertz zum 70. Geburtstag," 13.

Part II

GREAT PERFORMANCES

Chapter 7

THE SPIRIT IN BIBLICAL INTERPRETATION: BASIL OF CAESAREA AND MODERN DISCUSSION OF MEANING AND SIGNIFICANCE

Darren Sarisky

I

What is the role of the Holy Spirit in biblical interpretation? How does divine action on the part of the third person of the Trinity relate to what human readers do when they wrestle with biblical words and phrases in an effort to make sense of them and to respond fittingly? This is a perennial question for Christians, and certainly a theme on which Kevin J. Vanhoozer has written much. He has characteristically weighed in via speech-act philosophy, onto which he has grafted his pneumatology. Essentially Vanhoozer has been saying that the Spirit's function is to catalyze proper reception of and response to the biblical Word. As we honor Vanhoozer now that he is coming to his sixty-fifth birthday, it is possible to note some shifts in the details of other areas of his theology that might well prompt shifts in what he has been saying about the Spirit. This essay will turn first to Vanhoozer, exploring how his thinking has evolved and how he has characterized the Spirit's place in hermeneutics. Having done that, the next step will be to reflect on the Spirit as a subject in its own right, with special reference to an early Christian theologian who helped to develop the view of the Spirit that came to be accepted by all Christians subscribing to the creed of Nicaea. This theologian is Basil of Caesarea, one of the Cappadocian fathers from the fourth century. There are in Basil's pneumatology insights worth retrieving, which may enrich thinking about the Spirit's role in reading even today.

II

For the early Vanhoozer, as for the vast majority of evangelical scholars a generation older than him,[1] drawing a sharp distinction between a biblical text's

---

1. For instance, see these widely read textbooks: Grant R. Osborne, *The Hermeneutical Spiral: A Comprehensive Introduction to Biblical Interpretation*, 2nd ed. (Downers

meaning and its significance is absolutely fundamental to proper reading. This hermeneutical touchstone derives from a literary scholar named E. D. Hirsch, Jr. For him, meaning is identified with authorial intention: it is what the sequence of textual signifiers represents—not what the author planned to do in a text yet did not actually accomplish, but what the author actually did in employing a set of words to convey a message.[2] Interpreters may not always be able to ascertain with complete certainty what the meaning of a text is, but in principle the meaning is determinate and stable, unlike the text's significance. Significance refers to the relationship between the (fixed) meaning and any other context to which a reader might relate the text.[3] Keeping these two terms distinct means that significance depends on meaning, but meaning is in no way contingent on the text's significance to a reader. Chaucer, for instance, meant by his account of the Wife of Bath in the *Canterbury Tales* simply what he intended in telling that tale. What he meant is not a function of whatever readers in the present day might make of her as a character, or however they might relate to the experiences she recounts. Distinguishing these two ways of thinking about a text is indispensable to providing the only workable criterion for assessing different readings of a text, since a text has to represent *someone's* meaning—either the author's or that of the throng of squabbling critics, whose disputes are interminable as a matter of empirical fact. We do and should judge the validity of interpretations. The sole condition of that possibility is to link meaning with authorial intention, while refusing to conflate that with the text's history of reception.

Vanhoozer adheres closely to Hirsch's distinction, while providing a more complex, and ultimately theological, rationale for holding to it (and offering an account that is more oriented to speech-act theory and less indebted to other philosophical sources, such as Husserl's account of consciousness). At one level, Vanhoozer's rationale is metaphysical. As he says,

> The distinction between meaning and significance is, at root, a corollary of the belief in the reality of the past. For the realist, one cannot change the past simply by interpreting it differently. The way Jesus was in history, for example, does not change at the behest of our changing interpretations. The meaning of Jesus is independent of our attempts to express his significance.[4]

The basis here for keeping meaning and significance conceptually separate is metaphysical in its appeal to reality not being driven or created by perception. The two are different. There is also an ethical angle to this same point, which is that

---

Grove: InterVarsity, 2006), 7; Walter C. Kaiser Jr. and Moises Silva, *An Introduction to Biblical Hermeneutics: The Search for Meaning* (Grand Rapids: Zondervan, 1994), 41.

2. E. D. Hirsch Jr., *Validity in Interpretation* (New Haven: Yale University Press, 1967), 8.
3. Ibid.
4. Kevin J. Vanhoozer, *Is There a Meaning in This Text? The Bible, the Reader, and the Morality of Literary Knowledge* (Grand Rapids: Zondervan, 1998), 263.

the only way for readers to respect the alterity of the text they are engaging—a basic obligation of listening—is to recognize that there is something to listen *to*, or to engage *with*.[5] There must be something invariant that they are trying to access via interpretation, and the name for that is textual meaning. The theological dimension is not hard to discern, for it is already suggested by the block quotation immediately above. It is utterly necessary not to confuse meaning and significance for any text. But if that text is the Bible—a work testifying to the reality of God by, in a real sense, allowing readers to hear God's voice—then allowing that voice simply to be what it is, and responding appropriately, requires having a category for what the text is expressing. Failure to retain a place for textual meaning in the case of the Bible entails beginning to comingle one's own voice with God's and thus to commit idolatry in interpretation. In addition to these metaphysical, ethical, and theological perspectives, there is also an epistemological vantage point on interpretation. While there is a meaning that the text is conveying, doing justice to its full richness in the Bible's case requires more than one interpretive grid and a plurality of actual readings.[6] Divine transcendence entails that even beginning to understand the reality of Scripture's subject matter necessitates many different approaches to the text and also many embodiments of these styles of reading.

If meaning and significance are not the same, what is the Spirit's role in the Bible's interpretation? Vanhoozer writes, "The Spirit's role, I will argue, is not to change the meaning but to *charge* it with significance."[7] Building on classical Christian Trinitarian theology, which appropriates to the Spirit bringing to completion the acts of God, including God's communicative acts of self-disclosure,[8] Vanhoozer associates pneumatology with the process whereby a reader relates textual meaning to ever-new contexts. The Spirit opens the reader's eyes to how she ought to bring the meaning of the text to bear on her particular circumstances. In the terminology of speech-act theory, the Spirit is responsible for rendering effectual the text's perlocutions. The words an author writes can do things. In uttering and recording words on a page, an author can greet another, make a promise, or warn a reader to abstain from a certain course of action. What is done through words is the illocutionary value that they bear. What is brought about via these actions is the perlocutionary aspect. For instance, readers receive the greeting they have been offered, they accept the promise the author makes, or they heed the warning that was issued. Thereby the Spirit makes the speech acts contained in the Bible

---

5. Ibid., 367–441.

6. Vanhoozer's critique of fundamentalism is that the movement does not recognize this: ibid., 424–7.

7. Ibid., 421.

8. Ibid., 456. This should not be understood as a simple relay race, in which each person's action is independent of another's, whereby each one runs a leg and then hands off the work to another. The persons of the Trinity act together because they are one God. This apportioning of specific acts to one person is a limited appropriation that reflects patterns in the biblical text.

effective in the lives of its readers. Tying the Spirit to perlocution means that the Spirit's role pertains strongly to the later stage of interpretation, when the reader is attempting to discern what to do with textual meaning, and not obviously to the earlier stage of establishing meaning itself.[9] In this way, and in this way alone for the early Vanhoozer, the Spirit is active in the interpretation of the discourse that the Spirit originally inspired.

Initially, then, significance depends on meaning, while meaning is in no way reciprocally dependent on significance. The Spirit's work is associated with significance, leaving the determination of meaning essentially independent of pneumatology. Thus, in this early period, in which Vanhoozer engaged heavily with philosophical sources, the crucial initial stage of biblical reading is not in any obvious sense a spiritual exercise.

III

Things change, however, as Vanhoozer comes into more sustained conversation with theological sources—in what the introduction to this edited volume fittingly identifies as the periods when he becomes more theological and practices theological reading of Scripture. In his reflections on what makes for a theological commentary, he quietly but unambiguously repudiates the distinction between meaning and significance—or at least the strong version of this distinction that was so central at the beginning of his career. Without mentioning this distinction in so many words, but by asking whether interpretation involves a strictly sequential relationship between ascertaining meaning and only *then* applying it, he makes clear that such an order places the reader's theological commitment *after* the early, determinative stages of interpretation have already occurred, thus rendering faith commitments irrelevant for much of the process.[10] While bracketing out theological commitment does not require a reader to deny beliefs she may hold, it does require those beliefs to become inoperative or "merely notional" as Vanhoozer

---

9. There are some nuances on this point in Kevin J. Vanhoozer, "The Spirit of Understanding: Special Revelation and General Hermeneutics," in *Disciplining Hermeneutics*, ed. Roger Lundin (Grand Rapids: Eerdmans, 1997), 163–4. Here the Spirit convicts the reader that these are the words of God that bear authoritative witness to Jesus Christ. But this has less to do with how to read the text than it does with acknowledging that this is indeed the sacred text that must be read. Perhaps there is something about how to read embedded in the point that this text is a witness to the Word, but that aspect of what Vanhoozer says is not developed significantly in this context.

10. Kevin J. Vanhoozer, "Theological Commentary and the 'Voice from Heaven': Exegesis, Ontology, and the Travail of Biblical Interpretation," in *On the Writing of New Testament Commentaries: Festschrift for Grant R. Osborne on the Occasion of His 70th Birthday*, ed. Stanley E. Porter and Eckhard J. Schnabel, Texts and Editions for New Testament Study (Leiden: Brill, 2013), 275–76.

calls them.¹¹ As an alternative, what is required is broadening what counts as the context of a biblical passage. Not just the historical past should be included; in some way, the text's canonical context also counts, as do the creedal context (how the creedal text guides interpretation) and the catholic context (the history of the text's reception in the church).¹² The price of setting these later materials decisively to the side, claiming that they cannot count in proper interpretation—insisting instead that history in the sense of a closed sequence of causes and effects rather than the history of salvation is the proper background for reading the Bible—is being de facto committed to neglecting God's activity in those wider contexts.¹³ This stance creates a strange dissonance for any believing biblical interpreter. Divine activity becomes marginalized within the practice of interpretation.

To the best of my knowledge, Vanhoozer nowhere in his corpus deals head-on with a question that readers who note this shift have no choice but to face: Even if the reasons for abandoning the strongest possible version of the meaning/significance distinction are very strong, what of the original rationale for installing it? From his later perspective, what does Vanhoozer make of the basic reason he had for insisting that this distinction is fundamental? Recall how important this distinction initially appeared to be:

> Without this basic distinction between meaning and significance, subsequent distinctions—between exegesis and eisegesis, understanding and overstanding, commentary and criticism—will be difficult, if not impossible, to maintain. ... Bereft of intrinsic meaning, a text becomes a screen on which readers project their own images or a surface that reflects the interpreter's own face.¹⁴

But is listening to the text, and receiving its message without unduly mingling the text's message with one's own voice, possible without a robust version of this distinction?

The role of readerly subjectivity in interpretation, or what initially seems to come under that heading, expands once there is no longer a crisp distinction between meaning and significance. In his recent essay on theological commentary, Vanhoozer notes an ongoing discussion about a so-called subjective element in any version of theological interpretation.¹⁵ That is, no articulation of theological reading is going to command a universal consensus, because each version is built around a theological framework that is somewhat distinctive as compared with other versions (e.g., Roman Catholic theological reading will have a different

---

11. Ibid., 272.
12. Ibid., 276.
13. The main target here is biblical scholars who are skeptical of theological reading as it is typically known. But essentially this critique is an exercise in self-criticism of his own earlier stance.
14. Vanhoozer, *Is There a Meaning in This Text?*, 263.
15. Vanhoozer, "Theological Commentary," 275.

ecclesiology than an evangelical Protestant type would), and the ideas do different sorts of work (e.g., a Roman Catholic theological reading, at least that which follows official teaching, will assign greater weight to ecclesiology, making the magisterium's reading determinative). Vanhoozer apparently has come to terms with this lack of consensus. Just because there are disagreements on what shape theological reading should take—there are and will continue to be into the foreseeable future—it is better to involve a well-considered set of theological commitments within interpretation than to set them aside entirely, thereby becoming a methodological naturalist. Involving these commitments, even as there are some disagreements about them, is not really a matter of projecting one's own image onto the text. The commitments made operational are one's best attempt to testify to God's work in the world, and they can always be revised where that proves necessary. This seems to be the resolution to which Vanhoozer has come in pushing aside the rigid meaning/significance distinction.

Does eliminating a strict version of the distinction imply an expanded role for the Spirit in interpretation? Let us assume that it is worth insisting that the Spirit brings to completion the acts God undertakes in the economy of salvation—as will become clear later in the essay, a major working assumption of Nicene Trinitarian theology. Assume also, if only for the sake of argument, that the Spirit is still to be linked with the text's significance. If significance does not depend on meaning rather than the other way around, and if a proper reading relates the text to instantiations of its later significance—in the canon, the creed, and the catholic tradition—then meaning is already shot through with significance. This is what it means for the distinction not to be absolute. Then does grasping meaning need to involve the Spirit, by virtue of the Spirit's (still assumed) link with significance? Should the Spirit have more of a role even at the most rudimentary levels of interpretation, especially as the point is being underscored that theology's role in the practice of interpretation should not be cramped? There are hints here and there in Vahoozer's work that he wants to say more than he was saying early on. For instance, he notes approvingly how John Owen says that the Spirit enables us to see what is there in Scripture, perhaps indicating a fundamentally expanded role for the Spirit.[16] Yet the basic structure for mapping Trinitarian theology onto speech-act theory remains in place and orients how he treats this topic. Even in his later work, Vanhoozer says that the Father initiates or produces speech; the Son executes or is himself what the Father does in speaking; and the Spirit completes and perfects the divine work as a matter of "perlocutionary prowess."[17] How does

---

16. Kevin J. Vanhoozer, "The Spirit of Light after the Age of Enlightenment: Reforming/Renewing Pneumatic Hermeneutics via the Economy of Illumination," in *Spirit of God: Christian Renewal in the Community of Faith*, ed. Jeffrey W. Barbeau and Beth Felker Jones (Downers Grove: IVP Academic, 2015), 159–60.

17. Ibid., 162. The association between the Spirit and perlocution remains fairly stable across Vanhoozer's corpus, including in his two more recent monographs. See Kevin J. Vanhoozer, *The Drama of Doctrine: A Canonical-Linguistic Approach to Christian Theology*

7. Basil and the Spirit in Biblical Interpretation 119

this relate to the comment drawing upon Owen? The Spirit still seems restricted by this scheme to bringing about effects in the hearer and reader, being involved at the end of reading rather than right from the beginning. Is this philosophical framework perhaps cramping a fuller deployment of theological doctrine?

IV

In reflecting further, maybe it will help to draw on a source from outside of our immediate context. The next section will turn to one of the Cappadocian fathers, Basil of Caesarea (*c.* 330–379), who contributed significantly to the pneumatology that became enshrined in the Nicene-Constantinopolitan Creed of 381. In so doing, this essay takes seriously its placement in the Great Performances section of this volume. It is worth engaging with, even deferring to, such classic theological texts, which have the capacity to enrich debate in the present. C. S. Lewis writes that such older texts can correct the characteristic temptations of our own age.[18] Lewis is certainly correct to state that theologians today will not see what is in their own blind spot if they read only material from their contemporaries.[19] When he goes on to say that authors of older texts made as many mistakes as we do, only different errors,[20] he neutralizes the apprehension readers may understandably feel when engaging with a text that is hallowed in its classic status and composed in an unfamiliar idiom. Yet Lewis's statement could also be misleading. As long as one does not assume that the church lost its way in the fourth century, believing instead that the expansion of the clause on the Spirit contained in the original Nicene Creed of 325 was a proper step when it was taken in 381, then the main texts that moved the church to make that decision deserve at least the benefit of the doubt on precisely this issue. At any rate, that is the working assumption here.

Even if it does turn out—per my ensuing argument—that there are ways to enrich what is being said about the Spirit's role in interpretation by drawing

---

(Louisville: Westminster John Knox, 2005), 199, in which he writes, "The Spirit's special role is to make Christ's communicative action—in particular, the commissioned canonical testimony of the apostles—efficacious, transforming communication into a species of communion." Similarly, Vanhoozer, *Remythologizing Theology: Divine Action, Passion, and Authorship*, Cambridge Studies in Christian Doctrine (Cambridge: Cambridge University Press, 2010), 374, states in summary fashion: "The Spirit, I submit, has perlocutionary power: the capacity to bring about the appropriate communicative effects." This includes the moment of understanding, yet understanding has a perlocutionary inflection here, meaning to grasp a warning as a warning or a promise as such. The terminology does not offer immediate help in relating the Bible to its subject matter.

18. C. S. Lewis, "Introduction," in *St. Athanasius on the Incarnation: The Treatise De Incarnatione Verbi Dei* (Crestwood, NY: St. Vladimir's Seminary, 1953), 4.

19. Ibid., 5.

20. Ibid.

upon a classical theological source, still Vanhoozer's "first theology" agenda can accommodate the necessary changes. First theology is a way of speaking about which ideas are the most important in doing constructive theological work. Does one "start with" God and then move to Scripture? Or does one begin rather with the Bible and then build out of it a doctrine of God? The point of first theology is to eschew any supposed starting point that is itself isolated from the wider framework of Christian thought and life. According to first theology, God and Scripture are part of a single problem, as is the interpretation of Scripture.[21] Theologians should not consider Scripture apart from its relation to God, as if they can or should try to build from a neutral position that reflects no commitment of any kind from them. Nor should they consider God apart from how he manifests himself through biblical discourse, the interpretation of which ought to reflect these prior views. First theology is relevant to the present issue as one of Vanhoozer's major organizing rubrics for bringing God and interpretation together, with real focus and determination. Thus, the question under discussion—whether there might be an expanded role for the Spirit in interpretation—is a question that he has a framework to entertain.

V

The figure in focus, Basil of Caesarea, received the best education in rhetoric and Greek literature available in his day before becoming an ascetic and a leader of the church in a crucial period. After finishing his studies in Athens, he took part in several ascetic communities and then settled into his family's estate with the intent of withdrawing from the world and living a singularly focused Christian life. He invited his friend Gregory of Nazianzus to join him, and the two put together a collection of Origen's writings entitled *Philocalia*. The edited work focuses on the will and, importantly for our topic, biblical interpretation. In due course, Basil was drawn away from his retreat and took up a leadership position; he was ordained and eventually made bishop in Caesarea. Basil's surviving writings include many sermons, sets of instructions for the running of ascetic communities, several letters, and two treatises focused around doctrine, one on the person of Christ and the another on the status of the Spirit.[22] This latter work is arguably his most

---

21. Kevin J. Vanhoozer, "First Theology: Meditations in a Postmodern Toolshed," in *First Theology*, 16.

22. There have been several excellent studies of his theology published in recent years: Mark DelCogliano, *Basil of Caesarea's Anti-Eunomian Theory of Names: Christian Theology and Late-antique Philosophy in the Fourth Century Trinitarian Controversy*, Supplements to Vigiliae Christianae: Texts and Studies of Early Christian Life and Language (Leiden: Brill, 2010); Volker H. Drecoll, *Die Entwicklung der Trinitätslehre des Basilius von Cäsarea: Sein Weg vom Homöusianer zum Neonizäner*, Forschungen zur Kirchen- und Dogmengeschichte (Göttingen: Vandenhoeck & Ruprecht, 1996);

mature piece of theology. It has had the most impact on subsequent Christian theology, as its conclusion regarding the Spirit is essentially identical to the expanded affirmation on the Spirit that made its way into the Creed of 381. All of his writings are utterly saturated with biblical texts.[23]

Basil's main work in pneumatology, *On the Holy Spirit*, was written in direct response to a dispute about the proper form of the liturgy, a question posed to him by a younger Christian named Amphilochios. Is it acceptable to put the Spirit on the same level as the Father and the Son, as in the formula, "Glory to God the Father with the Son, together with the Holy Spirit"?[24] Ascribing glory to the Spirit in this way, by putting him on the same plane with the Father and Son, seems to suggest that all three share the same status, even that they are all on par in their very being. The intimation is ultimately that they are all three divine. Is this appropriate, Amphilochios wondered, or does this coordinated form of the doxology go too far in what it conveys? Would it be better, instead, to utilize only a doxological form stressing how the Father, Son, and Spirit act in concert to mediate grace to human beings, giving glory to God the Father "through the Son in the Holy Spirit"?[25] This arrangement of the Son and the Spirit in relation to the Father was less controversial in Basil's milieu, but he argues for the full propriety of both formats and contends that the form in question has a long history of usage, claiming in so doing that the Spirit has no lesser status than the Father and the Son. Some readers of Basil's treatise find him worryingly coy in framing his conclusion about the Spirit as he does, for he pulls back from employing the term *homoousion* (of the same substance or essence) with respect to the Spirit.[26] Scholars debate why Basil couches his conclusion without this terminology. It is possible that he seeks to avoid language that would alienate those wary of his conclusion and

---

Stephen M. Hildebrand, *The Trinitarian Theology of Basil of Caesarea: A Synthesis of Greek Thought and Biblical Truth* (Washington, DC: Catholic University of America Press, 2007); Andrew Radde-Gallwitz, *Basil of Caesarea, Gregory of Nyssa, and the Transformation of Divine Simplicity*, Oxford Early Christian Studies (Oxford: Oxford University Press, 2009).

23. See, e.g., several studies by Jean Gribomont: "La tradition johannique chez S Basile," in *Parola e spirito* (Brescia: Paideia Editrice, 1982), 847–66; "Le paulinisme de Saint Basile," in *Saint Basile, évangile et église*, ed. Enzo Bianchi, Spiritualité orientale et vie monastique (Bégrolles-en-Mauges, Maine & Loire: Abbaye de Bellefontaine, 1984), 192–200; "Les Règles Morales de Saint Basile et le Nouveau Testament," in *Saint Basile, évangile et église: mélanges*, ed. Enzo Bianchi, Spiritualité orientale et vie monastique (Bégrolles-en-Mauges, Maine & Loire: Abbaye de Bellefontaine, 1984), 146–56.

24. Basil, *On the Holy Spirit*, 1.3. I follow the translation from David Anderson (Crestwood, NY: St. Vladimir's Seminary, 1980).

25. Ibid.

26. For a recent discussion deeply sympathetic to Gregory of Nazianzus, see Christopher Beeley, *Gregory of Nazianzus on the Trinity and the Knowledge of God: In Your Light We See Light* (Oxford: Oxford University Press, 2008), 297–303.

therefore operates mostly with a strategic motivation.[27] It is also possible that his main concern is the inherent sanctity of the subject matter, prohibiting an open proclamation of the conclusion to those who lack the disposition to accept it.[28] Or maybe his motivation is a mixture of these two considerations. It is not the purpose of this essay to take sides on that question, but having the proper stance to consider questions of pneumatology becomes crucial in what follows.[29] It will not be possible to deal with *On the Holy Spirit* comprehensively, but I attempt to bring out the importance of some of Basil's main moves.

One of his key arguments for the Spirit's status is based upon the work the Spirit performs in the economy of salvation. Through the joint work of Father, Son, and Spirit, God reveals himself to human beings: "If we are illumined by divine power, and fix our eyes on the beauty of the image of the invisible God, and through the image are led up to the indescribable beauty of its source, it is because we have been inseparably joined to the Spirit of knowledge."[30] Here the Spirit is associated with illuminating power; as Basil frames it, the Spirit has this power "in himself."[31] The Spirit in turn directs attention to Jesus Christ, who is the initial object of vision. In the image of the Father, illuminated eyes are able to see not only the archetype but also the inherent beauty and attractiveness of the Father.[32] Only because of the perfect match between the image and the archetype can this imaging occur as it

---

27. Kathy Eden, *Hermeneutics and the Rhetorical Tradition: Chapters in the Ancient Legacy and Its Humanist Reception* (New Haven: Yale University Press, 1997), 42–52.

28. Andrew Louth, *Discerning the Mystery: An Essay on the Nature of Theology* (Oxford: Oxford University Press, 1983), 85.

29. My exposition of Basil builds upon my book *Scriptural Interpretation: A Theological Account*, Challenges in Contemporary Theology (Oxford: Wiley-Blackwell, 2013), 35–131.

30. Basil, *On the Holy Spirit*, 18.47.

31. Ibid.

32. Basil's emphasis on light in such contexts has provoked criticism from a major present-day theologian, Sarah Coakley. She finds it dissatisfying that Basil does so much with light imagery and so little with darkness motifs; she sees in Basil's brother, Gregory of Nyssa, a salutary stress on darkness as a way of speaking about the impossibility of ever achieving genuine knowledge of the transcendent God. See her *God, Sexuality, and the Self: An Essay "On the Trinity"* (Cambridge: Cambridge University Press, 2013), 138–40. Coakley makes this comment in her wide-ranging systematic theology and inevitably cannot provide detailed readings for all the pertinent passages. There is now a major study of Basil's distinctive mode of apophaticism in Lewis Ayres, "Apophasis and the Discipline of Theological Speech: The Case of Basil of Caesarea" (unpublished manuscript). He relates both Basil's ascetical texts and the homilies back to his more directly doctrinal work, arguing that for Basil there is indeed a rather substantial sense in which speech about God is necessarily destined to fail as a satisfactory account of its divine referent. For this reason, speech about the divine must ultimately yield to silence before the divine mystery. Coakley may well have a way to respond to this challenge, but the burden will now be on her to defend her reading.

does. This joint work of the divine persons has major theological consequences. It would be simplistic to say that Basil's argument is just that since the Father, Son, and Spirit are all involved in the same actions, they must all be divine. What Basil does is to read the way in which the Father, Son, and Spirit act in concert in their work of creating and redeeming against the background of a principle that specifies the significance of such activities: Actions find their place in a sequence where works reveal the power that causes them, and that power necessarily belongs to an entity of a specific sort.[33] That the Spirit works jointly with the Father and the Son, completing their action of illuminating human beings, implies that the Spirit has the same power as the other two; only beings of the same ontological order possess such power, even if that essence is itself incomprehensible, as the divine essence is.

The survey of the Spirit's joint actions together with the other persons draws heavily on the biblical witness, but what Basil's argument lacks—as it necessarily must, given what the biblical witness actually offers—is a direct, explicit, verbatim statement to the effect that the Spirit is indeed divine. That he does not and cannot ever provide. Certain biblical texts may approach this, but they do not finally grant it. So, especially in the face of demands for maximal certainty, Basil must explain how his conclusion about the Spirit derives from biblical texts and receives warrant from them. His final major move in the treatise is to deal with this issue. In ch. 27 of *On the Holy Spirit*, Basil takes as his task showing the sense in which the coordinated form of the doxology is biblical, "how its usage is in accord with Scripture."[34] The section has often been analyzed for what it seems to say about tradition, rather than the Bible,[35] but there is no disjunction between the two in Basil's own description of his aims or in the thrust of the passage itself.

Basil discusses a series of liturgical practices that Christians perform in the course of worship. These inculcate into them the scope of Scripture's message, even if they do not fully realize what is ultimately occurring. Some of these liturgical practices follow very closely the words of biblical passages, as with baptisms that invoke the name of the Trinity (see Mt. 28:19). Other practices do not receive precise verbal warrant in the text of the Bible; for instance, no single text indicates that those enrolling as catechumens should receive the sign of the cross, a common practice in Basil's day.[36] Whether or not the letter of the text offers such support is not ultimately the point, however. What matters more is that such practices reflect, in various ways, the overall scope or thrust of Scripture.[37] As enacted practices, they constitute lived glosses of the text: Thereby they not only represent what it

---

33. On this basic principle for pro-Nicene theologies, see Lewis Ayres, *Nicaea and Its Legacy* (Oxford: Oxford University Press, 2004).

34. Basil, *On the Holy Spirit*, 27.65.

35. Louth's comments on the treatise are lucid to be sure, but he treats the final section as mainly about tradition and fails to connect that theme up with biblical interpretation: *Discerning the Mystery*, 85–90.

36. Basil, *On the Holy Spirit*, 27.66.

37. Ibid., 7.16.

says, but they also draw the hearts and minds of those performing these symbolic actions into the whole sweep of the Bible in such a gentle and gradual way that not everyone is going to be cognizant of what is occurring. Basil cites the example of Christians praying facing east, another rite common in his day.[38] This practice does not have independent weight of its own, for it takes its cue from Gen. 2:8, a passage that speaks of God planting a garden in the east in a place called Eden. While everyone prays facing east, not everyone knows why, Basil explains. The rite's hidden intent is to accustom Christians to the idea that they are seeking paradise, this ancient land. What Basil is doing in this final section of his treatise, which is addressed to his apprentice Amphilochios, is to let him in on the inner rationale for the whole range of these liturgical practices. The reality of God is inherently overwhelming, and people must be accustomed to the Bible's subject matter bit by bit over time; otherwise, it will be entirely too much for them even to begin to experience.[39]

The rite of baptism is especially important for the case supporting the coordinated version of the doxology. This rite trains Christians to see God in a particular way. It is a picture of God's being and activity. How so? Baptism as a whole is tied closely to salvation. It is faith's fulfillment, it represents an initial enlightenment, and it ushers the Christian into a lifelong course of discipleship.[40] That is what the entirety of the rite signifies. Of course, though, as this rite is enacted in the service of worship, there are three separate immersions, each of which is connected with a person of the Trinity. The Father, the Son, and the Spirit are each named, highlighting the equal roles that they have in conversion. Each one performs the same action. Thus, according to Basil's power theology, which was mentioned earlier, they all have the same power or ability to save and can therefore be seen to share in one and the same essence. This major theological conclusion is inchoately present within a rite that would have been repeated many times before the eyes of worshippers. The practice of baptism in the name of the Father, Son, and Spirit, if not the correlation of a single immersion with each of them, is a clear response to Matthew 28, and the tacit theology of this custom is certainly a plank in Basil's cumulative argument for the propriety of the coordinated doxology.

The practices of the church are thus taken up into the pedagogy of the Spirit. The demand for proof texts, in the sense of explicit verbatim statements for a conclusion about the Spirit's status, is therefore rendered unnecessary, even positively out of

---

38. Ibid., 27.66.

39. Maurice Wiles make the point that even those accused of being dryly rational, and not at all liturgical, in their theological orientation and practice are often just indebted to a different sort of worship routine. He makes the valuable point that one must focus on which liturgy is relevant rather than simply whether worship is considered the context for engaging with God: "Eunomius: Hair-Splitting Dialectician or Defender of the Accessibility of Salvation?," in *The Making of Orthodoxy: Essays in Honour of Henry Chadwick*, ed. Rowan Williams (Cambridge: Cambridge University Press, 1989), 157–72.

40. Basil, *On the Holy Spirit*, 15.34–6.

place. What is important is seeing the overall scope of the text and having been drawn into it by virtue of liturgical formation. It is beyond anything Basil himself ever says to claim that "the tradition of the Church *is* the Spirit, that what is passed on from age to age in the bosom of the Church is the Spirit, making us sons in the Son, enabling us to call on the Father, and thus share in the communion of the Trinity."[41] Yet there is a close relationship between liturgical practices and the Spirit's work. The ecclesial practices that train Christians in how to think about the Spirit are responses that enable a reading of the text with respect to its ultimate subject matter. In a sense, then, Basil is recommending that scriptural texts should be read in relation to other scriptural texts if the reader is to engage with their subject matter. Making the liturgy this important to biblical interpretation is not a view to which all evangelicals will be accustomed. Yet a lack of familiarity is by no means a reason to reject the view, for there may well be ways in which it proves to be a resource for contemporary hermeneutical reflection.[42] Being willing to stretch oneself to consider Basil's argument is the way to "keep the clean sea breeze of the centuries blowing through our minds,"[43] as C. S. Lewis says, by allowing old books to challenge our settled notions.

It would not be accurate to paraphrase Basil in terms of the meaning/significance distinction. Basil is not saying that the text of the Bible, and specifically the meaning of its passages about the Spirit's status, cannot be accessed except by those who accept the significance they have for themselves. He does not operate with this distinction in the first place. Yet he is saying something close: that reading about the Spirit is only possible in the Spirit. What is necessary to arrive at the truth about the Spirit's standing is to be indwelt and illumined by him, since this allows for the contemplation of the Spirit, who is the text's subject matter. Relating the text and its subject matter requires nothing less than this illuminated contemplation—which is correlative to having gained a sense of Scripture's scope from the tradition that trains Christians in Scripture's enactment.

---

41. Louth, *Discerning the Mystery*, 88. This phrasing from Louth is characteristically unguarded, for it could easily be read as implying that the Spirit is identified with the church to the point that there is nothing more to the Spirit than what one sees in the ecclesial community. The Spirit should not be linked this closely with the ecclesial community. What Basil says, however, certainly accords with Paul Griffiths's point that any form of religiously engaged reading will not ultimately be intelligible outside of that religious tradition, depending as it does on the resources of the tradition rather than treating the individual as the final court of appeals for justifying a religious belief: *Religious Reading: The Place of Reading in the Practice of Religion* (Oxford: Oxford University Press, 1999), 74.

42. For further detail on how this might work, see Sarisky, *Scriptural Interpretation*, 224–32.

43. Lewis, "Introduction," 5.

VI

On this basis, it is now possible to return to Vanhoozer's theology and to address the hanging question of an expanded role for the Spirit in interpretation. Vanhoozer ties the Spirit mainly to the perlocutionary aspect of biblical language, that is, the text's effectiveness in attaining its communicative goal—for instance, that a reader would accept an assertion the Bible makes regarding the Spirit. The Spirit may do this by disabusing us of prejudices that prevent us from receiving the text's message.[44] Within this mapping of speech-act theory onto Trinitarian theology, however, there is little about perceiving as opposed to believing; it is difficult from within this framework to speak of the Spirit's hermeneutical efficacy in relation to the reader's effort to perceive the text's content. The framework pushes the Spirit's action further on in the process. The Spirit ought to bring to completion even whatever work comes first, not just the process as a whole. The application of speech-act philosophy to biblical hermeneutics has certainly proven to be worthwhile; but, where this philosophical-theological correlation cramps what ought to be said, it proves its usefulness to be limited, so it should be revised or relegated to the background. Moving in this direction is facilitated by abandoning the strong version of the meaning/significance distinction and allowing commitment to theological truths to become operative right from the start of interpretive work on biblical texts.[45]

The role of the Spirit that is more fundamental than responding fittingly to the text is reading it with reference to its subject matter, or relating the textual signifiers to what is signified. A Trinitarian theology of illumination, in which the Spirit is the light in which God reveals himself, requires that this light indwell readers so that they might know the matter of the text in the nuanced sense that is possible when what is known is God while the knower is a human creature. Basil's explication of the Spirit's work within the economy of salvation makes this clear. Yet making this point by no means limits the Spirit's ministry to perception alone. Allowing a fitting response to the text is also part of the Spirit's hermeneutical efficacy, as Vanhoozer rightly contends. But the diachronic and social pertinence of this ministry should be underlined. It is not only that the Spirit endows an individual reader with the ability to do what the text requires of her. Rather, the Spirit has been at work in the community of readers, conferring on them the ability to respond rightly to the text. This work of the Spirit, in turn, has salutary effects on readers immersed in this tradition by forming their prior understanding of the God to whom the text directs its readers' attention.

---

44. Vanhoozer, "The Spirit of Understanding," 234.

45. Whether a softer version of the meaning/significance distinction might prove viable is a topic for another time.

Chapter 8

AUGUSTINE AND SCRIPTURE

Gregory W. Lee

Introduction

Augustine's engagement with Scripture is intimately interwoven with his spiritual journey.[1] As he recounts in *Confessions*, Augustine's relationship with the Bible began on a bad note. When he was 19 years old, he discovered a (now lost) text of Cicero called *Hortensius*, which encouraged readers to love wisdom. Having been raised by a Christian mother, Augustine first sought this wisdom in Scripture.[2] Yet the Bible available to Augustine was an early and rough translation, before the publication of Jerome's Vulgate, and Augustine was a rising teacher of rhetoric. Judging the prose of the Bible to be inferior to that of the Roman greats, Augustine turned to Manichaeism, which rejected the OT and filtered the NT through the writings of Mani. Augustine would call himself a Manichee for about a decade before rejecting the sect. But Manichean objections to the OT would vex Augustine for many years after his conversion to the "Catholic" faith.

One stimulus toward Augustine's conversion was his encounter with Ambrose, the bishop of Milan, whose allegorical interpretation of the OT assured Augustine of the intellectual viability of the Catholic faith. Years later, when Augustine was ordained as priest, he requested extended time to study the Scriptures before assuming office.[3] To this point, Augustine's writings had been more philosophical in orientation. They would now take a decidedly biblical cast. As bishop, Augustine preached thousands of sermons on Scripture. Many of his greatest treatises consist of extended analyses of the biblical text. Many of his most influential ideas derive

---

1. Michael Cameron, *Christ Meets Me Everywhere: Augustine's Early Figurative Exegesis*, Oxford Studies in Historical Theology (Oxford: Oxford University Press, 2012). I am grateful to Michael Graves, Han-luen Kantzer Komline, and Darren Sarisky for feedback on an earlier draft of this chapter.

2. *Confessions* 3.5.9. Unless otherwise referenced, all primary texts cited in this chapter are available in English translation from WSA.

3. *Letter* 21.

from exegetical observations. Biblical exposition was arguably Augustine's central work as a bishop and theologian.

Augustine's interaction with Scripture reveals a series of stimulating positions on the historicity of the text, the weight of tradition, authorial intent, and the narrative of Scripture, each of which rewards evangelical consideration today. I treat each topic in turn.

History and Contradictions

Augustine's affirmation of the Bible's historicity often exceeds the level of interest and detail of contemporary evangelical practice. Yet many of his strategies for addressing historical quandaries might strike modern readers as quite strange. Let us consider some illustrative examples.

One extended instance is *Agreement among the Evangelists*, written in AD 400 against Roman opponents of Christianity who claimed that the Gospels disagree with each other.[4] Augustine defends the harmony of the Gospels with each other as well as with the intentions of Jesus, who commissioned their writing.[5] Matthew and John witnessed Jesus' adult words and actions and were able to secure "totally reliable information and completely trustworthy evidence" about his birth, infancy, and childhood.[6] Mark and Luke were not direct eyewitnesses but still received divine authority to write their Gospels.[7] As Augustine enjoins, the reader must "not ever suppose that any one of all four evangelists has lied or has fallen into error from such a holy and high authority."[8]

The core of *Agreement among the Evangelists*, Books 2–4, addresses every potential contradiction Augustine perceives in the Gospels, beginning with Matthew[9] and continuing with Mark,[10] Luke,[11] and John.[12] In his treatment of this material, Augustine defends the following principles. First, omissions do not count as contradictions.[13] The Gospels were written in the order presented, and each author was aware of the preceding texts.[14] Omissions do not reflect the authors' ignorance of earlier material but their desire to avoid redundancy. Second, the Gospels often arrange the same events in differing chronological sequence. These

---

4. *Agreement among the Evangelists* 1.7.10.
5. Ibid., 1.35.54.
6. Ibid., 1.1.1.
7. Ibid., 1.1.2. See also 4.8.9.
8. Ibid., 3.13.43.
9. Ibid., 2–3.
10. Ibid., 4.1.1–7.8.
11. Ibid., 4.8.9–9.10.
12. Ibid., 4.10.11–20.
13. Ibid., 2.5.16. See also 2.5.14, 2.17.34, 2.19.47, 2.41.88, 2.42.90.
14. Ibid., 1.2.3–4.

differences are themselves divinely inspired, reflecting the order in which the Holy Spirit brought these events to the authors' minds.[15] Third, some apparent contradictions suggest similar events that occurred multiple times.[16] Augustine appeals to this possibility with regard to the multiple accounts of Jesus' cleansing the temple,[17] and the relation between Matthew's sermon on the mount and Luke's sermon on the plain,[18] among other instances.[19] Finally and most importantly, the Gospel writers cared more about meaning and truth than exact words, which we should not think of as some kind of "deified sound (*consecratis sonis*)."[20] The truth of the Gospels is not found "in mere words (*uerborum*) but in the things themselves (*rerum*)."[21]

> The truth of the Gospel is from the word of God, which remains eternal and unchangeable above all that is created. It is spread abroad through the creation of temporal signs and through human language and has the highest level of authority. Therefore one should not suppose that one of [the evangelists] is deceitful if, in their account of something they saw or heard, several people remember it in not exactly the same way or in not exactly the same words but nonetheless describe the same thing; nor if the order of the words is different; nor if some words are in place of others that nonetheless indicate the same thing; nor if something is not said, either because it did not occur to the writer or because it could be inferred from other things that were said; nor if one decides to mention something for the sake of the narrative and, in order to keep the chronological order in place, only touches on part of something rather than explaining it entirely; nor if the person who has the authority to write the narrative should add not something to the subject but rather some words in order to illuminate and explain his meaning; nor if, although he presents the subject well, he tries but does not succeed in remembering and expressing the exact words he heard with complete accuracy.[22]

Similar strategies appear in *Reply to Faustus* and an oft-cited correspondence with Jerome about Galatians 2.[23] The former addresses the now deceased Manichean

---

15. Ibid., 2.21.51–2. See also 2.19.44, 2.26.59. For an intriguing account of how the Spirit directed Matthew to include a perplexing reference to Jeremiah, see 3.7.28–31.
16. Ibid., 2.29.69, 2.30.77.
17. Ibid., 2.67.129.
18. Ibid., 2.19.44–7.
19. Ibid., 2.50.105, 2.64.124.
20. Ibid., 2.66.128.
21. Ibid., 2.12.28.
22. Ibid., 2.12.28. See also 2.12.27, 2.19.44, 2.24.55–25.57, 2.28.66–7, 2.46.95, 2.46.97, 2.62.121, 2.77.147, 3.2.8, 3.4.14. In 3.13.48, Augustine suggests, drawing on Romans 9, that God inserted apparent contradictions into the Gospels to blind the wicked and to purify the righteous.
23. The key arguments are in *Letters* 28, 40, 75, and 82.

bishop who features in *Confessions* 5. Against Faustus's attacks, Augustine denies the possibility of Scripture contradicting itself and attributes apparent errors to manuscript issues.[24] "If something [in the Bible] strikes a person as absurd, it is not permissible to say, 'The author of this book did not have the truth,' but, 'Either the manuscript is defective, or the translator made a mistake, or you do not understand.'"[25] So also for the incident in Antioch when Paul rebukes Peter for acting as a Jew. At least on Augustine's account, Jerome depicted Paul's remarks as a useful lie: Paul did not think Peter had sinned, but he chastised Peter to mollify those who were offended by Peter's behavior. Augustine rejects this interpretation because it would cast doubt on the rest of Scripture as well.[26] He also writes, "I most firmly believe that none of authors [of the canonical books] erred in writing anything. And if I come upon something in those writings that seems contrary to the truth, I have no doubt that either the manuscript is defective or the translator did not follow what was said or that I did not understand it."[27]

Thus, Augustine aligns with evangelical sensibilities on the basic historicity of the Bible. Yet some of his strategies for defending its historicity differ significantly from those of evangelicalism, at least in its popular forms. Two examples concern the Greek OT and the earliest chapters of Genesis. In the correspondence mentioned above, Augustine and Jerome also squabbled over the authority of the LXX vis-à-vis the Hebrew text.[28] Jerome favored translating the Vulgate from the Hebrew, while Augustine thought Jerome should base his work on the Greek. Augustine would later soften his position, affirming in *City of God* that the Hebrew and the Greek were equally inspired.[29] Yet this position still left questions about apparent conflicts between the two texts. Augustine concludes that discrepancies should be attributed to the Holy Spirit, who inserted them into the texts to teach us hidden mysteries. In the Hebrew, for instance, Jonah announces that Nineveh will be overturned in forty days (Jon. 3:4). In the Greek, that number is three days. Augustine sides with the Hebrew on the historical matter but affirms the LXX account as signifying the Gentiles' conversion through Christ, who was raised on the third day but ascended on the fortieth day after that.[30] By ascribing the Spirit's work to both the Hebrew and the Greek texts, Augustine adopts an understanding of inspiration even more expansive than many evangelicals'.

Augustine's interpretation of Genesis has received much attention.[31] His earliest effort to interpret the text, a commentary against the Manichees, allegorizes the text

---

24. *Reply to Faustus* 3.5.
25. Ibid., 11.5. See also 11.8, 32.19.
26. *Letter* 28.3.3.
27. *Letter* 82.1.3.
28. See especially *Letters* 28, 71, 75, 82. See also *De doctrina christiana* 2.15.22.
29. *City of God* 18.42–4.
30. Ibid., 18.44.
31. Jules M. Brady, "St. Augustine's Theory of Seminal Reasons," *The New Scholasticism* 38 (1964): 141–58; Augustine, *La Genèse au sens littéral en douze livres (I-VII)*, trans. P. Agaësse and A. Solignac, Bibliothèque Augustinienne: Oeuvres de Saint Augustin 48

in a manner reminiscent of Origen. Later, as Augustine becomes more committed to the literal sense, he pens his fullest treatment of this material, *The Literal Commentary on Genesis*. Augustine takes Genesis 2–3 quite literally, affirming the reality of an actual paradise, its actual rivers, Adam and Eve as actual people, and the Tree of Life and the Tree of the Knowledge of Good and Evil as actual trees.[32] Yet he does not believe the six days of creation represent twenty-four hour blocks of time.[33] He interprets them instead as *rationes seminales* or *causales*—immaterial, causal principles that were created simultaneously by God and would subsequently determine the development of all created things.[34] In *Scandal of the Evangelical Mind*, Mark Noll leveraged Augustine's treatment of Genesis 1 for an argument against fundamentalist approaches to the chapter, stressing his openness to scientific inquiry and his affirmation of reason and experience as tools for the hermeneutical task.[35] Augustine's example remains relevant to present discussions of the creation narrative.

The Weight of Tradition

In contemporary discussions of Scripture and tradition, Augustine is commonly included in the latter. But Augustine did not have the hindsight to see himself in those terms, and he understood his own work to be reliant on his predecessors'. In general, Augustine considered the content of tradition to be identical to the content of Scripture,[36] and he believed that the "Catholic" church deserved the benefit of the doubt by Christians and non-Christians who were unsure whether to trust its teachings.[37] Yet he also stressed the unique authority of Scripture and departed from tradition when he perceived it to be in error.

(Paris: Institut d'Études Augustiniennes, 2000 [1972]), 653–68; Michael Fiedrowicz, "Introduction," in Saint Augustine, *On Genesis*, WSA I/13, 155–66.

32. *The Literal Meaning of Genesis* 8.1.1–7.14.

33. Ibid., 4.18.33, 4.26.43–28.45, 4.35.56, 5.1.1–3.6.

34. Ibid., 5.5.12–16, 5.11.27–12.28, 5.23.44–46, 6.10.17–11.19, 6.14.25–18.29.

35. Mark A. Noll, *The Scandal of the Evangelical Mind* (Grand Rapids: Eerdmans, 1994), 202–3, which quotes at length Augustine, *The Literal Meaning of Genesis* 1.19.39.

36. On this "coincidence" view of Scripture, tradition, and the church, see Anthony N. S. Lane, "Scripture, Tradition and Church: An Historical Survey," *Vox Evangelica* 9 (1975): 37–55.

37. I take this to be the point of Augustine's controversial statement in *Answer to the Letter of Mani Known as The Foundation* 5.6, "In fact I would not believe the gospel if the authority of the Catholic Church did not move me." For fuller discussion of this quotation, see A. D. R. Polman, *The Word of God according to St. Augustine* (Grand Rapids: Eerdmans, 1961), 198–208. Calvin's interpretation, with which I substantially agree, is in *Institutes of the Christian Religion* 1.7.3.

Augustine's treatment of the Trinity illustrates this balance. Though Augustine began writing *De trinitate* only a couple of decades after the Council of Constantinople, he already presupposes its authority. Augustine introduces *De trinitate* by writing,

> The purpose of all the Catholic commentators I have been able to read on the divine books of both testaments, who have written before me on the trinity which God is, has been to teach that according to the scriptures Father and Son and Holy Spirit in the inseparable equality of one substance present a divine unity; and therefore there are not three gods but one God.[38]

He then describes the immanent relations and economic distinctions between the divine persons in the terms codified by the Niceno-Constantinopolitan Creed. The Father, Son, and Spirit are distinct in that the Father has begotten the Son, the Son has been begotten of the Father, and the Spirit belongs to both the Father and the Son. So, too, it was the Son who was born of the Virgin Mary and died on the cross; the Spirit who descended in the form of a dove upon Jesus and in tongues of fire on Pentecost; and the Father who blessed Jesus at the baptism by John and on the mountain of the transfiguration. Augustine concludes, "This is also my faith inasmuch as it is the Catholic faith."[39]

As the treatise continues, Augustine furnishes scriptural evidence for the Trinity as well as interpretive principles for reading the Bible. Some detractors cite passages like Jn 14:28, "The Father is greater than I," as evidence that the Son is ontologically inferior to the Father. Augustine responds with "a canonical rule (*canonicam regulam*)" that is "scattered through the scriptures, and marked out by learned Catholic expositors of them."[40] Taken from Phil. 2:6-7, this rule teaches that Jesus can be understood both according to the form of God by which he is coequal with the Father, and according to the form of a servant by which he is less than the Father (and less than himself, since he is God). All passages that teach the Son's unity and equality with the Father should be referred to the form of God. All passages that teach the Son's limitation or inferiority should be referred to the form of the servant. Finally, some passages teach that the Son comes from the Father—a relationship that, according to Nicene decree, does not mean that the Son is less than the Father.

Augustine does not invent the hermeneutical distinction between passages about the Son's humanity and passages about his divinity. This interpretive practice has precedent in Athanasius and the Cappadocian fathers as an element of a "pro-Nicene" theology.[41] Yet Augustine believes that the rule is found in Scripture itself,

---

38. *De trinitate* 1.4.7.
39. Ibid. See also *Unfinished Literal Commentary on Genesis* 1.1–2.
40. *De trinitate* 2.1.2. See also 1.7.14, 1.11.22.
41. On the definition of "pro-Nicene," see Lewis Ayres, *Nicaea and its Legacy: An Approach to Fourth-Century Trinitarian Theology* (Oxford: Oxford University Press, 2004), 236–40.

and he invites readers to challenge his theology of the Trinity where it needs correction.[42] Augustine is not an infallible authority. He seeks simply "*to meditate on the law of the Lord*, if not *day and night*, at least at whatever odd moments I can snatch" (Ps. 1:2) and to trust that God will reveal to him whatever he has gotten wrong.[43] Still, he offers no indication that he would entertain revisions to the creed, and his invitation for correction is best understood with reference to his Trinitarian speculations as opposed to the dogmatic formulations he has inherited.

The most significant instance when Augustine breaks from precedent occurs in the Donatist controversy, the stubbornest challenge of his bishopric. This controversy began at the beginning of the fourth century when a priest named Caecilian was ordained bishop of Carthage against the objections of a rigorist community that claimed one of the ordinands was a *traditor* ("traitor") who had denied Christ during the recent persecution of Christians by the Roman Empire.[44] The "Donatists" (as Augustine called this group) considered every community in fellowship with Caecilian to be so tainted by *traditio* that they rebaptized converts to their own community. Augustine, by contrast, did not rebaptize Donatists who became "Catholics" (as Augustine called his own community), affirming the validity of baptism among the Donatists even as he denied its fruitfulness for salvation.[45]

The problem for Augustine was Cyprian, a third-century martyr and bishop of Carthage esteemed by both the Catholics and the Donatists.[46] Cyprian had defended the practice of rebaptizing heretics and schismatics against the opinion of Stephen, the bishop of Rome, and pronounced on this matter at a council held in Carthage in 256. In arguing against rebaptism, Augustine found himself in the awkward position of claiming Cyprian's legacy while rejecting his judgment. Augustine's strategy involves three elements.

First, Augustine downplays the authority of Cyprian's judgment on rebaptism. As Augustine argues, the earliest custom of the church, perhaps going back to the apostles themselves, was to avoid repeating baptism.[47] This practice was changed by Agrippinus, one of Cyprian's predecessors as bishop of Carthage. Cyprian followed African practice without investigating the issue thoroughly. But he was

---

42. *De trinitate* 1.3.5, 3.prooem.2.

43. Ibid., 1.3.5.

44. For an overview of the Donatist controversy, see Richard Miles, ed., *The Donatist Schism: Controversy and Contexts*, Translated Texts for Historians, Contexts (Liverpool: Liverpool University Press, 2016).

45. *Baptism* 3.14.19–15.20, 4.17.24.

46. Recent studies of Augustine's interaction with Cyprian include Matthew Alan Gaumer, *Augustine's Cyprian: Authority in Roman Africa*, Brill's Series in Church History and Religious Culture 73 (Leiden: Brill, 2016); Han-luen Kantzer Komline, "Grace, Free Will, and the Lord's Prayer: Cyprian's Importance for the 'Augustinian' Doctrine of Grace," *AugSt* 45 (2014): 247–79.

47. *Baptism* 2.7.12–9.14.

also humble and would have responded to correction about rebaptism in the same way that Peter did when he was corrected by Paul about Jewish circumcision.[48] Cyprian only stuck with African custom because he never came across an effective argument against it.

Second, Augustine stresses Cyprian's willingness to remain in fellowship with bishops who rejected rebaptism.[49] According to Augustine, Cyprian respected the right of bishops to disagree with him. He did not think any bishop should set himself up as "the bishop of bishops" or force others to obey his own opinion. Cyprian thus embodied the opposite spirit of the Donatists, who spurn fellowship with the Catholics in their sectarian pride. What matters from Cyprian's legacy is not his position on rebaptism but his example of love, as manifest in his commitment to church unity. By accepting Donatist baptism, Augustine argues, Catholics have a stronger claim than the Donatists to Cyprian's legacy.

Finally, Augustine establishes principles for adjudicating sources of theological authority. The regional Council of Carthage where Cyprian issued his judgment was overturned by a "plenary council (*plenarium concilium*)," the Council of Arles of 314.[50] To establish this point, Augustine defends a theological hierarchy.[51] Bishops' letters are open to refutation by the wisdom of other people, the authority of other bishops, or councils. Councils may be regional or plenary; the latter trump the former. Even plenary councils can be corrected by later councils when "what had been hidden is revealed and what was concealed is recognized through the test of time."[52] Finally, the canon of Scripture "is thus so superior to all the later writings of the bishops that it cannot in any respect be subject to doubt or debate. Whatever is written in it establishes whether a thing is true or right."[53]

In practice, Augustine tends to defer to his predecessors. He does not present his writings as innovative, and he is keen to assert his continuity with earlier authorities, especially when his views are under attack.[54] He believes that Scripture should be interpreted according to the rule of faith and the authority of the church,[55] and that the Niceno-Constantinopolitan Creed coincides with

---

48. Ibid., 2.1.2.

49. Ibid., 2.1.2–5.6.

50. Ibid., 2.7.12–9.14. Cf. 1.7.9, 1.18.28, 2.4.5. As the translators comment in their note on 1.7.9, "Although described by Augustine as though it were a universal or ecumenical council, [the Council of Arles] was in fact attended only by about forty bishops or their representatives, all from the West." Augustine, *The Donatist Controversy I*, trans. Maureen Tilley and Boniface Ramsey, WSA, 400 n. 17.

51. *Baptism* 2.3.4.

52. Ibid.

53. Ibid. For similar judgments, see *Reply to Faustus* 11.5; *Nature and Grace* 61.71; *Letter* 82.1.3.

54. See, e.g., *The Gift of Perseverance* 19.48–50.

55. *On Genesis: A Refutation of the Manichees* 2.2.3; *De doctrina christiana* 3.2.2.

the content of Scripture. Though he breaks from Cyprian's position on rebaptism, Augustine stresses his continuity with an earlier tradition against rebaptism as well as his fidelity to the greater part of Cyprian's legacy, namely, Cyprian's commitment to love. Still, Augustine believes that all theological sources may in principle be questioned except for Scripture itself, which he considers an insuperable authority over his own works, the writings of Cyprian and other bishops, and councils of different kinds.

Authorial Intent

Augustine's position on authorial intent is complex.[56] On the one hand, he identifies human authorial intent with divine authorial intent and encourages interpreters to pursue the former in order to gain the latter. "The aim of [Scripture's] readers is simply to find out the thoughts and wishes of those by whom it was written down and, through them, the will of God, which we believe these men followed as they spoke."[57]

On the other hand, Augustine believes that authorial intent can encompass more than one meaning. As he writes in *Confessions* 12 concerning Genesis 1, Augustine wants to understand Moses's intent because he believes that Moses wrote by the inspiration of the Spirit.[58] But Moses may have intended multiple meanings. As Augustine writes, if two readers offered different interpretations of the first verses of Genesis, he would respond,

> Why not both, if both are true? And if there is a third possibility, and a fourth, and if someone else sees an entirely different meaning in these words, why should we not think that [Moses] was aware of all of them, since it was through him that the one God carefully tempered his sacred writings to meet the minds of many people, who would see different things in them, and all true?[59]

Moreover, the Spirit may have intended meanings beyond what Moses had in mind.

> Finally, Lord, what if human vision is incomplete? Does this mean that anything you intended to reveal by these words to later generations of readers … was hidden from your good Spirit, who will, I pray, lead me into the right land? Is this not the case even if the man through whom you spoke to us had perhaps only one of the true meanings in mind? If he did, by all means let that one which

---

56. This section condenses fuller treatments of the same material from my *Today When You Hear His Voice: Scripture, the Covenants, and the People of God* (Grand Rapids: Eerdmans, 2016), 203–6, 214–17.
57. *De doctrina christiana* 2.5.6.
58. *Confessions* 12.30.41–32.43.
59. Ibid., 12.31.42.

he intended be taken as paramount. But as for us, Lord, we beg you to point out to us either that sense which he intended or any other true meaning which you choose, so that whether you take occasion of these words to make plain to us the same thing that you showed him, or something different, you still may feed us and no error dupe us ... For this is the assurance on which I make my confession: that if I manage to expound the sense intended by the writer who served you, that will be correct and the best course I could take, and that I must endeavor to do; but if I do not succeed in that, I may at least say what your Truth wills to reveal to me through the words of Moses, since it was your Truth who communicated to him also whatever he willed.[60]

The goal of interpretation is truth, which we can trust Moses to have communicated. But Moses may have intended multiple meanings, and God can communicate truths through Moses's words that Moses did not originally intend. The reader can profit from many interpretations so long as they align with God's truth.

Another lens on authorial intent arises in Augustine's account of his conversion, which is recounted in *Confessions* 8 and gestures toward a connection between Scripture and divine speech.[61] Augustine's conversion is the climactic moment of five interlocking stories, each of which underscores Scripture's power to move the soul. The first concerns Marius Victorinus, a prominent rhetorician-philosopher who became interested in Christianity after "reading holy scripture and intensively studying all the Christian writings," but initially refused to be baptized because he feared the opinions of others.[62] Some time later, Scripture emboldened him to profess his faith: "He drank in courage from his avid reading and came to fear that he might be disowned by Christ before his holy angels if he feared to confess him before men and women."[63] Spurred by Jesus' admonition (Mk 8:38; Lk. 9:26; 12:8-9), Victorinus joined the catechumenate and received baptism, much to the joy of the Christian community in Rome.

The next two stories appear in Ponticianus's account of his colleagues' conversions. Two officials in Trier were walking in the gardens when they came across a copy of *The Life of Antony*. Antony had converted when he heard a reading in church about the rich young man and felt convicted to renounce his wealth. Now, reading this story about Antony, one of the officials discerned his own call to renounce secular pursuits.

> He directed his eyes back to the page, and as he read a change began to occur in that hidden place within him where you alone can see; his mind was being

---

60. Ibid., 12.32.43. See also *The Literal Meaning of Genesis* 1.21.41.

61. Note the prominence of this example in Nicholas Wolterstorff, *Divine Discourse: Philosophical Reflections on the Claim That God Speaks* (Cambridge: Cambridge University Press, 1995).

62. *Confessions* 8.2.4.

63. Ibid.

stripped of the world, as presently became apparent. The flood tide of his heart leapt on, and at last he broke off his reading with a groan as he discerned the right course and determined to take it.[64]

His colleague immediately followed suit. In this dual account, then, Mt. 19:21 converts both Antony and Ponticianus's colleagues.

Finally, *The Life of Antony* reappears in the garden of Milan, just prior to the conversions of Augustine and his friend, Alypius. Augustine believed that he must become sexually continent in order to become a Christian,[65] but he could not imagine renouncing the desires of his flesh. Having exhausted his power to overcome his own will, Augustine hears the voice of a child singing, "*Tolle lege, tolle lege*," which he interprets as "a divine command to open the Book [of Paul's writings] and read the first passage I chanced upon."[66] Antony then comes to mind, for "he happened to arrive when the gospel was being read, and took the words to be addressed to himself when he heard, *Go and sell all you possess and give the money to the poor: you will have treasure in heaven. Then come, follow me.* So he was promptly converted to you by this plainly divine message."[67] The rest of Augustine's story hinges on Rom. 13:13.

> Stung into action, I returned to the place where Alypius was sitting, for on leaving it I had put down there the book of the apostles' letters. I snatched it up, opened it and read in silence the passage on which my eyes first lighted: *Not in dissipation and drunkenness, nor in debauchery and lewdness, nor in arguing and jealousy; but put on the Lord Jesus Christ, and make no provision for the flesh or the gratification of your desires.* I had no wish to read further, nor was there need. No sooner had I reached the end of the verse than the light of certainty flooded my heart and all dark shades of doubt fled away.[68]

Alypius then reads beyond Romans 13 to Rom. 14:1, "Make room for the person who is weak in faith," hears in this passage a command to join Augustine in continence, and also converts.[69]

Scripture thus catalyzes every instance of conversion in *Confessions* 8. The story of the rich young ruler leads to Antony's conversion. Antony's example prompts Ponticianus's colleagues to convert as well. The story of their conversion triggers Augustine's turn to Paul's writings, which results in both Augustine's and Alypius's conversions. Meanwhile, Victorinus's conversion, which was also inspired by

---

64. Ibid., 8.6.15.
65. On this matter, see F. B. A. Asiedu, "Following the Example of a Woman: Augustine's Conversion to Christianity in 386," *VC* 57 (2003): 276-306.
66. *Confessions* 8.12.29.
67. Ibid.
68. Ibid.
69. Ibid., 8.12.30.

Scripture, paved the way for Augustine's conversation with Ponticianus in the first place.

In all these examples, Augustine attests to Scripture's privileged status with respect to divine speech. Though he recounts two instances of divine speech in his own conversion, the first through the child and the second through Paul, only the latter releases him from the bondage of sin. Divine influence operates specially through biblical locutions. Augustine also highlights the Word's ability to address the contemporary reader. Jesus' words to the rich young ruler surge from the Gospels to confront concentric layers of readers several centuries later. Romans 13 becomes for Augustine a command to continence, though he acknowledges not all Christians share this calling, and Romans 14 becomes for Alypius a command to the same. The same God can speak through Scripture differently to different people. Augustine's depiction of Scripture affirms the authority and fixity of the literal sense while also indicating the freedom and spontaneity of God's speech.

The Narrative of Scripture

Augustine is one of the most celebrated storytellers in the history of theology. The most recognized instance of his narrative gifts is *Confessions*, where Augustine recounts his dramatic conversion. Yet his most enduring legacy involves a story so influential that its impact is hardly perceived: the narrative of the Bible itself. It is hard for Western readers to appreciate that Genesis 1–3 has not always inspired the same interpretation. In the second century, Irenaeus depicted Adam and Eve as childlike creatures at the beginning of humanity's development into spiritual maturity.[70] In the third century, Origen traced humanity's roots to the descent of preexistent spirits into material bodies. It is Augustine to whom the Western tradition owes its understanding of Adam and Eve as mature bodily agents whose disobedience plunged humanity into a curse that only Christ could reverse.

Still, Augustine's narrative of Scripture involves more than creation-fall-redemption. Augustine divides the story of Scripture into seven stages, a number that corresponds to the days of creation. The first runs from Adam to the flood, the second from the flood to Abraham, the third from Abraham to David, the fourth from David to the exile in Babylon, the fifth from the exile to the incarnation, and the sixth from the incarnation to Christ's return. The seventh is our eschatological rest, the ultimate sabbath.[71]

---

70. For a comparison between Irenaeus's and Augustine's accounts of the fall, see John C. Cavadini, "Two Ancient Christian Views of Suffering and Death," in *Christian Dying: Witnesses from the Tradition*, ed. George Kalantzis and Matthew Levering (Eugene, OR: Cascade, 2018), 94–114.

71. *City of God* 22.30.

Augustine's fullest development of this story is found in *City of God*, but a more manageable counterpart is *Instructing Beginners in the Faith*.[72] This little text explains how to introduce catechumens to Christianity. Central to the process is the "historical exposition (*narratio*)" of Scripture.[73] In order to explain Scripture well, the teacher must perceive the big picture. The purpose of Scripture is to promote love for God and neighbor, and Scripture accomplishes this end by directing us to Christ. "Indeed, everything that we read in the holy scriptures that was written before the coming of the Lord was written for the sole purpose of drawing attention to his coming and of prefiguring the future Church."[74] According to Augustine's succinct summary, "In the Old Testament is concealed the New, and in the New Testament is revealed the Old."[75]

The twofold love commandment is closely related to the incarnation.

> Christ came so that people might learn how much God loves them, and might learn this so that they would catch fire with love for him who first loved them, and so that they would also love their neighbor as he commanded and showed by his example—he who made himself their neighbor by loving them when they were not close to him but were wandering far from him.[76]

By eliciting our love, Christ heals us of our worst vices.

> Nothing is more opposed to love than envy, and since the origin of envy is pride, the same Lord Jesus Christ, God-man, is at the same time the evidence of divine love toward us and the example of human humility among us. In this way the swelling of our arrogance, great as it is, could be reduced by an even stronger antidote.[77]

Teachers should therefore recount the historical exposition so that "your listener by hearing it may believe, by believing may hope, and by hoping may love."[78]

Augustine believes that teachers should introduce catechumens to the entire storyline of the Bible. He instructs teachers "to give a general summary sketch of all the content in such a way that a certain number of quite remarkable events are selected, ones that our listeners find particularly appealing and that constitute the

---

72. Johannes van Oort, *Jerusalem and Babylon: A Study into Augustine's* City of God *and the Sources of His Doctrine of the Two Cities* (Leiden: Brill, 1991), 175–98.

73. *Instructing Beginners in Faith* 1.1. For discussion and bibliography about *narratio*, see Augustine of Hippo, *Instructing Beginners in Faith*, trans. Raymond Canning (Hyde Park, NY: New City), 53 n. 2.

74. *Instructing Beginners in Faith* 3.6.

75. Ibid., 4.8.

76. Ibid.

77. Ibid.

78. Ibid.

critical historical turning points (*in ipsis articulis constituta sunt*)."[79] It is better to unfold fewer events in greater depth than to rush through too much material, which would tire and confuse newcomers to the faith.

Augustine models this practice by providing two sample expositions of Scripture, one longer and one shorter. The longer treats creation; the fall; the flood; the calling of Abraham and the formation of Israel; the exodus; the giving of the law; the establishment of Israel in Jerusalem; the captivity in Babylon; the rebuilding of the temple; the life, death, resurrection, and ascension of Christ; Pentecost and the establishment of the early church; persecution by certain Jews; Paul's conversion and ministry to the Gentiles; and—to move past the biblical period—persecution by unbelieving Gentiles, the death of the martyrs, the conversion of earthly rulers, and the rise of heresies and schisms.[80] Throughout his treatment of OT events, Augustine explains how they relate to Christ and the church. Noah's ark, for instance, prefigures God's salvation of the church from the destruction of the world through the wood of the cross.[81] The captivity in Babylon illustrates a time when the church would be subject to earthly rulers yet still submit to and pray for them.[82]

This narrative is the framework for the principles Augustine sets forth in *De doctrina christiana* for reading Scripture.[83] Augustine famously distinguishes in this text between signs (*signum/signa*) and things (*res/res*). Signs are things that refer to something else.[84] All signs are things, but not all things are signs. Signs are signs because they *signify*. The distinction between signs and things corresponds to another distinction between using (*uti*) and enjoying (*frui*).[85] We enjoy things when we pursue them for their own sake; we use things when we pursue them for the sake of something else. God alone is to be enjoyed; all other things are to be used in the sense that we pursue them from our love for God.[86] Humans constitute a special case; our "use" of others means loving them as we love ourselves.[87] But our love for humans should still be oriented to God, whom we are to love with all our heart, mind, and strength—far more than we love ourselves.

---

79. Ibid., 3.5. For discussion and bibliography about *articulus*, see Augustine, *Instructing Beginners in Faith*, 64 n. 19.

80. *Instructing Beginners in Faith* 18.29–24.44.

81. Ibid., 19.32.

82. Ibid., 21.37.

83. Two recent works that draw on *De doctrina christiana* for insights on the theological interpretation of Scripture are James A. Andrews, *Hermeneutics and the Church: In Dialogue with Augustine* (Notre Dame: University of Notre Dame Press, 2012); Darren Sarisky, *Reading the Bible Theologically*, Current Issues in Theology (Cambridge: Cambridge University Press, 2019).

84. *De doctrina christiana* 1.2.2.

85. Ibid., 1.3.3–4.4.

86. Ibid., 1.5.5.

87. Ibid., 1.22.20–1.

Augustine's suggestion that we may "use" other humans has spawned an enormous scholarly literature.[88] But the reason Augustine raises these matters seems clear enough. First, he believes the purpose of Scripture and the purpose of the Christian life are the same: to promote love for God and neighbor.[89] One implication of this principle is that we should not castigate minor misinterpretations of the Bible. Mistakes can be forgiven so long as our readings of the text promote love. On the flip side, any reading that does *not* promote love constitutes a mistake. "Anyone who thinks that he has understood the divine scriptures or any part of them, but cannot by his understanding build up this double love of God and neighbor, has not yet succeeded in understanding them."[90]

Second, love constitutes the hermeneutical key for discerning whether a word should be read literally (as a *res*) or figuratively (as a *signum*).[91] When we encounter texts that do not promote love, we should interpret them as referring to something else. Such interpretation will always direct us toward Christ and his body, the church. For Christ is the ultimate thing (*res*), in the sense that he is God, and he is the ultimate sign (*signum*), in that he directs us to the Father.[92]

Augustine's hermeneutic of love is thus redemptive-historical, attentive to textual detail, and centered on Christ. It also corresponds to Augustine's treatment of Scripture in *Confessions*, which is where this chapter began. As Augustine recounts, it was pride that prompted his dismissal of Scripture and prevented him from seeing its inner riches.[93] It was also pride that kept the philosophers from considering the possibility of God's entering physical reality.[94] But it is Christ who has reversed this curse as the embodiment of humility and the mystery of Scripture, the mediator between God and humanity, who restores and kindles our loves.

Conclusion

When I applied for my position at Wheaton College, Kevin J. Vanhoozer, my former professor at Trinity Evangelical Divinity School, was a member of the

---

88. Eric Gregory provides a comprehensive evaluation of the literature in *Politics and the Order of Love: An Augustinian Ethic of Democratic Citizenship* (Chicago: University of Chicago Press, 2008), 319–50. For a recent treatment of similar themes, see Sarah Stewart-Kroeker, *Pilgrimage as Moral and Aesthetic Formation in Augustine's Thought* (Oxford: Oxford University Press, 2017).

89. *De doctrina christiana* 1.35.39–36.41.

90. Ibid., 1.36.40.

91. Ibid., 3.5.9–10.14.

92. For a lovely treatment of this theme, see Rowan Williams, "Language, Reality and Desire in Augustine's *De doctrina*," *Journal of Literature and Theology* 3 (1989): 138–50.

93. *Confessions* 3.5.9.

94. Ibid., 7.9.13–15.

Wheaton faculty. During an interview, he asked me whether Augustine's views aligned with evangelical understandings of Scripture. My answer here remains the same as what I said then: *sic et non*. Augustine confesses the authority of Scripture above other norms, he prioritizes human authorial intent in the interpretive task, and he defends the historicity of the text, even attributing textual discrepancies to scribal errors. Yet he believes that apparent contradictions should direct us to spiritual meaning, he cares less about verbal minutiae than meaning and truth, he includes the divine author in authorial intent, and he exercises allegorical liberties that would make many evangelicals cringe.

What I did not think to say then is what this chapter concludes: Augustine's doctrine of Scripture resonates warmly with Vanhoozer's own. Both embrace historical truth and hermeneutical sensitivity, original words and extended meanings, Scripture's magisterial authority and tradition's ministerial hand. Even more, both are deeply invested in narrative—read: dramatic—readings of Scripture that climax in Christ. Vanhoozer's work bears an Augustinian cast because both draw from a common well: a commitment to catholicity and a spirit of humility, rooted in Christ and his Spirit. No contemporary evangelical theologian has better modeled these virtues than Kevin Vanhoozer, whose work I am honored to celebrate here.

Chapter 9

THOMAS AQUINAS AND THE BOOK OF JEREMIAH

Matthew Levering

Is it true, as the Catholic theologian Hans Urs von Balthasar says, that "in Jeremiah, it is a struggle *between* God and the prophet that comes into the forefront" and that "Jeremiah is essentially *sad*, unlike any other of the prophets"?[1] This question will receive different answers depending upon the exegetical approach one takes. In what follows, I examine the approach taken by Thomas Aquinas in his *Commentary on Jeremiah*. Aquinas wrote this cursory, literal commentary while in his mid-twenties studying under Albert the Great in Cologne, prior to becoming a Master of the Sacred Page in Paris.[2] During the same period, he also wrote a cursory, literal commentary on the book of Isaiah.[3] He continued to teach

---

1. Hans Urs von Balthasar, *The Glory of the Lord: A Theological Aesthetics*, vol. 6: *Theology: The Old Covenant*, trans. Brian McNeil, C.R.V, and Erasmo Leiva-Merikakis, ed. John Riches (San Francisco: Ignatius, 1991), 257–8.

2. For background, see Jean-Pierre Torrell, O.P., *Saint Thomas Aquinas*, vol. 1: *The Person and His Work*, trans. Robert Royal (Washington, DC: Catholic University of America Press, 1996), ch. 2; cf. 337. For further discussion of Aquinas's approach to biblical commentary, see also Matthew Levering, Piotr Roszak, and Jörgen Vijgen, "Introduction," in *Reading Job with St. Thomas Aquinas*, ed. Matthew Levering, Piotr Roszak, and Jörgen Vijgen (Washington, DC: Catholic University of America Press, 2020), ix–xxx; Daniel Keating and Matthew Levering, "Introduction," in St. Thomas Aquinas, *Commentary on the Gospel of John*, vol. 1: *Chapters 1–5*, trans. Fabian Larcher, O.P., and James A. Weisheipl, O.P., ed. Daniel Keating and Matthew Levering (Washington, DC: Catholic University of America Press, 2010), ix–xxx; John F. Boyle, "Authorial Intention and the *Divisio textus*," in *Reading John with St. Thomas Aquinas: Theological Exegesis and Speculative Theology*, ed. Michael Dauphinais and Matthew Levering (Washington, DC: Catholic University of America Press, 2005), 3–8.

3. For an excellent introduction to what Aquinas understood by the "literal" sense—including his view (indebted to Augustine and the patristic tradition) that complex biblical texts can have multiple literal senses intended by the divine and human authors—see Scott W. Hahn and John Kincaid, "The Multiple Literal Sense in Thomas Aquinas's Commentary

Scripture for the remainder of his relatively short life (he died at 49 or 50 years old), and he wrote full-length commentaries on the book of Job, all the Pauline epistles (including Hebrews), the Gospel of Matthew, and the Gospel of John. In his *Summa Theologiae*, he quotes roughly 2,200 times from the Pauline epistles and Hebrews, and he quotes 40 percent of the verses contained in these letters.[4] In the *secunda pars* alone of the *Summa Theologiae*, he quotes from over half the chapters of the entire OT.[5] In the *Summa Theologiae* and *Summa contra Gentiles*, there are around twenty-five thousand quotations from the Bible.[6] Aquinas is indeed a biblical master.

In what follows, I examine Aquinas's commentary on three passages in the book of Jeremiah where the prophet cries out to God or undergoes severe personal tribulation: Jer. 15:10-21; 20:7-18; and 37–38. As my friend Kevin J. Vanhoozer remarks with reference to Jer. 1:4-10, "The prophets and apostles were acutely aware of the obligation to deliver a 'word of God' that was not their own."[7] Jeremiah faithfully endures the consequences of delivering such a word, though he complains about it rather forcefully. Elsewhere, Vanhoozer states, "The word of God is indeed nourishing: 'Your words were found, and I ate them, and your words became to me a joy and the delight of my heart' (Jer 15:16)."[8] In this very context, Jeremiah wishes that he had never been born, so burdensome to him is the word of God (Jer. 15:10).

Clearly, Jeremiah's life offers a preeminent instance of what Vanhoozer, indebted to von Balthasar, calls *"theo-drama."*[9] Vanhoozer argues that for the theologian, "The model of *drama* brings into focus the centrality of communicative action,

---

on Romans and Modern Pauline Hermeneutics," in *Reading Romans with St. Thomas Aquinas*, ed. Matthew Levering and Michael Dauphinais (Washington, DC: Catholic University of America Press, 2012), 163–82. Some contemporary scholars have exaggerated the plasticity included in the notion of multiple literal senses. Aquinas's commentary on the literal sense of Jeremiah is an effort to understand the plain sense of the text, illumined canonically by parallel texts from the whole of Scripture.

4. For further discussion, see my *Paul in the Summa Theologiae* (Washington, DC: Catholic University of America Press, 2014).

5. See my "Supplementing Pinckaers: The Old Testament in Aquinas's Ethics," in *Reading Sacred Scripture with Thomas Aquinas: Hermeneutical Tools, Theological Questions and New Perspectives*, ed. Piotr Roszak and Jörgen Vijgen (Turnhout, Belgium: Brepols, 2015), 349–73.

6. See Jean-Pierre Torrell, O.P., *Aquinas's Summa: Background, Structure, and Reception*, trans. Benedict M. Guevin, O.S.B. (Washington, DC: Catholic University of America Press, 2005).

7. Kevin J. Vanhoozer, *The Drama of Doctrine: A Canonical-Linguistic Approach to Christian Theology* (Louisville: Westminster John Knox, 2005), 142.

8. Kevin J. Vanhoozer, *Hearers and Doers: A Pastor's Guide to Making Disciples through Scripture and Doctrine* (Bellingham: Lexham, 2019), 79.

9. Vanhoozer, *Drama of Doctrine*, 35; cf. 17.

both human and divine."[10] I focus on Jeremiah's complaints and tribulations in order to explore this communicative action. The drama consists in the great costliness of the dignity of bearing God's Word. Certainly, Jeremiah embodies what Vanhoozer identifies as the "*performance* practice … of corresponding in one's speech and action to the word of God."[11] He remains faithful to the God whose word he has to deliver, and he remains faithful to the word that he delivers, by being willing to suffer for it. But what are we to make of his complaints?

Christians such as Vanhoozer and Aquinas hear God's Word canonically. For example, Vanhoozer notes that "Acts 8 depicts Philip initiating the Ethiopian eunuch into a prototypical canonical practice: reading the Scriptures 'figurally' or typologically in light of the person and work of Jesus Christ."[12] The canon is central to Vanhoozer's theodramatic understanding of how to interpret (hear) and perform (do) God's Word. In turning to the dramatic laments and tribulations of Jeremiah, I hope to learn from Aquinas how to hear Jeremiah rightly and how to act upon this word. Aquinas argues that Jeremiah's laments reflect profound sadness but not any disjunction or conflict between God and Jeremiah. By reading Jeremiah with Aquinas, I hope to learn how to hear Jeremiah rightly and how to act upon his words, along paths that resonate with Vanhoozer's canonical and theodramatic reading of Scripture.

Jeremiah 15:10-21

Some of Jeremiah's most bitter words appear in Jer. 15:10-21. Not only does he bemoan his birth, but also, after praising God for the joy and delight of his word, he speaks to God in an accusatory fashion. He tells God, "I sat alone, because your hand was upon me, for you had filled me with indignation. Why is my pain unceasing, my wound incurable, refusing to be healed? Will you be to me like a deceitful brook, like waters that fail?" (Jer. 15:17-18).

How does Aquinas interpret Jeremiah's bitter lament? He reads it in light of the book of Lamentations. He connects Jer. 15:17 specifically with Lam. 3:15: "He has filled me with bitterness, he has sated me with wormwood." Taken as a whole, Lamentations 3, which Aquinas understood to be spoken by Jeremiah, puts Jeremiah 15 in the shade in terms of the intensity and detail of the lament. The wrath of God against his people Israel, according to Lamentations 3, has brought the prophet (speaking on behalf of all Israel) to an interior place of "darkness without any light" (3:2). Israel has "become the laughingstock of all peoples," and Israel (and/or the prophet) "has forgotten what happiness is" (3:14, 17). Yet Lamentations 3 ends with a lengthy affirmation of God's continuing faithfulness and compassion. Aquinas sees the same dialectic in Jeremiah 15. In Jer. 15:15, the

10. Ibid.
11. Ibid., 16.
12. Ibid., 119.

prophet offers up a prayer of hope: "O Lord, you know; remember me and visit me, and take vengeance for me on my persecutors." Aquinas observes that Jeremiah is here pointing to "the comfort of divine consolation" as well as to the "effect of mercy."[13] The effect of mercy involves having one's deficiencies filled up, which happens when God "remembers" one. Thus, in Jer. 15:17 as read in context and in light of Lamentations 3, Aquinas perceives both agony and hope.

Regarding the agony, Aquinas recognizes that in Jer. 15:18, the prophet wonders in dismay "at the sting of the pain inflicted."[14] The prophet cannot understand why God allows such pain to persist. After all, Jeremiah has lifted up many heartfelt prayers, and Jeremiah has not been alone, since he has friends among the people of Israel. These prayers, fueled by grace, are surely good and meritorious acts, worthy of reward rather than ongoing punishment. Aquinas suggests that Jeremiah is saying, "How is it that this trouble has not receded after such prayers, and so many merits?"[15] More broadly, Aquinas recognizes that Jeremiah may be speaking not on his own behalf but on behalf of the whole people of Israel. Along these lines, Aquinas draws a connection to Jer. 30:12, where God says of the people of Israel, "Your hurt is incurable, and your wound is grievous." This verse does indeed strike a very similar note to what we find in Jer. 15:18. Aquinas notes that Jewish commentators read Jer. 15:18 precisely in this corporate fashion. He states, "According to the Jews, he [Jeremiah] speaks in the person of Jerusalem."[16]

Insofar as Jer. 15:18 is not simply a reflection of Jeremiah's interior state but rather articulates the political situation of the people of Israel facing exile, Jeremiah's own personal suffering no longer stands out quite as boldly. Jeremiah's agony is real, but it is also a prophetic act of standing in the place of the whole people of Israel on whose behalf he speaks. Aquinas also thinks that Jeremiah means to suggest that the pain will pass, even though at present it feels "incurable." Thus, Aquinas does not entertain the possibility that Jeremiah thinks that God really will fail him. In part, this seems to be because of the divine consolations and confidence in God portrayed by other verses in Jeremiah 15, Jeremiah 30–31, and Lamentations 3.

Jeremiah 20:7-18

Jeremiah 20 contains additional complaints directed by Jeremiah toward God. On the one hand, some verses of Jeremiah 20 praise God and show confidence in him.

---

13. Thomas Aquinas, *Commentary on Jeremiah*, ch. 15, lect. 4. All translations come from the S.T.L. thesis of Benjamin Martin, completed in 2019 at the University of St. Mary of the Lake. This translation will appear in the series being edited by the Aquinas Institute for the Study of Sacred Doctrine.
14. Ibid.
15. Ibid.
16. Ibid.

For example, Jeremiah proclaims that "the Lord is with me as a dread warrior; therefore my persecutors will stumble, they will not overcome me. They will be greatly shamed, for they will not succeed. Their eternal dishonor will never be forgotten" (Jer. 20:11). There is even a moment when Jeremiah breaks into a song of praise: "Sing to the Lord; praise the Lord! For he has delivered the life of the needy from the hand of evildoers" (Jer. 20:13).

The very next verse, however, contains the most direct possible denunciation of the prophet's own existence. Far from praising God for having chosen him to bear God's Word, Jeremiah has this to say: "Cursed be the day on which I was born! The day when my mother bore me, let it not be blessed! Cursed be the man who brought the news to my father, 'A son is born to you,' making him very glad" (Jer. 20:14-15). Jeremiah goes on to insist that the man who proclaimed his birth would have done better to kill him through an abortion in the womb. He curses the man who failed to perform the abortion: "Let that man be like the cities which the Lord overthrew without pity" (Jer. 20:16). Jeremiah concludes with a plaintive cry intended for God. He asks, "Why did I come forth from the womb to see toil and sorrow, and spend my days in shame?" (Jer. 20:18).

Even this does not sum up the whole of the complaint that Jeremiah delivers to God. Talking directly to God, he suggests that God was not forthright to Jeremiah about the prophet's mission. He states, "O Lord, you have deceived me, and I was deceived; you are stronger than I, and you have prevailed" (Jer. 20:7). Still, Jeremiah is compelled inwardly to continue to proclaim God's Word. If he tries to suppress God's Word rather than speaking it, it burns inside him and insists upon coming out. He explains, "If I say, 'I will not mention him, or speak any more in his name,' there is in my heart as it were a burning fire shut up in my bones, and I am weary with holding it in, and I cannot" (Jer. 20:9). Yet, once he does speak God's Word, his life becomes even more miserable. He becomes a "laughingstock" (Jer. 20:7). He comments that "the word of the Lord has become for me a reproach and derision all day long" (Jer. 20:8). No one believes his prophecies about the approaching devastation. But, although they do not believe him, they do see him as dangerous. Therefore, they plot against his life. In fact, his own friends, embarrassed and alarmed by their association with him, most want him silenced. As he reports, "'Denounce him! Let us denounce him!' say all my familiar friends, watching for my fall" (Jer. 20:10). They hope that Jeremiah will deliver a deceptive prophecy; if this happens, they plan to take strong revenge upon him for all the threats he has spoken.

How does Aquinas interpret these complaints spoken directly to God? Let me begin with Jeremiah's cursing of his own birth, a more vigorous cursing than the one discussed above. Aquinas remarks that, at first glance, speaking in such a way to God seems to be evidence of moral failure. After all, he points out, in Rom. 5:3-5 Paul explains that we (namely, those who have been justified and sanctified, so as no longer to be in a state of sin) "rejoice in our sufferings, knowing that suffering produces endurance, and endurance produces character, and character produces hope, and hope does not disappoint us, because God's love has been poured into our hearts through the Holy Spirit who has been given to us." If Jeremiah complains rather than rejoices in his sufferings, then it seems that this situation proves Jeremiah's unrighteousness.

Aquinas brings forward still further theodramatic concerns. God is the Creator of the day (Genesis 1). Each and every day is a creature of God. By cursing one of God's creatures—by wishing that it had never existed—one is actually cursing the Creator. It is a sin to curse God. Moreover, Jeremiah curses the man who delivered him from his mother's womb rather than aborting him. But had the man aborted him, this action would have been the grave sin of killing the innocent. Jeremiah therefore sins not only by cursing God but also by cursing a man for not aborting him.

Responding to these concerns, Aquinas points out that the book of Job presents a parallel to Jeremiah's speech against God. When Job undergoes horrific afflictions—the loss of his property and his children—"Job did not sin or charge God with wrong" (Job 1:22). When Job suffers a gruesome disease and his body is covered entirely "with loathsome sores," Job's wife advises him, "Curse God, and die" (Job 2:7, 9). Job still does not complain against God. But after seven days of sitting among the ashes with his three friends, who were shocked and horrified by how awful he looked, "Job opened his mouth and cursed the day of his birth. And Job said: 'Let the day perish wherein I was born, and the night which said, "A man-child is conceived." Let that day be darkness! ... Why did I not die at birth, come forth from the womb and expire?'" (Job 3:1-4, 11).

Quoting Job 3:3 and 3:11, Aquinas argues that Jeremiah is "[giving] us to understand his own sense of horror, hyperbolically speaking, and weariness at his own life because of the difficulties which he was suffering."[17] In speaking in such a hyperbolic fashion to God, Jeremiah is not blaspheming or sinning. After all, it is reasonable to complain about tribulations. Naturally speaking, it is no sin to hate evils of every kind. It would be a sin only if one hated evils insofar as those evils draw one toward the good that God wills. Paul is right that the saints glory in their sufferings, but the saints do so only in a certain respect: namely, sufferings are good because they produce endurance, character, and hope. Sufferings are not good in themselves, however, and so Jeremiah is firmly within his rights to bemoan them. Aquinas makes clear that if we were meant to understand that Jeremiah's bitter complaints about his sufferings indicated a sinful loss of hope, then Jeremiah would not urge us in the same context to "praise the Lord" (Jer 20:13).

Has Aquinas thereby removed all real drama from Jeremiah's complaint against God regarding the misery of his life as a prophet? I do not think so. With regard to the horrors experienced by Jeremiah, Aquinas points back to Jer. 15:10: "Woe is me, my mother, that you bore me, a man of strife and contention to the whole land!" Aquinas also directs attention to 1 Macc. 2:7, where Mattathias Maccabeus, the patriarch of the family, responds to King Antiochus's effort forcibly to stamp out Jewish Torah observance by proclaiming in agony, "Alas! Why was I born to

---

17. Ibid., ch. 20, lect. 3.

see this, the ruin of my people, the ruin of the holy city, and to dwell there when it was given over the enemy, the sanctuary given over to aliens?"

Recall that Mattathias was living in a time when any Jew who was found observing Torah was put to death. We read in 1 Macc. 1:60-61 that, in accord with King Antiochus's decree, the soldiers in charge (joined by many apostate Israelites) "put to death the women who had their children circumcised, and their families and those who circumcised them; and they hung the infants from their mothers' necks." Far from domesticating the theodrama, therefore, Aquinas compares Jeremiah's situation with one of Israel's gravest moments of spiritual and physical peril and destruction. No wonder Jeremiah cried out to God so bitterly. His fellow Jews were not listening to the word that God had given him; rather than listening they wanted to be revenged upon him, and they made his life a misery. Jeremiah knew that the result was to be the destruction of God's own temple, the expulsion of the Davidic king, and the exile of all Judah to Babylon. No wonder he mourns profoundly and confronts God.

Similarly, at the time of King Antiochus's decree, although Mattathias does not confront God, he and his five sons "tore their clothes, put on sackcloth, and mourned greatly" (1 Macc. 2:14). In the book of Job, the character of Job can only endure so much before he curses the day of his birth. Jeremiah does what Job does. Jeremiah does so with even more reason than Job had. After all, Job faced only personal humiliation and death. Jeremiah faces not only those things but also—surely even worse—the destruction of God's temple and the exile of God's people due to their failure to listen to the word of God that has been given to Jeremiah.

Note that Aquinas makes these points simply by quoting the biblical verses; in this very brief commentary, he does not expand upon the quotations, although his meaning is generally clear. Another example of this procedure comes in his comments on Jer. 20:7: "O Lord, you have deceived me, and I was deceived; you are stronger than I, and you have prevailed." To suggest what Jeremiah has in mind, Aquinas quotes Paul's statement to his opponents in 2 Cor. 12:16: "I was crafty, you say, and got the better of you by guile." Given that the word "deceived" can mean "seduced," Aquinas suggests that Jer. 20:7 has in view something like Paul's "guile." Such "guile" consists in the allurements of persuasion, consolations, and promises. These are all present in the book of Jeremiah. The word that God gives to Jeremiah includes not only terrible judgment and threats of devastation but also highly comforting promises about Israel's eventual destiny.

In this regard, Aquinas draws attention to Jer. 4:10: "Then I [Jeremiah] said, 'Ah, Lord God, surely you have utterly deceived this people and Jerusalem, saying, "It shall be well with you"; whereas the sword has reached their very life.'" The implied point is that the deception referred to in Jer. 4:10 and 20:7 is complex, because although indeed "the sword has reached their very life," nonetheless in fact "it shall be well" with God's people in the future. On the one hand, the prophet has been sent to speak words to which the people will not listen, even though God is giving them the opportunity to repent. On the other hand, the prophet has also been sent to speak words of eschatological consolation, foretelling the restoration of all Israel and the gathering of all nations to the Lord in Jerusalem (see, e.g., Jer.

3:15-18). Thus, if God has exercised deception or guile vis-à-vis Jeremiah, it is not the kind of deception or guile that lacks underlying truth. On the contrary, God will accomplish his consolations and promises. In this sense, God has rightly deceived or seduced Jeremiah, difficult as the experience may be: The consolations and promises contained in the word given to Jeremiah are worth the pain of preaching a word that is not immediately heard, and thereby temporarily becoming "a laughingstock" and enduring "reproach and derision" (Jer. 20:7-8).[18] Yet this experience is still deeply painful to Jeremiah, who has been "deceived" in the sense that he surely hoped that his prophetic word of warning would be heeded.

Aquinas also states that "the Lord prevails by correcting."[19] By means of a string of biblical verses, he argues that God's prevailing over Jeremiah consisted in keeping Jeremiah from falling into the pride and injustice of the people. Aquinas quotes Isa. 8:11, where Isaiah testifies that "the Lord spoke thus to me with his strong hand upon me, and warned me not to walk in the way of this people," and Hos. 2:6, where God (speaking about Israel) says, "I will hedge up her way with thorns; and I will build a wall against her, so that she cannot find her paths." God does this for Israel's good, just as God put his "strong hand" upon the prophet Isaiah for Isaiah's good. Isaiah too had been required to deliver a terrible prophecy,

---

18. See also R. E. Clements's historical-critical remarks on Jer. 20:7:

> Jeremiah accuses God in a shocking and almost blasphemous way of having deceived him (the Hebrew verb implies a meaning 'to seduce, lead astray'). ... In what sense can we understand Jeremiah's claim that God had "deceived" or "seduced" him? The reference is undoubtedly intended to be understood in relation to the prophet's sense of call to his high task. (*Jeremiah* [Atlanta: John Knox, 1988], 121)

On the one hand, Clements notes that some commentators have understood Jeremiah's meaning to be as follows: "How was it that God had deceived Jeremiah into believing and proclaiming that a disastrous future awaited Judah, wrought by a 'foe from the north,' when this had still, at the time of Jeremiah's complaint, not happened?" (ibid.). Clements argues, to the contrary, that

> Jeremiah's sense of having been deceived and misled by God was not because his prophecies appeared to lack fulfillment but because they lacked any adequate response in the hearts and minds of his hearers. What Jeremiah looked for was to be taken seriously as the mouthpiece of God, to be listened to, and to be able to evoke a deep and genuine repentance in the hearts of his people. This had not happened at all; instead his sombre warnings had been turned into the opportunity for mockery and ill-treatment. ... He reasoned that if God had truly called him to be a prophet it was God's responsibility also to ensure that his calling as a prophet was respected and acknowledged by those to whom he testified. (ibid., 122)

19. Aquinas, *Commentary on Jeremiah*, ch. 20, lect. 3.

namely, the rise of "the king of Assyria and all his glory," leading to conquest and terrible trouble (Isa. 8:7). The final biblical quotation that Aquinas offers in this section illustrates God's prevailing "by holding one fast with love."[20] Aquinas quotes Hos. 11:4: "I led them with cords of compassion, with the bands of love." If Jeremiah has been "deceived" or "seduced" into preaching God's Word to a people who will reject it (thus causing Jeremiah much bitter suffering, both in terms of personal persecution and in terms of his awareness of the terrible consequences of the rejection), Jeremiah has also consistently been—as he well knows—the beloved of God, gifted with God's true word of love for his people.

Aquinas's quotation of 2 Cor. 12:16 (above) can be further unpacked. Like Jeremiah, Paul is enduring the bitter sadness of not having his word heard, as well as suffering humiliation from the people who were supposed to hear it. Just as Jeremiah contends with false prophets, Paul has to defend his apostleship over against people whom he mocks as "superlative apostles" (2 Cor. 12:11). Like Jeremiah, Paul has given all that he has for the benefit of the very people who are not listening to him. Paul states, "I will most gladly spend and be spent for your souls. If I love you the more, am I to be loved the less?" (2 Cor. 12:15).

The theodramatic power of Jeremiah's bitter lament, then, involves profound mourning and dismay over what is happening both to himself and to the people who are rejecting the word of God. At the same time, Aquinas carefully avoids reading Jeremiah's bitter lament as though Jeremiah despaired or as though he were renouncing his prophetic task as not worth it. In a certain sense Jeremiah was "deceived," but not fundamentally so, because God "prevailed" not only by keeping him on the right path but also by promising to accomplish the restoration of all that was being destroyed by the people's rejection of Jeremiah's prophetic word. Even so, Aquinas recognizes the theodramatic strain placed upon Jeremiah (whose plight Aquinas compares in this section to that of Job, Mattathias Maccabeus, Isaiah, and Paul), due to both the rejection of his prophetic word and the consequent calamities that befell God's people.

Jeremiah 37–38

The tribulations endured by Jeremiah included physical assault and mortal threat. In a moment of extreme tension under King Zedekiah, when Judah was being pinched between the armies of Egypt and Babylon (and Jeremiah was prophetically urging King Zedekiah not to side with Egypt), Jeremiah was seized by soldiers on the false accusation that he was deserting to the Babylonians. We read that "the princes were enraged at Jeremiah, and they beat him and imprisoned him" (Jer. 37:15). Somewhat later, the princes of Judah went even farther. Enraged by the content of his prophetic discourse, they asked King Zedekiah to put him to death: "Let this man be put to death, for he is weakening the hands of the soldiers who are left in this city, and the hands of all the people, by speaking such words

---

20. Ibid.

to them. For this man is not seeking the welfare of this people, but their harm" (Jer. 38:4). They cast him into a waterless well, without food or ability to escape. Jeremiah's friends managed to get the permission of king to retrieve him. This rescue did not weaken Jeremiah's boldness in proclaiming God's Word. Rather, at the king's secret request, Jeremiah spoke the word of the Lord to the king, to the effect that if the king did not surrender to the Babylonians, "this city shall be given into the hand of the Chaldeans, and they shall burn it with fire, and you shall not escape from their hand" (Jer. 38:18). For his pains, Jeremiah remained imprisoned "until the day that Jerusalem was taken" (Jer. 38:28).

Let me briefly examine how Aquinas comments upon these tribulations. He notes that in Jeremiah 37, Jeremiah's "persecution is spoken of in three ways."[21] These three ways are capture, flagellation, and imprisonment. Canonically, Aquinas connects the flagellation or beating of Jeremiah with Acts 8 and Heb. 11:36. Again, given the intentional brevity of his commentary, Aquinas simply cites these biblical texts, but they can be unpacked. What happens to Jeremiah due to the word of the Lord is comparable to what happens to the deacon Stephen when he is stoned for proclaiming God's Word (Acts 7:54–8:1), and comparable also to what happens to the church due to the persecution inflicted by Saul before he became Paul. In Acts 8:3, we read that "Saul laid waste the Church, and entering house after house, he dragged off men and women and committed them to prison." Jeremiah, too, is dragged off and put in prison. The connection between Jeremiah in his testimony (including, for Aquinas, his testimony to the new covenant in Jeremiah 31) and the first followers of Christ in their testimony is important. There is a link between the sufferings endured by God's faithful people at these periods of salvation history.

This is the very point made by Heb. 11:36, quoted by Aquinas in explicating the beating endured by Jeremiah. Although Heb. 11:36 does not refer explicitly to Jeremiah, it comes in a section of Hebrews that extols the faithful suffering of members of God's people Israel prior to the coming of Jesus Christ. Hebrews 11:36 states with regard to the faithful Israelites, "Others suffered mocking and scourging, and even chains and imprisonment." Jeremiah suffering mocking, beating, and imprisonment. In this way, Jeremiah is here identified by Aquinas as one of the faithful Israelites praised by Hebrews 11. This canonical connection underscores that the truth of Jeremiah's prophecy is connected with his truthful performance of God's Word, namely, his willingness to endure suffering for it.

Aquinas comments on Jeremiah's imprisonment by drawing a connection to "the pit," a connection available only through the Vulgate translation of Jer. 37:15.[22] He quotes Ps. 88:4: "I am reckoned among those who go down to the pit." Since

---

21. Ibid., ch. 37, lect. 5.

22. Aquinas employed more than one version of the Vulgate. Since modes of historical criticism—with attendant emphasis on learning and commenting on the biblical text in its original languages—did not develop until the Renaissance (Erasmus being a primary exemplar), the main task in Aquinas's day was attempting to comment upon an accurate version of the Vulgate.

"the pit" in the Psalm quoted by Aquinas means Sheol—the realm of the dead—one can see here the understanding of death as an imprisonment. Christ breaks the chains of this imprisonment. Although Aquinas does not mention Christ here, the connection is evident, especially given Christ's words in Lk. 22:37: "For I tell you that this Scripture [Isa. 53:12] must be fulfilled in me, 'And he was reckoned with transgressors.'"

Regarding the capture of Jeremiah, Aquinas cites Lam. 3:52: "I have been hunted like a bird by those who were my enemies without cause." The translation found in the Vulgate is somewhat different, but the point is the same: The speaker has been chased and captured. The next verse of Lamentations 3 states, "they flung me alive into the pit" (3:53). This fits with Jeremiah's fate.

Once liberated from the prison and brought into the presence of King Zedekiah, Jeremiah does not hesitate, in reply to the king's request, to give the king a harsh word from God: "You shall be delivered into the hand of the king of Babylon" (Jer. 37:17). Aquinas indicates that this boldness is the mark of true prophets. He cites 1 Kgs 14:6: "I am charged with heavy tidings for you." In this parallel text, the heavy tidings are from the prophet Ahijah, and they are delivered to King Jeroboam of the northern kingdom (Jeroboam led the successful rebellion of the ten northern tribes against the rule of Solomon's son Rehoboam). The tidings proclaim that due to Jeroboam's sins, his entire house shall be cut off and he will have no descendants. This canonical resonance illuminates Jeremiah's faithful "performance" of God's Word, given that Jeremiah, too, has to communicate an ominous word to his king.

What about Jeremiah's being cast into the waterless well? Aquinas draws a connection here between the persecution of Jeremiah and the persecution of Jesus. He does so not directly but by means of a (deutero-)canonical link: Wis. 2:12, where the lawless and godless men say, "Let us lie in wait for the righteous man, because he is inconvenient to us and opposes our actions." Aquinas cites this verse as a commentary upon Jer. 38:4, in which the princes of Judah call for the death of Jeremiah. When King Zedekiah responds by handing him over, Aquinas makes the link to Jesus explicit by noting that Zedekiah thus "is not excused, even though he sinned less."[23] Here Aquinas cites Jesus' words to Pilate, "You would have no power over me unless it had been given you from above; therefore he who delivered me to you has the greater sin" (Jn 19:11).

Commenting on Jeremiah's descent into the waterless well, Aquinas cites Ps. 88:6: "You have put me in the depths of the Pit, in the regions dark and deep." As noted above, he has already cited this Psalm. The connection to Christ's death and the significance of the liberation of Jeremiah from the pit are left implicit. Yet Aquinas takes advantage of the meaning of "Ebedmelech" ("servant of the king") to link Ebedmelech with "Paul, a servant of Jesus Christ" (Rom. 1:1). Just as Ebedmelech serves Jeremiah, so Paul serves Christ. Christ, like Jeremiah, descends into the pit and ascends from it. Aquinas, as often in this commentary, contents himself with simply citing Rom. 1:1 as a commentary upon Jer. 37:7-8. In this

---

23. Aquinas, *Commentary on Jeremiah*, ch. 38, lect. 1.

brief way, he makes the Christological link clear between Ebedmelech's service to Jeremiah (bearer of the Word) and that of the apostles to Christ (the Word incarnate).

In his commentary on Jeremiah 37–38, therefore, Aquinas both gives due regard to Jeremiah's own experience of persecution and connects these chapters with the tribulations and ministry of Christ and his followers. In this way, Jeremiah's tribulations take on a richer hue without losing their literal meaning as the sufferings of Jeremiah. Rather than being a post-biblical imposition upon the text of Jeremiah, the connections to Christ and his followers can be seen already in certain ways in the NT. For example, commenting upon 1 Cor. 9:16—"Woe to me if I do not preach the gospel!"—Roy Ciampa and Brian Rosner compare Paul's "woe" to Jeremiah's laments (e.g., in 15:10). Admittedly, by contrast to Aquinas, they think that Jeremiah, unlike Paul, rejects his suffering because he has not yet perceived the value of suffering.[24] David Pao and Eckhard Schnabel offer another example when they note that Jesus' remark in Lk. 13:33, "it cannot be that a prophet should perish away from Jerusalem," connects Jesus' death with the "attempt … made on Jeremiah's life in Jerusalem."[25]

The connections identified by these evangelical scholars only involve the most explicit links. But it seems to me that Vanhoozer's canonical-linguistic and performative understanding of Scripture, exegesis, and doctrine opens up space for the kind of interpretation that guides Aquinas's entrance into the meanings of the Book of Jeremiah. Certainly, Vanhoozer supports "the Protestant Reformers' habit of following typological *trajectories* (i.e., the broad sweep of redemptive history), as opposed to compiling allegorical *inventories* (i.e., a list of detailed correspondence)."[26] These typological trajectories are important to Aquinas for illuminating the experience and testimony of Jeremiah.

---

24. Roy E. Ciampa and Brian S. Rosner, "1 Corinthians," in *Commentary on the New Testament Use of the Old Testament*, ed. G. K. Beale and D. A. Carson (Grand Rapids: Baker Academic, 2007), 722.

25. David W. Pao and Eckhard J. Schnabel, "Luke," in *Commentary on the New Testament Use of the Old Testament*, 336.

26. Kevin J. Vanhoozer, "Ascending the Mountain, Singing the Rock: Biblical Interpretation Earthed, Typed, and Transfigured," in *Heaven on Earth? Theological Interpretation in Ecumenical Dialogue*, ed. Hans Boersma and Matthew Levering (Oxford: Blackwell, 2013), 215–16; cf. 218–19 for a more detailed explanation of his position, which amounts to support of typology where the biblical narrative (taken as a whole) renders it reasonable. See also Richard B. Hays, *Echoes of Scripture in the Gospels* (Waco: Baylor University Press, 2016); Don C. Collett, *Figural Reading and the Old Testament: Theology and Practice* (Grand Rapids: Baker Academic, 2020).

Conclusion

As Vanhoozer says, "Ezekiel and Jeremiah were also bibliovores: 'Eat this scroll' (Ezek 3:1; Jer 15:16). ... To practice biblical authority involves more than giving it lip service. It is rather to eat, pray and love the songs, stories, laws and other parts of Scripture."[27] In this sense, Aquinas too was a bibliovore, as I hope is evident from the above. As a theologian, his way of reading Scripture was deeply doctrinal: What he found in the NT and knew from the church's teachings shaped what he heard when he read the OT. At the same time, he allowed what he found in the OT to shape his reading of the NT, because he appreciated the historical specificity of Jeremiah's faithful and painful bearing of God's Word.

As a Catholic, I believe that all doctrine must be biblical. It is not enough for a doctrine to be "not unbiblical," in the sense of not being present in Scripture but also not being explicitly contradicted by Scripture. I also hold that it is not necessarily easy to determine what counts as a biblical doctrine—in other words, to identify what doctrines are present in Scripture. Scripture itself teaches a variety of ways of identifying what is a biblically warranted doctrine.[28] For example, Jesus and Paul arrive at doctrinal conclusions along exegetical paths that modern biblical scholars do not countenance. The Gospel of John teaches that the Holy Spirit's guidance of the community into all truth will be another mode of determining whether a particular doctrine is biblical. Of course, almost all Catholic doctrine derives not from Rome, but from the Greek East—and most exceptions to this, such as the *filioque*, also did not originate in Rome. For Catholics, it is clear that Scripture teaches that the community will retain the apostolic structure of church order, in which Peter (and thus his successors in the "apostolic" church) has a leading role in securing the church's unity around biblically warranted doctrine. This does not mean that either Peter or his successors make no significant mistakes. Catholics hold only that Peter and his successors do not err when they teach doctrine in a solemn and definitive manner, invoking the biblical promises.

I mention all this because the history of theological controversy is enough to make Protestant, Catholic, and Orthodox theologians throw up their hands and say, "Woe is me, my mother, that you bore me, a man of strife and contention to the whole land!" (Jer. 15:10). Contention over the word of God is painful. The words of another bibliovore, Katherine Sonderegger, ring true. She states, "Jeremiah has encountered the I AM, and it is the end of him. The wrenching laments of this prophet, unlike any other in Scripture, sear us who stand close by this fire, to listen and to watch."[29] The power of God's Word should sear all of us who

---

27. Kevin J. Vanhoozer, "Three Ways of Singing *Sola*: Scripture as Light, Compass and Script," in *Pictures at a Theological Exhibition: Scenes of the Church's Worship, Witness and Wisdom* (Downers Grove: IVP Academic, 2016), 97.

28. See Matthew Levering, *Was the Reformation a Mistake? Why Catholic Doctrine Is Not Unbiblical*, with a Response by Kevin J. Vanhoozer (Grand Rapids: Zondervan, 2017).

29. Katherine Sonderegger, *Systematic Theology*, vol. 1: *The Doctrine of God* (Minneapolis: Fortress, 2015), 223–4.

perceive, with Jeremiah, the terrible troubles that befall God's people in this world, under the judgment of God. In this context, Aquinas's canonical interpretation helps us to hear, in Jeremiah's laments and tribulations, the testimony that Israel and the church offer to Jesus Christ, our shared "refuge in the day of evil" (Jer. 17:17). As Vanhoozer says, "There is theodrama wherever there is divine address awaiting human response."[30] God has addressed us in Jesus Christ and in his prophet Jeremiah. Let all bibliovores respond, "Amen!"—not only in words but also in deeds that faithfully bear God's Word of judgment, mercy, and grace to the whole world.

---

30. Kevin J. Vanhoozer, *Faith Speaking Understanding: Performing the Drama of Doctrine* (Louisville: Westminster John Knox, 2014), 24.

Chapter 10

JOHN CALVIN AND THE THEOLOGICAL INTERPRETATION OF SCRIPTURE

Scott M. Manetsch

In 1534–5, John Calvin wrote a brief preface for his cousin Pierre Olivétan's French Bible. In the preface, Calvin acknowledged that though this Bible translation lacked the royal privilege to print it, and was thus illegal, nevertheless the "King of Kings" had authorized its publication. Calvin then pivoted to make this memorable admission: "But I desire only this: that the faithful people be permitted to hear their God speaking and to learn from [his] teaching."[1] Here, at the outset of his career as a religious reformer, Calvin points toward his vocational identity as one called to teach God's Word so that "people from all classes" might make "progress in God's school."[2] Moreover, this striking statement illustrates Calvin's central theological conviction that God himself speaks through the sacred Scriptures and their proclamation. More than a chronicle of the history of the Jews, more than a compilation of ancient religious wisdom, the OT and NT are divine oracles, the very words of God, announced to his covenant people throughout history, past, present, and future.

Over the next thirty years, John Calvin's role as pastor and professor of the Genevan church involved daily, intensive interaction with the biblical text. In addition to preaching as many as 220 sermons a year, Calvin gave academic lectures on Scripture twice a week and oversaw a public Bible study (known as the *Congrégation*) for ministers, professors, and educated lay people that met each Friday morning.[3] Beginning with his Romans commentary in 1540, Calvin published commentaries and lectures on nearly every book of the NT, and on more than half of the books of the OT.[4] For Calvin, commentary writing was of

---

1. Calvin's Latin Preface to Olivétan's Bible, in Calvin, *Institutes of the Christian Religion* (1536), trans. and annotated by Ford Lewis Battles (Grand Rapids: Eerdmans, 1975), 374.
2. Ibid.
3. For Calvin's public ministry of the word, see Scott Manetsch, *Calvin's Company of Pastors: Pastoral Care and the Emerging Reformed Church, 1536–1609* (New York: Oxford University Press, 2012); Elsie Anne McKee, *The Pastoral Ministry and Worship in Calvin's Geneva* (Geneva: Droz, 2016).
4. See W. de Greef, *The Writings of John Calvin*, trans. Lyle Bierma (Grand Rapids: Baker, 1993), 93–109.

strategic importance because, in addition to helping people read Scripture, it left for posterity a faithful exposition of right doctrine that would continue to edify and preserve the true church. Thus, in the dedicatory epistle to his lectures on the Minor Prophets (1559), Calvin judged his efforts as a commentator so fruitful and useful for the church that he intended "to spend the remainder of my life in this kind of labor, as far as my continued and multiplied employments will allow."[5]

This essay will survey the exegetical method and theological principles underlying John Calvin's ministry as an interpreter of Scripture. To be sure, Calvin's method of interpretation has received extensive scholarly attention in recent years.[6] My analysis will draw on this literature, while giving special focus to select passages from Calvin's exegetical writings, including the dedicatory prefaces and author's *arguments* that introduce most of his published commentaries; his comments on Genesis 1–3, Psalm 119, Matthew 1–2, and Galatians 4; and his lectures on Jeremiah. While this essay will cover much familiar ground, it will place special emphasis on the theological foundations and assumptions of Calvin's hermeneutics, and (briefly) assess these theological principles in light of the contemporary movement known as the theological interpretation of Scripture (TIS).

Calvin's Exegetical Method

John Calvin's reading of the Bible was shaped extensively by the values and priorities of an educational reform movement known as northern humanism. This pedagogical program entailed the mastery of the humane letters (*studia humanitatis*), the cultivation of eloquence, the recovery of ancient texts, and the careful study of the Christian Scriptures in their original languages of Hebrew and Greek.[7] Frequently, the humanist commitment to return *ad fontes*—to a more pristine form of Christianity and a more accurate version of the Christian

---

5. CTS 26: xix. The Latin text is found at CO 17:447.

6. Some of the most important studies include T. H. L. Parker, *Calvin's Old Testament Commentaries* (Edinburgh: T&T Clark, 1986); Parker, *Calvin's New Testament Commentaries*, 2nd ed. (Louisville: Westminster John Knox, 1993); David Steinmetz, *Calvin in Context* (New York: Oxford University Press, 1995); David Puckett, *John Calvin's Exegesis of the Old Testament* (Louisville: Westminster John Knox, 1995); Richard A. Muller and John Thompson, eds., *Biblical Interpretation in the Era of the Reformation* (Grand Rapids: Eerdmans, 1996); John Thompson, "Calvin as Biblical Interpreter," in *The Cambridge Companion to John Calvin*, ed. Donald McKim (Cambridge: Cambridge University Press, 2004), 58–73; David Puckett, "Calvin, John," in *Dictionary of Major Biblical Interpreters*, ed. Donald McKim (Downers Grove: IVP Academic, 2007); Sujin Pak, *The Judaizing Calvin: Sixteenth-Century Debates over the Messianic Psalms* (New York: Oxford University Press, 2010).

7. See Timothy George, *Reading Scripture with the Reformers* (Downers Grove: IVP Academic, 2011), 52–61.

Scriptures—involved sharp criticism of the traditional Western church and a call for religious renewal. To a significant degree, then, the Protestant reformation was predicated upon advances in sacred philology, including new lexical aids and biblical commentaries, as well as superior editions of the Hebrew Bible and Greek NT.[8]

Calvin lays out his exegetical method in a famous passage found in the dedication to his Romans commentary (1540). Here Calvin argues that the best mode of expounding Scripture is with "lucid brevity" (*perspicua brevitas*). The biblical interpreter is responsible to explain the "mind of the writer" (both human and divine) in such a way that the plain or genuine meaning of the Hebrew or Greek text is laid bare without tiring the reader with unnecessary detail.[9] Faithful biblical interpretation must always promote the "common good of the Church."[10] With his method, Calvin intends to strike a middle path between the approach taken by Philipp Melanchthon, whose commentary on Romans limits itself to random "common places" (*loci communes*), and the method of Martin Bucer, whose exegetical work is so "verbose" and exhaustive that "he does not know how to stop writing."[11] Calvin scrupulously followed this exegetical method in the biblical commentaries and lectures that he published over the next twenty-five years. In a passage found in his lectures on Jeremiah, which appeared in 1563, the Genevan reformer articulated once again his priority that biblical exegesis be concise, capture the author's intention, and serve the good of the church: "More things might be said," he writes, "but I study brevity as far as I can; and I trust that I have briefly included what is sufficient for the understanding of this passage." Indeed, "this subject might be more copiously handled; but I merely explain what the Prophet means, and also show the import of his doctrine, and how it may be applied for general instruction."[12]

What exegetical strategies does Calvin employ to determine the intention or "mind" of the biblical author? The reformer works through the text of Scripture verse-by-verse, chapter-by-chapter. He gives careful attention to the Hebrew or Greek grammar of the select pericope as he defines terms, identifies verbal forms and syntactical arrangements, and explains various figures of speech such as hyperbole, personification, paradox, simile, and synecdoche. Calvin also emphasizes the importance of understanding the genre as well as the literary, theological, and canonical context of a passage. Based on his assumption of the unity of the biblical canon, Calvin frequently employs the principle of *analogia scriptura*—Scripture interprets Scripture—to clarify the meaning of obscure words and phrases. Moreover, Calvin is not averse to drawing from Latin and

---

8. See Jaroslav Pelikan, *The Reformation of the Bible, The Bible of the Reformation* (New Haven: Yale University Press, 1996).

9. CNTC 8:1 (CO 10:402).

10. CNTC 8:3 (CO 10:404).

11. Ibid.

12. CTS 18:12, 24–5 (CO 38:61, 69).

Greek literature outside the biblical narrative to clarify the historical, geographical, scientific, and cultural setting of Scripture.[13] Thus, for example, Calvin supplements his description of the ancient city of Babylon by consulting the writings of Strabo, Pliny, Aristotle, and Jerome.[14] It is interesting to note that in addition to employing these interpretive strategies, Calvin is often intentional in signaling them to his reader. Thus, for example, in a comment on Gal 4:19, Calvin informs his audience that "the diminutive is an expression, not of contempt, but of endearment."[15] Likewise, in discussing the Hebrew words "image" and "likeness" in Gen. 1:26, Calvin reminds his readers that "it was customary with the Hebrews to repeat the same thing in different words."[16] For Calvin, the task of a commentator is not only to explain the biblical text but to demonstrate to readers how they might interpret it as well.

A point often overlooked is the importance that Calvin attaches to a person's character and motivation in the study of Scripture. The reformer warns his readers against those who treat the interpretation of Scripture as a kind of sport; who delight in defaming others; or whose work is marked by ambition, hatred, sloth, or a love for novelty and speculation. By contrast, faithful interpreters are teachable, sober, discrete, reverent, honest, and concerned for the common good.[17] They display earnest affection for God's Word and meditate upon it continually.[18] Calvin also believes that God frequently uses personal suffering and hardship to help students of Scripture grasp more fully the design of the biblical authors.[19] For Calvin, spiritual maturity and moral character are necessary for the proper interpretation of Scripture. In a comment on Hos. 14:9, Calvin notes, "Whoever then wishes to be truly wise, he must begin with the fear of God and with reverence for his Word; for where there is no religion, men cannot certainly understand anything aright."[20]

Calvin believes that Scripture needs to be studied in conversation with Christian interpreters both ancient and contemporary. In a letter addressed to Wolfgang Musculus of Bern explaining the purpose of Geneva's weekly public Bible study (the *Congrégation*), Calvin notes that "the fewer discussions of doctrine we have together, the greater the danger of pernicious opinions," for "solitude leads to great abuse."[21] This concern informs Calvin's work as a commentator, as he regularly engages the exegetical conclusions of patristic authors (such as Tertullian, Jerome, Augustine, Ambrose, and Chrysostom), Jewish rabbis (including David Kimchi),

---

13. See Randall Zachman, "Gathering Meaning from the Context: Calvin's Exegetical Method," *JR* 82 (2002): 1–26.
14. CTS 21:234–6 (CO 39:463–4).
15. CNTC 11:82 (CO 50:234).
16. CTS 1:94 (CO 23:26).
17. CNTC 8:4 (CO 10:405); CNTC 1:viii (CO 45:711).
18. CTS 11:474, 476 (CO 32:256–57).
19. CTS 8:xlviii (CO 31:33).
20. CTS 26:505 (CO 42:511).
21. Calvin to Wolfgang Musculus, October 22, 1549, in CO 13:434.

and contemporary writers (such as Erasmus, Melanchthon, Bullinger, Bucer, and Musculus). Calvin does not usually identify these authors by name; rather, his normal practice is to enumerate alternative readings proposed by a variety of (unnamed) interpreters, which he then evaluates and either rejects or incorporates into his own interpretation. In this respect, a number of observations are in order. First, Calvin is especially critical in his evaluation of Jerome and his Latin (Vulgate) translation of the Scripture. References to Jerome are frequently punctuated with disparaging asides such as "Jerome explains very absurdly," or "Jerome's comment makes no sense at all."[22] Second, Calvin appears open to divergent exegetical perspectives and sometimes admits having changed his view because of them. Hence, in a comment on Gal 4:25, the reformer concedes that "although I once held the opposite opinion, I now agree with Chrysostom and Ambrose."[23] Third, the Genevan reformer believes that consensus in the interpretative tradition is important—but not decisive. Commenting on Jer. 26:23, he notes, "The common consent of almost all interpreters also influences me, from which I wish not to depart, except necessity compels me, or the thing itself makes it evident that they were mistaken."[24] Fourth, Calvin does not hesitate to propose original readings that diverge from the interpretive tradition. For example, as the reformer seeks to identify the author of the inscriptions to Isaiah's prophecy, he comments that "not one of the commentators whose writings I have hitherto perused answers this question. For my own part, though I cannot fully satisfy my mind, yet I shall tell what I think."[25] Finally, as Calvin interprets Scripture in conversation with other commentators, he displays a high degree of confidence that he can determine the "natural" or "genuine" meaning of the text in accordance with the intention of the biblical author. In a remarkable statement from the preface to his lectures on Jeremiah, Calvin boasts that "if Jeremiah himself were now alive on earth, he would add ... his recommendation [to my work]"; for Jeremiah "would acknowledge that his prophecies have been explained by me not less honestly than reverently" and that "they have been usefully accommodated to present circumstances."[26] Calvin's extensive interaction with patristic and contemporary commentators indicates his suspicion of biblical interpretation that occurs in isolation, without attention to the exegetical tradition or concern for Christian consensus. Biblical interpretation is always a ministry of the church, undertaken for the church.

---

22. CTS 20:182 (CO 39:20); CNTC 1:xiii (CO 45:3). David Puckett shows that Calvin's Latin translations of the Scripture differed significantly from Jerome's translation. See Puckett, *John Calvin's Exegesis*, 58.

23. CNTC 11:87 (CO 50:239).

24. CTS 19:345 (CO 38:537).

25. CTS 13:xxxii (CO 36:24).

26. CTS 17:xxiii (CO 20:77).

Calvin's Theological Interpretation of Scripture

For Calvin, faithful biblical interpretation requires more than explaining the grammar, syntax, and literary and historical context of a passage of Scripture. A distinctively Christian hermeneutic also requires consistent reflection on the theological and dogmatic dimensions of the Bible's central storyline, namely, God's covenant of grace with his chosen people, which finds its fulfillment in the incarnation, sacrificial death, and glorious resurrection of Jesus Christ. These theological themes, along with their ethical entailments, are woven tightly into the fabric of Calvin's commentaries and biblical lectures. At the same time, Calvin envisions a close, yet distinct, relationship between his exegetical writings and his more dogmatic works. In the preface to his 1539 edition of the *Institutes*, the reformer alerts the reader to the fact that, henceforth, his *Institutes* will serve as a collection of common places (*loci communes*) where he will treat larger doctrinal themes and theological debates that would otherwise be too unwieldy and burdensome for his commentaries.[27] Calvin believes that this division of labor—where his *Institutes* supplements his exegesis, and his exegesis informs his *Institutes*—will allow him to keep his commentaries concise and clear, while at the same time providing readers with a larger theological horizon for the right interpretation of Scripture. True to his word, Calvin as commentary-writer scrupulously follows the principle of *perspicua brevitas*, oftentimes directing his readers to the *Institutes* to help them discern the theological substance of the biblical pericope under study. For Calvin, theological discourse and exegesis are two parts of one whole, yet the right order of teaching requires that they be examined in different literary genres.

A somewhat different matter pertains to the theological foundations that undergird Calvin's work as an interpreter of Scripture. What are the theological assumptions and principles that Calvin brings to his work as a biblical exegete? Here I have space to consider only five theological aspects of his hermeneutic: (1) the divine inspiration and authority of Scripture, (2) the Holy Spirit's role in Scripture's inspiration and interpretation, (3) the unity of Scripture, (4) the literal meaning of Scripture, and (5) the usefulness of Scripture. As will become clear, despite Calvin's firm commitment to a "historical-literal" reading of God's Word, his exegetical approach remained traditional or "premodern" in its approach to the authorship, interpretation, and use of Scripture.

The Inspiration and Authority of Scripture

Even as Calvin embraced the commitments of northern humanism, his doctrine of Scripture remained conventional, located within the broad Augustinian tradition that viewed the OT and NT as a unified canon of Scripture, divinely inspired and without error in their original form.[28] Calvin affirmed the sixty-six books of the

---

27. See Parker, *Calvin's New Testament Commentaries*, 89–90.

28. See Augustine's classic statement, *Reply to Faustus*, XI.5, in NPNF, 4:180. This Augustinian tradition is described well by John Woodbridge, "*Sola Scriptura*: Original Intent, Historical Development, and Import for Christian Living," *Presbyterion* 44, no. 1 (2018): 7–11, 16–19.

Christian canon, although he admitted ignorance of the authorship of some of those books (e.g., Joshua, Hebrews) and believed that others were written with the help of an amanuensis (e.g., Mark, 2 Peter). While Calvin recognized the significant role that human authors played in the writing of Holy Scripture as they contributed their unique life experiences and literary styles, he nevertheless insisted that they were "sure and genuine scribes of the Holy Spirit" through whom God communicated heavenly doctrine to his people.[29] Calvin's conviction that the very words of Scripture are God's inspired revelation is witnessed frequently throughout his commentaries. He often conflates the agency of the biblical author with that of the Holy Spirit: "I now return to the design of Moses, or rather the Holy Spirit, who has spoken by his mouth."[30] In a similar fashion, Calvin describes the biblical author Mark as a divinely appointed witness, who "publish[ed] nothing except by the previous dictation of the Holy Spirit."[31] For Calvin, Scripture has both a human and divine author. In his comments on 2 Tim. 3:16, Calvin notes that the doctrine of biblical inspiration

> is a principle which distinguishes our religion from all others, that we know that God has spoken to us, and are fully convinced that the prophets did not speak at their own suggestions, but that, being organs of the Holy Spirit, they only uttered what they had been commissioned from heaven to declare.[32]

As a result of their divine origin, the reformer believed that the canonical Scriptures were without error in their original autographs. In his commentary on Psalm 119, Calvin praised God's Word (and the divine law) as "an unerring light," "an inestimable treasure," "the certain and unerring rule," the "certain and infallible truth," and "unchangeable forever."[33] Elsewhere, Calvin acknowledges that, whereas the prophets and apostles were fallible as to their persons, the truths they recorded in Scripture were "pure" and "free from every imperfection." Accordingly, the doctrine taught by the prophet Jeremiah "was free from every defect, for the Holy Spirit guided his mind, his thoughts, and his tongue, so that there was in it nothing human."[34] At the same time, Calvin the exegete occasionally identified errors in the received text, which he attributed either to faulty translation or to errant transmission.[35] So too, he recognized that in Scripture the Spirit of

---

29. See Calvin, *Institutes of the Christian Religion*, ed. J. T. McNeill and F. L. Battles (Philadelphia: Westminster, 1960), IV.viii.9 (p. 1157). See further Manetsch, *Calvin's Company of Pastors*, 158–9.

30. CTS 1:59 (CO 23:7).

31. CNTC 1:xiii (CO 45:3).

32. CTS 42:248–9 (CO 52:383).

33. CTS 11:480, 482, 485; 12:11, 29, 36 (CO 32:260–2, 273, 282–3, 286–7).

34. CTS 18:290 (CO 38:231).

35. Hence, in his comments on Mt. 27:9, Calvin notes, "How the name Jeremiah crept in, I confess that I do not know, nor do I give myself much trouble to inquire" (CNTC 3:177; CO 45:749). For a copyist error, see his comments on Mt. 1:6; CNTC 1:60 (CO 45:60–1).

God accommodates divine truth to the limited capacities of finite human beings; God through the human authors frequently uses "baby talk" when addressing men and women so that they might better understand his divine word. Thus, for example, in his comments on Gen. 2:8, Calvin argues that when Moses states that "God planted a garden in ... Eden" he was adopting "a simple and uncultivated style" to suit "the capacity of the vulgar. For since the majesty of God ... cannot be expressed, the Scripture is wont to describe it according to the manner of men."[36] Nevertheless, Calvin insisted that divine accommodation in no way impugned the reliability of sacred Scripture; God's Word is entirely truthful and completely trustworthy. Calvin insists that "nothing is more firm or certain than the teaching of Scripture," and on that support Christians must "confidently rest."[37]

Related to Calvin's doctrine of divine inspiration is his understanding of Scripture's authority. Because Scripture is God's word, it deserves the highest place of authority in the church. The Word of God "is like the Lydian stone" by which the church "tests all doctrines," Calvin observes. Indeed, "all controversies should be decided by the Word."[38] Moreover, the Spirit's central role in God's action of revelation ensures that God's Word is clear in what it teaches and sufficient to accomplish the purpose for which it was intended, namely, the salvation of God's people. Calvin has no patience for Roman Catholic apologists who claim to revere Holy Scripture but criticize it as being obscure, ambiguous, or inadequate. In doing so, they deny Scripture's authority and effectively ignore what the prophets and apostles have written.[39] For Calvin, God's Word "is the only true asylum of salvation."[40]

The Holy Spirit's Role in Scripture Interpretation

The Princeton theologian Benjamin Warfield once described John Calvin as the "theologian of the Holy Spirit."[41] This designation seems justified when one considers the crucial role that Calvin assigns to the Holy Spirit in his doctrines of the inspiration and illumination of Scripture. As I have already noted, Calvin

---

36. CTS 1:113 (CO 23:36). For the doctrine of accommodation in Calvin and the Christian tradition, see Glenn Sunshine, "Accommodation Historically Considered," in *The Enduring Authority of the Christian Scriptures*, ed. D. A. Carson (Grand Rapids: Eerdmans, 2016), 238–65.

37. CTS 44:xix–xx (CO 14:37).

38. Calvin, *John Calvin-Jacopo Sadoleto, A Reformation Debate*, ed. John Olin (reprint, Grand Rapids: Baker, 1987), 61, 86. See also Mark Thompson, "*Sola Scriptura*," in *A Systematic Summary of Reformation Theology*, ed. Matthew Barrett (Wheaton: Crossway, 2017), 145–87.

39. CTS 44:xix (CO 14:36–7).

40. CTS 44:xix (CO 14:36).

41. Cited in I. John Hesselink, *Calvin's First Catechism. A Commentary* (Louisville: Westminster John Knox, 1997), 177.

believes in the dual authorship of Scripture: the Holy Spirit infallibly communicates God's truth through the writings of human authors. Although Calvin nowhere lays out his doctrine of inspiration in detail, his exegetical writings demonstrate that he recognizes human agency in the composition of holy writ, even as he is not averse to stating that the Holy Spirit *dictated* divine truth to the human authors.[42] For Calvin, the fact that Scripture is inspired by the Holy Spirit means that God has revealed his will *and himself* to the church; indeed, God is truly present with his people as the Scriptures are taught and received in faith.[43]

The Holy Spirit also enables men and women to hear and receive the biblical message. Calvin believes that one of the ministries of the Spirit is to testify to the divine nature of Scripture: it is by "the inward revelation of the Holy Spirit" that Christians recognize Scripture as God's Word, and receive it as truthful and "unchangeable forever."[44] So too, it is by the Spirit's illumination that people understand God's Word. The Holy Spirit softens hardened hearts and enlightens darkened minds so that men and women are able to understand and love the message of Scripture, and empowered to obey it. As Calvin notes, "In vain does divine truth sound in our ears, if the Spirit of God does not effectively pierce into our hearts."[45] The Holy Spirit is thus rightly called the "Spirit of understanding" and the "teacher" in Christ's school, the church.[46] For Calvin, therefore, the faithful interpretation and reception of Scripture occurs through the profound ministries of the Holy Spirit, ever at work in the hearts and minds of both exegetes and audience. Word and Spirit are inseparable in Calvin's theological hermeneutic.

The Unity of Scripture

As with other premodern Christian interpreters, Calvin believed that the sixty-six books of the OT and NT formed a single book and communicated a single redemptive story.[47] This was the story of God's gracious covenant with his chosen but rebellious people, which found fulfillment in the incarnation, sacrificial death, and glorious resurrection of Jesus Christ. Calvin's covenantal perspective included a number of foundational theological assumptions that shaped his exegetical work. These principles included his conviction that the old covenant, with its regulations and ceremonies, pointed to spiritual realities that were fulfilled in Christ; that, throughout human history, sinful men and women were accounted as righteous on the basis of God's boundless grace, received through faith in the promised

---

42. See, e.g., CTS 3:xiv (CO 24:5–6); CTS 7:xviii (CO 25:421–2).

43. CTS 20:197 (CO 39:30). See further Mark Beach, "The Real Presence of Christ in the Preaching of the Gospel: Luther and Calvin on the Nature of Preaching," *Mid-America Journal of Theology* 10 (1999): 77–134.

44. CTS 12:29 (CO 32:283).

45. CTS 12:14 (CO 32:275).

46. CTS 11:424 (CO 32:228); CTS 1:87 (CO 23:22).

47. For Calvin's view of the unity of Scripture, see Puckett, *John Calvin's Exegesis*, 37–45.

mediator, Jesus Christ; that the church, as the company of God's elect, has existed since God created the first human parents in the garden of Eden. Hence, in his comments on Gal 4:1, Calvin asserts that the "company of believers" in the old covenant

> held the same doctrine as ourselves, were joined with us in the true unity of faith, placed reliance with us on the one mediator, called on God as their Father, and were governed by the same Spirit. All this leads to the conclusion that the difference between us and the ancient fathers lies not in substance but accidents. In all the chief points of the testament or covenant we agree.[48]

Calvin's belief in the unity of Scripture brought with it important implications for his exegesis. For one, biblical interpreters must read across the canon of Scripture, allowing clear passages to help interpret that which is unclear (the *analogia Scriptura*). So too, prophecies, figures, and types in the OT must be read in light of their fulfillment in the NT. Additionally, the Hebrew Scriptures belong to the Christian church, and must be studied, explained, and proclaimed as God's timeless revelation to his covenant people. Most importantly for Calvin, "Scripture should be read with the aim of finding Christ in them,"[49] for, the "hope of the godly has ever reposed in Christ alone."[50]

The Literal Meaning of Scripture

John Calvin's defense of the literal sense of Scripture, along with his harsh assessment of allegorical readings of the sacred text, runs as a leitmotif throughout his exegetical writings. From Calvin's perspective, biblical interpretation in the Christian tradition had taken a wrong turn with Origen, who introduced an allegorical method of exegesis that advanced foolish subtleties and speculation over the clear teaching of Scripture. Following Origen's example, nearly all medieval interpreters had discounted the literal sense of Scripture in search of deeper mysteries, twisting Scripture this way and that to fit their vain imaginations. The reformer believed that this allegorical tradition was nothing less than a satanic trick to confuse Christian readers and render "the doctrine of Scripture ambiguous and destitute of all certainty and firmness."[51] Exegetes must put aside those "deadly corruptions" and "pretended expositions that lead us away from the literal sense."[52] For Calvin, then, the antipode of allegorical interpretation was what he called the literal, genuine, pure, or simple meaning of the Scripture, one that reflected the intention of the human and divine authors of holy writ. This, he believed, was the

---

48. CNTC 11:71 (CO 50:234–5).
49. CNTC 4:139 (CO 47:125).
50. Calvin, *Institutes* (1559), II.vi.3 (p. 345).
51. CTS 1:114–15 (CO 23:37).
52. CNTC 11:85 (CO 50:237).

most natural and straightforward reading of the text, based upon a careful study of the grammar, and historical and literary context of the passage. An example of Calvin's approach is seen in his exegesis of Jer. 16:16—"I will send for many fishermen"—which medieval commentaries often interpreted as referring to the twelve apostles. Calvin finds this reading "wholly foreign to the subject." Rather, the context of Jeremiah makes clear that the "fishermen" are an allusion to the Babylonians, who will hunt down and capture the disobedient Jews of the Southern Kingdom.[53] Another example is found in Calvin's treatment of Gen. 1:7—"'waters above the firmament'"—which some allegorists had interpreted as referring to angels in heaven. Calvin argues that this interpretation violates Moses's clear intention; the prophet is simply describing the order of nature in a manner that best accommodates the understanding of "the rude and unlearned" who perceive that rain comes down as from the reservoir of heaven.[54]

Calvin could not discount allegory entirely, however, for the apostle Paul himself sometimes engaged in figurative readings of OT passages. An instructive example is seen in Calvin's treatment of Gal. 4:24—a passage where Paul identifies the struggle between Sarah (and her son Isaac) and Hagar (and her son Ishmael) as an allegory (*allēgoria*) of the conflict between spiritual freedom found in the gospel and spiritual bondage found in the Jewish law. Calvin acknowledged that this passage, on the surface, might seem to give warrant to Origen's allegorical fancies. However, closer examination shows that Paul has not distorted the genuine meaning of the OT narrative, for Abraham's household (through Sarah and Isaac) was *literally* God's church, and, as such, it served as a type or anagoge of the Christian church of Paul's own day; both were founded upon God's gracious gospel. From Calvin's perspective, then, Paul was, technically speaking, not employing an allegory at all; rather, he was drawing a figure that accorded with the literal sense (*sensus literalis*) of Moses's historical narrative.[55]

As this example indicates, Calvin sometimes approved of figurative or typological readings of the biblical text—although he invariably linked such interpretations with (what he saw as) the literal meaning of the biblical author. Oftentimes, Calvin resorted to typological or Christological readings when the straightforward meaning of a passage raised historical or theological problems. Thus, for example, in his comment on Jer. 30:10—"Jacob will again have peace and security, and no one will make him afraid"—Calvin notes that since "this did not happen to the Jews, we must again conclude that this prophecy cannot be otherwise interpreted than of Christ's kingdom."[56] Even so, Calvin was more reticent than most other Protestant commentators in adopting figurative or Christian readings of OT passages. This can be illustrated in the way Calvin departs from common "Christian" readings of Genesis 1–3. In these chapters he

---

53. CTS 18:322–3 (CO 38:251).
54. CTS 1:79–80 (CO 23:18).
55. CNTC 11:84–6 (CO 50:236–8).
56. CTS 20:20 (CO 38:622).

rejects the idea that the plural form of the divine name *Elohim* denotes the three persons of the Trinity[57]; he contests the conclusion that the Garden of Eden is a figure of celestial bliss[58]; and he argues that the so-called *protoeuangelion* in Gen. 3:15 refers to the posterity of Eve in general (and especially the Christian church), rather than to Jesus Christ or the Virgin Mary.[59] On the other hand, Calvin agrees with the judgment of Augustine and Eucherius that the Tree of Life mentioned in Gen. 2:9 was "a figure of Christ, inasmuch as he is the Eternal Word of God."[60] As Sujin Pak has shown in her study of Calvin's interpretation of the Messianic Psalms, the reformer consistently restricts "the christological possibilities in the text" by requiring that any Christological reading "have a clear and intimate tie with the basic plain, historical reading of the text," a strategic move that renders "typological or figural readings deeply tied to the literal sense."[61] These elements of Calvin's hermeneutic—his commitment to authorial intention and the literal sense of Scripture; his cautious stance toward figurative or Christian readings of OT passages; *and* his belief in the unity of the Bible's redemptive story—constituted a dynamic approach to biblical interpretation whereby the reformer paid careful attention to the historical message and moral lessons of the Jewish patriarchs and prophets, while at the same time giving priority to the theological arcs of biblical revelation that anticipated, and were fulfilled, in the life and ministry of Jesus Christ and the NT church.

The Usefulness of Scripture

A final feature of Calvin's hermeneutic, and one that is frequently overlooked, is his conviction that the interpretation of Scripture should be profitable for those who receive it by faith. The Scriptures were given not only to God's people in the distant past but to believers of every age. In his commentaries, Calvin frequently reminds readers that they themselves are the recipients of God's revelation and must respond to it. The author of Psalm 119 "exhorts *us*," "assures *us*," "instructs *us*," "teaches *us*."[62] In the preface to his commentary on 1 and 2 Timothy, Calvin notes that "there is nothing in [these epistles] that is not highly applicable to *our* times, and hardly anything that is necessary in the building of the Church that may not likewise be drawn from them."[63] Because Scripture is a timeless treasure that God has given to his people, its message necessarily bears fruit and is profitable for those who receive it in faith. Throughout Calvin's exegetical and theological writings one frequently encounters such words as profitable (*frugiferens*), fruitful

---

57. CTS 1:70–1 (CO 23:15).
58. CTS 1:114–15 (CO 23:37).
59. CTS 1:171 (CO 23:71).
60. CTS 1:117 (CO 23:38).
61. Pak, *The Judaizing Calvin*, 138.
62. CTS 11:444, 445, 447 (CO 32:240–1); CTS 12:35 (CO 32:286). Emphases added.
63. CTS 42:xi (CO 13:18). Emphasis added.

(*fructeux*), useful (*utilis*), or usefulness (*usus*), highlighting the fact that when Scripture is faithfully taught and received it brings about spiritual growth and health for individual Christians and the church as a whole. In the preface to his Psalms commentary, Calvin notes, "I have labored faithfully to open up this treasure for the use of all the people of God" that it might be "profitable to others."[64]

In what ways does Calvin expect that right interpretation of Scripture will prove profitable? Scripture provides good examples to imitate and bad ones to avoid. It teaches us sound doctrine and instructs us in piety, right worship, and moral discipline. Scripture protects God's people from the deceptions of Satan, providing them with spiritual weaponry to battle heretics and the Roman Antichrist. Scripture builds up Christ's church. So too, Scripture refreshes the souls of Christian believers and makes them happy. In the preface to Calvin's lectures on Hosea, the sixteenth-century editor Jean Budé summarized the reformer's interpretive approach this way: after laying bare "the mind of the Prophet," Calvin briefly shows "the use and application of the doctrine, so that no one, however ignorant, can mistake the meaning; in short, he so unfolds and opens the subjects and fountains of true theology, that it is easy for anyone to draw from them what is needful to restore and refresh the soul."[65] For Calvin, then, God's Word is not only a repository of propositional truths but also a sacred space where God meets with his people, instructing and communing with them so that they might flourish in him. For that reason, Calvin insists, "it is an intolerable profanation of the law of God, to draw out of it nothing that is profitable."[66]

Conclusion: Calvin and TIS

Having outlined Calvin's theological hermeneutics, I would like in conclusion to consider briefly some differences and similarities between the reformer's theological approach to Scripture and the central commitments of the contemporary movement known as the theological interpretation of Scripture (TIS). Because this movement consists of "a family of interpretive approaches"[67] and includes a variety of perspectives that are not always congenial with one another, our comparison will be based on presentations of TIS found in the writings of evangelical scholars such as Kevin J. Vanhoozer, Daniel Treier, and J. Todd Billings, as well as early assessments provided by evangelical interpreters such as Gregg Allison and D. A. Carson.[68]

---

64. CTS 8: xlviii–xlix (CO 31:33).
65. CTS 26:xxvii–xxviii (CO: 42:87–8).
66. CTS 43:13–14 (CO 52:245).
67. Gregg Allison, "Theological Interpretation of Scripture: An Introduction and Preliminary Evaluation," *Southern Baptist Journal of Theology* 14, no. 2 (2010): 29.
68. Kevin J. Vanhoozer, "Introduction: What Is Theological Interpretation of the Bible?" in *Dictionary for Theological Interpretation of the Bible*, ed. Kevin J. Vanhoozer (Grand Rapids: Baker Academic, 2005); Vanhoozer, "Ten Theses on the Theological Interpretation

At the heart of evangelical presentations of TIS is the concern to "bridge the gap between biblical studies and theology, which grew wide with the ascendancy of critical approaches to Scripture."[69] While not rejecting historical-critical methods per se, evangelical practitioners of TIS insist that the meaning of Scripture is found primarily *in* the biblical text, rather than *behind* the text (through historical reconstructions) or *in front of* the text (as a reflection of personal identity or cultural location).[70] Defenders of TIS take seriously the theological nature of the Bible and seek to read it as divine discourse through which the triune God reveals himself and accomplishes salvation for his people both past and present.[71] They insist that because the OT and NT convey a unified story of God's redemptive plan, the OT must be read in light of God's fuller revelation in Jesus Christ.[72] For proponents of TIS, the goal of interpretation is to achieve not simply doctrinal understanding but communion with the living God in fellowship with his church. As Billings summarizes, faithful biblical interpretation "is nothing less than a part of our life of participation in Christ through the Spirit, a means by which God nurtures our love to God and neighbor."[73] At the same time, evangelical scholars who practice TIS seek to recover many of the commitments and practices of premodern exegesis: They argue that the Bible should be recognized as authoritative divine revelation. They insist that Scripture should be interpreted in light of the Christian tradition, that is, in conversation with ancient commentators and the rule of faith. Finally, like many premodern exegetes, evangelical proponents of TIS believe that a canonical reading of Scripture, one where Christ's life and ministry "recapitulates the story of Adam and Israel," requires a more expansive understanding of the literal or historical sense that includes typological and allegorical readings of God's sacred Word.[74]

Calvin's theological hermeneutic runs against the grain of several of the assumptions and approaches advocated by TIS. Evidently, as a premodern exegete, Calvin is rarely self-critical of the ways his social, confessional, or cultural

---

of Scripture," *Modern Reformation* 19, no. 4 (July/August 2010); Daniel J. Treier, *Introducing Theological Interpretation of Scripture: Recovering a Christian Practice* (Grand Rapids: Baker Academic, 2008); J. Todd Billings, *The Word of God for the People of God: An Entryway to the Theological Interpretation of Scripture* (Grand Rapids: Eerdmans, 2010). For helpful evaluations of TIS, see also Allison, "Theological Interpretation," 28–36; D. A. Carson, "Theological Interpretation of Scripture: Yes, But…," in *Theological Commentary: Evangelical Perspectives*, ed. R. Michael Allen (London: T&T Clark, 2011), 187–207.

69. Promotional statement for Treier's book, *Introducing Theological Interpretation of Scripture*, at worldcat.org/identities/lccn-n2003118091 (accessed January 6, 2020).

70. Vanhoozer, "Introduction," 19–20.

71. Billings, *Word of God*, xii–xv.

72. Vanhoozer, "Ten Theses"; Billings, *Word of God*, 179.

73. Billings, *Word of God*, 195.

74. Ibid., 179. On their treatment of typology and allegory, see Treier, *Introducing Theological Interpretation of Scripture*, 47–9; Billings, *Word of God*, 172–9.

"location" affects his exegetical conclusions. Hence, for many modern readers, his approach lacks the epistemic humility expected of faithful biblical interpreters. This is especially the case as Calvin regularly populates his exegesis with harsh attacks against his theological opponents, especially Roman Catholics. In addition, Calvin is more restrictive and cautious than at least some proponents of TIS in the manner in which he defines the literal sense and draws Christological and figurative readings from OT texts.[75] For Calvin, the allegorical sense represents a hostile takeover of sacred Scripture, not a legitimate reading strategy based on associations beyond the historical-literal meaning of the passage itself. Finally, Calvin's valuation of church tradition, and his trust of ancient commentators, is more ambivalent and critical than at least some proponents of TIS.[76] The reformer consistently demands that the judgments of patristic, medieval, and contemporary commentators, as well as the analogy of faith (*analogia fidei*), be ruled by the literal, straightforward reading of Scripture.

In other important ways, however, Calvin's exegetical priorities are closely aligned with evangelical presentations of TIS. Together they believe in the divine inspiration, authority, and unity of the Christian Scripture. They share the conviction that the Bible should be read theologically in light of the historical-redemptive message of God's grace as fulfilled in the life and ministry of Jesus Christ. The OT writings should be interpreted with Christ as their *scopus* or goal. Calvin and advocates of TIS also emphasize the importance of reading Scripture in conversation with the larger church tradition, and in the context of the worshipping community. They agree that the Bible is fundamentally the church's book; consequently, its interpretation and exposition must be *useful* for the Christian church in every age. Perhaps most importantly, Calvin and evangelical proponents of TIS such as Vanhoozer, Treier, and Billings share the conviction that God speaks to and communes with his people through the faithful interpretation of his word. As Calvin notes in his lectures on Jeremiah, "There is, then, no reason for us to seek anything better, when God is present with us by his word; for we have a sure testimony of his presence whenever true and faithful teachers rise up."[77] Such is the high calling and glorious privilege to which biblical interpreters of every age are called.

---

75. On this aspect, see the assessment of Carson, in "Theological Interpretation of Scripture: Yes, But . . .," 198–200.

76. On this aspect, see the assessments of Carson in ibid., 197–8, and Allison, "Theological Interpretation of Scripture," 32–3.

77. CTS 20:197 (CO 39:30).

Chapter 11

"THE WHOLE SCOPE AND TENOR OF SCRIPTURE": HERMENEUTICS, WHOLENESS, AND HOLINESS IN WESLEYAN THEOLOGICAL INTERPRETATION OF SCRIPTURE

Thomas McCall

Introduction

It is no secret that Wesleyan theology is marked by a pervasive doctrinal pluralism. There are "neo-orthodox" Wesleyan theologies, "radically orthodox" Wesleyan theologies, "paleo-orthodox" Wesleyan theologies, and starkly heterodox Wesleyan theologies of various varieties.[1] Similarly, biblical scholarship in the Methodist tradition is widely variegated. Biblical scholars and theologians alike often read the Bible in ways very different than the ways that the Wesleys and many of the early Methodists read and interpreted Scripture. In this essay, I revisit—and defend—an important element of the older approach to Scripture.

Wholeness, Holiness, and Hermeneutics

John Wesley was strongly committed to reading Scripture in a holistic manner.[2] He thought that the Bible had one, unified meaning. He made appeal to the "whole

---

1. For a sense of the breadth of approaches (as exemplified in approaches to Christology), see Jason Vickers and Jerome VanKuiken, eds., *Methodist Christology: From the Wesleys to the Twenty-First Century* (Nashville: GBHEM, 2020). I here echo Thomas Noble's endorsement of this book.

2. On Wesley's biblical interpretation, see Randy L. Maddox, "John Wesley – A Man of One Book," in *Wesley, Wesleyans, and Reading Bible as Scripture*, ed. Joel B. Green and David F. Watson (Waco: Baylor University Press, 2012), 3–18; Maddox, *Responsible Grace: John Wesley's Practical Theology* (Nashville: Abingdon, 1994), 36–40; Kenneth J. Collins, "Scripture as a Means of Grace," in *Wesley, Wesleyans, and Reading Bible as Scripture*, 19–32.

scope and tenor" of Scripture.³ This was no idle matter for Wesley, nor was it a cliché to which he paid mere lip service. To the contrary, he relied upon canonical interpretation in various treatises, doctrinal formulations, and even sermons.⁴ This commitment is not arbitrary. The wholeness and unity of Scripture, for Wesley, is grounded in the holiness of Scripture as the Word of God. As Scott J. Jones puts it, for "Wesley, the Bible's unity stems from the fact that it has a single ultimate author."⁵ This means, as Jones explains, that "for Scripture to be interpreted according to the intent of the author, one must consult the entire Book."⁶ Thus, "no particular part of Scripture can be fully understood without reference to the whole of Scripture."⁷

Many theologians and biblical scholars in the historic Wesleyan tradition are in broad agreement with Wesley.⁸ But in the past century many biblical scholars have turned away from canonical readings and overtly theological interpretations to pursue what Joel Green calls "scientific exegesis" (roughly, historical-critical biblical scholarship).⁹ George Lyons expresses this commitment to historical-critical studies, along with the corresponding suspicion of theological interpretation, when, in his presidential address to the Wesleyan Theological Society, he states that "loyalty to the primacy of Scripture gives Wesleyans a deep dissatisfaction with the easy conclusions of church dogma, even Wesleyan dogma."¹⁰

Recently, however, some prominent Wesleyan voices are calling for biblical interpreters in the broad Methodist tradition to recover overtly theological exegesis that is canonically shaped. Robert W. Wall says that "Scripture sets before us a word about God."¹¹ Further, he says that "the Bible's different collections were arranged to perform together as an integral whole."¹² Richard B. Hays is forthright: "Scripture is about God, and it has a deep coherence."¹³ There is a dramatic coherence to Holy Writ; the Bible tells "a coherent story, a complex but coherent dramatic narrative

---

3. E.g., John Wesley, "Predestination Calmly Considered," in *The Works of John Wesley*, vol. X (Grand Rapids: Zondervan, n.d.), 211.

4. E.g., John Wesley, "Justification by Faith," in *Wesley's 52 Standard Sermons* (Salem, OH: Schmul, 1988), 43–4.

5. Scott J. Jones, *John Wesley's Conception and Use of Scripture* (Nashville: Abingdon, 1995), 197.

6. Ibid.

7. Ibid., 199.

8. E.g., Thomas Ralston, *Elements of Divinity* (Nashville: Abingdon, 1919), 694–700.

9. Joel B. Green, "Contribute or Capitulate? Wesleyans, Pentecostals, and Reading the Bible in a Post-Colonial Mode," *Wesleyan Theological Journal* 39, no. 1 (2004): 77.

10. George Lyons, "Biblical Theology and Wesleyan Theology," *Wesleyan Theological Journal* 30, no. 2 (1995): 23.

11. Robert W. Wall, "John's John: A Wesleyan Theological Reading of 1 John," *Wesleyan Theological Journal* 46, no. 1 (2011): 131.

12. Ibid., 115.

13. Richard B. Hays, "The Future of Scripture," *Wesleyan Theological Journal* 46, no. 1 (2011): 30.

that runs from Genesis to Revelation."[14] This means that Scripture "must be read from front to back, starting with the Old Testament and moving to the New Testament. But we must also read it from back to front."[15] Hays is well aware, of course, of the diversity within the Bible. He knows that the diversity pertains not only to form but also to material content; not only is the Bible made up of drastically different literary genres and styles, but it also contains diverse perspectives. He is aware of this diversity in ways that Wesley likely was not, and he knows that any serious account of biblical interpretation cannot look away from this or avoid it. Nonetheless, he insists on the reality of a deep, canonical unity.

So, given the diversity, what grounds the claims of canonical unity? Hays makes his position clear: The Bible contains one unified message because it has one author. The genuine variety should be recognized and accepted as such, but we should also see that there is a deep, underlying unity at the level of canon. Putting these elements together—both the undeniable diversity and the theologically grounded unity—leads Hays to conclude that there are *multiple meanings* as well as *one ultimate meaning*. And putting these elements together leads Hays to a striking hermeneutical conclusion: "Scriptural texts do not necessarily have a single meaning limited to the intent of the original author."[16] Instead, we should affirm that there are "multiple meanings and that these meanings are given by God, who is the author of the meanings."[17] There is—or at least may be—a meaning intended by the original author of, say, Exodus 3 or Isaiah 53. The meaning of the passage within the OT context is to be understood in relation to the intention of the initial (human) author, and we are to make progress on understanding this intention by study of the relevant historical and literary contexts. But, while important, the meaning that is indexed to the intent of the original (human) author does not exhaust the meaning of the passage. For, given the divine authorship of the whole canon, passages such as Exodus 3 or Isaiah 53 may come to contain additional meaning. This additional meaning does not replace the "original" meaning, but it is no less valid. So, while study of the various historical contexts (and, of course, grammar) remains important, such study does not represent the interpretive ceiling.

"Fantasies," "Delusions," and the "Blanket of Canon": Some Common Criticisms

It is something of an understatement to say that the approach exemplified by Wesley and retrieved by Hays faces opposition. Their approach to reading the Bible as the Word of God from God for the people of God attracts criticism. Indeed, this

---

14. Ibid., 28.
15. Ibid., 29.
16. Ibid., 30.
17. Ibid.

approach to Scripture is the object of criticism from both the theological "left" and "right." Consider the following statements.

(1) From Walter C. Kaiser Jr.:

> There lurks in evangelical thought the occultic idea that a hidden meaning lay just outside the purview of the human authors of the Old Testament that can be unlocked now that we have the New Testament. This is damaging to the case for inspiration and for unity of Scripture. It posits that there exists somewhere in cyberspace a meaning that cannot be reached by the grammatico-historical interpretation of the text. But since it is not in the words, grammar, or syntax of the sentences or paragraphs, it must be located between the lines. If that is so, then it is not graphe – that is, what is "written" – that is said to be inspired by God (2 Tim. 3:16–17) but rather what is not written.[18]

(2) From John H. Walton:

> Biblical authority is tied inseparably to the author's intention. God vested his authority in a human author, so we must consider what the human author intended to communicate if we want to understand God's message. Two voices speak, but the human author is our doorway into the room of God's meaning and message. That means that when we read Genesis, we are reading an ancient document and should begin by using only the assumptions that would be appropriate for the ancient world.[19]

(3) From John Goldingay:

> Let us grant that the doctrine of the Trinity is a (even the) logical outworking within a Greek framework of the implications of statements of the more Greek-thinking writers within the NT. That means that it is two stages removed from most of the NT narratives (because they are narrative, they are less inclined to think in Greek forms). Further, it is three stages removed from most biblical narrative (which was written before Bethlehem and Pentecost made trinitarian thinking possible, let alone necessary). If one starts from biblical narratives and asks after their theological freight, the vast bulk of their theological implications does not emerge within a trinitarian framework. ... For all its truth and fruitfulness, the doctrine of the Trinity seriously skews our theological reading of Scripture.[20]

---

18. *Recovering the Unity of the Bible: One Continuous Story, Plan, and Purpose* (Grand Rapids: Zondervan, 2009), 217.

19. *The Lost World of Adam and Eve: Genesis 2–3 and the Human Origins Debate* (Downers Grove: IVP Academic, 2015), 15.

20. John Goldingay, "Biblical Narrative and Systematic Theology," in *Between Two Horizons: Spanning New Testament Studies and Systematic Theology*, ed. Joel B. Green and Max Turner (Grand Rapids: Eerdmans, 2000), 130–1.

Taken together, we can see the following claims emerge:

(MC1) There is only one meaning in a given text, and it is the meaning that was intended by the original author (and/or what would have been understood by the original audience).

Here we need not get too hung up on the familiar debates over authorial intention. Many proponents of (MC1) would likely hold out for authorial intention and insist that the *right* interpretation secures the proposition that was the intended communication of the original author (as well, of course, as any other illocutionary acts performed by the author). But since most of these authorial-intention interpreters would agree that understanding the context of the original audience is vital to understanding the author's intentions, for present purposes we can consider (MC1) as it stands.

(MC2) The only way to determine that (singular) meaning is via the historical-grammatical exegetical method.

On (MC2), some version of the historical-grammatical exegetical method is *the* proper way to approach the interpretive task. Proponents may disagree among themselves on the precise methodological details; they may squabble over exactly *what* constitutes good, historically grounded interpretation. Some may include more mainstream historical-critical considerations, while others may think that we should hold these at arm's length. The common thread, however, is the commitment to the necessity of historical considerations as well as the importance of grammatical considerations. Without an understanding of the historical context (which is to be gained from detailed study of the relevant ancient Near Eastern, Graeco-Roman, and Second Temple contexts and includes archaeological work as well as philological and sociological considerations), the statements of the Bible simply cannot be rightly understood. Without such knowledge, we could not know how the original audience would have received the message of these texts, and thus we could not know what the author was trying to convey. Without understanding the historical setting, there is little hope of understanding the language; without comprehending the language, there is no hope of understanding the message of the text. Or so the claim goes.

This brings us to the next main claim.

(MC3) Theological interpretation that prioritizes Christological and Trinitarian interpretations and that privileges creedal norms or the *regula fidei* (or *analogia fidei*) is at best an unhealthy distraction and at worst a barrier to proper understanding.

Goldingay admits that the Rule of Faith "provides a horizon from within which we may come to understand the Scriptures, and it may open our eyes to see things within the horizons of the Scriptures themselves."[21] But he rejects the notion that it is "the definitive hermeneutical framework for understanding the Scriptures," and he concludes that the *regula fidei* has "been a disaster for the hearing of the First Testament."[22] He thus allows that "theological interpretation is proper exegesis," but he also forcefully rejects the conviction of Craig G. Bartholomew that "any theological interpretation worth its salt must be Christocentric" as well as the statement of Francis Watson that "Christian faith ... is necessarily christocentric: for in Jesus Christ the identity of God, the creator who is also the God of Israel, is definitively disclosed in the triune name of Father, Son, and Holy Spirit for the salvation of humankind."[23] Against Watson, Goldingay does "not see much danger in an autonomous First Testament," but he sees "much danger" in the "christocentric interpretation" that "makes it harder for the Scriptures to confront us when we need to be confronted."[24] Walton ties this concern quite tightly to the foregoing one, and he judges traditional theological interpretation to be inferior to the type of historical-grammatical exegesis that he favors because "the church fathers had no access to the ancient world. They were lacking the resources that have been recovered today through archeological excavation. Over a million cuneiform texts now offer us unparalleled access to important information about the ancient world in which the Old Testament was written."[25]

Turning to NT scholarship, we can see similar concerns in the Jesus Seminar's reference to the "smothering cloud of the historic creeds."[26] N. T. Wright worries that "pre-critical" interpretations make it all too easy for the theological interpreter to "inflict his or her own point of view onto unwilling material."[27] He warns "the church" that it is "living in a fool's paradise" if it does not practice biblical

---

21. John Goldingay, *Do We Need the New Testament? Letting the Old Testament Speak for Itself* (Downers Grove: IVP Academic, 2015), 173.

22. Ibid.

23. Ibid., 160. Bartholomew's statement is found in "Listening for God's Address: A *Mere* Trinitarian Hermeneutic for the Old Testament," in *Hearing the Old Testament: Listening for God's Address*, ed. Craig G. Bartholomew and David J. H. Beldman (Grand Rapids: Eerdmans, 2012), 3. Watson's is found in *Text and Truth: Redefining Biblical Theology* (Grand Rapids: Eerdmans, 1997), 185.

24. Goldingay, *Do We Need*, 165.

25. Walton, *Lost World of Adam and Eve*, 205.

26. Robert Funk, Roy W. Hoover, and the Jesus Seminar, *The Five Gospels: The Search for the Authentic Words of Jesus* (New York: Macmillan, 1993), 7. See also Paul M. Casey, *From Jewish Prophet to Gentile God: The Origins and Development of New Testament Christology* (Louisville: Westminster John Knox, 1991), 163.

27. N. T. Wright, *Jesus and the Victory of God*, Christian Origins and the Question of God vol. 2 (Minneapolis: Fortress, 1996), 104. C. Stephen Evans notes the rather pejorative manner of Wright's use of "pre-critical," in "Methodological Naturalism in Historical Biblical Scholarship," in *Jesus and the Restoration of Israel*, ed. Carey C. Newman (Downers Grove: InterVarsity, 1999), 189–90.

interpretation that is properly attentive to history.[28] He says that tradition-oriented Christian readers are "capable of all kinds of fantasies and anachronisms in reading the Gospels, and to pull the blanket of canon over our heads and pretend that we are safe in our private, fideistic world is sheer self-delusion."[29]

These claims seem to be widely held. They are also held with tenacity and conviction. It is worth noting at the outset that these seem to be *brought to* the biblical text rather than *derived from* it. This is merely an observation rather than a criticism. Moreover, there is much to appreciate and affirm in the helpful work of these scholars. For instance, surely Goldingay and Wright are correct that it is all too easy to miss vitally important elements of the biblical account; if we think that we have already captured all the truth in our creedal and canonical summaries, then we are likely to miss much that is crucial. But there is also good reason to think that the considerations in their favor are not decisive. In some cases, the claims are ambiguous, and when disambiguated we see that they either amount to uncontroversial platitudes that are hardly relevant or else they appear to be flawed. In other cases, there simply is good reason to think that the claims are mistaken.

(Hermeneutical) Holiness and Wholeness Reconsidered

Consider (MC1). This claim tells us that *the* meaning is one that is historically contextualized and temporally located. It denies that the text can rightly be understood as communicating more than one meaning. A text "cannot mean what it never meant" (as the old cliché has it), and the meaning of that text is fixed by the author's intention in the original communicative event. The author meant one thing, and that is what the contemporary interpreter seeks to discover. What (MC1) denies is the possibility (and thus, of course, the actuality) of there being different meanings; whether these supposed multiple meanings are "layered" at different levels or independent of one another, they simply are not possible. A text has a sole determinate meaning, and that meaning is identical to the author's intention.

Yet this claim is not obvious, and, indeed, there are reasons to consider the possibility that (MC1) is not only under-supported but false. Recent work in the philosophy of language may be helpful here; in particular, considerations raised by John Perry (and others) are relevant. As background, it will help to get clear on the differences between "utterances" and "tokens." Perry explains,

> The term "token" is used in two different ways in the literature: for the act of speaking, writing, or otherwise using language and for an object that is produced

---

28. N. T. Wright, "Five Gospels But No Gospel: Jesus and the Seminar," in *Authenticating the Activities of Jesus: New Testament Tools and Studies, Volume XXVIII.2*, ed. Bruce Chilton and Craig Evans (Leiden: Brill, 1999), 119.

29. N. T. Wright, "Jesus and the Identity of God," *Ex Auditu* (1998): 49.

by, or at least used in, such an act. I use "utterance" in the first sense. Utterances are intentional acts. The term "utterance" often connotes spoken language, but as I use it an utterance may involve speech, writing, typing, gestures or any other sort of linguistic activity. I use "token" in the second sense, in the way Reichenbach used it when he said a certain token was to be found on a certain page of a certain copy of a book. Tokens, in this sense, are traces left by utterances.[30]

Applied to our case, when we are talking about the act of communication or *writing* (however exactly this is to be understood with respect to doctrines of inspiration, authorship, etc.) we are talking about *utterances*, and when we are talking about the biblical text or *writings* we are talking about *tokens*. For present purposes, we are interested in the tokens (the Bible as we have it) rather than the initial utterances (the process whereby the Bible came to be).

Perry goes on to discuss how one and the same token may be used in various ways. He does so by describing a rather mundane domestic situation:

> My wife Frenchie and I were once Resident Fellows in a dormitory at Stanford, eating with students each evening in the cafeteria. If she went to dinner before I returned, she would write on a small blackboard on the counter, "I have gone to the cafeteria," and set it on the table near the front door of our apartment. I would put it back on the counter. There was no need for her to write out the message anew each time I was late; if the blackboard had not been used for something else in the interim, she could simply move it from the counter back to the table. Frenchie used the same token to say different things on different days.[31]

Now consider a day in which Perry is early or on time but Frenchie is late. Perry could use the same token to communicate to Frenchie that he had gone to dinner. This would be yet another—and different—use of the same token to express a different truth.

Sometimes the same token is used to convey different meanings at different times. Perry asks us to consider the following scenario:

> Suppose there is a sign in a flying school, intended to warn would-be pilots: "Flying planes can be dangerous." The flying school goes bankrupt; the manager of a park near the airport buys the sign and puts it next to a sign that

---

30. John Perry, "What Are Indexicals?" in *The Problem of the Essential Indexical and Other Essays*, expanded ed. (Stanford: Center for Study of Language and Information, 2000), 318, cited in Scott Williams, "Indexicals and the Trinity: Two Non-Social Models," *Journal of Analytic Theology* 1 (2013): 80.

31. Perry, "What Are Indexicals?" 319, cited in Williams, "Indexicals and the Trinity," 80.

prohibits walking on high tightropes. In its new use the sign is a token of a type with a ... different meaning than in its original use.[32]

A bit of further reflection helps us to see that one token can be used to convey different meanings and to communicate different propositions at the same time. Sometimes statements or utterances are expressed in tokens that are intentionally multifaceted and thus sometimes (at least initially) ambiguous. Consider how Bilbo Baggins greets Gandalf.

> "Good morning!" said Bilbo, and he meant it. The sun was shining, and the grass was very green. But Gandalf looked at him from under long bushy eyebrows that stuck out further than the brim of his shady hat. "What do you mean?" he said. "Do you wish me a good morning, or mean that it is a good morning whether I want it or not; or that you feel good this morning; or that it is a morning to be good on?" "All of them at once," said Bilbo.[33]

Bilbo claims that he means "all of them at once." But "I wish you a good morning" is neither equivalent to nor reducible to "It is a good morning," and neither is equivalent to nor reducible to "I feel good this morning" or "It is a morning on which to be good." These are very different claims. Yet they are all carried or conveyed by the same token, and indeed they are all *intended* by Bilbo.

The upshot is that one and the (numerically) same token may be used by different people to convey different propositions. And one and the same token may be used by the same author to convey different propositions. The different propositional claims can be made simultaneously. On the other hand, they can be made sequentially; indeed, they can be temporally indexed in a way that is responsive to the differing contexts. They may be "layered" in the sense that one meaning is foundational to another and the meanings build upon one another. Or they may be relatively independent. As the example of Bilbo and Gandalf shows, the same, or at least much the same, could be said of other speech acts as well.

I am not suggesting that these illustrations map directly or neatly onto issues of biblical interpretation. But the major insights are valid and seem very relevant. If this is correct, then there is reason to doubt (MC1). It simply is not obvious that there is only one meaning or a singular proposition (or set thereof) that is conveyed by the text. Multiple propositional claims may be communicated by the same token, and these may all be intended by the author. Moreover, an appropriate and authorially intended meaning may be temporally indexed in a way that is intended to be received by later recipients—even if this is unavailable to the original audience. Without endangering authorial intention (and without demeaning the importance of historical inquiry in the interpretive process), we

---

32. Perry, "What Are Indexicals?" 319, cited in Williams, "Indexicals and the Trinity," 80–1.

33. Cited in Williams, "Indexicals and the Trinity," 82.

can see that there may be multiple legitimate meanings. Thus, there is reason to hold (MC1) at arm's length.

Without (MC1), the support for (MC2) is diminished. One may continue to think that historical considerations are very helpful and indeed important. But, if there is not just one meaning that is obviously and inextricably linked to the immediate historical context, if instead there may be meanings available to later interpreters, then other factors—such as canon and creed—are also important. One may think, in other words, that historical study is not sufficient for a full and adequate understanding—even if it remains necessary. Furthermore, if we are not hampered by (MC1) and (MC2), then any solid support for (MC3) becomes hard to find. If later interpretations—even those that are canonically shaped and creedally normed—are viable as more complete understandings of the biblical texts, then we have no reason to be innately suspicious of Christological and Trinitarian theological interpretation.

With this in mind, let us return to Walton's statement that traditional theological interpretation is inferior to his preferred approach, which seeks to recover the intention of the human author through historical-grammatical exegesis that prizes the study of ancient Near Eastern documents. He notes that premodern interpreters did not have the one million or so cuneiform documents uncovered by archaeological study. Surely this is true; Wesley did not have access to the rocks and pottery shards from which we can learn about the historical context of the OT. But so what? In addition to wondering exactly how many of these one million or so artifacts one must have mastered to be a competent interpreter of Holy Scripture, we might also wonder exactly how such study is decisive for an understanding that is canonically shaped and creedally formed.

What happens if, following centuries of Christian theology, we factor the dual authorship of Scripture into these considerations? Here the well-known work of Nicholas Wolterstorff is helpful. Wolterstorff distinguishes between notions of "appropriated discourse," "deputized discourse," and "double agency discourse."[34] In cases of appropriated discourse, one author writes (or otherwise states) something that another author "appropriates" or takes on as her own. Seeing it, the second author says something akin to "that is exactly what I mean!" or "my thoughts exactly" or "I concur wholeheartedly."[35] This is distinct from "deputized discourse."[36] In deputized discourse the one person speaks *for* another as an ambassador does for a head of state. In such cases, it is the ambassador who does it, but she does so as one authorized—that is, deputized—by the head of state. She represents the head of state, and her words carry that weight and authority. Both modes are distinct from

---

34. See also Anthony C. Thiselton, "Speech-Act Theory and the Claim That God Speaks: Nicholas Wolterstorff's *Divine Discourse*," *Scottish Journal of Theology* 50, no. 1 (1997): 97–110.

35. Nicholas Wolterstorff, *Divine Discourse: Philosophical Reflections on the Claim that God Speaks* (Cambridge: Cambridge University Press, 1995), 51–4.

36. Ibid., 42–51.

"double agency discourse," which is more like a secretary composing a statement for a president. Of course, such composition *can* take the form of dictation, but it need not. Instead the secretary "may *know* what the executive wants to say to one and another person, and compose letters accordingly."[37] As Wolterstorff explains, the "crucial thing is that the secretary 'know the mind' of his superior."[38] He notes that there may be variations in the mode and degree of superintendence as well as "variations in the mode of authorization."[39]

One need not agree with all that Wolterstorff says to see the relevant point: In each of these cases, one author may use another to communicate some proposition (or, again, to perform other speech acts). In cases of deputized discourse and double agency discourse, it is entirely possible for one author to mean exactly what the other author means *and* to mean something further. And, as we have seen, there indeed may be more than one intended meaning. Perhaps Author-1 understands and intends all such meanings; Author-1 intends a meaning that is readily understandable to the immediate audience but also intends a meaning for the audience on the other side of significant divine action (e.g., Bethlehem, Golgotha, and Pentecost). But maybe Author-2 only understands and intends one meaning. Perhaps the meaning intended by Author-2 is the one that is most immediately relevant; maybe it is the one that makes readiest sense in his own social and intellectual location. As such, it would be the one most discernible for late modern readers via historical methods. But it would not necessarily be the *only* warranted meaning, nor would it even be the only one grounded in authorial intention.

There is nothing "occultic" about this claim. The meaning is not hidden "in cyberspace," nor is it located "between the lines." To the contrary, it is intended by the author, and conveyed by the same token—the words on the page. Consider Walton's claims from (2) above. He says that because "God vested his authority in a human author," then "we must consider what the human author intended to communicate if we want to understand God's message." His claim that "God vested his authority in a human author" is both ambiguous and unsupported, but neither does it follow that the intention of the human author must be identical to that of the divine author. In addition, while it is obviously true that to read Genesis is to read an ancient document, the conclusion that we can only interpret "by using the assumptions that would be appropriate in the ancient world" does not follow from the mere observation that Genesis is very, very old. To be fair, Walton says that we should "begin" this way, and maybe he does not intend his statement to serve as a moratorium on theological interpretation of an authorially intended meaning that goes far beyond what the original human author intended. If so, however, it is not at all clear why he would proceed as he does or come to the conclusions that he reaches. At any rate, more clarification would be welcome.

37. Ibid., 39.
38. Ibid.
39. Ibid., 41.

Some biblical scholars and theologians may worry that what I suggest here would open the door to all manner and species of vicious interpretive pluralism. They may be concerned that to allow for multiple legitimate interpretations would be to open a hermeneutical Pandora's Box. But it simply is not the case that "anything goes." Several considerations are relevant. First, as I have said, nothing here discounts the importance of the "historical-grammatical" method, which can help us to arrive at (what has historically been called) the "literal meaning." Second, some candidates for interpretation can be eliminated simply because they are inconsistent with those that we judge to have been established rightly. Two (or more) purported interpretations cannot both (or all) be true if they are either contradictory or contrary. If some proposition P is *contradictory* to some proposition Q, then it is possible that either P or Q is true but not possible for both P and Q to be true, and it is not possible that both P and Q are false. If P and Q are contradictory, then they are "mutually exhaustive as well as mutually inconsistent."[40] They cannot both be true and they cannot both be false. If some proposition P is *contrary* to some proposition Q, then it is not possible that both P and Q are true. If P is true, then Q cannot be true. And if Q is true, then P cannot be true. They are mutually exclusive but not mutually exhaustive. It is not possible that both P and Q are true. But it is not necessary that either P or Q is true, that is, both P and Q could be false. What this means for our discussion is decisive: Any two purported interpretations that are actually (rather than only *apparently*) either contrary or contradictory cannot both be true. Suppose, then, that we have very good reason to hold some interpretive proposal I. Suppose that I seems to be firmly established by good historical-grammatical interpretation. Now suppose further that we are presented with some additional interpretive proposal I^*. When we look at I and I^* together, they appear to be inconsistent. What is to be done? Well, we should first make sure that I and I^* are *actually* (rather than only apparently) inconsistent. If closer analysis reveals that they are really inconsistent (either contrary or contradictory), then we perhaps should revisit the exegetical warrant for I. Maybe I is not as secure as we had at first assumed. But maybe it is, and our further investigation reveals that the exegetical warrant is even stronger than we initially thought. In that instance we have good reason to reject I^*; if we have strong support for I, and if we rightly conclude that I^* is contrary (or contradictory) to I, then we have grounds to conclude that I^* is mistaken. But we *do not* have reason to conclude that I is the *only* legitimate interpretation.

Conclusion

In this essay I have worked to defend an important element of traditional Wesleyan hermeneutics—an element, gratefully, that is being rediscovered by some excellent

---

40. Laurence R. Horn, "Contradiction," *Stanford Encyclopedia of Philosophy*. Available online: https://plato.stanford.edu/entries/contradiction/ (accessed June 12, 2018).

Wesleyan biblical scholars and theologians. I have argued in support of (a version of) the notion of *sensus plenior*, and, more broadly, in favor of intentionally theological interpretation of Scripture that is canonically shaped.

These Wesleyans have an ally in the work of Kevin J. Vanhoozer. He has labored long and hard in the "defense of the author," and he has been a foremost advocate of "theological interpretation of Scripture." Moreover, he has, at various times and in sundry ways, made cautious use of insights drawn from analytic philosophy of language. This Wesleyan is both indebted and grateful.

Nothing that I have said should be taken to demean the value of historical studies for biblical interpretation. Not at all. History matters a great deal to the Christian faith; Christianity is, after all, founded upon God's actions in human history. The grand story of the Christian faith—from creation through covenant to Christ and finally to the consummation and reconciliation of all things—is a story of what has happened, what is happening now, and what will happen. So of course history matters, and we should gratefully receive and use all the tools at our disposal. History matters, and grammar matters. Insights from the ancient Near East and the Mediterranean world should be valued. Using such tools, we can glean very helpful insights. Understanding how the "original audience" would have received a saying or text remains very important. Historical-grammatical interpretation is valid and should be valued, and it is a very good place to start.

But there is no good reason to think that such important work exhausts the interpretive process, or that "whatever the original audience would have thought" is the ceiling or the *telos* of hermeneutics. Nor is there any good reason to think that the way to proceed is by insisting that we first must lock down the meaning of some discrete text via historical study and then move on to the next text and lock down its meaning via historical study—and then get around to doing theology only after we have done this enough times and only on the basis of those insights gleaned from such study. Indeed, such limitations seem arbitrary. And they threaten to inhibit our reception of the full biblical message. If we believe in the holiness of the divine author, then we will believe in the wholeness of the divine revelation. And we will be grateful.

Chapter 12

"FANTASTIC!" KARL BARTH, AMERICAN EVANGELICALS, AND THE STRANGE NEW WORLD OF THEOLOGY

Stephen M. Garrett

Introduction: Evangelical Theology Coming to America

In April 1962, Karl Barth delivered the first five lectures of his *Einführung in die evangelische Theologie* at the University of Chicago's Divinity School. An African American theological colleague greeted him at the airport and "with a subtle smile" said, "How do you like that strange place called the United States?" Barth was evasive, downplaying any pretension of what he might "know" about America. After his return to Basel, though, he did have "impressions." One word seemed to say it all: "*fantastic!*"[1] While in Chicago, Barth met with the Rev. Billy Graham, whom he previously encountered nearly two years prior in Switzerland. Barth's first meetings with Graham, along with Carl F. H. Henry, came just before Graham's multi-city evangelistic tour through Berne, Zürich, Basel, and Lausanne. Barth recollected that Graham was a "jolly good fellow" with whom "one can talk easily and openly," not something he expected of a "trumpeter of the gospel."[2]

In a letter to his son, Christoph, in September 1960 and at a meeting with Swiss Methodist pastors months later, Barth indicated that he was perplexed and actually rather appalled "when he went to hear him let loose in the St Jacob stadium" where Graham held his two-day revival crusade in Basel. Barth thought Graham "acted like a madman," for "what he presented was certainly not the gospel." It was "the gospel at gun-point." Graham compromised God's freedom, according to Barth, by neutering God's act in Christ with a horizontal human decision; no numerical

---

1. Karl Barth, *Evangelical Theology: An Introduction*, trans. Grover Foley (Grand Rapids: Eerdmans, 1979), v–vii. Emphasis added.

2. Eberhard Busch, *Karl Barth: His Life from Letters and Autobiographical Texts*, trans. John Bowden (Grand Rapids: Eerdmans, 1994), 446, 458–9. See also Carl F. H. Henry, "Graham Challenges Swiss Throngs to Decision," *Christianity Today*, September 26, 1960. Available online: https://www.christianitytoday.com/ct/1960/september-26/graham-challenges-swiss-throngs-to-decision.html (accessed February 20, 2021).

success could legitimize turning the gospel into law or "push[ing] it like an article for sale."[3]

In the September 26, 1960, issue of *Christianity Today*, Henry recounted Graham's interactions with Barth and concerns about his supposed commitment to universal salvation. If evangelism were to have a positive effect on Swiss life, then the distinction between "saved" and "lost," which a "call to decision" implies, must be maintained.[4] For Graham and Henry, the matter was one of human responsibility, of a personal relationship with Jesus Christ. Despite these disagreements, Henry and Graham readily acknowledged that Barth's theology was not the sole problem. Rudolf Bultmann's liberal theology was also a detriment, which Henry credited Barth for countermanding by encouraging the Swiss to study the Bible.[5]

Since these early, reluctant, and indeed skeptical encounters, a notable shift has occurred among American evangelicals toward a more amenable reception of Barth, sometimes called "the Barthian Turn."[6] While engagement ranges across the doctrinal spectrum, Barth's doctrine of the Word of God has received by far the most attention, with significant implications for evangelical hermeneutics. To be sure, it was Barth's reverence for Holy Scripture, for "The Strange New World within the Bible,"[7] that drew the attention of American evangelicals. Yet Barth's doctrine of the Word of God encompassed more than merely a doctrine of Scripture. It situated Scripture and its attendant doctrines like revelation, inspiration, illumination, and authority with respect to God's triunity—at heart of which was Barth's Threefold Form of the Word of God. In short, what Scripture is *cannot be separated* from who God is.

The more American evangelicals engaged with Barth's doctrine of the Word of God, the more they were ushered into another "strange new world," a resurgent Trinitarian theology that envisions a rapprochement with Scripture as part of the triune God's action in the world. This "strange new world" initially disrupted American evangelical theology as the likes of Cornelius Van Til from the 1940s to the 1960s and Henry in the 1970s and early 1980s challenged Barth based on the doctrine of revelation, albeit with little consideration for how God's triunity bears on Scripture's ontology or dogmatic location. Others like Bernard Ramm, Geoffrey Bromiley, and Donald Bloesch in the 1970s through the 1990s pressed Barth on his understanding of revelation and Scripture but did so while engaging his Christology and pneumatology. Despite their friendlier engagement with Barth,

---

3. Busch, *Karl Barth*, 446.

4. Henry, "Graham Challenges Swiss." See Barth's lecture fragments to *CD* IV/4 regarding divine encounter and human responsibility.

5. Henry, "Graham Challenges Swiss."

6. James R. A. Merrick, "Have Evangelicals Changed Their Minds about Karl Barth? A Review Essay with Reference to the Current Crisis in Evangelical Identity," *Evangelical Review of Theology* 32, no. 4 (2008): 355–68.

7. Karl Barth, "The Strange New World within the Bible," in *The Word of God and the Word of Man*, trans. Douglas Horton (Boston: Pilgrim, 1928), 28–50.

tensions remained as evangelical theology found it difficult to reconcile Barth's ontology of Scripture with any direct sense of its being the trustworthy Word of God.[8] As Kevin J. Vanhoozer entered this conversation, he sought to account for evangelical concerns while learning from Barth about locating Scripture within God's triune economy.[9] His efforts made a significant contribution to the landscape of this strange new world as evangelical theology matured while manifesting further differences concerning God and Scripture.

To substantiate this account, first I will sketch the contours of Barth's doctrine of the Word of God in light of his sociocultural milieu. Then, through a "Yes-No" dialectic, I will examine the aforementioned engagement with Barth's doctrine of the Word, noting the continuity and discontinuity while bringing into relief the underlying dogmatic concerns. It will become evident, then, how evangelical theology not only found itself in a doctrinal stalemate with Barth concerning Scripture's ontology but also found itself amidst a renaissance in Trinitarian theology. As Vanhoozer attempts to address the stalemate, he creatively rearticulates an account of Scripture in light of God's triunity as being-in-communicative-action. In so doing, he contributes to more robust theological discourse regarding God, Scripture, and hermeneutics, encouraging American evangelicals to go beyond Barth rather than simply turning toward or against him.

---

8. Karl Barth's reception among American evangelicals is a kaleidoscope of responses influenced by sociocultural conditions and theological commitments. Philip Thorne argues for two basic patterns of reception, orthodox-apologetic and mediating approaches, amidst a mosaic of traditions with familial resemblances: Northern Fundamentalist, Holiness-Pentecostal, Reformed Confessional, and Southern Evangelical (*Evangelicalism and Karl Barth: His Reception and Influence among North American Evangelical Theology* [Eugene, OR: Pickwick, 1995]). Donald Dayton assesses Barth's reception under the rubric of "sibling rivalry" among reformed confessionalists, revivalists/pietists, and fundamentalists ("Karl Barth and Evangelicalism: The Varieties of Sibling Rivalry," *Theological Students Fellowship Bulletin* 8, no. 5 [1985]: 18–23). While the five central figures of this essay reflect elements of the above, they are situated chronologically in a dialectical chiasm to highlight dogmatic concerns leading to a Trinitarian renaissance. Ramm is a pivotal, transitional figure that illuminates further difference even as the fundamentalist-modernist controversy subsided.

9. See, initially, Kevin J. Vanhoozer, "God's Mighty Speech Acts: The Doctrine of Scripture Today," in *A Pathway into the Holy Scripture*, ed. D. F. Wright and P. Sattherwaite (Grand Rapids: Eerdmans, 1994), 143–81; more recently and directly, Vanhoozer, "Triune Discourse: Theological Reflections on the Claim that God Speaks (Parts 1 and 2)," in *Trinitarian Theology for the Church: Scripture, Community, Worship*, ed. Daniel J. Treier and David Lauber (Downers Grove: IVP Academic), 25–78. For other contemporary engagements, see Sung Wook Chung, ed., *Karl Barth and Evangelical Theology: Convergences and Divergences* (Grand Rapids: Baker Academic, 2006); David Gibson and Daniel Strange, eds., *Engaging with Barth: Contemporary Evangelical Critiques* (London: Continuum, 2008); Bruce L. McCormack and Clifford B. Anderson, eds., *Karl Barth and American Evangelicalism* (Grand Rapids: Eerdmans, 2011).

Karl Barth's Doctrine of the Word of God

At the outbreak of the First World War on August 1, 1914, nearly one hundred German intellectuals signed a manifesto in support of Kaiser Wilhelm II's war policy. Barth was dismayed as nearly all his former professors signed the manifesto. How could theological scholarship capitulate to such ideology and change itself "into intellectual 42mm cannons"?[10] While this capitulation compelled Barth to reject the Romantic theology of his teachers, seeds of doubt were already sown during his pastorate at Safenwil and through conversations with his dear friend Eduard Thurneysen. Thurneysen suggested while they were together on holiday that "what we need for preaching, instruction and pastoral care is a 'wholly other' theological foundation." Barth spoke of deciding to "learn our theological ABC all over again, beginning by reading and interpreting the writing of the Old and New Testaments, more thoughtfully than before."[11]

In his turn to Scripture, Barth discovered a "strange new world," the world of "God's absolutely unique existence, power and initiative, above all in his relationship to men"—in short, "the Godness of God."[12] This notion drove Barth to consider God first rather than as an afterthought meant to justify human endeavor. Human beings cannot assert, as pietists did, "God's standpoint [as] their own partisan standpoint and therefore no individual or group simply stands on God's side over against others. Rather, in solidarity, together, they all share the responsibility before God!" Moreover, Barth insisted, contra his liberal heritage, that human attempts at sociocultural reform remain within created possibilities. The Kingdom of God, however, "creates something completely new in the world." It is not an "escape into the safe heights of pure ideas but an entry into the need of the present world, sharing in its sufferings, its activity and its hope."[13]

In 1924, during lecture preparation on dogmatics at the University Göttingen, Barth discovered the patristic notion of anhypostatic-enhypostatic Christology. This Christology highlighted that the second Person of the Trinity, the Logos, took on human flesh in its entirety, entering into a "divine incognito," unrecognizable and indiscernible to humanity. The incomprehensible God veils himself even as he unveils himself in and through human flesh, granting faith to human beings who would know him only in and through Christ.[14] This discovery allowed Barth to retain the critical distance between God and humanity while grounding it in Christology rather than eschatology. Revelation was not constrained to the event of the cross; rather, "the dialectic of veiling and unveiling on its objective side could comprehend the whole of the incarnate existence of the Mediator."[15]

10. Busch, *Karl Barth*, 81.
11. Ibid., 97.
12. Ibid., 119.
13. Ibid., 100.
14. Bruce L. McCormack, *Karl Barth's Critically Realistic Dialectical Theology: Its Genesis and Development 1909–1936* (Oxford: Oxford University Press, 1995), 327.
15. Ibid., 328.

The Godness of God and his newfound Christology transformed Barth's understanding of dogmatics. Whereas nineteenth-century dogmatics established human conditions for making faith possible, Barth began with God. Yet, if God is incomprehensible, how could dogmatics, no less preaching, even begin to speak of God? Speaking of God, Barth surmised, is only possible because God spoke first—*Deus dixit*. The Word of God in the form of revelation "denotes the Word of God itself in the act of being spoken in time." It is preeminent and "is the condition which conditions all things without itself being conditioned." It is God's original, independent address and does not require human hearers. God's speaking is identical with God so that "God's speech is really God's act." This form of the Word of God "does not differ from the person of Jesus Christ nor from the reconciliation he accomplished in Him." If the Word of God is to be known, the Word creates human beings to receive this address. Hence, "to say revelation is to say 'the Word became flesh'" so that it may be perceived by human beings who receive the Word of God, not as its possession, but in faith and obedience.[16]

The Word of God in the form of God's Word written attests to the divine event of revelation, then and there. Those who received this revelation in the concrete reality of Jesus of Nazareth, in whom is summed up all the history of Israel, were the prophets and the apostles as witnesses. As such, "revelation engenders the Scripture which attests it," says Barth, "as the commission or burden laid on the prophets and apostles ..., as the event of inspiration in which they become speakers and writers of the Word of God."[17] The event of revelation makes the Bible the Word of God. "The Bible is God's Word," says Barth, "to the extent that God causes it to be His Word, the extent that He speaks through it." Holy Scripture is the witness of the prophets and the apostles brought about by their encounter with *Deus dixit*. God's free act of speaking in and through the Bible defines what the Bible *is* as God's Word. Yet what the Bible is cannot be separated from what it *becomes* "by which he causes it to be true to us and for us here and now that the biblical word of man is His own Word."[18] As Bruce McCormack says, the Bible as Holy Scripture, "as defined by the will of God as expressed in his act of giving it to the church," is a being-in-becoming, which "means that where and when the Bible *becomes* the Word of God, it is only becoming what it already is."[19]

To hear the Bible as revelation in this way makes the form of the Word of God as church proclamation possible and indeed necessary. The Word of God written, as prophetic and apostolic testimony, is how the church remembers God's past revelation and "is thus summoned and guided to proclamation and empowered for it." Church proclamation is "real proclamation, i.e., the promise of future revelation, only as the repetition of the biblical witness to past revelation" just as "the Bible is

16. Karl Barth, *CD* I/1, 119–20, 134.
17. Ibid., 115.
18. Ibid., 110.
19. Bruce L. McCormack, "The Being of Holy Scripture Is in Becoming: Karl Barth in Conversation with American Evangelical Criticism," in *Evangelicals and Scripture: Tradition, Authority, and Hermeneutics*, ed. Vincent Bacote, Laura C. Miguelez, and Dennis L. Okholm (Downers Grove: InterVarsity, 2004), 55–75 (66).

real witness, i.e., the factual recollection of past revelation, only in its relation to this past revelation attested in it."[20] In other words, the Bible is really God's Word only as it bears witness to revelation just as proclamation is really God's Word as it really promises revelation. Like the Bible, church proclamation has a divine being-in-becoming. This becoming depends not on human experience or reaction but rather on God's freedom to use church proclamation so that people hear in faith and obedience. In becoming what it already is as God's Word, then, church proclamation is a place of divine action, so long as it adheres to its commission, theme, and criterion established by revelation.[21]

Barth was careful to nuance what he meant by the Word of God; do these three forms entail three different Words of God? *Nein!* The Word of God "is one and the same whether we understand it as revelation, Bible, or proclamation. There is no distinction of degree or value between the three forms." Proclamation is the Word of God as it faithfully sets forth the revelation attested in Scripture. The Bible is the Word of God as it witnesses to revelation. Revelation is the Word of God as God's direct address in the person of Jesus Christ and never in some abstracted form but only indirectly through Scripture and proclamation.[22] As for this God of revelation, Barth reasons, "God's Word is God Himself in His revelation. For God reveals Himself as Lord and according to Scripture this signifies for the concept of revelation that God Himself in unimpaired unity yet also in unimpaired distinction is Revealer, Revelation, and Revealedness."[23] The doctrine of revelation begins with the triune God, yet the doctrine of the Trinity is church dogma, developed in exegetical reflection upon the biblical witness to revelation. To grapple with the threefold Word of God is to grapple with the triune God himself, with important implications for hermeneutics that are evident in Barth's theological interpretation of Scripture.[24]

The "Yes and No" of American Evangelical Reactions

American evangelical reception of Barth's doctrine of the Word of God has ranged from exclusion to embrace.[25] Some of the harshest and earliest criticisms

---

20. Barth, *CD* I/1, 111, 117.
21. Ibid., 117–18.
22. Ibid., 121.
23. Ibid., 295.
24. See Mary Kathleen Cunningham, *What Is Theological Exegesis? Interpretation and Use of Scripture in Barth's Doctrine of Election* (Philadelphia: Trinity Press International, 1995); Richard E. Burnett, *Karl Barth's Theological Exegesis: The Hermeneutical Principles of the Römerbrief Period* (Grand Rapids: Eerdmans, 2001); Donald Wood, *Barth's Theology of Interpretation* (Aldershot: Ashgate, 2007).
25. Evangelicalism is a notoriously slippery term. See especially Gerald R. McDermott, "Introduction," in *The Oxford Handbook of Evangelical Theology*, ed. Gerald R. McDermott

came from Cornelius Van Til and Carl F. H. Henry; others like Bernard Ramm and Geoffrey Bromiley were more measured; still others like Donald Bloesch were more amenable. As each affirmed various aspects of Barth's doctrine while rejecting others, their underlying concerns highlighted questions concerning the who and whatness of God. Accordingly, American evangelicals were immersed in the Trinitarian renaissance of the twentieth century,[26] which led toward theological maturity but also illuminated internal differences.

Cornelius Van Til

Cornelius Van Til, in light of Barth's celebrated "coming to America," issued a clarion call to defend against this "new and concerted attack" on biblical Christianity.[27] Given his acerbic criticisms, it can be difficult to take seriously Van Til's apparent affirmations of Barth's thinking about Scripture's revelatory nature, Christ's virgin birth, the objective character of Christ and his work, and even Christ's bodily resurrection.[28] Van Til remained radically opposed because Barth's "activist concept of revelation controls all his thinking."[29] Barth understood Jesus of Nazareth and Scripture as the Word of God only indirectly, denying any direct revelation in history to preserve God's freedom. This denial meant that Jesus and the Bible only become and bear witness to revelation but never are revelation, undermining biblical authority and ultimately the historicity of the resurrection.[30]

Van Til's primary dogmatic concern was evident in Barth's use of the terms *Geschichte* and *Historie*.[31] On Van Til's account, *Historie* for Barth involved "the facts of the world as the neutral historian sees them" while *Geschichte* was the realm of revelation. The resurrection involved *Historie* in that Jesus was seen, felt, and heard; yet the resurrection was not *Historie* but *Geschichte* as the foundation of the Christian faith where God is God, Christ is the God-man, and humanity is fully itself in Christ.[32] This distinction dispensed with direct revelation, according to Van Til, undermining the certainty, dependability, and continuity of revelation. Today it is widely believed that Van Til misunderstood Barth's use of these terms, in that Barth was making an epistemological rather than ontological distinction: The

---

(Oxford: Oxford University Press, 2010), 1–16; Bruce Hindmarsh, *The Spirit of Early Evangelicalism: True Religion in a Modern World* (Oxford: Oxford University Press, 2018).

26. For debates about this renaissance, see Michael Allen's chapter on the Trinity later in this volume.

27. Cornelius Van Til, *Christianity and Barthianism* (Philadelphia: P&R, 1962), vii. Note the symmetry with J. Gresham Machen's *Christianity and Liberalism* (New York: Macmillan, 1923).

28. Cornelius Van Til, *Karl Barth and Evangelicalism* (Philadelphia: P&R, 1964), 13.

29. Van Til, *Christianity and Barthianism*, 107.

30. Ibid., 13–29, 408–11, 438–9.

31. Ibid., 430.

32. Ibid., 14.

resurrection occurred in created time, in this concrete world (*Historie*); yet what we know of God acting to raise Christ from the dead is only accessible by the illumination of the Holy Spirit (*Geschichte*).[33] If Van Til properly understood Barth's distinction, might he have elucidated how his Trinitarian presupposition connected Christologically and pneumatologically with God's Word written?

Carl F. H. Henry

Like Van Til, Carl F. H. Henry focused on Barth's doctrine of revelation. For Henry, revelation is rational and propositional, its truthfulness discernible in human language and concepts, especially in the words of Scripture.[34] Henry commended Barth for his authoritative use of Scripture throughout *Church Dogmatics*. Henry acknowledged development in Barth's theology of the Word of God, appreciating how he ascribed objectivity to divine revelation, providing "a basis for genuine ontological statements."[35] Yet Henry viewed Barth as wildly inconsistent when Barth concluded, "God gives Himself to man entirely in His revelation. But not in such a way as to give Himself as a prisoner of man." Thus, said Henry, "God remains so intellectually imprisoned within his voluntary self-disclosure that not even inspired prophets and apostles can or do convey objective ontological information about God as he truly is in himself." Barth problematically belied any notion of "theologically objective information, that is, universally shareable truths, about [God's] intrinsic nature," especially in relation to Scripture.[36]

While Henry deemed Barth's doctrine of revelation inconsistent and irrational, he deepened his dogmatic concerns regarding Scripture. For Henry, God's self-disclosure must be directly identified with the human words and concepts of Scripture in order to say that the Bible is the Word of God and thus cognitively and propositionally intelligible. To do otherwise invites skepticism and anti-intellectualism, undermining biblical authority.[37] Barth appeared to diminish "the inspiration or inspiredness which the New Testament ascribes to Scripture (2 Tim. 3:16)" in favor of the present; despite good intentions, Barth followed a Kierkegaardian "irrationalism" rooted in an "existential faith in God's self-revelatory confrontation."[38] How can we say anything reliable about God, if the Bible "becomes" revelatory only when God sees fit for it to do so? Nonsense![39] Henry's criticisms draw our attention to concerns regarding God's unity of action. If the Spirit leads us into truth, how might his present activity relate to God's past self-disclosure, not to mention the promise to do so in the future?

---

33. Barth, *CD* I/1, 324–33; cf. *CD* III/2, 446.
34. Carl F. H. Henry, *God, Revelation and Authority*, 6 vols. (Waco: Word, 1976–83), 1.282.
35. Ibid., 5.129, 366.
36. Ibid., 5.129.
37. Ibid., 2.287.
38. Ibid., 1.62, 187.
39. Ibid., 4.267. See also 4.196–200 regarding "Barth on Scriptural Errancy."

Bernard Ramm

Bernard Ramm's interaction with Barth's doctrine of the Word marks a noticeable shift among American evangelicals. Contra Van Til and Henry, Ramm saw Barth as subscribing to an objective revelation rather than an existential or subjectivist rendering because the Word of God is the subject matter of Scripture. In short, "The Word is in the words."[40] This notion implies a divine speaking in that "the product of special revelation as speaking is thereby carried over as writing" and thus "the creation of a Scripture is but the extension of the modality of the divine speaking" as the "inscripturated Word of God" wrought by the Spirit.[41] Ramm did gently criticize the event character of Barth's doctrine of revelation as being incomplete: "To speak of revelation of a Person and not of truths is to speak ... nonsense. God is given in revelation as a Person, *but along with truths of God.*" Thus, "revelation is event *and* interpretation, encounter *and* truth, a Person *and* knowledge."[42]

Ramm arrived at this conclusion because of deep concern that evangelicals failed to respond appropriately to the Enlightenment, a failure that manifested itself in the fundamentalist/modernist controversy and more specifically in evangelical responses to higher criticism. Ramm was well aware of Van Til's and Henry's criticisms that Barth succumbed to modernism and so undermined Scripture's coherence and authority. He concurred that "Barth's thesis" about the Word of God "creates a *diastasis* (distance), an interval between the Word of God and the text of Holy Scripture." Ramm, however, saw Barth thinking Christologically about Scripture's divine-human ontology. Following Barth, he thought incarnationally at this point, as the revelatory Word of God must be discerned in the "culturally conditioned" human text through the process of interpretation.[43] What, then, might be the implications that follow from this diastasis for the inspiration and truthfulness of Scripture?

Geoffrey Bromiley

Geoffrey Bromiley had deep appreciation for Barth's theology, crediting him for retrieving the Bible's proper authority for theological discourse in the face of modern liberal theology and higher criticism. Bromiley praised Barth for ascribing Scripture's authority to God rather than human achievement, for "God Himself is the true source of authority in the things of God; Scripture is authoritative because it is divinely authorized by Him who is always both subject and object." [44] Nevertheless,

---

40. Bernard Ramm, *After Fundamentalism: The Future of Evangelical Theology* (San Francisco: Harper & Row, 1983), 92–94.

41. Bernard Ramm, *Special Revelation and the Word of God* (Grand Rapids: Eerdmans, 1961), 135, 161, 167.

42. Ibid., 159–60.

43. Ramm, *After Fundamentalism*, 89–94.

44. Geoffrey Bromiley, "The Authority of Scripture in Karl Barth," in *Hermeneutics, Authority, and Cannon*, ed. D. A. Carson and John D. Woodbridge (Grand Rapids: Zondervan, 1986), 292.

Bromiley raised several concerns about how Barth attempted to safeguard Scripture's authority, wondering whether he actually diminished it. Is the Bible "authoritative because God inspired it once and for all, or is it authoritative only ad hoc as God inspires it when heard or read?" Despite Barth's emphasis on the Holy Spirit speaking uniquely in Scripture and the necessity of approaching Scripture with reverence, Bromiley contended that Barth's "presentation leaves serious questions as to the scope, meaning, and solid objectivity of the authority that he proclaimed."[45]

Bromiley's dogmatic concern involved whether Barth's doctrine eclipsed past inspiration with an overemphasis on the present. To be sure, Barth's focus on "the present act of inspiring serves as a valuable reminder that God is no deistic or absentee God who has simply placed His authority elsewhere by a past act." This presentness reveals that the "divine author of the Bible is the living God, who as Spirit still speaks and rules in and through the written word." As such, the Bible is not a scientific textbook but "has unique authority precisely because its divine author Himself speaks through it to call, judge, enlighten, regenerate, and save."[46] Despite this presentness, Bromiley questioned whether the divine commands of Scripture, for example, "have any real authority unless God speaks through them." Compounding this question, "there may be no coincidence of the living voice of the Spirit and the permanent record of the commands," leveling biblical authority to that of church tradition.[47] Without continuity between God's past inspiration and present inspiring, what is implied about God's reliability to speak faithfully in the future or to make good in the present on promises made in Scripture?

Donald Bloesch

Donald Bloesch embraced Barth's doctrine of the Word of God, calling evangelicals to build their theology on "the living Word of God as apprehended by faith and interpreted by the church" in contrast with the "evangelical rationalism" of Carl F. H. Henry and the "existentialist theology" of Paul Tillich.[48] Bloesch followed Barth's distinction by affirming "the priority of revelation over Scripture and their indissoluble unity by the action of the Spirit." Hence, he championed God's sovereignty so that "he is free to speak his Word in his own way and time" along with "the primacy of biblical revelation over church tradition and religious experience and at the same time … the rightful place for historical investigation of Scripture."[49] Nevertheless,

---

45. Ibid., 291.
46. Ibid., 292–3.
47. Ibid., 292.
48. Donald Bloesch, *A Theology of Word and Spirit: Authority and Method in Theology*, Christian Foundations (Downers Grove: InterVarsity, 1992), 203, 251–53.
49. Donald Bloesch, "Karl Barth: Appreciation and Reservations," in *How Karl Barth Changed My Mind*, ed. Donald McKim (Grand Rapids: Eerdmans, 1986), 126–27. See also Bloesch, *Holy Scripture: Revelation, Inspiration, and Interpretation*, Christian Foundations (Downers Grove: IVP Academic, 1994), 177.

Bloesch demurred from Barth's Christological objectivism, the idea that the object of theological discourse is not "the relation of humanity to God in religious experience (as in Schleiermacher) but the relation of God to humanity in Jesus Christ," because Barth's "unmistakable objectivistic bent ... tends to undercut the necessity for personal faith and repentance." What might be the implications of human agency for participating in the kingdom of God?[50]

Beyond this demurral lay Bloesch's dogmatic concern for the doctrine of the Holy Spirit. Bloesch acknowledged that Barth's doctrine of the Word "expanded the role of the Spirit to include not only the subjective possibility of revelation but the vibrant reality of revelation as well."[51] Barth was adamant, though, "that the basis of faith lies outside of ourselves in God's self-revelation in Jesus Christ"—response to the gospel being one of recognition and obedience rather than faith and repentance, "basically ethical rather than soteriological in significance."[52] Bloesch saw faith as "correlative with God's self-revelation in Jesus Christ" and as "a work of the Spirit in the interiority of our being," so that "the truth of the gospel is not only announced from without but also confirmed from within" by the Spirit. This led Bloesch to a theology of Word and Spirit whereby "both revelation and salvation have to be understood as objective-subjective" rather than one or the other.[53] How, then, might Bloesch's notion of Word and Spirit affect evangelical hermeneutics and the pursuit of holiness?

The Strange New World of (Trinitarian) Theology

As American evangelicals wrestled with Barth's doctrine of the Word of God, the more they were confronted with questions concerning God's triune identity. No longer were questions being raised merely about Scripture's inspiration and truthfulness; rather, questions surfaced about how God's triunity *secures* Scripture's authority for making theological claims. Continuing to wrestle with Barth's doctrine challenged American evangelicals to foreground assumptions about God in relation to questions about Scripture's ontology, biblical interpretation, theological method, the role of tradition, and so forth—and thus, eventually, to go beyond Barth.

Among others, Kevin Vanhoozer has attempted to address the longstanding tension between Barth and American evangelicals. Drawing on Nicholas Wolterstorff's critique of Barth, Vanhoozer says that the crux of the matter lies between God's sovereign freedom (Barth) and fixed, propositional revelation (evangelicals). To resolve this "doctrinal standoff," Vanhoozer ministerially

---

50. Bloesch, "Karl Barth: Appreciation and Reservations," 128–9.

51. Donald Bloesch, *The Holy Spirit: Works and Gifts*, Christian Foundations (Downers Grove: InterVarsity, 2000), 277.

52. Bloesch, "Karl Barth: Appreciation and Reservations," 128.

53. Bloesch, *A Theology of Word and Spirit*, 15.

employs speech-act theory, which "pinpoints the crucial equivocation: does 'communication' (i.e. revelation) include the reader's response or not?" Vanhoozer avoids the either/or dichotomy implicit in the standoff in favor of a both/and: "the Bible has its *being* in its locutions and illocutions, yet the Bible *becomes* what it is when the illuminating Spirit ministers those locutions and illocutions in order to bring about the divinely intended perlocutionary effects." Barth reminds evangelicals of the importance of the Spirit's illumination in understanding Scripture—the perlocutionary effect—while evangelicals remind Barthians that understanding is inseparable from the verbal content of textual locutions and illocutions because God has freely and reliably tied himself to these texts.[54]

Vanhoozer juxtaposes Barth's Trinitarian theology of the Word with Wolterstorff's understanding of divine discourse, "to set forth an evangelical, gospel-centered account of the Trinity and Scripture."[55] He reflects on the significance Scripture gives to divine speech (e.g., Exodus 3, John 1, Hebrews 1) and expands our understanding of language beyond simply a medium to convey information. Rather, God "uses language not merely to inform but also to form and transform, permit and forbid, cajole and console." God speaking in and through Scripture, then, is not only about revelation but also about relationship, a covenant relationship whereby "the people of God gain understanding of who God is, who they are, what God is doing in the world and what they can do in order rightly to participate in the action."[56] Yet who is this God who speaks in such multivalent ways?

Since the economy "reflects" the immanent life of the Godhead, Vanhoozer concludes that God's being is in conversation as one "unified action with three dimensions." Not only does each of the three persons have speaking parts, but the persons also talk among themselves. Vanhoozer surmises that "this inner-trinitarian conversation is perfect: there is complete union, and thus communion, between the communicants, in glorious contrast to the incomplete and broken nature of most human communicative ventures."[57] While acknowledging that his communicative analogy treads on social and psychological analogies of the Trinity, he propounds a "rhetorical analogy" in line with the dogmatic tradition, while appropriating Aristotelian rhetorical categories so that "the Father takes responsibility for the ethos of discourse, the Son for the logos of discourse, and the Spirit for the pathos of discourse." Ethos relates, then, to the speaker's moral character, the logos to the message's form and content, and pathos to effects on hearers. Scripture is "a work of triune rhetoric whose purpose is to shape the church's identity and solicit the church's participation in God's being-in-conversation."

---

54. Kevin J. Vanhoozer, "A Person of the Book? Barth on Biblical Authority and Interpretation," in *Karl Barth and Evangelical Theology: Convergences and Divergences*, ed. Sung Wook Chung (Grand Rapids: Baker Academic, 2006), 55–9.

55. Vanhoozer, "Triune Discourse," 51.

56. Ibid., 51–4.

57. Ibid., 54–8.

Hence, Vanhoozer relocates Scripture from the usual locus of revelation into the broader "economy of triune communication" that embraces both revelation and redemption, concluding that "the Trinity is our Scripture Principle."[58] This interplay between the doctrines of the triune God and Scripture has contributed both to the development of the theological interpretation of Scripture and to intra-evangelical debates over classical theism and alternatives such as open theism.

One such example involves John Franke's conception of God as a relational plurality-in-unity and unity-in-plurality based on intratrinitarian love between the Father, the Son, and the Spirit. The reciprocal nature of this love as "expressed and received" binds the Father, Son, and Spirit together in unity and "in this sense, through all eternity, God is the social Trinity, the community of love."[59] God's love also characterizes his mission as he extends himself into the world (*missio Dei*), seen in the covenant with Israel, culminating in the life, death, and resurrection of Jesus Christ, and continuing through the Spirit who empowers the community of faith to embody the gospel in concrete witness. With this in mind, revelation "can be understood as an outworking of the mission of God in the accomplishment of this creative intention" to redeem and renew.[60] The missional character of revelation and his relational theism lead Franke to emphasize Scripture's pneumatological location within the triune economy—as an instrument of the Spirit to bring about new creation, with an eschatological realism involving participation in the divine fellowship of love.

Conclusion: Verbo crescent verba deficient

John Webster made an astute observation regarding the necessity to connect the "quantitative elements of biblical economy ... to their cause in the fullness of God's own life" in order to avoid emaciated theological discourse.[61] By engaging Barth's doctrine of the Word of God, American evangelicals found themselves amid the "strange new world" of Trinitarian theology that highlighted the interplay between God, Scripture, and hermeneutics. Thus, evangelical theology matured yet encountered new differences on how to "rightly divide the word of truth" (2 Tim. 2:15) even as the fundamentalist-modernist debates subsided. Accordingly, Webster's remarks offer sage advice, as these matters

---

58. Ibid., 51, 58–68, 76. See Kevin J. Vanhoozer, *Remythologizing Theology: Divine Action, Passion, and Authorship*, Cambridge Studies in Christian Doctrine (Cambridge: Cambridge University Press, 2010), 181–294, for a fuller post-Barthian, Thomistic account of God's being-in-communicative-action as "the one who lights and lives in love."

59. John R. Franke, *The Character of Theology: An Introduction to its Nature, Task, and Purpose* (Grand Rapids: Baker Academic, 2005), 65–7.

60. Ibid., 68–72.

61. John Webster, *The Domain of the Word: Scripture and Theological Reason* (London: T&T Clark, 2012), vii–viii.

can only be settled "metaphysically," that is, by working out what the text is, who we are as its interpreters and what ends we are to pursue as we read it. The core of such an account is, of course, the doctrine of the triune God, who alone is the *ratio essendi et cognoscendi* of all creatures; its near edge is Christian teaching about the resurrection of Jesus.[62]

Among other factors, evangelical engagement with Barth's doctrine of the Word of God brought such concerns to the forefront.

The crux of the conversation seems to hinge on the tension captured by the phrase, *finitum non capax infiniti*—the finite is incapable of containing the infinite. American evangelicals across the spectrum seem to agree that only God can resolve this tension, yet they diverge over how God does so. While Vanhoozer and Barth concur that the triune God speaks, Vanhoozer's account of God's speech goes beyond Barth's, not only expanding our understanding of language but also contending for the adequacy of finite human language for divine speaking. Such adequacy is rooted in the Incarnation because it checks our tendency to pit divine transcendence against human finitude. The Incarnation ultimately dissolves "the line between divine and discourse" since Jesus himself not only speaks human words but also quotes Scripture.[63] Does the Incarnation, though, *dissolve* the line between divine and discourse? It seems that the divine-human nature of the Incarnation, with its veiling and unveiling, is wrapped in *mystērion*, the revealing of the eternal secret of God—the unfathomable riches of divine love once hidden in the Word and now made known by the Spirit in Christ (Rom. 11:12-32; 1 Cor. 2:1-16; Eph. 3:3-10; Col. 1:24–2:5).[64] I wonder, then, if American evangelicals' understanding of God and Scripture would benefit by further contending with Barth's "divine incognito" as the One who was "made known as the Unknown, speaking in eternal silence."[65]

Pressing beyond Barth, this eternal silence and secrecy now revealed by God's speech act is not only what is made known in Scripture about the gospel of Christ and what is accomplished through his death and resurrection. The eternal God is revealed yet hidden in the "unsearchable riches" of Christ (Eph. 3:8-9) "in whom are hidden all the treasures of wisdom and knowledge" (Col. 2:3). These unsearchable riches of wisdom suggest, by way of the resurrection, the transfiguring of all things so that those who dwell in Christ by faith, strengthened by the Spirit, come "to know also the love of Christ which surpasses all knowledge; that you may be filled

---

62. Ibid., 33.
63. Vanhoozer, "Triune Discourse," 54.
64. See Markus Bockmuehl, *Revelation and Mystery in Ancient Judaism and Pauline Christianity* (Grand Rapids: Eerdmans, 1990); Louis Bouyer, *The Christian Mystery: From Pagan Myth to Christian Mysticism*, trans. Illtyd Trethowan (London: T&T Clark, 1990).
65. Karl Barth, *The Epistle to the Romans*, 6th ed., trans. Edwyn C. Hoskyns (Oxford: Oxford University Press, 1968), 98; cf. Barth, "The Speech of God as the Mystery of God," *CD* I/1, 162–86.

unto the fullness of God" (Eph. 3:16-19). Thus, "if the word was silent previously it is now, according to revelation, so rich and luxuriant (hyperbole, *perisseuein*) that further speech and utterance fails, and we are reduced to a knowledge of how greatly love surpasses knowledge." This self-giving, abundant love goes beyond thought into action, "not our own act but God's act in us."[66] Contemplation becomes integral to God's speech act, rooted in the intratrinitarian discourse of the Godhead. Christ maintains the vision of the Father as he carries out his mission, for the Son cannot *do* anything except for what he *sees* the Father doing (Jn 8:38; 15:19). This temporal interplay reflects the immanent life of the Trinity that "ever at rest and at work, ever beholds itself and continues the missions within the Godhead." As such, "Christ's contemplation consists in his being the Word of the *Father*, his action in his being the *Word* of the Father" that culminates in his passion. These normative movements of action and contemplation by Word and Spirit form the pattern in which the Christian life participates to make contemplation and action "interpenetrate more and more."[67]

Such active contemplation and contemplative action regarding the unsearchable riches of Christ evoke awe and wonder, a "seeing" in the midst of "hearing and doing." Theological interpretation of Scripture becomes a sanctifying practice of encountering the resurrected Christ in the Spirit, part of what Barth calls a "rational wrestling with the mystery." [68] Scripture's ontology is seen more as *sacramentum*, moving interpreters beyond mere textual-historical interrogation to sapiential performance *in actione contemplativus*, the fruitfulness of which is a subversive, counterintuitive existence in church and world. Such existence seeks to resist capitulating to the machinations of any ideology and to heal the alienation so prevalent today.[69] In the end, as the Word of God increases, our words decrease (Jn 3:30), ushering us into the eternal silence of the awe-ful love of the Father, Son, and Spirit that surpasses all knowledge.

---

66. Hans Urs von Balthasar, "The Word and Silence," in *The Word Made Flesh*, trans. A. V. Littledale with Alexander Dru, vol. 1, *Explorations in Theology* (San Francisco: Ignatius, 1989), 145–6.

67. Hans Urs von Balthasar, "Action and Contemplation," in *The Word Made Flesh*, 234.

68. Barth, *CD* I/1, 368.

69. See Willie James Jennings, *The Christian Imagination: Theology and the Origins of Race* (New Haven: Yale University Press, 2011) and my visual commentary on Jn 15:1-17, "Subversive Horticulture" in the *Visual Commentary of Scripture*. Available online: https://thevcs.org/subversive-horticulture (accessed February 19, 2021).

Part III

THEODRAMA TODAY

Chapter 13

BAPTIZED BIBLICAL INTERPRETATION: THE PLACE AND FUNCTION OF THE CREED

Scott R. Swain

Introduction

What has baptism to do with biblical interpretation? The question does not concern how various views of the nature and proper subjects of baptism inform our hermeneutical perspectives—though that is an interesting question in its own right! The question concerns how being baptized in God's triune name (Mt. 28:19) might make us more fluent readers of divine discourse in Holy Scripture. What promise does baptism hold for biblical interpretation?

Patristic, medieval, and Protestant orthodox interpreters of Scripture agreed that the creed confessed by believers in baptism or, in the case of those baptized in infancy, as a consequence of baptism provided the Christian with a proper orientation and framework not only for the Christian life but also for the interpretation of Holy Scripture. More recent interpreters have been less sanguine about the promise of the church's baptismal creed for biblical interpretation.

The worries are numerous. Some worry that the creed imposes unwarranted constraints on the Enlightenment ideal of free and rational inquiry vis-à-vis the biblical text.[1] The creed limits the interpreter's freedom. Others, less concerned with preserving Enlightenment ideals, nevertheless worry that the creed allows later ecclesiastical developments to guide biblical interpretation rather than the historical, literary, and theological categories of the Bible itself.[2] The creed threatens to distort the interpreter's perspective. Both worries express a deeper, underlying concern that the creed unduly predetermines interpretive conclusions.[3] The creed

---

1. John Barton, "Historical-critical Approaches," in *The Cambridge Companion to Biblical Interpretation*, ed. John Barton (Cambridge: Cambridge Unviersity Press, 1998), 16–19.

2. D. A. Carson, "Systematic Theology and Biblical Theology," in *New Dictionary of Biblical Theology*, ed. Desmond Alexander and Brian Rosner (Downers Grove: InterVarsity, 2000), 89–104.

3. William Wrede, "The Task and Methods of 'New Testament Theology,'" in *The Nature of New Testament Theology*, ed. Robert Morgan (London: SCM, 1973), 69.

blocks us from discovering the meaning of the biblical text and thus from realizing the goal of biblical interpretation, that is, understanding.

As we will see more fully below, the first two worries are fairly easily addressed. The creed is not a constraint on our freedom. The creed is an expression of "evangelical freedom," the freedom for which Christ has set us free (Gal. 5:1). The creed is the free confession of faith evoked by God's gracious work in and through the gospel. Moreover, the creed, far from distorting scriptural teaching, is a faithful summary of divine discourse in Holy Scripture and a means of embracing the One who addresses us therein. For these reasons, the creed has a key role to play in biblical interpretation.

The third worry, however, expresses a legitimate concern that is not always accounted for in recent approaches to creedal biblical interpretation.[4] Does the creed unduly predetermine interpretive conclusions? Preunderstanding cannot, indeed should not, be avoided in biblical interpretation. But there are helpful and unhelpful preunderstandings. There are those that we should embrace because they dispose us to discerning the meaning of Scripture; and there are those that we should avoid because they foreclose a faithful hearing of God's Word, turning the act of interpretation into mere reflection of what we already know, mere repetition of judgments we only seek to confirm in our "readings" of Scripture.[5] The burden of the proponent of baptized biblical interpretation is to show how the creed informs a helpful preunderstanding for interpreting divine discourse in Holy Scripture.

What follows is a theological account of baptized biblical interpretation that seeks to address the first two concerns, while avoiding the problem rightly identified in the third concern. First, we will consider the place of the church's baptismal creed in relation to Scripture. Second, we will consider the function of the creed in interpreting Scripture.

The Place of the Creed in Relation to Divine Discourse in Holy Scripture

Gospel, Baptism, Faith, and Confession

In Rom. 6:17-18, Paul interrupts his larger argument regarding baptism and the moral implications of the gospel with an outburst of gratitude: "But thanks be to

---

4. The proposal of the late Robert W. Jenson, for all its brilliance, raises an eyebrow precisely at this point. By identifying the creed as the Christian "critical theory" for interpreting Scripture, Jenson introduces a tension between the creed and the plain sense of Scripture, suggesting that the creed is necessary for discerning what is and is not admissible from Scripture. See Robert W. Jenson, *Canon and Creed* (Louisville: Westminster John Knox, 2010), ch. 9, esp. p. 81.

5. Healthy preunderstanding poses "questions" to the text that it hopes *the text* will "answer" at the conclusion of the interpretive "quest." Unhealthy preunderstanding poses "questions" that contain their "answers" *within the questions themselves* before embarking on the interpretive "quest" (Jean-Yves Lacoste, "More Haste, Less Speed in Theology," *IJST* 9, no. 3 [2007]: 273).

God, that you who were once slaves of sin have become obedient from the heart to the pattern of teaching to which you were committed, and, having been set free from sin, have become slaves of righteousness" (ESV, alt.). Paul's exclamation celebrates God's grace. In this case, Paul is not celebrating the grace expressed in God's eternal purpose of salvation before the ages began (Eph. 1:4-6; 2 Tim. 1:9). Nor is he celebrating the grace expressed in God's accomplishment of salvation in the incarnation, death, resurrection, and enthronement of Jesus Christ as Lord at his right hand (2 Cor. 8:9; Gal. 2:20; Eph. 1:19-23). In Rom. 6:17-18, Paul is celebrating the grace expressed in God's application of salvation to elect sinners: the grace poured out in the Holy Spirit, announced in the preaching of the gospel, and applied in the rite of baptism. These graces too are occasions for awe, wonder, and gratitude: "Thanks be to God."

These divine graces are occasions for gratitude because by them God has brought the Roman Christians into a state of evangelical freedom. Those "who were once slaves of sin" have been "set free from sin." The outpouring of the Spirit, the preaching of the gospel, and baptism have brought about freedom *from* the tyranny of sin and, as Paul will elaborate in the next chapter, freedom from the tyranny of sin as experienced under the conditions of the Mosaic law (Rom. 7:1-6).

According to the apostle, evangelical freedom involves more than freedom from the sinful "powers that oppress our agency"; evangelical freedom has a positive form as well.[6] Evangelical freedom is freedom *for* life with the triune God. Through baptism, we have been transferred from the thralldom of sin, its fruitless ways, and its deadly end into the kingdom of God's beloved Son and into a fruitful life of righteousness and sanctification whose end is eternal life (Rom. 6:21-23). Being set free from the bondage of sin brings with it being bound in covenant to the triune God.[7] Thus, Paul describes our relationship to our new Lord in covenantal terms of marriage (Rom. 7:4) and our relationship to our new God in covenantal terms of adoption (Rom. 8:14-17).

In order to appreciate fully the shape of evangelical freedom brought about by God's grace in baptism and the new covenant bond that is formed thereby, we must consider another feature of Paul's thanksgiving in Rom. 6:17-18, namely, the relationship between divine and human action. In the act of baptism, we are passive. We have *been* baptized (Rom. 6:2); we *were* committed or "handed over" to something or someone in the act of baptism (Rom. 6:17). The significance of our passive reception of the rite of baptism is not to be missed. One can no more baptize oneself than one can save oneself: *God's* gracious agency, in and through baptism, effects evangelical freedom, binding us to himself through the Son and by the Spirit. That said, the divine grace that is active in and through baptism does

---

6. Oliver O'Donovan, *Entering into Rest: Ethics as Theology, Vol. 3* (Grand Rapids: Eerdmans, 2017), 8.

7. The movement of freedom *from* slavery *into* covenant echoes the movement of the first exodus narrated in Exodus 1-24, where Exodus 1-18 narrates Israel's emancipation from slavery and Exodus 19-24 narrates Israel's covenantal engagement with God.

not operate in contrast to or in competition with human agency.[8] The divine grace that is operative in and through baptism awakens human agency.[9] This agency, in turn, has both subjective and objective poles: You "have become obedient from the heart to the standard of teaching to which you were committed."

Paul describes the subjective pole of evangelical freedom as an act of "obedience," a "harkening" that proceeds "from the heart." No doubt an allusion to OT promises regarding the new covenant (e.g., Deut. 30:6; Jer. 31:33; Ezek. 36:26-27), Paul's language also reflects his earlier statement regarding the purpose of his apostolic mission: "to bring about the obedience of faith" (Rom. 1:5). Corresponding to the subjective pole of evangelical freedom, Paul describes the objective pole of evangelical freedom as a "pattern," "standard," or "outline" of teaching. The obedience of faith, according to Paul, is not a general attitude of trust or credulity. The obedience of faith, according to Paul, has an object.

What is the object of faith, the "pattern of teaching" to which the Roman Christians were handed over in baptism? It cannot be something delivered by Paul to the Roman Christians since he had not met them and he did not baptize them (Rom. 1:8-15). The pattern of teaching, then, must be something known to both the apostle and the Roman Christians. Based upon the broader context of Romans in particular, as well as broader patterns of apostolic preaching in general, we may surmise that the pattern of teaching is closely related to the gospel itself, "which Paul believed to be common to himself and other Christian missionaries."[10] This is how Basil understands Rom. 6:17. In baptism, the baptizand is handed over "to the mold of doctrine according to the Gospel."[11] In Paul's case, this mold has a Trinitarian, Christological shape.

In Rom. 10:8-9, Paul says "the word of faith" that he "proclaims" calls for faith in the heart and confession on the lips. The object of evangelical faith and confession, according to Paul, is "that Jesus is Lord" and "that God raised him from the dead." That Christological claims such as these belong to the "pattern of teaching" to which Christians are handed over in baptism fits well with the context of Romans 6, where the apostle ties what the Roman Christians already know about baptism to Christ's death and resurrection and to the free gift of eternal life in Jesus Christ our Lord. This understanding of the "pattern of teaching" is consistent, furthermore,

---

8. The language of non-contrastive, noncompetitive divine agency is Kathryn Tanner's, from *God and Creation in Christian Theology: Tyranny or Empowerment?* (Minneapolis: Fortress, 2005).

9. On the passive/active dynamics of baptism and their implications for the Christian life, see Grant Macaskill, *Living in Union with Christ: Paul's Gospel and Christian Moral Identity* (Grand Rapids: Baker Academic, 2019), ch. 3.

10. C. H. Dodd, *The Apostolic Preaching and its Developments: Three Lectures with an Appendix on Eschatology and History* (New York: Harper, 1949), 17.

11. Basil, *On Baptism*, 1.2, in *Saint Basil: Ascetical Works*, trans. M. Monica Wagner, The Fathers of the Church: A New Translation (Washington, DC: Catholic University of America Press, 1950), 358.

with Paul's initial summary of his apostolic gospel in Rom. 1:1-6 that, among other things, proclaims Jesus Christ as a crucified and risen Lord (1 Cor. 15:1-3).

Romans 1:1-6 suggests yet another element for inclusion in the apostolic "pattern of teaching." The central subject matter of the gospel, according to Paul, is Jesus' identity as God's "Son" (Rom. 1:2; 8:29, 32). The gospel that Paul proclaims not only announces Jesus' Davidic lineage, death, resurrection, lordly enthronement at God's right hand, and future coming as judge—all in fulfillment of the OT Scriptures.[12] The gospel that Paul proclaims also identifies Jesus by his relation to God his Father,[13] an identification consistent with broader apostolic patterns of baptismal teaching (Mt. 28:19; 1 Cor. 6:11; Eph. 4:4-6; Tit. 3:4-7) and with Jesus' identification as God's Son at his baptism (Mt. 3:17; Mk 1:11; Lk. 3:22; Jn 1:24).

This brings us back to Rom. 6:17-18. The object of evangelical faith and confession is not only Jesus as Lord: born, crucified, risen, enthroned, and coming again. The object of evangelical faith and confession is also Jesus as God's Son and God as Father—specifically, God as the Father of our Lord Jesus Christ (Rom. 15:6) and God as our Father through Spirit-endowed union and communion with Jesus Christ, God's Son: "For all who are led by the Spirit of God are sons of God. For you did not receive the spirit of slavery to fall back into fear, but you have received the Spirit of adoption as sons, by whom we cry, 'Abba! Father!'" (Rom. 8:14-15). If the preceding line of argument is correct, then the "pattern of teaching" associated with baptism—the object of the Christian's baptismal faith and confession—has both a Christological and a Trinitarian shape. By the Spirit, baptized persons confess, "Jesus is Lord." By the Spirit, baptized persons call upon God as "Father."[14] In doing so, baptized persons exhibit obedience from the heart to the pattern of teaching to which they have been delivered in baptism. "Thanks be to God" (Rom. 6:17).

We conclude our discussion of gospel, baptism, faith, and confession in Paul observing that, in addition to freedom *from* sin and freedom *for* life in covenant fellowship with the triune God, evangelical freedom also includes freedom to confess faith in the triune God *with* others. The form of agency awakened by the Spirit through the gospel and baptism is a shared form of agency.[15] Evangelical freedom is fully realized when "with one voice" we "glorify the God and Father of our Lord Jesus Christ" (Rom. 15:6), when we join our voices "with all those who in every place call upon the name of our Lord Jesus Christ, both their Lord and ours"

---

12. Dodd, *Apostolic Preaching*, 17.

13. Wesley Hill, *Paul and the Trinity: Persons, Relations, and the Pauline Letters* (Grand Rapids: Eerdmans, 2015).

14. Note the close connection between the Spirit, confessing Jesus as Lord, and baptism in 1 Cor. 12:3 and 12:13, and between the Spirit, calling upon God as Father, and baptism in Gal. 3:27 and 4:6.

15. "To be free is not merely to *have* an agent's point of view on the world, but to *share* one" (Oliver O'Donovan, *Finding and Seeking: Ethics as Theology, Vol. 2* [Grand Rapids: Eerdmans, 2014], 61).

(1 Cor. 1:2). Authentic Christian confession—awakened by the Spirit through the preaching of the gospel and baptism (1 Cor. 12:3; Gal. 4:6)—is a *Trinitarian, Christological, shared* confession.

Traditio and Redditio: The Rule of Faith and the Creed

In Paul's grateful astonishment at what God had accomplished in and among the Roman Christians through baptism, we have traced a train of thought involving four elements: gospel, baptism, faith, and confession. Moreover, we have seen that gospel and baptism, along with the obedient faith and confession they elicit, exhibit a Trinitarian and Christological pattern. Had we opportunity, we could trace similar trains of thought in other NT writings. Instead we must look beyond the NT era to consider ways these four elements, along with analogous Trinitarian and Christological patterns, are received and transmitted in early Christian preaching and catechesis.

At a synodical gathering in Hippo in 393, Augustine, recently ordained as a priest, delivered a lecture to the gathered bishops on a (for us unidentifiable) baptismal creed. Augustine opens his lecture stating that the apostolic faith "makes demands on both our tongues and our hearts," citing Rom. 10:10. The apostolic faith, though "vast," is well summarized in the "few words" of the baptismal creed. The creed is useful, Augustine argues, for accomplishing a number of ends: from catechizing beginners, to refuting "the deceitful cleverness of heretics," to leading the mature into a deeper understanding of the faith. Almost in passing, Augustine refers to the ancient practice of "handing on" the apostolic faith to new converts (*traditio*) who, in turn, "recite" the faith back in their baptismal creed (*redditio*).[16] This practice of *traditio* and *redditio* provides a meaningful context for appreciating the place of gospel, baptism, faith, and confession in early Christian preaching and catechesis.

For Augustine and other church fathers, the authority of the Lord himself, voiced in the prophetic and apostolic Scriptures and preserved by faithful bishops and presbyters, guarantees the validity of the Trinitarian faith received, handed on, and recited in early Christian summaries of faith.[17] According to Athanasius, the Lord laid "the foundation of the Church" when he commissioned the apostles

---

16. Augustine, *Faith and the Creed*, 1.1 in *On Christian Belief*, WSA, 155.

17. Irenaeus, *Against Heresies*, 1.9.4; 1.10.1-2; 3.1.1; 3.2.1-2 in ANF 1 (reprint Grand Rapids: Eerdmans, 1996), 330–1, 414–15; Clement of Alexandria, *Strom.* 7.15–16 in ANF 2 (Grand Rapids: Eerdmans, 1951), 549–54; Athanasius, *Letters to Serapion*, 1.28.1 in *Works on the Holy Spirit: Athanasius the Great and Didymus the Blind* (Yonkers, NY: St Vladimir's Seminary, 2011), 96; Augustine, *Enchiridion on Faith, Hope, and Charity*, 1.4–5 in *On Christian Belief*, 274–5; Augustine, *On Christian Doctrine*, 3.2.2 in NPNF 2 (reprint Grand Rapids: Eerdmans, 1993), 556–7. For discussion of the function of church leadership in preserving apostolic teaching, see Jenson, *Canon and Creed*, ch. 8; Carl R. Trueman, *The Creedal Imperative* (Wheaton: Crossway, 2012).

to baptize the nations in the triune name.[18] Basil too cites dominical warrant for the Trinitarian faith handed down in baptism, quoting Mt. 28:19: "Our baptism accords with exactly what the Lord handed down: it is in the name of the Father, and of the Son, and of the Holy Spirit."[19] For these fathers, "The Lord and the Scriptures"[20] guarantee the Trinitarian faith's status as genuine "tradition"—the social and historical transmission of apostolic truth (1 Cor. 15:1-3; 2 Tim. 1:13-14; 2:2), as opposed to mere "custom"—the social and historical repetition of habits inherited from our ancestors (1 Pet. 1:18).[21] According to Irenaeus, this is precisely what Gnostic summaries of faith lack: they were not announced by the prophets, taught by the Lord, or handed down by the apostles.[22]

Grounded in dominical authority, expressed in Holy Scripture, and preserved by faithful leaders, *traditio* and *redditio* identify the dual drumbeat of early Christian preaching and catechesis, the "call" and "response" of the gospel announced in preaching, sealed in baptism, and received and confessed by the faithful. Identifying these two moments helps us better appreciate some of the distinctions, commonalities, and relationships between two primary forms of early Christian preaching and catechesis, namely, the rule of faith and the creed.

According to Everett Ferguson, the distinction between rule of faith and baptismal creed follows the distinction between *traditio* and *redditio*. "The rule of faith summarized the preaching and teaching of the evangelists and teachers in the church, that is, the objective faith of the church; and the baptismal confession was the faith professed by candidates at baptism, which was the subjective acceptance of, and identification with, the gospel that had been taught."[23] The distinct functions of rule of faith and baptismal creed in early Christian "call" and "response" also explain the different forms they take. While the rule of faith tends to appear in flexible forms within and across various patristic authors, the baptismal creed, though initially exhibiting a degree of diversity, developed in a more fixed direction in order to serve the liturgical, doctrinal, and polemical advantages of having a shared confession of faith.[24]

These distinctions notwithstanding, various forms of the rule of faith and the baptismal creed evince common "building blocks," quarried from Holy Scripture.

---

18. Athanasius, *Letters to Serapion*, 1.28.4 in *Works on the Holy Spirit*, 97.

19. Basil, *Against Eunomius*, 3.5 in *Saint Basil of Caesarea against Eunomius*, The Fathers of the Church: A New Translation (Washington, DC: Catholic University of America Press, 2011), 192.

20. Tomas Bokedal, *The Formation of the Christian Biblical Canon: A Study in Text, Ritual and Interpretation* (London: Bloomsbury Academic, 2014).

21. Cyprian: "Custom without truth is the antiquity of error" ("Epistle 73," 9 in ANF 5 [Grand Rapids: Eerdmans, 1951], 386).

22. Irenaeus, *Against Heresies*, 1.8.1.

23. Everett Ferguson, *The Rule of Faith: A Guide* (Eugene, OR: Cascade, 2015), 67-8.

24. Ferguson, *Rule of Faith*, 39, 68; Wolfram Kinzig and Markus Vinzent, "Recent Research on the Origin of the Creed," *JTS* 50 (1999): 535-59.

Binitarian and Trinitarian patterns, drawn from texts such as 1 Cor. 8:6 and Mt. 28:19, often structure both forms. Furthermore, especially in their second and third articles, various forms of the rule of faith and the baptismal creed contain elements drawn from the basic outline of apostolic preaching summarized in Scripture. These elements include Jesus' conception and birth, death, burial, resurrection, ascension and enthronement, and second coming, as well as promises of forgiveness of sins, resurrection of the body, and eternal life.[25] The Trinitarian and Christological teaching of Scripture provides the basic building blocks of the rule of faith and the baptismal creed.

These two patristic forms of "handing on" and "confessing" the apostolic faith may thus be regarded as "biblical" in two senses. The *acts* of handing on and confessing the faith themselves follow from the Lord's command in the prophetic and apostolic Scriptures. Moreover, the *building blocks* of which these forms are composed derive from the Scriptures as well. *Traditio* and *redditio* in rule of faith and baptismal creed are *scripturally prescribed actions* performed with *scripturally derived content*.[26] We will return to this observation below.

We should also note that the tendency toward a fixed form of baptismal creed, a tendency that enters a new stage of development in the production and eventual ecumenical reception of the Nicene Creed, is a fitting application of the apostolic ideal of confessing the faith "with one voice" (Rom. 15:6).[27] The catholic confession of the Trinitarian and Christological faith proclaimed in the Scriptures fulfills a deep evangelical impulse: that all those in every place would call upon the name of the Lord (1 Cor. 1:2).

Scripture and Creed: God's "Yes" and the Church's "Amen"

We have identified four elements that belong in a theological account of the relationship between Scripture and creed: gospel and baptism, faith and confession. We have also indicated the biblical bases of these four elements. The presence of scriptural mandate and the possession of scriptural building blocks, however, do not fully establish what it means to say that these processes and products of apostolic and ecclesiastical tradition are biblical. In order to establish fully the biblical bona fides of these four elements, we must address the question: What is the "whole" that gives fuller biblical meaning to these various "parts"? What is the scripturally inspired "score" that turns these four "notes" into a fitting hymn of

---

25. Dodd, *Apostolic Preaching*; Ferguson, *Rule of Faith*, 34–5; Kinzig and Vinzent, "Recent Research," 547, 555–6.

26. According to the Leiden Synopsis, the Apostles' Creed is among the traditions "that are found in the sacred writings" "by virtue of *isodunamia* or equivalence, being of the same kind, and in harmony with Holy Scripture" (Dolf te Velde, ed., *Synopsis Purioris Theologiae*, Latin Text and English Translation, Vol. 1: Disputations 1–23 [Leiden: Brill, 2015], 4.26, 29).

27. The Council of Chalcedon (451) uses the Pauline language "with one voice" to confess its agreement with the faith of Nicaea.

praise to God? Addressing this question will complete our theological account of the place of the creed in relation to divine discourse in Holy Scripture and lay the foundation for our discussion of the function of the creed in biblical interpretation.

Irenaeus criticized the Gnostics for their atomistic use of biblical teaching. According to Irenaeus, Gnostics used biblical terms, and even performed biblically prescribed motions,[28] but they used those terms and performed those motions within a manifestly unbiblical framework of meaning and action. The Bishop of Lyon offers two illustrations that help us appreciate the importance of relating biblical parts to the larger biblical whole. In one illustration, he compares Gnostics to persons who fabricate stories by rearranging Homeric verses. Such persons take Homeric verses out of their original literary context and place them within a literary "hypothesis" of their own construction.[29] The result is a new story with new characters, with lines originally spoken by one Homeric character being put into the mouth of another.[30] In another illustration, Irenaeus compares Gnostics to persons who transform the image of a handsome king into the image of a dog or a fox.[31]

According to Irenaeus, anyone well acquainted with the Scriptures will recognize Gnostic stories for what they are: fabrications.[32]

Clement of Alexandria offers a similar illustration, in his case drawn from music, to identify the unifying principle of the prophetic and apostolic Scriptures. Clement locates "the concord and harmony" of "the law and the prophets, and the apostles along with the Gospel" in "the *covenant* delivered at the coming of the Lord."[33] As we saw above, Paul uses covenant language to describe conversion (obedience from the heart) and covenant imagery to portray our relation to God in Christ (adoption, marriage). Following Clement's observation and Paul's example, I suggest that the concept of "covenant" provides a fitting score within which the various notes of gospel, baptism, faith, and confession achieve "concord and harmony" with the dual drumbeat of *traditio* and *redditio*.

Covenant is a theme of architectonic significance in Holy Scripture. God relates to human beings through various covenants, such as the Abrahamic, Mosaic

---

28. The Gnostics also performed baptisms (Irenaeus, *Against Heresies*, 1.23.5).

29. In classical rhetoric, the term "hypothesis" described the overarching "plot or outline of a drama or epic" (John Behr, *The Way to Nicaea*, The Formation of Christian Theology, vol. 1 [Crestwood, NY: St Vladimir's Seminary, 2001], 32).

30. Irenaeus, *Against Heresies*, 1.9.4.

31. Ibid., 1.8.1.

32. John Behr describes the difference between Irenaeus's rule of faith and the Gnostics' hypotheses: "Irenaeus' appeal to tradition is thus fundamentally different to that of his opponents. While they appealed to tradition precisely for that which was not in Scripture, Irenaeus, in his appeal to tradition, was not appealing to anything that was not also in Scripture" (Behr, *Way to Nicaea*, 45).

33. Clement of Alexandria, *Strom.* 6.11; 6.15 in ANF 2 (Grand Rapids: Eerdmans, 1951), 499–502, 506–11.

Davidic, and new covenants. The Father makes covenant promises to the Son (Psalms 2, 110; Gal. 3:16) and appoints the Son as Mediator of the new covenant (Heb. 9:15; 12:24), bringing all covenant promises to fulfillment in and through him (1 Cor. 1:20). God issues covenant commands and makes covenant promises to his people, above all, promising to be their God (Gen. 17:7-8; Lev. 26:12; 2 Cor. 6:18; Rev. 21:3, 7). In turn, God calls his people to covenant loyalty and obedience and, in response to God's call, his people pledge their covenant allegiance to God (Gen. 4:26; 12:8; Exod. 19:8; 24:7; Isa. 44:3-5; Joel 2:32; Rom. 10:13).

Divine discourse in Holy Scripture is covenantal discourse. Covenant is how God does things with words. Moreover, as Kevin J. Vanhoozer argues, Scripture as a whole may be understood as God's covenantal speech act aimed at accomplishing a covenantal end, namely, union and communion between God and his people through the gospel of Jesus Christ.[34] God in Scripture promises, "I will be a Father to you, and you shall be sons and daughters to me, says the Lord Almighty" (2 Cor. 6:18), and this promise, like all God's promises, finds its "Yes" in Jesus Christ (2 Cor. 1:20; Gal. 4:4-7).

Furthermore, God employs covenantal means in bringing about his covenantal end. Those means include preaching, baptism, faith, and confession. William Perkins explains,

> The means of applying God's blessings and graces unto man are twofold: some respect God himself and some respect man. Those which respect God are such whereby God, on his part, offers and conveys his mercies in Christ unto man. Of this sort are the preaching of the Word, baptism, and the Lord's Supper—and these are as it were the hand of God whereby he reaches down and gives unto us Christ with all his benefits. The other means of applying on man's part are those whereby the said benefits are received. Of this sort, there is only one, namely faith, whereby we believe that Christ, with all his benefits, belongs unto us. And that is the hand of man whereby he receives Christ as he is offered or exhibited by God in his Word and sacraments.[35]

In preaching and baptism, the *traditio* of Christian ministry, God utters his covenantal "Yes" to his people. In faith and confession, the *redditio* of the church, God's people utter their covenantal "Amen to God for his glory" (2 Cor. 1:20). This, then, is the place of the creed in relation to divine discourse in Holy Scripture: The creed is the "Amen" of God's covenant people that answers to God's covenant "Yes"

---

34. Kevin J. Vanhoozer, "From Speech Acts to Scripture Acts: The Covenant of Discourse and the Discourse of the Covenant," in *After Pentecost: Language and Biblical Interpretation*, ed. Craig Bartholomew, Colin Greene, and Karl Möller (Grand Rapids: Zondervan, 2001), ch. 1.

35. William Perkins, *A Reformed Catholic*, in *The Works of William Perkins, Vol. 7* (Grand Rapids: Reformation Heritage, 2019), 58-9.

in Jesus Christ as testified in Scripture, proclaimed in the gospel, and sealed in baptism.

This, at last, is what it means to say that gospel, baptism, faith, and confession are biblical. Understood within a covenant framework, gospel and baptism (*traditio*), along with faith and confession (*redditio*), may be understood as scripturally authorized *means* of conveying and embracing scripturally authorized *truth*—Christ himself clothed with the promises of the gospel—for a scripturally authorized *end*: covenant union and communion between God and his people. In terms of Irenaeus's analogy of the handsome king, the Trinitarian and Christological "pattern of teaching," derived from Scripture and summarized in rule of faith and baptismal creed, *frames* the scriptural portrait of the handsome king (Prov. 25:11). The preaching of the gospel and baptism *convey* the handsome king. The church, by her faith and confession, *embraces—kisses*—the handsome king (Song 1:2).

The Function of the Creed in the Interpretation of Divine Discourse in Holy Scripture

Having located the creed relative to Scripture within the divine economy of covenant discourse, it is time to address briefly the function of the creed in the interpretation of Holy Scripture. As we will see, the creed functions as an introduction—but *only* as an introduction—to the interpretation of Scripture.

The Creed as Introduction to Holy Scripture

As the church's "Amen" to God's "Yes" uttered in Scripture and conveyed in gospel and baptism, the creed is a fitting entryway to interpreting divine discourse in Holy Scripture.[36] The creed serves as an introduction to biblical interpretation in at least four ways.

First, because its teaching derives from Scripture, the creed *identifies Scripture's primary ascriptive subject*, the "three-personed God" (John Donne).[37] Learning to identify the primary ascriptive subject of Scripture is essential if interpreters are to get beyond observing mere "features" in the text to perceiving the "face" of the handsome king who reveals himself therein.[38] Second, the creed *summarizes*

---

36. For ways in which a "hypothesis" functioned as a "first principle" of inquiry in ancient philosophy and later in patristic biblical interpretation, see Behr, *Way to Nicaea*, 31–40.

37. Jenson, *Canon and Creed*, 45. The scribal practice of using "*nomina sacra*" fulfills a similar function in this regard. See Bokedal, *Formation and Significance*, ch. 3.

38. Rowan Williams describes certain characteristically modern approaches to knowing on analogy with patients who have suffered brain injuries that "leave people with the capacity to recognize features but not faces" (*Being Human: Bodies, Minds, Persons* [Grand Rapids: Eerdmans, 2018], 54). Certain characteristically modern approaches to biblical

Scripture's plan of salvation (cf. Eph. 1:10). The creed relays what Irenaeus calls "the order and connection of the Scriptures" concerning "the operation and dispensation of God connected with human salvation."[39] Third, the creed *sets boundaries for interpretation*. The prophetic and apostolic writings set a boundary on what the church may and may not believe, do, and say and therefore upon what the reader may and may not expect to discover in the process of scriptural interpretation (Deut. 4:2; 12:32; Rev. 22:18-19).[40] As a summary of the prophetic and apostolic writings, the creed identifies the main boundaries set by the plain sense of biblical teaching, guarding interpreters from heretical conclusions.[41]

The creed did not fall ready-made from the sky. The creed is the product of an *interpretive tradition* and can only be fully appreciated in that light.[42] This is not merely about the creed's historical development but also a pedagogical point. As the product of a culture of scriptural interpretation,[43] fourth, the creed *identifies certain interpretive skills that we must acquire to become competent readers of the biblical text* (Heb. 5:11-6:2). Those skills include "prosopological exegesis" (the ability to identify properly unnamed speech agents within the text, especially the persons of the Trinity),[44] "partitive exegesis" (the ability to distinguish and relate the Son's two natures and modes of action),[45] and "figural exegesis" (the ability to relate properly the persons, institutions, and events of the OT to the persons, institutions, and events announced in the apostolic gospel).[46] The creed identifies some of the fundamental elements of a well-formed hermeneutical curriculum.

---

interpretation suffer a similar malady. Attention to the creed could well aid in recovering from this hermeneutical affliction.

39. Irenaeus, *Against Heresies*, 1.8.1; 1.10.3.

40. On this "canonical principle," see Bokedal, *Formation and Significance*, 292-5.

41. Augustine, *On Christian Doctrine*, 3.2.2; Ferguson, *Rule of Faith*, 77-80.

42. Khaled Anatolios, *Retrieving Nicaea: The Development and Meaning of Trinitarian Doctrine* (Grand Rapids: Baker Academic, 2011), 1, 11, 33-5.

43. As Kevin J. Vanhoozer observes, this culture of interpretation is at work *within* Scripture, going back to the Lord himself and his apostles, before it is at work *on* Scripture in the interpretation of the early church (*The Drama of Doctrine: A Canonical-Linguistic Approach to Christian Theology* [Louisville: Westminster John Knox, 2005], 194-7).

44. Matthew W. Bates, *The Birth of the Trinity: Jesus, God, and Spirit in New Testament and Early Christian Interpretations of the Old Testament* (Oxford: Oxford University Press, 2015); Madison N. Pierce, *Divine Discourse in the Epistle to the Hebrews: The Recontextualization of Spoken Quotations of Scripture* (Cambridge: Cambridge University Press, 2020).

45. John Behr, *The Nicene Faith, Part One: True God of True God*, The Formation of Christian Theology: Vol. 2 (Crestwood, NY: St Vladimir's Seminary, 2004), 208-15; R. B. Jamieson, "1 Corinthians 15:28 and the Grammar of Paul's Christology," *NTS* 66 (2020): 187-207.

46. John J. O'Keefe and R. R. Reno, *Sanctified Vision: An Introduction to Early Christian Interpretation of the Bible* (Baltimore: Johns Hopkins University Press, 2005); Richard B. Hays, *Echoes of Scripture in the Gospels* (Waco: Baylor University Press, 2016); Matthew

Only an Introduction: Reading in Faith, Love, and Hope

While the creed serves as a fitting introduction to biblical interpretation, informing the right kind of preunderstanding for engaging divine discourse in Holy Scripture, the creed is *only* an introduction to biblical interpretation. The faith expressed in the creed is only the first step in the interpretive itinerary: "When a mind is filled with the beginning of that faith which works through love, it progresses by a good life even toward vision, in which holy and perfect hearts know that unspeakable beauty, the full vision of which is the highest happiness."[47] The faith expressed in the creed is the "root" of interpretive agency that works through love in hope of acquiring understanding.[48]

What is true of Christian agency in general is true of Christian interpretive agency in particular: faith works through love (Gal. 5:6). "Love asks; love seeks; love knocks; love reveals; love, finally, remains in what has been revealed."[49] Love's quest for understanding is fulfilled by giving *attention* to Holy Scripture: "*Hear*, O Israel" (Deut. 6:4; emphasis added). Having received the ears of faith through the preaching of the gospel (Rom. 10:17), faith devotes its loving attention to interpreting the scriptural text.[50]

Like faith, love has an object. In the case of biblical interpretation, the specific object of our loving attention presents itself to us by means of a text—*this* text, Holy Scripture. Because God speaks *here*, by means of these appointed and anointed ambassadors, the prophets and apostles, by means of these historical and literary particularities, addressing all times and places from these specific times and places, faith devotes its loving attention to these words.

More specifically, love's object is the one God who presents himself to us in Scripture: "Hear, O Israel: The Lord our God, the Lord is one. You shall love the Lord your God with all your heart and with all your soul and with all your might" (Deut. 6:4-5). This, above all, is why our loving attention to the particularities of Holy Scripture is necessary. The Lord is not one god among other gods, one of the ordinary things with which we interact in the ordinary course of life. He is the holy Trinity: the Father, the Son, and the Holy Spirit (1 Cor. 8:5-6; Eph. 4:4-6). The

---

W. Bates, *The Hermeneutics of the Apostolic Proclamation: The Center of Paul's Method of Scriptural Interpretation* (Waco: Baylor University Press, 2019).

47. Augustine, *Enchiridion*, 1.5.

48. For the notion of faith as the "root" of agency, see Oliver O'Donovan, *Self, World, and Time: Ethics as Theology, Vol. 1* (Grand Rapids: Eerdmans, 2013), ch. 6. For fuller exploration of the interrelations between faith, love, and hope, see O'Donovan, *Finding and Seeking* and *Entering into Rest*.

49. Augustine, *The Catholic Way of Life and the Manichean Way of Life*, 1.17.31, in *The Manichean Debate*, WSA, 46.

50. According to Gadamer, in interpretation "what one has to exercise above all is the ear" (cited in Anthony C. Thiselton, *Hermeneutics: An Introduction* [Grand Rapids: Eerdmans, 2009], 2).

holy Trinity *is* and *acts* in his own unique and unparalleled way (Deut. 4:32-40). Therefore, he can be known and loved truly only if we set aside our idolatrous conceptions and longings and *listen* to his voice as he presents himself *here*, in the prophetic and apostolic writings.

Biblical interpretation requires giving our loving attention to the words of Scripture in all their historical, literary, and theological particularity. "Exegesis," according to Eugene Peterson, "is loving the one who speaks the words enough to get the words right. It is respecting the words enough to use every means we have to get the words right. Exegesis is loving God enough to stop and listen carefully to what he says."[51] For this reason,

> Good interpretation never struggles *against* the text, reading, as the fashion is, "against the grain," deconstructing the textual surface and showing it up as a confidence trick. Good interpretation never tries to bargain with the text, forging a compromise between what it says and what we would like to hear from it. It never supplements the text, overlaying it with independent reflections that head off on their own devices, never invokes a higher wisdom to cover the text's nakedness. Interpretation is the cheerful acceptance of the text's offer of more than lies on its surface, its invitation to come inside, to attune ourselves to its resonances and its dynamics, its suggestions and its logic.[52]

Careful exegetical attention to the words of Scripture is how Christian interpretive agency, rooted in faith, works through love in biblical interpretation.

Such loving attention is self-involving. Specifically, the summons to attend to Holy Scripture in love is a summons to *self-denial*. If we would follow Jesus by following his Word in his prophetic and apostolic emissaries, we must deny ourselves and take up our cross (Mt. 16:24). What does this mean in the context of biblical interpretation?

In all our exegetical asking, seeking, and knocking on the scriptural door of understanding, we (rightly) *hope to find*. We hope to find wisdom, power, and life. "You search the Scriptures because you think that in them you have eternal life" (Jn 5:39). "Jews demand signs and Greeks seek wisdom" (1 Cor. 1:22). However, the word that delivers wisdom, power, and life to those who seek them is a "word of the cross" (1 Cor. 1:18), which cuts against the grain of our often malign and misguided expectations and, only in crucifying them, delivers in the person of a crucified and risen Lord all that we had hoped to find—and that only on his terms. "They bear witness about me" (Jn 5:39). "He is your life" (Deut. 30:20; Jn 14:6), "Christ the power of God and the wisdom of God" (1 Cor. 1:24). Holy Scripture addresses all sorts of questions posed by hermeneutical preunderstanding. It is in this sense a book that realizes the universal expectations of all human beings. But it addresses these questions only insofar as it announces the fulfillment of Israel's

---

51. Eugene H. Peterson, "Caveat Lector," *Crux* 32 (1996): 6.
52. O'Donovan, *Finding and Seeking*, 136.

Scriptures in the crucifixion and resurrection of God's incarnate Son and in the life of fellowship he opens up to us with his Father in the Spirit. *This* book announcing *this* God and *this* gospel alone is the ground of universal hope and joy.[53]

The promise that lies at the end of the quest for interpretive understanding, of course, is that in finding the crucified and risen Lord of Scripture, and in finding all things in him, we will also find *ourselves*: "whoever will lose his life for my sake will find it" (Mt. 16:25). On the other side of the self's crucifixion in and with Christ is the self's resurrection: the self reformed by the pattern of teaching to which it has been delivered in baptism (Rom. 6:17).[54]

Conclusion: Beyond Scripture, Creed, and Interpretation

In the quest for interpretive understanding, baptized readers may hope to find true understanding of God, world, and self in this life in and through Holy Scripture. However, this quest, initiated in faith, traversed in love, and abounding in hope, will only be fully realized when faith becomes sight: "For now we see in a mirror dimly, but then face to face" (1 Cor. 13:12). "So, then, brothers and sisters, we feed on hope now, but there is no real life for us other than the life that is promised us in the future. Here our experience is of groaning, temptations, miseries, and dangers; but in the world to come our soul will praise the Lord as he deserves to be praised."[55]

"Until the day dawns," the prophetic and apostolic Scriptures are "a lamp shining in a dark place," to which we do well to "pay attention" (2 Pet. 1:19). The creed orients faith's loving attention to Scripture under the promise of finding theological understanding. As the church's covenantal "Amen" to God's covenantal "Yes" in Jesus Christ, the creed also gives form to the praise that, though imperfect in this life, will be perfected in the world to come when, with all the ransomed saints of God from every tribe and language and people and nation (Rev. 5:9), we will behold the face of our handsome king (Tit. 2:13) and we "will praise the Lord as he deserves to be praised."

---

53. Lacoste, "More Haste, Less Speed," 269–75.
54. Ibid., 280–2.
55. Augustine, *Expositions of the Psalms (Enarrationes Psalmos): 121–150*, WSA, 476.

Chapter 14

THE TRIUNE GOD

Michael Allen

Introduction

Reading the Bible well involves dealing with its subject matter, namely, the triune God, for the living and true God is present in and through its literary multiformity. Thinking about hermeneutics in a manner that is biblically rooted demands attention to the doctrine of the Trinity. The Trinity serves as a focal point and a nexus, a lodestar for our contemplation and a searchlight for our pathways. Thus, the supposed modern revival of interest in Trinitarian theology warrants analysis.[1] Beginning with the work of Karl Barth and Karl Rahner, both Protestants and Roman Catholics of all stripes have given themselves to engage this doctrine's material form and methodological significance.[2]

This supposed revival may not be truly vivifying; much of its purported historical assessment has been shown subsequently to be rather uninformed. Not surprisingly a good many of its material judgments are thereby malformed, even at key junctures.[3] Even so, it has helped to reemphasize the centrality of God's

---

1. Exemplary instances of the so-called revival are Christoph Schwöbel, ed., *Trinitarian Theology Today: Essays on Divine Being and Act* (Edinburgh: T&T Clark, 2000); Stanley J. Grenz, *Rediscovering the Triune God: The Trinity in Contemporary Theology* (Minneapolis: Fortress, 2004). The former volume includes an essay-length synopsis from John Zizioulas, whose work has been perhaps the most frequently cited text in the so-called revival: *Being as Communion: Studies in Personhood and the Church* (Crestwood, NY: St. Vladimir's Seminary, 1997).

2. My account will restrict itself to Protestant developments, simply for the sake of scope. Assessment of Karl Rahner's Trinitarian theology (from the Roman Catholic world) and John Zizioulas's application of Trinitarian theology (from the East) would be requisite for any complete exposition.

3. Summary of the historical reassessment exceeds the bounds of this essay yet warrants mention. For a synopsis of so-called new canon historiographic research, see the perceptive essay by Michel Rene Barnes, "The Fourth Century as Trinitarian Canon," in *Christian Origins: Theology, Rhetoric, and Community*, ed. Lewis Ayres and Gareth

works as the place whereby God is made present and known; hence, an emphasis upon the economy or the economic Trinity has been a first principle in much recent Trinitarianism. Similarly, it has paired this economic focus with a second principle, namely, that the doctrine of the Trinity cannot be isolated but must also be employed in shaping other doctrines and concerns; hence the proliferation of Trinitarian theologies of this, that, and the other. In this essay, I will explore ways in which these two principles shape a Trinitarian reading of the Bible productively, at least if they are handled wisely and without overreaching. In one sense the Trinitarian theology of Kevin J. Vanhoozer has brought much of twentieth-century reflection on the Trinity to a transition: offering a chastened account of the economy of the gospel and then applying that theology to the task of practical wisdom in what he deems a theodramatic form, contributing in each regard. This essay examines these two principles of recent Trinitarian formulation, in each case offering brief suggestions for how they might best be put to hermeneutical use.

Principle 1—The Turn to the Economy: The Supposed Revival

Theologies in the twentieth century turned emphatically, sometimes exclusively, to the economy of God's works. In an attempt to avoid speculation, they began with the missions of the incarnate Son of God (the Word) and the *Paraclete* (the Spirit), from which alone could any judgments about God's inner life be ventured. To grasp this foundational turn to the divine economy, the Trinitarian theologies of Karl Barth, Jürgen Moltmann, and finally Kevin J. Vanhoozer will be assessed.

Karl Barth: The God Who Elects to Self-Reveal

Karl Barth's doctrine of God was offered as a salve to a wounded Protestant body. That body manifested symptoms such as a theologically weakened backbone incapable of standing up to National Socialism in the 1930s or to the prior war efforts in the 1910s, but the roots of the malady went far deeper. Weakness in liberal theology stemmed from missteps in earlier orthodox dogmatics, especially

---

Jones (London: Routledge, 1998), 47–67, as well as monograph-length analyses including Lewis Ayres, *Nicaea and Its Legacy: An Approach to Fourth-Century Trinitarian Theology* (Oxford: Oxford University Press, 2004); John Behr, *Formation of Christian Theology*, Vol. 1: *The Way to Nicaea*, and Vol. 2: *The Nicene Faith* (Crestwood, NY: St. Vladimir's Seminary, 2001–4); plus a host of specific studies on various figures (including Arius, Athanasius, Basil, Gregory of Nyssa, Gregory Nazianzus, Augustine, and Thomas Aquinas) and a range of topics (divine simplicity, eternal generation, inseparable operations, the *filioque*, *perichoresis*, patristic exegesis, divine impassibility, aseity, and the divine processions). For perspective on the claims of the so-called revival, see Stephen R. Holmes, *The Quest for the Trinity: The Doctrine of God in Scripture, History, and Modernity* (Downers Grove: IVP Academic, 2012).

regarding the doctrine of God. "We stand here before the fundamental error which dominated the doctrine of God of the older theology and which influenced Protestant Orthodoxy at almost every point. For the greater part this doctrine of God tended elsewhere than to God's act in revelation, and for the greater part it also started elsewhere than from there."[4] Barth was a student of the post-Reformation Reformed dogmatics, viewing them as personally invaluable for his preparation as a university professor in the early 1920s. Yet he deems them to have made a misstep at just this point, namely, beginning to study God elsewhere than his self-revelation (whether later historical work shows Barth's judgment here to be valid or not has been and should be debated).

For himself, Barth begins the doctrine of God otherwise. "It is by the grace of God and only by the grace of God that it comes about that God is knowable to us."[5] But what does that divine grace for knowledge of God involve? "God reveals Himself. He reveals Himself through Himself. He reveals Himself."[6] The triune God reveals himself; in revealing himself, he graciously does all that is needed for humans to know him; and in thus providing all, he reveals himself to be triune: Revelation yes, but also Revealer and Revealedness.

Divine self-revelation does not remain nebulous or abstract, however, as Barth ties it more specifically to the coming of the incarnate Word of God and the sending of his promised Holy Spirit. "If God gives Himself to man to be known in the revelation of his Word through the Holy Spirit, it means that He enters into the relationship of object to man the subject."[7] That Word is the singular revelation of God, and "therefore our first and decisive transcription of the statement that God is, must be that God is who He is in the act of His revelation."[8] Barth scholars continue to debate just how deep that material judgment goes—whether divine being in the act of divine self-revelation means that there is no anterior divine life or not[9]—but the broader point has kick-started a modern emphasis upon the divine economy of Word and Spirit as the matrix within which God makes himself to be known. Similarly influential (albeit, in hindsight and with the benefit of more recent studies in the primary sources, historically questionable) was Barth's historical judgment that this economic emphasis constitutes a turn not merely

---

4. Karl Barth, *CD*, II/2, 261.
5. Barth, *CD*, II/1, 69.
6. Barth, *CD*, I/1, 296.
7. Barth, *CD*, II/1, 9.
8. Ibid., 262.
9. See especially Bruce McCormack, "Grace and Being: The Role of God's Gracious Election in Karl Barth's Theological Ontology," in *The Cambridge Companion to Karl Barth*, ed. John Webster (Cambridge: Cambridge University Press, 2000), 92–110; Paul Molnar, *Divine Freedom and the Doctrine of the Immanent Trinity*, 2nd ed. (London: T&T Clark, 2017). I have addressed the matter in "Eternal Generation after Barth," in *Retrieving Eternal Generation*, ed. Fred Sanders and Scott R. Swain (Grand Rapids: Zondervan Academic, 2017), 226–40.

from liberal platitudes that identified culture with divine spirit but also from Protestant orthodox dogmatics that conflated Christ and Divine Wisdom with the capacities of human rationality.

Jürgen Moltmann: The Suffering Trinity and Divine Reciprocity

The project of Barth (and that of Karl Rahner) both identified problems in faith and practice and sought to refashion Trinitarianism without abstractions, largely by grounding their efforts upon the divine economy. Later theologians would take up the task and extend it farther. While a host of figures might be considered here (including Wolfhart Pannenberg, Eberhard Jüngel, Robert Jenson, Colin Gunton, and Stanley Grenz), Jürgen Moltmann has most vigorously and widely illustrated the trajectory.

Moltmann shares a sense that something has gone amiss. He juxtaposes an approach to the doctrine of God via God as "the supreme substance" with an alternative affirmation wherein "God is the absolute subject."[10] Yet Moltmann finds both approaches lacking: "In distinction to the trinity of substance and to the trinity of subject we shall be attempting to develop a social doctrine of the Trinity" and in so doing will draw on "panentheistic ideas."[11] To grasp the negations as well as the appeal of panentheism, we must appreciate his concern for the works of God.

What of the economy in Moltmann's social approach? "The New Testament talks about God by proclaiming in narrative the relationships of the Father, the Son and the Spirit, which are relationships of fellowship and are open to the world."[12] Fellowship within the Godhead appears in the triune God's works of creation and of new creation, the moments in the divine economy. Indeed, unity "lies in their fellowship, not in the identity of a single subject."[13] Moltmann has no place for divine substance and resolves all Trinitarian unity in these interpersonal relations. These divine works also reveal God's openness to the world, which picks up on the influence of panentheism. He defines "Christian panentheism" much later as "the idea that the world is inherent in the nature of God himself from eternity. For it is impossible to conceive of a God who is not a creative God."[14] This creative and open portrait of God brings with it vulnerability: "The relationship between God and the world has a reciprocal character, because this relationship must be seen as a living one."[15]

---

10. Jürgen Moltmann, *The Trinity and the Kingdom of God: The Doctrine of God*, trans. Margaret Kohl (London: SCM, 1981), 10–12.
11. Ibid., 19.
12. Ibid., 64.
13. Ibid., 95 (see also 157).
14. Ibid., 106.
15. Ibid., 98.

This reciprocity runs two ways, positively and negatively. Positively, "if God is love, then he does not merely emanate, flow out of himself; he also expects and needs love."[16] Negatively, this need for reciprocal concern opens God up to suffer. A Christological example illustrates this approach to divine limitation: "If we are to understand the suffering of Christ as the *suffering of the passionate God* – it would seem more consistent if we ceased to make the axiom of God's apathy our starting point and started instead from the axiom of God's passion."[17] Here a material turn to the divine economy has led to a more revisionary approach, precisely because the divine economy has been interpreted with God operating as a figure among other figures, neither as a substance nor as an Absolute figure or subject above all others; rather God's being has been interpreted panentheistically as always creative and thus as always limited and passible (in what Moltmann calls the "self-humiliation of God"[18]).

Moltmann's emphases on divine vulnerability and passibility as perceived in the divine economy could be seen in the work of others, from Jon Sobrino to Paul Fiddes. One might debate whether some interpreters or improvisers upon the approach of Barth, such as Robert Jenson and Bruce McCormack, do not also wind up logically in much the same place. At the turn of the millennium, this turn to the economy seemed to lead to a revisionary doctrine of God, which would be juxtaposed to the God of Protestant liberalism and post-Reformation orthodoxy (as in Barth), to the modern piety and scholastic theologies of the Roman Catholic churches (as in Rahner), and even to the catholic tradition of the fathers that was now seen to be Hellenized (as in Moltmann). With the work of Moltmann and others, the economic Trinity has led to a radical revision of the divine attributes and of the task of Christian theology as a whole.

Kevin Vanhoozer: Communicative Theism and the Project of Remythologizing

We have already alluded to ways in which the historiographic judgments of this supposed Trinitarian revival have been questioned. The so-called Hellenization thesis has been challenged.[19] Former understandings of post-Reformation

---

16. Ibid., 99.

17. Ibid., 22 (emphasis original). For more on this subject, both divine passibility and patripassianism, see JürgenMoltmann, *The Crucified God: The Cross of Christ as the Foundation and Criticism of Christian Theology*, trans. R. A. Wilson and John Bowden (London: SCM, 1974).

18. The language of self-humiliation, though, distinguishes an inward life (wherein such "inward self-humiliation" occurs) from the outward economy (wherein "outward incarnation" manifests the inward move), at least at places in Moltmann's argument; see *Trinity and the Kingdom of God*, 118–19.

19. See, e.g., Andrew Radde-Gallwitz, *Basil of Caesarea, Gregory of Nyssa, and the Transformation of Divine Simplicity*, Oxford Early Christian Studies (Oxford: Oxford University Press, 2009); Sarah Coakley, ed., *Re-thinking Gregory of Nyssa*, Directions in Modern Theology (Oxford: Blackwell, 2005).

orthodoxy have been overturned.[20] Much of recent Trinitarian theology just will not do. Yet the focus upon the economy, begun by Barth and Rahner and shorn of the excesses of Moltmann and others, has not simply been tossed aside in more recent years—and for good reason. No one has shown a constructively critical approach to upholding the emphasis upon the economy apart from that kind of iconoclasm more than Kevin Vanhoozer. His stated goal in *Remythologizing Theology* is "to explore the ontology of the one whose speech and acts propel the theodrama forward."[21] He does not ditch the priority of the economy: "The proper starting point for a doctrine of God is thus the biblical depiction of God as a speaking subject whose breathed ('Spirited') voice is expressed supremely in the Christological Word made flesh and secondarily in the canonical polyphony that in turn presents Jesus Christ."[22] Economy takes in neither only incarnation and passion nor even simply Pentecost but also the apostolic emissaries and their ecclesiastical instruments, the writings that serve as the canonical voice of Jesus Christ. Vanhoozer expands the divine economy, then, to include the performative speech acts of making Scripture holy: past, present, and future. Whereas Rahner expanded in the direction of existential transcendentals, Vanhoozer pushes toward what he calls a "communicative theism" fixed upon canonical Scripture.

What sort of Trinitarianism flows from this question? Who and what must God be to speak thus? Here Vanhoozer speaks of "remythologizing" as a means of rebutting the attempt (post-Bultmann) to disentangle the divine being and presence from the so-called mythos of sacred Scripture.

> To remythologize theology we must focus not on the being of God considered in the abstract but on the identity of God considered in the historically and canonically concrete. God is not a story, however; hence to remythologize also entails seeking the implicit logos in the mythos, and that means reflecting on the 'what' of the divine "who." Theology must do more than retell the old, old story, but it need not follow that we have to choose between narrative and metaphysics. On the contrary, the way forward is to develop a theological ontology whose basic framework and categories are generated by (or, if borrowed from elsewhere, revised in light of) the divine self-presentation in the gospel of Jesus Christ and its canonical attestation.[23]

In so doing Vanhoozer speaks of how "God's being is in communicating" himself and his speech. Vanhoozer addresses what he calls "kenotic-perichoretic relational

---

20. See especially the four volumes of Richard A. Muller, *Post-Reformation Reformed Dogmatics: The Rise and Development of Reformed Orthodoxy, ca. 1520 to ca. 1725*, 2nd ed. (Grand Rapids: Baker Academic, 2003).

21. Kevin J. Vanhoozer, *Remythologizing Theology: Divine Action, Passion, and Authorship*, Cambridge Studies in Christian Doctrine (Cambridge: Cambridge University Press, 2010), xiv.

22. Ibid., 24.

23. Ibid., 182–3.

ontotheology" (his term for what Moltmann and others such as Philip Clayton are proposing), seeking to counter the recent affirmations of divine passibility. Over against the supposedly vulnerable and empathetic God that has dominated recent theology, Vanhoozer suggests that "only the communicating God can help."[24] Such a God must be seen in the economy, though not merely in incarnation and passion and those depths of humiliation but also in resurrection and ascension and Christ's exalted session on high.[25] Vanhoozer's argument here reminds one of the quip from the late Herbert McCabe, namely, that "the temptation to attribute suffering to God as God, to the divine nature, is connected with a failure to acknowledge that it is really God who suffers in Jesus of Nazareth."[26]

A range of questions remain with his project. Does Vanhoozer's description of Trinitarian communicative theism most fully express the kind of communicative project revealed in the economy and the Scriptures? Where he says that "the three persons are distinct communicative agents that share a common communicative agency,"[27] one might question whether that is not exactly backward. Would it not better reflect their communicative action and the biblical breadth of God-speech (especially inclusive of texts such as Rom. 8:12-17) to say they are one communicative agent active in distinct communicative agencies? Such would perhaps parallel classical language of inseparable operations and of the one divine will more smoothly while also affirming the singular covenantal plan of God, adopting women and men into the family of God via union by grace with the eternal, now incarnate Son of God, in whom all such communication occurs by the Spirit.[28]

Such questions noted, Vanhoozer's project should nonetheless be appreciated as an exegetically infused recalibration of the modern turn to the economy, taking in more of that divine economy (including not only the full span of God's Christological works, not least the heavenly session, but also the scriptural instruments employed directly by God in making his own goods common through human speech acts). Vanhoozer does not merely turn to the narrative elements of the biblical drama but also attends to passages that provide a metaphysical context within which that drama fits.[29] Reading the Bible for the Trinity involves not merely picking up the divine character(s) in the story but also reading all the breadth of that inscripturated Word.

---

24. Ibid., 504.

25. Ibid., 501.

26. Herbert McCabe, "The Involvement of God," in *God Matters* (London: Mowbray, 1987), 51.

27. Vanhoozer, *Remythologizing Theology*, 247.

28. In this regard I construe the communicative agency of the three in Rom. 8:12-17 differently than Sarah Coakley, *God, Sexuality and the Self: An Essay 'On the Trinity'* (Cambridge: Cambridge University Press, 2013), 100–51 (esp. 111–21).

29. See also Matthew Levering, *Scripture and Metaphysics: Aquinas and the Renewal of Trinitarian Theology*, Challenges in Contemporary Theology (Oxford: Blackwell, 2003); Wesley Hill, *Paul and the Trinity: Persons, Relations, and the Pauline Letters* (Grand Rapids: Eerdmans, 2015).

Doing so necessarily alerts the reader to the unique character of the triune God of Israel, who is near and yet other, whose way is in our midst and yet wholly unfamiliar. While Trinitarian theology is to be gleaned from the economy, that economy takes the form not only of redemptive-historical acts (say, virgin birth through Pentecost) but also of their redemptive-historical canon (the scriptural witness of prophets and apostles), which illuminates not only a major plotline but also its metaphysical context. If the economy fills the verses of the triune God's scriptural hymn, then the recurring chorus (apart from which the varied stanzas make little sense) is the metaphysics of God and creation revealed just as pointedly in biblical verse.

Principle 2—The Call for Practical Wisdom: Trinitarian Theologies of This, That, and the Other

The supposed turn to the Trinity has also involved a marked emphasis upon the value of viewing other subjects in a Trinitarian manner. Supposedly Christian faith and practice could subtract all Trinitarian reference, Karl Rahner had said, without suffering any real change.[30] Similarly, Robert Jenson said that "God's first debility in the Enlightened West is that he has become useless."[31] Immanuel Kant surely laid the groundwork for such claims as he averred that "absolutely nothing can be acquired for practical life from the doctrine of the Trinity."[32] In contrast to this worry about a discrete and insular doctrine of the Trinity, twentieth- and twenty-first-century theologians have sought to employ the Trinity as a lens for perceiving reality in its multifaceted nature.

If such a worry were ever really justified (and there are reasons to doubt at least the extent of its applicability[33]), today increasing swathes of doctrine, ethics, and exegesis cannot be accused of having a discrete and insular Trinitarianism. The second emphasis of recent Trinitarian theology has been its insistence that the Trinity opens up space for viewing other topics more holistically, serving hermeneutically not only for reading the Bible but also for constructing a coherent, authentically Christian faith and practice.[34] To explore the application of Trinity as

---

30. Karl Rahner, *The Trinity*, trans. Joseph Donceel (London: Herder & Herder, 1970), 10–11.

31. Robert W. Jenson, "The Christian Doctrine of God," in *Keeping the Faith: Essays to Mark the Centenary of Lux Mundi*, ed. Geoffrey Wainwright (London: SPCK, 1989), 27.

32. Immanuel Kant, "Der Streit der Fakultäten," in *Werke in sechs Bänden*, ed. W. Weischedel (Dormstadt: Wissenschaftliche Buchgesellschaft, 1964), 50.

33. Fred Sanders, *The Deep Things of God: How the Trinity Changes Everything*, 2nd ed. (Wheaton: Crossway, 2017).

34. Ironically this trend arose simultaneous to what has been a widespread castigation of Augustine's Trinitarian theology (see, e.g., John Zizoulas, *Communion and Otherness: Further Studies in Personhood and the Church* [London: T&T Clark, 2006], esp. 33-4; Colin Gunton, "Augustine, the Trinity, and the Theological Crisis of the West," *SJT*

a lens for viewing other biblical concerns, Miroslav Volf, Sarah Coakley, and then Kevin Vanhoozer will be considered.

Miroslav Volf: Trinitarian Politics

Frequently, Trinitarian theology in the vein of Moltmann—what may trade under the name of "social Trinitarianism"—has been employed for cultural or sociopolitical purposes. A range of theologians have offered such analysis: Catherine LaCugna, John Zizioulas, Jon Sobrino, Leron Shults, and Stanley Grenz, to name but a few prominent voices. Volf, a student of Moltmann, took up the ecclesiological imprint of the Trinity in *After Our Likeness: The Church as the Image of the Trinity*.[35] His aim was blunt: "I have tried to develop a nonhierarchical but truly communal ecclesiology based on a nonhierarchical doctrine of the Trinity."[36] He did not deem the link controversial at the time; in fact, he could note that "today, the thesis that ecclesial communion should correspond to trinitarian communion enjoys the status of an almost self-evident proposition."[37]

Now Volf alerts us to the "limits of analogy."[38] He also admits that "within interpersonal relations there is nothing that might correspond to the numerically identical divine nature."[39] And he notably points to the "strict impossibility of human correspondence to perichoresis."[40] But he proceeds to describe the "catholic self," arguing that "every person is a catholic person insofar as that person reflects in himself or herself in a unique way the entire, complex reality in which the person lives."[41] This catholic personhood comes only within relationships and

---

43, no. 1 [1990]: 33–58; for critical, historiographic pushback, see Lewis Ayres, "Augustine, The Trinity and Modernity: Colin Gunton's *The One, the Three and the Many*," *AugSt* 26 [1995]: 127–33). This inverse relationship is ironic given that Augustine's *de Trinitate* provides the paradigmatic example of looking at the Trinity (as revealed in the economy [books 1–4] and named via creedal terminology [books 5–7]) as well as looking along the Trinity at creaturely realities (books 8–15). See Rowan Williams, "*Sapientia* and the Trinity," in *Collectanea Augustiniana: Mélanges T. J. van Bavel*, ed. Bernard Bruning, Mathijs Lamberigts, and J. van Houtem, BETL XCII-A (Louvain: Leuven University Press, 1990), 317–32; Michael Hanby, *Augustine and Modernity*, Radical Orthodoxy (London: Routledge, 2003); Matthew Drever, "The Self before God? Rethinking Augustine's Trinitarian Thought," *HTR* 100, no. 2 (2007): 233–42.

35. Grand Rapids: Eerdmans, 1998. See also Volf, "'The Trinity Is Our Social Program': The Doctrine of the Trinity and the Shape of Social Engagement," *Modern Theology* 14, no. 3 (1998): 403–23.

36. Volf, *After Our Likeness*, 4.

37. Ibid., 191.

38. Ibid., 198–200.

39. Ibid., 204.

40. Ibid., 210, 213.

41. Ibid., 212, 213.

cannot be experienced in isolation.⁴² Furthermore, this personal reality is a gift of the Spirit, for "it is not the mutual perichoresis of human beings, but rather the indwelling of the Spirit common to everyone that makes the church into a communion corresponding to the Trinity, a communion in which personhood and sociality are equiprimal."⁴³

For Volf, then, "the church reflects in a broken fashion the eschatological communion of the entire people of God with the triune God in God's new creation."⁴⁴ While he tries not merely to make but to manifest the analogical limits of this fit between divine and human communion, much more might be asked.⁴⁵ Not least would be examination of ways in which the divine nature has to function in any such correspondence, given that the divine nature and will exist in a fashion that drastically outstrips any creaturely commonality. Human unity is not on the order of divine unity and singularity; it merited saying, "Hear, O Israel, the LORD your God, the LORD is one" (Deut. 6:4). Volf's Trinitarian approach to community typifies recent trends to use the doctrine, or at least slivers of the doctrine, as a map for a distinctive politics.

Sarah Coakley: Gender, Transforming Desire, and the Trinity

Not all applications of Trinity to other issues provide such a smooth transition from the divine to the ideals of human flourishing regnant today. The Trinity can function as a lens that challenges as well as validates Christian thought in other arenas. The first of a projected four-volume systematic theology by Anglican theologian and philosopher of religion Sarah Coakley—the whole project titled *On Desiring God*—fixes upon the Trinity, though not discretely and definitely not atomistically. Coakley begins by claiming that "no cogent answer to the contemporary Christian question of the Trinitarian God can be given without charting the necessary and intrinsic entanglement of human sexuality and spirituality in such a quest: the question of right contemplation, right speech about God, and right ordering of desire all hang together."⁴⁶

Coakley pushes back on the "doctrinal criticism" of an earlier generation of Anglican divines (typified by Maurice Wiles) by noting that "the modern textbook account of the development of the doctrine of the Trinity has largely obscured these crucial points of connection, often by concentrating more on philosophical issues of coherence than on the fathers' biblical exegesis or ascetical exercise."⁴⁷

---

42. Ibid., 280.

43. Ibid., 213.

44. Ibid., 235.

45. See the trenchant critique in Mark A. Husbands, "The Trinity Is Not Our Social Program: Volf, Gregory of Nyssa, and Barth," in *Trinitarian Theology for the Church: Scripture, Community, Worship*, ed. Daniel J. Treier and David Lauber (Downers Grove: IVP Academic, 2009), 120–41.

46. Sarah Coakley, *God, Sexuality, and the Self: An Essay "On the Trinity"* (Cambridge: Cambridge University Press, 2013), 1–2.

47. Ibid., 3.

She turns then to mine resources rarely related to Trinitarian theology, not least the ascetical treatises of Gregory of Nyssa and other fathers of the church, and she seeks to explore what it means that God is the object of our desires, which overlap and entangle themselves with other desirings (inclusive of, though not subsumed by, sexual desires). In so doing she seeks to reestablish systematic theology as a life-giving discipline by showing how it plays a role in the transformation of human desire, and how the doctrine of the Trinity makes sense of that transformative experience at a basic level (what she calls "explicitly prayer-based access to the workings of the divine").[48]

Her *théologie totale* wagers that systematic theology "does not convey the hubristic idea of a totalizing discourse that excludes debate, opposition, or riposte; but on the other hand, it does not falter at the necessary challenge of presenting the gospel afresh in all its ramifications – systematically unfolding the connections of the parts of the vision that is set before us."[49] Thus, systematic theology, viewed as a rational and ordered path to the purgation of desire via prayer-based access to the triune God, forwards the feminist cause: by challenging the "idolatrous desire to know all that fuels 'onto-theology,'" by undercutting the "imperious desire to dominate that inspires 'hegemony,'" and by transforming the "'phallocentric' desire to conquer that represses the feminine."[50] In Coakley's hands, then, a systematic theology of the Trinity evokes the dispossession of meeting God, specifically the triune God who enlivens us (by the Spirit) in a way that intensifies and simultaneously purges our desire.[51] This kind of Trinitarianism challenges hubris and weaponized power—not least in its misogynistic forms—not by dulling the edges of the Creator-creature distinction but by dispossessing humans of any control. In this regard, Coakley's feminist project continues a path that stands a good bit askance from identity politics or the mainstream of that movement in any of its waves.[52]

Crucial to Coakley's project is a kenotic approach to Christology that emphasizes the self-emptying of God within which Christians participate.[53] Thus, the call to empty our voices (in silent prayer) as a means of more deeply emptying

---

48. Ibid., 6; on the transformation of desire, see esp. 11–22.

49. Ibid., 11.

50. Ibid., 51–2.

51. On the simultaneity and pairing of intensification and purgation of desire, see ibid., 13.

52. On her project vis-à-vis mainstream feminism, see Sarah Coakley, *Powers and Submissions: Spirituality, Philosophy, and Gender*, Challenges in Contemporary Theology (Oxford: Blackwell, 2002). My analysis would differ starkly from Linn Marie Tonstad, *God and Difference: The Trinity, Sexuality, and the Transformation of Finitude*, Gender, Theology, and Spirituality (New York: Routledge, 2017), though Tonstad's concern to avoid what she terms "corrective projectionism" remains needful, even if not exactly applicable as a critique of Coakley (esp. 13–14, 17).

53. See especially Coakley, "Kenosis and Subversion: On the Repression of 'Vulnerability' in Christian Feminist Writing," in *Powers and Submissions*, 3–38 (see 16–25 for her disentangling various iterations of kenosis throughout history).

our weak and wayward desires finds roots in Trinitarian and Christological thought, although this humiliating form and the rather narrow breadth of that Christological root might be questioned. The exalted Christ in his heavenly session does not yet play a significant role in Coakley's Trinitarian reasoning (though that may emerge in later volumes). Even so, those and other hesitations aside, it should be appreciated that a Trinitarian schema grounds this ascetical and feminist project, the latter facet of which really finds its own way only because of that Trinitarian and Christological mooring.

Kevin Vanhoozer: Theodramatic Wisdom

Kevin Vanhoozer has also shown how the Trinity may be employed as a lens for other theological concerns. Throughout his works he has taken the language of drama to frame the task of Christian discipleship, wherein fittingness shapes the formation of women and men who follow the stage prompts and the script (not to mention the guidance of the Director) as participants in the company of the gospel.[54] He continues to speak of the economy of God, addressing the sending of the Son and of the Holy Spirit: "The purpose of the two missions, then, is communion and community: a sharing in the truth and love – the very life – of God."[55]

Vanhoozer offers what he calls a "directive" theory of doctrine that leads to wisdom.[56] To that end, his book offers "new metaphors for theology (dramaturgy), Scripture (the script), theological understanding (performance), the church (company), and the pastor (director)."[57] To what end? "The task of theology is to enable hearers and doers of the gospel to respond and to correspond to the prior Word and Act of God, and thus to be drawn into action."[58] The beneficial emphasis of Vanhoozer's argument lies in relating Scripture overtly and theologically to the acts of God. We are drawn into participating in a play that has a script given by a Figure who not only authors but also immerses himself in the drama. Thus, the self-dispossessive posture heralded by Coakley finds an epistemological prompt here, as

---

54. See especially Kevin J. Vanhoozer, *The Drama of Doctrine: A Canonical-Linguistic Approach to Christian Theology* (Louisville: Westminster John Knox, 2005); Vanhoozer, *Faith Speaking Understanding: Performing the Drama of Doctrine* (Louisville: Westminster John Knox, 2014). These performances are prompted by the *Theo-Drama* of Hans Urs von Balthasar and the influence of his doctoral supervisor: see Nicholas Lash, "Performing the Scriptures," in *Theology on the Way to Emmaus* (London: SCM, 1986), 37–46. The language of theodrama has also been taken up recently by David F. Ford, *The Future of Christian Theology* (Oxford: Blackwell, 2011), 23–4, and Ben Quash, *Theology and the Drama of History*, Cambridge Studies in Christian Doctrine (Cambridge: Cambridge University Press, 2005).

55. Vanhoozer, *Drama of Doctrine*, 70.
56. Ibid., xii, xiii, 22.
57. Ibid., xii.
58. Ibid., 44.

the Christian receives not only their stage prompt but also their very being in the Word of the Lord. Similarly, the version of communal leveling that is spoken to those who natively measure worth by their power, as in Volf's argument, here finds a more highly directed and concretely bounded foundation for unitive community.

Vanhoozer has used the Trinity as a lens for other things in the past: for grasping speech-act theory in *Is There a Meaning in This Text?*, and even for thinking more specifically of the inspiration and interpretation of Holy Scripture as "triune discourse."[59] His most developed application of Trinitarian thought—employing the divine economy as the matrix for a directive approach to doctrine—matches his approach to the economy in *Remythologizing Theology*, namely, tying the missions of Word and Spirit in redemptive history to the agency of Word and Spirit in the prophetic ministry of God's Holy Word. While other applications of the Trinitarian lens are crucial and its enunciation in *Drama of Doctrine* is not the most effusive, Vanhoozer's pairing of Trinitarian reasoning and exegetical protocols is a most promising contribution for theological method and biblical hermeneutics, further showing how God's triune splendor might cast light upon other facets of Christian theology and ethics.

Principled Steps for Future Trinitarian Theology and Hermeneutics: A Brief Conclusion

In "Meditation in a Tool-Shed," C. S. Lewis spoke of the difference between "looking at" something and "looking along" that same thing. It is one thing to look at the overwhelming vibrancy of a skylight pouring like a laser beam into a darkened shed; it is altogether different to stand in that beam as it functions like a floodlight upon other things.[60] Recent Trinitarian theology has sought to extend both facets of thinking the Trinity: looking at who God is by means of his self-revelation in the divine economy, while also looking through this Trinitarian self-revelation to see how all things hold together in God. Thus, Vanhoozer's project brings to a head these major trends in modern theology: a reassertion of the particular deity who is illumined as triune and a reassertion of the significance of God's triune character for everything else. Here the one (living and true, triune God) and the many (all arenas of life made new by this triune gospel of Christ) are shown to be unified.

---

59. Kevin J. Vanhoozer, *Is There a Meaning in This Text? The Bible, the Reader, and the Morality of Literary Knowledge* (Grand Rapids: Zondervan, 1998); Vanhoozer, "Triune Discourse: Theological Reflections on the Claim that God Speaks (Parts 1 and 2)," in *Trinitarian Theology for the Church: Scripture, Community, Worship*, ed. Daniel J. Treier and David Lauber (Downers Grove: IVP Academic, 2009), 25–78. See also "Introduction: Evangelical Hermeneutics in Dialogue with Kevin J. Vanhoozer," by Daniel J. Treier in the present volume.

60. C. S. Lewis, "Meditation in a Toolshed," in *God in the Dock* (Grand Rapids: Eerdmans, 1970), 230–4. Kevin J. Vanhoozer appeals to Lewis's distinction in "First Theology: Meditations in a Postmodern Toolshed," in *First Theology: God, Scripture and Hermeneutics* (Downers Grove: InterVarsity, 2002), ch. 1.

In future doctrinal and exegetical work, perhaps more attention should be paid to the interstices between the two—that is, to how looking at conjoins with looking along. If the supposed turn to Trinitarian theology in the late twentieth century involved a renewed verve in looking at the triune God as revealed in the divine economy as well as a new focus upon looking along the Trinity to grasp other realities in its light, then perhaps what is now needed most is a refocusing upon contemplative wisdom as a fundamental theological vocation.[61] This refocusing would alert Scripture readers that more is happening in those texts than the mere transmission of a redemptive history and that God is revealed there as more than another character. A reassertion of theology's contemplative role would also remind us that the triune God has bearing on all things but is never to be used for the sake of anything else. While it is not only rightful but necessary to develop a theological and thus Trinitarian perspective on every facet of life, the application of Trinitarian jargon to projects of our own devising flirts with idolatry and can fall afoul of the third commandment, namely, taking the Lord's name in vain. Only beholding the Lord's majestic beauty in worship and learning via contemplation can guard us, by God's grace, from weaponizing Trinitarian language as a religious ornament for our academic and practical pursuits.

Recent Trinitarian theology, in both exegetical and doctrinal forms, manifests the practical turn of a wider culture. Pragmatism does not merely influence laypersons, who sit before Scripture asking "what does this mean to me?" It also pressures the intellectual underpinnings of modern Christian theology by accentuating the active life and the works of God for us and with us. In so doing it opens up the reality that Scripture offers us good news (*evangelium*) of a God who is not far off (Jer. 23:23). Yet we must also beware lest this pressure should foreclose other theological ventures, such as the contemplative task of knowing and loving God in and of himself, God for God's own sake, God as only God is in the eternal divine life.[62] As we read Holy Scripture and participate in the dramatic practice of Christian doctrine, may our watchfulness for God's action in our midst and God's relevance to our action be matched by our attentiveness to God himself.

---

61. For examples, see Levering, *Scripture and Metaphysics*, 23–46; Levering, "Friendship and Trinitarian Theology: A Response to Karen Kilby," *IJST* 9, no. 1 (2007): 39–54; Katherine Sonderegger, *Systematic Theology*, vol. 1: *The Doctrine of God* (Minneapolis: Fortress, 2015), esp. 19, 24, 456; John Webster, *God without Measure*, vol. 1: *God and the Works of God* (London: T&T Clark, 2015), on which see Michael Allen, "Toward Theological Theology: Tracing the Methodological Principles of John Webster," *Themelios* 41, no. 2 (2016): 236 n. 106; and especially Coakley, *God, Sexuality, and the Trinity*, 18–30, 43–52.

62. Of significance in this regard would be places where Thomas Aquinas addressed the contemplative task: e.g., *Summa Theologica*, 1a.1.4, reply and especially 2a2ae.180.4, reply. In her projected second volume, Sarah Coakley will take up the task of contemplation more directly as well.

Chapter 15

HOW GOD DOES THINGS WITH WORDS IN THE CHURCH

Michael Horton

For the word of God is living and active ...Heb. 4:12[1]

In his widely acclaimed *Remythologizing Theology*, Kevin J. Vanhoozer's "deepest wish" is to "complete Paul Ricoeur's 'second Copernican Revolution' that dethrones the autonomous knowing subject in order to hearken to the one whose creative word forms, informs, and transforms us."[2] In honor of Kevin, this essay focuses

---

1. By way of further introduction, "*Practice* gives the words their sense" (Ludwig Wittgenstein, *The Wittgenstein Reader*, ed. Anthony Kenny [Oxford: Blackwell, 1994], 304). And in the words of this chapter's protagonist, "This presupposition of the *textuality* of faith distinguishes *biblical* faith ('Bible' meaning book) from all others. In one sense, therefore, texts do precede life. I can name God in my faith because the texts preached to me have already named God" (Paul Ricoeur, *Figuring the Sacred: Religion, Narrative and Imagination*, trans. Mark I. Wallace [Minneapolis: Fortress, 1995], 218).

2. Kevin J. Vanhoozer, *Remythologizing Theology: Divine Action, Passion, and Authorship*, Cambridge Studies in Christian Doctrine (Cambridge: Cambridge University Press, 2012), xv. Evangelical hermeneutics and homiletics have interacted sympathetically with Gadamer, especially in Anthony C. Thiselton, *The Two Horizons: New Testament Hermeneutics and Philosophical Description* (Grand Rapids: Eerdmans, 1980); John R. W. Stott, *Between Two Worlds: The Art of Preaching in the Twentieth Century* (Grand Rapids: Eerdmans,1982). Surprisingly, though, Ricoeur is less engaged in evangelical and Reformed circles, apart from Vanhoozer and Dan R. Stiver, *Theology after Ricoeur: New Directions in Hermeneutical Theology* (Louisville: Westminster John Knox, 2001). Nicholas Wolterstorff should also be mentioned: *Divine Discourse: Philosophical Reflections on the Claim that God Speaks* (Cambridge: Cambridge University Press, 1995), especially ch. 4. Through seminars with Wolterstorff (1996–8) I encountered speech-act theory and Ricoeur; ever since I have drawn on his work in an ad hoc manner (e.g., in *Covenant and Eschatology: The Divine Drama* [Louisville: Westminster John Knox, 2002]). Vanhoozer had already written a doctoral dissertation on Ricoeur under Nicholas Lash, published as *Biblical Narrative in the*

on Paul Ricoeur's contribution to theological hermeneutics and especially to the concept of the church as "creature of the word" (*creatura verbi*).

The son of pious Huguenot parents, Paul Ricoeur (1913–2005) was only 2 years old when his father was killed in the First World War. His mother died soon afterward, leaving him in the care of his paternal grandparents (and an aunt) who were also actively involved in the French Reformed Church. Ricoeur's interest in hermeneutics was sparked early on by Bible studies that were a lively part of the family's life. After having been a POW in the Second World War, he taught in the Protestant faculty at the University of Strasbourg and eventually was awarded the chair of philosophy at the Sorbonne, with a young Jacques Derrida as his assistant from 1960 to 1965. From 1970 to 1985 he accepted a triple appointment in philosophy, social theory, and divinity (replacing Paul Tillich) at the University of Chicago. Ricoeur did not merely happen to be a believer who did philosophy; he considered his religious convictions essential to the whole realm of discourse on which he touched.

Professionally, Ricoeur helped to create an intersection between continental and analytic traditions of philosophy after Ludwig Wittgenstein's later work. Phenomenology emphasizes that we understand the world not merely as a collection of external objects but as part of our world toward which we have certain intentions. With his simple but provocative *How to Do Things with Words*, J. L. Austin formulated the basic outlines of speech-act theory, arguing with Wittgenstein that meaning is found not in words themselves but in the actions for which they are used. Language is rich, social, multivalent, and context-dependent.[3] At the same time, interpretation is not just free play, Ricoeur argues. We cannot read the author's mind, but we have a text before us. "If it is true that there is always more than one way of construing a text, it is not true that all interpretations are equal ... The text is a limited field of possible constructions." He adds, "It is always possible to argue against an interpretation, to confront interpretations, to arbitrate between them and to seek for agreement, even if this agreement remains beyond our reach."[4]

Philosophy of Paul Ricoeur: A Study in Hermeneutics and Theology (Cambridge: Cambridge University Press, 1990). Vanhoozer also draws insightfully on Ricoeur in *The Drama of Doctrine: A Canonical-Linguistic Approach to Christian Doctrine* (Louisville: Westminster John Knox, 2005).

3. 2nd ed., ed. J. O. Urmson and Marina Sbisà (Cambridge, MA: Harvard University Press, 1975). Most basically, Austin argues that in performing one act (*locutionary*, such as writing a sentence), one performs another (*illocutionary*, such as promising, warning, asserting, etc.), which effects yet another (*perlocutionary* effect, such as assurance, fear, assent, etc.).

4. Paul Ricoeur, "The Model of the Text: Meaningful Action Considered as a Text," in *From Text to Action: Essays in Hermeneutics, II*, trans. Kathleen Blamey and John B. Thompson, Studies in Phenomenology and Existential Philosophy (Evanston: Northwestern University Press, 2007), 160.

Ricoeur judged, "I think we are at a moment that I would qualify as being beyond the linguistic turn ... Two factors, I believe, have facilitated this surpassing of the linguistic turn: on the one hand, the recognition that discourse is an action; on the other hand, and in a contrary sense, the recognition that human action is a speaking action."[5] My purpose here is not to evaluate Ricoeur's wider project, much less to adjudicate his relative orthodoxy, but to focus on two of his pregnant insights for preaching.

How God Does Things with Words: Background to Ricoeur's Theological Hermeneutics

The biblical consciousness is shaped by events of discourse with a personal God. While Hebraic culture was founded by hearing the word, Hellenistic culture concentrated on metaphors of vision for the act of knowing.[6] The tendency in our Greek heritage is to move from the inside out: inner thoughts of private individuals expressed externally and publicly. The biblical emphasis, however, moves in the other direction: A word comes to us all, publicly, and changes us all, deeply and inwardly, into the kind of community that it calls into being. Jewish theologian Jon Levenson explains that for Israel, the rabbinic Passover liturgy calls upon each individual to see himself or herself as one who has come out of Egypt with that liberated generation:

> The present generation makes history their story, but it is first history. They do not determine who they are by looking within, by plumbing the depths of the individual soul, by seeking a mystical light in the innermost reaches of the self. Rather, the direction is the opposite. What is public is made private. History is not only rendered contemporary; it is internalized. One's people's history becomes one's personal history. ... One does not *discover* one's identity, and one certainly does not forge it oneself. He *appropriates* an identity that is a matter of public knowledge. Israel affirms the given.
>
> The given that is affirmed in the covenant ceremony is not a principle; it is not an idea or aphorism or an ideal. Instead, it is the consequence of what are presented as the acts of God ... Israel began to infer to and to affirm her identity by telling a story.[7]

---

5. Ricoeur, *Figuring the Sacred*, 105.

6. See e.g. Walter Ong, S.J., *Presence of the Word* (New Haven: Yale University Press, 1967); Oswald Bayer, *Living by Faith: Justification and Sanctification* (Grand Rapids: Eerdmans, 2003), 47. For further discussion and sources, see Michael Horton, *The Christian Faith: A Systematic Theology for Pilgrims on the Way* (Grand Rapids: Zondervan Academic, 2011), 35–186.

7. Jon D. Levenson, *Sinai and Zion: An Entry into the Jewish Bible* (Minneapolis: Winston, 1985), 38–9.

"To be sure," Levenson adds, "the story has implications that can be stated in propositions. For example, the intended implication of the historical prologue is that YHWH is faithful, that Israel can rely on God as a vassal must rely upon his suzerain. But Israel does not begin with the statement that YHWH is faithful; she infers it from a story," which depends on the particulars of time and place.[8]

God's speech not only describes, refers, explains, and asserts timelessly true propositions but also (even primarily) *accomplishes* every errand on which it is sent by the Father, in the Son, through the Spirit (Isa. 55:11). God's Word kills and makes alive (Ezekiel 37). Not only creation and Israel's formative events but also the new creation is the result of God's speech. The new birth is not something that we decide to activate based on a gospel presentation. Rather, just as the prophet's word raises the dead, the gospel proclaimed today is the primary means through which the Spirit gives faith (Rom. 10:14-18; cf. 1 Pet. 1:23; Jas 1:18). "For God, who said, 'Let light shine out of darkness,' has shone in our hearts to give the light of the knowledge of the glory of God in the face of Jesus Christ" (2 Cor. 4:6). "So faith comes from hearing, and hearing through the word of Christ" (Rom. 10:17). Our response, too, is verbal and public: "For with the heart one believes and is justified and with the mouth one confesses and is saved" (v. 10). This is why we need preachers who are sent (v. 14). Believing what we hear places us under the authority of the speaker. The Hebrew prophets complained that God's Word had been sidelined in favor of "idols that cannot speak" (Ps. 115:5; Hab. 2:18; 1 Cor. 12:2). Since God works by speaking, with transforming effects that must be heard to be believed, a religion based on law and promise *must* be grounded in the verbal rather than the visual. Even the signs and seals of the covenant are visible ratifications of the covenantal promise.

The Protestant Reformation renewed this emphasis on the church as *creatura verbi* and the word of God as "sacramental"—a means of grace. Not only the written word but also (even especially!) "the *preached* word is the Word of God."[9] "Calvin felt no antagonism between what we may call the 'pedagogical' and the 'sacramental' functions of the word," notes B. A. Gerrish.[10] Stephen H. Webb represents the Reformation as the "re-vocalization of the cosmos." "This was a verbosity caused not by the need to explain an image or to make a moral point. Rather, it was a verbosity that intended *to convey grace through sound.*"[11] It is "covenantal speech, active and full of life," Webb observes concerning Calvin's

---

8. Ibid., 39.

9. Second Helvetic Confession, ch. 1, in *Book of Confessions* (Louisville: PCUSA General Assembly, 1991).

10. B. A. Gerrish, *Grace and Gratitude: The Eucharistic Theology of John Calvin* (Minneapolis: Augsburg Fortress, 1993), 84–85. The Westminster Larger Catechism explains that God blesses the reading "but especially the preaching of the Word of God" as a means of grace since by it the Spirit confronts sinners in their self-enclosed existence, "driving them out of themselves and drawing them unto Christ" (Q/A. 155).

11. Stephen H. Webb, *The Divine Voice: Proclamation and the Theology of Sound* (Grand Rapids: Brazos, 2004), 106, emphasis added.

view. "Even in its stuttering, God's Word has the power to give what it asks. God's Word called the world into being, and it continues to uphold the world through the speech of the Spirit-filled church."[12]

So it is not surprising that renewed emphasis on this biblical approach to speech as the medium of God's mighty deeds would find greater hermeneutical resources in Wittgenstein, Austin, and Ricoeur than in Leibniz, Schleiermacher, and A. J. Ayer. According to Northrop Frye, we have gone from viewing language as a "living and active" medium of revelation to mere metaphor, then metonymy, and finally, description.[13] With each phase, the unity of subject and object begins to be pulled apart. But for Friedrich Nietzsche and his heirs, signs refer merely to other signs in unending play, never reaching a signified.[14]

In opposition to such epistemological and hermeneutical skepticism, conservative evangelicals have sometimes defended a distinctly modern (even positivist) view of language. Following his mentor Gordon H. Clark, Carl F. H. Henry insisted that the truth conveyed in Scripture consists entirely of propositional statements.[15] According to Henry, "A proposition is a statement that is either true or false; it is a rational declaration capable of being believed, doubted, or denied."[16] In fact, "In this self-disclosure God unveils his very own mind."[17] Historical narratives, parables, and metaphors "become fully intelligible only if they express thought, ideas, beliefs—in short, propositions."[18] Such propositions

---

12. Ibid., 159.

13. Northrop Frye, *The Great Code: The Bible and Literature* (San Diego: Harcourt, 1982). See also Jean Baudrillard, "The Map Precedes the Territory," in *The Truth About the Truth: De-confusing and Re-constructing the Postmodern World*, ed. Walter Truett Anderson (New York: TarcherPerigree/Penguin, 1995), 71–89.

14. Friedrich Nietzsche, "On Truth and Lies in a Nonmoral Sense," in *The Portable Nietzsche*, trans. Walter Kaufmann (New York: Viking, 1976), 46–7:

> "Truth" is a mobile army of metaphors, metonyms, and anthropomorphisms—in short, a sum of human relations which have been enhanced, transposed, and embellished poetically and rhetorically, and which after long use seem firm, canonical, and obligatory to a people: truths are illusions about which one has forgotten that this is what they are; metaphors which are worn out and without sensuous power; coins which have lost their pictures and now matter only as metal, no longer as coins.

15. Following Gordon Clark (e.g., *Language and Theology* [Phillipsburg: Presbyterian and Reformed, 1980], 92–97), Henry went so far as to deny the analogical account of predications involving God and creatures. We must know at least some things *exactly* as God knows them if we are to know with certainty at all. See Carl F. H. Henry, *God, Revelation, and Authority* (Waco: Word, 1976–83), 1:237–38.

16. Henry, *God, Revelation, and Authority*, 3.456; cf. 96.

17. Ibid., 3.457.

18. Ibid., 3.446.

are "timelessly true as is the truth of mathematics."[19] Furthermore, "Regardless of the parables, allegories, emotive phrases and rhetorical questions said by those writers, their literary devices have a logical point which can be propositionally formulated and is objectively true or false."[20] A command like "Thou shalt not kill" is not a proposition, but it can be stated propositionally as "murder is wrong."[21]

It is not surprising that many who have experienced an impersonal, individualistic, and non-sacramental view of the divine word would seek after visual ritual and drama as therapy against "the domestication of transcendence" from both liberal and conservative quarters.[22] Deeply influenced by the biblical and Reformation emphasis on the preached gospel and sacraments as the word of God, Ricoeur argues that these are not our means of conjuring, mimicking, or even representing transcendence but the means through which the transcendent God makes himself present among us and to us in judgment and grace.[23] In opposition to a lecture hall or a theater, the setting of preaching is more like the wardrobe through which Aslan draws us in to his new creation. We will not learn much from Ricoeur about what the Bible *is* (the doctrine of Scripture).[24] However, he is a superb resource for recovering the emphasis on what God *does* with words.

Ricoeur for Preachers

If for higher critics the real world (i.e., factual history) lies somewhere in the murky past *behind* the Bible and for some conservatives it lies *above* the Bible, in the ideas that must be separated from the dross of narrative, poetry, metaphor, and

---

19. Ibid., 3.464.
20. Ibid., 4.453.
21. Ibid., 3.477. While surely the prohibition *may* be stated thusly, what is lost is substantial: the character of the command as a summons or claim by one person (Yahweh) on others (us). Once we reduce truth to propositional statements, the only illocutionary act that God's Word can have is informing. Its perlocutionary effect is made dependent on what the subject does with the information or exhortation rather than on the divine speaker (the Father), what is said (the gospel of Christ), and the quickening power of the Spirit.
22. I draw this wonderful phrase from William C. Placher, *The Domestication of Transcendence: How Modern Thinking About God Went Wrong* (Louisville: Westminster John Knox, 1996).
23. Paul had something like this in mind, I believe, in Romans 10 with his contrast between "the righteousness that is by works" and "the righteousness that is by faith."
24. Despite his similarities to Barth, even here Ricoeur cannot be easily classified. His reticence to make a one-to-one correspondence between the Bible and the Word of God is not the former's binding to history, but just the opposite: "Revelation is a historical process, but the notion of sacred text is something antihistorical. I am frightened by this word 'sacred'" (*Figuring the Sacred*, 72). As on other points of Christian doctrine, one will do better to consult Vanhoozer's *Drama of Doctrine*.

so forth, for Ricoeur its ultimate meaning is to be found *in front of* the text, as the Bible (especially in preaching and sacrament) projects a new world for us to enter. To be sure, the Bible includes history, morality, powerful feeling, and propositional statements. However, it primarily (and in this respect uniquely) discloses a world. The similarities with Karl Barth's brilliant 1928 essay, "Strange New World," are striking.[25]

We are not standing over the text, dissecting and mastering it, using it as a quarry for our life projects. Even as we interpret, we ourselves are being interpreted. The text is working on us even more than we are working on it. By "world-projection" Ricoeur means something like Heidegger's idea of language as the "house of being." Van Gogh's "peasant shoes" (1886) are not mere footwear; they disclose a world, a form of life.[26] We do not merely use language to describe our inner thoughts or intentions but already indwell it as the world that gives rise to the very possibility of thought in the first place.[27] Like Gadamer, Ricoeur does not isolate meaning in the text alone; there are indeed horizons of the text and the interpreter. However, Ricoeur eschews Gadamer's sanguine theory of a *fusion* of horizons. Instead of being generated by a calm conversation between text and reader, textual meaning for Ricoeur is more like a confrontation, a *clash* of horizons. After all, we systematically distort even our own horizon. Like Adam, he said, we are all "responsible and captive, or rather ... responsible for being captive."[28] There are two areas where Ricoeur is especially relevant for preachers: his treatment of Scripture as narrative and his negotiation between theologies of manifestation and of proclamation.

Christianity and Narrative

While many theorists (including some Christians) blame secularization on a loss of shared rituals, Ricoeur considers narrative (especially preaching) the glue that holds the diverse genres of Scripture and therefore the Christian community together. The "inevitability of the divine plan and the contingency of human action" create the tension that forms a great narrative structure—and the kerygma

---

25. The translated essay is published in *The Word of God and the Word of Man* (Gloucester, MA: Peter Smith, 1958). Similarly, see Barth's unjustly overlooked *Homiletics* (Louisville: Westminster John Knox, 1991).

26. Martin Heidegger, "On the Origin of a Work of Art," in *Basic Writings* (New York: Harper Perennial, 2008), 139-212.

27. This is what Charles Taylor (also indebted to the phenomenological tradition) describes richly as the "preconditions of belief" (*A Secular Age* [Cambridge, MA: Harvard University Press, 2007], 529-723) and seems close to Michael Polanyi's "tacit" or "subsidiary awareness" in *Personal Knowledge: Toward a Post-Critical Philosophy* (Chicago: University of Chicago Press, 1974), esp. 55-63.

28. Paul Ricoeur, *The Symbolism of Evil*, trans. Emerson Buchanan (Boston: Beacon, 1986), 101.

embedded in it.²⁹ Of course, there are *stories* in other religious texts. But the Bible *is* a story wrapped around God's covenantal promise. Over against the disintegrating moves of higher critics, Ricoeur sees the Bible as a canon, "one vast 'intertext'" with an unfolding plot.³⁰ The laws and the narratives cannot be pulled apart, as is often done in higher criticism.³¹

"Not just any theology whatsoever can be tied to the narrative form, but only a theology that proclaims Yahweh to be the grand actor in a history of deliverance. Without a doubt it is this point that forms the greatest contrast between the God of Israel and the God of Greek philosophy." Biblical theology "speaks of God in accord with the historical drama instituted by the acts of deliverance reported in the story." In other words, it is "a theology in the form of *Heilsgeschichte* [the history of salvation]."³² It is precisely this Christocentric, redemptive-historical interpretation of Scripture in terms of promise and fulfillment that Gadamer (the lapsed Lutheran) claimed was superior to modern hermeneutics.³³

While narrative ties everything together, Ricoeur warns that a merely narrative theology is as reductive as other modern approaches.³⁴ There is a "time" to the wisdom literature, for instance, that is not narrative time.³⁵ If the Bible were only a narrative, it would simply slip into the past. The laws and doctrines give it a permanence, while the narratives ground the laws and doctrines "in its theology of the covenant in speaking of God's faithfulness."³⁶ This implies, by the way, that the reliability of the laws and doctrines is just as essential as the narrative itself.

The specific covenants provide the context for God's relationship to his people.³⁷ They also provide a "cumulative aspect" to biblical time and the identity of Israel's God.³⁸ The old is always at work even in the new, as the new covenant is still

---

29. Ricoeur, *Figuring the Sacred*, 183.

30. Ibid., 171. Comparisons may be made with Brevard Childs's "canonical" approach.

31. Ibid., 172.

32. Ibid., 40. Like many biblical scholars and theologians with whom he sympathized, Ricoeur offers a false choice between narrative theology and metaphysics. Although he is correct to emphasize that God's self-identification with a particular character in an unfolding plot is crucial, it is unclear why this emphasis must exclude technical terms like "being," "essence," etc., which are fundamental to orthodox theology.

33. Hans-Georg Gadamer, *Truth and Method*, 2nd ed. (New York: Continuum, 1991), 292.

34. This fact points up Ricoeur's aversion to reductionism. He is not particularly fond of "schools": narrative, phenomenological, speech act, history-of-religions, etc.—and, in this case, what was then a new program identified with the narrative theology of Hans Frei and other "Yale School" scholars. This is one of the reasons why it is difficult to place him, but also why diverse readers can find something astonishing in his analysis.

35. Ricoeur, *Figuring the Sacred*, 178.

36. Ibid., 173.

37. One of the best examples of Ricoeur's integration of the covenant motif is "The Category of 'Before God': The Covenant," in *Symbolism of Evil*, 50–3.

38. Ricoeur, *Figuring the Sacred*, 173.

talking about "a new exodus, a new desert, a new Sinai, a new Zion, a new Davidic descendance, and so on ... A few centuries later, the early church will turn this procedure into a hermeneutic and find in it the basic structures of its typological reading of the Old Testament"—a retrospective and prospective dialectic already at work in the OT itself.[39]

If the Bible were merely a catalog of timelessly true doctrines and laws, biblical faith would hardly belong to history. But prophecy and eschatology keep the history from standing still.[40] Despite certain Bultmann-like expressions that both Gadamer and Ricoeur share with Heidegger, Ricoeur objects strenuously to the existentialist theologian's false dichotomies, especially between kerygma and myth. "The equation we are seeking to reconstruct between a narrativized kerygma and a kerygmatized narrative seems indeed to have its rationale in the identity proclaimed between the Christ of faith and the Jesus of history."[41] The narrative is not a *bridge to* the historical Jesus. Rather, "It is *in narrative* that [the Gospel writer] interprets the identity of Jesus."[42]

Ricoeur defends fundamental unity between hermeneutics, Christology, and soteriology. Modern diffidence shown toward the Jesus of history is largely the result of rejecting the depths of humanity's sinful condition and the need for justification by grace alone. Kant's interpretation of Romans 5 "is certainly a Pelagian interpretation of the phrase 'in Adam,'" he judges.[43] Thus, "Kant manifests no interest for the Jesus of history, as we would put it today. The only thing that is important philosophically is the Christ of faith elevated to an idea or an ideal." It's all ethics, which has no room for Christ or justification.[44] Genuine semiotic analysis would never make the "kernel"-"husk" dichotomy of higher criticism (especially Bultmann), since in narrative interpretation the events and commentary/interpretation are inextricably linked.[45]

The events reported in Scripture name God: the God who raised Jesus from the dead.[46] Once more the narrative is not merely the context in which certain divine attributes (propositions) are revealed, though that is true enough. Rather, the narrative itself reveals who God is: a "who"—a character in a story—rather than a "what"—a substance of certain qualities.[47] "The word 'God' says more than the

---

39. Ibid., 176. The argument thus far is quite similar to Hans W. Frei, *The Eclipse of Biblical Narrative: A Study in Eighteenth and Nineteenth Century Hermeneutics* (New Haven: Yale University Press, 1974), yet with a more expansive view of narrative's essential integration with other parts of Scripture.

40. Ricoeur, *Figuring the Sacred*, 176.

41. Ibid., 185.

42. Ibid., emphasis added.

43. Ibid., 81.

44. Ibid., 85–6.

45. Ibid., 158.

46. Ibid., 225.

47. Again Ricoeur overreacts to scholastic treatments of God's being and attributes as "the God of the philosophers." Yet his point is well taken, that God reveals himself not only in propositions (doctrines) but in the action of the narrative itself.

word 'being' because it presupposes the entire context of narratives, prophecies, laws, wisdom, writings, psalms, and so on."[48] "God" is never abstracted from the creative and saving events: the God *of* Abraham, Isaac, and Jacob.[49] "Some may say that the relation between the Christological ground and this mediation through the whole of history of the names of God is circular. Certainly it is circular. But this circle must be courageously assumed. Everything, in one sense, begins with the cross and resurrection."[50]

But at some point we have to ask, Is the story *true*? Like Barth and Frei, Ricoeur's evasion of such questions is motivated not by a higher-critical agenda but by the reduction of truth to a revelatory event. And I think that he improves on Barth and Frei in his nuanced critique of modern dichotomies between truth and myth, fact and value, history and interpretation.[51] In particular, Ricoeur rejects the opposition between kerygma and myth that Bultmann represents. We cannot take refuge in existential truths that have no connection to history. Above all, we do not stand over the Bible as its autonomous interpreter. "Faith is the attitude of the one who accepts being interpreted at the same time that he or she interprets the world of the text. Such is the hermeneutical constitution of the biblical faith, ... resisting all psychologizing reductions of faith." He adds,

> The feeling of absolute dependence would remain a weak and inarticulated sentiment if it were not the response to the proposition of a new being that opens new possibilities of existence for me. Hope, unconditional trust, would be empty if it did not rely on a constantly renewed interpretation of sign-events reported by the writings, such as the exodus in the Old Testament and the resurrection in the New Testament. These are the events of deliverance that open and disclose the utmost possibilities of my own freedom and thus become for me the word of God. Such is the properly hermeneutical constitution of faith.[52]

All historical writing involves fiction—not "made-up stories"—but interpreted facts.[53] A narrative is not just a chronology, a catalog of propositional statements. A myth is the overarching story that makes sense of us, our world, and the meaning of it all: the *pax Romana*, Christendom, Enlightenment, Democracy, Communism. Each system champions a particular *mythos* of who we are, why we are here, and where we are (or should be) going. Stories are social. They break us out of our self-enclosed individual existence and make us part of a community. *Indeed, the*

---

48. Ricoeur, *Figuring the Sacred*, 228.
49. Ibid.
50. Ibid., 231.
51. Vanhoozer interacts with this issue in *Biblical Narrative in the Philosophy of Paul Ricoeur*, 11–12, 91–4, 101–3, 176–8, 192–3, 238–9.
52. Ricoeur, *Figuring the Sacred*, 47.
53. This is the main burden of Paul Ricoeur, *Time and Narrative*, 3 vols., trans. Kathleen McLaughlin and David Pellauer (Chicago: University of Chicago Press, 1984–8).

proclamation of the biblical narrative forms not merely a common community but a sacred communion: the body of Christ.

There is a world of myth in which actual historical events are unimportant. At the other extreme, there is calculative reasoning, where we live and work most of the time. Where does God fit in all of this? According to Mark I. Wallace, Ricoeur's writing is characterized "by a fragile hope that in the borderlands beyond calculative reason there might be a world of transcendent possibilities (mediated through the text) that can refigure and remake the world of the reader."[54] Here I suggest that we are closer to the world of C. S. Lewis in his articulation of "The Myth That Became Fact."[55]

As Wallace points out, "The concept of plot—or rather 'emplotment,' as [Ricoeur] prefers—is the linking idea that holds together both forms of writing."[56] Certain elements associated with fiction are present in historical writing, just as fiction is never isolated from real life. A human life (*ipse*-identity: selfhood that has a stable yet developing answer to the question, "Who am I?") thus "storied" is itself a kind of historical fiction.[57] The Bible, especially in preaching, projects a world that we may enter to discover new possibilities for existence: "emplotment."[58] Instead of a sovereign reader coming to master the text or to find resources for a self whose identity is already settled, Ricoeur declares, "It is the text, with its universal power of world disclosure, which gives a self to the ego."[59]

This emphasis on the sovereignty of the text (with its divine summons) over the reader stands in stark contrast with the Enlightenment's emphasis on the autonomous self and especially with the sovereignty of the reader in Roland Barthes's 1968 essay, "The Death of the Author." Again, the Bible is unique in this respect. God's Word does not merely invite us to think something or do something; much less is it the self-expression of pious souls or the holy church. Rather, it comes from God and has "the power to set forth the new being it proclaims." Ricoeur refers to "a word that is *addressed to us rather than our speaking it*, a word that *constitutes us rather than our articulating it*—a word *that speaks*."[60] He adds, "This is what I call the world of the text, the world probably belonging to this unique text."[61]

The theological implications are considerable: The first task of hermeneutics is not to give rise to a decision on the part of the reader but to allow the world of being that is the "issue" of the biblical text to unfold. Thus, above and beyond

---

54. Mark I. Wallace, "Introduction," in Ricoeur, *Figuring the Sacred*, 2.

55. C. S. Lewis, "*Myth Became Fact*," in *God in the Dock: Essays on Theology and Ethics* (Grand Rapids: Eerdmans, 1970).

56. Wallace, "Introduction," 11.

57. Ricoeur, *Figuring the Sacred*, 13.

58. Ibid., 41.

59. Paul Ricoeur, *Interpretation Theory: Discourse and the Interpretation of Meaning* (Fort Worth: Texas Christian University, 1976), 95.

60. Ricoeur, *Figuring the Sacred*, 66, emphases added.

61. Ibid., 43.

emotions, disposition, belief, or nonbelief is the proposition of a world that in the biblical language is called a new world, a new covenant, the kingdom of God, a new birth.[62] "These are the realities unfolded before the text, which are certainly for us, but which begin from the text," its "objective" meaning or reference. This is revelation, which includes me and my world in it and its world.[63]

Of course, we cannot comprehend the miracle of how the Spirit creates a new world through the word. But, in one of the most relevant passages for preaching, Ricoeur explains,

> In effect, what progressively happens in the Gospel is the recognition of Jesus as being the Christ. We can say in this regard that the Gospel is not a simple account of the life, teaching, work, death, and resurrection of Jesus, but the communicating of an act of confession, a communication by means of which the reader in turn is rendered capable of performing the same recognition that occurs inside the text.[64]

He adds, "The narrative of the life and death of Jesus is organized in such a way that the knowledge unveiled right at the beginning should be appropriated by the actors themselves and, beyond them, by the reader. It is the work of the text to do this."[65]

Through preaching, *we* are swept into the story. The confrontation between Jesus and Martha at Lazarus's tomb, where he brings her to the confession that he is the Resurrection and the Life (Jn 11:25), happens to us. Jesus himself speaks through his word of judgment and grace. The Spirit produces the perlocutionary effect through proclamation. It belongs to "the nature of proclamation," says Ricoeur, "to reverse the relation from written to spoken."[66]

Relocating the Sacred: Manifestation vs. Proclamation

Ricoeur also challenges Mircea Eliade's dichotomy between "religions of the sacred" and "religions of proclamation," taken for granted by many scholars. Especially since the Romantic era, Protestantism has often been represented as contributing to the "disenchantment" of the cosmos: The word drove out the sacred, we are told.[67] Some, like Charles Taylor, even argue that the Reformation was simply the

---

62. Ibid., 44.
63. Ibid.
64. Ibid., 162.
65. Ibid., n. 1. I would rephrase this as "the Spirit through the text …"; there is little if any pneumatology in Ricoeur's formulations of the text's power to unfold a new world—and to bring hearers into it.
66. Ibid., 71.
67. Taking the phrase from Friedrich Schiller, Max Weber argued the case in *The Sociology of Religion* (trans. Ephraim Fischoff [Boston: Beacon, 1963]) and *The Protestant Ethic and the Spirit of Capitalism* (trans. Talcott Parsons [New York: Scribner, 1958]). The flaws in Weber's method, research, and analysis are numerous. Nevertheless, the "Weber Thesis" continues to be taken for granted by nonspecialists across a variety of fields.

outworking of the anti-sacred impulses of the Hebrew prophets.[68] Influenced by Max Weber, Mircea Eliade (1907–1986) deployed this contrast in order to affirm "the sacred" over "proclamation." Eliade argued that rituals participate in the hierophanies (manifestations of the gods).[69] Hierophanies are "breakthroughs" of the divine into the world, though in the biblical world of the Hebrew prophets and early Christians this is identified with "idolatry," Eliade acknowledged.[70] Ricoeur took the thesis seriously but realized that biblical faith makes a cunning sleight of hand at this point.

At first, Ricoeur seems to adopt Eliade's dichotomy but, unlike Eliade, favors the Bible's hermeneutics of proclamation over hierophanies. The idols cannot even speak, as the prophets mock.[71] A hermeneutics of proclamation is *disruptive*. God is always doing "new things," things that have never even been heard of. The cosmic sacredness of all things in the Canaanite cults contrasts sharply with Hebrew prophets.[72]

"The universe of the sacred," Ricoeur argues, "is internally 'bound.'" It is an eternal circle. Even the sacred celebrations are tied closely to the calendar of natural turning of the seasons. For example, Persephone, the goddess-queen of the underworld and wife of Hades, comes back to life every spring. But the biblical faith is tied uniquely to a series of unrepeatable events of promise and fulfillment: God's saving acts of the past (Passover, Exodus, Conquest) that are linked eschatologically to an even greater future reality (Golgotha, the resurrection, and ascension, as well as Pentecost and Christ's return). In placing us within this story through preaching and sacrament, the Spirit creates Christ's ecclesial body. For this very reason, as Gerhard von Rad (on whom Ricoeur depends) notes, a genuinely historical consciousness emerged for the first time in Israel.[73]

---

68. The arguments cannot be summarized, much less engaged, in the scope of this essay. It is a relatively common thesis, arguing that the Reformation's "war on the idols" extended to an all-out offensive against the sacred. Taylor even acknowledges that the roots of Reformation iconoclasm are in the Hebrew prophets and that the Bible as a whole represents an assault on "the sacred." "To draw on this power, you have to leap out of the field of magic altogether, and throw yourself on the power of God alone. This 'disenchanting' move is implicit in the tradition of Judaism, and later Christianity" (*A Secular Age*, 74).

69. Wendy Doniger, "Foreword," to Mircea Eliade, *Shamanism: Archaic Technologies of Ecstasy* (Princeton: Princeton University Press, 2004), xiii. See also Eliade, *Myth of the Eternal Return: Cosmos and History*, trans. Willard R. Trask (Princeton: Princeton University Press, 1971).

70. Mircea Eliade, *Myth and Reality*, trans. Willard R. Trask (New York: Harper & Row, 1983).

71. Ricoeur, *Figuring the Sacred*, 49–50.

72. Ibid., 55.

73. Gerhard von Rad, *Theology of the Old Testament*, trans. D. M. G. Stalker (Louisville: Westminster John Knox, 2001), vol. 1. Throughout this volume the "promise-fulfillment" pattern dominates von Rad's method. See also the excellent introduction by Walter Brueggemann on just this point in *Theology of the Old Testament: Testimony, Dispute, Advocacy* (Minneapolis: Fortress, 2012), xviii–xxviii.

In contrast with the bounded cosmos of pagan myth and ritual, the biblical cosmos is paradoxical, which means that it throws off our expectations about what will always be. "The paradoxical universe of the parable, the proverb, and the eschatological saying on the contrary, is a 'burst' or an 'exploded' universe."[74] For example, one thinks of Nathan's parable that draws David out into the open, with the punch line, "You are that man" (2 Sam. 12:7). This is precisely how Jesus' parables work as well: Even as he is telling them, the Pharisees he addresses are carrying out the plot, realizing that he is talking about them—yet he is also talking to us. If we reduce these parables to propositional statements, they lose this interpersonal effect.

"I will say first of all that with the Hebraic faith the word outweighs the numinous," Ricoeur says. Even in Isaiah's vision of the Holy One, the face is hidden and the emphasis falls on the dialogue: The prophet is *summoned* and in the process is transformed from being paralyzed by his unworthiness to being forgiven and empowered to bring God's Word to the people. Drawing again on von Rad, Ricoeur says, "The whole of Israel's theology is organized around certain fundamental discourses." Even hymns, wisdom, and laws "are grafted onto the polarity of tradition [founding acts] and prophecy [criticism of Israel's self-confident presumption]." Torah smashes the idols. "A theology of the Name is opposed to any hierophany of an idol. Hearing the word has taken the place of a vision of signs."[75]

But theologians like Bultmann and Harvey Cox rush to the other extreme, making much of this war on the sacred in support of their "secular theology."[76] Ricoeur rejects this reaction. Instead, we need "some mediation between the sacred and the kerygma."

> I am surprised to see how many critical thinkers, whose suspicious nature is elsewhere limitless, capitulate before what they take to be the verdict of modernity and adopt the ideology of science and technology in a most naïve fashion ... Modernity is neither a fact nor our destiny. It is henceforth an open question.[77]

So away with the rhetoric that biblical faith is archaic![78] "Stripped of any ritualization, can the repetitive moments of life be anything other than an image of damnation? ... Is Christianity without the sacred possible?"[79]

Disturbed by this loss of the sacred in our culture, still others pursue "the retreat of the sacred into the unconscious," which is just as atheistic as the

---

74. Ricoeur, *Figuring the Sacred*, 60.
75. Ibid., 56.
76. Ibid., 61.
77. Ibid., 63.
78. Ibid.
79. Ibid., 64.

elevation of science and technology. "Indeed, this retreat is just the dark side of the same phenomenon, the counterpart of the Enlightenment." Christianity must resist this retreat, realizing that "kerygmatic religion is virtually antisacral" in that non-biblical sense.[80] This proclamation provokes experiences, to be sure. Not just experiences of "crisis and decision, as in the many theologies of crisis," he adds, alluding to Bultmann. Rather, "They are also experiences of culmination, as in the parable of the pearl of great price where 'finding the inestimable' constitutes the supreme joy."[81]

What has Ricoeur done here? He has exposed the shallowness of *both* the approach that thinks valuing the sacred requires returning to pagan theurgy[82] *and* one that rejects the sacred as if this could hold forth any hope of affirming the world. Instead, Ricoeur agrees with the biblical writers (and the Reformers) that the sacred is not *abolished* by the word but, on the contrary, all of the gravity of the sacred shifts away from the cosmos and hierophanies to the word and the sacraments. Both sacralizing nature and rejecting the sacred avoid the authentic intervention of the Word-made-flesh, who confronts us now in the sacred event of preaching and sacrament. Although there is still sacred space and time, says Ricoeur, the biblical emphasis is ethical, covenantal, and theological rather than aesthetic and mystical. Against a cosmic theology of sacred nature "the battle had to be merciless, without any compassion," as in the sarcastic polemic of the prophets.[83] By means of ordinary events and speech, ordinary events and speech are radically altered.

Only if one misunderstands the word of God—what is and especially what it does—can a "religion of proclamation" be seen as anything other than a genuine (and, with biblical proclamation, *the* genuine) "religion of the sacred." True, the word breaks away from the numinous, *but only to take over its functions*.

> There would be no hermeneutic if there were no proclamation. *But there would be no proclamation if the word were not powerful; that is, if it did not have the power to set forth the new being it proclaims*. A word that is addressed *to us* rather than *our speaking it*, a word that *constitutes us* rather than *our articulating it*—a word that speaks—does not such a word reaffirm the sacred just as much as abolish it?[84]

There is no inherent opposition between hearing and seeing, hierophany and word, manifestation and proclamation, in Scripture. Word and manifestation are finally

---

80. Ibid., 62.
81. Ibid., 61.
82. In *History and Truth*, 11, Ricoeur contrasts the Neoplatonist heritage with that of Irenaeus. It would be interesting at this point to put Ricoeur in conversation with John Milbank and other representatives of Radical Orthodoxy.
83. Ricoeur, *Figuring the Sacred*, 56.
84. Ibid., emphases added.

reconciled in John's Prologue, Ricoeur observes. "The Word became flesh and we beheld his glory" (Jn 1:14). Even the cosmogonic myths of the gods are exploited for Yahweh and the incarnation, subverted and taken captive to the history of deliverance.[85] Thus, for all his iconoclasm Ricoeur appears to argue similarly with C. S. Lewis (among many others) that the gospel is not anti-mythical or anti-sacred but the true myth and the genuinely sacred event that breaks through our self-enclosed existence. In fact, he says, "The subtle equilibrium between the iconoclastic virtualities of proclamation and the symbolic resurgence of the sacred has expressed itself throughout the history of Christianity as a dialectic of preaching and sacraments ... The sacrament, we could say, is *the mutation of the sacred ritual into the kerygmatic realm*."[86]

There is not first of all an individual or a community and then a word that it speaks to express inner thoughts, feelings, or agendas. The word creates and defines the self and the community that hears it. This socializing effect of the word of God not only works vertically (from God to us) but also unites horizontally, into one body, people from all nations and generations. "You preach on canonical texts, but not on profane; the community would be completely changed if you chose a modern poet to do a sermon, or if you took the Bhagavad Gita into the church," says Ricoeur. This point merits reflection, not only for those who actually *do* bring the Bhagavad Gita into the pulpit, but also for those who think that movie clips or reviews of one's summer reading will be more relevant that the gospel texts. "This is a crisis of the community because its own identity relies on the identity of the text. ... Preaching is the permanent reinterpretation of the text that is regarded as grounding a community; therefore, for the community to address itself to another text would be to make a decision concerning its social identity. A community that does that becomes another kind of community."[87]

Conclusion

Ricoeur is not an aloof theorist. Since his earliest days he found the word in preaching and sacrament to be the "strange new world" worth inhabiting in troubling times. He defined himself as "a listener to Christian preaching" on the presupposition "that this speaking is meaningful, that it is worthy of consideration, and that examining it may accompany and guide the transfer from the text to life where it will verify itself fully."

---

85. Ibid.: "The new Zion prophetically inverts the reminiscence of the sacred city, just as the Messiah who is to come projects into the eschatological future the glorious royal figures of divine unction. And for Christians, Golgotha becomes a new *axis mundi*. Every new language is also the reemployment of an ancient symbolism."
86. Ibid., 67, emphasis added.
87. Ibid., 70.

Can I account for this presupposition? Alas, I stumble already. I do not know how to sort out what is here "unravelable" situation, uncriticized custom, deliberate preference, or profound unchosen choice. I can only confess that my desire to hear more is all these things, and that it defies all these distinctions. But if what I presuppose precedes everything I can choose to think about, how do I avoid the famous circle of believing in order to understand and understanding in order to believe? I do not seek to avoid it. I boldly stay within this circle in the hope that, through the transfer from text to life, what I have risked will be returned a hundredfold as an increase in comprehension, valor, and joy. Shall I tolerate the fact that thinking, which aims at what is universal and necessary, is linked in a contingent way to individual events and particular texts that report them? Yes, I shall assume this contingency, so scandalous for thinking, as one aspect of the presupposition attached to listening. For I hope that once I enter into the movement of comprehending faith, I shall discover the very reason for that contingency, if it is true that the increase in comprehension that I expect is indissolubly linked to testimonies to the truth, which are contingent in every instance and rendered through certain acts, lives, and beings ... This presupposition of the textuality of faith distinguishes biblical faith ("Bible" meaning book) from all others. In one sense, therefore, texts do precede life. I can name God in my faith because the texts preached to me have already named God.[88]

The alternative is not reason, he continues, but a different presupposition of faith, the "I think" which becomes "the principle of everything that is valid." "The idea of a subject that posits itself thus becomes the unfounded foundation, or, better, the foundation that founds itself, in relation to which every rule of validity is derived. In this way, the subject becomes the supreme 'presupposition.'"[89] Only Christian preaching can overcome this—a presupposition that is finally the antithesis of a self-founding. "Listening excludes founding oneself," giving up our claim to "mastery, sufficiency, and autonomy. The Gospels' statement that 'Whoever would save his life will lose it' applies to this giving up. This double renouncing of the absolute 'object' and the absolute 'subject' is the price that must be paid to enter into a radically nonspeculative and prephilosophical mode of language."[90]

---

88. Ibid., 218.
89. Ibid., 223–4.
90. Ibid., 224.

Chapter 16

THE DRAMA OF (IMPUTATION) DOCTRINE: ORIGINAL GUILT AS BIBLICAL AND SYSTEMATIC THEOLOGY

Hans Madueme

A lifetime ago when I was a medical student, I fell in love with theology—irresistibly and irrevocably. After completing a residency in internal medicine some years later, I left my medical career to attend seminary. At that time, my extended family thought I was losing my mind (and earning potential), but several factors played into my decision to move to Trinity Evangelical Divinity School. One was my experience with Kevin J. Vanhoozer's *Is There a Meaning in This Text?* This was a book on a mission! I resonated with the central query that has driven much of the literary output throughout his illustrious career: "What does it mean to be 'biblical'?"[1] That question inspired Kevin's "God in Biblical and Systematic Theology" doctoral seminar, where we pondered how "to negotiate the 'ugly ditch' between" exegesis and theological construction (quoting the course syllabus). This basic conundrum was far from the mind of church fathers for whom exegesis and theology were as one; but, in the modern era, such questions haunt systematic theologians. Threading that needle, Kevin writes elsewhere that doctrine "is faithful to biblical discourse not when it simply repeats the same terms in different contexts but when it renders the same judgments by using different terms."[2]

Original guilt is a doctrine that has fallen on hard times in academia. As I define it, "original guilt" means that descendants of Adam and Eve are guilty and

---

1. Kevin J. Vanhoozer, *Is There a Meaning in This Text? The Bible, the Reader, and the Morality of Literary Knowledge* (Grand Rapids: Zondervan, 1998), 9.

2. Kevin J. Vanhoozer, "Is the Theology of the New Testament One or Many? Between (the Rock of) Systematic Theology and (the Hard Place of) Historical Occasionalism," in *Reconsidering the Relationship between Biblical and Systematic Theology in the New Testament: Essays by Theologians and New Testament Scholars*, ed. Benjamin Reynolds, Brian Lugioyo, and Kevin J. Vanhoozer (Tübingen: Mohr Siebeck, 2014), 17–38. See also *The Drama of Doctrine: A Canonical-Linguistic Approach to Christian Theology* (Louisville: Westminster John Knox, 2005), 324–53, indebted to David S. Yeago, "The New Testament and the Nicene Dogma: A Contribution to the Recovery of Theological Exegesis," *Pro Ecclesia* 3, no. 2 (1994): 152–64.

justly condemned for Adam's first sin.³ Roman Catholic theologians have largely abandoned the notion of inherited guilt. For example, before he became Pope Benedict XVI, then Cardinal Ratzinger reinterpreted original guilt as damaged relationships: "When the network of human relationships is damaged from the very beginning, then every human being enters into a world that is marked by relational damage."⁴ His dislike of the hard edges of the Augustinian doctrine reflects much recent Catholic scholarship on original sin.⁵

The situation is no different among some Protestant theologians, like Wolfhart Pannenberg, who writes, "It is impossible for me to be held jointly responsible, as though I were a joint cause, for an act that another did many generations ago and in a situation radically different from mine."⁶ Oliver Crisp is equally candid: "It is immoral because it is necessarily morally wrong to punish the innocent, and I am innocent of Adam's sin (I did not commit his sin or condone it). It is also immoral because the guilt of one person's sin does not transfer to another (I am not guilty of committing Adam's sin)."⁷ Their basic charge is this: earlier theologians, swayed by Augustine, coaxed Rom. 5:12-21 into a dogmatic procrustean bed. However, modern exegetes have demonstrated that there is no such doctrine of original guilt in Romans or anywhere else in the Bible. Original guilt is a house built on exegetical sand.

Despite these dire criticisms, Kevin's canonically focused theological interpretation can help rehabilitate the doctrine of original guilt. Accordingly, this chapter will argue that original guilt is a very biblical doctrine—*biblical* not merely in terms of faithful exegesis of biblical texts but also in how it synthesizes a range of canonical judgments. My first task is to lay out the imputation of Adam's sin as the right reading of Rom. 5:12-21 and 1 Cor. 15:21-22. I then develop a wider canonical and doctrinal basis for imputed guilt in light of infant baptism and infant death. Finally, I conclude that the immediate imputation of Adam's guilt lies near the heart of the gospel.

The Imputation of Adam's Sin

Romans 5:12 teaches original guilt, according to Augustine. "Through the bad will of that one man all sinned in him," the African bishop argued, "when all were

---

3. We are liable to punishment *because* we are culpable for Adam's sin. For the relevance of the medieval concepts of *reatus poenae* and *reatus culpae*, see John Murray, *The Imputation of Adam's Sin* (Nutley: P&R, 1977), 71–95.

4. Joseph Cardinal Ratzinger, "*'In the Beginning . . .': A Catholic Understanding of the Story of Creation and the Fall*, trans. Boniface Ramsey (Grand Rapids: Eerdmans, 1995), 73.

5. E.g., see Tatha Wiley, *Original Sin: Origins, Developments, Contemporary Meanings* (Mahwah: Paulist, 2002), esp. 243 n. 9.

6. Wolfhart Pannenberg, *Anthropology in Theological Perspective*, trans. Matthew O'Connell (New York: T&T Clark, 1985), 124.

7. Oliver Crisp, "On Original Sin," *IJST* 17, no. 3 (2015): 257.

that one man, and on that account each individual contracted from him original sin."[8] Condemnation, he wrote elsewhere, "pervades the whole mass of humanity."[9] Death is universal because all of humanity sinned collectively *in Adam* and shares in his guilt. The human race was seminally present in Adam, like Levi in the body of Abraham (Heb. 7:9-10). Adam's sin was ours too. As penalty for their role in Adam's first sin, his descendants inherit innate, moral corruption.

Pelagius, of course, disputed Augustine's realism, arguing instead that Rom. 5:12 denies both inherited guilt and corruption. In the Pelagian scheme, sin is not innate depravity antecedent to our actions; people are independent of Adam and sin in their own persons. The early church rightly rejected this view, siding with Paul's insistence that Adam's sin brought condemnation and death to all (Rom. 5:15-19; 1 Cor. 15:21-22). Although medieval theologians modified Augustine's realism, they typically accepted original guilt.[10]

Romans 5:12-21 without Original Guilt

Recent Bible scholars have jettisoned any concept of an alien guilt in Paul. Thus, Joseph Fitzmyer argues that ἥμαρτον in v. 12 "should not be understood as 'have sinned collectively' or as 'have sinned in Adam', because they would be additions to Paul's text."[11] All sinned in their own persons, *not* in Adam, consistent with Paul's use of ἥμαρτον elsewhere (e.g., Rom. 2:12; 3:23; 5:14, 16, etc.).[12] Joseph Fitzmyer seems to deny the possibility of theologically interpreting a word in terms that are not explicit in its narrow linguistic meaning. Most readers would rightly demur from such a restrictive exegetical principle. Nonetheless, if we deny that all sinned *in Adam*, then whence the universality of sin? Charles Cranfield offers an elegant solution: all sin "in their own persons ... as a result of the corrupt nature inherited from Adam."[13] Sin is not merely external imitation of Adam, as Pelagius held; Adam's sin had an internal effect, "the fruit of the desperate moral debility and corruption which resulted from man's primal transgression and which all succeeding generations of mankind have inherited."[14] However, Cranfield's

---

8. Augustine, *Marriage and Desire* II.5.15 (WSA 2:61).

9. Augustine, *Nature and Grace* 8.9 (WSA 1:229).

10. Wiley, *Original Sin*, 76–88.

11. Joseph Fitzmyer, *Romans* (New York: Doubleday, 1993), 417.

12. Fitzmyer also argued from Rom. 5:12 that all sin *because* all died; see ibid., 416, and "The Consecutive Meaning of ΕΦ'Ω in Romans 5.12," *NTS* 39 (1993): 321–39. On why his reading is implausible, see Thomas R. Schreiner, "Original Sin and Original Death: Romans 5:12-19," in *Adam, the Fall, and Original Sin: Theological, Biblical, and Scientific Perspectives*, ed. Hans Madueme and Michael Reeves (Grand Rapids: Baker Academic, 2014), 273–4.

13. C. E. B. Cranfield, "On Some Problems in the Interpretation of Romans 5.12," *SJT* 22 (1969): 331.

14. Ibid., 337. Similarly, Richard N. Longenecker, *The Epistle to the Romans: A Commentary on the Greek Text*, NIGTC (Grand Rapids: Eerdmans, 2016), 590.

interpretation has to add an extra step to Paul's argument in Rom. 5:12-21. After all, Paul repeatedly draws a *direct* connection between Adam's sin and death (vv. 15, 16, 17, 18); yet, as Douglas Moo notes, Cranfield insinuates a middle term: "one man's trespass *resulted in the corruption of human nature, which caused all people to sin, and so* brought condemnation to all men."[15] Although there is little reason to think that Paul makes this inference, recent theologians have cashed in on the "corruption-only" position.

Oliver Crisp is a case in point. In dialogue with Huldrych Zwingli, Crisp argues that everyone inherits a defective moral condition from Adam—but without guilt. I am not culpable for inheriting this moral disease, "though it will lead to my death without the interposition of divine grace, just as some inherited conditions lead to death without medical intervention."[16] On this view, fallen human beings *will* inevitably sin.[17] Suffering from original corruption "yields condemnation irrespective of actual sin." As Crisp explains, "possession of original sin will lead to death and exclusion from the presence of God without the application of the relevant treatment: in this case, salvation through Christ."[18] Thomas McCall likewise endorses the corruption-only argument.[19] Corruption-only proponents favor the position, he writes, because "there is ample evidence for corruption—a corruption of the human nature that is deep and vast beyond telling. But on the other hand, they typically do not find such evidence for original guilt. Furthermore, they often argue that the doctrine of original guilt is utterly contrary to true justice."[20]

Yet the corruption-only account falters under scrutiny.[21] Crisp thinks that Adam's fall saddles humanity with a morally corrupt condition, a condition for which we are not culpable, but that same condition leads inevitably to human sinning ("sinning" for which we *are* culpable). This position is incoherent. If the fall caused original corruption, for which we bear no guilt, then any actual

---

15. Douglas Moo, *The Letter to the Romans*, 2nd ed., NICNT (Grand Rapids: Eerdmans, 2018), 353.

16. Oliver Crisp, "Sin," in *Christian Dogmatics: Reformed Theology for the Church Catholic*, ed. Michael Allen and Scott Swain (Grand Rapids: Baker Academic, 2016), 213.

17. Crisp puts it more precisely in order to account for premature infant death or mentally impaired persons: "The moral corruption of original sin makes it inevitable that all fallen human beings will actually sin on at least one occasion, if they live long enough and are appropriate subjects for the ascription of moral responsibility and culpability" ("On Original Sin," 261–2; original italics removed).

18. Ibid., 262.

19. In addition to Zwingli, McCall discerns a precedent in Arminius (Keith Stanglin and Thomas McCall, *Jacob Arminius: Theologian of Grace* [Oxford: Oxford University Press, 2012], 149–50).

20. Thomas McCall, *Against God and Nature: The Doctrine of Sin* (Wheaton: Crossway, 2019), 160–61.

21. My thinking has been shaped by Julius Müller, *The Christian Doctrine of Sin*, trans. William Urwick, 5th ed. (Edinburgh: T&T Clark, 1868), 2:307–57.

sins—which, as the theory goes, inevitably arise from that corruption—are themselves caused *necessarily* by the fall, for which we bear no guilt. If I have no personal guilt for my corrupt state, then the Lord cannot judge me guilty for actual sins arising necessarily from said state (in fact, naming them "sins" is a mistake).[22] One might try to neutralize this inference by arguing, against Crisp, that actual sins do not arise inevitably from original corruption. Perhaps an individual's free will can resist the power of internal corruption. Alas, that move traps you on the horns of a dilemma. On the one hand, the universality of sin exposes human "free will" as a paper tiger that is consistently (and mysteriously) *powerless* to block the expression of internal corruption. On the other hand, if human beings do have genuine incompatibilist freedom, then human sinlessness is a live option (or, if it is not, the universality of sin is again inexplicable).

Crisp insists that his corruption-only hamartiology is legitimately Reformed, in light of the Zwingli association. But Zwingli's conception of original corruption was an anomaly among Lutheran and Reformed theologians. Without ignoring the substantial diversity within the "Calvinist" tradition, Zwingli's account is marginal to the classical Reformation doctrine.[23] Original sin as corruption-only has more affinities with a Roman Catholic than Reformed theology of sin. Luther and most of the other Reformers, following Augustine, decreed concupiscence as culpable sin, yet medieval theologians saw concupiscence as the "tinder of sin" (*fomes peccati*), the punishment for original sin but not sin itself (so, too, the Council of Trent).[24] The seventeenth-century Remonstrants agreed that original corruption was a punishment for Adam's sin but insisted that his descendants incurred no guilt. The Apology for the Remonstrants explains that "it is contrary to justice and equity, that any one should be charged as guilty, for a sin that is not his own, or that he should be judged to be really guilty who in respect to his own individual voluntariness is innocent, or, rather, not guilty."[25] Zwingli notwithstanding, the

---

22. Responding to a similar objection, Crisp claims elsewhere that "moral approbation or blame attaches to *actions* an agent performs, not (or not necessarily) to the moral nature with which a person is created" ("A Moderate Reformed Response," in *Original Sin and the Fall: Five Views*, ed. J. B. Stump and Chad Meister [Downers Grove: IVP Academic, 2020], 142).

23. Crisp argues that Zwingli's account shares key features with the doctrine of original sin depicted in the Anglican *Thirty-Nine Articles of Religion* (1563) and the *Belgic Confession* (1561), in "Retrieving Zwingli's Doctrine of Original Sin," *Journal of Reformed Theology* 10 (2016): 357–60. In fact, Crisp may be misreading both confessions, neither of which supports his claim. See Hans Madueme, "An Augustinian-Reformed Response," in *Original Sin and the Fall: Five Views*, 136.

24. According to the Westminster Assembly, reflected in its Westminster Standards, original corruption *entails* guilt; see Robert Letham, *The Westminster Assembly: Reading Its Theology in Historical Context* (Phillipsburg: P&R, 2009), 205.

25. Simon Episcopius, *Apologia pro Confessione sive Declaratione Sententiae eorum, Qui in Foederato Belgio vocantur Remonstrantes, super praecipuis Articulis Religionis Christianae: Contra Censuram Quatuor Professorum Leidensium* (n.p., 1629),

theological pedigree of Crisp's thesis appears to be primarily in the medieval Catholic and Arminian traditions.[26]

Henri Blocher carves out a mediating position between Augustine and Pelagius. Based on Rom. 5:13-14, he thinks that God cannot judge sin without established law. "Sin cannot be imputed" unless an explicit divine command is broken. As isolated individuals, Blocher explains, we humans "have no standing with God, no relationship to his judgment"—entire generations between Adam and Moses who, unlike Adam, never violated a divine command would be (as it were) "floating in a vacuum."[27] Yet "death reigned from the time of Adam to the time of Moses" (Rom. 5:14).[28] Since death is the result of sin (Rom. 5:12), how were the sins of pre-Mosaic generations imputed *as transgression* when no law had been given? According to Blocher, Adam is the missing link, the legal head who makes possible "*the imputation, the judicial treatment, of human sins.* His role thus brings about the condemnation of all, and its sequel, death."[29] Blocher continues, "Before the law of Moses was promulgated, sin was imputed and therefore death reigned owing to the relationship of all humans to Adam, the natural and legal head or mediator."[30] In virtue of Adam's natural headship, every descendant is born with a will that opposes God and is thus guilty. "Being born sinners is not a penalty, or strictly the result of transference, but simply an existential, spiritual, *fact* for human beings since Adam."[31] Alien guilt is irrelevant, for everyone sins in his or her own person.[32]

Against Blocher's thesis, Rom. 2:14-15 seems to deny Adam as the basis for imputing pre-Mosaic sins. Paul writes that those who lived before Moses "are a law for themselves, even though they do not have the law, since they show that the requirements of the law are written on their hearts." Blocher anticipates this objection:

> If this provides a way other than that of Adamic dependence, leading to the same end (imputation of human sins), then my proposal must be withdrawn.

84-5. The translation is from William G. T. Shedd, *A History of Christian Doctrine*, 2 vols. (New York: Scribner, 1863), 2:184.

26. For a similar judgment, see Leslie, "Original Sin," 346-7.

27. Henri Blocher, *Original Sin: Illuminating the Riddle*, New Studies in Biblical Theology (Leicester: Inter-Varsity, 1997), 77.

28. Unless otherwise noted, Scripture quotations are from the NIV®. Copyright © 1973, 1978, 1984, 2011 by Biblica, Inc.™

29. Blocher, *Original Sin*, 77.

30. Ibid.

31. Ibid., 129.

32. Adam's headship permits God to judge human iniquity *as transgression* of his commandments; however, Adam's primal sin plays no causal role in human sinning—as Blocher concludes, "I see no necessity for the idea that alien guilt was transferred (that is, that Adam's particular act was reckoned to the account of all)" (ibid., 130).

But I venture to suggest that it is not "another" way; rather, it is the same way described from another angle. Being related to God through Adam, the covenant head, is equivalent to having the law written on one's heart; they are two sides of the same coin.[33]

Blocher's argument has similarities with both Pelagian and Augustinian approaches, since each person sins in his or her own self (no one sins in Adam nor is Adam's guilt imputed), and each person sins in his or her own self *ab initio* and is thus guilty from birth. In reply, I cannot accept his exegesis of Rom. 5:13-14 for a number of crucial reasons (see more below). Furthermore, he seems to underestimate Paul's insistence that Adam's sin—not merely his headship—causes our condemnation and death (Paul emphasizes the point five times, Rom 5:15-19).[34] The causal link between Adam's sin and our own sin damages Blocher's thesis.

Blocher appeals to Adam's headship to explain why everyone is born in a state of guilt and willful enmity toward God. Once Adam fell, we were all born sinners due to "the organic solidarity of the race."[35] Ironically, Blocher does not escape the alleged problems with an alien guilt. His proposal still leaves us sinning from the beginning—*and that sin is guilt-bearing*. Even without the *peccatum alienum*, then, his proposal retains the very thing that has rankled critics since Pelagius. Hence Blocher's defensive remark: "An inborn state, or *habitus*, of guilt without any prior deliberation at a 'neutral' stage will be denounced by some as intolerably unjust. The root of this reaction, however, is clearly the absolutization of individual freedom."[36] Indeed! Yet I wonder if the pot is calling the kettle black. His denial of original guilt is odd given his own position. At any rate, the *peccatum alienum* has far more biblical support than Blocher recognizes—as I shall argue.

Once More on Imputed Guilt

The objections to original guilt are hard to square with Paul's reasoning in Rom. 5:12-21 and 1 Cor. 15:21-22.[37] Adam's fall brought sin into the human experience, and that sin inaugurated physical and spiritual death.[38] In the wake of Adam's sin, all people die because we all sinned individually (ἐφ' ᾧ πάντες ἥμαρτον). The one man's trespass leads not only to death (vv. 15, 17) but also to judgment and condemnation (vv. 16, 18). More pointedly: "through the disobedience of the one

33. Ibid., 80.
34. Cf. Schreiner, "Original Sin and Original Death," 176.
35. Blocher, *Original Sin*, 129.
36. Ibid., 131.
37. For a helpful survey of the main exegetical issues, see McCall, *Against God and Nature*, 176–84.
38. Moo, *Romans*, 348: "We are not forced to make a choice between [spiritual and physical death]. Paul frequently uses 'death' and related words to designate a 'physico-spiritual entity,' – 'total death,' the penalty incurred for sin."

man the many were made sinners" (v. 19). As Douglas Moo sums up, "'all sinned' must be given some kind of corporate meaning: sinning not as voluntary acts of sin in one's own person, but sinning in and with Adam."[39] In short, Adam's sin and human sinning are part of a deeper reality.

Although Augustine may have erred on some details, he saw this deeper reality, that Adam's posterity is guilty and justly condemned for his first sin. Against his Augustinian realism, however, I root original guilt in Adam's role as a federal head. Adam and Christ as representatives of humanity loom large in the parallelism of Rom. 5:15-21. Just as Adam's trespass brought the reign of death, so too the obedience of Christ unlocks God's astonishing grace (v. 15). The one sin ends in judgment and condemnation, but the gift of Christ enables justification (v. 16). One man brought death, whereas grace and righteousness abounded through one man (v. 17). Paul keeps piling on the symmetrical contrast: Adam's disobedience brings our sin, condemnation, and death, whereas Christ's righteousness brings justification, righteousness, and eternal life (vv. 18-19). Adam's sin effects our condemnation, just as Christ's righteousness effects our justification. Jesus is a federal head like Adam, who was a pattern or type of Christ (v. 14). God appointed both men to act in place of those they represented. Let us call this *imputation*.

Federalism holds that we all became sinners when Adam sinned. Adam's sin was imputed to us. Adam's sin and guilt are our sin and guilt.[40] However, Blocher takes issue with federalism's exegesis of Rom. 5:13-14: "There remains a slight tension," he writes, "between Paul's wording, 'they did not sin after the likeness of Adam's transgression', and the Reformed emphasis that they sinned in Adam."[41] In addition, Paul's emphasis on the period between Adam and Moses sits awkwardly with federal theology's precept that *all* people sinned in Adam.[42]

Blocher is right to fault the older federalists.[43] Nevertheless, federalism as such pledges no fealty to what seems to be a misreading of Rom 5:13-14. Adam died because he disobeyed God's direct command (v. 12). Everyone before Moses died too, even though God had not yet handed down any law. If Paul is saying that

---

39. Ibid., 354.

40. Charles Hodge famously argued that imputing the guilt of sin meant "the judicial obligation to satisfy justice" (*Systematic Theology* [New York: Scribner's, 1898], 2:194). He was wrong (even the great ones stumble!). The imputation of Adam's sin includes both penalty *and* guilt (Rom. 5:19, "the many were made *sinners*").

41. Blocher, *Original Sin*, 75.

42. Federal theologians have often interpreted Rom. 5:14—"those who did not sin by breaking a command"—as referring to infants or the mentally impaired. E.g., see John Murray, *The Epistle to the Romans*, vol. 1 (Grand Rapids: Eerdmans, 1959), 190–1.

43. With most contemporary exegetes, I disagree with the traditional Augustinian and federal grammatical reading of ἥμαρτον in v. 12, i.e., that we all sinned *in Adam*; defending the latter, see Murray, *Romans*, 178–87. Cf. Francis Turretin, *Institutes of Elenctic Theology*, trans. George Musgrove Giger (Phillipsburg: P&R, 1992), 1:617–18; however, in the broader context of vv. 13–21, sinning in and with Adam is the right *theological* interpretation.

the absence of law implies the absence of any formal sin, why did they all die? Recall that Paul has already said in v. 13 that sin was in the world before Moses (and see Rom. 2:12); thus, he cannot mean that their sins were not reckoned as sin *in any sense*. Those pre-Mosaic generations all died, and death results from *sin*. "Paul's point," Thomas Schreiner explains, "is that their sins, though still punishable by death, were not technically counted against them in the same way as sin was counted against Adam."[44] They died because they sinned against God. Although people disobeyed God's direct commands after Moses instituted the law, the post-Mosaic scene differed from Adam pre-fall. Since God's covenant with Israel was with a sinful people, Adam's sin had already corrupted the human race. Far from jeopardizing federalism, the fact that the generation before Moses did not transgress "as did Adam" actually *supports* it. They did not sin as did Adam because Adam's sin was the fountainhead. He was *sui generis*, the head of the human race. Typologically, he was the chosen representative, anticipating the one to come, Jesus Christ the righteous antitype.

Early Reformed theology understood the transmission of sin as natural propagation from Adam to his descendants. The realistic union had priority and guilt followed the corruption inherited from Adam. John Calvin, for example, commenting on Rom. 5:17, remarks that "by Adam's sin we are not condemned by imputation alone, as though we were punished only for the sin of another; but we suffer his punishment, because we also ourselves are guilty; *for as our nature is vitiated in him, it is regarded by God as having committed sin*."[45] Peter Martyr Vermigli described Adam "as a certaine common lumpe or masse, wherein was conteined all mankind: which lumpe being corrupted, we cannot be brought forth into the world, but corrupted and defiled."[46] As Robert Letham demonstrates, hereditary depravity and our realist connection to Adam were emphasized by other sixteenth- to early-seventeenth-century Reformers, among them Martin Bucer, Heinrich Bullinger, Wolfgang Musculus, William Perkins, Robert Pollock, Johannes Piscator, and Amandus Polanus (and reflected, too, in the Irish Articles of Religion, the Canons of Dort, and the Leiden Synopsis).[47]

The later shift from mediate to immediate imputation was part of the Reformed development of doctrine at the turn of the seventeenth century. As the covenant of works rose to prominence, Reformed divines increasingly emphasized Adam's role as the federal head of humanity. Francis Turretin, the apogee of these shifts in Reformed orthodoxy, wrote,

---

44. Schreiner, *Romans*, 284.

45. John Calvin, *Commentaries on the Epistle of Paul the Apostle to the Romans*, ed. and trans. John Owen (Edinburgh: Calvin Translation Society, 1849), 210, emphasis added.

46. Peter Martyr Vermigli, *The Common Places of the Most Famous and Renowned Doctor Peter Martyr*, trans. Anthonie Marten (London: Henrie Denham, Thomas Chard, William Broome, and Andrew Maunsell, 1583), 242, cited in Letham, *Westminster Assembly*, 211.

47. For historical documentation, see Letham, *Westminster Assembly*, 198–223.

> For the bond between Adam and his posterity is twofold: (1) natural, as he is the father, and we are his children; (2) political and forensic, as he was the prince and representative head of the whole human race. Therefore the foundation of imputation is not only the natural connection which exists between us and Adam ... but mainly the moral and federal (in virtue of which God entered into covenant with him as our head). Hence Adam stood in that sin not as a private person, but as a public and representative person—representing all his posterity in that action and whose demerit equally pertains to all.[48]

Although mediate imputation is a species of original guilt, it suffers from the same liability as the corruption-only position. If corruption is a consequence of divine punishment—and what else could it be?—then guilt must precede or coexist with it. Otherwise, all human beings through no fault of their own are born condemned with concupiscence, and thus the worry of divine injustice looms large. Building on the truths of mediate imputation, federalism as I defend it fully accepts the natural, biological, seminal union that we have with Adam. God appointed Adam, the first man, to represent all humans, that is, his genealogical descendants; genealogical descent, then, is the *necessary* ground for federal headship. As John Murray noted, "On the representative construction natural headship and representative headship are correlative, and each aspect has its own proper and specific function."[49] Herman Bavinck was also federalist and Augustinian: "Federalism certainly does not rule out the truth contained in realism; on the contrary, it fully accepts it. It proceeds from it but does not confine itself to it."[50] Although the imputation of Adam's sin rests on a physical unity with Adam, its justification lies in a deeper, moral unity with Adam as the federal head.[51]

Original Guilt as a Whole-Bible Doctrine

Original guilt is not merely an exegetical conclusion from Rom. 5:12-21 and 1 Cor. 15:21-22; it is also a whole-Bible doctrine that condenses a range of canonical judgments about the human condition.[52] Already in Augustine we see that original

---

48. Turretin, *Elenctic Theology*, 1:616.
49. Murray, *Imputation*, 37-8.
50. Herman Bavinck, *Reformed Dogmatics*, ed. John Bolt, trans. John Vriend (Grand Rapids: Baker Academic, 2003–8), 3:104.
51. Alas, I cannot engage here the important objections to imputed guilt. For a longer version of this essay that does so, see my "Mea Culpa: An Apology for Original Guilt," *Mid-America Journal of Theology* (forthcoming).
52. On the exegesis vs. doctrine distinction, see Ben Dunson, "Do Bible Words Have Bible Meaning? Distinguishing between Imputation as Word and Doctrine," *WTJ* 75 (2013): 239–60.

guilt has much wider theological warrants than Rom. 5:12.[53] The widespread practice of infant baptism proves original guilt; why else baptize infants?

Infant Baptism and Original Guilt

Augustine beat this drum relentlessly with copious citations from all corners of the Bible. Christ died for the ungodly (Rom. 5:6) and was a physician for the sick, not the healthy (Lk. 5:31-32).[54] If Jesus came to save his people from their sins, infants are among those beneficiaries (Mt. 1:21).[55] They too descend from Eve who was deceived (Gen. 3:1-6), and they too are cursed with a body of death (Rom. 7:24). The only antidote is the forgiveness of sins (Tit. 2:11).[56] Since babies need their sins forgiven (Mt. 26:28), they share that original guilt.[57] The grace of Christ in baptism delivers infants from the devil (Col. 1:13).[58] These texts are only a drop in the sea of biblical warrants throughout Augustine's writings. The logic of Scripture was irresistible: the possibility of redemption extends to the human race, which includes infants. They need baptism, Augustine concluded, to erase the guilt of Adam's sin.

Augustine defended baptismal regeneration; the water literally washed away the infant's guilt by the power of the Holy Spirit. The Council of Trent would give its stamp of approval to this sacramental doctrine: "If any one denies, that, by the grace of our Lord Jesus Christ, which is conferred in baptism, the guilt of original sin is remitted; or even asserts that the whole of that which has the true and proper nature of sin is not taken away ... let him be anathema."[59] Baptismal regeneration remains official Catholic dogma.

Christians, however, should reject baptismal regeneration. Baptism cannot erase sin nor can it secure union with Christ. We are justified by faith. Abraham was counted righteous when he believed the Lord (Gen. 15:6). Salvation comes by faith in Christ (e.g., Jn 3:14-16; 1 Jn 5:1; Gal. 3:9). Baptismal regeneration is

---

53. However, one should not downplay the significance of Rom. 5:12 in Augustine's thinking. As Gerald Bonner notes, "It is clear ... from the very magnitude of the list of recorded citations, that Augustine regarded Romans 5,12 as being of palmary significance in his theology" ("Augustine on Romans 5,12," in *Studia Evangelica*, vol. IV: Papers Presented to the Third International Congress on New Testament Studies Held at Christ Church, Oxford, 1965, ed. Frank L. Cross [Berlin: Akademie-Verlag, 1968], 246).

54. Augustine, *The Punishment and Forgiveness of Sins* I.19.24 (*Answer to the Pelagians*, WSA 1:46-7).

55. Augustine, *Unfinished Work in Answer to Julian* V.29 (WSA 3:554).

56. Augustine, *The Punishment and Forgiveness of Sins* I.28.56 (*Answer to the Pelagians*, WSA 1:66).

57. Augustine, *Unfinished Work in Answer to Julian* V.9 (*Answer to the Pelagians*, WSA 3:521-2).

58. Augustine, *Marriage and Desire* I.20.22 (*Answer to the Pelagians*, WSA 2:42-3).

59. Philip Schaff, *The Creeds of Christendom* (Grand Rapids: Baker, 1985), 2:87.

antithetical to justification by grace through faith (Eph. 2:8-9), having the form of godliness but denying its power. As the Westminster divines put it, "The justification of believers under the old testament was, in all these respects, one and the same with the justification of believers under the new testament."[60] The countless baptized infants who grow up without any evidence of genuine faith testify against baptismal regeneration. As Charles Hodge wrote,

> Regeneration is no slight matter. It is a new birth; a new creation; a resurrection from spiritual death to spiritual life. It is a change, wrought by the exceeding greatness of God's power, analogous to that which was wrought in Christ, when He was raised from the dead, and exalted to the right hand of the majesty on high. It cannot therefore remain without visible effect. It controls the whole inward and outward life of its subject, so that he becomes a new man in Christ Jesus. The mass of those baptized, however, exhibit no evidence of any such change.[61]

Although Augustine was wrong about baptismal regeneration, however, he was right about original guilt. Strictly speaking, no infant is innocent; all infants are guilty in the courtroom of heaven. Christ's atonement is glad tidings indeed.

In Reformed federalism, by contrast, infants are sinful from conception (Ps. 51:5) and incur original guilt from God's imputation of Adam's sin to each of his descendants. All infants face eternal damnation unless they are born again, unless Christ atones for their sins and justifies them by grace through faith. In the Roman Catholic tradition, following Augustine, baptism communicates the grace of regeneration *ex opere operato*, thereby objectively purifying the stain of original guilt. Anti-sacramental traditions hold a symbolic view of baptism that has no bearing on the presence (or absence) of original guilt. Against both these options, a Reformed account sees baptism as a sign and seal of the covenant of grace. In the OT, circumcision was given to male infants as the sign of the Abrahamic covenant: "This is my covenant with you and your descendants after you, the covenant you are to keep" (Gen. 17:10). After this promise was fulfilled in Acts 2:39 ("The promise is for you *and your children*"), circumcision as the covenant sign was replaced with baptism of male *and female* infants, reflecting the richer, wider, deeper blessings of the new covenant (Col. 2:11-12).

Baptism signifies a trove of covenant blessings, including union with Christ in his death and resurrection. As Paul says, "we were all baptized by one Spirit so as to form one body" (1 Cor. 12:13, cf. Rom. 6:3-6; Gal. 3:27-28). Baptism also stands in for the remission of sins (Acts 2:38; 22:16; 1 Pet. 3:21) and the cleansing of our

---

60. WCF 11.6, in *The Westminster Confession of Faith and Catechisms as Adopted by the Presbyterian Church in America with Proof Texts* (Lawrenceville: Christian Education & Publications Committee of the Presbyterian Church in America, 2007), 55–6.

61. Hodge, *Systematic Theology*, 3:603.

moral corruption by the Spirit (e.g., Jn 3:5; Tit. 3:5; 1 Cor. 6:11).[62] "In the New Testament," Anthony Lane points out, "salvation, union with Christ, forgiveness, washing, regeneration and receiving the Holy Spirit are all attributed to baptism."[63] Baptism itself, however, is a sign and seal pointing visibly to the grace of God received by faith.[64] Regeneration can occur at baptism, or even earlier, perhaps in the womb (Lk. 1:41), or years afterwards; only God knows at what point he regenerates a person by his Word and Spirit.[65]

Original guilt reminds us that children are sinners like everyone else (even if they have committed no actual sins). The children of believers are included in the covenant of grace. They need Christ to atone for their guilt before God. As J. Mark Beach declares, "those who are united with Christ, according to divine promise, are the objects of God's saving mercy and so likewise the proper subjects of baptism—believers and their children."[66] In the waters of baptism, God extends to infant sinners the promise (the sign!) of salvation, regeneration, union with Christ, and the forgiveness of sins.[67]

Sin, Death, and Original Guilt

Original guilt reflects the biblical understanding of human death. Infants die because they are already sinners. Augustine thought so. "Why do little ones also die if they are not subject to the sin of that first human being? Are the little ones, then, rescued from the kingdom of death in any other way than by him in whom all will be brought to life?"[68] His rhetorical questions presuppose death as the consequence of sin.

Modern theologians are not so sure. According to David Fergusson, for example, Scripture rejects the idea that physical death is a punishment for sin: "Indeed," he says, "the prevailing view seems to be that death as a return to the dust is the

---

62. The cited passages depict regeneration as washing with water; it is reasonable to think that baptism signifies the same reality. On the remission of sins, John Murray remarks that baptism represents "purification from the guilt of sin by the sprinkling of the blood of Christ" (*Christian Baptism* [Phillipsburg: P&R, 1980], 5).

63. Anthony N. S. Lane, *Justification by Faith in Catholic-Protestant Dialogue: An Evangelical Assessment* (New York: T&T Clark, 2002), 187, cited in Robert Letham, *Systematic Theology* (Wheaton: Crossway, 2019), 713.

64. See Murray, *Christian Baptism*; Letham, *Systematic Theology*, 705–23; Bavinck, *Reformed Dogmatics*, 4:521–39.

65. Letham, *Systematic Theology*, 715.

66. J. Mark Beach, "Original Sin, Infant Salvation, and the Baptism of Infants: A Critique of Some Contemporary Baptist Authors," *Mid-America Journal of Theology* 12 (2011): 79.

67. Reformed Baptists who affirm original guilt will disagree with my analysis of infant baptism. E.g., see Jeffrey D. Johnson, *The Fatal Flaw of the Theology behind Infant Baptism* (Conway: Free Grace, 2017).

68. Augustine, *Answer to Julian* I.6.24 (*Answers to the Pelagians*, WSA 2:284).

natural lot of human beings who organically came from the dust."[69] J. Richard Middleton argues that death in Genesis 2 and 3 is "the antithesis of flourishing," *not* "the contrast between mere existence and the extinction of existence; nor does it refer to immortality versus mortality."[70] Similarly, John Zizioulas recoils at the idea that death is God's punishment for Adam's sin, for then "God himself introduced this horrible evil which he then tried through his Son to remove." Zizioulas contends that creation was "from the beginning in a state of mortality—owing to its having had a beginning—and awaiting the arrival of man in order to overcome this predicament."[71] These examples reflect the common opinion that Adam's sin did not bring about physical death.

Scripture opposes this way of reasoning. At the outset of the canonical narrative, after Adam's fall, God metes out death as part of a judicial *curse* (Gen. 3:17-19): "for dust you are and to dust you will return." Rendering death natural to God's creation strips the curse of all meaning. Some have suggested that the curse is *premature* death (not death per se); however, vv. 17-18 imply a long life of toilsome labor that culminates in death.[72] As John Stott writes, "The Bible everywhere views human death not as a *natural* but as a *penal* event. It is an alien intrusion into God's good world, and not part of his original intention for humankind."[73] Human life is from God's Spirit (Gen. 2:7). Death is antithetical to creation; it is the absence of life, separation from God. Breaking the law is punishable by death: "Anyone who strikes a person with a fatal blow is to be put to death" (Exod. 21:12; also Lev. 20:2, 9-13, 15-16, 27; Deut. 22:21, 24; *passim*). God himself inflicts the death of the wicked, as he did at Sodom and Gomorrah (Genesis 18–19) and among the Canaanites (Num. 21:2-3; Josh. 6:17, 21), the Amalekites (1 Sam. 15:1-9), the Hittites, the Hivites, the Amorites, the Perizzites, the Jebusites, and so on (e.g., Deut. 20:16–18). Death as a *natural* function of creaturely being clashes with such biblical narratives in their portrayal of death as divine *punishment*. The wages of sin, Scripture says, is death (Rom. 6:23). Death is the last enemy (1 Cor. 15:26). Isaiah prophesies a day when death will be no more (Isa. 25:8). One day our tears will be wiped away forever (Rev. 21:4). The logic of salvation's drama falls to pieces if mortality is native to God's original creation.

This sin-death nexus emerges in the work of Christ.[74] Christ's physical death is central to the atonement. He died for our sins according to the Scriptures (1

---

69. David Fergusson, *Creation* (Grand Rapids: Eerdmans, 2014), 38.

70. J. Richard Middleton, "Reading Genesis 3 Attentive to Human Evolution: Beyond Concordism and Non-Overlapping Magisteria," in *Evolution and the Fall*, ed. William Cavanaugh and James K. A. Smith (Grand Rapids: Eerdmans, 2017), 79.

71. John D. Zizioulas, *The Eucharistic Communion and the World*, ed. Luke Ben Tallon (New York: Continuum, 2011), 173.

72. Geerhardus Vos, *Biblical Theology: Old and New Testaments* (Grand Rapids: Eerdmans, 1948), 48.

73. John R. W. Stott, *The Cross of Christ* (Leicester: IVP, 1986), 65.

74. In this paragraph, I am drawing on Stephen Lloyd, "Chronological Creationism," *Foundations* 72 (May 2017): 76–99.

Cor. 15:3); we were reconciled by his physical body through death (Col. 1:22). As the apostle says, Jesus bore our sins on his body on the tree, "so that we might die to sins and live for righteousness; 'by his wounds you have been healed'" (1 Pet. 2:24). Death entered the world through the first Adam (Rom. 5:12), but it was in dying—being obedient to death on a cross (Phil. 2:8)—that the last Adam secured our justification, sanctification, and glorification. Sin also lies behind the suffering and decay that herald death. Jesus' healing miracles reversed sin's effects on human lives. Christ's death, Isaiah says, atoned for human suffering and disease (Isa. 53:4; Mt. 8:17). To be sure, reimagining death as intrinsic to the world *as created* resonates with post-Darwinian scientific sensibilities, but this revisionism pays a steep price, driving a wedge between Christ as creator and Christ as redeemer. Are we to believe that death was part of the Son's original creation, only for him then to defeat it at the cross (1 Cor. 15:55), that disease and death are natural processes, even though Jesus miraculously healed the sick and raised the dead throughout his earthly ministry? This convoluted logic undermines orthodox Christology and pits creation and redemption against each other.

If sin causes suffering and death, then it raises a dilemma: Infants are not guilty of any personal sins. Nonetheless, many infants have suffered and died throughout history. If they are sinless, why do they experience death? I suggest that they have an original guilt imputed from Adam. Difficult pastoral questions immediately press in, and here I speak with halting lips. Scripture gives us grounds to be confident that covenant children are elect; Peter reiterates that the promise is to believing parents *and their children* (Acts 2:39). In the case of premature death, the child's imputed guilt is forgiven based on Christ's atonement. I am agnostic, however, on the fate of uncovenanted children who die in infancy—entrusting them to the Lord's righteous judgment.

My argument that infant death implies original guilt is controversial. Other explanations are available. Adam Harwood, for instance, draws on Gen. 6:5-6 and 2 Sam. 12:23 to deny that original guilt causes infant death. Instead, he says, "infants are sometimes subject to the sweeping consequences of God's judgment against the sinful behavior of their parents."[75] Jesse Couenhoven argues likewise that infant death is the collateral damage of sin being in the world: "many parts of the creation suffer and die without sin."[76] Infant death is a symptom of living in a fallen world. As *partial* explanations, I happily endorse such accounts. However, they fare poorly as *ultimate* explanations given the respective roles of the OT sacrificial system and Christ's atonement.

The sacrificial system allowed God to dwell among sinful people—despite the consuming fire of his holiness (Deut. 4:24). Without atoning sacrifices, God was liable to destroy sinners (Exod. 33:3). This sacrificial ritual, like other rituals of

---

75. Adam Harwood, *The Spiritual Condition of Infants: A Biblical-Historical Survey and Systematic Proposal* (Eugene, OR: Wipf & Stock, 2011), 55.

76. Jesse Couenhoven, *Stricken by Sin, Cured by Christ: Agency, Necessity, and Culpability in Augustinian Theology* (Oxford: Oxford University Press, 2013), 212 n. 39.

the time, assumes the principle of a covenant household. Anyone included in the patriarchal household was covered. Much like the circumcision of the patriarch covered the females in the family, so also the sacrifices of the adults covered the children (e.g., in Lev. 10:14 children were included in the fellowship offerings). In his discussion of various sacrifices, Gordon Wenham confirms that individuals sacrificed for themselves and their families, which obviously included infants.[77] These sacrifices anticipated the spotless sacrifice of Christ and his atonement for our sins (Heb. 10:1-4). In a nutshell: Atonement, by definition, entails the guilt of the recipient. Since the sacrifices in the OT were offered for all, including babies, and Christ's atonement in the NT covers infant sinners, it follows that infants have Adam's imputed guilt.

Conclusion

In conclusion, let us circle back to an earlier point: Original guilt preserves divine justice. Sin entered the world through Adam (Rom. 5:12). God was just to punish him for the transgression since he disobeyed a direct command. Adam brought on himself the irreversible corruption of human nature and lost fellowship with God. As a result, *all* Adam's descendants are subsequently born into the same condition as fallen Adam—morally corrupt, destitute of any righteousness, condemned to suffering and death. While it is true that we have corporate solidarity with Adam and thus suffer from the consequences of his sin, God himself condemned all humanity for that first transgression in Eden: "through the disobedience of the one man the many were made sinners" (Rom. 5:19). At this point, Blocher rightly asks,

> Can we see how it is *right*, under the righteous God's sovereign rule, that Adam's descendants find themselves deprived of the gift of divine fellowship, and therefore enmeshed in a destructive disorder at all levels of their nature, which affects heredity; and that they find themselves the slaves of their own pride, greed, lies and fears, under the tyranny of the Evil One?[78]

God cannot punish us without just cause: "Will not the Judge of all the earth do right?" (Gen. 18:25). As Andrew Leslie notes, "the universal imposition of punishment needs a legal foundation in some real sin, otherwise it is profoundly unjust."[79] Adam's federal headship *is* that legal foundation, the imputation of his sin its juridical consequence. God is just to condemn the entire human race because he counted us guilty of Adam's sin.

---

77. Gordon Wenham, "The Theology of Old Testament Sacrifice," in *Sacrifice in the Bible*, ed. Roger Beckwith and Martin Selman (Grand Rapids: Baker, 1995), 85.
78. Blocher, *Original Sin*, 129.
79. Leslie, "Original Sin," 352.

Original guilt permeates the biblical drama. For the hermeneutical purposes of this volume, original guilt illustrates the import of the Westminster Confession of Faith 1.6 for the drama of doctrine: God's revelation for our salvation and holiness involves both what is explicitly stated in Scripture and what may be rightly deduced from it. Scripture recounts the story of God redeeming humanity. "For God so loved the world that he gave his one and only Son, that whoever believes in him shall not perish but have eternal life" (Jn 3:16). Our sins are individually forgiven (Ps. 32:1-2). All of humanity stands guilty before God; Jews and Gentiles alike are all under sin (Rom. 3:9); all have sinned and fall short of the glory of God (Rom. 3:23). Is this canonical drama profoundly unjust? If the imputation of Adam's sin is unjust, then the imputation of Christ's righteousness is also unjust (Rom. 5:12-21). If Adam cannot be the federal head for our guilt, then Christ cannot be the federal head for our righteousness. In Christ's propitiatory sacrifice, God imputes our guilt to him and his righteousness to us (2 Cor. 5:21). The drama is just this: Original guilt and justification—paradoxically—are the twin daughters of redemption.[80]

---

80. Thanks to Robert Erle Barham, John Bush, Cam Clausing, Bill Davis, Jonathan King, Flavien Pardigon, and Stephen Williams for their comments on an earlier draft.

Chapter 17

"BORN OF WATER AND THE SPIRIT": DIVINE AGENCY IN INTERPRETATIONS OF JOHN 3 AND BAPTISM IN ACTS

Elizabeth Y. Sung

This study examines the conception of divine and human agency that is present in some patristic interpretations of Jn 3:5 and baptisms in Acts, especially Acts 10. It offers an alternative account in light of contemporary evangelical scholarship on those texts. Kevin J. Vanhoozer's articulation of the drama of Christian doctrine influences this effort to engage with patristic readings of Scripture as a biblical, ecumenically engaged Protestant theologian.

A basic premise of Vanhoozer's "canonical-linguistic theology" is that "we come to know God by attending to the uses to which language of God is put in Scripture itself. Scripture's own use of Scripture is of particular interest."[1] Thus, "canonical-linguistic theology ... takes its primary bearings from the Scriptures themselves, making what we call canonical practices the norm for the church's speech and thought of God."[2] Theology's task is both exegetical and conceptual: it attends to and renders explicit the patterns of communicative action and the judgments that "subsist in the particular [biblical] texts and their particular literary and historical contexts."[3] Patterns of canonical judgments that obtain across the Scriptures are "canonical paradigms"—normative canonical practices—which "give us a handle on those communicative practices and habits that make up the canon ... to make it easier to participate in and continue them in our own idioms."[4]

Vanhoozer's approach is not only canonical but also catholic in vision. The "*canonical* principle" affirms that "there is an original point of reference that stands over against the history of mission and the history of theology: the apostolic testimony to the history of Jesus Christ. ... The supreme authority for any version of Christianity is Scripture, the divinely commissioned testimony to what God was doing in Jesus Christ." The "*catholic* principle" recognizes that "no

---

1. Kevin J. Vanhoozer, *The Drama of Doctrine: A Canonical Linguistic Approach to Christian Theology* (Louisville: Westminster John Knox, 2005), 22.
2. Ibid., 330–1.
3. Ibid., 341.
4. Ibid., 301.

one version of Christianity ... is equal to the original; rather, we come more fully to appreciate the meaning and significance of the original as we ... contextualize it into ... everyday life ... and attend to other attempts at contextualization."[5] The desideratum remains grasping the canonical practices that give doctrinal direction to everyday life: "the canonical dialogue ... in and between the canonical books themselves ... is both catalyst and norm for the ensuing [faithful and fitting] performance in the history of the church."[6]

The present study engages patristic treatments of Jn 3:5 and baptisms in Acts along these lines. Irenaeus, Tertullian, Cyprian, and Chrysostom reflect a common view of the meaning of "born of water and the Spirit" and its bearing on baptisms in Acts. This view regarding the relation of Spirit-baptism, ecclesial baptism, and salvation reflects an implicit pattern of judgments about divine and human agency that may be inadequate to "the logic of scriptural discourse."[7] The alternative proposed here builds on recent treatments of Jn 3:3-8 and its OT background to highlight a distinct canonical emphasis on divine agency in Spirit-baptism as the climax of God's promised salvation. As we shall see, the proposed alternative is more canonically apt to the baptism accounts in Acts as well, regarding both their narrative sequence for baptism in relation to the giving of the Spirit and their similar emphasis on unique divine agency. Ultimately, this study will have implications for both the theology of baptism and the canonical and catholic drama of doctrine.

A Patristic Paradigm

The patristic passages selected below are not the earliest indications of belief in the salvific effects of church baptism. However, they are noteworthy exemplars of biblical exegesis; in homilies, treatises, polemical writings, and epistles, these eminent second-, third-, and fourth-century church fathers quote Jn 3:5 and comment on its meaning. Together they represent how a paradigm of "baptismal regeneration" could emerge from engaging with this key biblical text.

Irenaeus (c. 130–c. 202)

In a comment on Naaman's cleansing from leprosy in 2 Kings 5, Irenaeus draws a parallel with Christian baptism: "As we are lepers in sin, we are made clean, by means of the sacred water and the invocation of the Lord, from our old transgressions; being spiritually regenerated as new-born babes, even as the Lord has declared: Unless a man be born again through water and the Spirit, he shall not

---

5. Ibid., 322.
6. Ibid., 331.
7. David S. Yeago, "The New Testament and the Nicene Dogma: A Contribution to the Recovery of Theological Exegesis," *Pro Ecclesia* 3, no. 2 (1994): 152.

enter into the kingdom of heaven. John 3:5."[8] Notably, "born again through water and the Spirit" refers to baptism; administered in Christ's name, "by means of the sacred water," it brings about salvific effects: cleansing from defilement and new birth "through ... the Spirit."

Two passages in *Against Heresies* expound the two gifts of ecclesial baptism. In the first, a discussion of Jesus' healing of the man born blind by directing him to wash off the mud smeared over his eyes (Jn 9:1-41), Irenaeus refers twice to "the laver of regeneration" needed after the fall, stating "that regeneration which takes place by means of the laver ... confer[s] life." [9] The new birth and cleansing from sins come by the instrumentality of ecclesial baptism. This model of divine and human agency in salvation is aptly designated "baptismal regeneration."

Irenaeus also employs "baptism for the remission of sins" as an equivalent expression for the "cleansing of transgressions by means of the sacred water." In a discussion of Cornelius's conversion in Acts 10, Irenaeus reproduces in full Peter's message about Jesus of Nazareth, leading to this declaration: "To Him give all the prophets witness, that, through His name, every one that believeth in Him does receive remission of sins" (v. 43). Acts 10 shows, Irenaeus concludes, that Peter "bare witness to them that Jesus Christ was the Son of God, the Judge of quick and dead, into whom he did also command them to be baptized for the remission of sins."[10]

However, a discrepancy exists between Peter's and Irenaeus's claims concerning the remission of sins. Whereas Peter asserts that "everyone who *believes in [Christ]* receives remission of sins through his name" (v. 43), Irenaeus recasts Peter's final words as a "command ... to *be baptized for* the remission of sins" (vv. 46b-48), indicating that Peter ordered them to undergo baptism in order to receive forgiveness—an interpretation consistent with baptismal regeneration. But the Gentiles received the Holy Spirit as a divine *fait accompli* (v. 44). Only afterward were they baptized, per Peter's instructions (v. 48).

Acts 10 does not specify the relation of remission of sins to receipt of the Spirit, but the following chapters elaborate what the bestowed Spirit entailed. After hearing Peter's initial report to the church in Jerusalem, they praise God: "So, then, even to Gentiles God has granted repentance that leads to life" (Acts 11:18). Peter provides the fullest accounting at the Council of Jerusalem: "God, who knows the heart, showed that he accepted them by giving the Holy Spirit to them ... for he purified their hearts by faith. ... We believe that it is through the grace of our Lord Jesus that we are saved, just as they [too already] are" (Acts 15:8, 9, 11). Acts 10:1-48; 11:1-18; and 15:1-19 present a unified account of the conversion of Cornelius's household. When God imparted the Spirit to them, it signified their effective reception of his concomitant gifts (penitent faith in Christ, forgiveness of sins, hearts purified by faith, and life) and his full acceptance of them, which constituted their "salvation" by the grace of Christ (Acts 15:1, 11). On the Lukan paradigm of

---

8. Irenaeus, "Fragment 34," in *Fragments of the Lost Writings of Irenaeus*, in ANF 1:574.
9. Irenaeus, *Against Heresies* 5.15.3, in ANF 1:543.
10. Ibid., 3.12.7, in ANF 1:432–3.

divine and human agency, they were "saved" apart from ecclesial baptism (and circumcision). Thus, while Peter indeed directed the new believers to be baptized with water in the name of Jesus Christ (Acts 10:48), it was not "for the remission of sins." The Lukan pattern tells against the baptismal regeneration model.

Tertullian (c. 155–c. 220)

Two passages from Tertullian's treatise *On Baptism* present important aspects of his view. The first states that Christ's baptism is a "celestial baptism giving both the Holy Spirit and remission of sins." Moreover, Christ "would baptize in the Spirit and fire—of course because true and stable faith is baptized with water unto salvation."[11]

Tertullian also addresses objections that faith is sufficient without baptism. To the contrary:

> The law of baptism has been imposed and the formula prescribed: "Go," he says, "teach the nations, baptizing them into the name of the Father and of the Son and of the Holy Spirit." The comparison of this law with that definition, "Unless one has been reborn of water and Spirit, he shall not enter into the kingdom of the heavens," has tied faith to the necessity of baptism.
>
> Accordingly, all therefore who became believers used to be baptized. Then it was, too, that when Paul believed, he was baptized; and this is the meaning of the precept which the Lord had given him when smitten with the plague of loss of sight, saying, "Arise, and enter Damascus; there it shall be demonstrated to thee what thou oughtest to do"—to wit, be baptized, which was the only thing lacking to him. That point excepted, he had sufficiently learnt and believed "the Nazarene" to be "the Lord and Son of God."[12]

These claims are instructive. Baptism in the triune God's name is a "law." John 3:5 gives its "definition": One is "reborn of water and Spirit." Christ's "law" and "definition" "tie faith to the necessity of baptism." Paul's baptism also demonstrates its necessity; although he "believed" the Lord Jesus, it was imperative that he be baptized (Acts 9:18). Baptism is a "sacrament" (or an "obligation of faith"),[13] a "sealing act" mandatory for believers.

Tertullian's systematizing is helpful, but his argument for the "necessity" of baptismal regeneration (Jn 3:5) in Paul's case is not secured by Acts 9:17-18: It is possible that Paul received the Spirit's infilling concurrently with his restored vision, prior to his baptism (v. 18). Thus, the claim that Paul's baptism demonstrates

---

11. Tertullian, *On Baptism* 10.5–6, in ANF 3, cited in Jaroslav Pelikan, *The Emergence of Catholic Tradition (100–600)* (Chicago: University of Chicago Press, 1971), 164.

12. Tertullian, *On Baptism* 13, in ANF 3:676, cited in Joel C. Elowsky, ed., *John 1–10*, ACCSNT 4a (Downers Grove: IVP, 2006), 112.

13. Ibid.

its necessity for his salvation is not clearly established. While Tertullian aptly observes that the Lord's command to baptize disciples comprises a "law," imposing it as "necessary," much depends on how "law" and "necessity" are construed.

Cyprian (c. 200–258)

In a letter informing the Bishop of Rome of a conciliar decision concerning persons previously baptized by heretical groups now seeking admission to the Catholic Church, Cyprian explains that laypersons "dipped abroad outside the Church" in "profane water"

> ought to be baptized, for the reason that it is a small matter to "lay hands on them that they may receive the Holy Ghost," unless they receive also the baptism of the Church. For then finally can they be fully sanctified, and be the sons of God, if they be born of each sacrament; since it is written, "Except a man be born again of water and of the Spirit, he cannot enter into the kingdom of God." For we find also, in the Acts of the Apostles, that this is maintained by the apostles, and kept in the truth of the saving faith, so that when, in the house of Cornelius the centurion, the Holy Ghost had descended upon the Gentiles who were there, fervent in the warmth of their faith, and believing in the Lord with their whole heart; and when, filled with the Spirit, they blessed God in divers tongues, still none the less the blessed Apostle Peter, mindful of the divine precept and the Gospel, commanded that those same men should be baptized who had already been filled with the Holy Spirit, that nothing might seem to be neglected to the observance by the apostolic instruction in all things of the law of the divine precept and Gospel.[14]

The conciliar decision now rests on a different construal of Jn 3:5. While the sacrament of baptism is needed, it is inadequate. The "baptism of the Church" does not confer the Holy Spirit, who comes subsequently via the imposition of hands, as the quotation of Acts 8:17 indicates.[15] Hence, the church must administer two sacraments to complete the initiation of salvation.

This interpretation translates "born of water and spirit" (*gennēthē ex hudatos kai pneumatos*) as "born *again* of water and [born again] *of the* Spirit": it adds a

---

14. Cyprian, Epistle 71.1, in ANF 5:378–9.
15. Based on the paradigm of Spirit-baptism in Acts, the occasions wherein the Spirit was bestowed in conjunction with the imposition of hands are best understood as exceptional: God withheld the Spirit, giving the apostles opportunity to verify that these non-Jewish groups' professed faith in Christ was genuinely in continuity with his teaching. Delayed Spirit-bestowal is not the normal pattern in either Luke-Acts or Paul (Rom. 8:9-11), who consistently teaches that people receive the Spirit "when they believe" the gospel and call upon Christ for salvation (Eph. 1:13-14; Gal. 3:2, 5-6; Rom. 10:6-13). A rite of confirmation, positing the Spirit's conferral with a prelate's imposition of hands, has a precedent in Acts 8, but it is an exception to the ordinary pattern of Spirit-baptism upon personal confession of Christ—"conversion," discussed below.

second preposition and an article modifying "spirit," whereas the construction is anarthrous and the preposition "of" governs both "water and "spirit," designating a single object.[16] Thus, this interpretation, treating "water" and "spirit" disjunctively in terms of two births, is grammatically dubious. Accordingly, Cyprian's extended theological reasoning—that the phrase "born of water and spirit" indicates that full salvation is effected only when one is "born of each sacrament"—is problematic.

It is puzzling that Cyprian cites Acts 10 as an authoritative precedent for administering baptism and confirmation to converts and returnees from heretical groups. These practices scarcely needed explanation in his context. However, the recommended procedure reverses the sequence recounted in Acts 10 (receipt of the Spirit, followed by baptism). Moreover, Cornelius's household received the Holy Spirit (with all this entailed) in a single sweep, by a decisive divine action apart from ministrations by apostolic or clerical hands.

Like Irenaeus, Cyprian appeals to the Cornelius case for biblical support. Unlike Irenaeus, however, he does not specify that Peter's purpose in ordering that they be baptized was to procure forgiveness of their sins. Instead, he emphasizes that nothing should be omitted in carrying out "the apostolic instruction in all things of the law of the divine precept and Gospel."

John Chrysostom (c. 347–407)

In a homily on Jn 3:5, Chrysostom explains the meaning of "Unless a man is born of water and the Spirit, he cannot enter the kingdom of God":

> That the need of water is absolute and indispensable, you may learn in this way. On one occasion, when the Spirit had flown down before the water was applied, the Apostle did not stay at this point, but, as though the water were necessary and not superfluous, observe what he says; "Can any man forbid water, that these should not be baptized, which have received the Holy Ghost as well as we?"
>
> What then is the use of the water? ... In Baptism are fulfilled the pledges of our covenant with God; burial and death, resurrection and life; and these take place all at once. For when we immerse our heads in the water, the old man is buried as in a tomb below, and wholly sunk forever; then as we raise them again, the new man rises in its stead.[17]

Chrysostom's sermon on Jn 3:6 further explicates this "great mystery" that unfolds in baptismal water, which is analogous to the womb as the medium incubating

---

16. So Murray J. Harris, "Appendix: Prepositions and Theology in the Greek New Testament," *NIDNTT* 3.1178, cited in Linda Belleville, "'Born of Water and Spirit': John 3:5," *Trinity Journal* 1 NS (1980): 125–41 (135); also George R. Beasley-Murray, *John*, WBC (Waco: Word, 1987), 48; J. Ramsey Michaels, *The Gospel of John*, NICNT (Grand Rapids: Eerdmans, 2010), 182–4.

17. John Chrysostom, Homily XXV on John iii.5, in NPNF 1, 14:86–89.

the new person. "Born of water and of the Spirit" describes the new "fabric of our nature": "in the water [the believer] is fashioned and formed ... all at once. ... [F]rom the time that the Lord entered the streams of the Jordan, the water ... gives forth ... reasonable and Spirit-bearing souls."[18] The OT depictions of supernatural life and the many miraculous events "accomplished by water ... proclaimed beforehand, as by a figure, the Birth and the purification" that Jesus inaugurated with his own baptism.[19]

With his predecessors, Chrysostom insists that baptism is "absolute[ly] ... indispensable." Like Cyprian, he appeals to Acts 10:47 as evidence that, even in Cornelius's case, baptism with water is "not superfluous." Again, though, he neglects the Lukan sequence in which God enacted his covenantal promises— signified in giving the Spirit as proof of the Gentiles' salvation, as Peter and other circumcised believers came to recognize (Acts 10:44-47; 11:15-18; 15:11)—apart from baptism.

An Alternative Proposal

Tertullian's formulation encapsulates baptismal regeneration as a patristic paradigm. Christ's "definition" of baptism, being "born of water and spirit" (Jn 3:5), complements his prescription of baptism as a "law" by disclosing its rationale: Without the cleansing from sin and sanctification by the Spirit it conveys, one cannot "enter the kingdom of God." Christ's teaching, therefore, "ties faith to the necessity of baptism." Tertullian's casual comment that Christ "would baptize in the Spirit and fire—*of course because true and stable faith is baptized with water unto salvation*"[20] indicates that this conception of the relation of Spirit-baptism, ecclesial baptism, and salvation seemed axiomatic. Baptismal regeneration became the "logical-consensual"[21] patristic paradigm for the reception of salvation.

The difficulties noted above suggest, however, that we should explore a different possibility for relating divine-human action in Jn 3:5 to the narrative sequence in Acts. An alternative construal of "born of water and spirit" follows, in light of its immediate context, its OT background, and then other intracanonical connections.

Jesus' explanation of the birth "from above" (v. 3) consists in three affirmations: one must be "born of water and spirit" (v. 5); "what is born of the Spirit is spirit" (v. 6); and "the wind blows where it wills ... but you do not know where it comes from, or where it goes. So it is with all born of the Spirit" (v. 8). On a *prima facie* reading Jesus utters, in rapid succession, three terse, opaque

---

18. John Chrysostom, Homily XXVI on John iii.6, in NPNF 1 14:90, cited in *John 1–10*, ACCSNT 4a, 114.
19. Ibid.
20. Tertullian, *On Baptism*, 8.1, 10.5, in ANF 3, cited in Pelikan, *Catholic Tradition*, 166. Emphasis added.
21. Thomas Oden, *Life in the Spirit* (New York: HarperCollins, 1992), 103.

sayings, loosely strung together into a *non sequitur*. The first task, then, is to clarify the meaning of each statement and then to indicate how the three claims hang together.

D. A. Carson's treatment of the three assertions is foundational for our alternative proposal. First, following Linda Belleville's study, which concludes that "water" refers to Ezek. 36:26-27 and "spirit" to the impartation of God's nature as *pneuma* (Jn 4:24), he notes that although this exact phrase does not appear in the OT, "the ingredients are there."[22] Thus, for "born of water and spirit" in v. 5,

> most important of all is Ezekiel 36:25-27, where water and spirit come together so forcefully, the first to signify cleansing from impurity, and the second to depict the transformation of heart that will enable people to follow God wholly. And it is no accident that the account of the valley of dry bones, where Ezekiel preaches and the Spirit brings life to dry bones, follows hard after Ezekiel's water/spirit passage. The language is reminiscent of the 'new heart' expressions that revolve around the promise of the new covenant (Je. 31:29ff.).[23]

Because "born of water and spirit" designates a single referent, "the article and the capital 'S' ... should be dropped: the focus is on the impartation of God's nature as 'spirit' [cf. 4:24], not on the Holy Spirit as such. [It] signals a new begetting, a new birth that cleanses and renews, the eschatological cleansing and renewal promised by the Old Testament prophets."[24] Accordingly, on Jesus' second assertion—"what is born of the Spirit is spirit" (v. 6)—Carson concludes, "It is God's Holy Spirit who produces a new nature, a spirit-nature where 'spirit' is related to the sphere of God and things divine (as in [John] 4:24)."[25]

Third, then, on Jesus' analogy between the wind and those born of the Spirit (v. 8), he states,

> The point is that the wind can be neither controlled nor understood by human beings. ... How is this relevant to the nature of the new birth? ... The person who is "born of the Spirit" can be neither controlled nor understood by persons of but one birth. As the "water and spirit" birth is grounded in Ezekiel 36:25-27 ... so there may be an allusion here to Ezekiel 37. There God's breath/Spirit (*rûaḥ/pneuma*) comes upon the valley of dry bones and the dry bones are revived; God's people come to life. Thus it is with everyone born of the Spirit: they have their "origin and destiny in the unseen God" (Fenton, p. 54).[26]

Hence, Jesus rebukes "Israel's Teacher" (v. 9):

---

22. D. A. Carson, *The Gospel According to John*, PNTC (Grand Rapids: Eerdmans, 1991), 194 n. 2, citing Belleville, "'Born of Water and Spirit'."
23. Carson, *John*, 195.
24. Ibid., 194–5.
25. Ibid., 196.
26. Ibid., 197–8.

From his study of Scripture, his grasp of the distance between human beings and God, and the axiom that like produces like [Nicodemus] should have understood the need for a God-given new birth, and God's promise that he would give his people a new heart, a new nature, clean lives and a full measure of the Spirit on the last day. That is why Jesus told Nicodemus he should not be surprised.[27]

Building on Belleville's clarification that "born of water" (Jn 3:5) refers to Ezek. 36:25 and Carson's observation that Jn 3:5 and 8 may allude to Ezekiel 37, we can go even further: Jesus' discourse on the birth "from above" in Jn 3:5-8 is tied even more tightly to Ezekiel 36 and 37. What conceptual background and line of reasoning would unite the three principal assertions in Jesus' discourse about the birth "from above"? These enigmatic pronouncements form a coherent train of thought when we recognize that with these statements Jesus references not only Ezek. 36:24-28 but also 37:1-14 (and secondarily 39:21-29).

John 3:5: "Born of Water and Spirit"

Carson aptly observes that "the full construction 'born of water and of the Spirit' is not found in the Old Testament."[28] The reason it does not appear there is that Jesus himself coins this peculiar collocation, conveying a substantive, original insight.

Jesus' first assertion—redescribing the "birth from above" (*gennēthē anōthen*) in v. 3 with the novel expression "born of water and spirit" (*gennēthē ex hudatos kai pneumatos*) in v. 5—indicates that both Ezekiel 36 and 37 are in view. "Born" and "water and spirit" name these chapters' most memorable ideas. Jesus yokes them together, making them the literary-theological counterpart of a diptych—a composition created by joining two panels displaying a single subject—so that they must be read together. Just as significantly, by placing "born" in the leading position, Jesus invokes Ezekiel 37 and reverses these chapters' sequence. This reversal is not arbitrary: he assigns Ezekiel 37 precedence because its chief idea is birth, and birth has conceptual primacy in this two-part portrait.

"Born [of]" (Jn 3:5) invokes the idea writ large over Ezek. 37:1-14: Birth signifies coming to life. The prophetic vision (vv. 1-10), set in a "Death Valley" strewn with bones, depicts this particular birth as a resurrection that Yahweh announces he will bring about: "I will cause *rûaḥ* ("breath," "spirit") to enter you, and you shall live" (v. 5). God's declared purpose—to bring the dead to life by conferring *rûaḥ*—is stated four more times: Having disclosed this intention, he instructs Ezekiel to address, summon, and command *hārûaḥ* ("the breath"/"the spirit") to enter the physically rebuilt but inert bodies of the slain, which come to life when *rûaḥ*, having arrived from "the four winds" (*'arba' rûḥôt*), blows upon (*nāpaḥ*) them (vv. 9-10).

---

27. Ibid., 197.
28. Ibid., 194.

The vision's meaning is supplied in vv. 11-14: God declares that he will enact his promise, bringing his scattered, rebel people up from their graves. Notably, whereas the vision speaks of "caus[ing] *rûaḥ* to enter" them and instilling "the breath" in them, the full import of this revivification is that "I will put My Spirit [*rûḥî*] in you and you shall live" (v. 14). Not only will God infuse a new life-power into individuals who are as good as dead, but he also will do so by endowing them with his Spirit.

Thus, "born of water and spirit" conjoins the primary motif of Ezekiel 37 ("birth": coming to life) and the key words of Ezek. 36:25-26 ("water and spirit," per Belleville)—but in reverse order. Jesus inverts them for logical reasons. Birth in ch. 37 is the initiation of life by God's act of putting his Spirit in his people. When further elaborated in ch. 36, birth entails the emergence of a new person whose inner condition must be changed to live fittingly within the new world she enters by being born. In interpretations of John 3 it appears that scant attention has been paid to the anchorage of *gennēthē* ("born") in Ezekiel 37, yet with this reordered literary-conceptual diptych of v. 5 Jesus lays the groundwork for vv. 6 and 8.

John 3:6: "What Is Born of the Spirit Is Spirit"

Jesus' second assertion—*to gegennēmenon ek tou pneumatos pneuma estin* (v. 6)—is his interpretation of Ezek. 36:26-27. There Block observes that the descriptions and the prepositions used with "a new spirit" (*rûaḥ*) and "a new heart" (*lēb*) differ, concluding that the promised "new spirit" in v. 26 is, in fact, "My Spirit" (v. 27).[29] However, Jesus' own rendering summarizes their import as "what is born of the Spirit is spirit," clarifying that God's Spirit (Ezek. 36:27) and the "new spirit" (Ezek. 36:26) remain distinct. While Carson's statement that "the Holy Spirit produces a new nature, a spirit-nature where 'spirit' is related to the sphere of God and things divine"[30] leaves too much unspecified, since "nature" admits of many senses, he rightly notes the distinction.

Hence, the most plausible understanding of "what is born of the Spirit is spirit" (Jn 3:6)—the dominical interpretation of Ezek. 36:26-27—is that the "new [human] spirit" (*rûaḥ*/*pneuma*) singles out the will as distinct from the all-inclusive "heart" (*lēb*) in Ezek. 36:26. This "new [human] spirit" is described in terms of a changed inclination to keep all of God's ways, stemming from the placement and subsequent movements of God's Spirit within the person (Ezek. 36:27). Both the Holy Spirit and the regenerate individual's new disposition are gifts received from God. Jesus points to Ezekiel 36, indicating that none of Nicodemus's qualities or accomplishments as an erudite religious leader qualify him for the kingdom of God; he must undergo a radical, complete transformation that he himself cannot effect.

---

29. Daniel I. Block, *The Book of Ezekiel: Chapters 25–48*, NICOT (Grand Rapids: Eerdmans, 1997), 356.

30. Carson, *John*, 196.

John 3:8: "The Wind Blows Where It Wills . . . so It Is with All Born of the Spirit"

Jesus' third statement—still addressing Nicodemus's original query about how such things can happen—draws an analogy: "The wind blows where it wills, and you hear the sound of it, but you do not know where it comes from or where it is going; so it is with all born of the Spirit" (v. 8). Commentators frequently interpret this verse as an extended comparison that Jesus makes to describe those born "from above": it indicates, for example, their freedom from domination by the world, their inexplicability to the world, and/or their origins and ultimate home with God.

However, with Ezekiel 37/36 as the background, Jn 3:8 more likely refers to the prophetic vision in which, at Yahweh's instruction, Ezekiel summons "the breath" to appear from "the four winds" (Ezek. 37:9). When it enters the reassembled physical bodies, they come to life (Ezek. 37:10). Here the prophet possesses privileged information: he knows where "the breath" comes from (the four corners of the earth). Even so, he does not understand how these lifeless bodies become a host of living, breathing people. Jesus' statement in Jn 3:8 may be an *a fortiori* comparison between the exceptional case (Ezekiel, who knew from where and why *hārûaḥ* came: to instill life) and ordinary people. "You do not know ... where it is going" may simply complete the description of the wind that is the basis for the analogy.

If so, the primary referent is not believers as such, but the birth "from above." Jesus says that those undergoing it do not understand what is unfolding in the moment, but after the Spirit comes upon them, they find that, mysteriously, their entire disposition toward God has changed. Conversion and regeneration are unpredictable and incomprehensible to both recipients and observers because the initiation of life and the implanting of God's Spirit within the person who believes "into Christ" is enacted by God himself. Thus, there is no need to postulate other meanings for Jn 3:8 on grounds extraneous to Ezekiel 37/36. This suggestion has the virtue of being grounded in this textual diptych. It also hews closely to Jesus' subject: a new birth from the Spirit.

The conversation with Nicodemus tapers off after Jesus reproves him in Jn 3:9. Had Nicodemus grasped the signals pointing to Ezekiel 37/36, Jesus could have expanded his discourse. His final statement, "So it is with all who are born of the Spirit" (Jn 3:8), names an essential feature of Ezekiel 36 and 37 that does not appear in Jn 3:5-8 because further elaboration would have been fruitless. Reckoning with this element is nonetheless crucial for understanding the relation of Christ's baptism with the Spirit and ecclesial baptism as represented in Acts. This essential element is the climactic, unilateral divine action that characterizes the giving of God's Spirit.

Two major motifs knit Ezekiel 37 and 36 together. The first is the concept of birth underpinning 37:1-14 (birth *qua* the inception of life), on which 36:25-29 elaborates (birth *qua* the emergence of a new person, entering a new realm). The second pertains to a genuinely new element in Ezekiel that is explicitly stated in both chapters: God's promise, "I will put my Spirit [*rûḥî*] in you" (Ezek. 36:27; 37:14;

cf. 11:15-20 where—given its restatement in Ezek. 36:24-28—it is conspicuously absent). The promised results of Yahweh's putting his Spirit in his people begin with (first) "you will live" (Ezek. 37:14), and (second) "I will move you to follow my decrees and be careful to keep my laws" (Ezek. 36:27). The penultimate results of this holistic restoration are that "the nations will know" this is Yahweh's doing ("I, Yahweh, have spoken and I will do it"; Ezek. 36:36), and Israel "will know that I, Yahweh, have spoken, and I have done it, declares Yahweh" (Ezek. 37:14). Then the ultimate result is living in fullness with Yahweh their God (Ezek. 36:28), within the "everlasting covenant of peace" he establishes, where he puts his dwelling place among them forever (Ezek. 37:24-28).

These results are echoed in the prophecy of Israel's salvation after Gog's defeat in Ezek. 39:25-29, which culminates in this statement: "I will no longer hide my face from them, for *I will have poured out my Spirit on the people of Israel*, declares the Lord Yahweh." Block comments on this sole reference to "pouring the divine Spirit" on people in Ezekiel: "The divine Spirit poured out on the nation serves as a sign and seal of the covenant. The poured-out Spirit represents Yahweh's mark of ownership ... [serving] as permanent seal of the covenant of peace (*bĕrît šālôm*) and the 'eternal covenant' (*bĕrît 'ôlām*) mentioned in 37:26."[31]

In Ezekiel, then, God's outpouring of his Spirit is the climax of his saving acts, "the definitive event by which Yahweh claims and seals the ... nation as his own."[32] While Block distinguishes on historical grounds between God's actions described in Ezekiel 36 and 37 (pertaining to the nation's revitalization) and that depicted in Ezek. 39:29, the New Testament portrayal of this outpouring combines them. Most crucially, then, Ezekiel treats as God-given the initiation of life, the removal of sins and cleansing from impurities and idols, a changed disposition toward God, and the placing of God's Spirit in people. God emphatically declares in advance that he alone will accomplish this: "I, Yahweh, have spoken and I will do it" (Ezek. 36:36); "Israel will know that I, Yahweh, have spoken, and I have done it, declares Yahweh" (Ezek. 37:14). This effective inception of salvation is due to divine agency alone.

Divine Agency in the Spirit's Outpouring

Elsewhere in the OT, God's outpouring of the Spirit, which marks the onset of the eschatological age (Isa. 44:3), is further clarified as an outpouring on "all flesh" who call on the Lord, therein receiving salvation (Joel 2:22-28). The Servant of Yahweh, himself Spirit-anointed, is the agent of this outpouring, making all things new (Isa. 42:1-4; 61:1-2).

The OT idiom of "pouring out the Spirit" shifts in the New Testament to "baptism with the Spirit." The agent who "baptizes with the Holy Spirit"—Yahweh (Joel 2:28-29/Acts 2:17-18)—is further specified, as Jesus' Father (Acts 1:4-5) and as Jesus himself, who is attested at the outset of his ministry as the Spirit-anointed

---

31. Block, *Ezekiel*, 488.
32. Ibid.

Messiah who baptizes "with the Spirit" (Jn 1:33; Mk 1:8). Luke employs both idioms ("baptism with the Spirit" and "pouring out the Spirit") to describe its actualization on the Day of Pentecost (Acts 1:4-5; 2:2-4, 17-18, 32-33). The original band of believers is the first to be "baptized with the Holy Spirit and with fire" (Mt. 3:11; Lk. 3:16; Acts 2:2-4). Peter publicly announces that God the Father and his designated Messiah Jesus ("Lord and Christ") act in concert to "pour out the Spirit" on those who call upon his name for salvation (Acts 2:17-18, 32-33, 21).

Hence, the anticipated outpouring of the Spirit and Christ's baptism with the Spirit refer to the same reality, which we have designated "Spirit-baptism." In the New Testament, both idioms signify the salvation-constituting, life-initiating event whereby the Father and the Son (with special reference to his messianic role) effectively bestow the Holy Spirit at the inception of the penitent believer's life in Christ and transfer him into "the kingdom of light ... the kingdom of the Son" beloved by the Father (Col. 1:12-13).

Pauline statements further confirm this distinctive pattern—the life-conferring, salvific event of Spirit-baptism that God alone effects—to which Jesus points in Jn 3:5-8. Second Corinthians 1:21-22 asserts, "Now it is God who makes both us and you stand firm in Christ. He anointed us, set his seal of ownership upon us, and sent his Spirit into our hearts as a deposit, guaranteeing what is to come." Titus 3:3-7 highlights the relation of Spirit-baptism to justification and adoption:

> But when the kindness and love of God our Savior appeared, he saved us, not because of righteous things we had done, but because of his mercy. He saved us through the washing of rebirth and renewal by the Holy Spirit, whom he poured out on us generously through Jesus Christ our Savior, so that, having been justified by his grace, we might become heirs having the hope of eternal life.

The "deposit" of the Holy Spirit is the crowning sign and tangible "seal" of the believer's permanent incorporation into covenanted life in the kingdom of God, as a member of his people. So, as we return to the Lukan account of Cornelius's conversion, the pattern of "Spirit-baptism"—as the culminating act that signifies the effective inception and reception of salvation—involves the work of God alone.

Spirit-Baptism and Ecclesial Baptism

It is time to draw the multiple lines of investigation together. As we have seen, patristic theologians interpreted Jn 3:5 in relation to church baptism. "Born of water and [of] [the] Spirit" describes the saving benefits conferred with the church's administration of baptism in Christ's name, perhaps combined with confirmation. Consecrated water is the "indispensable" medium, per Chrysostom as quoted above, through which the mysterious transformation takes place within an institutionalizing sacramental framework, as Cyprian's instructions indicate: "The water ought to be first cleansed and sanctified by the bishop that it may be able to wash away in its baptism the sins of the one who is baptized."[33] While these church fathers were right to read Jn 3:5 in relation to other canonical texts and particularly the baptisms of Paul and Cornelius, evangelical exegetes and biblical theologians can better attend to the pattern of divine agency in such passages. Particularly in the epochal case of Cornelius's household (Acts 10:34-48; 11:15-18; 15:1, 5-11), the patristic paradigm of baptismal regeneration struggles with the Lukan sequence that reflects this larger pattern. Luke's account describes the Gentiles' "salvation" (Acts 15:1, 11) as consisting in God's granting of "repentance that leads to life" (Acts 11:18): by believing in the Lord Jesus, they received forgiveness of sins (10:43; 11:17), and "God purified their hearts by faith" (15:9). The coming of the Holy Spirit upon them (10:44-46; 11:15-17), Peter concludes, plainly "showed that [God] accepted them ... [and they] are saved" (15:8, 11)—before and apart from church baptism.

Moreover, the pattern of sole divine agency from Acts 10 is not exceptional: It applies to Gentiles and Jews alike, as Peter and the circumcised believers recognize with increasing clarity (10:44-46; 11:15-17; 15:8-11). Paul's apostolic commission in Acts 26:13-18 expands the scope and universalizes the framework. The Lord Jesus told him he was "sending" him to his "own people and ... the Gentiles ... to open their eyes and turn them from darkness to light, and from the power of Satan to God, so that they may receive forgiveness of sins and a place among those who are sanctified by faith in me." The result associated with conversion ("turning to light and to the power of God") here—being ingrafted into the people of God—corresponds to the significance of the outpoured Spirit in Ezek. 39:29, signifying God's ratification of the covenantal relationship. Thus, the Spirit-baptism of Cornelius's household not only confirms the pattern noticed elsewhere but even clarifies it with the sharpest possible ontological distinction: God himself bestows all of the gifts that comprise salvation, which culminated in the Spirit's outpouring—apart from the ministrations of human hands.

Such canonical patterns of divine agency authorize, says Kevin Vanhoozer, the primacy that John Webster gives to "the triune God's communicative presence and activity. ... Scripture, interpretation, the church, and tradition alike [are] creaturely elements in a divine economy in which Son and Spirit are the primary agents."[34] Thus, Webster insisted that "God's work and the work of the church are fundamentally distinguished."[35] Accordingly, God's saving gifts are not necessarily conferred in ecclesial baptism understood as its instrumental or effective cause. Rather, since in Ezek. 37:26 the poured-out Spirit himself is "a sign and ... permanent seal of

---

33. Cyprian, Letter 70.1, in *Fathers of the Church: A New Translation* (Washington, DC: Catholic University of America Press, 1947–), 51:259, cited in Kenneth Stevenson and Michael Glerup, eds., *Ezekiel, Daniel*, ACCSOT 13 (Downers Grove: IVP, 2008), 118.

34. Kevin J. Vanhoozer, "A Mere Protestant Response," in Matthew Levering, *Was the Reformation a Mistake? Why Catholic Doctrine Is Not Unbiblical* (Grand Rapids: Zondervan, 2017), 214–15.

35. John Webster, *Word and Church* (Edinburgh: T&T Clark, 2001), 196.

the covenant of peace ... and the 'eternal covenant,' "[36] baptism is itself a sign, a concrete pointer to an inwardly accomplished and appropriated reality, effected by God himself.

Of course, God's bestowal of "the repentance that leads to life," accompanied by the reception of the Holy Spirit, can coincide with the occasion of baptism. Gregory of Nazianzus reminds us, says Oden, that "it is presumptuous to assume that human insight can identify precisely how, when, or why the Spirit works to bring life."[37] As Peter observed, Cornelius's household was "saved" (Acts 15:11) when "God, who knows the heart, ... purified their hearts by faith" and "showed that he accepted them by giving the Holy Spirit" (Acts 15:8-9). But the meaning, rationale, and "necessity" of church baptism—which Tertullian rightly observes is a dominical "law"—does not lie in Cyprian's dictum *salus extra ecclesiam non est* ("there is no salvation outside of the church") premised on an appeal to Jn 3:5 stating that the church's sacraments alone confer the gifts preparing baptisands to enter the kingdom of God,[38] but elsewhere. Indeed, Cyprian's own interpretation of "necessity" in the case of Acts 10 can be very helpful, perhaps suggesting that he held a more nuanced view. Beyond such "necessity" as a sign of God's saving work, baptism of course serves other pedagogical and practical purposes as well.[39]

Conclusion

Kevin Vanhoozer has asserted that "theology's main task is to assist the church to remain faithful to the gospel as Scripture articulates it. The reference point and norm for all the church believes, says, and does is the Word of God written."[40] In keeping with the "canonic" and "catholic" principles of his canonical-linguistic approach, this study has endeavored to clarify the relationship of Spirit-baptism, ecclesial baptism, and salvation as Scripture portrays it. Any interpretative claim should be weighed for its consistency with canonical judgments throughout the rest of Scripture, in both particular parts and the whole of the canonical dialogue. In the present case, patristic proponents of baptismal regeneration were right in seeking to relate Jn 3:5 and Acts 10, but their paradigm does not fit "the logic of scriptural discourse" when it comes to the sole divine agency promised in the climactic outpouring of the Holy Spirit. An alternative biblical-theological approach to Jn 3:3-8 highlights this pattern of divine agency in light of its rootage in Ezekiel 37 and 36. The pattern running across Ezekiel, John, Acts, and Paul

---

36. Block, *Ezekiel*, 488.
37. Oden, *Life in the Spirit*, 169.
38. Cyprian, Epistle 72.21, in ANF 5:384–5.
39. For a concise outline of the major traditions, see Ted A. Campbell, *Christian Mysteries* (Eugene, OR: Wipf and Stock, 2005).
40. Vanhoozer, "Mere Protestant Response," 215.

establishes normative "canonical practices" for the relation of Spirit-baptism, ecclesial baptism, and salvation.

If these arguments are accepted, they introduce tensions that—even for traditions whose confessional statements and historic liturgies subscribe to baptismal regeneration—can nevertheless be productive if taken as an opportunity to pursue theological understanding in its "catholic" sense: *ecclēsia kath holēs*, "according to the whole" people of God (Acts 9:31), via the "canonical" sense of Scripture. There is an opportunity to pursue *catholicity* by engaging new contexts and reexamining inherited views while reckoning with the human condition—including as it does the noetic effects of the fall and the culturally limited character of our understanding. There is an opportunity to pursue *canonicity* as individual and communal expressions of faith lead us to pursue further study of Scripture, seeking the normative canonical practices exemplified in it.

Here it is important to maintain the essential distinction between having saving faith and being able to express it in ways that are conceptually adequate to biblical teaching.[41] With respect to the latter, bearing in mind the categorical distinctions between dogma, doctrine, and opinion can shape one's sense of proportion and spiritual disposition in engaging with other traditions and viewpoints. John Wesley's conception of "a catholic spirit" admirably captures the latter, and Vanhoozer's summation is helpful: Distinguishing between essential beliefs and nonessential opinions, Wesley held that "as to all opinions *which do not strike at the root of Christianity*, we think and let think."[42] Respecting the individual conscience before God on nonessential matters, Wesley's "catholic spirit is his generosity of spirit to all Christians who have hearts right with God."[43] Mindful that we presently know only in part and see through a glass darkly, we are called to keep in step with the Lord Jesus, always seeking to promote others' good, in his way of loving them (1 Corinthians 13).

---

41. Ibid., 199.

42. From Albert C. Outler, *John Wesley* (New York: Oxford University Press, 1964), 92, cited in Vanhoozer, "Mere Protestant Response," 198.

43. Vanhoozer, "Mere Protestant Response," 200.

Chapter 18

SCRIPTURE IN SOUND

Jeremy Begbie

No one has done more than Kevin J. Vanhoozer to show the potential of drama to enrich biblical interpretation. By inviting us into the world of script, stage, and actor, he has refreshed and advanced evangelical hermeneutics while meeting head-on some of modernity's (and postmodernity's) most pointed challenges. Here, however, I am concerned with another art form, one of which our honored theologian is an extremely able practitioner, namely, music. Those who have been fortunate enough to hear Vanhoozer at his Steinway may have wondered why he has not drawn on his musical expertise more fully in his writing. In any case, here I explore what the medium of music might offer to the biblical interpreter. What follows are improvisations on Vanhoozerian themes, which I hope are faithful to the man himself.

I aim to show that music has the capacity to disclose aspects of our interpretive engagement with Scripture that may otherwise remain hidden or forgotten, and that are highly pertinent in the current hermeneutical climate. I will demonstrate this, first, with respect to music's aurality—music as a *heard* art form—and second, with respect to a sonic phenomenon heavily implicated in music: *resonance*. I am working from the assumption that music offers a unique way of coming to terms with the world we inhabit, of interacting with our fellow humans and the physical environment at large. As such, it has the capacity to enlarge our perception of virtually anything we encounter, from the mood of a person to the rhythms of nature. I take this to be highly relevant to theology, not least to biblical hermeneutics.

There are clearly dangers lurking here. The most obvious is treating music as if it were an independent source of revelation that can provide theological criteria of truth more ultimate and more determinative than those given in the testimony of Scripture. This is a perennial temptation. Music has a habit of becoming too big for its theological boots, especially in post-Enlightenment culture, and especially when it is contrasted with language. So, for example, it will be said that of all art forms music is the least reducible to words, and that this is its supreme theological virtue: It is not only a paradigmatic model of what communion with God entails but a superlative vehicle of it. However, as well as radically inflating the capacities of music, this seriously overlooks the intrinsic role of language in the dynamic of God's salvific and reconciliatory action, and of Scripture's language in particular. What is needed is a way of maintaining a resolute orientation to Scripture, and to the theodrama Scripture engages, yet *within that orientation* allowing music to do its own nonverbal work in helping us discover and experience that theodrama more fully. That is what is being attempted here.

Hearing the Word?

Rowan Williams reminds us that

> before [the Bible] is read in private, it is heard in public. Those of us who assume that the normative image of Scripture reading is the solitary individual poring over a bound volume, one of the great icons of classical Protestantism, may need to be reminded that for most Christians throughout the ages and probably most in the world at present, the norm is listening.[1]

Evangelicalism is rightly known for its stress upon listening: *hearing* God's Word. *Deus dixit*. God has spoken. God speaks, and his Word is to be heard. Interpreting Scripture is an exercise in audition before anything else. (Vanhoozer's appropriation of "speech-act" theory speaks to just this conviction.) Of course, reading Scripture aloud and preaching from Scripture have always been part of public worship. But what seem to have been underexplored by evangelicals are the consequences for biblical interpretation of the fact that the texts of the NT (and we will restrict ourselves to the NT here) were written in the expectation that they would be heard more than they would be read, and certainly heard aloud much more than they would be read silently. The majority of early Christians encountered these texts through hearing, especially (although not exclusively) within corporate worship.[2] This was a culture that was pervasively oral and

---

1. Rowan Williams, "The Bible Today: Reading & Hearing," transcript of The Larkin-Stuart Lecture, April 16, 2007. Available online: https://www.anglican.ca/news/archbishop-of-canterbury-church-needs-to-listen-properly-to-the-bible/ (accessed February 17, 2021).

2. The NT references to texts being read "seem rather clearly to reflect the reading of texts (from manuscripts) in early Christian circles, similarly to the references to, and visual depictions of, texts read in non-Christian social gatherings of the time" (Larry W. Hurtado, "Oral Fixation and New Testament Studies? 'Orality', 'Performance' and Reading Texts in Early Christianity," *NTS* 60, no. 3 [2014]: 339). There is much disagreement over the extent to which reading took the form of "dramatic performance." See Werner H. Kelber, *The Oral and the Written Gospel: The Hermeneutics of Speaking and Writing in the Synoptic Tradition, Mark, Paul, and Q* (Bloomington: Indiana University Press, 1997); Whitney Shiner, *Proclaiming the Gospel: First-Century Performance of Mark* (Harrisburg: Trinity, 2003); David Rhoads and J. Dewey, "Performance Criticism: A Paradigm Shift in New Testament

auditory: "For the overwhelming majority of people in the ancient world, texts were experienced in an oral context."[3] Silent reading was known and practiced in the Roman era, but relatively uncommon compared with reading aloud. Texts were often dictated to a scribe rather than written directly, and those who could read typically did so aloud, even when in private: "Reading effectively became a way of speaking the text, and speaking effectively became a way of reading and interpreting it."[4] Further, although the ability to read rudimentary texts (e.g., signs, numbers) was widespread in the Roman Empire, only a minority could cope with texts of the NT's sophistication, making the arts of hearing and speaking all the more important for the early church.[5]

This is not to say that the texts themselves were regarded as having minor or secondary importance. And we need to admit that we know little of what the texts would have actually sounded like when read.[6] Nonetheless, the pervasiveness of aural reception historically is undeniable and, I believe, worth taking seriously, especially in academic theological circles. Evangelical scholars make much of "hearing" God's Word in the Bible, but typically as a metaphor for something like "understanding" or "heeding." Hearing Scripture in a literal sense—perceiving

---

Studies," in *From Text to Performance: Narrative and Performance Criticisms in Dialogue and Debate*, ed. K. R. Iverson (Eugene, OR: Cascade, 2014), 1–26. For vigorous criticism of this strand of scholarship, see Hurtado, "Oral Fixation and New Testament Studies?" and the response by Kelly R. Iverson, "Oral Fixation or Oral Corrective? A Response to Larry Hurtado," *NTS* 62, no. 2 (2016): 183–200. This approach is not to be confused with Vanhoozer's "performance interpretation," where "performance" has a different and much wider sense. See Kevin J. Vanhoozer, *The Drama of Doctrine: A Canonical-Lingustic Approach to Christian Theology* (Louisville: Westminster John Knox, 2005), ch. 5.

3. Iverson, "Oral Fixation or Oral Corrective?" 198. "In the ancient world, in the Middle Ages and as late as the sixteenth and seventeenth centuries, the sort of reading implicit in many texts was oralized (as was their actual reading). The 'readers' of those texts were listeners attentive to a reading voice" (Guglielmo Cavallo and Roger Chartier, "Introduction," in *A History of Reading in the West*, ed. Guglielmo Cavallo and Roger Chartier [Oxford: Polity, 1999], 4).

4. Carol Harrison, *The Art of Listening in the Early Church* (Oxford: Oxford University Press, 2013), 5.

5. Iverson, "Oral Fixation or Oral Corrective?" 189–92. We should bear in mind that at this time, we are dealing with *scriptio continua* (i.e., texts with no gaps between words), making education in reading with understanding all the more crucial.

6. Some have attempted "sound analyses" of biblical texts. See, e.g., Dan Nässelqvist, *Public Reading in Early Christianity: Lectors, Manuscripts, and Sound in the Oral Delivery of John 1–4* (Leiden: Brill, 2016); Margaret Ellen Lee and Bernard Brandon Scott, *Sound Mapping the New Testament* (Salem, OR: Polebridge, 2009); Margaret Ellen Lee, *Sound Matters: New Testament Studies in Sound Mapping* (Eugene, OR: Cascade, 2018). These studies seem to have received scant attention from scholarly guilds, making them hard to evaluate.

spoken words—is rarely treated as integral to interpretation.[7] Much of what comes under "hermeneutics" these days appears to assume by default an "author-silent reader" paradigm. Even when "interpretive communities" are mentioned, they appear to be highly literate and do most of their actual reading outside a concrete communal context.

I am not suggesting that the oral-aural axis is intrinsically superior to silent reading, or that there is no place for reading silently. But I am proposing that we recover the distinctiveness of the experience of hearing texts read aloud in real time, for the sake of a more faithful hermeneutics and a deeper sense of what Christian hermeneutics is about. One way of doing this is to examine an art form that depends more than any other upon audition: music.

On the face of it, comparing the hearing of music with the hearing of Scripture might seem odd. The sound patterns of music do not normally direct our attention with consistency and clarity to particular ideas, physical entities, events, and so forth. Music does not possess terms that "refer" in this way. It cannot make assertions. Even when music mimics objects, or uses leitmotifs for particular people or ideas, the notes usually make very good sense without these things having to come to mind.[8] Its notes become meaningful for us in the first instance because they are dynamically and intrinsically related to each other. And their resulting relation to extra-musical realities will be of a different sort than designative reference. Language, on the other hand, makes little sense unless at least *some* of its terms are taken as focusing our attention on specific, extra-linguistic states of affairs.

True as all this may be, the two media are by no means incomparable in all respects. The experience of hearing or listening to music can throw into sharp relief some key differences between hearing a text read to (or by) us and reading it silently, which in turn have important implications for biblical interpretation.[9] For the sake of space, here I focus on music's *temporal* character.

---

7. John Webster, for instance, in "Scripture, Reading, and the Rhetoric of Theology," offers a penetrating treatment of "texts and the reading of texts" in "the culture of the Gospel" (*The Culture of Theology*, ed. Ivor J. Davidson and Alden C. McCray [Grand Rapids: Baker Academic, 2019], 63–80 [64]). But in his account of what happens when "the church reads the Bible" (67), nothing is said about the gains (or losses?) in reading it aloud, or about the fact that if "church" means gathered congregation, "reading Scripture" is invariably done through speech. And nothing is said about the texts themselves being originally intended for public reading.

8. The birdsong imitated at the end of the second movement of Beethoven's "Pastoral" Symphony, for example, can be musically intelligible even if we have never heard birds singing.

9. Three qualifications are needed. (1) I am assuming a scholarly setting for "interpretation," leaving texts interpreted in, for example, worship to one side. (2) For our purposes, the distinction between hearing music (simply being aware of it) and listening to it (attending *to* it) is not crucial. Occasionally, I shall speak of *perception* to cover both. (3) I shall make the (albeit artificial) assumption that nothing is being heard *except* the music. To consider how music interacts with nonmusical sounds would take us too far afield.

Going with the Flow

The perception of music is time-laden through and through. The only way a song makes any sense at all is when it is heard in and through time. We need to "go with it," to be carried along, pulled into carefully timed note patterns. The meaning is in the movement. Of course, we might say much the same about hearing a poem or a watching a play, but music's engagement with time is far more intense. A poem or play includes words that designate, orienting our attention clearly to extra-verbal objects. Music lacks such terms, as we have said, so its possibilities for meaning depend to a far greater extent upon the careful timing of notes in relation to each other.

Obvious as all this may seem, music theorists and analysts have found it extremely hard to cope with music's "thick" temporality. Much musical analysis has fixated on the written score, so that, as music theorist Nicholas Cook puts it,

> performance is seen as the translation into ongoing, experienced time of something that is not in itself temporal. Scores represent pieces of music as spatial configurations (you can flip the pages forwards and backwards), and music theory mainly consists of the elaboration of non-temporal models.[10]

But, as many studies have shown, a score can be radically misleading if taken as an image or map of the music *as perceived*.[11] The same goes for diagrams of musical structure. This is why in recent decades many have recommended more "kinetic" and embodied modes of analysis that do justice to music's ebbing and flowing, its emotional peaks and troughs—its "aural shape" (John Rink) as heard by real people in real time.[12]

What has all this to do with biblical hermeneutics? Many years ago, the Scottish theologian T. F. Torrance chided biblical scholars for not taking the time-embeddedness of Scripture's content seriously.[13] He felt that they tended to ignore what he called the "internal relations" within texts, and especially the temporal and spatial interrelations of recounted events. The result was fragmentation—parts divorced from wholes, events abstracted from intentions, theological concepts isolated from God's purposive actions in history. Torrance called for "kinetic" modes of thought in which temporal relations are never forgotten, intentions are not screened out, we avoid converting factual necessity (X happened) into logical

---

10. Nicholas Cook, *Beyond the Score: Music as Performance* (Oxford: Oxford University Press, 2013), 23.

11. See Nicholas Cook, *Music, Imagination, and Culture* (Oxford: Oxford University Press, 1990), chs. 1.2 and 1.3; Jerrold Levinson, *Music in the Moment* (Ithaca: Cornell University Press, 1997).

12. John Rink, "Review of Wallace Berry, 'Musical Structure and Performance,'" *Music Analysis* 9, no. 3 (1990): 319–39.

13. See e.g. Thomas F. Torrance, *Theological Science* (Oxford: Oxford University Press, 1969), 65, 87, 209, 40, 71, and especially 153–4.

or ontological necessity (X had to happen), and instead we "penetrate into the living happening behind the factual necessity and appreciate it as far as possible from within its own movement."[14]

The links between this and what we observed in music analysis should be clear. Indeed, there are strong parallels even between the way time itself is being conceived (or misconceived) in each case. Cook contrasts the "structuralist model" of musical analysis, in which an atemporal object passes through time, with the "rhetorical model," in which "time is a dimension of musical material, so that ... music is not *in* time, as with the structuralist model, but rather *of* time."[15] The importance of recovering just this latter outlook for hermeneutics was one of Torrance's key concerns.

Some of Torrance's points were doubtless overplayed, but he had an unerring eye for the issues that really mattered and he identified damaging currents in hermeneutics that have by no means disappeared. Much of Vanhoozer's work can be seen as a valiant attempt to counter just these currents, not least when they appear in forms of evangelicalism that tend toward static propositionalism. Hence his interest in narrative hermeneutics, and in the more comprehensive category of drama which can embrace human (and divine) actions and intentions.

My key point is that all this will be far more evident if a text is read aloud than silently—which is to say, "musically." Of course, this applies especially to narratives, and above all to narratives that recount a sequence of historical events. Consider, for example, the narrative of Jesus' passion, death, and resurrection as presented in each of the four Gospels. In his profound study *Between Cross and Resurrection*, Alan Lewis highlights two different ways of reading the story of Good Friday to Easter: "as a story whose ending is *known*, and as one whose ending is discovered only *as it happens*."[16] The NT gives us both: the "overview" perspective of those who know Friday and Saturday were not the last word (as in many of Paul's letters), and the perspective of those who went through Friday and Saturday without knowing the outcome (as in the Gospel accounts of Jesus' suffering and death).[17] Ignore the latter and we risk ascribing victory to the resurrection alone, forgetting that sin and evil were defeated *in* and *through* the Son's immersion in the humiliation and death of Friday. The cross is "*both* the disastrous finale to Christ's life as it sounds on the story's first hearing *and* as the first episode in a three-day event of triumph."[18] Lewis's phrase "first hearing" is telling. Most first hearers were just that,

---

14. Thomas F. Torrance, *Space, Time, and Resurrection* (Grand Rapids: Eerdmans, 1976), 93.

15. Cook, *Beyond the Score*, 126. Emphasis original.

16. Alan E. Lewis, *Between Cross and Resurrection: A Theology of Holy Saturday* (Grand Rapids: Eerdmans, 2001), 33. Emphases original.

17. Of course, the Gospels' passion accounts contain intertextual references to "the bigger picture," but the marked slowing down of the narrative pace, the portrayal of the guilt of the disciples, and the inexorable isolation of Jesus himself all ensure that there is no downplaying of the awfulness of these events for those who took part in them.

18. Lewis, *Between Cross and Resurrection*, 33. Emphases original.

hearers of a story as read to them; and for Jews who did not know the ending, the notion of a crucified Messiah would have been repulsive. Even for those who did know it, the way the Gospel accounts rub our noses in the Messiah's degradation would have jarred, to say the least. Today, thankfully, in some churches the story of the Passion is read aloud without a break, often on Good Friday.[19] Hearers are made to resist a premature grasp for Easter, or the amalgamation of cross and resurrection into a timeless and abstract concept. They are required to go with the story's flow, move through its transitions (and not over them), enter it as their story, and to do so slowly (reading aloud is generally slower than reading silently), letting the horror have its full sway. Might there not be good reasons for scholarly interpreters to do the same, as a hermeneutical habit?

One area where all this becomes especially telling is at the interface between hermeneutics and doctrine. The "overview" perspective, after all, is just what doctrine aspires to provide. Vanhoozer speaks of doctrines "providing summary statements of the story line of the Bible," thus giving us a dramatic framework for understanding the drama of redemption and giving us direction for our active participation in it.[20] The perennial temptation, however, is to treat doctrine as a substitute for the drama, as if the gospel were essentially an atemporal entity that unfortunately got entangled in time (akin to "the essence" of symphony being equated with a visual map of its form). The regular practice of reading Scripture aloud could be a healthy way of discouraging just these moves.

One last matter regarding the temporality of music is worth spotlighting. Rowan Williams describes music as the most "contemplative" of the arts, "*not because it takes us into the timeless but because it obliges us to rethink time.*"[21] By this he means that it gives us an experience of time that we do not control, one that is not ours to command but which can nonetheless be enormously enriching. This will probably be most evident when we listen attentively to music, but any perception of music *as music* requires that we take things at *its* speed, allowing ourselves to be caught up in *its* configurations of time-embedded relations. In this respect it reminds us of another obvious but crucial difference between hearing a biblical text read (read *to* us in this case) and reading it silently. In the former case, we are not in charge. We cannot go back or skip forward. Applied to Scripture, this can be a much-needed reminder of the irreversible and integrated flow of the

---

19. Against the notion that sections or segments are where music's meaning is most concentrated, Cook argues that performance (and listening) "is to a very large extent an art of *transitioning* – in other words, it is oriented to precisely the horizontal dimension of music that the spatialised, hierarchical models of theorist's analysis de-emphasise" (Cook, *Beyond the Score,* 46; emphasis added).

20. Kevin J. Vanhoozer, "At Play in the Theodrama of the Lord: The Triune God of the Gospel," in *Theatrical Theology: Explorations in Performing the Faith,* ed. Wesley Vander Lugt and Trevor A. Hart (Eugene, OR: Cascade, 2014), 26–7.

21. Rowan Williams, "Keeping Time," in *Open to Judgement: Sermons and Addresses* (London: Darton, Longman & Todd, 1994), 248. Emphasis original.

theodrama it renders. It is God's drama before it is ours—a drama for us to join, not recompose.

Resonance Realism

In the words of Ian McGilchrist, "We neither discover an objective reality nor invent a subjective reality ... there is a process of responsive evocation: the world 'calling forth' something in me that in turn 'calls forth' something in the world."[22] From the theology of time we turn to epistemology, and to another way in which music can inform hermeneutics. As we might expect, for Vanhoozer, epistemology is to be shaped by the form and content of God's dramatic self-disclosure in and through Scripture. "Theological epistemology is not something one does 'before' doing theology. It is not a method for knowing God but a way of thinking about methods of knowing in light of God's triune self-revelation."[23] Knowledge, then, in its highest form is a form of faithful participation in the economy of this divine self-communication.[24] And what kind of knowledge is this? In *Is There a Meaning in This Text?* Vanhoozer recommends "critical realism," an "interpretive rationality that does not presuppose either absolute foundations or a value-free standpoint on the one hand, or arbitrary and value-laden readings on the other. ... The critical realist must be able to say 'There is literary knowledge' (viz. determinate meaning and correct interpretation), but I am not certain that I have it."[25] In his later *The Drama of Doctrine* he speaks of "aspectual realism."[26] That there are many different literary genres in Scripture may be due to different levels of complexity in the reality being engaged, but perhaps different forms are also needed to highlight different *aspects* of reality. This aspectual realism takes two forms. That "certain frames or schemes are indispensable for knowing certain aspects of reality" Vanhoozer calls "moderate realism"; that we need a plurality of literary forms to do justice to the different aspects of the theodrama he calls "well-versed realism." In all these cases the "realist" pole remains: the inevitability of our being immersed in theories and schemes, and the unavoidability of multiple literary forms in Scripture, do not preclude epistemic access through these media to what lies beyond them.[27]

---

22. Iain McGilchrist, *The Master and His Emissary: The Divided Brain and the Making of the Western World* (New Haven: Yale University Press, 2009), 133.

23. Kevin J. Vanhoozer, "[Common Places]: Reading Notes: Theological Epistemology," Zondervan Academic blog, May 19, 2016. Available online: https://zondervanacademic.com/blog/common-places-reading-notes-theological-epistemology (accessed February 21, 2021).

24. Vanhoozer, *Drama of Doctrine*, 302.

25. Kevin J. Vanhoozer, *Is There a Meaning in This Text? The Bible, the Reader, and the Morality of Literary Knowledge* (Grand Rapids: Zondervan, 1998), 300–1.

26. Vanhoozer, *Drama of Doctrine*, 289–90.

27. Ibid., 289.

Resonant Knowing

I propose that a highly fruitful way of elucidating this kind of realism is through *resonance*—a phenomenon appropriated by a number of fields in recent years.[28] It comes in many types but the basic dynamic is of one thing "setting off" another. When an object is subjected to regular impulses at a frequency equal (or very close) to its natural ("resonant") frequency, it will start vibrating. Here we concentrate on resonance as we might encounter it in a musical context.

Imagine a violinist trying out a new violin: She draws the bow across a single string and a rich sound returns. The wood of the instrument vibrates, ringing on after the string has stopped vibrating. She begins to play a scale slowly, listening for where the resonances are strongest. Some notes sound "thin," others "thick." Occasionally, the whole instrument seems to come alive. The stronger the resonance, the more the wood "speaks back," and the more the instrument in its integrity and uniqueness is opened out to her.

The bearing of such a scenario for epistemology has been drawn out in a remarkable article entitled "Resonance Realism" by mathematician John Puddefoot, in which he expands upon the thought of Michael Polanyi (1891–1976), the Hungarian-British scientist.[29] According to Polanyi, all knowing employs tacit ("subsidiary") awareness as a means to achieving a more explicit ("focal") awareness. No knowledge is final and complete, since every human act of knowing presupposes a range of tacit awareness that can never be exhaustively articulated. In the above example, the player focally attends to the violin in order to find out where it is strong and weak. But to do this she relies upon (without focusing upon) a whole range of subsidiaries: sound quality, the force with which she presses the bow, experience with other instruments, the wisdom of teachers, and so on. Her bodily, social, linguistic, and cultural embeddedness is inescapable, but not in such a way that she gains no knowledge of the wood: It is *with* and *through* these subsidiaries that she attains a deeper focal awareness of the violin. "The essential point about resonance realism," Puddefoot explains, "is that it places the central criterion of our contact with reality on the boundary between the constructed world of human sense, culture and language and the discovered world 'out there' of which we can have no direct unmediated knowledge."[30] "When we 'hit the mark' something comes back to us, an echo, and we tune our theories by searching for

---

28. See, e.g., Hartmut Rosa, *Resonance: A Sociology of the Relationship to the World* (Medford, MA: Polity, 2019); Jean-Luc Nancy, *Listening*, trans. Charlotte Mandell (New York: Fordham University Press, 2007); Veit Erlmann, *Reason and Resonance: A History of Modern Aurality* (New York: Zone, 2010); Krzysztof Burdzy, *Resonance: From Probability to Epistemology and Back* (London: Imperial College, 2016); Jürgen Goldstein, "Resonance – a Key Concept in the Philosophy of Charles Taylor," *Philosophy & Social Criticism* 44, no. 7 (2018): 781–3.

29. John C. Puddefoot, "Resonance Realism," *Tradition and Discovery* 20, no. 3 (1993): 29–38.

30. Ibid., 31.

resonances with the world that sharpen and increase the volume of that echo. It is this that gives us our sense of reality, of being on the track of the real."[31]

This phenomenon of resonance, I suggest, both enacts and provides a model of the basic epistemological outlook Vanhoozer recommends for biblical hermeneutics. More than that, it extends and amplifies it. Five points may be made about this.

First, resonance realism provides a particularly strong way of *avoiding the false polarity between objectivism and subjectivism*. At every point the violinist relies upon her senses, her body's clues, mental processing, and years of encultured training. She never attains an unmediated, direct "hold" on the reality of the wood. On the other hand, the very fact that she goes on testing for resonance speaks of her assumption that she is in touch with a rich reality independent of her.

Like Vanhoozer, Puddefoot holds that "our knowing is always by means of the contingent language and theory of a particular culture and history in a particular world-line, a language, theory, culture and history that we have constructed."[32] Our knowing is always partial (we are finite, temporally and spatially located) and fallible (we are prone to distorting what we encounter). It is thus always corrigible and revisable. But we persist in searching for fuller and wider resonances in the belief that there are mind-independent realities to which we have access, which call forth our attention and respect. This model is as apt for biblical hermeneutics as for any other field of enquiry. Scriptural language, bound up with patterns of social and cultural life, and our own similarly implicated hermeneutical discourse, never give us an indubitable, exhaustive hold on the Bible's theodrama. But this does not commit us to presuming that these languages by their very nature deny us trustworthy access to the theodramatic realities they render.

Second, resonance realism *draws attention to the ongoing, "eschatological" dimension of knowing*: reality always outstrips what can be apprehended *now*. This provisionality is exacerbated by sin, but at root it is a function of our temporal finitude, the fact that we cannot stand *outside* time and wholly grasp something that exists *in* time. Just as the violinist always goes on seeking further resonance, so the process of biblical interpretation is never over, and this is especially so, of course, insofar as we are engaging with God's uncontainability by time.

Third, resonance realism gives us a trenchant way of throwing into relief *the poverty of a simple correspondence theory of truth*—of the sort that claims that a belief, statement, or idea can count as true to the extent that it is isomorphic with an object. Vanhoozer's realism eschews any such "mirroring" picture.[33] But that picture still lurks behind much theological epistemology and, as our model shows, it is deeply flawed. In the case of the violinist testing an instrument, there is no formal "match" between the string and the wood, yet the string evokes a sound which nonetheless discloses something of the wood's own nature. Similarly, Puddefoot writes,

---

31. Ibid.
32. Ibid., 32.
33. Indeed, he rewrites the notion of "correspondence" (*The Drama of Doctrine*, 298).

> We do not pretend – at least, we should not pretend – that [a] tuning-fork in some sense "corresponds" with that with which it resonates; on the contrary, we know that it bears no essential resemblance to it, only that it evokes an echo which tells us something about the intrinsic nature of the world.[34]

In any case, correspondence theories of truth are prone to an infinite regress. Testing the "match" of, say, an idea to an object implies that we can extricate ourselves from the idea and compare it with the object "as it really is." But this new stance vis-à-vis the object will surely need to be tested for *its* "match" with the object by extricating ourselves from *it*, and so on *ad infinitum*. There is simply no way of jumping out of ourselves in this way. We are always immersed in our beliefs, theories, and language; always shaped by history, social setting, and culture: "Testing is performed through conversation, theory and experimentation, not by comparing conversation, theory and experiment with something else."[35] The model of resonance is superbly equipped to throw this dynamic into relief. And it is a dynamic that is surely basic to biblical interpretation; there can never be wholesale disengagement from the contingencies of the biblical texts, or from our own. Indeed, it belongs to the very witness of these texts that we are creatures, not gods.

On the other hand—our fourth point—resonance realism makes clear that *we can, and should, compare the different strengths of what "sounds back" from reality.* Resonance realism holds that the single criterion by which a theory or statement is to be judged is whether it produces better resonances than others. It thus resists the pull of subjectivism. In interpreting a biblical text, there is a host of resonances to be alert to: internal coherence, consonance with other texts, explanatory power, fruitfulness in our lives, and so forth. The relative strength of these we can and should compare: That is basic to the process.

Fifth, resonance realism can help us to counter the model of *a detached, disembodied, observing subject confronting an essentially inert object*, a scheme that has notoriously skewed much modern epistemology and biblical hermeneutics. From the start we are encouraged to think instead of an embodied knower. The perception of sonic resonance is bodily through and through, involving many organs and cavities (not only the ears). The sub-Christian portrayal of the knower as an essentially immaterial, disengaged intellect has no place here. From the other side, the model evokes an object that is anything but inactive. The wood "sounds back" to the enquiring violinist. The reality discovered is not a formless "other" being compelled to conform to our interrogation, but declares itself according to its nature, calling back to us in often surprising ways. The momentum is responsive. Indeed, we could perhaps extend this and speak of the primary call as coming *from* beyond us. Polanyi offers a remarkable comment in this respect:

> This is, in fact, my definition of external reality: reality is something that *attracts our attention* by clues which harass and beguile our minds into getting ever

---

34. Puddefoot, "Resonance Realism," 31.
35. Ibid., 36.

closer to it, and which, since it owes this attractive power to its independent existence, can always manifest itself in still unexpected ways.[36]

Again, as a way of construing the process of interpreting a biblical text this could hardly be more appropriate, especially insofar as we believe that Scripture mediates the speech acts of a calling, attracting God.

Musical Resonance

We have been looking at resonance in one of its most basic forms, as occurring between two sounding objects. But, although testing a violin is geared toward playing music, we have not actually said anything about music itself as resonant, and how this might speak to biblical hermeneutics. I have space to point to only one set of possibilities here, concerning resonance as something that happens not only *within* music but also *between* music and its physical and social environment. In what is probably the most thorough treatment of the model of resonance yet available, the German sociologist Hartmut Rosa writes, "The peculiar quality of music lies in its ability to produce a highly specific form of relating to the world."[37] Music has "no content of its own" nor does it provide a "cognitive reference point"; rather, it "negotiates the quality of the relation [to the world] itself,"[38] turning into sound what happens or could happen *between* self and world. Here we explore what this self-world resonance might signal about the capacities of language in human life, and thus about language in biblical hermeneutics.

Much recent scholarship has exercised itself with the origins of music in relation to language.[39] The jury is still out on many issues, but some things command fairly widespread support. Music and language probably share a distant ancestor in evolutionary history: a primeval "musilanguage," an emotionally charged vocal expression from which emerged what we would now call music and language.[40]

---

36. Michael Polanyi, "The Unaccountable Element in Science," *Philosophy* 37, no. 139 (1962): 13-14; emphasis added. (Polanyi of course does not mean that external reality is *no more* than what attracts our attention. HIs point is about externality: Extra-human reality confirms its independence by attracting us.) The theme of call and response has been developed philosophically by many others; see, e.g., Jean-Louis Chrétien, *The Call and the Response* (New York: Fordham University Press, 2004).

37. Rosa, *Resonance*, 94.

38. Ibid.

39. See, e.g., Aniruddh D. Patel, *Music, Language, and the Brain* (Oxford: Oxford University Press, 2008); Ian Cross and Iain Morley, "The Evolution of Music: Theories, Definitions and the Nature of the Evidence," in *Communicative Musicality*, ed. Stephen Malloch and Colwyn Trevarthen (Oxford: Oxford University Press, 2008), 61-82.

40. Steven Brown, "The 'Musilanguage' Model of Music Evolution," in *The Origins of Music*, ed. Nils L. Wallin, Björn Merker, and Steven Brown (Cambridge, MA: MIT, 2001); Steven Brown, "A Joint Prosodic Origin of Language and Music," *Frontiers in Psychology* 8

One of the most lucid accounts comes from psychiatrist Ian McGilchrist, whose book *The Master and his Emissary* has become a classic. As McGilchrist observes, musilanguage would have been far more like what we would now call music than referential language, in that it would have relied upon pitch, intonation, volume, rhythm, and phrasing but would not yet have used terms that designate or denote. In this sense at least, we can say that language as we know it today grew out of music.[41]

The primary purpose of these primitive vocalizations, it seems, was emotional communication in the interests of social formation and cohesion.[42] This communication would have thoroughly implicated the body. We need to bear in mind that music activates the motor cortex of the brain even if we keep still when hearing it: "dance and the body are everywhere implied in [music]."[43] It has long been known that music depends for much of its emotional power upon our ability to read bodily movements and gestures that are inscribed into its sounds—movements and gestures associated with particular emotional states. This can make it an extraordinarily effective way of "inhabiting the body of another,"[44] of bonding with others without direct bodily contact.

In short, "Everything about human music suggests that its nature is sharing, non-competitive."[45] Here, so McGilchrist and others argue, we will best understand the roots of language. The particular type of language we now often think of as "language"—referential or denotative—arose not out of the need to communicate (musilanguage was doing that very well) but out of the need to *grasp*: to identify and distinguish things with precision and consistency, and in turn to manipulate objects and rearrange the world we inhabit. Language in this sense also gave us the ability to frame and organize ideas abstracted from the contingencies of time and space. Such designative language is by no means inherently harmful. Anything but. We depend upon it every day. The problems come when it is divorced from our bodily, social, and empathetic capacities, and McGilchrist believes that many of modernity's woes—including our social uprootedness and our tendency to

---

(2017): 1–20; Tim Ingold, *The Perception of the Environment: Essays on Livelihood, Dwelling and Skill* (London: Routledge, 2000), 408; Ian Cross, "The Evolutionary Basis of Meaning in Music: Some Neurological and Neuroscientific Implications," in *The Neurology of Music*, ed. Frank Clifford Rose (London: Imperial College, 2010), 1–15. For a semipopular presentation, see Steven J. Mithen, *The Singing Neanderthals: The Origins of Music, Language, Mind and Body* (London: Phoenix, 2006).

41. McGilchrist, *The Master*, 102–3.

42. Ian Cross, "Music and Communication in Music Psychology," *Psychology of Music* 42, no. 6 (2014): 814. See Daniele Schön and Benjamin Morillon, "Music and Language," in *The Oxford Handbook of Music and the Brain*, ed. Michael H. Thaut and Donald A. Hodges (Oxford: Oxford University Press, 2018), 408–9.

43. McGilchrist, *The Master*, 119.

44. Ibid., 122.

45. Ibid., 123.

instrumentalize other people—are linked to just this divorce. Language, he says, needs to be reminded of its roots. "If language began in music, it began in … functions which are related to empathy and common life, not competition and division; promoting togetherness, or, as I would prefer, 'betweenness.'"[46] Brain research suggests that even the most formal and strictly referential language depends and draws upon these embodied, communal, and empathetic dimensions.[47] Of course, a vast amount of the language that we use today is not of the naming, designative type; figurative language (e.g., metaphor) is one way in which language is reminded of its bodily, social, and affective rooting.[48]

McGilchrist's description of our "musical" relation to the world is very close to what we have described in terms of resonance: a bodily, responsive, noncoercive indwelling of our environment. His main interest is in the social resonance of music, but it is clear that he is thinking more widely than this: The same resonant dynamic could apply, *mutatis mutandis*, to the wider physical world. The ancient view of music as "tuning us in" to cosmic order now begins to make fresh sense.[49] It is not hard to transpose all this into a theological register: A resonant-musical relation to the world (social and nonhuman) is one in which we recognize our finite, embodied, and creaturely condition, as members of what Richard Bauckham calls "the community of creation."[50]

However, it is the implications for understanding *language* theologically that I want to underline, bringing us back to Vanhoozer. One of the trademarks of Vanhoozer's hermeneutics is a drive toward the relationality—resonance, indeed— that he sees undergirding all linguistic acts as God intended them to be. Against the backdrop of corrosive theories deeply cynical about the potential of any speech to mediate truth—and the no less corrosive modernist reduction of language to the transfer of units of information, encoded in designative words that supposedly "picture" reality, processed by disembodied minds for the purpose of greater control—he seeks to recover the close connection between communication and communion.[51] Thus, he can affirm, "*The design plan for language is to serve as the medium of covenantal relations with God, with others, with the world.*"[52] He distinguishes two dimensions: the interpersonal communion between speakers and "the objective bond between language and reality,"[53] the latter being a condition

---

46. Ibid.

47. See Cross, "Music and Communication," 814–15.

48. McGilchrist, *The Master*, 115–18. See Rowan Williams, *The Edge of Words: God and the Habits of Language* (London: Bloomsbury Continuum, 2014), 27–28 and ch. 4 *passim*.

49. Jeremy S. Begbie, *Resounding Truth: Christian Wisdom in the World of Music* (Grand Rapids: Baker Academic, 2007), ch. 3.

50. Richard Bauckham, *Bible and Ecology: Rediscovering the Community of Creation* (London: Darton, Longman & Todd, 2010).

51. "Language … should be seen as the most important means and medium of communication and communion" (Vanhoozer, *Is There a Meaning in This Text?*, 205).

52. Ibid., 206. Emphasis original.

53. Ibid.

of the former. Just this double-sided and rich view of language is needed to furnish a hermeneutics that will allow the biblical text to become—at its deepest level—a medium of reconciliation, of *koinonia* with the triune God. The consonances—dare I say it, resonances!—between this and what we have been proposing above hardly need to be spelt out.

In sum: I have argued that the kind of resonance that music affords between us and the physical world, and between us and other humans, speaks in its own way of the kind of responsive, covenantal, communality from which all language once derived and toward which it has been purposed by God. This will apply supremely to the language of Scripture and to the interpretative language we use to hear and live into its theodrama. I, for one, hope that our illustrious honoree will be drawn to explore these, and indeed, numerous hermeneutical openings that engaging with music provides. Surprises abound, even in the simplest sounds.

CONCLUSION

Douglas A. Sweeney

Kevin J. Vanhoozer came of age as the world's most thoughtful evangelicals were chafing under and outgrowing the sociocultural and hermeneutical mantle of American fundamentalism. During his undergraduate years at the post-fundamentalist Westmont College in California, he discovered that Alvin Plantinga had become one of the world's leading religious philosophers. As he studied at J. Gresham Machen's Westminster Seminary in suburban Philadelphia, he watched George Marsden (another Westminster graduate) publish *Fundamentalism and American Culture*.[1] And while he started on his doctorate at Cambridge University, he learned that Mark Noll and Nathan Hatch had just inaugurated the Institute for the Study of American Evangelicals at post-fundamentalist Wheaton College in Illinois. At about the same time, demographers reported that there were now more Christians living outside the West than in Europe and North America. Evangelical success across the two-thirds world meant that the church's center of gravity now lay in northwest Africa. The horizons of mainstream evangelical leaders had expanded quite dramatically in only a few decades. And the posture of many of them toward the world at large proved increasingly cosmopolitan as well.

On the eve of these changes, nearly all evangelical theologians in the United States had harbored sectarian attitudes about the world. Having recently departed from more liberal Protestant precincts, they were circling the wagons, defending the faith once delivered, and resisting the corruptions of the secular society. But in the late 1970s, while at Westmont College, Vanhoozer attached himself to Robert H. Gundry, an up-and-coming, innovative, middle-age professor, who taught him not to run from but learn about the world. So in navigating seminary and doctoral research, he gave himself to learning as much as he could about philosophy, literature, and the arts, exploring the knowledge of God in the light of history and culture. He continued to prioritize questions and concerns most important to his colleagues in the evangelical movement. But he studied those subjects in relation to a broader range of resources and intellectual trends than

1. George M. Marsden, *Fundamentalism and American Culture: The Shaping of Twentieth-Century Evangelicalism, 1870–1925* (New York: Oxford University Press, 1980).

was common among his evangelical peers. Consequently, he has come to play a far more influential role than most others in helping fellow evangelicals come to terms with late modernity.

As Vanhoozer has explained on many occasions, his intellectual journey has been fueled by the question, "What does it mean to be biblical?" Though his evangelical forebears usually dealt with this question in terms of literal, inductive, propositional construals of the contents of the Bible (defending fundamentalist readings of the meanings intended by the human authors of Scripture), Kevin himself has come to deal with it more broadly in terms of theological construals of what the Lord says and does (via Scripture's human authors) through the wide array of genres bound together in the Bible by its overarching story or redemptive-historical drama—interpreting what he calls the divine script given for performance by God's people. When Vanhoozer was in school, most interpreters of Scripture thought that textual meanings were fixed by discrete historical referents lying outside the text. But, of course, things have changed during the past fifty years, at least among the literati. And Vanhoozer has done more than anyone else to help us understand what it means to be biblical in a world where scholars disagree about this method—and even about the value of their hermeneutical vantage points for understanding Scripture. Our twenty-first-century world is much more patently diverse than ever before in human history and Kevin's calls for evangelical unity in diversity—informed as they are by an evangelical-catholic method of *ressourcement* and recovery of the common roots shared by his readers—have rallied more wise and faithful hearing and doing of Scripture than any others on offer in the academy today.

In *Hearing and Doing the Word: The Drama of Evangelical Hermeneutics in Honor of Kevin J. Vanhoozer*, we have gathered to respond to Vanhoozer's calls for unity and to demonstrate our friendship and fellowship in Christ—amid our obvious diversity—through collaborative engagement with Kevin on the Bible. The authors of this *Festschrift* are biblical, historical, and constructive theologians. They have all addressed themes that pervade Kevin's writings, extending them with help from their own scholarly work, and improvising responses to both Kevin and the questions he has raised in his oeuvre. Inasmuch as our honoree has pleaded many times for creative and collaborative engagement with the biblical text that is faithful to the Lord, respectful of tradition, and responsive to changes in the late modern world, we hope he will be pleased.

In Part One, "The Biblical Script," our contributors engage Kevin's interests in the canon. Iain Provan leads off with a fascinating argument about the hermeneutics of textual criticism. Using the work of textual scholars on the consonantal MT of the OT as a helpful case in point, he contends that all too often they have "failed to engage in sufficiently deep thought about initially puzzling texts before proposing emendations to them." They have dismissed received texts too hastily, that is, in favor of revisions "that permit texts to make immediate sense to the text critic, without pursuing with sufficient rigor the possible senses of the text as it stands as a piece of ancient literary art." Provan prompts them to recognize that critical methods ought to fit the character of texts. Our approach to ancient manuscripts needs to be guided by the nature of their contents, "which means that the excellent text critic requires always to be, at the same time, an accomplished literary critic."

Phil Long looks at recent efforts to respect the literary nature of canonical materials by noting what they communicate "implicitly," reading "between the lines" of biblical texts. Long appreciates these efforts, admitting from his own work on 1 and 2 Samuel that a lot of what is taught to us in the Bible is communicated obliquely, indirectly. "But here is the rub," he avers. "Attempts to read between the lines can go astray, particularly when interpreters are insufficiently attentive to the lines themselves. In the opinion of the present writer, some recent interpretations that have sought to read between the lines have, in fact, read *outside the lines*—that is, outside the boundary lines established by what the text explicitly says." Long goes on in his essay to demonstrate that such transgressions occur frequently and to explain that they are dangerous for biblical theology. He then offers useful guidelines for reading between the lines in a manner regulated by the text.

Karen Jobes examines the use of the Septuagint in Hebrews with assistance from Vanhoozer's work on Scripture as God's speech act. Beginning with the declaration in Heb. 1:2 that God's Son is, in part, a new speech act of God ("In the past God spoke to our ancestors through the prophets at many times and in various ways, but in these last days he has spoken to us by his Son"), she interprets this epistle as a divine locution in which God deploys the Greek OT to speak of a new covenant in Christ—thus advancing a novel use of the law and the prophets. This suggests, according to Jobes, that the Greek OT bears divine authority even and especially when it differs from the Hebrew. Or, to put this again in terms of speech-act theory,

> the production of the Greek versions of the Hebrew Scriptures by uninspired translators does not fall outside the purview of God's purposes. And if the Holy Spirit can coopt fallible English translations as efficacious enough to make conversion to Christ and a life of faith possible today, then cooption of the fallible LXX into a new divine speech act should not scandalize us.

Robert Gundry presents evidence for what he calls the Gospel of John's "backdating" of many of the events in Jesus' life as reported in the three synoptic Gospels. He then asks about the implications of this for Vanhoozer's understanding of theodrama and this drama's performance in the church's life today. Is John's Gospel as accurate as Matthew's, Mark's, and Luke's? Should it be harmonized with them on the level of chronology? Or does it represent a somewhat different genre of Scripture, one that Gundry calls "narratival fiction"? What is implied in all of this for the meaning and performance of the Gospel of John? Gundry calls for the recognition of multiple theodramas in the canon of the Bible, and he challenges Vanhoozer to account for this plurality, helping Christians today to make good on this diversity as we play our parts in the script God has given us.

Graham Cole provides a canonical interpretation of the devil in relation to what Vanhoozer calls the Bible's theodrama. Along the way, he provides an excellent example of biblical theology on a major theme of Scripture. Cole identifies Satan as the Lord's chief antagonist throughout the biblical canon, the character who does more than anyone else to give rise to its crisis and propel its plot forward. In the end, though, writes Cole, Satan proves to be a poor match for Jesus Christ, the Son of God and hero of our story. Satan's reach exceeds his grasp. He is conquered by the Savior. As the conflict is resolved and the canon brought to a close, the devil and his minions are "ejected from the theater."

Bob Yarbrough calls attention to Vanhoozer's frequent emphasis on Christian martyrdom, interpreting it in relation to the history of reflection on such costly suffering, especially in the long-neglected work of Martin Albertz, an NT scholar who was jailed by the Nazis and narrowly escaped being killed for his witness. Yarbrough reminds us that ninety thousand Christians die annually for testifying to Jesus and commends both Albertz and Vanhoozer for their efforts to address this reality theologically. Comparing Vanhoozer and his work to the scholarship of Albertz, he concludes that both men are faithful witnesses (μάρτυρες/mártyres) to Jesus. Both invite their fellows to the kind of faithful witness that has often led to death. Both champion a traditional Christian faith in late modernity, defying those conventions of the secular academy that contradict the gospel. And both commend a model of ecclesial commitment that will leave a lasting legacy of faithfulness and fortitude for thousands of their students around the world.

In Part Two, "Great Performances," our writers mine church history for models of engagement with the canon of holy writ that align with Kevin's view of what it means to be biblical. Darren Sarisky deploys the work of Basil of Caesarea to engage Vanhoozer on the question of the Spirit's role in biblical interpretation. Pointing out that Vanhoozer has usually emphasized the Spirit's role in catalyzing the hearing and the doing of the Word, Sarisky asks his former teacher to account more fully for the ways in which the Spirit also helps people of faith to establish the meaning of the biblical texts themselves. Trinitarian theology "in which the Spirit is the light in which God reveals himself," Sarisky emphasizes, "requires that this light indwell readers so that they might know the matter of the text in the nuanced sense that is possible when what is known is God while the knower is a human creature." The Spirit not only "endows an individual reader with the ability to do what the text requires of her" but also shapes her "prior understanding of the God to whom the text directs ... attention."

Greg Lee addresses Augustine's engagement with the Bible in view of modern evangelical approaches. He looks at questions of historicity, the weight of tradition in relation to the Scriptures, authorial intent, and the narrative of Scripture, asking whether Augustine's views align with the views of evangelicals. "*Sic et non*," quips Lee.

> Augustine confesses the authority of Scripture above other norms, he prioritizes human authorial intent in the interpretive task, and he defends the historicity of the text, even attributing textual discrepancies to scribal errors. Yet he believes that apparent contradictions should direct us to spiritual meaning, he cares less about verbal minutiae than meaning and truth, he includes the divine author in authorial intent, and he exercises allegorical liberties that would make many evangelicals cringe.

Lee concludes with a tribute to this volume's honoree, submitting that Augustine's doctrine of Scripture "resonates warmly with Vanhoozer's."

Matthew Levering looks at Thomas Aquinas on the book of Jeremiah, asking whether, in the end, Jeremiah should be seen as a person who struggled against the Lord and despaired. He interprets Jeremiah as a case of theodrama and assesses his tribulations and complaints in the language of communicative action. He demonstrates that Aquinas viewed Jeremiah's laments as instances of sadness but not conflict with God. "The theodramatic power of Jeremiah's bitter lament," he writes, "involves profound mourning and dismay over what is happening both to himself and to the people who are rejecting the word of God. At the same time," however, "Aquinas carefully avoids reading Jeremiah's bitter lament as though Jeremiah despaired or as though he were renouncing his prophetic task." God prevailed over the sadness of the so-called weeping prophet "not only by keeping him on the right path but also by promising to accomplish the restoration of all that was being destroyed by the people's rejection of Jeremiah's prophetic word."

Scott Manetsch surveys Calvin's interpretation of the Bible and compares Calvin's methods to those most prominent today among scholars like Vanhoozer who champion the theological interpretation of Scripture (TIS). Manetsch makes clear that, for Calvin, "faithful biblical interpretation requires more than explaining the grammar, syntax, and literary and historical context of a passage of Scripture. A distinctively Christian hermeneutic also requires consistent reflection on the theological and dogmatic dimensions of the Bible's central storyline." But Manetsch also contends that the reformer's exegesis "runs against the grain of several of the assumptions and approaches advocated by TIS." Calvin is more cautious with respect to the literal sense, offering Christological interpretations of OT texts with great care and more sparingly than many do today. And "Calvin's valuation of church tradition, and his trust of ancient commentators, is more ambivalent and critical than at least some proponents of TIS. The reformer consistently demands that the judgments of patristic, medieval, and contemporary commentators, as well as the analogy of faith (*analogia fidei*), be ruled by the literal, straightforward reading of Scripture."

Tom McCall reviews and defends what he refers to as a classically Wesleyan, theological reading of the whole canon of Scripture, one at odds with purportedly more "scientific" readings now common among John Wesley's denominational heirs. Wesley himself affirmed the unity of Scripture, says McCall, on the basis of its status as the very Word of God. He applied himself to the languages and history in and through which God reveals his Word to us. McCall, too, avows that grammatical-historical investigation of the Bible is "a very good place to start" for those who want to increase in the knowledge and likeness of God. But it is not a good place to end, he claims. Canonical and explicitly theological understanding of the Scriptures is required. Disciples must read the Bible whole with an awareness of the variegated, interconnected meanings of its texts. "If we believe in the holiness of the divine author," he argues, "then we will believe in the wholeness of the divine revelation."

Steve Garrett looks at evangelical engagement with Barth and his Trinitarian doctrine of the Word of God. Barth challenged Americans to deal with Scripture's character in light of the doctrine of God. Vanhoozer, writes Garrett, has done this admirably without gainsaying his evangelical commitment to the Bible as God's Word. He has dealt with the Bible in view of the doctrine of the Trinity and the economy of communication/redemption. Along the way, he has contributed a robust treatment of "God, Scripture, and hermeneutics, encouraging American evangelicals to go beyond Barth rather than simply turning toward or against him."

In Part Three, "Theodrama Today," our authors perform variations on some of Kevin's themes in an effort to enhance his directions for the hearing and the doing of the Word in the late modern world. Scott Swain revisits an age-old theological question but addresses it in relation to contemporary concerns. "What has baptism to do with biblical interpretation?" he asks today's readers. Or more specifically, in what ways should Trinitarian doctrine professed during baptism—presumably in the Apostles' Creed—inform our exegesis? Ancient and early modern interpreters agreed that the creed "provided the Christian with a proper orientation and framework not only for the Christian life but also for the interpretation of Holy Scripture." But many late modern Christians have dissented from this view. They oppose the imposition of ancient doctrine on the biblical work of better-read, late modern exegetes. Swain attempts to quell their fears, suggesting that when the creed shapes a "helpful preunderstanding" of exegesis by summarizing the witness of the canon (at least as understood by most Christians through the centuries), it can play a key and salutary role in our present engagement with the Bible.

Michael Allen examines two principles of recent Trinitarian formulation—the late modern focus on the economic Trinity and the relationship of Trinitarian doctrine to our thinking on other doctrines and concerns—making suggestions about the ways in which these principles might best be put to hermeneutical use with Vanhoozer's help. Allen ends his essay with a rousing call to refocus our Trinitarian energy on the task of promoting Christian wisdom in our worship and contemplation of the Lord. "While it is not only rightful but necessary to develop a theological and thus Trinitarian perspective on every facet of life," writes Allen,

> the application of Trinitarian jargon to projects of our own devising flirts with idolatry and can fall afoul of the third commandment, namely, taking the Lord's name in vain. Only beholding the Lord's majestic beauty in worship and learning via contemplation can guard us, by God's grace, from weaponizing Trinitarian language as a religious ornament for our academic and practical pursuits.

Michael Horton mines the writings of the Frenchman Paul Ricoeur, one of Kevin's favorite sources, to examine "how God does things with words in the church," especially through preaching. He finds two main themes in Ricoeur to be especially relevant: his work on Scripture as narrative and the distinction he draws between theologies of manifestation and proclamation. "The proclamation of biblical narrative," writes Horton after Ricoeur, gives shape to the church, which is a creature of the Word. The implications of this notion, furthermore, are "considerable: The first task of hermeneutics is not to give rise to a decision on the part of the reader but to allow the world of being that is the 'issue' of the biblical text to unfold." Then through preaching, consequently, "we are swept into the story." We do not precede the Word. "There is not first of all an individual or a community and then a word that it speaks to express inner thoughts, feelings, or agendas." Rather, "the word creates and defines the self and the community that hears it."

Hans Madueme resuscitates another ancient theological question, whether all of humanity is justly held guilty and condemned for Adam's sin. This doctrine, like the creed treated earlier by Swain, has fallen on hard times as a guide to making sense of what the Bible says today. But Madueme defends it by employing a Vanhoozer-style, canonical-linguistic interpretation of Scripture texts like Rom. 5:12-21 and 1 Cor. 15:21-22. He contends that the notion of original guilt is biblical "not merely in terms of faithful exegesis of biblical texts, but also in how it synthesizes a range of canonical judgments." So after laying out an Augustinian construal of his key biblical texts, Madueme examines theological support for his doctrine in the theory lying behind infant baptism, a heartrending analysis of the spiritual condition of those who die in infancy, and the forensics of the doctrine of justification. He concludes that his doctrine of the immediate imputation of Adam's guilt to his posterity "lies near the heart of the gospel."

Lisa Sung treats the doctrine of baptism from yet another angle. She compares patristic readings of Jesus' well-known teaching that "unless one is born of water and the spirit, he cannot enter the kingdom of God," with a handful of modern readings of the same passage. She engages in her own grammatical-historical exegesis of Jn 3:3-8, interpreting this passage in relation to Ezekiel 36–37 and the baptisms mentioned in the Acts of the Apostles. She affirms Kevin's commitment to the primacy of Scripture in the formulation of doctrine and the need for canon sense in making exegetical judgments. And she claims, contra her reading of the fathers Irenaeus, Tertullian, Cyprian, and Chrysostom regarding baptismal regeneration, that salvation commences with repentance and faith, not the practices associated with baptism.

In a series of variations on Vanhoozer's major themes, Jeremy Begbie explores some of the ways in which music can aid the interpretation of Scripture, especially as we reflect on its aurality and resonance. In view of its aurality, Begbie reminds us that the first people of faith knew Scripture more as read and heard aloud than read silently. He affirms, of course, the value of unspoken Bible reading by those with literacy and access but suggests that modern exegetes need to "recover a sense of the distinctiveness of the experience of hearing texts read aloud in real time." Such hearing reminds auditors "of the irreversible and integrated flow of the theodrama it renders. It is God's drama before it is ours," Begbie offers, "a drama for us to join, not re-compose." Regarding resonance, Begbie contends that this phenomenon can amplify Vanhoozer's notes on biblical hermeneutics in five main ways: helping us to avoid the false polarity between exegetical objectivism and subjectivism; attracting due attention to the eschatological dimension of human knowing ("reality always outstrips what can be apprehended *now*"); underscoring problems in simplistic correspondence or picture theories of truth; moving us past subjectivism by demonstrating the benefit of comparing varied values that sound back from reality; and counteracting the still-too-common paradigm of a "detached, disembodied, observing" interpreter confronting an essentially inert Bible. "In sum," concludes Begbie,

> I have argued that the kind of resonance that music affords between us and the physical world, and between us and other humans, speaks in its own way of the kind of responsive, covenantal, communality from which all language once derived and toward which it has been purposed by God. This will apply supremely to the language of Scripture and to the interpretative language we use to hear and live into its theodrama.

* * *

We hope that the cumulative effect of these theological tributes will be to bless our dear friend and faithful colleague, Kevin Vanhoozer, for his field-changing work on the interpretation of Scripture—and to further that work in creative ways, thereby honoring our brother by walking in his steps. Careful readers will have seen by now that Kevin is an inspiration to all within these pages. We affirm his commitment to evangelical unity through learned, wise, and loving exegesis of the Bible for performance by the church. We share his passion for the practices of *ressourcement* and recovery of the common roots that bind us all together. We have sailed together with him from the straits of sectarian, post-fundamentalist opposition to most other Christians into the deep blue sea of evangelical-catholic orthodoxy and ecumenical witness. And we pray with Kevin that the Lord will bless his people with both knowledge and wisdom (*scientia* and *sapientia/phronesis*) for the hearing and the doing of the Word in our day.

We conclude with canonical direction from St. Paul, asking God to guide us firmly on our quest

> to equip the saints for the work of ministry, for building up the body of Christ, until all of us come to the unity of the faith and of the knowledge of the Son of God, to maturity, to the measure of the full stature of Christ. We must no longer be children, tossed to and fro and blown about by every wind of doctrine, by people's trickery, by their craftiness in deceitful scheming. But speaking the truth in love, we must grow up in every way into him who is the head, into Christ, from whom the whole body, joined and knit together by every ligament with which it is equipped, as each part is working properly, promotes the body's growth in building itself up in love. (Eph. 4:12-16, NRSV)

All of us together say, "Amen."

PUBLICATIONS BY KEVIN J. VANHOOZER

Authored Books

Biblical Narrative in the Philosophy of Paul Ricoeur: A Study in Hermeneutics and Theology. Cambridge: Cambridge University Press, 1990. [Translated into Japanese and Chinese]

Is There a Meaning in This Text? The Bible, the Reader, and the Morality of Literary Knowledge. Grand Rapids: Zondervan, 1998. [Translated into Korean, Portuguese, Romanian, Indonesian, and Russian; 2nd ed., 2009]

First Theology: God, Scripture and Hermeneutics. Downers Grove: IVP Academic, 2002. [Translated into Korean and Portuguese]

The Drama of Doctrine: A Canonical-Linguistic Approach to Christian Theology. Louisville: Westminster John Knox, 2005. [Translated into Spanish, Portuguese, and Korean; named best theology book in the *Christianity Today* 2006 book awards]

With A. K. M. Adam, Stephen Fowl, and Francis Watson. *Reading Scripture with the Church: Toward a Hermeneutic for Theological Interpretation.* Grand Rapids: Baker Academic, 2006.

Remythologizing Theology: Divine Action, Passion, and Authorship. Cambridge Studies in Christian Doctrine. Cambridge: Cambriidge University Press, 2010.

Faith Speaking Understanding: Performing the Drama of Doctrine. Louisville: Westminster John Knox, 2014. [Translated into Korean and Portuguese; named theology book of the year in the *Christianity Today* 2015 book awards]

With Owen Strachan. *The Pastor as Public Theologian: Reclaiming a Lost Vision.* Grand Rapids: Baker Academic, 2015. [Translated into Korean and Portuguese]

With Daniel J. Treier. *Theology and the Mirror of Scripture: A Mere Evangelical Account.* Studies in Christian Doctrine and Scripture. Downers Grove: IVP Academic, 2015.

A Trindade, as Escrituras e a Função do Teólogo. Contribuições Para Uma Teologia Evangélica. Brazil: Vida Nova, 2015.

Pictures at a Theological Exhibition: Scenes of the Church's Worship, Witness and Wisdom. Downers Grove: IVP Academic, 2016. [Translated into Portuguese]

Biblical Authority after Babel: Retrieving the Solas in the Spirit of Mere Protestant Christianity. Grand Rapids: Brazos, 2016. [Translated into Portuguese]

Hearers and Doers: A Pastor's Guide to Making Disciples through Scripture and Doctrine. Bellingham: Lexham, 2019.

Edited Books

The Trinity in a Pluralistic Age: Theological Essays on Culture and Religion. Grand Rapids: Eerdmans, 1996.

With J. Andrew Kirk. *To Stake a Claim: Mission and the Western Crisis of Knowledge.* Maryknoll: Orbis, 1999.

Nothing Greater, Nothing Better: Theological Essays on the Love of God. Papers from the Sixth Edinburgh Dogmatics Conference. Grand Rapids: Eerdmans, 2001.

The Cambridge Companion to Postmodern Theology. Cambridge: Cambridge University Press, 2003.

Dictionary for Theological Interpretation of the Bible. Grand Rapids: Baker Academic; London: SPCK, 2005. [Translated into Portuguese; named best book in biblical studies in the *Christianity Today* 2006 book awards; awarded second prize in "reference" in the Catholic Press Association book awards; named "Christian Book of the Year" by the Evangelical Christian Publishers' Association]

With James K. A. Smith and Bruce Ellis Benson. *Hermeneutics at the Crossroads*. Indiana Series in the Philosophy of Religion. Bloomington: Indiana University Press, 2006.

With Martin Warner. *Transcending Boundaries in Philosophy and Theology: Reason, Meaning and Experience*. Aldershot: Ashgate, 2007.

With Charles A. Anderson and Michael J. Sleasman. *Everyday Theology: How to Read Cultural Texts and Interpret Trends*. Grand Rapids: Baker Academic, 2007. [Translated into Korean and Chinese]

Theological Interpretation of the New Testament: A Book-by-Book Survey. Grand Rapids: Baker Academic, 2008.

Theological Interpretation of the Old Testament: A Book-by-Book Survey. Grand Rapids: Baker Academic, 2008.

With Benjamin E. Reynolds and Brian Lugioyo. *Reconsidering the Relationship between Biblical and Systematic Theology in the New Testament: Essays by Theologians and New Testament Scholars*. WUNT 2/369. Tübingen: Mohr Siebeck, 2014.

With Michael J. Thate and Constantine R. Campbell. *"In Christ" in Paul: Explorations in Paul's Theology of Union and Participation*. WUNT 2/384. Tübingen: Mohr Siebeck, 2014. [Reprint, Grand Rapids: Eerdmans, 2018]

Contributions to Books

"The Semantics of Biblical Literature: Truth and Scripture's Diverse Literary Forms." In *Hermeneutics, Authority and Canon*, edited by D. A. Carson and John Woodbridge, 49–104. Grand Rapids: Zondervan, 1986.

"Philosophical Antecedents to Ricoeur's *Time and Narrative*." In *On Paul Ricoeur: Narrative and Interpretation*, edited by David Wood, 34–54. London: Routledge, 1991.

"Christ and Concept: Doing Theology and the 'Ministry' of Philosophy." In *Doing Theology in Today's World*, edited by John D. Woodbridge and Thomas Edward McComiskey, 99–146. Grand Rapids: Zondervan, 1991.

"Bernard Ramm." In *Handbook of Evangelical Theologians*, edited by Walter A. Elwell, 290–306. Grand Rapids: Baker, 1993.

"The World Well-Staged? Theology, Hermeneutics, and Culture." In *God and Culture*, edited by D. A. Carson and John Woodbridge, 1–30. Grand Rapids: Eerdmans, 1993.

"The Hermeneutics of I-Witness Testimony: John 21:20–24 and the 'Death' of the 'Author.'" In *Understanding Poets and Prophets*, edited by A. Graeme Auld, 366–87. Sheffield: Sheffield Academic Press, 1993.

"God's Mighty Speech Acts: The Doctrine of Scripture Today." In *A Pathway into the Holy Scripture*, edited by P. E. Satterthwaite and D. F. Wright, 143–81. Grand Rapids: Eerdmans, 1994.

"The Reader in New Testament Study." In *Hearing the New Testament*, edited by Joel B. Green, 301-28. Grand Rapids: Eerdmans, 1995.
"Does the Trinity Belong in a Theology of Religions? On Angling in the Rubicon and the 'Identity' of God." In *The Trinity in a Pluralistic Age*, edited by Kevin J. Vanhoozer, 41-71. Grand Rapids: Eerdmans, 1997.
"Human Being, Individual and Social." In *Cambridge Companion to Christian Doctrine*, edited by Colin E. Gunton, 158-88. Cambridge: Cambridge University Press, 1997.
"The Word of God: Its Relevance Today." In *God, Family and Sexuality*, edited by David W. Torrance, 9-30. Carberry, UK: Handsel, 1997.
"The Spirit of Understanding: Special Revelation and General Hermeneutics." In *Disciplining Hermeneutics*, edited by Roger Lundin, 131-66. Grand Rapids: Eerdmans, 1997.
"Linguistics, Literary Theory, Hermeneutics, and Biblical Theology: What's Theological about a Theological Dictionary?" In *New International Dictionary of Old Testament Theology and Exegesis*, edited by Willem A. Van Gemeren, vol. 1, 15-50. Grand Rapids: Zondervan, 1997.
"Salvation." In *Dictionary of Biblical Imagery*, edited by Leland Ryken, James C. Wilhoit, and Tremper Longman III, 752-56. Downers Grove: InterVarsity, 1997.
"The Trials of Truth: Mission, Martyrdom, and the Epistemology of the Cross." In *To Stake a Claim*, edited by J. Andrew Kirk and Kevin J. Vanhoozer, 120-56. Maryknoll: Orbis, 1999.
"Paul Ricoeur." In *Dictionary of Historical Theology*, edited by Trevor A. Hart, 489-93. Grand Rapids: Eerdmans, 2000.
"Exegesis and Hermeneutics." In *New Dictionary of Biblical Theology*, edited by T. Desmond Alexander and Brian Rosner, 52-64. Downers Grove: InterVarsity, 2000.
"The Voice and the Actor: A Dramatic Proposal about the Ministry and Minstrelsy of Theology." In *Evangelical Futures: Conversations on Theological Method*, edited by John G. Stackhouse Jr., 61-106. Grand Rapids: Baker Academic, 2000.
"The Pattern of Evangelical Theology: Homage à Ramm." Foreword to Bernard Ramm, *The Evangelical Heritage*. Grand Rapids: Baker, 2000.
"'Jesus Christ': Who do we say that he is?" In *This We Believe: The Good News of Jesus Christ for the World*, edited by John N. Akers, John H. Armstrong, and John D. Woodbridge, 61-76. Grand Rapids: Zondervan, 2001.
"The Love of God: Its Place, Meaning, and Function in Systematic Theology." In *Nothing Greater, Nothing Better*, edited by Kevin J. Vanhoozer, 1-29. Grand Rapids: Eerdmans, 2001.
"Foreword" to J. Scott Duvall and J. Daniel Hays, *Grasping God's Word: A Hands-On Approach to Reading, Interpreting, and Applying the Bible*. Grand Rapids: Zondervan, 2001.
"From Speech Acts to Scripture Acts: The Covenant of Discourse and the Discourse of the Covenant," in *After Pentecost: Language and Biblical Interpretation*, edited by Craig Bartholomew, Colin Greene, and Karl Möller, 1-49. Grand Rapids: Zondervan, 2001.
"Theology and the Condition of Postmodernity: A Report on Knowledge (of God)." In *The Cambridge Companion to Postmodern Theology*, edited by Kevin J. Vanhoozer, 3-25. Cambridge: Cambridge University Press, 2003.
"Scripture and Tradition." In *The Cambridge Companion to Postmodern Theology*, edited by Kevin J. Vanhoozer, 149-69. Cambridge: Cambridge University Press, 2003.
"Praising God in Song: Beauty and the Arts." In *Blackwell Companion to Christian Ethics*, edited by Stanley Hauerwas and Samuel Wells, 110-22. Oxford: Blackwell, 2003.

"Evangelicalism and the Church: The Company of the Gospel." In *The Futures of Evangelicalism*, edited by Craig Bartholomew, Robin Parry, and Andrew West, 40–99. Grand Rapids: Kregel, 2004.

"The Atonement in Postmodernity: Of Guilt, Goats and Gifts." In *The Glory of the Atonement*, edited by Charles E. Hill and Frank A. James, 367–404. Downers Grove: InterVarsity, 2004.

"Into the Great 'Beyond': A Theologian's Response to the Marshall Plan." In I. H. Marshall, *Beyond the Bible: Moving from Scripture to Theology*, 81–95. Grand Rapids: Baker, 2004.

"Pilgrim's Digress: Christian Thinking on and about the Post/modern Way." In *Christianity and the Postmodern Turn: Six Views*, edited by Myron B. Penner, 71–103. Grand Rapids: Brazos, 2005.

"Disputing about Words? Of Fallible Foundations and Modest Metanarratives." In *Christianity and the Postmodern Turn: Six Views*, edited by Myron B. Penner, 187–200. Grand Rapids: Brazos, 2005.

"Lost in Interpretation? Truth, Scripture, and Hermeneutics." In *Whatever Happened to Truth?*, edited by Andreas J. Köstenberger and R. Albert Mohler Jr., 93–129. Wheaton: Crossway, 2005.

"Introduction: What Is Theological Interpretation of the Bible?" In *Dictionary for Theological Interpretation of the Bible*, edited by Kevin J. Vanhoozer, 19–25. Grand Rapids: Baker Academic, 2005.

"Intention/Intentional Fallacy." In *Dictionary for Theological Interpretation of the Bible*, edited by Kevin J. Vanhoozer, 327–30. Grand Rapids: Baker Academic, 2005.

"Providence." In *Dictionary for Theological Interpretation of the Bible*, edited by Kevin J. Vanhoozer, 641–5. Grand Rapids: Baker Academic, 2005.

"Ricoeur, Paul." In *Dictionary for Theological Interpretation of the Bible*, edited by Kevin J. Vanhoozer, 692–5. Grand Rapids: Baker Academic, 2005.

"Systematic Theology." In *Dictionary for Theological Interpretation of the Bible*, edited by Kevin J. Vanhoozer, 773–9. Grand Rapids: Baker Academic, 2005.

"Truth." In *Dictionary for Theological Interpretation of the Bible*, edited by Kevin J. Vanhoozer, 818–22. Grand Rapids: Baker Academic, 2005.

"Word of God." In *Dictionary for Theological Interpretation of the Bible*, edited by Kevin J. Vanhoozer, 850–4. Grand Rapids: Baker Academic, 2005.

"Theology and Apologetics." In *New Dictionary of Christian Apologetics*, edited by Gavin J. McGrath and W. C. Campbell-Jack, 35–43. Downers Grove: IVP Academic, 2006.

"Imprisoned or Free? Text, Status, and Theological Interpretation in the Master/Slave Discourse of *Philemon*." In A. K. M. Adam et al., *Reading Scripture with the Church*, 51–94. Grand Rapids: Baker Academic, 2006.

"Four Theological Faces of Biblical Interpretation." In A. K. M. Adam et al., *Reading Scripture with the Church*, 131–42. Grand Rapids: Baker Academic, 2006.

"'One Rule to Rule Them All'? Theological Method in an Era of World Christianity." In *Globalizing Theology*, edited by Craig Ott and Harold A. Netland, 85–126. Grand Rapids: Baker Academic, 2006.

"Ricoeur, Paul." In *Dictionary of Biblical Criticism and Interpretation*, edited by Stanley E. Porter, 327–38. London: Routledge, 2007.

"Once More into the Borderlands: The Way of Wisdom in Philosophy and Theology after the 'Turn to Drama.'" In *Transcending Boundaries in Philosophy and Theology*, edited by Kevin J. Vanhoozer and Martin Warner, 31–54. Aldershot: Ashgate, 2007.

"On the Very Idea of a Theological System: An Essay in Aid of Triangulating Scripture, Church, and World," in *Always Reforming: Explorations in Systematic Theology*, edited by A. T. B. McGowan, 125–82. Downers Grove: IVP Academic, 2007.

"What Is Everyday Theology? How and Why Christians Should Read Culture." In *Everyday Theology*, edited by Kevin J. Vanhoozer et al., 15–60. Grand Rapids: Baker Academic, 2007.

"The Triune God of the Gospel." In *The Cambridge Companion to Evangelical Theology*, edited by Timothy Larsen and Daniel J. Treier, 17–34. Cambridge: Cambridge University Press, 2007.

"Foreword" to John Owen, *Communion with the Triune God*, edited by Kelly M. Kapic and Justin Taylor. Wheaton: Crossway, 2007.

"The Apostolic Discourse and its Developments." In *Scripture's Doctrine and Theology's Bible*, edited by Markus Bockmuehl and Alan J. Torrance, 191–207. Grand Rapids: Baker Academic, 2008.

"A Person of the Book? Barth on Biblical Authority and Interpretation." In *Karl Barth and Evangelical Theology: Convergences and Divergences*, edited by Sung Wook Chung, 26–59. Grand Rapids: Baker Academic, 2008.

"Theological Method." In *Global Dictionary of Theology*, edited by William A. Dyrness and Veli-Matti Kärkkäinen, 894–7. Downers Grove: IVP Academic, 2008.

"Triune Discourse: Theological Reflections on the Claim that God Speaks (Parts 1 and 2)." In *Trinitarian Theology for the Church: Scripture, Community, Worship*, edited by Daniel J. Treier and David Lauber, 25–78. Downers Grove: IVP Academic, 2009.

"A Drama-of-Redemption Model." In *Four Views on Moving Beyond the Bible to Theology*, edited by Gary T. Meadors, 151–99. Counterpoints. Grand Rapids: Zondervan, 2009.

"Scripture and Hermeneutics." In *Oxford Handbook of Evangelical Theology*, edited by Gerald R. McDermott, 35–52. Oxford: Oxford University Press, 2010.

"C. S. Lewis and Scripture." In *The Cambridge Companion to C. S. Lewis*, edited by Robert MacSwain and Michael Ward, 75–88. Cambridge: Cambridge University Press, 2010.

"Enhancement in the Cathedral: Towards Whose Advantage? Wisdom from Theology." In *Why the Church Needs Bioethics*, edited by John F. Kilner, 105–24. Grand Rapids: Zondervan, 2011.

"Wrighting the Wrongs of the Reformation? The State of the Union with Christ in St. Paul and Protestant Soteriology." In *Jesus, Paul, and the People of God: A Theological Dialogue with N. T. Wright*, edited by Nicholas Perrin and Richard B. Hays, 235–58. Downers Grove: IVP Academic, 2011.

"Ezekiel 14. 'I, the Lord, Have Deceived That Prophet': Divine Deception, Inception, and Communicative Action." In *Theological Commentary: Evangelical Perspectives*, edited by R. Michael Allen, 73–98. London: T&T Clark, 2011.

"Atonement." In *Mapping Modern Theology*, edited by Kelly M. Kapic and Bruce L. McCormack, 175–202. Grand Rapids: Baker Academic, 2012.

"Theological Commentary and 'the Voice from Heaven': Exegesis, Ontology, and the Travail of Biblical Interpretation." In *On the Writing of New Testament Commentaries: Festschrift for Grant R. Osborne on the Occasion of His 70th Birthday*, edited by Stanley E. Porter and Eckhard J. Schnabel, 269–98. Texts and Editions for New Testament Study. Leiden: Brill, 2013.

"The Strange New Status Symbol of the Cross." In *If I Could Only Preach One Sermon*, edited by Johnson T. K. Lim. Singapore: Word N Works, 2013.

"Interpreting Scripture between the Rock of Biblical Studies and the Hard Place of Systematic Theology: The State of the Evangelical (Dis)union." In *Renewing the Evangelical Mission*, edited by Richard Lints, 201–25. Grand Rapids: Eerdmans, 2013.

"Augustinian Inerrancy: Literary Meaning, Literal Truth, and Literate Interpretation in the Economy of Biblical Discourse." In *Five Views on Biblical Inerrancy*, edited by J. Merrick and Stephen M. Garrett, 199–235. Counterpoints. Grand Rapids: Zondervan, 2013.

"Ascending the Mountain, Singing the Rock: Biblical Interpretation Earthed, Typed, and Transfigured." In *Heaven on Earth? Theological Interpretation in Ecumenical Dialogue*, edited by Hans Boersma and Matthew Levering, 207–29. Oxford: Blackwell, 2013.

"What is the Bible?" In *Theology Questions Everyone Asks*, edited by Gary M. Burge and David Lauber, 30–46. Downers Grove: IVP Academic, 2014.

"The Origin of Paul's Soteriology: Election, Incarnation, and Union with Christ in Ephesians 1:4 (with special reference to Evangelical Calvinism)." In *Reconsidering the Relationship between Biblical and Systematic Theology in the New Testament*, edited by Benjamin E. Reynolds et al., 177–211. Tübingen: Mohr Siebeck, 2014.

"Is the Theology of the New Testament One or Many? Between (the Rock of) Systematic Theology and (the Hard Place of) Historical Occasionalism." In *Reconsidering the Relationship between Biblical and Systematic Theology in the New Testament*, edited by Benjamin E. Reynolds et al., 17–38. Tübingen: Mohr Siebeck, 2014.

"At Play in the Theodrama of the Lord: The Triune God of the Gospel." In *Theatrical Theology: Explorations in Performing the Faith*, edited by Wesley Vander Lugt and Trevor Hart, 1–29. Eugene, OR: Cascade, 2014.

"In Bright Shadow." In *The Romantic Rationalist: God, Life, and the Imagination in the Work of C. S. Lewis*, edited by John Piper and David Mathis, 81–104. Wheaton: Crossway, 2014.

"From 'Blessed in Christ' to 'Being in Christ': The State of Union and the Place of Participation in Paul's Discourse, NT Exegesis, and Systematic Theology Today." In *"In Christ" in Paul*, edited by Michael J. Thate et al., 3–35. Tübingen: Mohr Siebeck, 2014.

"Three (or more) Ways of Triangulating Theology: On the Very Idea of a Trinitarian System." In *Revisioning, Renewing, and Rediscovering the Triune Center: Essays in Honor of Stanley J. Grenz*, edited by Derek J. Tidball, Brian S. Harris, and Heson S. Sexton, 31–58. Eugene, OR: Cascade, 2014.

"Christology in the West: Conversations in Europe and North America." In *Jesus without Borders*, edited by Gene L. Green, Stephen T. Pardue, and K. K. Yeo, 11–36. Grand Rapids: Eerdmans, 2015.

"Systematic Theology." In *Routledge Companion to Modern Christian Thought*, edited by Chad V. Meister and James K. Beilby, 713–27. London: Routledge, 2015.

"The Spirit of Light after the Age of Enlightenment: Renewing/Reforming Pneumatic Hermeneutics via the Economy of Illumination." In *Spirit of God: Christian Renewal in the Community of Faith*, edited by Jeffrey W. Barbeau and Beth Felker Jones, 149–67. Downers Grove: IVP Academic, 2015.

"Scripture and Theology: On 'Proving' Doctrine Biblically." In *Routledge Companion to the Practice of Christian Theology*, edited by Mike Higton and James Fodor, 141–59. London: Routledge, 2015.

"Improvising Theology According to the Scriptures: An Evangelical Account of the Development of Doctrine." In *Building on the Foundations of Evangelical Theology*, edited by Gregg R. Allison and Stephen J. Wellum, 15–50. Wheaton: Crossway, 2015.

"'Exegesis I Know, and Theology I Know, but Who Are You?' Acts 19 and the Theological Interpretation of Scripture." In *Theological Theology: Essays in Honour of John Webster*, edited by R. David Nelson, Darren Sarisky, and Justin Stratis, 289–306. London: T&T Clark, 2015.

With R. R. Reno. "Epilogue." In *Evangelicals and Catholics Together at Twenty: Vital Statements on Contested Topics*, edited by Timothy George and Thomas G. Guarino, 165–70. Grand Rapids: Brazos, 2015.

"May We Go Beyond What Is Written After All? The Pattern of Theological Authority and the Problem of Doctrinal Development." In *The Enduring Authority of the Christian Scriptures*, edited by D. A. Carson, 747–92. Grand Rapids: Eerdmans, 2016.

"Holy Scripture: Word of God; Word of Christ; Sword of the Spirit." In *Christian Dogmatics*, edited by Michael Allen and Scott R. Swain, 30–56. Grand Rapids: Baker Academic, 2016.

"Imagination in Theology." In *New Dictionary of Theology: Historical and Systematic*, 2nd ed., edited by Martin Davie, Tim Grass, Stepehn R. Holmes, John McDowell, and T. A. Noble, 441–3. Downers Grove: IVP Academic, 2016.

"Love of God." In *New Dictionary of Theology: Historical and Systematic*, 2nd ed., edited by Martin Davie et al., 535–6. Downers Grove: IVP Academic, 2016.

"Scripture, Doctrine of." In *New Dictionary of Theology: Historical and Systematic*, 2nd ed., edited by Martin Davie et al., 827–9. Downers Grove: IVP Academic, 2016.

"Systematic Theology." In *New Dictionary of Theology: Historical and Systematic*, 2nd ed., edited by Martin Davie et al., 885–6. Downers Grove: IVP Academic, 2016.

"Theological Method." In *New Dictionary of Theology: Historical and Systematic*, 2nd ed., edited by Martin Davie et al., 901–3. Downers Grove: IVP Academic, 2016.

"Truth." In *New Dictionary of Theology: Historical and Systematic*, 2nd ed., edited by Martin Davie et al., 925–7. Downers Grove: IVP Academic, 2016.

"The Pastor as Public Theologian." In *Becoming a Pastor Theologian*, edited by Todd Wilson and Gerald L. Hiestand, 37–51. Downers Grove: IVP Academic, 2016.

"From Bible to Theology: Learning Christ." In *Theology, Church, and Ministry: A Handbook for Theological Education*, edited by David S. Dockery, 233–56. Nashville: B&H, 2017.

"A Mere Protestant Response." In Matthew Levering, *Was the Reformation a Mistake? Why Catholic Doctrine Is Not Unbiblical*, 191–231. Grand Rapids: Zondervan, 2017.

"Doctrine." In *Evangelical Dictionary of Theology*, 3rd ed., edited by Daniel J. Treier and Walter A. Elwell, 251–3. Grand Rapids: Baker Academic, 2017.

"Language." In *Evangelical Dictionary of Theology*, 3rd ed., edited by Daniel J. Treier and Walter A. Elwell, 474–6. Grand Rapids: Baker Academic, 2017.

"Analytics, Poetics, and the Mission of Dogmatic Discourse." In *The Task of Dogmatics: Explorations in Theological Method*, edited by Oliver D. Crisp and Fred Sanders, 23–48. Grand Rapids: Zondervan, 2017.

"Foreword" to Jonathan King, *The Beauty of the Lord*. Bellingham: Lexham, 2018.

"*Sola Scriptura* Means Scripture *First*! A 'Mere Protestant' Dogmatic Account (and Response)." In *Sola Scriptura: Biblical and Theological Perspectives on Scripture, Authority, and Hermeneutics*, edited by Hans Burger, Arnold Huijgen, and Eric Peels, 333–56. Leiden: Brill, 2018.

"Continuing the Conversation: A Reformed Reflection." In *God's Two Words: Law and Gospel in Lutheran and Reformed Traditions*, edited by Jonathan A. Linebaugh, 220–38. Grand Rapids: Eerdmans, 2018.

"*Sola Scriptura*, Tradition, and Catholicity in the Pattern of Theological Authority," In *Worship, Tradition, and Engagement: Essays in Honor of Timothy George*, edited by David S. Dockery, James Earl Massey, and Robert Smith Jr., 109–28. Eugene, OR: Pickwick, 2018.

"Towards a Theological Old Testament Theology: A Systematic Theologian's Take on Reading the Old Testament Theologically." In *Interpreting the Old Testament Theologically: Essays in Honor of Willem A. VanGemeren*, edited by Andrew T. Abernethy, 293–317. Grand Rapids: Zondervan, 2018.

"Theology and Wisdom: Creation as Context; Christ as Content; Canon as Curriculum." In *Where Wisdom May Be Found: The Eternal Purpose of Christian Higher Education*, edited by Edward P. Meadors, 43–55. Eugene, OR: Pickwick, 2019.

"Expounding the Word of the Lord: Joseph Ratzinger on Revelation, Tradition, and Biblical Interpretation." In *The Theology of Benedict XVI: A Protestant Appreciation*, edited by Tim Perry, 66–86. Bellingham: Lexham, 2019.

"Redemption Accomplished: Atonement." In *The Oxford Handbook of Reformed Theology*, edited by Michael Allen and Scott R. Swain, 473–96. Oxford: Oxford University Press, 2020.

Articles

"A Lamp in the Labyrinth: The Hermeneutics of Aesthetic Theology." *Trinity Journal* 8, no. 1 (Spring 1987): 25–56.

"Hyperactive Hermeneutics." *Catalyst* 19 (April 1993): 3–4.

"From Canon to Concept: 'Same' and 'Other' in the Relation between Biblical and Systematic Theology." *Scottish Bulletin of Evangelical Theology* 12, no. 2 (Fall 1994): 96–124.

"Exploring the World; Following the Word: The Credibility of Evangelical Theology in an Incredulous Age." *Trinity Journal* 16, no. 1 (Spring 1995): 3–27.

"Why Study Theology? The Cash Value of Systematics." In *The 1996 Seminary and Graduate School Handbook*.

"Effectual Call or Causal Effect? Summons, Sovereignty, and Supervenient Grace." *TynBul* 49, no. 2 (1998): 213–51.

"Mapping Evangelical Theology in a Post-modern World." *Evangelical Review of Theology* 22, no. 1 (January 1998): 5–27.

"'But That's Your Interpretation': Realism, Reading, and Reformation." *Modern Reformation* 8, no. 4 (1999): 21–28.

"The Case Remains Unproven: A Response to Philip Clayton's 'The Case for Christian Panentheism.'" *Dialog* 38, no. 4 (Fall 1999): 281–85.

"Body-Piercing, the Natural Sense and the Task of Theological Interpretation: A Hermeneutical Homily on John 19:34." *Ex Auditu* 16 (2000): 1–29.

"What Has Vienna to Do with Jerusalem? Barth, Brahms, and Bernstein's Unanswered Question." *WTJ* 63, no. 1 (Spring 2001): 123–50.

"The Promise of Consensus: Towards a Communicative Hermeneutic." *Transmissio* (Spring 2001): 6–7.

"Worship at the Well: From Dogmatics to Doxology (and Back Again)." *Trinity Journal* 23, no. 1 (Spring 2002): 3–16.

"Discourse on Matter: Hermeneutics and the 'Miracle' of Understanding." *IJST* 7, no. 1 (January 2005): 5–37.

"Lost in Interpretation? Truth, Scripture, and Hermeneutics." *JETS* 48, no. 1 (March 2005): 89–114.

"The Joy of Yes: Ricoeur, Philosopher of Hope." *Christian Century* 122, no. 17 (August 23, 2005): 27–28.

"Ten Theses on the Theological Interpretation of Scripture." *Modern Reformation* 19, no. 4 (2010): 16–19.
"The Inerrancy of Scripture." *Knowing & Doing: A Teaching Quarterly for Discipleship of Heart and Mind* (Spring 2010): 4–5, 18–20.
"Forming the Performers: How Christians Can Use Canon Sense to Bring Us to Our (Theodramatic) Senses." *Edification: The Transdisciplinary Journal of Christian Psychology* 4 (2010): 5–16.
"Continuing the Dialogue: A Theological Offering." *Edification: The Transdisciplinary Journal of Christian Psychology* 4 (2010): 41–46.
"Interview with Kevin J. Vanhoozer: What Does it Mean to be Biblical? What Should Biblical Authority Look Like in the 21st Century?" *Edification: The Transdisciplinary Journal of Christian Psychology* 4 (2010): 75–78.
Op-ed on theological interpretation of Scripture. *Southern Baptist Journal of Theology* 14, no. 2 (Summer 2010): 78–80.
"Five Picks: Essential Theology Books of the Past 25 Years." *Christian Century* 127, no. 21 (October 19, 2010): 37.
"Translating Holiness: Forms of Word, Writ, and Righteousness." *IJST* 13, no. 4 (October 2011): 381–402.
"Love's Wisdom: The Authority of Scripture's Form and Content for Faith's Understanding and Theological Judgment." *Journal of Reformed Theology* 5, no. 3 (2011): 247–75.
"Ascending the Mountain, Singing the Rock: Biblical Interpretation Earthed, Typed, and Transfigured." *Modern Theology* 28, no. 4 (October 2012): 781–803.
"What Is Theological Interpretation of the Bible?" *Theology and Life* 35 (2012): 1–13.
"Does a Red-Faced God Sing the Blues? Emotions, Divine Suffering, and Biblical Interpretation." *Trinity Magazine* (2012).
"Vanhoozer Responds to the Four Horsemen of an Apocalyptic Panel Discussion on *Remythologizing Theology.*" *Southeastern Baptist Theological Review* 4, no. 1 (Summer 2013): 67–82.
"Ontology, Missiology, and the Travail of Christian Doctrine: A Conversation with Kevin Hector's *Theology Without Metaphysics.*" *Journal of Analytic Theology* 1 (2013): 108–19.
"Being in Christ: Ontology, Topology, and the Church as Eutopic Theater." *Criswell Theological Review* 13, no. 1 (2015): 3–21.
"Putting on Christ: Spiritual Formation and the Drama of Discipleship." *Journal for Spiritual Formation and Soul Care* 8, no. 2 (2015): 147–71.
"Analytic Theology as Sapiential Theology: A Response to Jordan Wessling." *Open Theology* 3 (2017): 539–45.
"Catholic but not Roman: To Celebrate the 500th Anniversary of the Reformation, the 'Reforming Catholic Confession' Calls Protestants to Unity." *Christianity Today* 61, no. 8 (October 2017): 64–65.
"Love without Measure? John Webster's Unfinished Dogmatic Account of the Love of God, in Dialogue with Thomas Jay Oord's Interdisciplinary Theological Account." *IJST* 19, no. 4 (October 2017): 505–26.
"Don't Call It 'Retro': Retrieval Theologians are Looking Back to Move Forward." *Didaktikos* vol. 2 (2018): 41–42.
"Letter to an Aspiring Theologian." *First Things* 285 (August/September 2018): 27–32.
"Core Exercises: How Focusing on our Theological Center Helps Us Remember Who We Are." *Christianity Today* 82, no. 9 (November 2018): 46–50.
"Staurology, Ontology, and the Travail of Biblical Narrative: Once More unto the Biblical Theological Breach." *Southern Baptist Journal of Theology* 23, no. 2 (Summer 2019): 7–33.
"Hocus Totus: The Elusive Wholeness of Christ." *Pro Ecclesia* 29, no. 1 (2020): 31–42.

WORKS CITED

Publications by Kevin J. Vanhoozer appear in a separate bibliography.

Albertz, Martin. *Die Botschaft des Neuen Testaments*. Zollikon-Zürich: Evangelischer Verlag, 1947–57.

Albertz, Martin. "Die Krisis der sogenannten neutestamentlichen Theologie." *Zeichen der Zeit* 8 (1954): 370–6.

Allen, Michael. "Eternal Generation after Barth." In *Retrieving Eternal Generation*, edited by Fred Sanders and Scott R. Swain, 226–40. Grand Rapids: Zondervan Academic, 2017.

Allen, Michael. "Toward Theological Theology: Tracing the Methodological Principles of John Webster." *Themelios* 41, no. 2 (2016): 217–37.

Allison, Gregg. "Theological Interpretation of Scripture: An Introduction and Preliminary Evaluation." *Southern Baptist Journal of Theology* 14, no. 2 (Summer 2010): 28–37.

Almond, Philip C. *The Devil: A New Biography*. Ithaca: Cornell University Press, 2014.

Alter, Robert. *The Art of Biblical Narrative*. New York: Basic, 1981.

Alter, Robert. *The David Story: A Translation and Commentary of 1 and 2 Samuel*. New York: Norton, 1999.

Anatolios, Khaled. *Retrieving Nicaea: The Development and Meaning of Trinitarian Doctrine*. Grand Rapids: Baker Academic, 2011.

Andrews, James A. *Hermeneutics and the Church: In Dialogue with Augustine*. Notre Dame: University of Notre Dame Press, 2012.

Aquinas, Thomas. *Commentary on Jeremiah*. Unpublished translation by Benjamin Martin. Edited by the Aquinas Institute. Emmaus Academic, forthcoming.

Aquinas, Thomas. *Summa Theologica*. Translated by the Fathers of the Dominican Province. 5 vols. Allen, TX: Christian Classics, 1981.

Aristotle: Poetics, Longinus: On the Sublime, Demetrius: On Style. Translated by Stephen Halliwell, W. Hamilton Fyfe, and Doreen C. Innes. Revised by Donald A. Russell. LCL 199. Cambridge, MA: Harvard University Press, 1995.

Asiedu, F. B. A. "Following the Example of a Woman: Augustine's Conversion to Christianity in 386." *VC* 57 (2003): 276–306.

Athanasius. *Letters to Serapion*. In *Works on the Holy Spirit: Athanasius the Great and Didymus the Blind*. Yonkers, NY: St. Vladimir's Seminary, 2011.

Attridge, Harold W. *Essays on John and Hebrews*. WUNT 264. Tübingen: Mohr Siebeck, 2010.

Attridge, Harold W. "God in Hebrews." In *The Epistle to the Hebrews and Christian Theology*, edited by Richard Bauckham, Daniel R. Driver, Trevor A. Hart, and Nathan MacDonalsd, 95–110. Grand Rapids: Eerdmans, 2009.

Augustine of Hippo. *Agreement among the Evangelists*. WSA I/15–16.

Augustine of Hippo. *Answer to the Letter of Mani Known as The Foundation*. WSA I/19.

Augustine of Hippo. *Baptism*. WSA I/21.

Augustine of Hippo. *City of God*. WSA I/6–7.

Augustine of Hippo. *Confessions*. WSA I/1.

Augustine of Hippo. *De doctrina christiana*. WSA I/11.

Augustine of Hippo. *De trinitate*. WSA I/5.
Augustine of Hippo. *The Donatist Controversy I*. WSA I/21.
Augustine of Hippo. *The Gift of Perseverance*. WSA I/26.
Augustine of Hippo. *Instructing Beginners in Faith*. Translated by Raymond Canning. Hyde Park, NY: New City, 2006.
Augustine of Hippo. *La Genèse au sens littéral en douze livres (I-VII)*. Translated by P. Agaësse and A. Solignac. Bibliothèque Augustinienne: Oeuvres de Saint Augustin 48. Paris: Institut d'Études Augustiniennes, 2000.
Augustine of Hippo. *Letters*. WSA II/1.
Augustine of Hippo. *The Literal Meaning of Genesis*. WSA I/13.
Augustine of Hippo. *Nature and Grace*. WSA I/23.
Augustine of Hippo. *On Genesis: A Refutation of the Manichees*. WSA I/13.
Augustine of Hippo. *Reply to Faustus*. In *NPNF* 1, vol. 4.
Augustine of Hippo. *Unfinished Literal Commentary on Genesis*. WSA I/13.
Austin, J. L. *How to Do Things with Words*. 2nd ed. Edited by J. O. Urmson and Marina Sbisà. Cambridge, MA: Harvard University Press, 1975.
Ayres, Lewis. "Apophasis and the Discipline of Theological Speech: The Case of Basil of Caesarea." Unpublished manuscript.
Ayres, Lewis. "Augustine, The Trinity and Modernity: Colin Gunton's *The One, the Three and the Many*." *AugSt* 26 (1995): 127–33.
Ayres, Lewis. *Nicaea and its Legacy: An Approach to Fourth-Century Trinitarian Theology*. Oxford: Oxford University Press, 2004.
Baird, William. *History of New Testament Research*. 3 vols. Minneapolis: Fortress, 1992–2013.
Bakhtin, Mikhail. *Art and Answerability: Early Philosophical Essays*. Edited by Michael Holmquist and Vadim Liapunov. Translated by Vadim Liapunov and Kenneth Brostrom. Austin: University of Texas, 1990.
Bakhtin, Mikhail. *The Dialogic Imagination*. Edited by Michael Holmquist. Translated by Caryl Emerson and Michael Holmquist. Austin: University of Texas, 1981.
Bakhtin, Mikhail. *Problems of Dostoevsky's Poetics*. Edited and translated by Caryl Emerson. Theory and History of Literature 8. Minneapolis: University of Minnesota, 1984.
Bakhtin, Mikhail. *Speech Genres and Other Late Essays*. Translated by Vern W. McGee. Austin: University of Texas, 1986.
Bakhtin, Mikhail. *Toward a Philosophy of the Act*. Edited by Vadim Liapunov and Michael Holquist. Translated by Vadim Liapunov. Austin: University of Texas, 1993.
Balthasar, Hans Urs von. *Explorations in Theology*, vol. 1: *The Word Made Flesh*. Translated by A.V. Littledale with Alexander Dru. Vol. 1 of *Explorations in Theology*. San Francisco: Ignatius, 1989.
Balthasar, Hans Urs von. *The Glory of the Lord: A Theological Aesthetics*, vol. 6: *Theology: The Old Covenant*. Translated by Brian McNeil, C.R.V, and Erasmo Leiva-Merikakis. Edited by John Riches. San Francisco: Ignatius, 1991.
Balthasar, Hans Urs von. *My Work in Retrospect*. Translated by John Saward. San Francisco: Ignatius, 1993.
Barnes, Michel René. "The Fourth Century as Trinitarian Canon." In *Christian Origins: Theology, Rhetoric, and Community*, edited by Lewis Ayres and Gareth Jones, 47–67. London: Routledge, 1998.

Barth, Karl. *The Epistle to the Romans*. 6th ed. Translated by Edwyn C. Hoskyns. Oxford: Oxford University Press, 1968.
Barth, Karl. *Evangelical Theology: An Introduction*. Translated by Grover Foley. Grand Rapids: Eerdmans, 1979.
Barth, Karl. *Homiletics*. Louisville: Westminster John Knox, 1991.
Barth, Karl. "The Strange New World within the Bible." In *The Word of God and the Word of Man*, translated by Douglas Horton, 28–50. Boston: Pilgrim, 1928.
Barth, Karl. *The Word of God and the Word of Man*. Gloucester, MA: Peter Smith, 1958.
Bartholomew, Craig G. "Listening for God's Address: A *Mere* Trinitarian Hermeneutic for the Old Testament." In *Hearing the Old Testament: Listening for God's Address*, edited by Craig G. Bartholomew and David J. H. Beldman, 3–19. Grand Rapids: Eerdmans, 2012.
Barton, John. "Historical-critical Approaches." In *The Cambridge Companion to Biblical Interpretation*, edited by John Barton, 9–19. Cambridge: Cambridge University Press, 1998.
Barton, John. *Reading the Old Testament*. London: Darton, Longman and Todd, 1984.
Basil of Caesarea. *Against Eunomius*. In *Saint Basil of Caesarea against Eunomius*. The Fathers of the Church: A New Translation. Washington, DC: Catholic University of America Press, 2011.
Basil of Caesarea. *On Baptism*. In *Saint Basil: Ascetical Works*, translated by M. Monica Wagner. The Fathers of the Church: A New Translation. Washington, DC: Catholic University of America Press, 1950.
Basil of Caesarea. *On the Holy Spirit*. Translated by David Anderson. Crestwood, NY: St. Vladimir's Seminary, 1980.
Bates, Matthew. *The Birth of the Trinity: Jesus, God, and Spirit in New Testament and Early Christian Interpretations of the Old Testament*. Oxford: Oxford University Press, 2015.
Bates, Matthew. *The Hermeneutics of the Apostolic Proclamation: The Center of Paul's Method of Scriptural Interpretation*. Waco: Baylor University Press, 2019.
Bauckham, Richard. *Bible and Ecology: Rediscovering the Community of Creation*. London: Darton, Longman & Todd, 2010.
Baudrillard, Jean. "The Map Precedes the Territory." In *The Truth About the Truth: De-confusing and Re-constructing the Postmodern World*, edited by Walter Truett Anderson, 71–89. New York: TarcherPerigree/Penguin, 1995.
Bavinck, Herman. *Reformed Dogmatics*. 4 vols. Edited by John Bolt. Translated by John Vriend. Grand Rapids: Baker Academic, 2003–8.
Bayer, Oswald. *Living by Faith: Justification and Sanctification*. Grand Rapids: Eerdmans, 2003.
Beach, J. Mark. "Original Sin, Infant Salvation, and the Baptism of Infants: A Critique of Some Contemporary Baptist Authors," *Mid-America Journal of Theology* 12 (2011): 47–79.
Beach, J. Mark. "The Real Presence of Christ in the Preaching of the Gospel: Luther and Calvin on the Nature of Preaching." *Mid-America Journal of Theology* 10 (1999): 77–134.
Beasley-Murray, George R. *John*. WBC. Waco: Word, 1987.
Beck, Richard. *Reviving Old Scratch: Demons and the Devil for Doubters and the Disenchanted*. Minneapolis: Fortress, 2016.
Beekmann, Sharon, and Peter G. Bolt. *Silencing Satan: Handbook of Biblical Demonology*. Eugene, OR: Wipf and Stock, 2012.

Beeley, Christopher. *Gregory of Nazianzus on the Trinity and the Knowledge of God: In Your Light We See Light*. Oxford: Oxford University Press, 2008.
Begbie, Jeremy S. *Resounding Truth: Christian Wisdom in the World of Music*. Grand Rapids: Baker Academic, 2007.
Behr, John. *The Nicene Faith, Part One: True God of True God*. The Formation of Christian Theology, vol. 2. Crestwood, NY: St. Vladimir's Seminary, 2004.
Behr, John. *The Way to Nicaea*. The Formation of Christian Theology, vol. 1. Crestwood, NY: St. Vladimir's Seminary, 2001.
Belleville, Linda. "'Born of Water and Spirit': John 3:5." *Trinity Journal* 1 NS (1980): 125–41.
Berlin, Adele. *Lamentations*. Old Testament Library. Louisville: Westminster John Knox, 2002.
Berlin, Adele. *Poetics and Interpretation of Biblical Narrative*. Sheffield: Almond, 1983.
Billings, J. Todd. *The Word of God for the People of God: An Entryway to the Theological Interpretation of Scripture*. Grand Rapids: Eerdmans, 2010.
Blocher, Henri. *Original Sin: Illuminating the Riddle*. New Studies in Biblical Theology. Leicester: Inter-Varsity, 1997.
Block, Daniel I. *The Book of Ezekiel: Chapters 25–48*. NICOT. Grand Rapids: Eerdmans, 1997.
Bloesch, Donald. *Holy Scripture: Revelation, Inspiration, and Interpretation*. Christian Foundations. Downers Grove: IVP Academic, 1994.
Bloesch, Donald. *The Holy Spirit: Works and Gifts*. Christian Foundations. Downers Grove: InterVarsity, 2000.
Bloesch, Donald. "Karl Barth: Appreciation and Reservations." In *How Karl Barth Changed My Mind*, edited by Donald McKim, 126–30. Grand Rapids: Eerdmans, 1986.
Bloesch, Donald. *A Theology of Word and Spirit: Authority and Method in Theology*. Christian Foundations. Downers Grove: InterVarsity, 1992.
Bockmuehl, Markus. "Bible versus Theology: Is 'Theological Interpretation' the Answer?" *Nova et Vetera* 9, no. 1 (2011): 27–47.
Bockmuehl, Markus. *Revelation and Mystery in Ancient Judaism and Pauline Christianity*. Grand Rapids: Eerdmans, 1990.
Bokedal, Tomas. *The Formation of the Christian Biblical Canon: A Study in Text, Ritual and Interpretation*. London: Bloomsbury Academic, 2014.
Bolt, Peter G., ed. *Christ's Victory over Evil: Biblical Theology and Pastoral Ministry*. Nottingham: Inter-Varsity, 2009.
Bonner, Gerald. "Augustine on Romans 5,12." In *Studia Evangelica*, vol. IV: Papers Presented to the Third International Congress on New Testament Studies Held at Christ Church, Oxford, 1965, edited by Frank L. Cross, 242–47. Berlin: Akademie-Verlag, 1968.
Bouyer, Louis. *The Christian Mystery: From Pagan Myth to Christian Mysticism*. Translated by Illtyd Trethowan. London: T&T Clark, 1990.
Bowald, Mark. "A Generous Reformer: Kevin Vanhoozer's Place in Evangelicalism." *Southeastern Theological Review* 4, no. 1 (2013): 3–9.
Boyd, Gregory A. *Satan and the Problem of Evil: Constructing Trinitarian Warfare Theodicy*. Downers Grove: IVP Academic, 2001.
Boyle, John F. "Authorial Intention and the *Divisio textus*." In *Reading John with St. Thomas Aquinas: Theological Exegesis and Speculative Theology*, edited by Michael Dauphinais and Matthew Levering, 3–8. Washington, DC: Catholic University of America Press, 2005.

Brady, Jules M. "St. Augustine's Theory of Seminal Reasons." *The New Scholasticism* 38 (1964): 141–58.

Briggs, Charles A. *The Book of Psalms*. ICC, vol. 2. Edinburgh: T&T Clark, 1907.

Briggs, Richard S. *Words in Action: Speech Act Theory and Biblical Interpretation: Toward a Hermeneutic of Self-Involvement*. Edinburgh: T&T Clark, 2001.

Bromiley, Geoffrey. "The Authority of Scripture in Karl Barth." In *Hermeneutics, Authority, and Cannon*, edited by D. A. Carson and John D. Woodbridge, 275–94. Grand Rapids: Zondervan, 1986.

Brown, Jeannine K. *Scripture as Communication: Introducing Biblical Hermeneutics*. Grand Rapids: Baker Academic, 2007.

Brown, Steven. "A Joint Prosodic Origin of Language and Music." *Frontiers in Psychology* 8 (2017): 1–20.

Brown, Steven. "The 'Musilanguage' Model of Music Evolution." In *The Origins of Music*, edited by Nils L. Wallin, Björn Merker, and Steven Brown, 271–301. Cambridge, MA: MIT, 2001.

Brueggemann, Walter. *First and Second Samuel*. Interpretation. Louisville: John Knox, 1990.

Brueggemann, Walter. *Theology of the Old Testament: Testimony, Dispute, Advocacy*. Minneapolis: Fortress, 2012.

Bultmann, Rudolf. "New Testament and Mythology: The Problem of Demythologizing the New Testament Proclamation (1941)." In *The New Testament and Mythology and Other Basic Writings*, edited and translated by Schubert M. Ogden, 1–44. Philadelphia: Fortress, 1984.

Burdzy, Krzysztof. *Resonance: From Probability to Epistemology and Back*. London: Imperial College Press, 2016.

Burnett, Richard E. *Karl Barth's Theological Exegesis: The Hermeneutical Principles of the* Römerbrief *Period*. Grand Rapids: Eerdmans, 2001.

Busch, Eberhard. *Karl Barth: His Life from Letters and Autobiographical Texts*. Translated by John Bowden. Grand Rapids: Eerdmans, 1994.

Calvallo, Guglielmo, and Roger Chartier. "Introduction." In *A History of Reading in the West*, edited by Guglielmo Cavallo and Roger Chartier, 1–36. Oxford: Polity, 1999.

Calvin, John. "Calvin's Latin Preface to Olivétan's Bible." In *Institutes of the Christian Religion* (1536), translated and annotated by Ford Lewis Battles. Grand Rapids: Eerdmans, 1975.

Calvin, John. *Institutes of the Christian Religion*. 2 vols. Edited by J. T. McNeill and F. L. Battles. LCC. Philadelphia: Westminster, 1960.

Calvin, John. *John Calvin-Jacopo Sadoleto: A Reformation Debate*. Edited by John Olin. Reprint, Grand Rapids: Baker, 1987.

Cameron, Michael. *Christ Meets Me Everywhere: Augustine's Early Figurative Exegesis*. Oxford Studies in Historical Theology. Oxford: Oxford University Press, 2012.

Campbell, Ted A. *Christian Mysteries*. Eugene, OR: Wipf and Stock, 2005.

Carson, D. A. *The Gospel According to John*. PNTC. Grand Rapids: Eerdmans, 1991.

Carson, D. A. "Systematic Theology and Biblical Theology." In *New Dictionary of Biblical Theology*, edited by Desmond Alexander and Brian Rosner, 89–104. Downers Grove: InterVarsity, 2000.

Carson, D. A. "Theological Interpretation of Scripture: Yes, But . . . ." In *Theological Commentary: Evangelical Perspectives*, edited by R. Michael Allen, 187–207. London: T&T Clark International, 2011.

Casey, Paul M. *From Jewish Prophet to Gentile God: The Origins and Development of New Testament Christology*. Louisville: Westminster John Knox, 1991.
Cavadini, John C. "Two Ancient Christian Views of Suffering and Death." In *Christian Dying: Witnesses from the Tradition*, edited by George Kalantzis and Matthew Levering, 94–114. Eugene, OR: Cascade, 2018.
Chrétien, Jean-Louis. *The Call and the Response*. New York: Fordham University Press, 2004.
Chrysostom, John. "Homily XXV on John iii.5." In NPNF 1, vol. 14.
Chung, Sung Wook, ed. *Karl Barth and Evangelical Theology: Convergences and Divergences*. Grand Rapids: Baker Academic, 2006.
Ciampa, Roy E., and Brian S. Rosner. "1 Corinthians." In *Commentary on the New Testament Use of the Old Testament*, edited by G. K. Beale and D. A. Carson, 695–752. Grand Rapids: Baker Academic, 2007.
Clark, Gordon. *Language and Theology*. Phillipsburg: Presbyterian and Reformed, 1980.
Clement of Alexandria. *Stromateis*. In ANF 2. Grand Rapids: Eerdmans, 1951.
Clements, R. E. *Jeremiah*. Atlanta: John Knox, 1988.
Coakley, Sarah. *God, Sexuality, and the Self: An Essay "On the Trinity."* Cambridge: Cambridge University Press, 2013.
Coakley, Sarah. *Powers and Submissions: Spirituality, Philosophy, and Gender*. Challenges in Contemporary Theology. Oxford: Blackwell, 2002.
Coakley, Sarah, ed. *Re-thinking Gregory of Nyssa*. Directions in Modern Theology. Oxford: Blackwell, 2005.
Collett, Don C. *Figural Reading and the Old Testament: Theology and Practice*. Grand Rapids: Baker Academic, 2020.
Collins, Kenneth J. "Scripture as a Means of Grace." In *Wesley, Wesleyans, and Reading Bible as Scripture*, edited by Joel B. Green and David F. Watson, 19–32. Waco: Baylor University Press, 2012.
Cook, Nicholas. *Beyond the Score: Music as Performance*. Oxford: Oxford University Press, 2013.
Cook, Nicholas. *Music, Imagination, and Culture*. Oxford: Oxford University Press, 1990.
Couenhoven, Jesse. *Stricken by Sin, Cured by Christ: Agency, Necessity, and Culpability in Augustinian Theology*. Oxford: Oxford University Press, 2013.
Cranfield, C. E. B. "On Some Problems in the Interpretation of Romans 5.12." *SJT* 22 (1969): 324–41.
Crisp, Oliver D. "A Moderate Reformed Response." In *Original Sin and the Fall: Five Views*, edited by J. B. Stump and Chad Meister, 140–9. Downers Grove: IVP Academic, 2020.
Crisp, Oliver D. "On Original Sin." *IJST* 17, no. 3 (2015): 252–66.
Crisp, Oliver D. "Retrieving Zwingli's Doctrine of Original Sin." *Journal of Reformed Theology* 10 (2016): 340–60.
Crisp, Oliver D. "Sin." In *Christian Dogmatics: Reformed Theology for the Church Catholic*, edited by Michael Allen and Scott Swain, 194–215. Grand Rapids: Baker Academic, 2016.
Cross, Ian. "The Evolutionary Basis of Meaning in Music: Some Neurological and Neuroscientific Implications." In *The Neurology of Music*, edited by Frank Clifford Rose, 1–15. London: Imperial College, 2010.
Cross, Ian. "Music and Communication in Music Psychology." *Psychology of Music* 42, no. 6 (2014): 809–19.
Cross, Ian, and Iain Morley. "The Evolution of Music: Theories, Definitions and the Nature of the Evidence." In *Communicative Musicality*, edited by Stephen Malloch and Colwyn Trevarthen, 61–82. Oxford: Oxford University Press, 2008.

Croy, N. Clayton. "Review of Candida Moss, *The Myth of Persecution: How Early Christians Invented a Story of Martyrdom*." *Review of Biblical Literature* 10 (2013). Available online: http://www.bookreviews.org/bookdetail. asp?TitleId=9158&CodePage=8587,9158 (accessed July 10, 2020).

Cullmann, Oscar. *Christ and Time: The Primitive Christian Conception of Time and History*. Translated by Floyd F. Filson. Philadelphia: Westminster, 1964.

Cunningham, Mary Kathleen. *What Is Theological Exegesis? Interpretation and Use of Scripture in Barth's Doctrine of Election*. Philadelphia: Trinity Press International, 1995.

Cyprian. "Epistle 71." In ANF 5.

Cyprian. "Epistle 72." In ANF 5.

Cyprian. "Epistle 73." In ANF 5.

Cyprian. "Letter 70." In *Fathers of the Church: A New Translation*, 51:259. Washington, DC: Catholic University of America Press, 1947–.

Dayton, Donald. "Karl Barth and Evangelicalism: The Varieties of Sibling Rivalry." *Theological Students Fellowship Bulletin* 8, no. 5 (1985): 18–23.

de Greef, W. *The Writings of John Calvin*. Translated by Lyle Bierma. Grand Rapids: Baker, 1993.

De La Torre, Miguel A., and Albert Hernandez. *The Quest for the Historical Satan*. Minneapolis: Fortress, 2011.

DelCogliano, Mark. *Basil of Caesarea's Anti-Eunomian Theory of Names: Christian Theology and Late-antique Philosophy in the Fourth Century Trinitarian Controversy*. Supplements to Vigiliae Christianae: Texts and Studies of Early Christian Life and Language. Leiden: Brill, 2010.

Dempster, Stephen G. "Geography and Genealogy, Dominion and Dynasty: A Theology of the Hebrew Bible." In *Biblical Theology: Retrospect and Prospect*, edited by Scott J. Hafemann, 66–82. Downers Grove: InterVarsity, 2002.

Docherty, Susan E. *The Use of the Old Testament in Hebrews*. WUNT 260. Tübingen: Mohr Siebeck, 2009.

Dodd, C. H. *The Apostolic Preaching and its Developments: Three Lectures with an Appendix on Eschatology and History*. New York: Harper, 1949.

Doniger, Wendy. "Foreword." In Mircea Eliade, *Shamanism: Archaic Technologies of Ecstasy*. Princeton: Princeton University Press, 2004.

Drecoll, Volker H. *Die Entwicklung der Trinitätslehre des Basilius von Cäsarea: Sein Weg vom Homöusianer zum Neonizäner*. Forschungen zur Kirchen- und Dogmengeschichte. Göttingen: Vandenhoeck & Ruprecht, 1996.

Drever, Matthew. "The Self before God? Rethinking Augustine's Trinitarian Thought." *HTR* 100, no. 2 (2007): 233–42.

Dunson, Ben. "Do Bible Words Have Bible Meaning? Distinguishing between Imputation as Word and Doctrine." *WTJ* 75 (2013): 239–60.

Duvall, J. Scott, and J. Daniel Hays. *Grasping God's Word: A Hands-On Approach to Reading, Interpreting, and Applying the Bible*. 3rd ed. Grand Rapids: Zondervan, 2012.

Edelman, Diana V. "Saul's Rescue of Jabesh-Gilead (1 Sam 11:1–11): Sorting Story from History." *ZAW* 96 (1984): 195–209.

Eden, Kathy. *Hermeneutics and the Rhetorical Tradition: Chapters in the Ancient Legacy and Its Humanist Reception*. New Haven: Yale University Press, 1997.

Eliade, Mircea. *Myth and Reality*. Translated by Willard R. Trask. New York: Harper & Row, 1983.

Eliade, Mircea. *Myth of the Eternal Return: Cosmos and History*. Translated by Willard R. Trask. Princeton: Princeton University Press, 1971.

Elowsky, Joel C., ed. *John 1–10*. ACCSNT 4a. Downers Grove: IVP, 2006.
Episcopius, Simon. *Apologia pro Confessione sive Declaratione Sententiae eorum, Qui in Foederato Belgio vocantur Remonstrantes, super praecipuis Articulis Religionis Christianae: Contra Censuram Quatuor Professorum Leidensium* (n.p., 1629).
Erickson, Millard J. *Christian Theology*. 3rd ed. Grand Rapids: Baker Academic, 2013.
Erlmann, Veit. *Reason and Resonance: A History of Modern Aurality*. New York: Zone, 2010.
Evans, C. Stephen. "Methodological Naturalism in Historical Biblical Scholarship." In *Jesus and the Restoration of Israel*, edited by Carey C. Newman, 180–205. Downers Grove: InterVarsity, 1999.
Ferguson, Everett. *The Rule of Faith: A Guide*. Eugene, OR: Cascade, 2015.
Fergusson, David. *Creation*. Grand Rapids: Eerdmans, 2014.
Fiedrowicz, Michael. "Introduction." In St. Augustine, *On Genesis*, translated by Edmund Hill, 155–66. Hyde Park, NY: New City, 2002.
Fitzmyer, Joseph. "The Consecutive Meaning of ΕΦ'Ω in Romans 5.12," *NTS* 39 (1993): 321–39.
Fitzmyer, Joseph. *Romans*. New York: Doubleday, 1993.
Ford, David F. *The Future of Christian Theology*. Oxford: Blackwell, 2011.
Franke, John R. *The Character of Theology: An Introduction to its Nature, Task, and Purpose*. Grand Rapids: Baker Academic, 2005.
Freedman, David N. "Acrostics and Metrics in Hebrew Poetry." *HTR* 65 (1972): 367–92.
Frei, Hans W. *The Eclipse of Biblical Narrative: A Study in Eighteenth and Nineteenth Century Hermeneutics*. New Haven: Yale University Press, 1974.
Frei, Hans W. *The Identity of Jesus Christ: The Hermeneutical Bases of Dogmatic Theology*. Reprint, Eugene, OR: Wipf and Stock, 1997.
Frei, Hans W. *Types of Christian Theology*. Edited by George Hunsinger and William C. Placher. New Haven: Yale University Press, 1992.
Frye, Northrop. *The Great Code: The Bible and Literature*. San Diego: Harcourt, 1982.
Funk, Robert, Roy W. Hoover, and the Jesus Seminar. *The Five Gospels: The Search for the Authentic Words of Jesus*. New York: Macmillan, 1993.
Gadamer, Hans Georg. *Truth and Method*. 2nd rev. ed. Translated by Joel Weinsheimer and Donald Marshall. New York: Crossroad, 1989.
Garrett, Stephen M. "Subversive Horticulture." In *Visual Commentary of Scripture*. Available online: https://thevcs.org/subversive-horticulture (accessed February 17, 2021).
Gaumer, Matthew Alan. *Augustine's Cyprian: Authority in Roman Africa*. Brill's Series in Church History and Religious Culture 73. Leiden: Brill, 2016.
George, Timothy. *Reading Scripture with the Reformers*. Downers Grove: IVP Academic, 2011.
Georghita, Radu. *The Role of the Septuagint in Hebrews: An Investigation of Its Influence with Special Consideration to the Use of Hab. 2:3–4 in Heb. 10:37–38*. WUNT 2/160. Tübingen: Mohr Siebeck, 2003.
Gerrish, B. A. *Grace and Gratitude: The Eucharistic Theology of John Calvin*. Minneapolis: Augsburg Fortress, 1993.
Gibson, David, and Daniel Strange, eds. *Engaging with Barth: Contemporary Evangelical Critiques*. London: Continuum, 2008.
Goldingay, John. "Biblical Narrative and Systematic Theology." In *Between Two Horizons: Spanning New Testament Studies and Systematic Theology*, edited by Joel B. Green and Max Turner, 123–42. Grand Rapids: Eerdmans, 2000.

Goldingay, John. *Do We Need the New Testament? Letting the Old Testament Speak for Itself*. Downers Grove: IVP Academic, 2015.
Goldstein, Jürgen. "Resonance – a Key Concept in the Philosophy of Charles Taylor." *Philosophy & Social Criticism* 44, no. 7 (2018): 781–3.
Goslinga, C. J. *Het eerste boek Samuel*. Commentaar op het Oude Testament. Kampen: J. H. Kok, 1968.
Green, Barbara. *Bakhtin and Biblical Scholarship*. Atlanta: SBL, 2000.
Green, Joel B. "Contribute or Capitulate? Wesleyans, Pentecostals, and Reading the Bible in a Post-Colonial Mode." *Wesleyan Theological Journal* 39, no. 1 (2004): 74–90.
Green, Joel B. *Seized by Truth: Reading the Bible as Scripture*. Nashville: Abingdon, 2007.
Green, Michael. *I Believe in Satan's Downfall*. London: Hodder and Stoughton, 1999.
Gregory, Brad S. *Salvation at Stake: Christian Martyrdom in Early Modern Europe*. Cambridge, MA: Harvard University Press, 1999.
Gregory, Eric. *Politics and the Order of Love: An Augustinian Ethic of Democratic Citizenship*. Chicago: University of Chicago Press, 2008.
Grenz, Stanley J. *Rediscovering the Triune God: The Trinity in Contemporary Theology*. Minneapolis: Fortress, 2004.
Gribomont, Jean. "Le paulinisme de Saint Basile." In *Saint Basile, évangile et église*, edited by Enzo Bianchi, 192–200. Spiritualité orientale et vie monastique. Bégrolles-en-Mauges, Maine & Loire: Abbaye de Bellefontaine, 1984.
Gribomont, Jean. "Les Règles Morales de Saint Basile et le Nouveau Testament." In *Saint Basile, évangile et église: mélanges*, edited by Enzo Bianchi, 146–56. Spiritualité orientale et vie monastique. Bégrolles-en-Mauges, Maine & Loire: Abbaye de Bellefontaine, 1984.
Gribomont, Jean. "La tradition johannique chez S Basile." In *Parola e spirito*, 847–66. Brescia: Paideia Editrice, 1982.
Griffiths, Paul. *Religious Reading: The Place of Reading in the Practice of Religion*. Oxford: Oxford University Press, 1999.
Gundry, Robert H. *Peter—False Disciple and Apostate according to Saint Matthew*. Grand Rapids: Eerdmans, 2015.
Gunkel, Hermann. *Die Psalmen*. Gottingen: Vandenhoek und Ruprecht, 1926.
Gunn, David M. *The Fate of King Saul: An Interpretation of a Biblical Story*. JSOTSup 14. Sheffield: JSOT, 1980.
Gunton, Colin E. "Augustine, the Trinity, and the Theological Crisis of the West." *SJT* 43, no. 1 (1990): 33–58.
Guthrie, George H. "Hebrews." In *Commentary on the New Testament Use of the Old Testament*, edited by G. K. Beale and D. A. Carson, 919–95. Grand Rapids: Baker Academic, 2007.
Hahn, Scott W., and John Kincaid. "The Multiple Literal Sense in Thomas Aquinas's Commentary on Romans and Modern Pauline Hermeneutics." In *Reading Romans with St. Thomas Aquinas*, edited by Matthew Levering and Michael Dauphinais, 163–82. Washington, DC: Catholic University of America Press, 2012.
Halpern, Baruch. *The Constitution of the Monarchy in Israel*. HSM 25. Chico: Scholars, 1981.
Halpern, Baruch. *David's Secret Demons: Messiah, Murderer, Traitor, King*. Grand Rapids: Eerdmans, 2001.
Halpern, Baruch. "The Uneasy Compromise: Israel between League and Monarchy." In *Traditions in Transformation: Turning Points in Biblical Faith*, edited by Baruch Halpern and J. D. Levenson, 59–96. Winona Lake: Eisenbrauns, 1981.

Hammann, Konrad. *Rudolf Bultmann—Eine Biographie*. Tübingen: Mohr Siebeck, 2009.
Hanby, Michael. *Augustine and Modernity*. Radical Orthodoxy. London: Routledge, 2003.
Harris, Murray J. "Appendix: Prepositions and Theology in the Greek New Testament." In *NIDNTT*, 3:1171–1215.
Harrison, Carol. *The Art of Listening in the Early Church*. Oxford: Oxford University Press, 2013.
Harwood, Adam. *The Spiritual Condition of Infants: A Biblical-Historical Survey and Systematic Proposal*. Eugene, OR: Wipf and Stock, 2011.
Hays, Richard B. *Echoes of Scripture in the Gospels*. Waco: Baylor University Press, 2016.
Hays, Richard B. "The Future of Scripture." *Wesleyan Theological Journal* 46, no. 1 (2011): 24–38.
Heidegger, Martin. "On the Origin of a Work of Art." In *Basic Writings*, 139–212. New York: Harper Perennial, 2008.
Henry, Carl F. H. *God, Revelation and Authority*, 6 vols. Waco: Word, 1976–83.
Henry, Carl F. H. "Graham Challenges Swiss Throngs to Decision." *Christianity Today*, September 26, 1960. Available online: https://www.christianitytoday.com/ct/1960/september-26/graham-challenges-swiss-throngs-to-decision.html (accessed February 17, 2021).
Hesselink, I. John. *Calvin's First Catechism. A Commentary*. Louisville: Westminster John Knox, 1997.
Hiebert, Paul G. *Anthropological Reflections on Missiological Issues*. Grand Rapids: Baker, 1994.
Hildebrand, Stephen M. *The Trinitarian Theology of Basil of Caesarea: A Synthesis of Greek Thought and Biblical Truth*. Washington, DC: Catholic University of America Press, 2007.
Hill, Wesley. *Paul and the Trinity: Persons, Relations, and the Pauline Letters*. Grand Rapids: Eerdmans, 2015.
Hindmarsh, Bruce. *The Spirit of Early Evangelicalism: True Religion in a Modern World*. Oxford: Oxford University Press, 2018.
Hirsch, E. D., Jr. *Validity in Interpretation*. New Haven: Yale University Press, 1967.
Hodge, Charles. *Systematic Theology*, vol. 2. New York: Scribner's, 1898.
Holmes, Stephen R. *The Quest for the Trinity: The Doctrine of God in Scripture, History, and Modernity*. Downers Grove: IVP Academic, 2012.
Horn, Laurence R. "Contradiction." *Stanford Encyclopedia of Philosophy*. Available online: https://plato.stanford.edu/entries/contradiction/ (accessed June 12, 2018).
Horton, Michael. *The Christian Faith: A Systematic Theology for Pilgrims on the Way*. Grand Rapids: Zondervan Academic, 2011.
Horton, Michael. *Covenant and Eschatology: The Divine Drama*. Louisville: Westminster John Knox, 2002.
Hurtado, Larry W. "Oral Fixation and New Testament Studies? 'Orality', 'Performance' and Reading Texts in Early Christianity." *NTS* 60, no. 3 (2014): 321–40.
Husbands, Mark A. "The Trinity Is Not Our Social Program: Volf, Gregory of Nyssa, and Barth." In *Trinitarian Theology for the Church: Scripture, Community, Worship*, edited by Daniel J. Treier and David Lauber, 120–41. Downers Grove: IVP Academic, 2009.
Ingold, Tim. *The Perception of the Environment: Essays on Livelihood, Dwelling and Skill*. London: Routledge, 2000.
Irenaeus. *Against Heresies*. In ANF 1.
Irenaeus. "Fragment 34." In *Fragments of the Lost Writings of Irenaeus*. ANF 1.

Iverson, Kelly R. "Oral Fixation or Oral Corrective? A Response to Larry Hurtado." *NTS* 62, no. 2 (2016): 183–200.
Jamieson, R. B. "1 Corinthians 15:28 and the Grammar of Paul's Christology." *NTS* 66 (2020): 187–207.
Jennings, Willie James. *The Christian Imagination: Theology and the Origins of Race*. New Haven: Yale University Press, 2011.
Jenson, Robert W. *Canon and Creed*. Louisville: Westminster John Knox, 2010.
Jenson, Robert W. "The Christian Doctrine of God." In *Keeping the Faith: Essays to Mark the Centenary of* Lux Mundi, edited by Geoffrey Wainwright, 25–53. London: SPCK, 1989.
Jobes, Karen H. "The Function of Paronomasia in Hebrews 10:5–7." *Trinity Journal* 13ns (1992): 181–91.
Jobes, Karen H. "Rhetorical Achievement in the Hebrews 10 'Misquote' of Psalm 40." *Bib* 72 (1991): 387–96.
Johnson, Jeffrey D. *The Fatal Flaw of the Theology behind Infant Baptism*. Conway: Free Grace, 2017.
Johnson, Todd M., Gina A. Zurlo, Albert W. Hickman, and Peter Crossing. "Christianity 2017: Five Hundred Years of Protestant Christianity." *IBMR* 41, no. 1 (January 2017): 41–52.
Johnson, Todd M., Gina A. Zurlo, Albert W. Hickman, and Peter Crossing. "Christianity 2018: More African Christians and Counting Martyrs." *IBMR* 42, no. 1 (January 2018): 20–28.
Jones, Scott J. *John Wesley's Conception and Use of Scripture*. Nashville: Abingdon, 1995.
Kaiser, Walter C., Jr. *Recovering the Unity of the Bible: One Continuous Story, Plan, and Purpose*. Grand Rapids: Zondervan, 2009.
Kaiser, Walter C., Jr., and Moisés Silva. *An Introduction to Biblical Hermeneutics: The Search for Meaning*. Grand Rapids: Zondervan, 1994.
Kant, Immanuel. "Der Streit der Fakultäten." In *Werke in sechs Bänden*, edited by W. Weischedel. Dormstadt: Wissenschaftliche Buchgesellschaft, 1964.
Kantzer Komline, Han-luen. "Grace, Free Will, and the Lord's Prayer: Cyprian's Importance for the 'Augustinian' Doctrine of Grace." *AugSt* 45 (2014): 247–79.
Keating, Daniel, and Matthew Levering. "Introduction." In St. Thomas Aquinas, *Commentary on the Gospel of John*, vol. 1: *Chapters 1–5*, translated by Fabian Larcher, O.P., and James A. Weisheipl, O.P., edited by Daniel Keating and Matthew Levering, ix–xxx. Washington, DC: Catholic University of America Press, 2010.
Keener, Craig S. *Miracles: The Credibility of New Testament Accounts*, 2 vols. Grand Rapids: Baker Academic, 2011.
Keener, Craig S. *Spirit Hermeneutics: Reading Scripture in Light of Pentecost*. Grand Rapids: Eerdmans, 2016.
Kelber, Werner H. *The Oral and the Written Gospel: The Hermeneutics of Speaking and Writing in the Synoptic Tradition, Mark, Paul, and Q*. Bloomington: Indiana University Press, 1997.
Kelhoffer, James A. *Persecution, Persuasion and Power: Readiness to Withstand Hardship as a Corroboration of Legitimacy in the New Testament*. WUNT 270. Tübingen: Mohr Siebeck, 2010.
Kelly, J. N. D. *Early Christian Doctrines*. 5th ed. London: Adam and Charles Black, 1977.
Kinzig, Wolfram, and Markus Vinzent. "Recent Research on the Origin of the Creed." *JTS* 50 (1999): 535–59.
Kirk, J. Andrew, and Kevin J. Vanhoozer, eds. *To Stake a Claim: Mission and the Western Crisis of Knowledge*. Maryknoll: Orbis, 1999.

Kistemaker, Simon. *The Psalms Citations in the Epistle to the Hebrews.* Amsterdam: Wed. G. van Soest, 1961.

Kittel, Rodolf. *Geschichte des Volkes Israel.* 7th ed. 3 vols. Gotha: Klotz, 1925.

Klein, William W., Craig L. Blomberg, and Robert L. Hubbard Jr. *An Introduction to Biblical Interpretation.* 3rd ed. Grand Rapids: Zondervan, 2017.

Kreeft, Peter. *Angels and Demons: What Do We Really Know about Them?* San Francisco: Ignatius, 1995.

Lacoste, Jean-Yves. "More Haste, Less Speed in Theology." *IJST* 9, no. 3 (2007): 263–82.

Lane, Anthony N. S. *Justification by Faith in Catholic-Protestant Dialogue: An Evangelical Assessment.* New York: T&T Clark, 2002.

Lane, Anthony N. S. "Scripture, Tradition and Church: An Historical Survey." *Vox Evangelica* 9 (1975): 37–55.

Lane-Mercier, Gillian. "Quotation as a Discursive Strategy." *Kodikas* 14 (1991): 199–214.

Lash, Nicholas. "Performing the Scriptures." In *Theology on the Way to Emmaus.* London: SCM, 1986.

Lee, Gregory W. *Today When You Hear His Voice: Scripture, the Covenants, and the People of God.* Grand Rapids: Eerdmans, 2016.

Lee, Margaret Ellen. *Sound Matters: New Testament Studies in Sound Mapping.* Eugene, OR: Cascade, 2018.

Lee, Margaret Ellen, and Bernard Brandon Scott. *Sound Mapping the New Testament.* Salem, OR: Polebridge, 2009.

Legaspi, Michael. *The Death of Scripture and the Rise of Biblical Studies.* Oxford: Oxford University Press, 2011.

Letham, Robert. *Systematic Theology.* Wheaton: Crossway, 2019.

Letham, Robert. *The Westminster Assembly: Reading Its Theology in Historical Context.* Phillipsburg: P&R, 2009.

Levenson, Jon D. *Sinai and Zion: An Entry into the Jewish Bible.* Minneapolis: Winston, 1985.

Levering, Matthew. "Friendship and Trinitarian Theology: A Response to Karen Kilby." *IJST* 9, no. 1 (2007): 39–54.

Levering, Matthew. *Paul in the Summa Theologiae.* Washington, DC: Catholic University of America Press, 2014.

Levering, Matthew. *Scripture and Metaphysics: Aquinas and the Renewal of Trinitarian Theology.* Challenges in Contemporary Theology. Oxford: Blackwell, 2003.

Levering, Matthew. "Supplementing Pinckaers: The Old Testament in Aquinas's Ethics." In *Reading Sacred Scripture with Thomas Aquinas: Hermeneutical Tools, Theological Questions and New Perspectives,* edited by Piotr Roszak and Jörgen Vijgen, 349–73. Turnhout, Belgium: Brepols, 2015.

Levering, Matthew. *Was the Reformation a Mistake? Why Catholic Doctrine Is Not Unbiblical,* with a Response by Kevin J. Vanhoozer. Grand Rapids: Zondervan, 2017.

Levering, Matthew, Piotr Roszak, and Jörgen Vijgen. "Introduction." In *Reading Job with St. Thomas Aquinas,* edited by Matthew Levering, Piotr Roszak, and Jörgen Vijgen, ix–xxx. Washington, DC: Catholic University of America Press, 2020.

Levinson, Jerrold. *Music in the Moment.* Ithaca: Cornell University Press, 1997.

Lewis, Alan E. *Between Cross and Resurrection: A Theology of Holy Saturday.* Grand Rapids: Eerdmans, 2001.

Lewis, C. S. *God in the Dock: Essays on Theology and Ethics.* Grand Rapids: Eerdmans, 1970.

Lewis, C. S. "Introduction." In *St. Athanasius on the Incarnation: The Treatise* De Incarnatione Verbi Dei. Crestwood, NY: St. Vladimir's Seminary, 1953.

Lindbeck, George A. *The Nature of Doctrine: Religion and Theology in a Postliberal Age*. Philadelphia: Westminster, 1984.

Lipiński, Edward. *Studies in Aramaic Inscriptions and Onomastics II*. Orientalia Lovaniensia Analecta 57. Leuven: Peeters, 1994.

Lloyd, Stephen. "Chronological Creationism." *Foundations* 72 (May 2017): 76–99.

Lods, Adolphe. *Israel from its Beginnings to the Middle of the Eighth Century*. Translated by S. H. Hooke. London: Kegan Paul, Trench, Trubner, 1932.

Long, V. Philips. *The Art of Biblical History*. Edited by M. Silva. Foundations of Contemporary Interpretation. Grand Rapids: Zondervan, 1994.

Long, V. Philips. "How Did Saul Become King? Literary Reading and Historical Reconstruction." In *Faith, Tradition and History*, edited by A. R. Millard, J. K. Hoffmeier, and D. W. Baker, 271–84. Winona Lake: Eisenbrauns, 1994.

Long, V. Philips. *The Reign and Rejection of King Saul: A Case for Literary and Theological Coherence*. SBLDS 118. Atlanta: Scholars, 1989.

Long, V. Philips. *1 and 2 Samuel*. TOTC. Downers Grove: IVP Academic, 2020.

Longenecker, Richard N. *The Epistle to the Romans: A Commentary on the Greek Text*. NIGTC. Grand Rapids: Eerdmans, 2016.

Louth, Andrew. *Discerning the Mystery: An Essay on the Nature of Theology*. Oxford: Oxford University Press, 1983.

Lyons, George. "Biblical Theology and Wesleyan Theology." *Wesleyan Theological Journal* 30, no. 2 (1995): 7–25.

Macaskill, Grant. *Living in Union with Christ: Paul's Gospel and Christian Moral Identity*. Grand Rapids: Baker Academic, 2019.

Machen, J. Gresham. *Christianity and Liberalism*. New York: Macmillan, 1923.

Maddox, Randy L. "John Wesley – A Man of One Book." In *Wesley, Wesleyans, and Reading Bible as Scripture*, edited by Joel B. Green and David F. Watson, 3–18. Waco: Baylor University Press, 2012.

Maddox, Randy L. *Responsible Grace: John Wesley's Practical Theology*. Nashville: Abingdon, 1994.

Madueme, Hans. "An Augustinian-Reformed Response." In *Original Sin and the Fall: Five Views*, edited by J. B. Stump and Chad Meister, 127–39. Downers Grove: IVP Academic, 2020.

Madueme, Hans. "Mea Culpa: An Apology for Original Guilt." *Mid-America Journal of Theology* (forthcoming).

Manetsch, Scott. *Calvin's Company of Pastors: Pastoral Care and the Emerging Reformed Church, 1536–1609*. New York: Oxford University Press, 2012.

Marsden, George M. *Fundamentalism and American Culture: The Shaping of Twentieth-Century Evangelicalism, 1870–1925*. New York: Oxford University Press, 1980.

Marshall, I. Howard. *Beyond the Bible: Moving from Scripture to Theology*. Grand Rapids: Baker Academic, 2004.

Marty, Martin E. *Dietrich Bonhoeffer's Letters and Papers from Prison: A Biography*. Princeton: Princeton University Press, 2011.

McCabe, Herbert. "The Involvement of God." In *God Matters*. London: Mowbray, 1987.

McCall, Thomas. *Against God and Nature: The Doctrine of Sin*. Wheaton: Crossway, 2019.

McCarter, P. Kyle. *I Samuel: A New Translation with Introduction and Commentary*. AB. Garden City, NY: Doubleday, 1980.

McCormack, Bruce L. "The Being of Holy Scripture Is in Becoming: Karl Barth in Conversation with American Evangelical Criticism." In *Evangelicals and Scripture: Tradition, Authority, and Hermeneutics*, edited by Vincent Bacote, Laura C. Miguelez, and Dennis L. Okholm, 55–75. Downers Grove: InterVarsity, 2004.

McCormack, Bruce L. "Grace and Being: The Role of God's Gracious Election in Karl Barth's Theological Ontology." In *The Cambridge Companion to Karl Barth*, edited by John Webster, 92–110. Cambridge: Cambridge University Press, 2000.
McCormack, Bruce L. *Karl Barth's Critically Realistic Dialectical Theology: Its Genesis and Development 1909-1936*. Oxford: Oxford University Press, 1995.
McCormack, Bruce L., and Clifford B. Anderson, eds. *Karl Barth and American Evangelicalism*. Grand Rapids: Eerdmans, 2011.
McDermott, Gerald R. "Introduction." In *The Oxford Handbook of Evangelical Theology*, edited by Gerald R. McDermott, 1–16. Oxford: Oxford University Press, 2010.
McGilchrist, Iain. *The Master and His Emissary: The Divided Brain and the Making of the Western World*. New Haven: Yale University Press, 2009.
McKee, Elsie Anne. *The Pastoral Ministry and Worship in Calvin's Geneva*. Geneva: Droz, 2016.
McKenzie, Steven L. *King David: A Biography*. Oxford: Oxford University Press, 2000.
Meadors, Gary T., ed. *Four Views on Moving Beyond the Bible to Theology*. Counterpoints. Grand Rapids: Zondervan, 2009.
Merk, Otto. *Biblische Theologie des Neuen Testaments in ihrer Anfangszeit: Ihre methodischen Probleme bei Johann Philipp Gabler und Georg Lorenz Bauer und deren Nachwirkungen*. Marburg: N. G. Elwert, 1972.
Merrick, James R. A. "Have Evangelicals Changed Their Minds about Karl Barth? A Review Essay with Reference to the Current Crisis in Evangelical Identity." *Evangelical Review of Theology* 32 no. 4 (2008): 355–68.
Michaels, J. Ramsey. *The Gospel of John*. NICNT. Grand Rapids: Eerdmans, 2010.
Middleton, J. Richard. "Reading Genesis 3 Attentive to Human Evolution: Beyond Concordism and Non-Overlapping Magisteria." In *Evolution and the Fall*, edited by William Cavanaugh and James K. A. Smith, 67–97. Grand Rapids: Eerdmans, 2017.
Middleton, J. Richard. "Samuel Agonistes: A Conflicted Prophet's Resistance to God and Contribution to the Failure of Israel's First King." In *Prophets, Prophecy, and Ancient Israelite Historiography*, edited by M. J. Boda, and L. M. W. Beal, 69–91. Winona Lake: Eisenbrauns, 2013.
Miles, Richard, ed. *The Donatist Schism: Controversy and Contexts*. Translated Texts for Historians, Contexts. Liverpool: Liverpool University Press, 2016.
Mithen, Steven J. *The Singing Neanderthals: The Origins of Music, Language, Mind and Body*. London: Phoenix, 2006.
Moberly, R. W. L. "Review of Kevin J. Vanhoozer, *Is There a Meaning in This Text?*" *ExpTim* 110, no. 5 (February 1999): 154.
Molnar, Paul. *Divine Freedom and the Doctrine of the Immanent Trinity*. 2nd ed. London: T&T Clark, 2017.
Moltmann, Jürgen. *The Crucified God: The Cross of Christ as the Foundation and Criticism of Christian Theology*. Translated by R. A. Wilson and John Bowden. London: SCM, 1974.
Moltmann, Jürgen. *The Trinity and the Kingdom of God: The Doctrine of God*. Translated by Margaret Kohl. London: SCM, 1981.
Moo, Douglas J. *The Letter to the Romans*. NICNT. 2nd ed. Grand Rapids: Eerdmans, 2018.
Mosebach, Martin. *The 21: A Journey into the Land of Coptic Martyrs*. Walden, NY: Plough, 2019.
Moss, Candida. *The Myth of Persecution: How Early Christians Invented a Story of Martyrdom*. San Francisco: HarperOne, 2013.

Muller, Richard A. *Post-Reformation Reformed Dogmatics: The Rise and Development of Reformed Orthodoxy, ca. 1520 to ca. 1725*. 2nd ed. Grand Rapids: Baker Academic, 2003.
Muller, Richard A., and John Thompson, eds. *Biblical Interpretation in the Era of the Reformation*. Grand Rapids: Eerdmans, 1996.
Müller, Julius. *The Christian Doctrine of Sin*. Translated by William Urwick. 5th ed. Edinburgh: T&T Clark, 1868.
Murray, John. *Christian Baptism*. Phillipsburg: P&R, 1980.
Murray, John. *The Epistle to the Romans*. Vol. 1. Grand Rapids: Eerdmans, 1959.
Murray, John. *The Imputation of Adam's Sin*. Nutley: P&R, 1977.
Nancy, Jean-Luc. *Listening*. Translated by Charlotte Mandell. New York: Fordham University Press, 2007.
Nässelqvist, Dan. *Public Reading in Early Christianity: Lectors, Manuscripts, and Sound in the Oral Delivery of John 1–4*. Leiden: Brill, 2016.
Neill, Stephen, and N. T. Wright. *The Interpretation of the New Testament 1861–1986*. 2nd ed. Oxford: Oxford University Press, 1988.
Newbigin, Lesslie. *The Finality of Christ*. Richmond: John Knox, 1969.
Niebuhr, H. Richard. *Christ and Culture*. New York: Harper, 1956.
Nietzsche, Friedrich. "On Truth and Lies in a Nonmoral Sense." In *The Portable Nietzsche*, translated by Walter Kaufmann. New York: Viking, 1976.
Noll, Mark A. *Between Faith and Criticism: Evangelicals, Scholarship, and the Bible in America*. New York: Harper, 1986.
Noll, Mark A. *The Scandal of the Evangelical Mind*. Grand Rapids: Eerdmans, 1994.
Noll, Stephen F. *Angels of Light, Powers of Darkness: Thinking Biblically about Angels, Satan, and Principalities*. Eugene, OR: Wipf and Stock, 1998.
Noss, Peter. *Martin Albertz (1883–1956)—Eigensinn und Konsequenz: das Martyrium als Kennzeichen der Kirche im Nationalsozialismus*. Neukirchen-Vluyn: Neukirchener Verlag, 2001.
Noss, Peter. "Theologische 'Leuchttürme' im Protestantismus und die Schicksale der Christen jüdischer Herkunft 1933–1945." In *Nationalprotestantische Mentalitäten: Konturen, Entwicklungslinien und Umbrüche eines Weltbildes*, edited by Manfred Gailus and Hartmut Lehmann, 307–42. Göttingen: Vandenhoeck & Ruprecht, 2005.
Oden, Thomas. *Life in the Spirit*. New York: HarperCollins, 1992.
O'Donovan, Oliver. *Entering into Rest: Ethics as Theology, Vol. 3*. Grand Rapids: Eerdmans, 2017.
O'Donovan, Oliver. *Finding and Seeking: Ethics as Theology, Vol. 2*. Grand Rapids: Eerdmans, 2014.
O'Donovan, Oliver. *Self, World, and Time: Ethics as Theology, Vol. 1*. Grand Rapids: Eerdmans, 2013.
O'Keefe, John J., and R. R. Reno. *Sanctified Vision: An Introduction to Early Christian Interpretation of the Bible*. Baltimore: Johns Hopkins University Press, 2005.
Oldridge, Darren. *The Devil: A Very Short Introduction*. Oxford: Oxford University Press, 2012.
Ong, Walter, S.J. *Presence of the Word*. New Haven: Yale University Press, 1967.
Osborne, Grant R. *The Hermeneutical Spiral: A Comprehensive Introduction to Biblical Interpretation*. 2nd ed. Downers Grove: InterVarsity, 2006.
Outler, Albert C. *John Wesley*. New York: Oxford University Press, 1964.

Packer, J. I. *Concise Theology: A Guide to Historic Christian Beliefs*. Wheaton: Tyndale, 1993.
Pak, Sujin. *The Judaizing Calvin: Sixteenth-Century Debates over the Messianic Psalms*. New York: Oxford University Press, 2010.
Pannenberg, Wolfhart. *Anthropology in Theological Perspective*. Translated by Matthew O'Connell. New York: T&T Clark, 1985.
Pao, David W., and Eckhard J. Schnabel. "Luke." In *Commentary on the New Testament Use of the Old Testament*, edited by G. K. Beale and D. A. Carson, 251–414. Grand Rapids: Baker Academic, 2007.
Parker, T. H. L. *Calvin's New Testament Commentaries*. 2nd ed. Louisville: Westminster John Knox, 1993.
Parker, T. H. L. *Calvin's Old Testament Commentaries*. Edinburgh: T&T Clark, 1986.
Patel, Aniruddh D. *Music, Language, and the Brain*. Oxford: Oxford University Press, 2008.
Pelikan, Jaroslav. *The Emergence of Catholic Tradition (100–600)*. Chicago: The University of Chicago Press, 1971.
Pelikan, Jaroslav. *The Reformation of the Bible, The Bible of the Reformation*. New Haven: Yale University Press, 1996.
Percival, Henry R, ed. *The Seven Ecumenical Councils*. NPNF, 2nd Series. Edited by Philip Schaff and Henry Wace, vol. 14. n.p.: Charles Scribner's Sons, 1900; reprint, Peabody: Hendrickson, 1999.
Perkins, William. *A Reformed Catholic*. In *The Works of William Perkins, Vol. 7*. Grand Rapids: Reformation Heritage, 2019.
Perry, John. "What Are Indexicals?" In *The Problem of the Essential Indexical and Other Essays*. Expanded edition. Stanford: Center for Study of Language and Information, 2000.
Peterson, Eugene H. "Caveat Lector." *Crux* 32 (1996): 2–12.
Pierce, Madison N. *Divine Discourse in the Epistle to the Hebrews: The Recontextualization of Spoken Quotations of Scripture*. Cambridge: Cambridge University Press, 2020.
Pitre, Brant. *Jesus and the Last Supper*. Grand Rapids: Eerdmans, 2015.
Placher, William C. *The Domestication of Transcendence: How Modern Thinking About God Went Wrong*. Louisville: Westminster John Knox, 1996.
Plantinga, Cornelius, Jr. *Not the Way It's Supposed to Be: A Breviary of Sin*. Grand Rapids: Eerdmans, 1995.
Polanyi, Michael. *Personal Knowledge: Toward a Post-Critical Philosophy*. Chicago: University of Chicago Press, 1974.
Polanyi, Michael. "The Unaccountable Element in Science." *Philosophy* 37, no. 139 (1962): 13–14.
Polman, A. D. R. *The Word of God according to St. Augustine*. Grand Rapids: Eerdmans, 1961.
Probst, Christopher J. *Demonizing the Jews: Luther and the Protestant Church in Nazi Germany*. Bloomington: Indiana University Press, 2012.
Provan, Iain. *1 & 2 Kings*. Understanding the Bible. Grand Rapids: Baker, 1995.
Provan, Iain. *Lamentations*. NCB. London: Marshall Pickering, 1991.
Provan, Iain. *The Reformation and the Right Reading of Scripture*. Waco: Baylor University Press, 2017.
Provan, Iain, V. Philips Long, and Tremper Longman III. *A Biblical History of Israel*. 2nd ed. Louisville: Westminster John Knox, 2015.

Puckett, David. "Calvin, John." In *Dictionary of Major Biblical Interpreters*, edited by Donald McKim, 287–94. Downers Grove: IVP Academic, 2007.
Puckett, David. *John Calvin's Exegesis of the Old Testament*. Louisville: Westminster John Knox, 1995.
Puddefoot, John C. "Resonance Realism." *Tradition and Discovery* 20, no. 3 (1993): 29–38.
Quash, Ben. *Theology and the Drama of History*. Cambridge Studies in Christian Doctrine. Cambridge: Cambridge University Press, 2005.
Rad, Gerhard von. *Theology of the Old Testament*, vol. 1. Translated by D. M. G. Stalker. Louisville: Westminster John Knox, 2001.
Radde-Gallwitz, Andrew. *Basil of Caesarea, Gregory of Nyssa, and the Transformation of Divine Simplicity*. Oxford Early Christian Studies. Oxford: Oxford University Press, 2009.
Rahner, Karl. *The Trinity*. Translated by Joseph Donceel. London: Herder & Herder, 1970.
Ralston, Thomas N. *Elements of Divinity*. Nashville: Abingdon, 1919.
Ramm, Bernard. *After Fundamentalism: The Future of Evangelical Theology*. San Francisco: Harper & Row, 1983.
Ramm, Bernard. *Special Revelation and the Word of God*. Grand Rapids: Eerdmans, 1961.
Ratzinger, Joseph Cardinal. *"In the Beginning . . .": A Catholic Understanding of the Story of Creation and the Fall*. Translated by Boniface Ramsey. Grand Rapids: Eerdmans, 1995.
Rhoads, David, and J. Dewey. "Performance Criticism: A Paradigm Shift in New Testament Studies." In *From Text to Performance: Narrative and Performance Criticisms in Dialogue and Debate*, edited by K. R. Iverson, 1–26. Eugene, OR: Cascade, 2014.
Ricoeur, Paul. *Figuring the Sacred: Religion, Narrative and Imagination*. Translated by Mark I. Wallace. Minneapolis: Fortress, 1995.
Ricoeur, Paul. *History and Truth*. Translated by Charles A. Kelbley. Evanston: Northwestern University Press, 1965.
Ricoeur, Paul. *Interpretation Theory: Discourse and the Interpretation of Meaning*. Fort Worth: Texas Christian University, 1976.
Ricoeur, Paul. "The Model of the Text: Meaningful Action Considered as a Text." In *From Text to Action: Essays in Hermeneutics, II*, translated by Kathleen Blamey and John B. Thompson, 144–67. Studies in Phenomenology and Existential Philosophy. Evanston: Northwestern University Press, 2007.
Ricoeur, Paul. *Oneself as Another*. Translated by Kathleen Blamey. Chicago: University of Chicago Press, 1992.
Ricoeur, Paul. *The Symbolism of Evil*. Translated by Emerson Buchanan. Boston: Beacon, 1986.
Ricoeur, Paul. *Time and Narrative*. 3 vols. Translated by Kathleen McLaughlin and David Pellauer. Chicago: University of Chicago Press, 1984–8.
Rink, John. Review of Wallace Berry, *Musical Structure and Performance*. *Music Analysis* 9, no. 3 (1990): 319–39.
Rosa, Hartmut. *Resonance: A Sociology of the Relationship to the World*. Medford: Polity, 2019.
Rudolph, Wilhelm. *Das Buch Ruth, Das Hohe Lied, Die Klagelieder, Kommentar zum Alten Testament*. Gütersloh: Gerd Mohn, 1962.
Russell, Jeffrey Burton. *Satan: The Early Christian Tradition*. Ithaca: Cornell University Press, 1987.
Ryken, Leland. *A Complete Handbook of Literary Forms in the Bible*. Wheaton: Crossway, 2014.

Sachs, John R. "Apocatastasis in Patristic Theology." *TS* 54 (1993): 617–40.
Salters, R. B. *Lamentations*. ICC. London: T&T Clark International, 2010.
Sanders, Fred. *The Deep Things of God: How the Trinity Changes Everything*. 2nd ed. Wheaton: Crossway, 2017.
Sarisky, Darren. *Reading the Bible Theologically*. Current Issues in Theology. Cambridge: Cambridge University Press, 2019.
Sarisky, Darren. *Scriptural Interpretation: A Theological Account*. Challenges in Contemporary Theology. Oxford: Wiley-Blackwell, 2013.
Schaff, Philip. *The Creeds of Christendom*. Grand Rapids: Baker, 1985.
Scharf, Kurt. "Martin Albertz zum 70. Geburtstag." In *Theologia Viatorum V: Jahrbuch der Kirchlichen Hochschule Berlin 1953-54*, edited by Harald Kruska. Berlin: Lettner-Verlag, 1954.
Schatz-Hurschmann, Renate. "Eine Frau ist immer im Dienst: Das Leben der Ilse Fredrichsdorff." In *Frauen in dunkler Zeit*, edited by Susi Hausammann, Nicole Kuropka, and Heike Scherer. Köln: Rheinland-Verlag, 1996.
Schenck, Ken. "God Has Spoken: Hebrews' Theology of the Scriptures." In *The Epistle to the Hebrews and Christian Theology*, edited by Richard Bauckham et al., 321–36. Grand Rapids: Eerdmans, 2009.
Schnabel, Eckhard. "The Persecution of Christians in the First Century." *JETS* 61, no. 3 (2018): 525–47.
Schön, Daniele, and Benjamin Morillon. "Music and Language." In *The Oxford Handbook of Music and the Brain*, edited by Michael H. Thaut and Donald A. Hodges, 389–416. Oxford: Oxford University Press, 2018.
Schreiner, Thomas R. "Original Sin and Original Death: Romans 5:12–19." In *Adam, the Fall, and Original Sin: Theological, Biblical, and Scientific Perspectives*, edited by Hans Madueme and Michael Reeves, 271–88. Grand Rapids: Baker Academic, 2014.
Schwöbel, Christoph, ed. *Trinitarian Theology Today: Essays on Divine Being and Act*. Edinburgh: T&T Clark, 2000.
Second Helvetic Confession. In *Book of Confessions*, ch. 1. Louisville: PCUSA General Assembly, 1991.
Shedd, William G. T. *A History of Christian Doctrine*. 2 vols. New York: Scribner, 1863.
Shiner, Whitney. *Proclaiming the Gospel: First-Century Performance of Mark*. Harrisburg: Trinity, 2003.
Smelik, Klaas A. D. *Saul, de voorstelling van Israels eerste Konig in de Masoretische tekst van het Oude Testament*. Amsterdam: Drukkerij en Uitgeverij P. E. T., 1977.
Sonderegger, Katherine. *Systematic Theology*, vol. 1: *The Doctrine of God*. Minneapolis: Fortress, 2015.
Spawn, Kevin L., and Archie T. Wright, eds. *Spirit and Scripture: Exploring a Pneumatic Hermeneutic*. London: T&T Clark, 2012.
Stafford, Tim. "The New Theologians." *Christianity Today* 43, no. 2 (February 8, 1999): 30–50.
Stanglin, Keith, and Thomas McCall. *Jacob Arminius: Theologian of Grace*. Oxford: Oxford University Press, 2012.
Steinmetz, David. *Calvin in Context*. New York: Oxford University Press, 1995.
Sternberg, Meir. *The Poetics of Biblical Narrative: Ideological Literature and the Drama of Reading*. Bloomington: Indiana University Press, 1985.
Sternberg, Meir. "Proteus in Quotation-Land: Mimesis and Forms of Reported Discourse." *Poetics Today* 3, no. 2 (1982): 107–56.

Stevenson, Kenneth, and Michael Glerup, eds. *Ezekiel, Daniel*. ACCSOT 13. Downers Grove: IVP, 2008.
Stewart-Kroeker, Sarah. *Pilgrimage as Moral and Aesthetic Formation in Augustine's Thought*. Oxford: Oxford University Press, 2017.
Steyn, Gert J. *A Quest for the Assumed LXX Vorlage of the Explicit Quotations in Hebrews*. FRLANT 235. Göttingen: Vandenhoeck & Ruprecht, 2011.
Stiver, Dan R. *Theology after Ricoeur: New Directions in Hermeneutical Theology*. Louisville: Westminster John Knox, 2001.
Stott, John R. W. *Between Two Worlds: The Art of Preaching in the Twentieth Century*. Grand Rapids: Eerdmans,1982.
Stott, John R. W. *The Cross of Christ*. Leicester: IVP, 1986.
Stuhlmacher, Peter. *Biblical Theology of the New Testament*. Edited and translated by Daniel P. Bailey. Grand Rapids: Eerdmans, 2018.
Sunshine, Glenn. "Accommodation Historically Considered." In *The Enduring Authority of the Christian Scriptures*, edited by D. A. Carson, 238–65. Grand Rapids: Eerdmans, 2016.
Tanner, Kathryn E. *God and Creation in Christian Theology: Tyranny or Empowerment?* Minneapolis: Fortress, 2005.
Taylor, Charles. *A Secular Age*. Cambridge, MA: Harvard University Press, 2007.
Tertullian. *On Baptism*. In ANF 3.
te Velde, Dolf, ed. *Synopsis Purioris Theologiae*, Latin Text and English Translation, Vol. 1: Disputations 1–23. Leiden: Brill, 2015.
Thiselton, Anthony C. *The First Epistle to the Corinthians: A Commentary on the Greek Text*. NIGTC. Grand Rapids: Eerdmans, 2000.
Thiselton, Anthony C. *Hermeneutics: An Introduction*. Grand Rapids: Eerdmans, 2009.
Thiselton, Anthony C. *Interpreting God and the Postmodern Self: On Meaning, Manipulation, and Promise*. Grand Rapids: Eerdmans, 1995.
Thiselton, Anthony C. *New Horizons in Hermeneutics: The Theory and Practice of Transforming Biblical Reading*. Grand Rapids: Zondervan, 1992.
Thiselton, Anthony C. "Speech-Act Theory and the Claim That God Speaks: Nicholas Wolterstorff's *Divine Discourse*." *Scottish Journal of Theology* 50, no. 1 (1997): 97–110.
Thiselton, Anthony C. *The Two Horizons: New Testament Hermeneutics and Philosophical Description*. Grand Rapids: Eerdmans, 1980.
Thompson, John. "Calvin as Biblical Interpreter." In *The Cambridge Companion to John Calvin*, edited by Donald McKim, 58–73. Cambridge: Cambridge University Press, 2004.
Thompson, Mark. "*Sola Scriptura*." In *A Systematic Summary of Reformation Theology*, edited by Matthew Barrett, 145–87. Wheaton: Crossway, 2017.
Thorne, Philip. *Evangelicalism and Karl Barth: His Reception and Influence among North American Evangelical Theology*. Eugene, OR: Pickwick, 1995.
Tonstad, Linn Marie. *God and Difference: The Trinity, Sexuality, and the Transformation of Finitude*. Gender, Theology, and Spirituality. New York: Routledge, 2017.
Torrance, Thomas F. *Space, Time, and Resurrection*. Grand Rapids: Eerdmans, 1976.
Torrance, Thomas F. *Theological Science*. Oxford: Oxford University Press, 1969.
Torrell, Jean-Pierre, O.P. *Aquinas's Summa: Background, Structure, and Reception*. Translated by Benedict M. Guevin, O.S.B. Washington, DC: Catholic University of America Press, 2005.
Torrell, Jean-Pierre, O.P. *Saint Thomas Aquinas*, vol. 1: *The Person and His Work*, translated by Robert Royal, ch. 2. Washington, DC: Catholic University of America Press, 1996.

Treier, Daniel J. "Christology and Commentaries: Examining and Enhancing Theological Exegesis." In *On the Writing of New Testament Commentaries: Festschrift for Grant R. Osborne on the Occasion of His 70th Birthday*, edited by Stanley E. Porter and Eckhard J. Schnabel, 299–316. Leiden: Brill, 2013.

Treier, Daniel J. "The Freedom of God's Word: Toward an 'Evangelical' Dogmatics of Scripture." In *The Voice of God in the Text of Scripture: Explorations in Constructive Dogmatics*, edited by Oliver D. Crisp and Fred Sanders, 21–40. Grand Rapids: Zondervan, 2016.

Treier, Daniel J. *Introducing Theological Interpretation of Scripture: Recovering a Christian Practice*. Grand Rapids: Baker Academic, 2008.

Treier, Daniel J. "Speech Acts, Hearing Hearts, and Other Senses: The Doctrine of Scripture Practiced in Hebrews." In *The Epistle to the Hebrews and Christian Theology*, edited by Richard Bauckham et al., 337–50. Grand Rapids: Eerdmans, 2009.

Treier, Daniel J. "Theological Hermeneutics, Contemporary." In *Dictionary for Theological Interpretation of the Bible*, edited by Kevin J. Vanhoozer, 787–93. Grand Rapids: Baker Academic, 2005.

Treier, Daniel J., and Craig Hefner. "Twentieth- and Twenty-First Century American Biblical Interpretation." In *The Oxford Handbook of the Bible in America*, edited by Paul C. Gutjahr, 129–48. New York: Oxford University Press, 2017.

Trueman, Carl R. *The Creedal Imperative*. Wheaton: Crossway, 2012.

Turretin, Francis. *Institutes of Elenctic Theology*. 3 vols. Translated by George Musgrove Giger. Phillipsburg: P&R, 1992.

Unger, Merrill F. *Biblical Demonology: A Study of Spiritual Forces Today*. Grand Rapids: Kregel, 1994.

Vanauken, Sheldon. *A Severe Mercy*. London: Hodder and Stoughton, 1992.

van Oort, Johannes. *Jerusalem and Babylon: A Study into Augustine's* City of God *and the Sources of His Doctrine of the Two Cities*. Leiden: Brill, 1991.

Van Overbeke, Marc. *Le langage en context: etudes philosophiques et linguistiques de pragmatique*. Edited by H. Perret. Amsterdam: John Benjamins, 1980.

Van Til, Cornelius. *Christianity and Barthianism*. Philadelphia: P&R, 1962.

Van Til, Cornelius. *Karl Barth and Evangelicalism*. Philadelphia: P&R, 1964.

Vermigli, Peter Martyr. *The Common Places of the Most Famous and Renowned Doctor Peter Martyr*. Translated by Anthonie Marten. London: Henrie Denham, Thomas Chard, William Broome, and Andrew Maunsell, 1583.

Vickers, Jason, and Jerome VanKuiken, eds. *Methodist Christology: From the Wesleys to the Twenty-First Century*. Nashville: GBHEM, 2020.

Volf, Miroslav. *After Our Likeness: The Church as the Image of the Trinity*. Grand Rapids: Eerdmans, 1998.

Volf, Miroslav. "'The Trinity Is Our Social Program': The Doctrine of the Trinity and the Shape of Social Engagement." *Modern Theology* 14, no. 3 (1998): 403–23.

von Rad, Gerhard. "The Form-Critical Problem of the Hexateuch." In *The Problem of the Hexateuch and Other Essays*, translated by E. W. Trueman Dicken, 1–78. New York: McGraw-Hill, 1966.

Vos, Geerhardus. *Biblical Theology: Old and New Testaments*. Grand Rapids: Eerdmans, 1948.

Wall, Robert W. "John's John: A Wesleyan Theological Reading of 1 John." *Wesleyan Theological Journal* 46, no. 1 (2011): 105–41.

Wallace, Mark I. "Introduction." In Paul Ricoeur, *Figuring the Sacred: Religion, Narrative and Imagination*. Translated by Mark I. Wallace. Minneapolis: Fortress, 1995.

Walton, John H. "A King Like the Nations: 1 Samuel 8 in Its Cultural Context." *Bib* 96 (2015): 179–200.

Walton, John H. *The Lost World of Adam and Eve: Genesis 2–3 and the Human Origins Debate*. Downers Grove: IVP Academic, 2015.

Ware, Bishop Kallistos. *How Are We Saved? The Understanding of Salvation in the Orthodox Tradition*. Minneapolis: Light and Life, 1996.

Watson, Francis. *Text and Truth: Redefining Biblical Theology*. Grand Rapids: Eerdmans, 1997.

Webb, Stephen H. *The Divine Voice: Proclamation and the Theology of Sound*. Grand Rapids: Brazos, 2004.

Weber, Max. *The Protestant Ethic and the Spirit of Capitalism*. Translated by Talcott Parsons. New York: Scribner, 1958.

Weber, Max. *The Sociology of Religion*. Translated by Ephraim Fischoff. Boston: Beacon, 1963.

Webster, John. *The Domain of the Word: Scripture and Theological Reason*. London: T&T Clark, 2012.

Webster, John. *God without Measure*, vol. 1: *God and the Works of God*. London: T&T Clark, 2015.

Webster, John. "Scripture, Reading, and the Rhetoric of Theology." In *The Culture of Theology*, edited by Ivor J. Davidson and Alden C. McCray, 63–80. Grand Rapids: Baker Academic, 2019.

Webster, John. *Word and Church*. Edinburgh: T&T Clark, 2001.

Wenham, Gordon. "The Theology of Old Testament Sacrifice." In *Sacrifice in the Bible*, edited by Roger Beckwith and Martin Selman, 75–87. Grand Rapids: Baker, 1995.

Wesley, John. "Justification by Faith." In *Wesley's 52 Standard Sermons*, 43–4. Salem, OH: Schmul, 1988.

Wesley, John. "Predestination Calmly Considered." In *The Works of John Wesley*, vol. X, 204–59. Grand Rapids: Zondervan, 1958.

The Westminster Confession of Faith and Catechisms as Adopted by the Presbyterian Church in America with Proof Texts. Lawrenceville: Christian Education & Publications Committee of the Presbyterian Church in America, 2007.

Wiles, Maurice. "Eunomius: Hair-Splitting Dialectician or Defender of the Accessibility of Salvation?" In *The Making of Orthodoxy: Essays in Honour of Henry Chadwick*, edited by Rowan Williams, 157–72. Cambridge: Cambridge University Press, 1989.

Wiley, Tatha. *Original Sin: Origins, Developments, Contemporary Meanings*. Mahwah: Paulist, 2002.

Williams, Rowan. *Being Human: Bodies, Minds, Persons*. Grand Rapids: Eerdmans, 2018.

Williams, Rowan. "The Bible Today: Reading & Hearing." Transcript of The Larkin-Stuart Lecture, April 16, 2007. Available online: https://www.anglican.ca/news/archbishop-of-canterbury-church-needs-to-listen-properly-to-the-bible/ (accessed February 17, 2021).

Williams, Rowan. *The Edge of Words: God and the Habits of Language*. London: Bloomsbury Continuum, 2014.

Williams, Rowan. "Keeping Time." In *Open to Judgement: Sermons and Addresses*. London: Darton, Longman & Todd, 1994.

Williams, Rowan. "Language, Reality and Desire in Augustine's *De doctrina*." *Journal of Literature and Theology* 3 (1989): 138–50.
Williams, Rowan. "*Sapientia* and the Trinity." In *Collectanea Augustiniana: Mélanges T. J. van Bavel*, edited by Bernard Bruning, Mathijs Lamberigts, and J. van Houtem, 317–32. BETL XCII-A. Louvain: Leuven University Press, 1990.
Williams, Scott. "Indexicals and the Trinity: Two Non-Social Models." *Journal of Analytic Theology* 1 (2013): 74–94.
Wink, Walter. Interview by Steve Holt. Available online: https://www.slideshare.net/smh00a/sojourners-walter-amp-june-wink-interview (accessed February 17, 2021).
Wink, Walter. *Naming the Powers: The Language of Power in the New Testament*. Philadelphia: Fortress, 1984.
Wittgenstein, Ludwig. *The Wittgenstein Reader*. Edited by Anthony Kenny. Oxford: Blackwell, 1994.
Wolterstorff, Nicholas. *Divine Discourse: Philosophical Reflections on the Claim That God Speaks*. Cambridge: Cambridge University Press, 1995.
Wood, Donald. *Barth's Theology of Interpretation*. Aldershot: Ashgate, 2007.
Woodbridge, John. "*Sola Scriptura*: Original Intent, Historical Development, and Import for Christian Living," *Presbyterion* 44, no. 1 (2018): 4–24.
Wrede, William. "The Task and Methods of 'New Testament Theology.'" In *The Nature of New Testament Theology*, edited by Robert Morgan, 68–116. London: SCM, 1973.
Wright, N. T. "Five Gospels But No Gospel: Jesus and the Seminar." In *Authenticating the Activities of Jesus: New Testament Tools and Studies, Volume XXVIII.2*, edited by Bruce Chilton and Craig Evans, 83–120. Leiden: Brill, 1999.
Wright, N. T. "Jesus and the Identity of God." *Ex Auditu* (1998): 42–56.
Wright, N. T. *Jesus and the Victory of God*. Christian Origins and the Question of God, vol. 2. Minneapolis: Fortress, 1996.
Würthwein, Ernst. *Der Text des Alten Testaments: Eine Einführung in die Biblia Hebraica*. 4th ed. Stuttgart: Wurttembergische Bibelanstalt, 1973.
Yarbrough, Robert W. *The Salvation Historical Fallacy? Reassessing the History of New Testament Theology*. Leiden: Deo, 2004.
Yeago, David S. "The New Testament and the Nicene Dogma: A Contribution to the Recovery of Theological Exegesis." *Pro Ecclesia* 3, no. 2 (1994): 152–64.
Zachman, Randall. "Gathering Meaning from the Context: Calvin's Exegetical Method." *JR* 82 (2002): 1–26.
Zizioulas, John. *Being as Communion: Studies in Personhood and the Church*. Crestwood, NY: St. Vladimir's Seminary, 1997.
Zizioulas, John. *Communion and Otherness: Further Studies in Personhood and the Church*. London: T&T Clark, 2006.
Zizioulas, John. *The Eucharistic Communion and the World*. Edited by Luke Ben Tallon. New York: Continuum, 2011.
Zurlo, Gina A., Todd M. Johnson, and Peter Crossing. "World Christianity and Mission 2020: Ongoing Shift to the Global South." *IBMR* 44, no. 1 (January 2020): 8–19.

CONTRIBUTORS

Michael Allen is Academic Dean and John Dyer Trimble Professor of Systematic Theology at Reformed Theological Seminary (Orlando, Florida, USA).

Jeremy Begbie is Thomas A. Langford Distinguished Professor of Theology at Duke University Divinity School (Durham, North Carolina, USA) and a senior member of Wolfson College and Affiliated Lecturer in the Faculty of Music at the University of Cambridge (England).

Graham A. Cole is Dean and Professor of Biblical and Systematic Theology at Trinity Evangelical Divinity School (Deerfield, Illinois, USA).

Stephen M. Garrett is Vice President of Curriculum for Global Scholars.

Robert H. Gundry is Scholar-in-Residence at Westmont College (Santa Barbara, California, USA).

Michael Horton is J. Gresham Machen Professor of Systematic Theology and Apologetics at Westminster Theological Seminary (Escondido, California, USA).

Karen H. Jobes is Gerald F. Hawthorne Professor Emerita of New Testament Greek and Exegesis at Wheaton College (Wheaton, Illinois, USA).

Gregory W. Lee is Associate Professor of Theology and Urban Studies and Fellow of the Center for Early Christian Studies at Wheaton College (Wheaton, Illinois, USA).

Matthew Levering holds the James N. and Mary D. Perry Jr. Chair of Theology at Mundelein Seminary, University of St. Mary of the Lake (Mundelein, Illinois, USA).

V. Philips Long is Professor Emeritus of Old Testament at Regent College (Vancouver, British Columbia, Canada).

Hans Madueme is Associate Professor of Theological Studies at Covenant College (Lookout Mountain, Georgia).

Scott M. Manetsch is Professor and Department Chair of Church History and the History of Christian Thought at Trinity Evangelical Divinity School (Deerfield, Illinois, USA).

Thomas McCall is Professor of Theology and Scholar-in-Residence at Asbury University (Wilmore, Kentucky, USA).

Iain Provan is Marshall Sheppard Professor of Biblical Studies at Regent College (Vancouver, British Columbia, Canada).

Darren Sarisky is Senior Research Fellow in Religion and Theology at the Australian Catholic University (Melbourne).

Elizabeth Y. Sung is Scholar-in-Residence at Regent College (Vancouver, British Columbia, Canada) and Visiting Researcher at the University of St. Mary of the Lake (Mundelein, Illinois, USA).

Scott R. Swain is President and James Woodrow Hassell Professor of Systematic Theology at Reformed Theological Seminary (Orlando, Florida, USA).

Douglas A. Sweeney is Dean and Professor of Divinity at Beeson Divinity School (Birmingham, Alabama, USA).

Daniel J. Treier is Gunther H. Knoedler Professor of Theology at Wheaton College Graduate School (Wheaton, Illinois, USA).

Robert W. Yarbrough is Professor of New Testament at Covenant Theological Seminary (St. Louis, Missouri, USA).

INDEX

Alter, Robert 37
analogia scriptura (analogy of Scripture) 159, 166
Aristotle 81, 89, 160
Augustine of Hippo 54, 100, 127–42, 160, 168, 210, 222, 229, 254–5, 257–8, 260, 262–5, 306–7
   Augustinian/Augustinianism 7, 142, 162, 254, 259–60, 262, 309
authorial intent 2, 8, 17–18, 114, 128, 135–42, 161, 168, 175–7, 179, 181–3, 304, 306

Balthasar, Hans Urs von 79, 143, 144
baptism 70, 124, 132–4, 136, 205, 271, 308–9
   ecclesial 272–4, 277, 281, 283–6
   regeneration through 263–4, 272–4, 277, 284–6, 309
   Spirit-baptism 272, 275 n.15, 277, 283, 285–6
Barr, James 4
Barth, Karl 11, 15, 80, 103, 187, 221, 222–4, 241
   on inspiration 188, 191, 194, 196
   on revelation 194–5
   on the Word of God 188–9, 190–2, 195–7, 199–200, 308
Basil of Caesarea 113, 306
being-in-becoming 191–2
Berlin, Adele 29, 37
Bible
   allegorical interpretation of 7, 127, 166
   authority of 5–6, 10–12, 15, 19, 76, 129, 131, 138, 142, 155, 162–4, 171, 176, 188, 193–7, 210–11, 271, 306
   divine inspiration of 7, 15, 54, 76–7, 83–4, 162, 164, 171, 180, 197, 233
      See also John Calvin
   as divine revelation 5, 10, 170, 185, 194, 307

   See also canon, Scripture
biblical theology 3, 7, 9, 12, 242, 305
Blocher, Henri 258
Bloesch, Donald 188, 193, 196–7
Bromiley, Geoffrey 188, 193, 195–6
Bucer, Martin 159, 161, 261
Bultmann, Rudolf 87, 102–3, 105–7, 188, 226, 243–4, 248–9

Calvin, John 157, 261. *See also Institutes*
   on biblical inspiration 163–5
   on doctrine of Scripture 162, 167
canon/canonical 1, 3, 10, 11, 77, 88, 91, 118, 134, 145, 159, 162, 166, 175, 179, 182, 304–9. *See also* Bible, Scripture
   interpretation of 156, 174, 305.
      See also biblical interpretation, Scripture
canonical-linguistic theology 10, 154, 271, 285, 309
Carson, D. A. 169, 278, 279
Childs, Brevard 4, 11, 242 n.30
Christology 18, 62, 96, 121, 123, 124, 132, 173 n.1, 188, 190, 191, 198–9, 201, 214, 217, 224, 226–7, 231, 232, 243–4, 267, 273, 292, 306, 310
   the incarnation 15, 16, 55, 56, 59, 61, 70, 85, 138, 139, 162, 165, 200, 207, 226–7, 250
   the Son as "divine incognito" 190, 200
   the Son as divine revelation 52–6
   See also Jesus Christ, God, Trinity
Chrysostom, John 160–1, 272, 276–7, 283, 309
Clement of Alexandria 213
Coakley, Sarah 122 n.32, 227 n.28, 229, 230–2, 234 n.62
Cyprian 100, 133–5, 272, 275–6, 277, 283, 285, 309

Eliade, Mircea 246–7

first theology 120
form criticism 25, 102
freedom, evangelical 206–9
Frei, Hans W. 4–6, 242 n.34, 243 n.39, 244

Gadamer, Hans-Georg 2, 3, 217 n.50, 236, 241–3
God
    doctrine of 4, 8, 12, 120, 199, 200, 308
    the Father 7, 52, 54–9, 68, 70–1, 73–5, 84–5, 86, 118, 121–2, 124, 132, 141, 166, 178, 198, 199, 201, 209, 211, 214, 217, 224, 238, 282–3
    revelation of 5, 85
    the Son. *See* Christology
    the Spirit. *See* Holy Spirit
    triunity of 7, 8, 10, 15–16, 54, 55, 170, 178, 188–9, 192, 197, 200, 205, 207, 209, 211, 221, 274, 294, 301. *See also* Christology, Jesus Christ, Holy Spirit, Trinity
Goldingay, John 176–9
Gregory of Nazianzus 120, 285
Gregory of Nyssa 90, 231

Halpern, Baruch 41
Hays, Richard 174–5
Henry, Carl F. H. 6, 187–8, 193–6, 239
hermeneutics/hermeneutical
    biblical 35, 75, 83–4, 125–6, 233, 287, 291, 296–8, 309
    hermeneutical philosophy 1, 4–10, 14–20, 113–14, 233
    theological 5, 8, 10–11, 18, 169, 131, 141–2, 162, 165, 168–70, 192, 197, 205, 217–18, 221–2, 236–9, 242–9, 269
    theory 2–4, 12, 17, 102, 175, 178, 185, 188, 287, 290–301
Hirsch, E. D., Jr. 2–3, 8, 17, 19, 114
historical-critical method 170
Holy Spirit 68, 74, 75, 147, 178, 193–4
    in biblical interpretation 7, 11, 16, 19, 54, 62, 113, 155, 162, 196
    doctrine of 197
    person of 74–5, 85, 107, 207, 211, 217, 223, 232, 263, 265, 273, 274, 275, 276, 278, 280, 282, 283, 284, 285
    role in Scripture's inspiration 84, 128–9, 130, 162–3, 164–5, 305
    See also God, Trinity
humanism 158, 162
    ad fontes 158
    Christian 5–8
    humane letters 158

illocution/illocutionary. *See also* locution, speech acts
    acts of 5, 9, 10, 35, 51, 52, 63, 77, 115, 177, 198, 240 n.21
    illocutionary intent 51–5, 58
    versus perlocution 9, 11, 115–16, 118, 119 n.17, 126, 198, 236 n.3, 241 n.21, 246
Institutes (Calvin's) 131 n.37, 162. *See also* John Calvin
interpretation, biblical 1, 2, 4, 5, 8, 11, 15, 16, 37, 51, 113, 159, 161–2, 166, 168, 170, 175, 181, 185, 197, 205, 287–8, 290, 296–7, 306–8. *See also* Bible, canon, Scripture
Irenaeus 138, 211, 213, 216, 272–4, 276, 309

Jerome 54, 129, 130, 160, 161
Jesus Christ. *See also* Christology
    followers of 94–6, 104, 107, 136, 188, 263, 274
    identity of 6, 122, 128–9, 132, 178, 207–9, 212, 226–7, 243
    revelation of 191–3, 197, 305
    speech of 3, 15, 51–6, 59, 61, 199–200, 214–15, 218, 246, 248, 278–84
    in theodrama 65–75, 83–7, 91, 97–8, 108, 139, 145, 153, 162, 165–71, 260–1, 267

Kelsey, David 4
kerygma/kerygmatic 241, 243, 244, 248, 249–50

Levenson, Jon 237–8
Lewis, C. S. 4, 85, 119, 125, 233, 233 n.60, 245, 250
literary criticism 4, 24, 30, 50

literary theory 5, 8
locution 7, 51–61, 138, 198, 305

meaning, textual 2, 115–16, 126, 161–2, 166–8, 170, 174–5, 177, 179, 181, 206, 233, 236, 241, 246, 253, 272, 294, 304, 306–7
and significance 114, 118, 126, 272
Melanchthon, Philipp 159, 161
Methodist/Methodism 173–4. *See also* John Wesley
Middleton, Richard 42, 266
Moltmann, Jürgen 222, 224–6, 227, 229

narrative, biblical 4, 6, 37, 41–3, 160, 176, 235, 245, 266, 308
Nicene Creed (325) 119
Nicene-Constantinopolitan Creed (381) 119, 132, 134, 212

ontology 16, 188–9, 195, 197, 201, 226
Origen 89–90, 100, 120, 131, 138, 166–7
original guilt (sin) 254
    doctrine of 254, 256
    and federalism 260–2, 264
    the imputation of Adam's 254–60, 260 n.40, 261–2, 267, 309
Owen, John 118–19

panentheism 224
perlocution. *See* illocution/illocutionary
Perry, John 179–81
perspicua brevitas (lucid brevity) 159, 162
philosophy of language 179, 185
Pitre, Brant 72–4
preaching 2, 16, 101, 150–1, 190–1, 207–15, 237–41, 245–51, 308

Ramm, Bernard 188–9, 193, 195
redditio 210–15
regula fidei (or *analogia fidei*) 171, 177–9, 307
ressourcement 305, 310
Ricoeur, Paul 2–6, 10, 17, 62, 76, 235–50, 308
Rudolph, Wilhelm 27–9

Scripture
    canonical reading of 80, 83, 145, 170, 174, 266, 307
    Christological reading of 167–8, 171, 177, 182, 208, 212, 307
    divine discourse in 8, 15, 170, 198, 205, 206–10, 213, 214, 215–19, 236
    as divine speech 51, 53, 54, 55, 58, 61, 63. *See also* divine speech acts
    doctrine of 16, 56, 60, 142
    synchronic reading of 37–8
    theological interpretation of 1, 2, 8, 12, 16, 17 n.37, 80, 157, 173, 174, 177–8, 182–3, 185, 192, 199, 254, 307
    unity of 7, 159, 162, 165–6, 168, 171, 174–5, 176, 307
    See also Bible, canon
sensus literalis (literal interpretation) 167
speech acts
    divine 51, 305. *See also* Christology, God, Holy Spirit, Jesus Christ, Trinity
    of the Father 51, 56, 57–9, 61, 118
    of the Son 7, 53, 51–5, 56–7, 59–60, 118–19
    of the Holy Spirit 55, 63, 106
    theory of 7–10, 14–15, 19, 51, 55, 77, 81, 113–15, 118, 126, 198, 233, 236, 288, 305
Sternberg, Meir 37–8, 42, 50, 52–3, 58

temporality 54, 291–3, 296
Tertullian 101, 160, 272, 274–5, 277, 285, 309
theodrama 12, 16, 20, 75–7, 79–81, 90, 145, 148–51, 222, 226, 288, 294–6, 305, 307, 309–10
theological interpretation. *See* Scripture
traditio 133, 210–15
Trinity
    as communicative 7–8, 15–16, 63, 108, 115, 198–9, 200, 227, 284
    doctrine of 12, 14–16, 19–21, 107–8, 123–5, 132–3, 168, 176–7, 182, 190–2, 208–12, 215–16, 221–2, 308
    economy of the 7–9, 51, 56–7, 62, 115, 118, 126, 188–9, 198–201, 222, 224–34, 306, 308
    social 199, 224–7, 229–30
    See also God, Holy Spirit
Trinity Evangelical Divinity School 4, 6, 9, 12, 141, 254

The University of Edinburgh 4, 8, 9, 14, 23

Van Til, Cornelius 188, 193–5
Volf, Miroslav 229–30, 233

Walton, John 176–8, 182–3
Webster, John 199, 284
Wesley, John 173–5, 182, 286, 307

Wheaton College 4, 141, 142, 303
Wolterstorff, Nicholas 15, 52, 182–3, 197–8, 235 n.2
Wright, N. T. 105, 178–9
Würthwein, Ernst 24

Zwingli, Huldrych 256–7

www.ingramcontent.com/pod-product-compliance
Lightning Source LLC
Chambersburg PA
CBHW072120290426
44111CB00012B/1721